successful in adjusting or adapting to competitive problems to those that have not. The third section examines generic or nonindustry specific U.S. policies in key functional areas such as trade, technology, finance, employment, and corporate governance.

This book offers no quick solutions. Rather, it identifies and evaluates current U.S. strategy, however implicit, diffuse, inconsistent, or passive that strategy may be; and shows it to be ineffective in the face of new competitive realities. The remedy, it concludes, will require reconsideration of some of our basic assumptions concerning the roles of government and private sector institutions.

While the findings of this study are sobering, the book's essential message is that Americans must acknowledge, understand, and learn to adapt to the changing locus and nature of international competition if they are going to continue to meet their goals.

Harvard Business School

Research Colloquium

Contributors

Joseph L. Bower

Harvey Brooks

William C. Crum

Davis Dyer

William F. Finan

Glenn R. Fong

Benjamin M. Friedman

Annette M. LaMond

George C. Lodge

Mark W. Love

Malcolm R. Lovell, Jr.

D. Quinn Mills

Stanley Nehmer

Malcolm S. Salter

Bruce R. Scott

Alan M. Webber

Philip A. Wellons

Alan Wm. Wolff

Michael Y. Yoshino

■■■U.S.■■■ COMPETITIVENESS in the WORLD ECONOMY

Edited by
Bruce R. Scott and George C. Lodge

92-2172

Harvard Business School Press
Boston, Massachusetts

Harvard Business School Press, Boston 02163
© 1985 by the President and Fellows of Harvard College.
All rights reserved.
Printed in the United States of America.

89   88   5   4   3

ISBN 0-87584-173-2 PBK
ISBN 0-87584-160-0

Library of Congress Cataloging in Publication Data

Scott, Bruce R.
  U.S. competitiveness in world economy.

  Includes index.
  1. United States—Foreign economic relations—Addresses,
essays, lectures.   2. Competition, International—Addresses,
essays, lectures.
I. Lodge, George C.   II. Title.
HF1455.S34 1984   338.973   84-15714
ISBN 0-87584-160-0
ISBN 0-87584-173-2 PBK

Contents

Foreword

Founded in 1908, the Harvard University Graduate School of Business Administration celebrated its seventy-fifth anniversary in the academic year 1983–84. We chose to take this opportunity to involve our faculty in thinking seriously about the challenges and opportunities ahead in important fields of management research and teaching.

Field-based empirical research, within and across organizations, has always been fundamental to Harvard Business School's ability to meet its objectives of educating business managers and helping to improve the practice of management. In some respects, we are creating a distinctive model of research. We have often broken through the bounds of traditional disciplines and methodologies to borrow whatever tools and concepts were needed for a particular inquiry. In addition, we have been less concerned with testing existing theory than with generating new insights. And while we often find ourselves drawn to problems that are broad in scope, we strive for results that are operationally significant to managers.

Because Harvard Business School faculty members are committed to pursuing research on the way business actually *does* function, as well as theoretical explorations of how it perhaps *should* function, they can give students and practitioners a vital perspective on the real world of professional practice. Their continuing close contact with operating businesses keeps Harvard Business School faculty at the frontiers of management practice. Research conducted by the faculty often yields insights that are of considerable practical benefit to managers in both day-to-day operations and longer-range planning.

In sponsoring the colloquium series of 1983–84, we hoped to set the course for research development over the next decade, and in particular to encourage greater emphasis on multiperson, multiyear studies of major issues. The complexity of many issues confronting business today almost requires that academicians find more effective forms of collaboration in doing our research. The problems we study are often beyond the capacity of any individual researcher.

In addition to encouraging a reshaping of researcher's work habits, the conferences promised to help strengthen the ties between Harvard Business School and the outside academic and business leadership communities. The series comprised sixteen conferences held at the Harvard Business School campus, each lasting two to five days. Papers were presented by eighty members of the HBS faculty and an approximately equal number of practitioners and academics from other institutions. Altogether, some 450 academics and practitioners were involved as discussants and participants.

Some of these colloquia focused on current research topics, such as U.S. competitiveness in the world economy, productivity and technology, global competition, and world food policy. Others concentrated on establishing agendas for the coming decade's research and course development in a particular field. Clearly, these were not tasks to be attempted in isolation. Rather we wanted to work jointly with others in business, government, and the academic world who could contribute and would themselves gain from the undertaking. The papers presented in this volume have all benefited from the thoughtful discussion they received at the colloquium.

This book is about important changes in the environment of the corporation. The authors carry forward a long-standing commitment by the school to the analysis of the political, social, and economic forces that shape and constrain the activities of corporate managers. Today those forces are more important than ever; consequently the school's research and teaching in this area have expanded and intensified.

Beyond exploring research findings in particular areas, we hoped that these colloquia would sustain and enliven the continuing dialogue between students and practitioners of management. From that melding of perspectives, we have found, insights emerge that can revitalize the education of future managers and refine current professional practice. In that spirit of cooperative endeavor, I am proud to introduce this collection of essays.

John H. McArthur
Dean of the Faculty
Harvard Business School

Acknowledgments

We wish to thank the following people, who generously gave their time reading and commenting on various drafts of the chapters: Robert H. B. Baldwin, Morgan Stanley; Professor Norman A. Berg, Harvard Business School; Dr. Carl E. Black, E. I. du Pont de Nemours; James Booe, Communications Workers of America; Thornton F. Bradshaw, RCA; Michael Brewer, Cummins Engine; Van W. Bussmann, TRW; Philip Caldwell, Ford Motor Company; Robert A. Charpie, Cabot Corporation; Professor George Eads, University of Maryland; Donald Ephlin, United Automobile Workers; Geza Feketekuty, Office of the U.S. Trade Representative; Murray Finley, Amalgamated Clothing and Textile Workers Union; Edmund L. Fitzgerald, Northern Telecom; Assistant Professor Marie-Therese Flaherty, Harvard Business School; Professor Emeritus Bertrand Fox, Harvard Business School; Dr. Ellen Frost, Westinghouse Electric; Dr. John H. Gibbons, Office of Technology Assessment; Professor Robert H. Hayes, Harvard Business School; Dr. Robert C. Holland, Committee for Economic Development; Donald Hughes, Burlington Industries; Edward Jefferson, E. I. du Pont de Nemours; Richard John, Department of Transportation; Howard W. Johnson, M.I.T.; William A. Klopman, Burlington Industries; Frederick Knickerbocker, Department of Commerce; Malcolm Lovell, The Brookings Institution; Bruce K. MacLaury, The Brookings Institution; Dr. Ruben F. Mettler, TRW; Professor David W. Mullins, Harvard Business School; Rudy Oswald, AFL-CIO; William J. Perry, Hambrecht & Quist; Peter Peterson, Peterson & Jacobs; Professor Michael E. Porter, Harvard Business School; Clyde Prestowitz, Department of Commerce; David Ragone, Case Western Reserve University; Howard Samuel, AFL-CIO; Henry B. Schacht, Cummins Engine; Norton Sloan, Cabot Corporation; Alexander B. Trowbridge, National Association of Manufacturers; Associate Professor Laura Tyson, University of California-Berkeley; Dr. Thomas Uhlman, Hewlett-Packard; Hans van der Ven, Hoogovens Bevernicks, Netherlands; Professor Ezra Vogel, Harvard University; Alan M. Webber, Harvard Business School; John A. Young, Hewlett-Packard; and Associate Professor John Zysman, University of California-Berkeley.

We wish to thank the Bertrand R. Fox Publication Fund for its support of the publication of this volume.

Ann Kester and Hans van der Ven were of particular assistance in the preparation of chapters 1 and 2. We wish also to thank officials at the Department of Commerce in 1982 who helped collect data for those chapters, in particular Rebecca Lambert, assistant deputy secretary, and Frederick Knickerbocker, executive director.

At Harvard Business School we are indebted to Dean John H. McArthur and Professor E. Raymond Corey, director of the Division of Research, for their leadership and support.

Bruce R. Scott
George C. Lodge

U.S. COMPETITIVENESS in the WORLD ECONOMY

Introduction

Bruce R. Scott
George C. Lodge

The following chapters were originally papers prepared for the Harvard Business School's colloquium entitled "U.S. Competitiveness in the World Economy," one of sixteen such meetings commemorating the school's seventy-fifth anniversary. The chapters describe and evaluate America's changing position in the world economy.

Without purporting to represent fully the views of each author, we believe the basic findings to be the following:

1. For some fifteen years the United States has been losing its capacity to compete in the world economy. This loss is particularly serious as the nation's dependence on international trade increases. The effects can be seen particularly in the manufacturing sector.
2. Declining U.S. competitiveness is evident in the performance pattern of several measures: a shift from decades of trade surpluses to substantial deficits, eroding market share in almost all sectors, and declining profitability since the late 1960s. In addition, real, after-tax earnings of American workers have been declining since they peaked in 1972.
3. The principal competitive challenge comes not from our traditional rivals in Western Europe, but from a new group of competitors in East Asia: Japan, South Korea, Taiwan, Singapore, and Hong Kong.
4. The competitive thrust of these new challengers comes not from favorable endowments of natural resources but from coherent national strategies through which each country mobilizes and shapes its productive capabilities to achieve economic growth and global competitiveness. These strategies emphasize work, saving, and investment to build a higher standard of living through increased productivity in

1

existing activities, and through accelerating the shift toward activities that promise above average growth and/or technical change.

5. The United States and most of the West European industrial democracies suffer by comparison from increasingly less competitive strategies. Although generally not explicit, their strategies emphasize more secure and equitable distribution of current income at the expense of increased market rigidities, and current consumption at the expense of investment for long-term benefits.

6. Unless the United States reexamines and modifies its basic economic strategy, it cannot expect to generate the performance necessary to finance its simultaneous commitments to leading the Western Alliance, increasing the domestic standard of living, and improving the distribution of income.

This study focuses on (1) the strategy by which the United States determines its place in the world economy, however implicit, diffuse, inconsistent, or passive that strategy may be, and (2) the inconsistency between ambitious goals and a short-term, distribution-oriented strategy. The issue is not whether the United States does or does not have a strategy, or should or should not have a strategy. It is clear that we do and that we must recognize and understand this strategy that concomitantly gives low priority to competitiveness and long-term development, and high priority to short-term distributional equity through a centralized system of income redistribution, entitlements, regulations, and subsidies for consumer goods from credit card purchases to housing. Perhaps most important, we must recognize that the U.S. economy can no longer be counted on to deliver the performance level required to meet the nation's goals and commitments. Either the goals need to be changed, reflecting more modest prospects for the American economy, or the strategy needs to be changed to increase the prospects for more robust performance in the future.

The conflict between ambitious military and social goals, coupled with the unrealistic notions of "supply-side" economics, have led to unprecedented peacetime budget deficits, high interest rates, capital inflows from abroad, and an overvalued dollar, which has greatly exacerbated our competitive problems. In our view, the overvalued dollar is first and foremost a reflection of an unrealistic U.S. strategy—a mismatch between ambitious goals on the one hand and the lack of political will to levy taxes to pay for them on the other.

This volume delineates U.S. strategy and its ineffectiveness in the face of competitive realities. Maintenance of such a strategy in the light of such obviously disappointing performance is not easily explained: indeed, many experts seem to deny the competitiveness problem rather than confront the issue. Some correctly claim, for instance, that the United States is not "deindustrializing" in absolute terms overall and, therefore, there is no cause for alarm. But U.S. goals and commitments surely require much better performance than the mere avoidance of decline.

Likewise, some claim the overvalued dollar is the essential problem, dwarfing all others. While the exchange rate surely has been the foremost competitive handicap since 1981, a pattern of decline seems to have emerged about 1968 and to have continued throughout the 1970s. Our focus is not on a short-term crisis but on longer-term decline like that which has characterized the United Kingdom for the last century.

A clear concept of national competitiveness is essential to diagnosing the problem. In this study, national competitiveness refers to a country's ability to create, produce, distribute, and/or service products in international trade while earning rising returns on its resources.[1] In adopting this definition, we have chosen the nation state—not the firm or industry—as the basic unit of analysis. Thus, U.S. competitiveness means the ability to employ U.S. resources, both human resources and capital resources, so that Americans earn increasing returns while in open competition with other countries. For example, if a U.S. firm moves some of its operations to Mexico or Taiwan to take advantage of lower cost labor, and if this can be done while the United States maintains something like full employment, the U.S. standard of living may be enhanced over the long term. If, however, such shifts occur during prolonged periods of high unemployment, the firms involved may benefit, but not necessarily the country.

. Although this volume addresses the competitive problems of the United States as a nation, plainly it is American companies that do the competing; they are in the front lines. Their failure to compete successfully, while remaining in this country, is to some extent the fault of managers who have been slow to invest and innovate; quick to move offshore before trying to improve the domestic situation; and prone to ask for sacrifices from others without recognizing that their own compensation levels are difficult to justify in light of their companies' performance. But these managerial shortcomings can neither be understood nor remedied unless they are viewed in the wider context of American strategy; they are part of a systemic pattern resting on old premises that need renovation.

Although competitiveness depends on both traded goods and services, this study focuses primarily on the former for several reasons. First, the volume of traded services is small relative to that of traded goods, particularly when allowance is made for dividends and other "service" payments on U.S. investments abroad. Many domestic services, such as government, retailing, and transportation, indirectly affect overall wage and productivity levels but cannot easily be replaced by imports. At the same time, services are also more difficult to export abroad (except for certain financial services) and may actually depend heavily on related manufactured products such as computers or communication equipment.[2] Thus, while the service sector has created millions of new jobs since 1970, our competitive core still largely lies in manufacturing, which in 1980 accounted for almost 70 percent of U.S. merchandise exports and over half of such imports.[3] Manufacturing also has traditionally yielded much higher wages and output per employee than the service sector.[4] As our aging work force grows more slowly in the future, raising our standard of living will depend increasingly on productivity gains rather than on expanding total employment, and manufacturing will, therefore, remain crucial.

To evaluate competitiveness we must judge the present and the future, not just measure the past. We must identify the critical forces that influence various industries and countries in areas such as research, innovation, investment, employment, production, and import-export decisions. Although the trade balance is an important and familiar index, for example, it is not sufficient by itself. The trade balance, or more precisely, the current account balance, measures international transactions in terms of the cash flows involved, not market share or incomes. To be competitive one must achieve or maintain some target level of market share and do so profitably—not at a loss or at an unsatisfactory income level.

American competitiveness is not an end in itself; it is a way to earn a rising standard of living and to generate the wealth to pay for our domestic and international commitments, both of which are linked to a prosperous world economy. It is neither in the United States' interest, nor that of the rest of the world, for America to seek to return to the level of economic dominance that it held in the 1950s. Rather we should establish reasonable goals for the competitiveness of our industries which are not incompatible with the reasonable expectations of our competitors. U.S. market share in traded manufactures might be expected to decline no more rapidly than U.S. share of world income, for example, and share in high technology areas or products might be expected to do considerably better.

In evaluating our prospects for future competitiveness, we must ask how the U.S. economic environment affects the capacity of firms to create, produce, distribute, and service products while paying rising real wages and maintaining a satisfactory return on capital employed in the United States. A century ago, such an analysis might have emphasized U.S. advantages in natural resources and in being the world's largest and richest domestic market. This emphasis would be much less appropriate today.

Since World War II, the shift of industrial activity toward science-based activities (for example, chemicals, electrical equipment, and electronics) means that national competitiveness depends increasingly on technology, capital investment, and labor skills, all of which can be shaped and mobilized if not "created." In addition, unlike natural resources, these man-made resources move readily across national boundaries. As a result, predicting future competitiveness increasingly hinges on assessing how national environments influence the creation of new technologies, where and how they are exploited, and who captures the returns. While business managers play an important role in the creation and exploitation of new ideas, for example, so do university scientists. The educational system, grants for research, and the incentives to take risks all play a role in stimulating creativity and are primarily shaped by government. Thus, one cannot evaluate future U.S. competitiveness without also considering the impact of U.S. government policies and institutions, since these shape the business environment more than natural resources do.

The U.S. advantage as the world's first "common market" has also shrunk dramatically, although it has not disappeared. The U.S. economy is now much more interdependent with other economies, with imports equaling 20 percent of manufactured output for the economy as a whole. The European Common Market is now larger than the U.S. market, although less truly a single market, and the Japanese market is roughly half as large, but growing much more rapidly.

The significance of our traditional natural advantages is thus greatly reduced, and our competitive position depends increasingly on *man-made* advantages. Competitiveness is more and more a matter of strategies, and less and less a product of *natural* endowments. For example, the United States has long been noted for high wage rates that were typically offset by greater productivity per worker. That productivity depended largely on higher levels of fixed investment per worker, a tribute not only to U.S. entrepreneurs but also to U.S. markets—notably the world's largest, best-functioning capital market. Several recent studies have shown, however, that the cost of capital in the United States is now much higher than in such key rival countries as Germany and Japan. These studies indicate that the cost difference is at least as great as the wage differences relative to these competitors, and that this difference—if allowed to continue—threatens the capacity of U.S.-based activities to maintain the necessary investment pace to keep up with competitors. Furthermore, the high cost of capital seems largely due to U.S. strategy, which has the effect of subsidizing consumer borrowing (mostly for housing) on the one hand and penalizing private savings through negative real returns on the other.

Unlike high wages, which permit those who work to enjoy a better standard of living, the high cost of capital does not necessarily benefit those who save. Tax sheltered savings, for example, may earn good returns, but if these are in housing, the "saver" may well pay a higher initial price than in an unsubsidized system. In addition, the saver may also buy a larger house than he or she otherwise might, implicitly increasing consumption—booked as investment in our accounting scheme—and reducing the funds available for investment in competitiveness. The United States uses more of its savings for households than its major competitors. In addition, we have established a firm hold on last place among industrial countries in terms of the personal savings rate. Thus, despite being the world's foremost capital market, American industry is handicapped by exceptionally high-cost funds. It is a competitive handicap entirely of our own making.

Evaluation of national competitiveness poses two basic questions: how and in what dimensions do we measure the competitiveness of a national economy, and what standards do we use in determining adequacy? For example, most analyses of competitiveness focus on the trade balance as the key indicator of performance. Is it, however, more important than other factors like market share, real incomes, profitability, and relative changes in productivity? We believe it is the performance pattern measured in several dimensions that is the key, not performance in a single dimension.

The significant measures are relative, not absolute. For example, while both the United States' standard of living and the manufacturing base have risen over the past several decades, the Europeans' and East Asians' have grown even more rapidly over the same period, outstripping any mere return to post–World War II normalcy. What performance level is satisfactory? Should we be satisfied with outperforming "underachievers" like the United Kingdom, or should we instead aim for a higher level of achievement?

To evaluate our overall performance we must compare it not only with our own past achievements and foreigners' accomplishments, but with our basic goals and commitments. Can we meet both our domestic aspirations and overseas obligations or should some of these be reduced to stay within our means? Conversely, can we significantly improve our competitiveness without requiring sacrifices from vested interest groups, and if not, how can such adjustments be accomplished in a democratic society?

These questions obviously raise diplomatic and political issues that can be clarified, but not resolved, by economic analysis. Since the end of World War II, for example, the United States has led a Western Alliance devoted both to containing Soviet aggression and to expanding international trade. While these endeavors have each been moderately successful to date, the United States has borne a disproportionate share of the cost, as the largest and richest member of the coalition. Unless we remain sufficiently competitive to maintain our economic strength, many American voters may question the defense spending and trade concessions that such leadership requires and ask whether the United States is not overextending itself. A retreat from some of the international commitments might follow, as happened in the United Kingdom.

If we wish to pursue our principal national and international goals, the competitiveness of our country—particularly its manufacturing base—becomes an urgent matter. At present, critical decisions about U.S. competitiveness—potentially determining which of our industries will live and which will die—are increasingly being determined by other countries whose national strategies are more dynamic and adaptive than ours. While this is sometimes related to their targeting or other so-called "unfair" trade practices, the analysis in this volume suggests that it is more a function of our own uncompetitive strategy and the theory or premises on which it rests. For example, while some countries tilt incentives toward promoting work, saving, and investment, the United States has increasingly tilted toward leisure, and borrowing to support additional consumption. While others offer incentives to exporting industries, U.S. policy favors industries sheltered from foreign competition, notably real estate. And, while others typically condition import relief and other forms of industrial intervention upon industry plans for rapid restructuring, the United States continues to grant protection with no quid pro quos for competitiveness. Setting our own house in order is thus at least as important as attempting to persuade other countries to modify their policies and practices.

In the process of planning this volume, discussing drafts of the papers in preliminary meetings, weighing the views expressed by colloquium participants, and by labor and business representatives since then, we have come to believe that one of the main issues is the set of premises, or the theory, on which the U.S. strategy is based. One of those premises is that the United States has only a confused, incoherent, passive, and largely ineffective

strategy. The various chapters in this volume point instead to a strategy that
has been surprisingly consistent in its domestic orientation and short-term
focus, despite the "incoherent" process through which it is formulated and—
as often as not—implemented. Our government has not been a passive
spectator or neutral arbiter of market forces; instead it has steadily steered
incentives away from work, saving, and investment toward leisure, borrowing, and consumption. Reestablishing a more neutral balance would be a
major step in the direction of competitiveness.

Perhaps the most basic premise is that the market system, guided only by
the invisible hand, gives the highest level of economic performance obtain-
able, consistent with a democratic society. Its corollary, first spelled out by
David Ricardo almost 170 years ago, that international specialization and
trade based on natural comparative advantages yields the highest level of
economic performance for the world economy as well as mutual gains for
all participating countries, deserves careful scrutiny. The following chapters
repeatedly question the validity of these premises. The issue is not whether
they have merit but whether they are still an adequate base for diagnosis and
policy, and whether they are an adequate basis for a strategy that is competitive with those of the East Asian challengers.

The book is divided into three main sections, followed by a concluding
chapter. The first section presents an overview of U.S. performance, and an
analysis of international competition among nations. The second section uses
four case studies to illustrate the variety of problems found in different
industries ranging from high to low technology, from growing industries to
mature and stagnant ones, and from industries that have been relatively
successful in adjusting or adapting to competitive problems to those that have
not. The third section examines "generic" or nonindustry-specific U.S. policies in key functional areas such as finance, government taxation and spending, trade, technology, employment, and corporate governance. Although
the chapters are written from somewhat different perspectives, each author
has attempted to place his or her analysis in a broader common context,
examining its relationship to U.S. strategy and to the country's intensifying
competition with others' strategies. The final chapter summarizes and examines the basic premises or assumptions that are called into question by
our competitive decline.

Each of the chapters adds a piece to a holistic analysis of U.S. competitiveness. None attempts an exhaustive study of a particular topic or industry.
It is the holistic nature of the analysis that is important, the attempt to place
the United States in its competitive context through examination of its policies

and a selection of industries. In a sense it is a "case study," in which the subject is USA, Inc. We hope the reader will share with us not only the exploration of the various pieces of the analysis, but the overriding sense of the whole: that is, the position of the United States relative to its key competitors and the key role of U.S. strategy in shaping that competitive position.

In the first chapter, Bruce R. Scott describes the declining competitiveness of U.S. manufacturing industries beginning in the late 1960s. The challenge, he points out, comes not from our traditional industrial rivals in the North Atlantic area, but from Japan and other East Asian nations. These countries, he notes in the second chapter, would not have achieved such progress without abandoning neoclassical Western trade theory, notably its emphasis on *static*, short-term, resource-based comparative advantage. Their adherence instead to a *dynamic* theory of comparative advantage has allowed these new competitors to design and implement economic strategies leading to higher rates of sustained growth than those countries that have depended on either the unassisted workings of the invisible hand or ad hoc political responses to "squeaky wheels" in their economies. He shows that these countries' national strategies are crucial to their success. The most successful competitors have adopted a developmental strategy that gives high priority to saving, investment, and growth, while the less successful have emphasized governmental policies to divide and distribute the economic pie. The winning strategies rest upon a national consensus shared by management and labor that restraining costs and consumption in the short run will lead to a higher standard of living in the long run.

The effects of such competitive national strategies on the American economy are shown in various chapters focusing on specific sectors. William F. Finan and Annette M. LaMond trace the development of the American semiconductor industry from its initial, almost fortuitous, nurturing by the Defense Department to its recent response to a concerted commercial challenge by the government and manufacturers of Japan. They conclude that unless we rebalance the scales soon to ensure U.S. firms access to capital, joint research and development, and product markets similar to that available to Japanese companies, the long-term competitiveness of the U.S. industry will erode, perhaps irreversibly. Similarly, Malcolm S. Salter, Alan M. Webber, and Davis Dyer show how persisting obsolete attitudes, institutional relationships, and work practices among government, company managers, and employees have stifled adequate productivity growth, quality control, and technological change in the American automobile industry. As a result,

U.S. firms that were the undisputed world leaders for half a century are no longer competitive and have little immediate prospect of regaining parity let alone global dominance. The profitability of their U.S. operations depends heavily on protection from imports.

Other chapters examine more successful governmental and industrial responses to foreign competition. Joseph L. Bower studies the petrochemical industry, in which American firms have adjusted part of their product portfolio to worldwide overcapacity more rapidly and more effectively than government-controlled or -regulated companies in Europe and Japan. Stanley Nehmer and Mark W. Love analyze the Multi-Fiber Arrangement, an international system of managed trade for textiles and apparel, which has actually increased the domestic competitiveness of many U.S. firms by stabilizing world markets and encouraging investment. They also suggest conditions under which the MFA concept could be applied to other industries involved in international trade disputes. Michael Y. Yoshino and Glenn R. Fong discuss the Defense Department's Very High Speed Integrated Circuit Program as an ongoing example of how government and business leaders can cooperate efficiently to achieve their complementary but distinct military and commercial interests.

Our chapters show that the United States has had a strategy, but that with a few notable exceptions it has been largely implicit, oriented toward consumers' short-term benefits and financed by borrowing. Philip A. Wellons analyzes differences in the cost, volume, and allocation of capital among various countries to see how these affect our national competitiveness. Benjamin M. Friedman looks at the recent but growing imbalance between governmental revenues and expenditures, which threatens to crowd private borrowers out of U.S. capital markets, thereby deterring much-needed investment and further exacerbating the competitiveness problem by keeping the dollar's real exchange rate high. Harvey Brooks describes trends in American technology and innovation that suggest our ability to commercially implement, though not discover, new ideas is falling behind Japan's. D. Quinn Mills and Malcolm R. Lovell consider recent developments, both here and abroad, that have undermined the relative competitiveness of American labor compared with that of newly industrialized countries. They project some of the choices that will face us in the future and explore ways to mitigate the adverse consequences of current trends by reforming labor-management relations and improving adjustment procedures.

These chapters document a tension between America's strategy, such as it is, and the pressures of increased competition in the world. Alan Wm. Wolff describes the conflicts in his chapter on U.S. trade policy. Traditionally

committed to the principles of free trade and the free market, both for
ideological reasons and because of a long-standing belief that American
interests are promoted by such principles, the United States increasingly finds
itself facing a new type of competition in which business and government
work together to achieve what might be called "managed competitiveness."
We are losing market share in key sectors to those who do not play by our
rules; we are unwilling to play by theirs; and it is clear that they are unwilling
to abdicate their strategies in favor of ours. In these circumstances, it is
imperative that the United States reexamine its premises and its traditional
strategy, no matter how discomforting such a reexamination might be.

The competitive diagnosis revealed in these papers raises fundamental
questions. How is national competitiveness best fostered? How should it be
reconciled with other socially desirable goals? Who should decide, and by
what process? In the final chapter, George C. Lodge and William C. Crum
summarize the major symptoms of declining U.S. competitiveness, list some
of the causes, consider certain responses made to date, and describe current
congressional proposals in this area. They then discuss the essential elements
of a more effective remedy and the tension between what must happen and
traditional assumptions about the roles of and relationships among government, big business, and labor.

Critics may chide us for failing to join in the current debate on "industrial
policy." We feel, however, that the term is poorly conceived and misleading.
Our description and analysis of the problems of American competitiveness
show clearly that any effective remedy must address the nation's strategy as
a whole: its goals, its priorities, and all of the policies that are used to
implement them—including policies only indirectly connected to government, such as those concerning managerial practices, employee wages, and
executive compensation.

The remedy must begin with sound macroeconomics, based on the premise
that each generation should earn its standard of living and not saddle future
generations with debts to support an artificial standard of living. It must
include a commitment to balance the needs of competitiveness and economic
development with the need for a fair division of the economic pie. To embark
on an "industrial policy" without meeting such conditions will surely risk
increased government involvement, which will further handicap U.S. industry while claiming to help it. The history of such efforts in France, Britain,
and other Western nations repeatedly shows that adopting an industrial policy
without first adopting a basic political commitment to competitiveness is
either useless or, more likely, counterproductive.

Finally, some readers may worry that this book is unduly preoccupied with the national interest of the United States and tacitly advocates a form of neomercantilism that ignores the inexorable trends toward global interdependence and integration.[5] They may feel that a preoccupation with U.S. problems will distract managers, public officials, and labor leaders from realizing the larger interests of the nation and the world. We believe, however, that to avoid the dangers of competitive nationalism and to achieve a more stable world order, the United States must recognize clearly what is happening to its economy because of foreign competition, see why it is occurring, and be aware of the likely consequences if we do not change our ways. Such self-knowledge is a prerequisite to the United States' understanding its self-interests and implementing enlightened policies, which, over the long run, can guard against both "giving the store away" and prompting an escalating trade war. Only after our competitive situation is clear can we effectively reconcile our needs with those of others to achieve a benign international order; only then can we consider specific policy recommendations for action.

1

U.S. Competitiveness: Concepts, Performance, and Implications

Bruce R. Scott

Since the mid-1960s, U.S. economic performance, and U.S. competitiveness in particular, has showed signs of weakening, as indicated by such measures as the trade balance, share of world markets in most major categories of manufactured goods, the profitability of American firms, and the real, after-tax earnings of American workers.

Most of our major competitors have been gaining on us in terms of real standard of living for more than twenty years. Is this evidence of a problem or of an abnormal lead enjoyed by the United States after the close of World War II? Recent U.S. performance has been less robust than in the 1950s and 1960s, but so has that of most of its competitors. U.S. performance is falling short of its goals and commitments, both domestic and foreign policy commitments, but so is the performance of its traditional European partner-competitors. A relatively new group of competitors in East Asia has continued to outperform all of the North Atlantic countries: will this continue or will they too slow down once they have caught up?

It is important to note at the outset that the issue is one of relative performance, not absolute decline. Even with the stagflation of the 1970s the United States experienced some growth in manufacturing labor force, capital stock, and output. It has not experienced absolute "deindustrialization."[1] The central issue is performance in relative terms: performance since about 1968 compared with the preceding decades, performance relative to our major competitors, and performance relative to U.S. goals and commitments.

Bruce R. Scott is Paul Whiton Cherington Professor of Business Administration at Harvard Business School. Contributions to this paper were made by Benjamin Friedman, George Lodge, Douglas Scott, Hans van der Ven, and Pierre Wack. Research assistance was provided by Ann Y. Kester and Hans van der Ven.

Our key competitors have changed over the period. While we continue to think of the traditional industrial democracies as our foremost competitors, this is no longer the case. Our key competitors are now in East Asia, and this seems almost certain to be increasingly the case for the remainder of this century. The performance of most of the industrial countries of Europe is not only weaker than ours but in some cases much weaker. Our most successful competitors are resource-poor countries, notably Japan and the new Japans of East Asia. These countries seem to have turned what was a competitive disadvantage according to traditional economic theory into an advantage.

The most serious challenge for American competitiveness is tied to its existing national goals and commitments. International commitments, such as containing the Soviet threat and fostering an open trading and monetary system, impose costs on the United States, as do domestic commitments to a rising standard of living and an improved distribution of income. Increasingly, the question must be asked whether the U.S. economy is strong enough and competitive enough to support those costs, whether it can find lower-cost strategies to meet them, or alternatively whether some of the commitments can be reduced. It is essential to realize that the problem is not merely the product of successive recessions like the one in the early 1980s, but rather a long-term secular weakening that appears to have begun in the late 1960s. Starkly put, the question is whether the United States is in the early stages of a decline similar to the United Kingdom's which, over the last century, led ultimately to a reduction in its political and military role and more recently to a loss of capacity to achieve a rising standard of living.

Evaluation of U.S. competitiveness requires careful interpretation of historical data, and of various explanations for what has happened. It requires a framework for interpreting the data that will allow us to make informed comparisons with other countries as a basis for making sound judgments about the prospects for future U.S. competitiveness. Inevitably an evaluation requires an excursion into economic theory, since theory provides the substance of the framework. As a start, however, it is important to understand what is meant by competitiveness at the level of the nation state, how it can be measured, and how it differs from competitiveness of enterprises domiciled within the country.

THE CONCEPT OF NATIONAL COMPETITIVENESS

National competitiveness refers to a nation state's ability to produce, distribute, and service goods in the international economy in competition with goods and services produced in other countries, and to do so in a way that earns a rising standard of living. The ultimate measure of success is not a "favorable" balance of trade, a positive current account, or an increase in foreign exchange reserves: it is an increase in standard of living. To be competitive as a country means to be able to employ national resources, notably the nation's labor force, in such a way as to earn a rising level of real income through specialization and trade in the world economy.

If the basic concept is simple, the measurement of performance is not. For example, competitiveness means *earning* a rising standard of living, not borrowing it. Obviously a rapid increase in borrowing will permit at least a short-term rise in the standard of living, for a country as for an individual. However, unless productivity rises even more rapidly than the borrowing, at some point the rate of borrowing must slow down, leaving the burden of debt-service payments without capital inflows to offset them. In these increasingly familiar circumstances, real incomes are likely to decline sharply, as they have throughout most of Latin America in the last few years. Thus, aggressive borrowing may be associated with a rising standard of living for a time, but there will come a day of reckoning. Evaluating performance over a reasonably long time period, measured in decades rather than shorter electoral periods, has advantages for unmasking the real fruits of a country's economic policy.

In addition, there are questions of income distribution. While the traditional focus is on labor and capital, there may also be differences among the incomes of those who work, the unemployed, those on public assistance, and the retired. While one might expect broadly similar trends among these groups, the last several decades have exhibited sharply divergent trends in how the economic pie is being divided among them. How is one to evaluate performance if the real incomes of the labor force are declining while those receiving transfer payments, financed by ever-increasing public debts, are rising? Is income to be measured in purely domestic terms, or in relation to some international standard? If the latter, how should one adjust for over- or undervalued currency rates? And how can one appraise present competitiveness as distinct from past performance?

This brief description of the issue suggests the wisdom of reviewing multiple measures, using a long time horizon, and attempting to relate U.S. performance to U.S. goals and commitments. The acid test of U.S. competitiveness is whether our economy has and is likely to continue to generate rising returns both to labor and capital while maintaining its various international commitments—particularly its commitment to an open trading system.

Foremost among the familiar measures of competitiveness is the trade balance, and second is its close relative, the current account. Both are important; each is like a corporate measure of cash flow—one measuring cash flow from goods, and the other from goods and services. Neither shows whether trade is being carried on at a profit or loss, nor whether real incomes are rising or falling. These balances are only two indicators—not necessarily the most important—which by themselves are much more a measure of past performance than indicators of future competitiveness.

If one attempts to think of competitiveness in present and future terms, and not just as measurement of the past, then the key indicators are much the same as for a company: market share; profitability; real incomes for employees; employment; productivity; relative unit cost levels both for capital and labor; and investment for the future in new technologies (R&D), new equipment, and enhanced skills for employees. Ordinarily the competitive challenge for a nation is to maintain or increase market share while enhancing wages and salaries as well as the returns to capital. This basic concept would be modified by the particular goals and commitments of each particular nation; for example, the U.S. commitment to help rebuild various economies after World War II or British decisions to dramatically scale back their international commitments to maintain domestic social priorities.

The challenge for the analyst is to fit together the various measurements into a theory that not only gives a sound appraisal of past performance, but also sheds some light on future prospects. Appraisal of U.S. competitiveness is complicated by the fact that the U.S. economy is so large that it affects the world economic system as a whole, as well as by the unnatural and undesirable degree of economic supremacy enjoyed by the United States in 1945. Some closing of the gap by other countries was explicitly sought by the United States and is not a sign of loss of competitiveness. At what point, and with what criteria is one to conclude that the closing of the gap has already—or soon will have—gone too far to be consistent with U.S. interests? The answer can only be relative and points to the most important dimension in our evaluation: the measurement of U.S. performance relative to U.S. goals and commitments.

The degree of competitiveness is manifested in the whole fabric of society—from the educational system to the infrastructure to the quality of life—and affects decisions both by individuals and by firms to enter, remain, or exit. However, the first symptoms of a problem are likely to be found where producers and consumers make choices at the margin, that is, to purchase tradable goods and services produced in the United States or elsewhere.

Export growth leads to increases in domestic investment, productivity, and employment; import growth means foreign suppliers are offering better value to consumers. In the case of the United States, "tradables" are overwhelmingly goods rather than services, and about two-thirds of the goods are manufactures (see figure 1-1). And, even with the rise in oil prices in the 1970s, it is manufactures, not oil, that dominate U.S. imports (see figure 1-2). Besides playing the leading role in tradables, manufactures are also the sector in which productivity has continued to grow (see figure 1-3). While the apparent stagnation in productivity in the service sector may reflect a very difficult problem of measurement—where services are valued at cost for want of a physical measure of output—productivity gains in manufacturing are also understated due to omission of improvements in product quality. The point is not to downplay the importance of services, but to note that a healthy manufacturing sector is a key both to international competitiveness and to a rising standard of living.[2]

Otto Eckstein stated the case for the importance of the manufacturing sector as follows:

> Beginning with our industrial revolution shortly before the Civil War, the growth of manufacturing industry has been the principal vehicle of U.S. eco-

Figure 1-1

U.S. Exports of Goods, 1970 and 1980

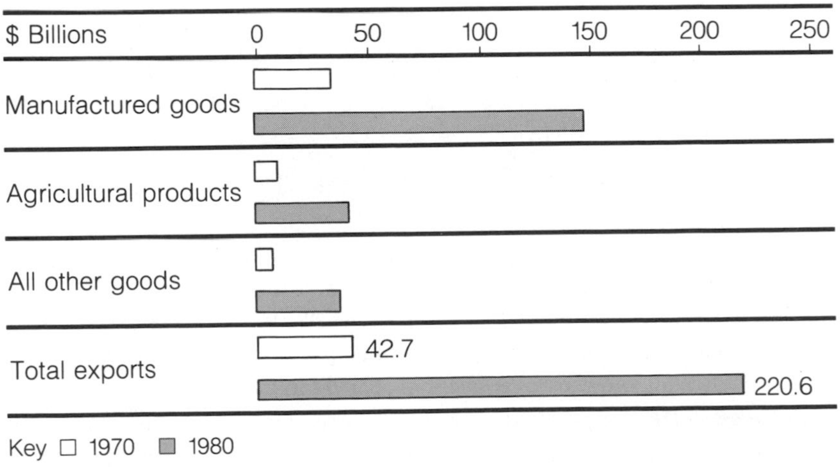

Key ☐ 1970 ■ 1980

Source: U.S. Department of Commerce
Note: Two-thirds of export growth in 1970s resulted from manufacturers.
Exports of manufacturers grew by $115 billion from 1970 to 1980, a fivefold increase. Agricultural exports rose $34.5 billion. This figure does not include services.

Figure 1-2

U.S. Imports of Goods, 1970 and 1980

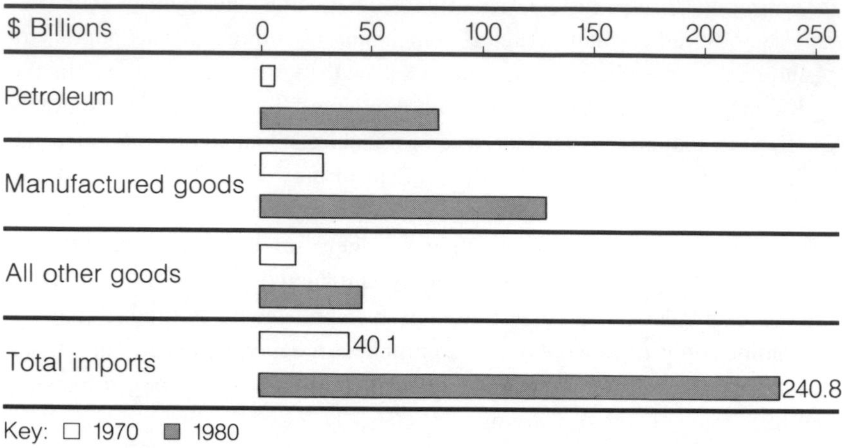

Key: □ 1970   ■ 1980

Source: U.S. Department of Commerce
Note: Half of U.S. import growth in the 1970s stemmed from manufacturers and about one
third from greater oil imports. Imports of manufacturers grew by $100 billion from 1970 t
1980. Petroleum imports rose $72 billion. This figure does not include services.

nomic growth. The increasing productivity in goods production made possible
by a capable labor force, innovative management, an exceptionally favorable
supply of natural resources and rapidly advancing technology, created a growth
of total output such as the world had never seen. A century-long industrial
development process raised U.S. living standards manyfold, made U.S. gross
national product nearly 40% of world output, and provided the nation with the
means to become the political leader and military protector of the western world
while concurrently meeting the social needs of its population.[3]

This chapter focuses on U.S. competitiveness in manufactures.

U.S. COMPETITIVE PERFORMANCE

To appreciate our declining competitiveness, we must note both America's
increased integration in the world economy and a broad pattern of loss of
leadership which stretches over a thirty-year period.

Between 1950 and 1980, for example, America's share of world GNP
dropped from 40 percent to 21.5 percent, its portion of world trade declined
from 20 percent to 11 percent, and its holdings of global gold and foreign
exchange reserves fell from 32 percent to 6 percent, even though its share
of world population only declined from 6 percent to 5 percent. While much
of this decline was both "inevitable" and desirable, it should be noted that—

at least since 1960—the U.S. share of world trade has declined more than its share of world GNP, as indicated in figures 1-4 and 1-5.

At the same time, the United States has become much more integrated into the world economy, with imports and exports each accounting for over 12 percent of domestic GNP in 1980, compared with less than 5 percent and

Figure 1-3

Output per Worker per Year in the Manufacturing and Nonmanufacturing Sectors, 1948-82 ($ thousands)

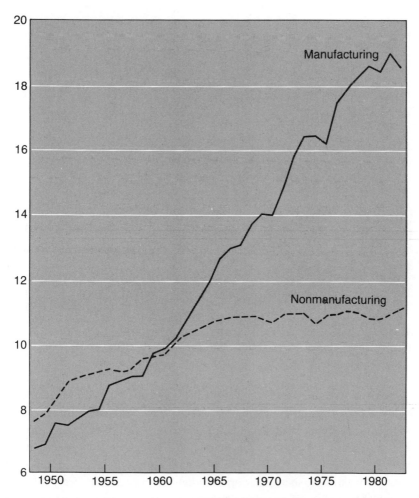

Source: Otto Eckstein, *The DRI Report on U.S. Manufacturing Industries* (New York: McGraw-Hill Book Company, 1984).

Figure 1-4

Shares of World GNP, 1960, 1970, 1980

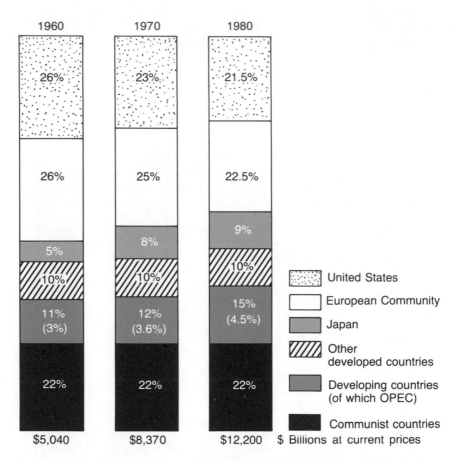

Source: U.S. Department of Commerce, International Trade Administration, *U.S. Competitiveness in the International Economy*, October 1981.

8 percent in 1960, respectively. The changes for manufactured imports and exports have been even more dramatic: in 1979 each exceeded 20 percent of domestic production, more than a fourfold increase for imports and a twofold jump for exports since 1960 (see figure 1-6). Over time, the imbalance in import and export growth has led to a deterioration in the trade balance and a weakening in U.S. shares in world markets. It has also adversely affected the profitability of the manufacturing sector and the well-being of its workers.

TRADE BALANCE

After remaining positive from 1893 until 1970, the merchandise trade balance turned negative in 1971 and has shown generally increasing deficits since then (see figure 1-7). While the overall trade balance was affected by sharp changes in commodity prices, particularly oil, the balance for manufactured goods shrank from a traditional strong surplus in the early 1960s to

Figure 1-5

Shares of World Trade, 1960, 1970, 1980

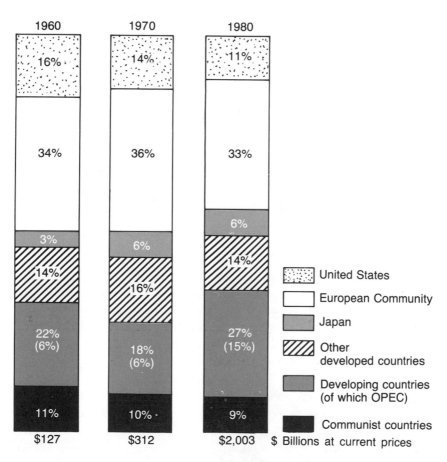

Source: U.S. Department of Commerce, International Trade Administration, *U.S. Competitiveness in the International Economy*, October 1981.

Figure 1-6

Relative Growth of Exports and Imports as a Share of Production, 1960-79

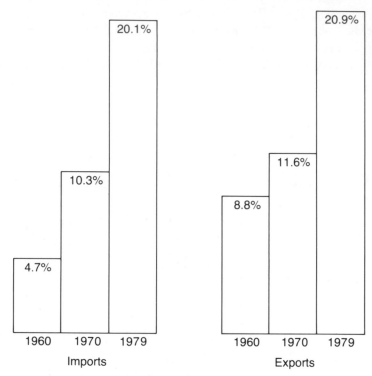

Source: U.S. Department of Commerce, International Trade Administration, *U.S. Competitiveness in the International Economy*, October 1981.

approximate balance by the late 1970s. The trade picture is far from uniformly negative, however. Investment income reflecting earnings on foreign direct investment and foreign loans has been a major contributor of foreign exchange (see figure 1-8). Net service income has also been traditionally positive, but it remains a small fraction of investment income.

Clearly the trade account has deteriorated; service earnings have not been enough to offset it; and investment income, while very significant and continually positive, is due more to our investments abroad than to America's desirability as a place in which to locate a plant or to do business. Likewise, writedowns of loans or concessionary interest rates seem likely to reduce the income to be derived from a considerable fraction of the LDC loans made by U.S. banks. Nonetheless, in examining the trade balance, the Council of Economic Advisers found reasons for reassurance.

The perception of diminished U.S. competitiveness stems not only from the trade deficit but from the impression that U.S. trade performance compares poorly with that of other countries, especially that of Japan. Japan runs a huge surplus in its manufactures trade, while the U.S. runs only a small one, and Japan also has a large surplus in its bilateral trade with the United States. . . . The main explanation of Japan's surplus in manufactures trade and in trade with the United States is that Japan, with few natural resources, incurs huge deficits in its trade in primary products, especially oil, and with primary producers, especially OPEC [see figure 1-11].[4]

According to the CEA the appropriate measure of competitiveness was not so much the overall balance in manufactured goods, in which the Japanese were steadily increasing their surplus with the United States in part to offset their shortage of raw materials, but rather in measurements of the merchandise balance's *composition* (see figure 1-9). Here, the council argued, the U.S. economy showed strength and was performing as trade theory indicated.

During the 1970s the United States developed an increasing surplus in areas in which it already enjoyed a comparative advantage and developed increasing deficits in areas in which it was at a disadvantage [see table 1-1].

Specialization of this kind is desirable both for the U.S. and for its trading partners. Specialization and trade raise the efficiency of the world economy as a whole by allowing each country to concentrate on doing what it does relatively well, and by allowing increased economies of scale.[5]

Figure 1-7

Trade Balance, United States, 1967-81

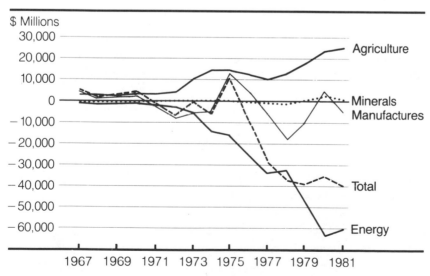

Source: Researcher's calculations based on data from CEPII

Figure 1-8

Structural Changes in the Current Account Balance

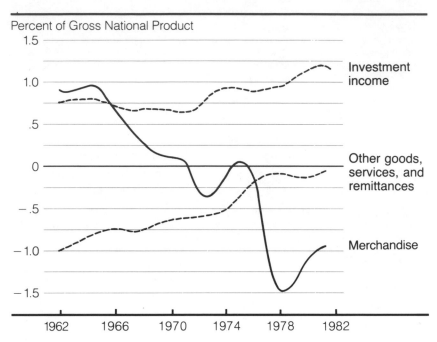

Source: U.S. Department of Commerce
Note: Data are sixteen-quarter weighted centered moving averages.

The CEA noted that U.S. advantages occur in research-intensive products, in resource-intensive products other than fuels, and in foreign investments. Trade in agricultural and mineral products also remains positive, with agricultural exports a particularly strong area (see figure 1-7). However, with agriculture directly accounting for about three million jobs and mining another million compared with some twenty million in manufacturing, the essential issue of U.S. competitiveness is obviously the performance of the latter.

A chart showing the evolution of U.S. trade balances by level of technology from 1962 through 1979 supports the CEA's belief that the United States is adjusting well (see figure 1-10). The CEA's conclusion that the U.S. pattern was good for the United States and the world is thus critically important both as an empirical observation and as an expression of theory. This chapter will review the data, the next chapter will consider the theory.

Figure 1-9

Composition of Trade, 1980

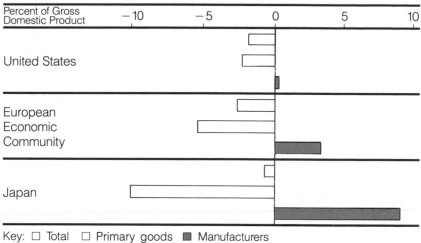

Key: □ Total □ Primary goods ■ Manufacturers

Source: Organization for Economic Cooperation and Development (OECD)

Table 1-1

U.S. Trade Balances by Sector as Percent of GDP, 1972 and 1979

Item	1972	1979
U.S. comparative advantage:		
Research-intensive manufactures	0.93	1.63
Resource-intensive products, other than fuels	.06	.67
Invisibles (services and investment income)	.40	1.44
U.S. comparative disadvantage:		
Nonresearch-intensive manufactures	−1.27	−1.44
Fuels	−.27	−2.41

Source: Council of Economic Advisers, *Economic Report of the President*, 1983, 58.

EXPORT MARKET SHARES FOR MANUFACTURED GOODS

Although the rapid growth of U.S. net export balances in high technology areas might seem at first to indicate comparative advantage, the United States has been losing market share in most of these categories to other industrialized competitors, though not as rapidly as it has been losing share in manufacturing as a whole. The U.S. share of manufactured exports, measured in

Figure 1-10

U.S. Trade Balances in R&D-intensive Manufactured Goods, Non-R&D-intensive
Manufactured Goods, and Transportation Equipment

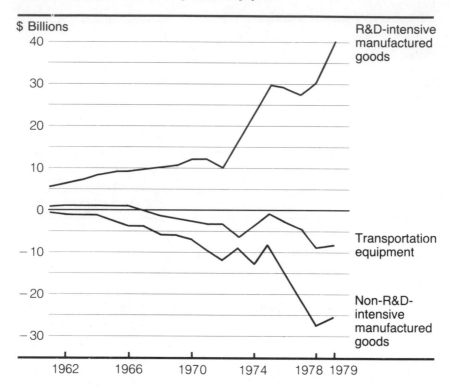

Source: *Science Indicators*, 1978; U.S. Department of Commerce; Domestic and International
Business Administration, *Overseas Business Reports*, August 1967, April 1972, April 1977,
June 1978, August 1979. 1979 data preliminary.
Note: R&D-intensive manufactured goods include chemicals, nonelectrical machinery, electrical
machinery, aircraft, professional, and scientific instruments. Transportation equipment refers to
motor vehicles and parts. Non-R&D-intensive includes food products, metals and fabrication,
other manufacturing.

terms of value, declined steadily from 1960 to 1980, with the most rapid
drop occurring from 1968 to 1973, or just prior to and along with the drop
in the dollar in the early seventies (see figure 1-11). U.S. share of high
technology exports had also declined using this measure (see figure 1-12).
Figure 1-13 breaks the comparison down further, taking the top ten high
technology categories for the years 1965, 1970, and 1980. This shows that
from 1970 to 1980, the United States (1) gained significant market share
only in agricultural chemicals (a relatively small category); (2) held share or

gained slightly in two categories (engines and plastics); and (3) lost share in the remaining seven, though it typically retained a high share (especially in aircraft and office machines). Thus, while America's net export balance for high technology products grew in absolute terms, reflecting aggregate increases in world trade, our competitiveness in these crucial areas actually eroded overall during the 1970s. The rise of the dollar since 1981 has brought an increase in terms of value and a drop in terms of volume, an issue to which we will return.

PROFITABILITY AND LIQUIDITY

Turning from market share to profitability reveals a further cause for concern. As indicated by figure 1-14, U.S. firms were experiencing declining profitability while they were losing market share. For most of the period since 1970 the return on total assets (before interest and taxes) in the manufacturing sector has shown little or no premium over the return on industrial

Figure 1-11

Market Shares of Manufactures, 1960-80

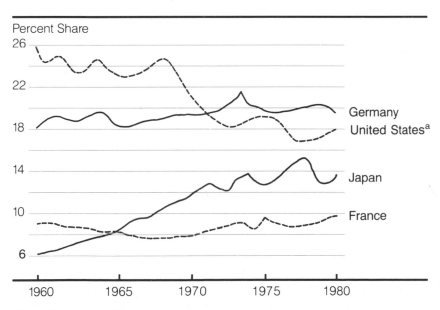

Source: Department of Commerce
Note: Exports from eighteen industrial countries
[a]Excluding imports to the United States

Figure 1-12

Market Shares of High Technology Manufactures

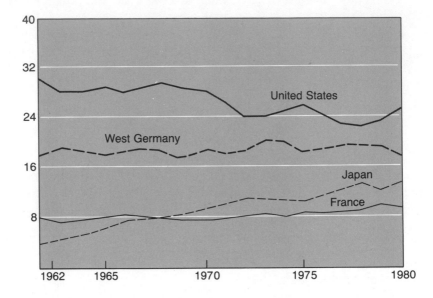

Source: U.S. Department of Commerce, International Trade Administration, from UN series D Trade Data.
Note: The industrial countries are: Austria, Belgium, Canada, Denmark, France, Italy, Japan, Luxembourg, Netherlands, Norway, Sweden, Switzerland, United Kingdom, United States, and West Germany.

bonds and, since 1979, the "risk premium" for being in business has been negative (see figure 1-15). In addition, the balance sheets of U.S. firms were deteriorating, and by 1982 they were the weakest since World War II (see figure 1-16). European and, to a lesser degree, Japanese firms also showed declining profitability during this period. Unfortunately, differences in accounting and reporting practices make direct comparisons difficult, both for profitability and balance sheet ratios. But the U.S. position has clearly deteriorated over time.

Not all of the deterioration can be attributed to international competition. In many industries, exports and imports are still a small share of total activity. However, for commodity products like oil, imports of 5-10 percent of internal demand may be enough to influence the price, as long as the market is open to additional imports. For less price-sensitive products the figure may well be higher, but with exports and imports averaging some 20 percent of domestic supply, some impact on prices from foreign competition must be accepted as a major force in most, if not all, industries.

Figure 1-13

U.S. Share of World High Technology Exports[a]

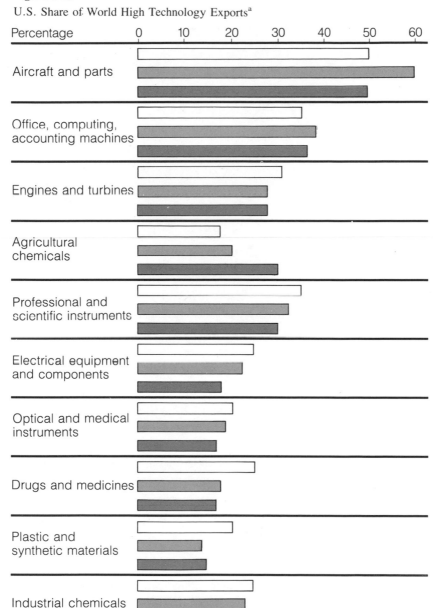

Key: ☐ 1965   ▨ 1970   ■ 1980

Source: U.S. Department of Commerce
[a]The world is defined as fifteen major industrial countries.

Figure 1-14

Rates of Return on Capital

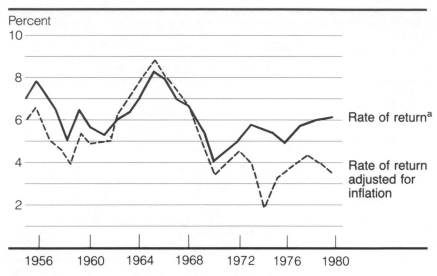

Source: U.S. Department of Commerce, Bureau of Economic Analysis, unpublished data.

Note: Rate of return = $\dfrac{\text{Corporate profit after taxes}}{\text{Net capital stock (including inventory) valued at current (replacement) costs}}$

[a]Rate of return on capital for nonfinancial corporations

Declining profitability of U.S. industry comes in part from price pressure by imports entering the U.S. market, and also in part from pressures to keep prices of exports competitive in a world market. Declining profitability was a particularly negative symptom in the 1970s, a decade when the dollar was depreciating against the currencies of most of our major trading partners. The dollar declined in real as well as nominal terms in the 1970s; U.S. costs declined in like measure, and profits should have risen sharply. The period 1977-79, when the dollar was thought to be sharply undervalued, should have been a bonanza—at least for exports and export profitability. Instead, the data suggest that profitability turned downward even before the 1980 recession and deteriorated dramatically in the face of recession followed by the rise of the dollar in 1981. This seems to indicate a productivity problem.

PRODUCTIVITY, INVESTMENT, AND EMPLOYMENT

Manufacturing productivity growth in the United States lagged behind such important competitors as Germany and Japan (see figure 1-17). While there

are probably many reasons for the weak U.S. performance, a low and
declining level of net capital formation appears to be a major factor. Gross
private investment actually rose in relation to GNP during the 1970s, along
with gross business spending for plant and equipment (see table 1-2). However, depreciation rose even more rapidly, reflecting both a shift of investment
away from plant toward equipment and the shorter economic life of equipment. As a result, net investment in plant and equipment fell from a high of
4 percent of GNP in the 1966-70 period, to 3.1 percent from 1971 to 1975,
and to 2.9 percent from 1976 to 1980 (see table 1-2). The decline was
widespread and was not the result of disaster in a few sectors (see table
1-3). The growth rate of net fixed investment per worker and per hour of
time worked deteriorated even more sharply, to .4 percent and .9 percent
respectively, compared with an average of 2.6 and 3 percent for the period
1951-80 (see table 1-4).

According to the Council of Economic Advisers:

> [T]he decline in the growth rate of the capital stock is understated by the net
> investment figures in [table 1-4]. The energy price shocks of 1973 and 1979
> hastened the obsolescence of a variety of past investments, which implies [that]

Figure 1-15

Rate of Return on Total Assets in Manufacturing, Corporate Bond Rate, and Prime
Rate, 1960-82

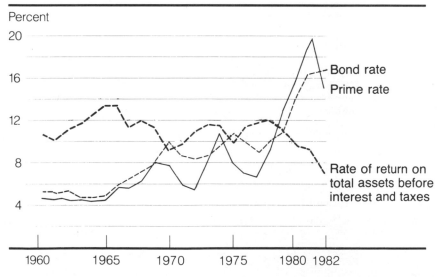

Source: Federal Trade Commission, *Quarterly Financial Report for Manufacturing Corporations*, various issues. Council of Economic Advisers, *Economic Report of the President*, February 1983.

Figure 1-16

Corporate Balance Sheets, 1955-82

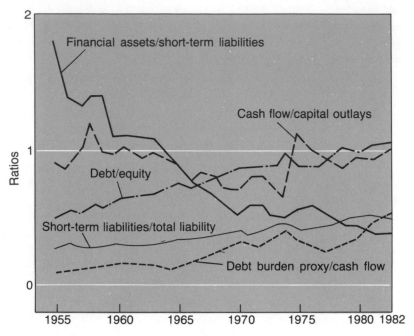

Source: Allen Sinai and Andrew Lin, "Business Liquidity, Reliquification, and Spending," Data Resources, Inc., July 1983, 122.

the actual depreciation was greater than the official statistics suggest. . . . In addition, it is important to recall that much of the investment in the 1970s took place in the energy-producing sector. The share of GNP devoted to net fixed nonresidential investment outside the energy sector averaged only 1.8% between 1975 and 1980.[6]

Concern for America's lagging levels of investment is also borne out by international comparisons (see table 1-5). As the CEA noted: "The share of U.S. gross domestic product (GDP) devoted to net fixed investment during the last decade was only 34% of the comparable share in Japan and 56% of the comparable share in Germany. No other major industrial nation devotes as small a fraction of total output to new investment as does the United States."[7]

Though pessimistic, this appraisal probably did not go far enough, because throughout its analyses of international competition the CEA limited its comparisons to the largest industrial countries, all but one of which are in the North Atlantic area. For example:

If U.S. workers. . .were to receive real wage increases equal to those granted in other countries while their productivity failed to increase at a comparable rate, U.S. industry would find itself increasingly uncompetitive. The fact is, however, that this did not occur, as the comparative experience of the United States and the European Economic Community illustrates.

From 1973 to 1980 output per manufacturing worker in the European Economic Community rose at an annual rate of 2.7%, but real compensation rose at a rate of 4.1%. By contrast, output per worker in the U.S. rose 1.1% annually,

Figure 1-17

Manufacturing Productivity: Japan, United States, and West Germany, 1965-81 (Index, 1965 = 100)

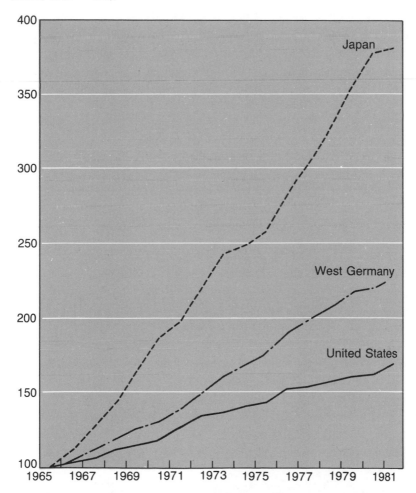

Source: Otto Eckstein, *The DRI Report on U.S. Manufacturing Industries* (New York: McGraw Hill Book Company, 1984).

Table 1-2
U.S. Gross and Net Investment, 1956–82 (% of GNP)

	1956–60	1961–65	1966–70	1971–75	1976–80	1981	1982
Gross private domestic investment	15.4%	15.3%	15.5%	15.7%	16.5%	16.0%	13.7%
Plant and equipment	9.9	9.5	10.6	10.4	11.2	11.8	11.4
Depreciation	7.3	6.6	6.6	7.3	8.3	9.0	9.4
Net investment	2.6	2.9	4.0	3.1	2.9	2.8	2.0
Residential construction	5.0	4.8	3.8	4.6	4.6	3.6	3.1
Inventory accumulation	0.6	1.0	1.1	0.7	0.7	0.7	−0.8

Source: U.S. Department of Commerce
Note: Data are averages (except for 1981 and 1982) of annual flows, as percentages of annual GNP. Detail may not add to total because of rounding.

while real compensation rose only 1.8% annually. In fact, until the recent rise in the dollar's exchange rate, it was workers in the European Economic Community, rather than those in the United States, who were probably pricing themselves out of the world market in spite of their relatively good productivity performance.[8]

The members of the European Economic Community are in worse competitive shape than the United States.[9] While the United States has suffered a drop in productivity growth, the major European economies have suffered a net loss of industrial jobs, including manufacturing jobs (see figure 1-18)—a loss that appears to start before 1973. We often forget that their rapid growth in earlier years came partly from undervalued exchange rates, particularly in Germany, and that undervaluation led to investments and jobs and growth that never should have been realized in the first place. For example, an undervalued exchange rate led to construction of plant capacity in Germany that with a more normal exchange rate would have been built elsewhere to begin with. The EEC's dramatic slowdown in economic growth and rise in unemployment to about a 10 percent average is in part the result of more normal competitive conditions, in part the result of noncompetitive strategies launched since World War II, especially in the high-growth era of the 1960s. While the CEA may be right in noting that the Europeans were pricing themselves out of the market, this does not mean that U.S. producers were not also.

AFTER-TAX EARNINGS OF WORKERS

Even with the recent recession, American's per capita income and output levels have risen in real terms and have remained ahead of those of most

Table 1-3
Annual Growth Rates of Real Net Capital Stock per Employee in Manufacturing, 1966–80

Industry Group	1966–70	1971–75	1976–80
1. Aircraft and parts	9.5%	1.0%	−4.3%
2. Office, computing, accounting	.9	4.0	0.9
3. Electronic components	8.9	7.6	−1.2
4. Drugs and medicines	3.1	2.7	2.6
5. Professional and scientific instruments	5.1	3.9	2.7
6. Engines and turbines	6.9	7.1	3.6
7. Plastics and synthetics	4.7	7.5	3.0
8. Electric industrial apparatus	8.9	3.6	2.1
9. Electrical transmission and distribution equipment	8.1	3.1	−0.6
10. Agricultural chemicals	7.7	5.8	3.0
11. Motor vehicles and equipment	7.1	11.4	12.8
12. Industrial chemicals	4.0	3.6	2.3
13. Farm machinery and equipment	7.2	1.1	5.6
14. Construction, mining, material handling	4.8	4.9	5.5
15. Industries not shown elsewhere	4.7	6.2	2.6
16. Electric equipment, n.e.c.[a]	4.9	7.6	3.0
17. Fabricated metal products	4.7	5.1	2.9
18. Transportation equipment, execept motor vehicles	4.4	4.0	3.6
19. Nonelectrical machinery, n.e.c.	5.6	3.8	1.5
20. Rubber and miscellaneous plastics	6.1	6.4	2.2
21. Radio and TV	13.3	11.3	5.0
22. Metalworking machinery	6.5	0.7	−0.4
23. Chemicals, n.e.c.	4.2	6.5	2.8
24. Stone-clay-glass products	3.8	4.8	3.5
25. Petroleum refining	4.3	4.9	2.0
26. Nonferrous metals	6.8	7.4	6.7
27. Ferrous metals	4.8	2.1	1.9
28. Textile mill products	4.8	7.3	3.2
29. Food and kindred products	3.3	5.3	4.2
All manufacturing	5.1	5.4	2.3

Source: CEC Associates, *Manufacturing Industry Time Series*. Data prepared for the U.S. Department of Commerce, Washington, D.C., July 1983.
[a] n.e.c. = not elsewhere classified

other industrialized nations (see table 1-6). In addition, despite inflation, real per capita disposable income has also followed an upward trend (see figure 1-19). On the other hand, the real per capita "spendable" (after-tax) earnings of American working people (excluding farmers) have been declining since

Table 1-4

Alternative Measures of Capital Formation, 1951–82

	Net Private Domestic Investment as Percent of GNP		Growth Rate of Net Capital Stock[a]	
Period	*Total Investment*	*Nonresidential Fixed Investment*	*Per Worker*[b]	*Per Hour*[b]
1951–55	7.2	2.9	3.1	3.5
1956–60	6.1	2.6	3.5	4.1
1961–65	6.7	2.9	2.5	2.4
1966–70	7.1	4.0	3.9	4.9
1971–75	6.4	3.1	2.2	2.6
1976–80	6.0	2.9	.4	.9
1951–80	6.6	3.1	2.6	3.0
1981	4.8	2.8	3.3	4.5
1982[c]	2.1	2.0	na	na

Source: U.S. Department of Commerce (Bureau of Economic Analysis), U.S. Department of Labor (Bureau of Labor Statistics), and Council of Economic Advisers.
[a]Real net private nonresidential fixed capital stock at year-end
[b]All persons in private business sector. Year-end obtained by averaging fourth quarter value with value for first quarter of subsequent year.
[c]Preliminary

Table 1-5

Comparison of Capital Formation in Six OECD Countries, 1971–80

	Investment as Percent of GDP			*Growth Rate of Output per Hour in Manufacturing*
Country	*Gross Investment*	*Gross Fixed Investment*	*Net Fixed Investment*	
France	24.2%	22.9%	12.2%	4.8%
Germany	23.7	22.8	11.8	4.9
Italy	22.4	20.1	10.7	4.9
Japan	34.0	32.9	19.5	7.4
United Kingdom	19.2	18.7	8.1	2.9
United States	19.1	18.4	6.6	2.5

Source: OECD

the all-time peak year of 1972 (see figure 1-19). According to Robert U. Ayres: "By the end of 1981, when the U.S. Department of Labor stopped compiling the figures, American nonfarm workers had 17 percent less spendable income than they had in 1972 and less than any time since 1959."[10]

Figure 1-18

Comparison of Manufacturing or Industrial Employment

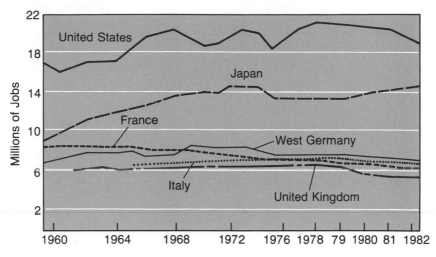

Source: OECD, *Main Economic Indicators*, September 1983.

Table 1-6

Gross National Product and GNP per Capita, Selected Countries, 1960–82

			GNP[a] (1980 prices)		GNP per Capita[a] (1980 prices)	
			Average Annual Growth Rates[a]			
	GNP 1982 ($bil.)	GNP per Capita 1982 ($)	1960–70	1970–82	1960–70	1970–82
United States	3,073	13,247	3.9%	2.6%	2.6%	1.6%
Germany	660	10,691	4.5	2.2	3.6	2.1
France	659[b]	12,277[b]	5.5	3.0[d]	4.4	3.0[d]
United Kingdom	473	8,481	2.9	1.3	2.3	1.3
Sweden	97	11,614	4.6	1.4	3.8	1.1
Japan	1,197	10,099	11.2	4.6	10.1	3.5
Korea	66	1,679	8.3	7.8	5.5	6.0
Singapore	13[c]	5,063[c]	9.2	8.3[d]	6.6	6.9[d]

Source: International Monetary Fund, *International Financial Statistics*, December 1982, November 1983.
[a]1980 prices, in national currencies.
[b]1981 statistics; exchange rate in 1981 was $5.43 francs per dollar. In 1982, the exchange rate was 6.57 francs per dollar; if per capita GNP in French francs remained unchanged in 1982, its equivalent in dollar terms would have been $10,146.
[c]1981 statistics
[d]1970–81

Figure 1-19

Trends in Real, After-Tax Incomes, United States, 1950-82

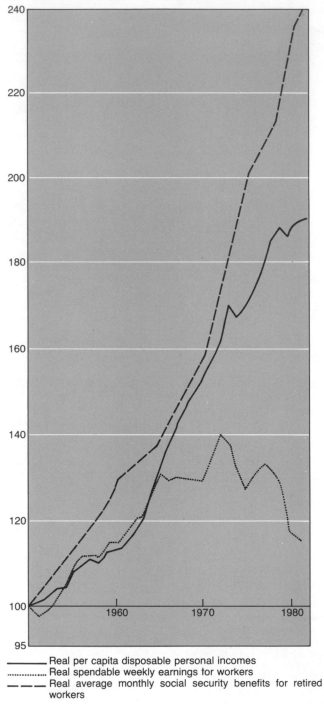

——————— Real per capita disposable personal incomes

·············· Real spendable weekly earnings for workers

— — — Real average monthly social security benefits for retired
workers

The striking difference between rising per capita disposable income for all Americans and declining real spendable earnings appears to be due to four main factors: increased participation in the labor force, the creation of a large number of low-paying service jobs, dramatic increases in real incomes for those not working (for example, those retired on social security), and the increased fraction of worker incomes absorbed by income and social security taxes. Participation in the labor force stood at 60.4 percent in 1970, up from 59.2 percent two decades earlier. During the 1970s it rose steadily and by 1982 it was at 64 percent, a new all-time high.[11]

As real spendable earnings for workers began to level off in the mid-1960s, the gap between the average take-home pay of workers and social security payments for retired workers shrank from more than 5 to 1 ratio to about 2 to 1 (see figure 1-20). Bracket creep and rising social security taxes cut take-home pay for those who worked, but not the incomes of those on social security. While the rise in retirement benefits is mostly a positive development, since 1972 the American economy has not been competitive enough to provide even stable take-home pay for its labor force.

An international comparison of earnings of manufacturing workers over the last two decades suggests that U.S. performance has been particularly unfavorable. While the manufacturing labor force in Japan, Germany, France, and even the United Kingdom experienced significant gains in real hourly earnings, their U.S. counterparts experienced only moderate increases which plateaued and then declined in the late 1970s (see figure 1-21). In Japan, nonagricultural workers have enjoyed almost a 25 percent gain in their real after-tax earnings since 1971, while average disposable income rose still more. In the United States, in contrast, nonagricultural workers suffered a decline in their real after-tax earnings (see figure 1-22).

The essential point is that the dramatic rise in real incomes for those on social security was not "earned"; it was achieved through the political process. The rising benefit levels reflected a series of decisions to increase benefits far more rapidly than contributions, and to index the benefits to prices rather than wages. The increased benefits were financed in part by declining military spending and then—in the 1980s—by public borrowing on a scale not previously witnessed in peacetime. In part, then, these rising incomes were being borrowed from the next generation. In this most important measure, Americans subject to the competitive pressures of the market-

---

Source: Based on statistics reported in *The Economic Report of the President*, Council of Economic Advisers, Washington, D.C., February 1982; *Supplement to Employment and Earnings, Revised Establishment Data*, Bureau of Labor Statistics, Washington, D.C., August 1981; and *Social Security Bulletin*, Social Security Administration, U.S. Department of Health and Human Services, Washington, D.C., May 1983.

Figure 1-20

Real Average Spendable Monthly Earnings for Workers and Real Monthly Social
Security Benefits for Retired Workers, 1950-82[a] (1972 dollars)

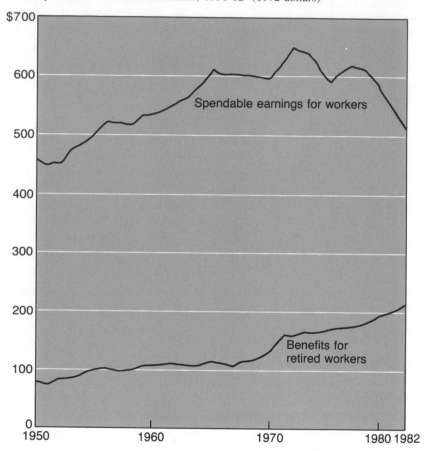

Source: Based on statistics reported in *Supplement to Employment and Earnings, Revised
Establishment Data*, Bureau of Labor Statistics, August 1981; and *Social Security Bulletin*,
Social Security Administration, U.S. Department of Health and Human Services, Washington,
D.C., May 1983.
[a]Series for spendable earnings stopped in 1981.

place were suffering declining incomes, while those receiving transfer payments continued to enjoy increases. Rising *average* incomes are thus not
indicative of U.S. competitiveness. Declining earnings in the competitive
sector and rising borrowed incomes for those insulated from the market
indicated weak performance on the one hand, and a consume now, pay later
strategy on the other, a point to which we will return in the next chapter.

Figure 1-21

Indexes of Average Real Hourly Earnings of Production Workers in Manufacturing, Selected Countries, 1960-81 (1960 = 100)

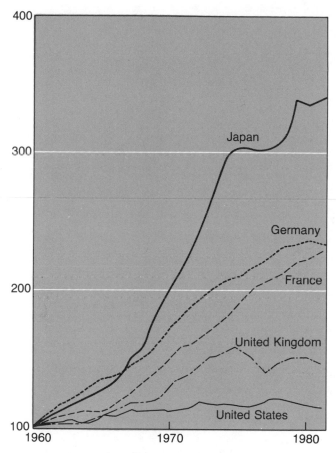

Source: *Handbook of Labor Statistics, 1980*, U.S. Department of Labor, Washington, D.C.; *Historical Statistics, 1960-1981*, OECD, Paris, 1983.

EXPLANATIONS FOR DECLINING U.S. PERFORMANCE

Broadly speaking, there are four major explanations for the deterioration of U.S. competitiveness. One view is that the exchange rate is the culprit: an overvalued dollar continues to overprice U.S. goods in world markets. Some but not all advocates of this explanation add that the yen is also undervalued, and therefore two adjustments are needed rather than just one.

Figure 1-22

Real Average Disposable Personal Income and Real Average Earnings for Nonagricultural Workers, United States and Japan, 1971-81 (1971 = 100)

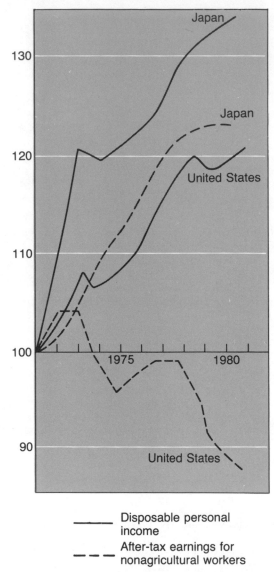

_____ Disposable personal income

_ _ _ After-tax earnings for nonagricultural workers

Source: Council of Economic Advisers, *Economic Report of the President*, Washington, D.C., February 1983. Economic Planning Agency, *Annual Report on National Accounts*, Tokyo, Japan, various editions. International Labor Office, *Yearbook of Labor Statistics*, Geneva, 1983. OECD, *Main Economic Indicators, Historical Statistics*, Paris, 1983.

Overvaluation results in part from macroeconomic mismanagement, that is, the budget deficits, tight money, and high interest rates since late 1980—but also in part from the dollar's role as a reserve currency and the fact that the United States is a safe haven for capital.[12]

Proponents of a second view assert that mismanagement of business enterprise is the heart of the problem: complacent managers of U.S. firms have allowed competitors, and particularly Japanese competitors, to pull ahead in cost or quality or both. American managers—who were leaders in introducing the divisionalized firm to manage diversified operations in the 1960s and who pioneered strategic planning in the 1970s—are alleged to be a growing source of competitive weakness. An excessive concern with analysis and planning, internal structure, and short-term results has pushed the interest in innovative manufacturing processes and high-quality products into the background.

A third group says that incoherent, noncompetitive U.S. policies and institutions are the major source of our problems. In terms of remedies, this group claims we need a coherent industrial policy as an essential step in competing with the "successful" industrial policies of other countries. Industrial policy is thus seen more as a sensible way to compete than as an unfair trade practice.

A fourth group emphasizes the need to learn from the economic strategies of some of our competitors, such as Japan, France, and Brazil. Business-government cooperation in such countries pits U.S. firms against government-backed competitors. As a result, the rules of the economic game are no longer the same, and U.S. companies are at a disadvantage.

Each of these views has some merit. The question is, how much? One approach to an answer is to attempt to rank the four in order of importance. While there is a logic to such an approach, such a ranking would be misleading at best. The essence of good analysis is to keep all four in mind as we compare a largely implicit U.S. economic strategy with the typically more explicit strategies of our competitors. To understand the problem, we need to see how all four (and other) causes affect one another, and not treat them as if they were separate, unrelated phenomena.

The analytic task of evaluating the extent and causes of relative decline is critically influenced by our choice of which countries we consider our most relevant competitors, and our theory of international specialization and trade. For example, if we see traditional North Atlantic rivals as our major competitors, the exchange rate obviously is a problem whose solution has a high priority. If we find our key competitors in East Asia, perhaps gradually spreading to include other newly industrializing countries, then the exchange rate seems much less important—and less easy—to correct. Evaluating the various explanations hinges on choosing the appropriate points of reference and the appropriate theory by which to interpret and weigh the evidence in the following.

MACROECONOMIC MISMANAGEMENT

Those who hold that an overvalued dollar is the crux of the problem typically argue that (1) the only competitiveness problem is the exchange rate; (2) the exchange rate results from an unfortunate mix of monetary and fiscal policies in the United States rather than from any particular policies pursued abroad; and (3) the essential remedy is to sharply reduce the deficits so that they will not absorb an inordinate share of net savings in a situation where steady monetary policy prevails. The CEA took this position in its 1983 report, noting that ". . . large projected U.S. trade deficits are a result of macroeconomic forces, particularly large budget deficits. The main sources of the U.S. trade deficit are not to be found in Paris or Tokyo, but in Washington."[13]

Having focused its review of U.S. competitiveness on comparisons with West European countries, to the neglect of those in East Asia, the CEA concluded that ". . . the overall performance of the United States . . . does not suggest a long-term problem of competitiveness. The shift from persistent trade surplus to persistent deficit which occurred over the last decade is, however, often misinterpreted as a sign of an inability to compete."[14]

Certainly an overvalued dollar has hurt U.S. trade, employment, and corporate profitability since 1981, and an overvalued dollar is likely to continue to do enormous damage to all three for as long as it persists. We need, however, to take a closer look at U.S. trade performance during the 1970s in relation to the changing exchange rate. Data from the International Monetary Fund suggest that there was already a problem in that decade. The U.S. share of world exports declined steadily in the 1960s, both in value and in volume (see figure 1-23), but the erosion in volume terms was reversed in 1971, presumably with the devaluation and subsequent floating of the dollar. The depreciation of the dollar by more than 20 percent between 1970 and 1979 allowed the United States to increase its market share in volume terms from less than 14 percent to more than 16 percent, while it continued to lose share in value terms (see figure 1-24).

Figure 1-23

U.S. Share of World Exports (volume share in 1960 U.S. dollars)

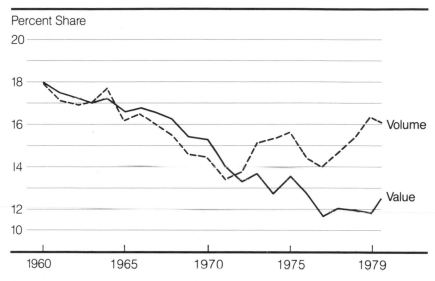

Source. International Monetary Fund, *International Financial Statistics*, as shown by U S Department of Commerce in "An Assessment of U.S. Competitiveness in High Technology Industries," February 1983.

Robert Lawrence has analyzed the impact of the exchange rate on U.S. trade during this period:

> Over the decade, U.S. relative export [prices] as measured by the IMF declined by 13.8%. In the absence of this decline, the equations imply that U.S. export volumes in 1980 would have been about 20% less than they actually were. Similarly, without the rise in relative prices of imports of 22%, the dollar value of U.S.-manufactured imports would have been about 21% higher.[15]

This analysis suggests that the United States would have recovered little, if any, market share in volume terms without the continuing slide of the dollar. Erosion of the dollar reduced U.S. costs in international markets. U.S. producers could use this opportunity either to reduce prices or raise profits or some combination of the two.

By reducing export prices, the United States gained market share by one measure, slowed the loss of share by another, and suffered declining profitability at the same time. Declining share and declining profitability, taken together, are unmistakable signs of weakness, not signs of healthy competitiveness.

Figure 1-24

Nominal and Real Effective Exchange Rate of the U.S. Dollar, 1973-83
(March 1973 = 100)

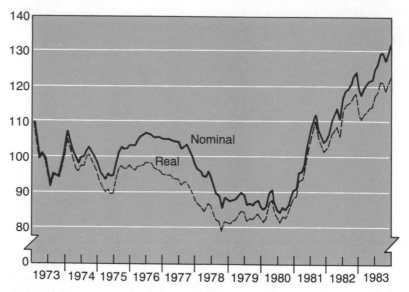

Source: Board of Governors of the Federal Reserve System. Excerpted from *Economic Report of the President*, Council of Economic Advisers, Washington, D.C., February 1984, 46.

This macroeconomic argument is important, but it has more bearing on the 1980s than on the 1970s. Loose monetary policy from 1977 to 1979 resulted in a worldwide glut of dollars, a negative interest rate in real terms, and an artificially low exchange rate, which disguised the increasing competitive weakness of U.S. industry. The overvalued dollar of the 1980s has exaggerated that weakness but is not its sole, or necessarily major, cause. Continued overvaluation of the dollar in the 1980s, however, will do untold damage to U.S. industry and to the employment prospects of the U.S. labor force. Many manufacturing operations that move overseas in search of lower cost locations will stay there even if the dollar returns to a more reasonable level.

COMPLACENT BUSINESS

Have some of the world's leading corporations become overly rigid in their manufacturing methods and unduly short-term oriented in their planning? Critics say yes and point to inadequate attention to product quality, insufficient product and process innovation, and an excessive emphasis on quarterly earnings per share—a very short-run measure of performance. Managerial shortcomings, they say, were in part a product of business school curricula that, like mutual fund managers, emphasized portfolio management and the buying and selling of businesses rather than the development and manufacture of products. This new school of management has appropriately been called "paper entrepreneurship."[16]

The poor performance of U.S. industry in terms of productivity growth seems to lend support to this argument. The United States was almost alone among industrial nations in increasing manufacturing employment in the 1970s while productivity improvement was far behind that of its competitors. This performance was so typical and so widespread, however, as to suggest that nearly all major companies somehow became complacent at about the same time, a possibility that implies more uniformity than one would expect. A recent "Report on U.S. Manufacturing Industries" by Data Resources, Inc., raises a similar doubt concerning the poor management theory as an explanation for declining U.S. competitiveness.[17]

Nevertheless, a growing body of case-study evidence supports this poor management theory, and many corporate executives will privately admit that their companies' performance deteriorated. Such testimony, though persuasive, is difficult to evaluate quantitatively. Together, however, the "insider" reports and the "outsider" analyses suggest that mismanagement has had a profound impact on the competitiveness of such significant industries as air conditioners, automobiles, machine tools, steel, and televisions.[18]

Once the issue has been identified and acknowledged, the question is whether the situation will improve. Again, there is no systematic evidence, but these same business executives indicate that the severity of the 1980-82 recession spurred their firms to initiate corrective actions. These ranged from emphasizing product quality and improved employee relations to sharply reducing white collar staff. Time is needed to see if these responses were a more or less normal reaction to recession or represent more fundamental change. Based on present indications it would seem that the reactions represent a good deal more than a "business as usual" response.

U.S. POLICIES AND INSTITUTIONS

Managements' ability to employ corrective measures will depend partly on factors in the U.S. business environment, including management of aggregate demand, the collective bargaining process, capital allocation, antitrust laws, educational policies, and environmental regulations. These factors affect our international competitiveness as well as our domestic corporate performance.

It is only in the last few years that there has been much serious debate about the competitive impact of U.S. policies and institutions. For decades we have essentially taken our overall competitiveness for granted. With competitiveness assumed if not necessarily assured, U.S. economic policy has been oriented to smoothing the business cycle, increasing economic security, and improving the distribution of income. "Supply-side" tax cuts like the one in 1964 must not be overlooked, but they have been relatively minor compared to the spending commitments inherent in the Employment Act of 1946, the Great Society programs of the 1960s, or the indexing of major entitlements to inflation during the Nixon administration.

Those who are now called industrial policy advocates have taken the lead in questioning the competitiveness of U.S. policies and institutions. They have correctly identified an existing but implicit industrial policy character-ized by ad hoc decision making, lack of an explicit strategy, and an adver-sarial set of relationships that inhibit development of an explicit strategy. They rightly point out that instead of dealing with our competitive problems by accelerating the adjustment process, the United States has responded with a mixture of protectionism at home and prosecution or threats of prosecution for unfair trade practices by foreigners. The need, they point out, is not only an explicit strategy, but one that is both coherent and achieved democratically through an open political process.[19]

Those who point to an implicit, incoherent industrial policy as the critical problem see the United States as lagging behind the Europeans as well as the Japanese. To wit: "In the United States, promotion of growth industries has been random, but in Japan, Germany, and France, policy has focused on reducing costs or promoting industries with the greatest promise of inter-national competitiveness."[20] Our "major trading partners, particularly Japan and West Germany" have also been more active in easing the movement of capital and labor out of declining industries.[21]

The principal reasons why the United States has failed to respond as rationally as its leading industrial competitors lies in a combination of ide-ology and politics. "For [these reasons] the United States has failed to acknowledge the practical choices confronting it and has clung instead to the notion that government can and should be neutral with regard to market adjustments."[22]

From our perspective, however, the problem is not so much the incoherence of U.S. policies as their emphasis on promoting growth through promotion of domestic demand (e.g., government spending and personal consumption) in contrast to other countries which aim to promote growth through external demand (e.g., exports and the investments necessary to support them), and the much higher priority given to a direct governmental role in distributing the pie than in baking more or better pie—or both. From our vantage point, the short-term, consumption-oriented bias in U.S. strategy, not the lack of coherence of its various components, is the bigger problem; this is so particularly because of the change we perceive in who U.S. competitors are.

Were we to continue to compare ourselves with the democracies of the North Atlantic—a group of distribution-oriented welfare states—then one could look for greater or lesser inconsistency in broadly similar strategies. If, however, we see our key competitors as East Asian, then inconsistencies among the components of our strategy pale compared with the differences in the basic thrust of the respective strategies.

THE EAST ASIAN CHALLENGE

Comparing ourselves with the Europeans as the basis of a competitive analysis is like General Motors comparing itself with Ford and Chrysler while disregarding Toyota and Nissan. Like GM, the United States must begin to include the East Asians in its comparative analyses. South Korea, Taiwan, Hong Kong, and Singapore, with a total population of about 70 million and a combined GNP of $125 billion (1980), have surpassed any of the large European economies in importance as a trading partner (see figure 1-25). Despite the various quotas and orderly marketing agreement we have imposed, these newly industrialized countries (NICs) now have a much larger trade surplus with the United States than does the EEC (see figure 1-26).

These countries, like Japan, industrialized very rapidly after a late start. Although South Korea and Taiwan began to industrialize before World War II, none was a significant industrial exporter even in 1960. Since then, however, their rise has been spectacular. Investment in these areas has risen more in the last two decades than in the older industrial countries (see table 1-7) and now represents a more significant share of GDP than investment in the traditional industrial countries of the North Atlantic area (see table 1-8).

Japan and the "new Japans" have become more important as U.S. export markets than any of the major European countries and likewise are a more

Figure 1-25

U.S. Trade by Selected Countries, 1960-82

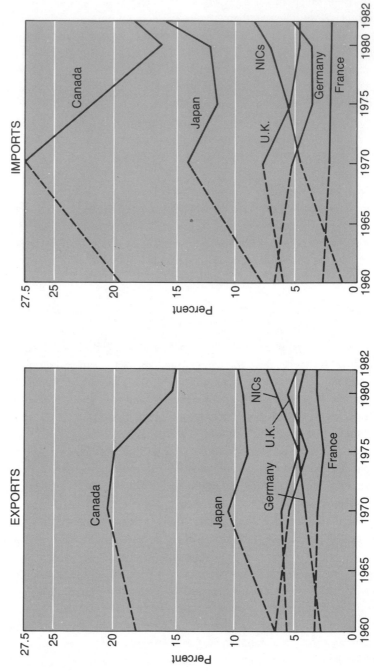

Source: International Monetary Fund, *The Direction of Trade Statistics*, various issues. U.S.
Bureau of Census, *Highlights of U.S. Export and Import Trade*, various issues.
Note: NICs = Taiwan, Hong Kong, Singapore, and South Korea.
Data not available for 1965; lines between 1960 and 1970 are approximations only.

Figure 1-26

U.S. Trade Balance in Manufactured Goods

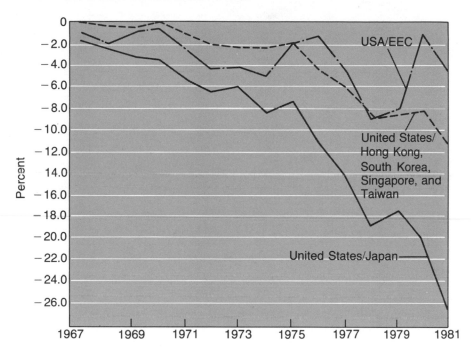

Source: Researcher's calculations based on data from CEPII

important source of U.S. imports. By 1982 the four NICs exported almost
twice as much to the United States as did Germany and four times as much
as France. Malaysia, the Philippines, and Thailand have also become important competitors in the U.S. market. While bilateral trade is far from the
only measure of competitiveness, and some of the shipments from East Asia
are part of the integrated supply networks of U.S. firms, these shipments
still reflect decisions to produce there and not here. Given the increasing
importance of our trade with East Asia and our increasing trade deficits there,
we should include these countries in our analyses. We must understand their
growing share of our market and their unceasing trade surplus with the U.S.
Japan is not our only problem.

The first step is to recognize that the pattern of exports from these East
Asian countries has changed rapidly, more rapidly than imaginable twenty
years ago. Figure 1-27 shows an extraordinary transition for South Korea

Table 1-7
Gross Domestic Investment (compound annual growth rate)

	1960–70	*1970–80*
West Germany	4.1%	1.6%
France	7.7	1.9
United Kingdom	5.0	.0
Italy	3.7	.5
Sweden	5.1	−.5
Belgium	6.0	1.5
Switzerland	3.9	−1.9
Denmark	7.9	−.6
United States	4.8	1.6
Canada	5.8	4.2
Japan	14.6	3.2
South Korea	23.6	13.4
Hong Kong	6.9	12.7
Singapore	20.5	6.7

Source: World Bank, World Development Report, 1982, table 4, 116–17.

Table 1-8
Gross Fixed Capital Formation/GDP, Selected Countries

	1960	*1970*	*1975*	*1980*
United States	17%	18%	17%	19%
Canada	22	21	24	23
France	20	23	23	22
West Germany	24	26	21	24
United Kingdom	16	19	20	18
Japan	30	36	32	32
South Korea	11	24	26	32
Hong Kong	26	19	19	28
Singapore	NA	33	35	39
Malaysia	11	16	25	26
Brazil	17	21	25	21

Source: United Nations, *Yearbook of National Accounts Statistics*, 1972, vol. 3, table 2A (for 1960); ibid. 1981, vol. 2, table 3 (for 1970, 1975, and 1980).

Figure 1-27

Manufactured Exports as Share of Country's Total Exports, 1960-79

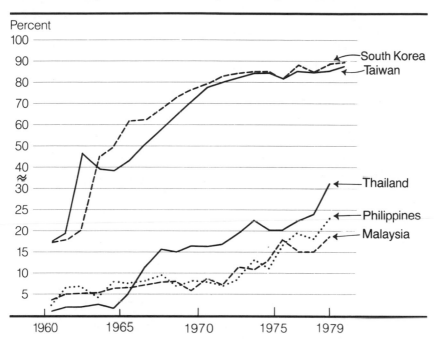

Source: Miyohei Shinohara, *Industrial Growth, Trade, and Dynamic Patterns in the Japanese Economy* (Tokyo: University of Tokyo Press, 1982), 88.

and Taiwan's manufactures, from less than 20 percent of exports in 1960 to more than 70 percent a decade later. Figure 1-28 shows the change in composition of those exports. Food, beverages, tobacco, and textiles are declining, while machinery exports are rising dramatically. If Thailand, Malaysia, and perhaps Indonesia and the Philippines follow this pattern of rapid industrialization, the newly industrialized countries of East Asia will soon have a population larger than the Common Market countries' and nearly three times larger than Japan's. It is their rapid growth in manufacturing (see table 1-9) coupled with their pattern of rapidly shifting their exports "upscale" that should concern us. Like Japan, this appears to represent not just new competition, but a new type of competition.

If these trading partners are able to adapt their production and export activities significantly more rapidly than we, they have the equivalent of a

Figure 1-28

Composition of Exports: South Korea, Hong Kong, Taiwan, and Singapore, 1957-78

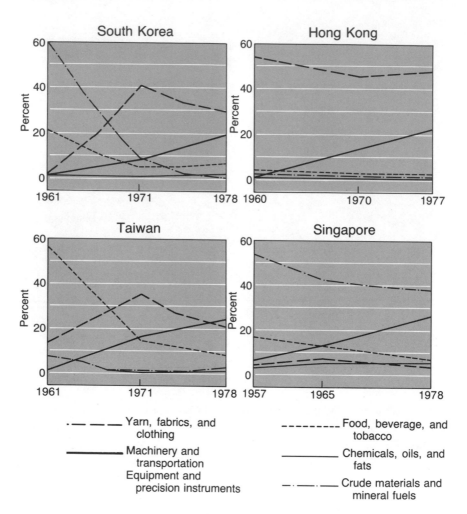

Source: Miyohei Shinohara, *Industrial Growth, Trade, and Dynamic Patterns in the Japanese Economy* (Tokyo: University of Tokyo Press, 1982).

Table 1-9
Average Annual Growth Rate in Manufacturing, Selected
Countries, 1960–80 (%)

	1960–70	*1970–80*
United States	5.3	2.9
Japan	11.0	6.4
Germany	5.4	2.1
France	6.6	3.6
United Kingdom	3.3	0.1
Taiwan	17.3[a]	13.3
Hong Kong	—	9.3
Singapore	13.0	9.6
South Korea	17.6	16.6
Indonesia	3.3	12.8
Philippines	6.7	7.2
Malaysia	—	11.8
Thailand	11.4	10.6

Source: The World Bank, *World Development Report* 1982 and 1983; The
World Bank, *World Tables*, 1980.
[a]Average of 1960–65 and 1965–70

better strategy. And if this is the case, we should inquire about the important
factors in their strategies. This is addressed in the next chapter.

JAPAN AS A SPECIAL CASE

Thus far we have considered Japan as the leading member of a group of
East Asian countries that seem to constitute a new set of competitors and
perhaps a new type of competition. As the earliest of this group to industrialize, and in many ways the model for the others, Japan should be distinguished from the traditional industrial countries of the North Atlantic area.
When grouped with France and Germany, Japan loses some of its most
salient characteristics. In addition, however, Japan has characteristics that
differentiate it from the "new Japans." For example, it has very little intrasectoral trade in its key export sectors. It exports in these sectors but has
almost no imports in return.

Figures 1-29, 1-30, and 1-31 show manufactured exports and imports for
France, Germany, and the United States, ranked as a share of exports. For
both France and Germany, passenger cars are the leading export, accounting

56

U.S. Competitiveness

Figure 1-29

Manufactured Exports and Imports as a Percentage of Total Exports, 1981: France

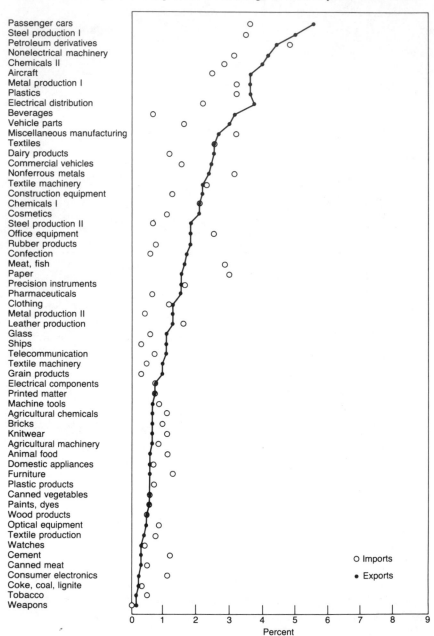

Source: Researcher's calculations based on data from CEPII

Figure 1-30

Manufactured Exports and Imports as a Percentage of Total Exports, 1981: Germany

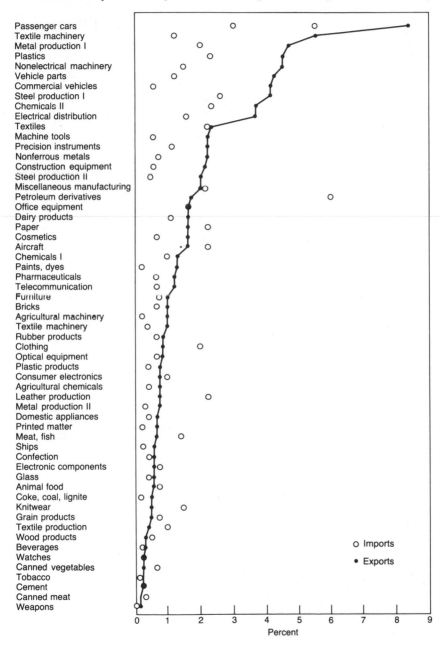

Source: Researcher's calculations based on data from CEPII

Figure 1-31

Manufactured Exports and Imports as a Percentage of Total Exports, 1981: United States

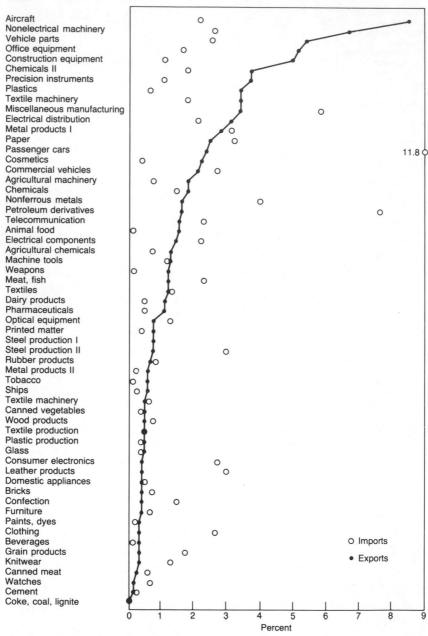

Source: Researcher's calculations based on data from CEPII

for over 6 percent of total manufactured exports in France and about 9 percent in Germany. For the United States the leading export is aircraft, accounting for about 9 percent of total exports. The important thing, however, is that passenger cars are also one of the highest import sectors in both France and Germany. Germans buy Peugeots and Renaults while French people buy Mercedes and BMWs. Distinctive product niches lead to active intrasectoral trade.

In France, five of the top ten import categories are among the top ten export categories. In Germany three of the top ten imports are in the top ten export categories, and all but commercial vehicles show imports at least equal to 1 percent of total exports. For the United States, the high import categories are more widely scattered, but again imports equal at least 1 percent of total exports in each of the top ten export categories.

The Japanese pattern is distinctly different (see figure 1-32). First, manufactured imports constitute a far lower percentage of total imports than is true for any other industrial country. As a result, to show imports by category as a share of total imports would require the use of a much smaller denominator than in the other countries. Therefore, to compare import patterns and intrasectoral trade it seemed essential to use total exports as a common denominator for all countries. With this common denominator, the second and probably more important point stands out. Japanese manufactured imports exceed 2 percent of manufactured exports in only three categories: nonferrous metals, petroleum derivatives, and processed meat and fish. All three derived from raw materials in short supply in Japan. In five categories, imports are between 1 percent and 2 percent of total exports, and in the remaining forty-eight they are 1 percent or less. In none of the top ten export categories are Japanese imports as much as 1 percent of total exports. The Japanese are exporting Toyotas, Datsuns, Hondas, Subarus, and so on but are not importing cars from France, Germany, the United Kingdom, or the United States.

The issue is not so much the relatively low level of manufactured imports as the fact that imports are a negligible factor in the overwhelming majority of the categories. Japan's pattern is hard to distinguish from a closed market. Those who claim otherwise note that Japan is a large market (though less than half the size of the United States), a strong producer of manufactured goods (as are France, Germany, and the United States), and a resource-poor country that must export manufactures (to a much greater degree than its large industrial rivals) to maintain its standard of living.

Some Americans continue to claim that this import pattern is predicted by neoclassical trade theory, meaning that Japan imports raw materials because

Figure 1-32

Manufactured Exports and Imports as a Percentage of Total Exports, 1981: Japan

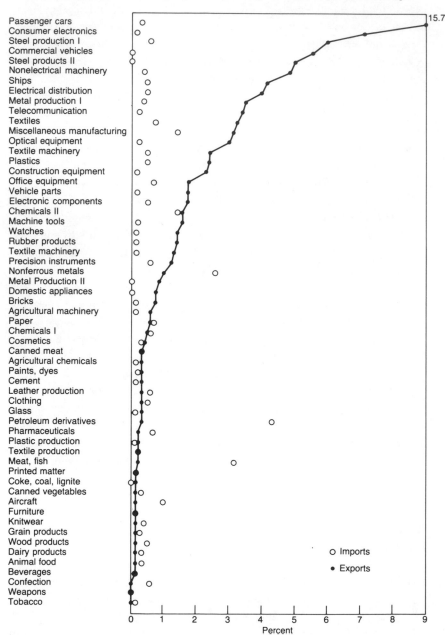

Source: Researcher's calculations based on data from CEPII

it must. However, the key question is why Japan, unlike other industrial countries, has such a low level of imports in nearly all sectors including its high export sectors. Why is there so little intraindustry specialization and trade?

Poverty of natural resources is not an adequate answer, as shown in the export-import analysis of the four "new Japans" (see figure 1-33). Grouped together, they show a pattern reminiscent of France, Germany, and the United States, and not of Japan. Textiles are the second-highest export category, for instance, and the highest import category. Many of the high-import categories are also above-average export sectors. Intraindustry trade occurs in these countries more or less as it does in the United States and Western Europe. They have trade barriers, of course, and do not have the industrial depth or breadth of the Japanese economy, so they must import more manufactured goods. A more detailed breakdown might show some highly selective barriers. But the basic point remains: a shortage of raw materials does not explain the paucity of intrasectoral trade in Japan. Japan is the exception.

The trade figures make the Japanese market look much less open than the other markets. The Japanese claim this is not the case, and since the early 1970s, there is much American literature that agrees. Nevertheless, as long as the situation persists, American business executives will feel, with some justification, that "if it looks like a duck and quacks like a duck, why not call it a duck?"

The fact that this unique condition has lasted more than a decade after the opening of the Japanese market merits careful study. Part of the explanation may lie in various institutional features such as the *keiretsu* groupings, which encourage intragroup integration and trade. There is a less formalistic legal system, which facilitates long-term working relationships based on a handshake rather than a fifty-page technical document. There are also close working relationships between business and government, which include a certain shared "vision" about which industries and products should have highest priority.

Japan also has a different business tradition that may derive from a cultural homogeneity not found in other industrial countries. In the United States companies can spring up almost overnight, while in Japan new companies must prove themselves. "If you want to do business with a Japanese, you have to prove reliability, quality, and seriousness of your intent. You can only prove these qualities over a period of time."[23] To foreigners who want to do business with Japan, the results of such attitudes seem like discrimination. On the other hand, when Nippon Telephone and Telegraph insists that bids meet both performance and design specifications but delays giving

Figure 1-33

Manufactured Exports and Imports as a Percentage of Total Exports, 1981: Hong Kong, South Korea, Singapore, and Taiwan

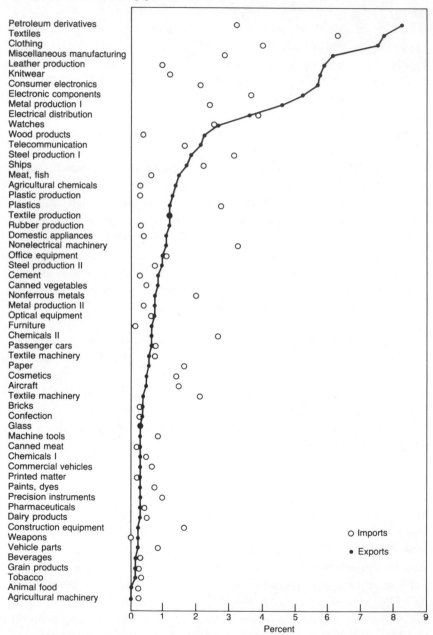

Source: Researcher's calculations based on data from CEPII

information to foreign firms about what the design specifications are, it most assuredly is.

The United States often fails to recognize discriminatory practices and to appreciate their competitive significance. The television case (see chapter 8), which dragged on for a decade before a consent decree was reached requiring the payment of $75 million for dumping and customs fraud, is a memorable example.

Our country's ineptitude in dealing with Japan is sometimes attributed to the "shocking ignorance" of top level U.S. diplomatic personnel, who focus on security relations with China and neglect economic relations with Japan.[24] Privately, several senior American diplomats have described the trade position of the U.S. embassy in Tokyo as hardly differing from Japan's, "almost as though it were flying their flag and not ours."

American inability to articulate which of its competitive problems are its own fault and which derive from unique features in the Japanese system is due partly to the low priority given to trade matters at the highest levels and partly to continued reliance on an obsolete theory of international trade that obscures some of the most significant elements of Japanese strategy. Evaluating the Japanese challenge requires that we distinguish successful Japanese business practices, such as their emphasis on quality and reliability, from unfair trade practices, however subtle or unsubtle they may be. It also requires that we see Japan as what Chalmers Johnson calls a "developmental state," one in which business and government work together in pursuit of shared interests, in contrast to the "regulatory state" that has characterized the U.S. business-government relationship since the 1890s.[25] If we do not appreciate differences in strategy and business-government relations, we shall continue to misperceive the meaning of Japan's actions, expend energy disagreeing among ourselves, and have little left to devote to solving crucial competitive problems.

SOME IMPLICATIONS FOR THE UNITED STATES

Our analysis has shown that the "new Japans" are growing very rapidly as industrial competitors and chalking up increasing trade balances with the United States. It also has shown that these countries are able to change their mix of exports very rapidly and move toward higher technologies. Although promoting "high tech" is much discussed as a possible strategy for the United States, the East Asians are, in fact, shifting their portfolios in this direction much more rapidly than any of the older industrial countries, including the United States, an issue that will be analyzed further in the next chapter. The implication is that the United States faces not only new competitors but a new form of competition, in which our key competitors adjust more rapidly than we do.

Other familiar aspects of this competition should be recalled. These new competitors have lower wages than the United States, from levels roughly half of ours in Japan down to one-tenth or less elsewhere. In addition, Japan also has a lower cost of capital (see table 1-10).

Japan and the four "new Japans" are high-investment countries. They now invest more as a share of GNP than the traditional industrial countries, and their investments and productivity are growing much more rapidly. If we had better data we might also find that their investment is more highly concentrated in the modern manufacturing sectors, and that their investment per worker in these modern sectors is rapidly catching up with the leaders. Thus, while their average productivity levels may remain far below that of the leading industrial countries, the gap is surely much narrower in some of the modern manufacturing sectors. And it is these sectors, not the averages, that should be our concern.

International competition is different from domestic or national competition. In domestic competition the company with the highest productivity will, other things being equal, be in the strongest position. This is not necessarily the case internationally. Exchange rates constitute an intervening variable that can substantially alter the terms of competition. If we ignore the capital account for a moment, exchange rates reflect average competitiveness in traded goods (exports and imports). If a country has a generally low level of productivity in the traded sectors, it can expect a "low" exchange rate, that is, one that yields a low standard of living compared with other countries. However, a company or industry that has above-average productivity for that country may benefit by the low exchange rate. Thus, even if the absolute productivity of firm *J* in Japan is much lower than that of firm *U* in the

Table 1-10
Average Weighted Cost of Capital to Industry

Country	1971	1976	1981
United States	10.0%	11.3%	16.6%
France	8.5%	9.4%	14.3%
West Germany	6.9%	6.6%	9.5%
Japan	7.3%	8.5%	9.2%

Source: U.S. Department of Commerce as quoted by Philip Wellons in chapter 10

United States, *J* may still benefit so much from the exchange rate that it can undersell the U.S. firm in the United States. The issue is one of relative productivity and prices within each country, and then productivity relative to one another as mediated by an exchange rate that presumably reflects a national average.

A study of Japanese and American productivity levels for 1973, for example, found that the American level was 17 percent higher on average in the manufacturing sector. At the same time, it found that Japanese levels were higher than their American counterparts in five industries.[26] Specifically, Japanese manufacturing productivity compared with America was estimated as follows:

On average	83%
Steel	105
General machinery	111
Electrical machinery	119
Transport equipment	124
Precision machinery	134

The differences are quite striking, for it is in these industries that Japan has most successfully invaded the American and other markets. (Table 1-11 shows the top five industries that contributed most to the Japanese net trade balance in 1980.) If the average was only 70 percent or 60 percent of the American level, the advantage of the high-productivity sectors would be still higher. As it is, these comparisons suggest that with a yen/dollar rate set in terms of the averages of the two countries, Japanese companies in these five industry groups should be able to sell at lower prices than their American counterparts and still make handsome profits. The exchange rate works so strongly in their favor that they should have impressive cash flows without subsidies.

Moreover, exchange rates are not determined only by the average productivity levels in each country's traded sectors. For example, interest rates matter and, as we have already seen, can artificially overvalue the dollar by attracting foreign capital to the United States. In addition, as a safe haven for capital and as the world's leading reserve currency, the United States may face the prospect of a dollar that has a more or less permanent tendency to be overvalued. Like Switzerland, we may have to learn to compete under such conditions rather than simply blame our failure on them.

Two other structural elements in the U.S. balance of payments further aggravate the price disadvantage of domestic firms in foreign markets. The

Table 1-11

Index of Import and Export Polarization: Japan, 1980

Top Five Surplus Categories		*Top Five Deficit Categories*	
Passenger cars	20.8	Agricultural products for industry	−9.7
Iron and steel	10.4	Nonferrous metals	−4.4
Television, radios, etc.	8.6	Other agricultural products	−4.1
Trucks, buses	6.9	Meat and fish products	−3.7
Tubes (including iron and steel wire, pipes and fittings, castings and forgings, unworked)	5.3	Cereals	−3.4
	$\overline{52.0}$		$\overline{-25.3}$

Source: Researcher's calculations based on data from CEPII
Note: Polarization is defined as the net trade balance for each product category, expressed as a
    percentage of Japan's total imports and exports divided by 2. Specifically,

$$\text{Pol}^{rt}_{ij} = \frac{\Sigma_j V^{rt}_{ij} - \Sigma_j V^{rt}_{ji}}{\Sigma_a \Sigma_j (V^{rt}_{ij} + V^{rt}_{ji})/2} \quad \text{where}$$

Pol^{rt}_{ij} = Polarization index
$\Sigma_j V^{rt}_{ij}$ = Exports of product r from zone i to the world.
$\Sigma_j V^{rt}_{ji}$ = Imports of product r by zone i from the world.
$\Sigma_a \Sigma_j (V^{rt}_{ij} + V^{rt}_{ji})/2\rho\epsilon$ = Total imports of manufactured products in zone i plus total exports of
    manufactured products from zone i, divided by 2.
        i = Japan

U.S. enjoys large net earnings on its foreign investments, some $30-40 billion
in recent years. Although a portion of these revenues are only imputed and
not actually remitted to the United States, they represent a potential claim
for dollars and add to its apparent strength. That some of these earnings may
never be collected—and some of the principal may be written off in years
ahead—suggests another area in which appearances of strength may mask
underlying realities. The resulting exchange rate, far from reflecting America's competitiveness as a source of internationally traded goods or services,
actually makes locally produced products more expensive—and less competitive—abroad.

The structure of imports affects relative exchange rates as well. The fast-
developing countries of East Asia are resource poor; they have created wealth
by building efficient manufacturing operations and not by inheriting a favorable set of circumstances. It is as though the poorer they have been in natural
resources, the better they have performed. In keeping with traditional notions
of comparative advantage, they must export manufactures to import necessary

raw materials. Their phenomenal success in manufacturing, however, has permitted an ever-increasing level of imports and a rapidly rising standard of living. Rises in raw material prices, and especially in the price of oil, add disproportionately to their import bill. This depresses their exchange rates, reduces their cost levels compared with their international competitors, and thereby adds to the profitability of those manufacturing operations that compete in world markets. Higher profits increase their investments and sustain their rapid productivity growth.

Contrary to traditional wisdom, richness in natural resources may be a handicap in today's international arena, which relies on creating value added in manufacturing. Specifically, U.S. industrial competition comes not from petroleum-rich countries able to reallocate the cash flow from their oil sector, as some portfolio models suggest. It comes from resource-poor countries that develop policies and institutions to carefully nurture what wealth they have, and from the growth of highly competitive firms in this favorable environment. For example, Iran and Venezuela have each had oil wealth for over fifty years, yet neither is a significant exporter of any manufactures other than oil products. South Korea with a population similar to Iran, and Taiwan with a population similar to Venezuela's came from far behind as industrial exporters in 1960 to absolutely dwarf Iran and Venezuela respectively in the 1970s (see table 1-12). The key is not so much natural wealth as a strategy for effective utilization of the resources at hand.

America's high net earnings on foreign investment and relatively low dependence on foreign oil benefit local consumers over the short run, since

Table 1-12
1960–82 Manufactured Exports of Selected Countries ($ billions)

	1960	*1970*	*1978*	*1980*	*1982*
Iran	0.020	0.10	0.17	0.11	1.14
South Korea	0.006	0.61	10.80	14.90	18.50
Venezuela	0.140	0.04	0.12	0.25	0.21
Taiwan	0.095	1.07	10.40	16.20	18.20
Latin America[a]	0.37	1.29	8.45	14.51	15.62

Source: The World Bank, *World Tables,* 1980 and 1983. Central Intelligence Agency, National Foreign Assessment Center, *Handbook of Economic Statistics,* October 1980. United Nations, *UN Selected Series of World Statistics,* February 1983. International Monetary Fund, *International Financial Statistics,* 1983. Roger Case, "The World Economy—The End of the Golden Age," The Associates, Santa Barbara, California, November 1983.
[a]Including Venezuela, Mexico, Brazil, Argentina, Columbia, Chile, Peru, Bolivia, Uruguay, and Paraguay.

both help satisfy our need for foreign exchange at a reduced cost in terms of shipping real goods and services abroad. Cheaper imports and lower dollar prices for American tourists abroad also provide tempting bargains. Ironically, however, from the point of view of U.S. industrial competitiveness, both aspects are liabilities. They give the United States a stronger exchange rate than it would otherwise have, higher costs for all U.S. operations, lower profitability, lower investment, reduced productivity gains, unemployment, and a lower growth rate in our standard of living.

TENTATIVE CONCLUSIONS '

This analysis of the U.S. competitive position in the world economy leads to seven basic conclusions.

1. The United States has a serious competitiveness problem. It is manifested in declining incomes for its labor force, declining market share in almost all major sectors of industrial activity, declining profitability, declining levels of investment per new worker, and unusually low rates of productivity growth. It is not just a problem created by the down phase of a business cycle; it appears to date roughly from the late 1960s. Nor is it a problem of a few key sectors: profitability and market share have declined over most, if not all, major industrial sectors, and manufacturing incomes have suffered even more than services.

2. The United States has a competitiveness problem when it is compared with a select group of countries, not across the board. The problem is particularly evident in comparisons between the United States and a relatively new group of competitors in East Asia, all of whom have been able to maintain much higher levels of investment and productivity growth than the United States for over two decades, through good times and bad. These competitors are now more important trading partners for the United States than the traditional big three European countries in terms of total trade volume. They are steadily increasing their share of U.S. markets and run a consistently favorable balance in manufactures with the United States, despite various restrictions on their goods.

3. The successful new competitors appear to represent not only more competition but a new, more effective type of competition. They have shown an ability to upgrade their export portfolios toward higher technology areas at an unprecedented speed. First Japan and more recently the East Asian NICs have created national systems that have fostered competitive strength through greater mobility of capital and labor. When coupled with their

outstanding capabilities to produce quality products and their long-standing advantages in labor costs, these nations appear to have achieved a superior competitive position that can, over time, be extended to successive new areas. It is not clear that any response by U.S. companies alone will make U.S. manufacturing operations competitive unless we are prepared to manage our country differently.

4. Japan appears to be a special case. Although it has opened its borders to trade, its trading pattern looks the most aggressive of any of the major industrial nations. Its exports are the most highly concentrated in a few sectors, and its import pattern is the most selective. One of the most often cited explanations, that of a shortage of natural resources, proves on closer inspection to be utterly unconvincing. The real reasons seem to be institutional, some of which lie deep in the structure of the Japanese system, and some of which represent less subtle manifestations of nontariff barriers. But a full appreciation of the Japanese trade pattern requires an understanding of Japan's developmental strategy and the economic theory on which it rests, which is the subject of the next chapter.

5. The United States does not appear to have a serious competitive problem with its traditional European rivals. On the contrary, the EEC countries' performance in recent years suggests that their problems are perhaps more severe and more deep seated than those of the United States.

Furthermore, the United States does not seem to have competitive problems with the newly rich, oil-exporting countries. Thus far none of these countries appears able to use its oil industry as a "cash cow" to support successful, internationally competitive industries other than those based on low-cost oil or gas as a key input.

6. The U.S. competitiveness problem can be attributed to a number of major factors, including the overvaluation of the dollar, the complacency of U.S. managers, the noncompetitiveness of U.S. policies and institutions, and the conscious and successful national strategies of a new group of East Asian nations.

While the exchange rate is sometimes cited as *the* cause, or the principal cause, the foregoing analysis suggests that the competitiveness problem manifested itself while the dollar was declining in the 1970s and continued even when the dollar was perhaps undervalued in the 1977-79 period. It also suggests that at least some "overvaluation" of the dollar in industrial competitiveness terms may be unavoidable for the foreseeable future, given the dollar's role as a reserve currency and the role of the United States as a safe haven. In this sense the United States may have an overvaluation problem like Switzerland's, though perhaps not as severe. If so, then competitiveness must mean competitiveness on the basis of an overvalued dollar; the exchange rate cannot always be used as an excuse.

7. Finally, in evaluating the relative importance of the various causal factors, ranking them as if they were independent of one another misses the essential point: the heart of the competitiveness issue lies in the differences between our strategy and those of our most successful competitors. Our key competitors are no longer the North Atlantic democracies whose political traditions and economic strategies are so close to our own. Instead, they are a new group of countries whose common strength is a development-oriented national strategy.

To understand and compare the respective strategies we need to review the assumptions behind each, the theories on which they are built, and the evidence on how similar or different they really are. This is the task of the next chapter.

2
National Strategies: Key to International Competition

Bruce R. Scott

The traditional industrial states of the North Atlantic area face a relatively new set of competitors and a new type of competition. The competitive challenge comes neither primarily from each other as it once did; nor does it come from nations with recently discovered great natural wealth, such as oil. It comes instead primarily from resource-poor countries, notably Japan and the "new Japans" of East Asia, which have consistently achieved more rapid increases in productivity, industrial output, and exports than the older industrial countries, despite a scarcity of natural wealth.

The critical element in this new competition is the effective participation of national governments in shaping respective business environments through what we will call a national strategy. Like a corporate strategy, a national strategy consists of goals, a concept of how to achieve those goals in a competitive environment, and a set of policies and institutions to implement the concept. While it is customary to analyze and compare national policies and institutions, it is the goals and the concept or "vision" of how to compete that drive the system. A comparison of national strategies must give due weight to the choice of goals and the creation of a vision of how to get there, as well as comparing policies and institutions.

National strategies are at least as distinctive as those of companies and follow a broadly similar pattern. Some companies are growth oriented, with a low-dividend payout to permit a maximum level of reinvestment in the business. Others have more modest growth aspirations and a higher payout

Bruce R. Scott is Paul Whiton Cherington Professor of Business Administration at Harvard Business School. Contributions to this paper were made by Benjamin Friedman, George Lodge, Douglas Scott, Hans van der Ven, and Pierre Wack. Research assistance was provided by Ann Y. Kester and Hans van der Ven.

of earnings. Likewise, some countries are growth oriented, with strong incentives to promote savings and investment and thus to reduce short-term consumption in favor of greater future returns. Other countries give higher priority to short-term consumer benefits and choose to promote consumption rather than savings. Typically such countries set minimum levels of income as a goal and guarantee such levels as an entitlement of citizenship or membership in the community. While all industrial countries do some of each, their goals and/or priorities are distinctly different, just as those of the "growth stock" differ from the "income producer/distributor."

In addition, national strategies differ in the degree to which they are resource versus opportunity oriented. Those that are resource oriented tend to see markets and competition guided by the invisible hand as the most effective way to develop those resources, with government in the role of referee and regulator. Those that are opportunity oriented see a role for the visible hand of government as supplementing market forces; *not* as a substitute, but as a supplement in shaping incentives to promote savings and/or discourage consumption, promote mobility of resources, and alter risk/reward relationships.

To speak of a company as having a strategy is obviously a simplification. To speak of a country as having one is a greater simplification, especially in a democratic country in which a government is hardly a unitary actor. In the U.S. context, in which there is a constitutionally mandated separation of powers designed to make coordination difficult, the concept may even seem far-fetched. Policymaking seems to be the outcome of the legitimate pulling and hauling of various groups seeking their own special interests.

Democratic governments, and perhaps the United States in particular, are constantly castigated for their inconsistencies and lack of coherence. And it has become fashionable in some quarters to blame internal inconsistencies or the lack of coherence of public policies as a fundamental source of disappointing performance in the United States. It is important to note, however, that all democratic governments—including the Japanese—have inconsistencies in their policies, though some may have more than others. The key differences in strategies do not appear to be between those that are more coherent and those that are less so, but between those that are growth/ productivity/opportunity oriented on the one hand and those that are distribution/security/resource oriented on the other. In other words, the broad orientations appear much more important than differing degrees of internal consistency. The subsequent chapters in this volume, for example, are eloquent testimony to the consistency of U.S. emphasis on economic security, short-term consumer interests, the adequacy of the invisible hand in the exploitation of resources, and the primary economic and social role of government as rule maker and referee in how the pie should be divided. Only when the issue is national defense do we find a clearly visible hand of government promoting the development and exploitation of opportunities, or the baking of the pie.

THE TRADITIONAL THEORY OF COMPARATIVE ADVANTAGE

Comparative advantage, free trade, and competition among firms are central features of theory behind the trading system built since World War II. It is a system in which all countries gain if each specializes in its areas of comparative advantage and exchanges products with other countries in the free market system. A much larger (world) market permits increased specialization, increased productivity, and higher incomes. Free trade among the fifty states allows productivity not possible in a single state, for example, and all states should gain in terms of a higher standard of living and improved welfare. In this system, firms should discover what can be produced best in a given locale, and governments should prohibit all forms of protection.

The theory of comparative advantage was first articulated by David Ricardo in 1817. He argued that England and Portugal would each gain by trading even if Portugal produced both wine and cloth more cheaply than England. If the British had less of a cost disadvantage in cloth, they should specialize in exporting cloth and import wine. The Portuguese should do the reverse. Both countries would be better off through specialization and trade in an open market than with a strategy of protection.

The theory was originally worked out for two commodities, wine and cloth, and a single measure of value—hours of labor. The basic idea is still one of the central pillars of Western economic theory. As stated in a current best-selling economics text, the theory is deceptively simple: ". . . countries export commodities whose production requires relatively intensive use of productive resources found locally in relative abundance."[1]

The theory is based on a number of important assumptions, including full employment, balanced current accounts, the existence of productive factors that are "homogeneous and mobile between sectors" and which can thus "costlessly be reallocated from one sector to another,"[2] and the comparability of knowledge and technology from one country to another. There are obvious problems with each of these assumptions; for example, the possibility of high and continuing levels of unemployment; frictional unemployment and/or retraining costs as labor shifts from one skill area or level to another; social costs as plants and sometimes whole communities are shut down while plants or even whole communities are built elsewhere; institutional factors that permit current accounts to remain substantially out of balance for extended periods of time; and different and unequal levels of knowledge and technology, some of which is proprietary to particular firms. Each of these abstractions from reality limits its applicability in some measure and thus calls for care in its use. However, there seem to be two additional abstractions that are not so much inevitable simplifications as distortions, which in the present international context cause the theory to obscure rather than illuminate some of the most important dynamics of international competition.[3]

As presently used in Western economics, the theory of comparative advantage assumes that "the law of increasing costs" prevails[4] and that productive resources are "found locally" rather than created. If resources are "found" and costs rise once they are fully utilized, then production levels are determined by natural endowments and they will tend to be self-limiting. Agricultural land is a good example: even a rich Portuguese vineyard will only yield so much wine. Increasing investments of fertilizer and labor have diminishing returns at some point. Much the same reasoning has been applied to industry, as though there will inevitably be diminishing returns and rising costs in the production of cloth as well.

The assumption is critical. Diminishing returns and rising costs mean that there are few if any natural monopolies other than public utilities, and that competition among numerous producers is the natural state of affairs. Any advantage a country has is both "natural" and "self-limiting." Given these assumptions, specialization and trade will yield higher incomes than the attempt to be self-sufficient, and it will be mutually beneficial given any reasonable distribution of the gains.

The resulting perspective is a positive-sum game based on an essentially static trade theory. Advantages rest largely on endowments that must be "found" rather than created, and one assumes rising costs as one exploits those resources more intensively. The fact that critical resources can be imported or created is overlooked, as is the possibility of continually declining costs (except temporarily in the case of an infant industry). The fact that a firm might continually cut prices to expand volume and in so doing drive all others out of the market is an example of monopolistic and antisocial behavior unjustified by economic reality. The fact that a nation might pursue a similar approach through an export promotion policy is likewise unjustified.

A static theory does make room for adjustment, but the adjustment process is assumed to operate smoothly at the margin so that the system remains in equilibrium. This is based on full employment and balanced current accounts, and the assumption that benefits are not only mutual but more or less symmetrical among countries. The theory leads to short-term analyses of incremental changes and to their mathematical modeling, not to longer-term analyses of major shifts in economic structure. In this it parallels the short-term, marginal analyses of costs and revenues that constitute so much of the theory of the firm, and that also underemphasize the role of major innovations and shifts in a firm's product portfolio.

CREATING COMPARATIVE ADVANTAGE

The challenge to traditional theory comes first and foremost from evidence that a number of countries have indeed succeeded in dramatically altering their comparative advantage, and secondarily from a limited number of documents that explain the theory that—over time—was worked out to guide a purposeful process of upgrading an industrial portfolio or creating comparative advantage. Before considering the alternative theory let us consider the evidence.

We can begin this inquiry by using the classification scheme shown in table 2-1, which organizes U.S. trade data in an analytic framework. Regina

Table 2-1
Description of Product Classes by Technology Classification, 1968–70

U.S. SIC Code	Position Description	Research Intensity Ratio (%)[a]
Technology-Intensive		
-372	Aircraft and parts	12.41
-357	Office, computing, and accounting machines	11.61
-361–2, 366–7	Electric transmission and distribution equipment, electrical industrial apparatus, communication equipment and electronic components	11.01
383–7	Optical and medical instruments, photos, watches	9.44

(continued)

Table 2-1 (*continued*)
Description of Product Classes by Technology Classification, 1968–70

U.S. SIC Code	Position Description	Research Intensity Ratio (%)[a]
-283	Drugs and medicines	6.94
-282	Plastic materials and synthetics	5.62
-351	Engines and turbines	4.76
-287	Agricultural chemicals	4.63
-345	Ordnance, except guided missiles	3.64
381–2	Professional, scientific, and measuring instruments	3.17
-281	Industrial chemicals	2.78
-365	Radio and TV receiving equipment	2.57
Non-Technology-Intensive		
352	Farm machinery and equipment	2.34
371	Motor vehicles and equipment	2.15
363–4, 369	Other electrical equipment and supplies	
353	Construction, mining, and related machinery	1.90
284–6, 289	Other chemicals	1.76
34	Fabricated metal products	1.48
30	Rubber and plastic products, n.e.c.[b]	1.20
354	Metalworking machinery and equipment	1.17
373–5, 379	Other transportation equipment	1.14
29	Petroleum and coal products	1.11
355–6, 358–9	Other nonelectrical machinery	1.06
21, 23–27, 31, 39	Other manufactures, n.e.c.	1.02
32	Stone, clay, and glass products	0.90
333–6, 3392	Nonferrous metals and products	0.52
331–2, 3391, 3399	Ferrous metals and products	0.42
22	Textile mill products	0.28
20	Food and kindred products	0.21
Total Manufacturing		2.36

Source: Regina Kelly, *The Impact of Technological Innovation on Trade Patterns,* U.S. Department of Commerce, Bureau of International Economic Policy and Research, ER-24, December 1977.
Note: SIC 1925 (guided missiles and space craft) was excluded from the calculation of the average intensity ratio of U.S. manufacturing because of its extremely high intensity ratio—almost seven times as high as the nearest product class—and its limited importance in U.S. trade flows.
[a]The ratio of applied R&D funds by product field to shipments by product class
[b]n.e.c. = not elsewhere classified

Kelly of the Commerce Department used National Science Foundation data
on R&D spending by industry category in the United States to arrange trade
data into twenty-six groupings, which were then ranked by R&D intensity.[5]
Using data from 1967 to 1970, the top three categories had R&D spending
in excess of 11 percent of sales; the lowest category showed R&D spending
at less than .5 percent of sales. The industries form a continuum, with no
easy break between high and low technology. This scheme, with its twenty-
six industry categories, helps us analyze U.S. specialization and adjustment.

Export specialization is revealed by those sectors having higher shares of
world export markets than the U.S. average. If all sectors clustered around
the average, there would be little specialization, at least at the twenty-six
industry level of aggregation. Clustering around the average would indicate
that the United States was not significantly stronger in any sectors.

As a high-wage and high technology society, we would expect to have
above-average share in high technology areas. Thanks to the world's richest
farm belt, we might expect above-average share in some of the agribusiness
areas as well. In the economist's language, we assume that the United States
has a comparative advantage in high technology exports and in agribusiness.
By definition, we must have a below-average share in some areas if we are
to have above-average share elsewhere. An assumed pattern of specialization
that reflects an assumed pattern of comparative advantage is shown in figure
2-1.

REVEALED COMPARATIVE ADVANTAGE

There is no exact way to gauge comparative advantage, but export data
give us an after-the-fact pattern called "revealed" (or, after-the-fact) comparative advantage. The curve on figure 2-1 suggests what the revealed
comparative advantage of the United States might look like.

An ideal pattern of adjustment would show the United States adding
relative market share in the higher technology categories and dropping it in
lower technology categories. Adjustment in this sense means "upgrading"
the export portfolio toward higher technology categories. This is in keeping
with a U.S. self-image as a technological leader and with the economic
necessities of a high-wage country shifting its exports to products presumably
requiring highly skilled labor. Over time, the curve might be expected to
shift in a clockwise rotation, with the export shares of the high technology
categories rising while those in low technology decline. In addition, there

Figure 2-1

Schematic Diagram of Revealed Comparative Advantage: United States, Circa 1970

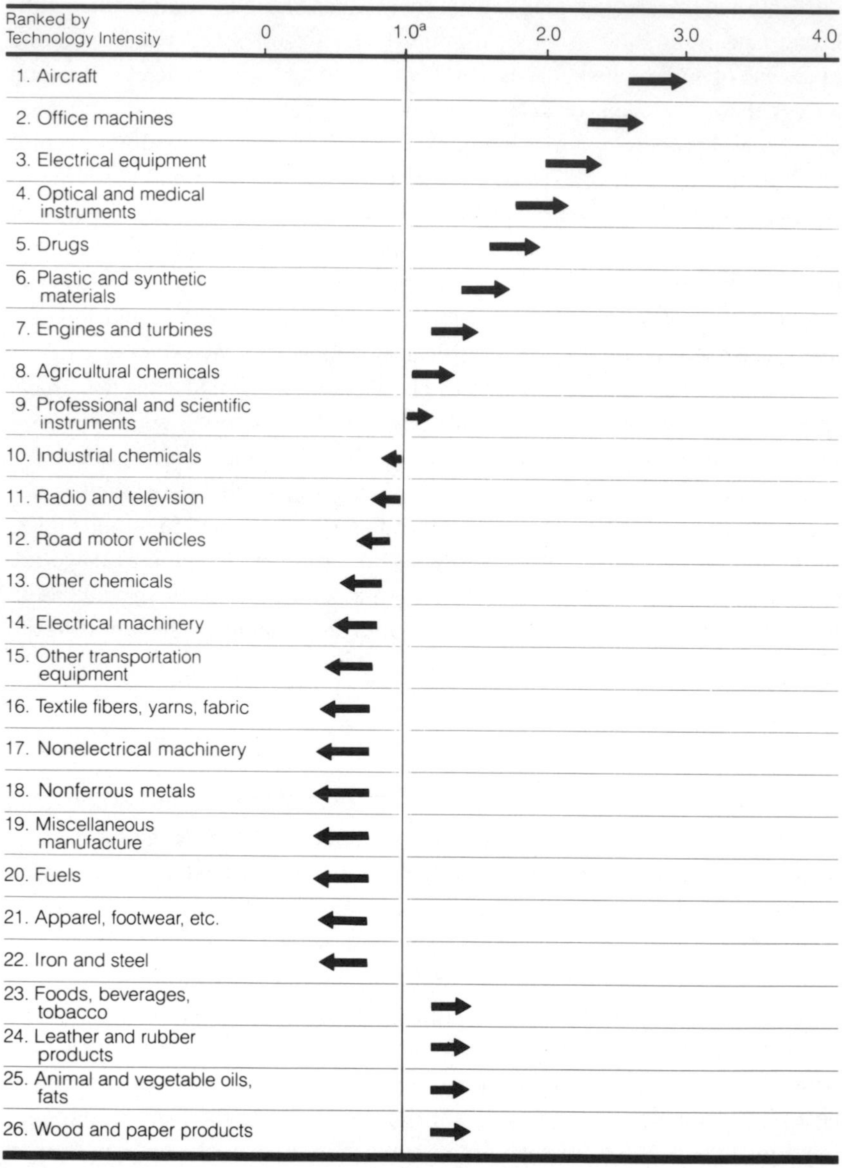

Ranked by Technology Intensity	0	1.0[a]	2.0	3.0	4.0
1. Aircraft				→	
2. Office machines			→		
3. Electrical equipment			→		
4. Optical and medical instruments			→		
5. Drugs		→			
6. Plastic and synthetic materials		→			
7. Engines and turbines		→			
8. Agricultural chemicals		→			
9. Professional and scientific instruments		→			
10. Industrial chemicals	←				
11. Radio and television	←				
12. Road motor vehicles	←				
13. Other chemicals	←				
14. Electrical machinery	←				
15. Other transportation equipment	←				
16. Textile fibers, yarns, fabric	←				
17. Nonelectrical machinery	←				
18. Nonferrous metals	←				
19. Miscellaneous manufacture	←				
20. Fuels	←				
21. Apparel, footwear, etc.	←				
22. Iron and steel	←				
23. Foods, beverages, tobacco		→			
24. Leather and rubber products		→			
25. Animal and vegetable oils, fats		→			
26. Wood and paper products		→			

[a]1.0=average share of world market in any given year

should be a similar shifting upscale within categories, a possibility that cannot be checked without more detailed data.

Figure 2-2, based on Commerce Department data rearranged to conform to this scheme, shows U.S. revealed comparative advantage in 1965 and 1980.[6] The solid vertical line represents the average U.S. share of the world market in any given year. The arrows show relative shares (above or below the U.S. average) for the years 1965 and 1980. If the arrow points right, the United States gained relative share; if it points left, the United States lost share. For example, aircraft and parts are an area of strong relative exports, or export specialization. In aircraft, the United States had more than double its average share in 1965 and nearly triple its average share by 1980. In office machines, it had nearly double its average share in 1980. In addition, the United States increased its relative share in both aircraft and office machines over the period.

The results shown in figure 2-2 resemble the curve shown in figure 2-1. The United States is strong and gaining strength in the top two categories; there is also relative strength near the bottom, in the agribusiness categories. Categories three through six are weaker than might be hypothesized, while agricultural chemicals show up as an area of uncharacteristic improvement. Radio and television seem surprisingly low, given their place on the technology chart, though their demise is hardly news. Motor vehicles also seem on the way down, though in this scheme they are hardly low technology.

The critical implication is that the data do not show a broad pattern of U.S. exports adjusting toward higher technology areas over this fifteen-year period. Although U.S. exports of high technology products grew more rapidly than low, markets grew at least as fast. Only aircraft, office machines, and agricultural chemicals showed the desired pattern on the high end, while fuels and animal and vegetable oils fit the desired pattern on the low end.[7]

If we analyze German and French exports using the same scheme (see figures 2-3 and 2-4), two things stand out. First, neither country shows as much specialization as the United States: the entries are closer to the average. Second, there is no pattern of upgrading toward high technology exports. In Germany the pattern seems, if anything, the reverse. Despite its well-deserved reputation for engineering and manufacturing skills, which should give Germany a "curve" much like that hypothesized for the United States, Germany seems to be losing comparative advantage in higher technology areas rather than holding even or gaining. France shows little change except in office machines and electrical machinery, with the former showing a decline in one of the high technology sectors.

Figure 2-2

Revealed Comparative Advantage: Manufactured Exports, United States, 1965 and 1980

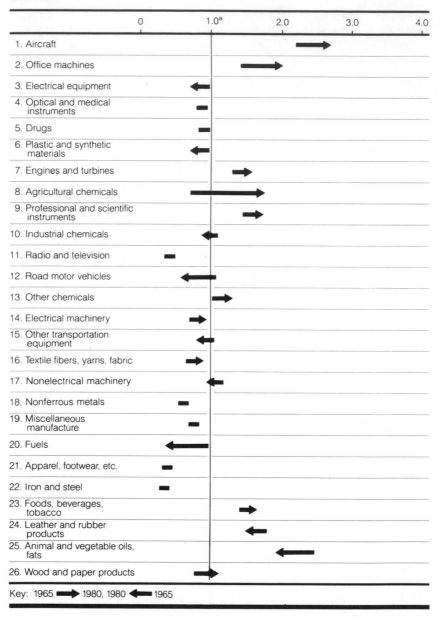

Source: Author's diagram based on data from table 23 in report prepared by the Office of International Trade Administration for the Cabinet Council on Commerce and Trade, October 1982.

Note: Comparative advantage is for 26 product categories relative to all merchandise exports.

[a]1.0=average share of world market in any given year

Figure 2-3

Revealed Comparative Advantage: Manufactured Exports, West Germany, 1965 and 1980

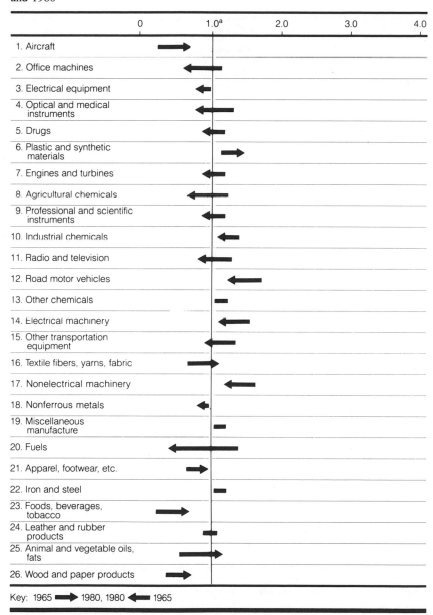

Key: 1965 ➡ 1980, 1980 ⬅ 1965

Source: Author's diagram based on data from table 23 in report prepared by the Office of International Trade Administration for the Cabinet Council on Commerce and Trade, October 1982.

Note: Comparative advantage is for 26 product categories relative to all merchandise exports.

[a]1.0=average share of world market in any given year

Figure 2-4

Revealed Comparative Advantage: Manufactured Exports, France, 1965 and 1980

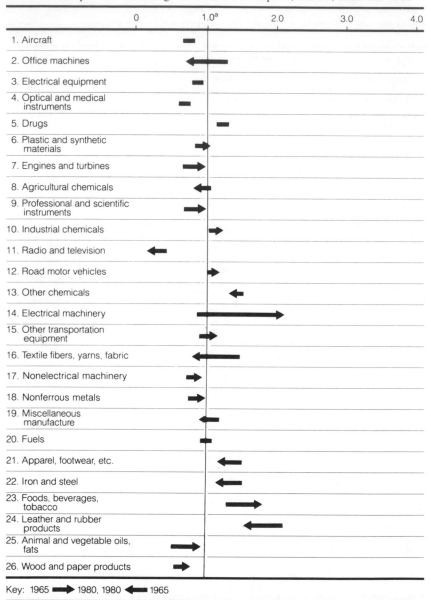

Key: 1965 ➡ 1980, 1980 ⬅ 1965

Source: Author's diagram based on data from table 23 in report prepared by the Office of International Trade Administration for the Cabinet Council on Commerce and Trade, October 1982.
Note: Comparative advantage is for 26 product categories relative to all merchandise exports.
[a]1.0=average share of world market in any given year

These two countries are often cited in American literature as having done better than the United States because of their active industrial policies. These data suggest, however, that neither has done as well as the United States, with its "less active" and "less coherent" industrial policy. These findings are consistent with the results of an EEC task force that found the community "does not manifest dynamic market leadership in any sector . . . [and that] the relatively small number and nature of the sectors in which the Community's share are growing . . . is cause for some concern."[8]

Figure 2-5 shows that the Japanese pattern is strikingly different. The magnitude of the changes indicates a much more rapid and far-reaching adjustment. In addition, the pattern reveals Japan gaining share in high technology areas and losing it in low ones. This becomes still clearer if the chemical industry is eliminated. It is the Japanese experience that demonstrates the upgrading of a national industrial portfolio over time.

Up through 1973, the Japanese chemical industry was a successful exporter, increasing from 5.1 percent of Japanese exports in 1955 to 6.4 percent in 1970 and 7.0 percent in 1975.[9] This pattern was upset by the oil price increase of 1973, because the Japanese petrochemical industry was based on naphtha, an oil derivative, while some of its competitors, notably those in the United States, were based in considerable measure on natural gas, a raw material whose price was regulated in the United States. With U.S. petrochemical producers enjoying an important cost advantage, the Japanese were at a disadvantage, and by 1979 chemicals had receded to 5.9 percent of Japanese exports.

REVEALED COMPARATIVE ADVANTAGE—A CLOSER LOOK

Before exploring how the Japanese have achieved their pattern, we should ask how many countries fit it and if it still holds when taking a closer look. Trade data compiled and carefully reconciled by CEPII, an agency established by the French government to study international competition and trade, permitted such an analysis.[10] Using the CEPII data base it was possible to analyze the patterns of revealed comparative advantage for a variety of countries during the period 1967 to 1980, based on fifty-seven categories instead of twenty-six.

We arranged the CEPII categories from high technology to low, following as best we could the rankings in the Commerce Department study. There was some guesswork, because the fifty-nine categories used by CEPII did not fit perfectly with the twenty-six categories used by the Commerce De-

Figure 2-5

Revealed Comparative Advantage: Manufactured Exports, Japan, 1965 and 1980

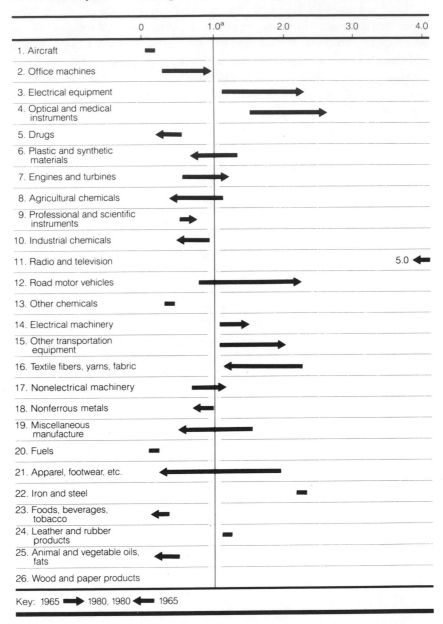

Key: 1965 ➡ 1980, 1980 ⬅ 1965

Source: Author's diagram based on data from table 23 in report prepared by the Office of International Trade Administration for the Cabinet Council on Commerce and Trade, October 1982.
Note: Comparative advantage is for 26 product categories relative to all merchandise exports.
[a]1.0=average share of world market in any given year

partment. We dropped two of the CEPII categories, coal and oil; they seemed more like raw materials than manufactured products. Also, using U.S. ranking of R&D spending to show technology intensity for all countries raised some questions. The point, however, is not which industry should rank number ten or eleven on the technology scale, but to have an approximate order to permit observation of general patterns. A computerized data base showing trade patterns among countries in fifty-odd industry categories was a valuable resource even with these qualifications.

Converting the CEPII data into a year-by-year analysis of revealed comparative advantage, it was found that there were very few abrupt swings or glitches; a particular category might go up or down but did so gradually. As a result, comparing the starting and finishing points gave a good sense of change over time. The analysis could be strengthened, however, by also showing the highs and lows for the period.

The results are shown in figures 2-6 through 2-10. The boxes show relative share in 1967 and the circles show the same for 1981. Where the circle is to the right of the box, the country has increased its relative export share in the category over the period. Showing the high and low share for each category during the entire period allows the reader to place the beginning and the end relative to these high and low points, and thus to have a sense of whether changes may still be in progress. Where a country has gained relative share during the period the circle has been blackened to allow the reader to look for a pattern in the data.

Although additional categories, plus high and low points, may make the patterns less obvious than in the graphs based on the Commerce Department data, careful inspection reveals that the results reflected by the CEPII data are similar to those of the Commerce Department and that the trends are continuing. Thus, with the CEPII data, the U.S. position is generally above average in the higher technology categories, and below average in the low technology categories until one reaches such agribusiness categories as paper, tobacco, animal feeds, canned vegetables, dairy products, and grain products (see figure 2-6). Cosmetics and printed matter stand out as higher than might be expected, while consumer electronics and watches appear much lower. But in terms of change, the United States has lost relative share in eleven of the top twenty categories and made significant gains in only three: aircraft, office equipment, and agricultural chemicals. Furthermore, in most of the categories experiencing decline, the position in 1981 was near the bottom for the period, suggesting that loss of relative share, or relative competitiveness, in high technology was continuing except for the same three categories shown in the Commerce Department data.

Figure 2-6

Revealed Comparative Advantage: Manufactured Exports, United States, 1967-81

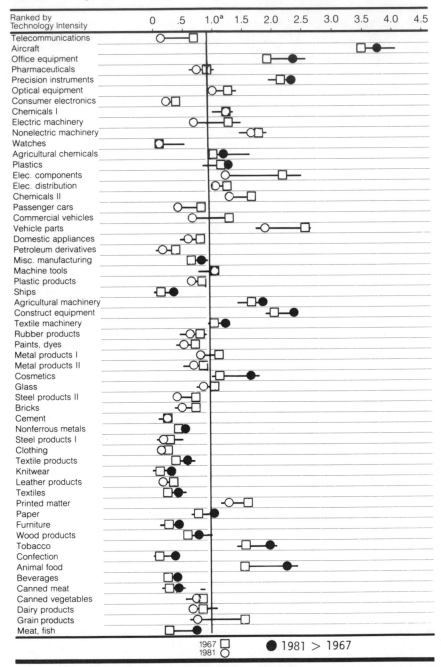

Source: Researcher's calculations based on data from CEPII
Note: Comparative advantage is for 57 product categories relative to total manufactured exports.
[a]1.0=average share of world market in any given year

Figure 2-7

Revealed Comparative Advantage: Manufactured Exports, Germany, 1967-81

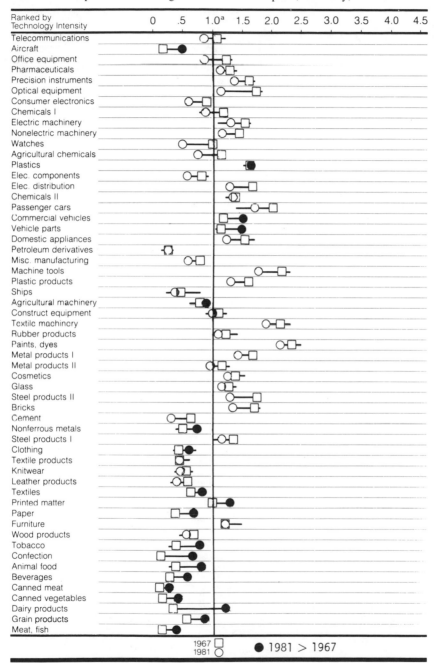

Source: Researcher's calculations based on data from CEPII
Note: Comparative advantage is for 57 product categories relative to total manufactured exports.
[a]1.0=average share of world market in any given year

Figure 2-8

Revealed Comparative Advantage: Manufactured Exports, France, 1967-81

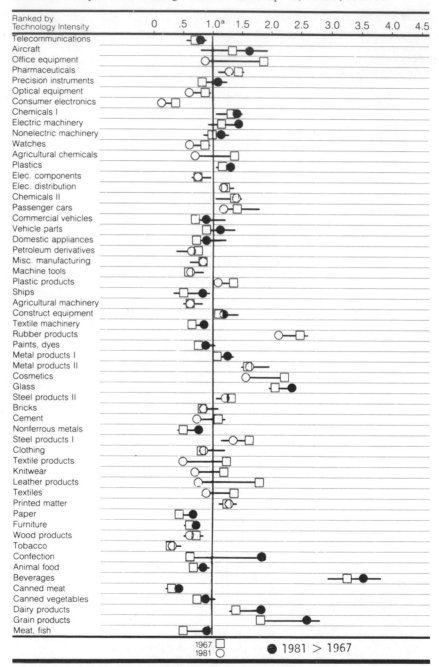

Source: Researcher's calculations based on data from CEPII
Note: Comparative advantage is for 57 product categories relative to total manufactured exports.
[a]1.0=average share of world market in any given year

Figure 2-9

Revealed Comparative Advantage: Manufactured Exports, United Kingdom, 1967-81

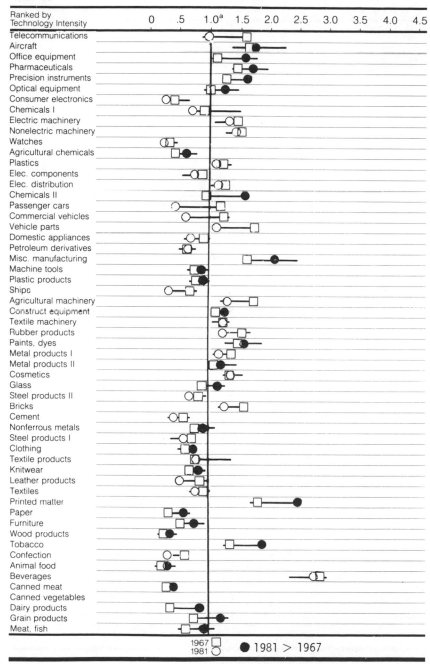

Ranked by Technology Intensity

0   .5   1.0ª   1.5   2.0   2.5   3.0   3.5   4.0   4.5

Telecommunications
Aircraft
Office equipment
Pharmaceuticals
Precision instruments
Optical equipment
Consumer electronics
Chemicals I
Electric machinery
Nonelectric machinery
Watches
Agricultural chemicals
Plastics
Elec. components
Elec. distribution
Chemicals II
Passenger cars
Commercial vehicles
Vehicle parts
Domestic appliances
Petroleum derivatives
Misc. manufacturing
Machine tools
Plastic products
Ships
Agricultural machinery
Construct equipment
Textile machinery
Rubber products
Paints, dyes
Metal products I
Metal products II
Cosmetics
Glass
Steel products II
Bricks
Cement
Nonferrous metals
Steel products I
Clothing
Textile products
Knitwear
Leather products
Textiles
Printed matter
Paper
Furniture
Wood products
Tobacco
Confection
Animal food
Beverages
Canned meat
Canned vegetables
Dairy products
Grain products
Meat, fish

1967 □
1981 ○   ● 1981 > 1967

Source: Researcher's calculations based on data from CEPII
Note: Comparative advantage is for 57 product categories relative to total manufactured exports.
ª1.0=average share of world market in any given year

Figure 2-10

Revealed Comparative Advantage: Manufactured Exports, Japan, 1967-81

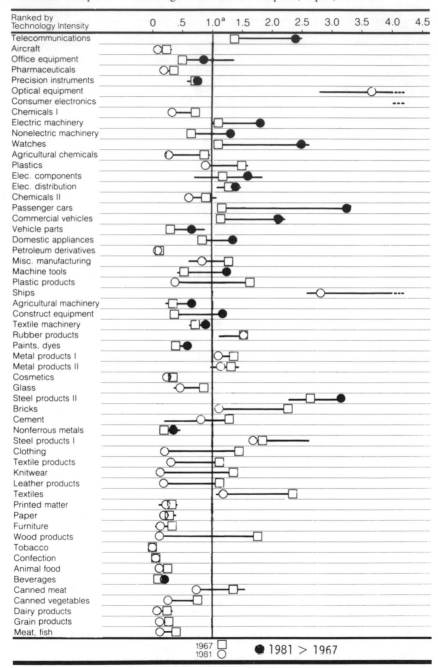

Source: Researcher's calculations based on data from CEPII
Note: Comparative advantage is for 57 product categories relative to total manufactured exports.
^a1.0=average share of world market in any given year

The German picture (figure 2-7) again shows less specialization than in the United States. More strikingly, Germany has also lost relative share in the high technology categories, with measurable losses in sixteen of the top twenty and measurable gains in only three. In addition, the Germans appear to be losing relative strength in passenger cars, machine tools, construction equipment, and rubber products. The German portfolio appears to be deteriorating to a striking degree, a phenomenon that could have unfavorable future implications for their capacity to earn their standard of living in the years ahead.

France also shows less specialization than the United States but relative decline in only seven of the top twenty categories and improvement in seven (see figure 2-8). At the other end of the scale there have been striking French gains in the agribusiness areas, as France, traditionally a high-cost producer, benefits from the common agricultural program (perhaps at the expense of its partners). The French pattern in general seems stronger than the German.

The United Kingdom (see figure 2-9) shows the modest degree of specialization characteristic of Germany and France, and deterioration in nine of its top twenty industries. However, it shows gains in seven. Since the United Kingdom was losing average market share during the period, this shift does not necessarily imply increased absolute share, much less increased competitiveness. It says the United Kingdom has done less badly in some high technology sectors than it has on average. The United Kingdom is also shifting its export mix toward low technology agribusiness areas, reducing its specialization, no doubt as a consequence of increased agricultural output subsidized by the Common Market.

But all four of the North Atlantic countries look more or less alike when compared with Japan. Again, we see much higher specialization, much greater adjustment, and the pattern of declining share in low technology areas and increasing share in high technology areas (see figure 2-10). Japan has added relative share in thirteen of the top twenty while losing in four, all of which are chemical based. Up until the oil shock of 1973, there was an almost textbook pattern of upgrading—dropping low technology sectors in favor of high. None of the older industrial countries shows a pattern remotely resembling Japan's, despite the theory that comparative advantage, coupled with the invisible hand, will automatically create such a pattern given open borders and international competition.

The significance of the "Japanese model" becomes clearer when we look at the pattern of those who have followed it—the "new Japans." Figure 2-11 shows the combined pattern of exports of South Korea, Taiwan, Hong Kong, and Singapore. These countries are grouped together in part because

Figure 2-11

Revealed Comparative Advantage: Manufactured Exports, Hong Kong, South Korea, Singapore, and Taiwan, 1967-81

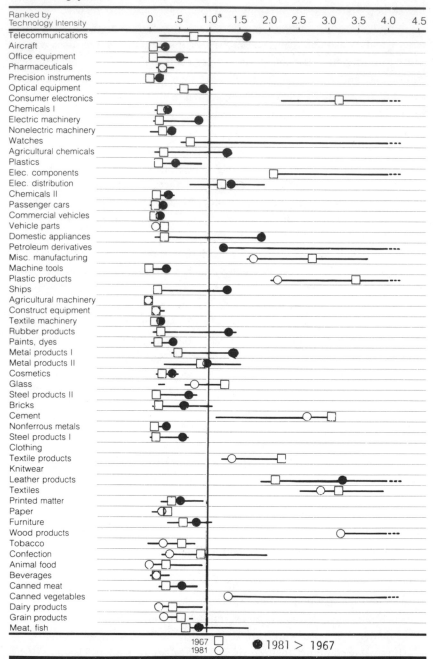

Source: Researcher's calculations based on data from CEPII
Note: Comparative advantage is for 57 product categories relative to total manufactured exports.
[a]1.0=average share of world market in any given year

their trade is overwhelmingly with the rest of the world rather than with each other, and in part because it enables the evaluation on an economic unit roughly comparable in size to one of the large European countries. Like Japan these countries show a high degree of specialization in their exports. Like Japan they also show a high degree of adjustment over time. And, like Japan, they show a pattern of gaining share at the high end and losing it at the low end. Obviously they are not as far up the scale as Japan: in thirteen of the top twenty categories they still have below-average share. But they show a decline in only one category, vehicle parts. The pattern is almost more striking than Japan's; in fifteen or twenty years they accomplished what the Japanese did in twenty-five or thirty. It is possible that in another decade a dramatic thrust toward higher technology exports and formidable competition from these newcomers will affect all the older industrial countries.

The pattern is all the more remarkable when coupled with the overall growth rate of exports. Thus, for the last twenty years these new Japans have had an extraordinary growth rate while at the same time shifting their export mix. Other countries such as Mexico and Brazil have also been able to shift their export mix somewhat toward higher technology sectors, but less dramatically than the new Japans. But as exporters of manufactured goods, neither Brazil nor Mexico is a major factor. In 1982, for example, Hong Kong, South Korea, and Taiwan *each* exported more manufactures than all the Latin American countries combined—Mexico and Brazil included.[11]

A DYNAMIC THEORY OF COMPARATIVE ADVANTAGE

One of the key innovations of the new East Asian competitors is a revised theory of comparative advantage, a theory focused on opportunity as well as resources, and one that shows how a country can mobilize whatever limited resources it has to seize opportunities. Instead of focusing on static factor endowments and rising (short-run) costs, it focuses on factor mobility and the possibility of declining long-run costs based on the learning curve as well as economies of scale. It is a theory that focuses on the opportunities for change through time—a dynamic theory of comparative advantage which supplements the traditional, static Western one.[12]

With the advantage of hindsight, it is obvious that the short-term and long-term growth and productivity prospects for cloth and wine were quite different in the original Ricardian example. For Portugal, the short-term advantage comes from specialization in wine; the long-term advantage comes from making a success in cloth, the "high-tech," high-growth, rapidly changing industry of the period. If the Portuguese follow the Western theory of comparative advantage, they are sacrificing long-term growth for short-term gains and implicitly accepting a lower standard of living than the British. Concluding otherwise implies that for some reason the Portuguese are "unable" to compete in textiles, a proposition much like the once popular notion that the Egyptians could not operate the Suez Canal. While there is still merit in the static theory, its implications for an economic strategy are likely to lead to second-rate performance at best.

In addition to recognizing the contrast between long-run and short-run gains, the dynamic theory recognizes that the benefits of the static system are not necessarily symmetrical. For example, those countries with a favored position in a high-growth, high value-added industry have an advantage over others. Those with advantages in low-growth industries or those with a low rate of technological change have "advantages" that are second rate in comparison. To stick with these natural advantages is to accept a lower rate of growth and technological development simply because it is a "natural state of affairs," for which, unfortunately, there is "no remedy."

A world of static comparative advantage and free trade favors the rich and the strong—those with natural resources and high levels of productivity in major growth industries. They can undersell newcomers in less-fortunate or less-developed countries and maintain their favored position. The issue is not so much "exploitation" of the weak as a "natural state of affairs" governed by an efficient, impersonal marketplace. And it should not be surprising that the leading advocates of free trade have been those who were the strong at the time, first the United Kingdom, then the United States, and then Germany. Free trade, like free competition, has political as well as economic content: taken literally it is a system that enhances the power of the powerful and makes it all the more difficult for the poor to catch up.

Assuming a connection between theory and national strategies, it should not be surprising that the foremost challenge to the world of static comparative advantage and free trade has come from those nations that were unwilling to accept the second-class citizenship implied by their lower standard of living. The driving motive is political more than economic: "The need for economic growth in a developing country has few if any economic springs. It arises from a desire to assume full human status by taking part in an industrial civilization, participation in which *alone* enables a nation or an individual to compel others to treat it as an equal."[13]

In a world of technological change, differential rates of growth in volume and productivity across industries, and declining costs—especially in the high technology, rapid-growth industries of the era—the rational choice for Por-

tugal, as for other less-developed countries, is to select growth industries
and to use the powers of government to supplement those of the market in
marshalling the resources necessary for entry and successful participation.
Portugal needs to think in terms of acquiring or creating strength in promising
sectors rather than simply accepting its existing mix of resources and attempting to exploit that "endowment" as efficiently as possible. *In short, the
Portuguese should specialize in textiles, not wine, regardless of whether their
costs are lower or higher than those prevailing in Britain at the time.*

Portugal should in some measure choose the industries in which it wishes
to participate and adapt its policies and institutions as required to participate
successfully. While it cannot be best at everything, it has considerable leeway
in choosing the industries in which it wishes to participate and in creating
the conditions necessary for successful participation. In other words, it has
a considerable measure of freedom to create the comparative advantages it
wishes, provided it has the will and ingenuity to create or borrow the
necessary mix of policies and institutions to achieve the cost and quality
positions required for success.

Miyohei Shinohara, former head of the economics section of the Japanese
Economic Planning Agency and longtime member of the Industrial Structure
Council, explains the need for a new view of comparative advantage as
follows:

> In modern economics it has been considered that in an economy of abundant
> labor and scarce capital, the development of labor-intensive production methods
> would naturally bring about a rational allocation of resources.
>
> On the other hand, in an economy with abundant capital and a shortage of
> labor, it has been taken for granted that capital-intensive industries would grow
> by becoming export industries. It has also been assumed that any measures
> taken contrary to this theorem would be going against economic principles, thus
> distorting resource allocation.
>
> If this reasoning is correct, the industrial policies adopted by MITI in the
> mid-1950s were wrong. Ironically, however, Japan's industrial policies achieved
> unprecedented success by going against modern economic theory.
>
> The problem of classical thinking undeniably lies in the fact that it is essen-
> tially "static" and does not take into account the possibility of a dynamic change
> in the comparative advantage or disadvantage of industries over a coming 10-
> or 20-year period. To take the place of such a traditional theory, a new policy
> concept needs to be developed to deal with the possibility of intertemporal
> dynamic development.[14]

The Japanese appear to have been the first to recognize that advantages
could be created through the mobilization of technology, capital, and skilled
labor not just to nurture a few infant industries to supply the domestic market
but as a way of nurturing the whole industrial sector toward areas of growth

and opportunity in the world market. Furthermore, government could create
policies and institutions that accelerated the attack of new sectors on the one
hand and the abandonment of declining or threatened sectors on the other.[15]
In so doing, the Japanese discovered or created a strategy of dynamic comparative advantage at the national level which in many ways parallels the
strategy of a diversified firm as it shifts resources from less promising to
more promising areas.

Once this visible hand or strategy was discovered, the label "Japan, Inc."
followed. This term, typically rejected in the U.S. academic community as
unduly simplistic, was found useful by business executives familiar with the
lack of tidiness of decision-making processes in large firms. As a consequence, when American academics and business executives meet to discuss
how the Japanese economy works and to assess its impact on the U.S.
economy, they often talk past one another. Businesspeople sense the Japanese
are doing something different but lack a theory to explain it. Much of the
academic community clings to a static theory that obscures what the Japanese
are doing, which leads inevitably to the conclusion that it involves nothing
new or different. Even though the Japanese have explicitly indicated that
rejecting Western theory was an essential ingredient in their growth strategy,
some of our leading experts refused to listen.

> Those who attribute Japan's economic success principally to MITI's industrial
> policy seem to be suggesting that without MITI the huge 30 to 35 percent of
> GNP that the Japanese invested in the past several decades would have gone
> mainly into such industries as textiles, shoes, plastic souvenirs, and fisheries.
> This is sheer nonsense. Given the quality of Japanese business executives, those
> massive investment funds probably would have wound up roughly where they
> actually did. And to the extent that there would have been differences, there is
> no reason to believe that MITI's influence, on balance, improved the choices
> in any major way.[16]

There have also been misunderstandings between some U.S. officials and
their Japanese counterparts, with the former alleging that Japanese industrial
policy was more significant than the latter were willing to acknowledge. This
problem was analyzed by Yoshizo Ikeda, senior adviser to the board of
Mitsui & Co., as follows:

> In my view, the real problem is a perception gap. Americans focus on the
> fact that the Japanese government is more successful than the U.S. government
> in promoting industry, while Japanese officials emphasize the fact that they have
> less power over the economy than they did several years ago. In order to close
> this perception gap, both sides must communicate more closely. The United
> States certainly needs to improve its understanding of Japanese policies. But

Japan also has a responsibility to explain its policies candidly and credibly. In my judgment, its failure to do so has contributed considerably to the friction over this issue.

My central theme . . . is that Japanese government industrial policies, although less powerful than in the past, continue to play an influential role in Japan's economic development. But this influence does not derive from dictatorial controls or unfair practices that violate international trade rules. Rather, it is based on effective policy implementation and a variety of cultural traits that enable the government and the private sector to cooperate effectively for the common good of the nation.[17]

In 1972, the Organization for Economic Cooperation and Development (OECD) published one of the early, formal explanations of the basic concepts underlying Japanese industrial policy based on a speech by the then MITI vice minister, as follows:

Should Japan have entrusted its future, according to the theory of comparative advantage, to these industries characterized by intensive use of labor? That would perhaps be a rational choice for a country with a small population of 5 or 10 million. But Japan has a large population. If the Japanese economy had adopted the simple doctrine of free trade and had chosen to specialize in this kind of industry, it would almost permanently have been unable to break away from the Asian pattern of stagnation and poverty, and would have remained the weakest link in the free world, thereby becoming a problem area in the Far East.

The Ministry of International Trade and Industry decided to establish in Japan industries which required intensive employment of capital and technology, industries that in consideration of comparative cost of production should be the most inappropriate for Japan, industries such as steel, oil refining, petrochemicals, automobiles, aircraft, industrial machinery of all sorts, and later electronics, including electronic computers. From a short-run, static viewpoint, encouragement of such industries would seem to conflict with economic rationalism. But, from a long-range point of view, these are precisely the industries where income elasticity of demand is high, technological progress is rapid, and labor productivity rises fast. It was clear that without these industries it would be difficult to employ a population of 100 million and raise their standard of living to that of Europe and America with light industries alone; whether right or wrong, Japan had to have these heavy and chemical industries.[18]

The Japanese, placed in a position similar to that of Portugal in Ricardo's famous example, rejected the notion of specializing in "wine" and chose "cloth" instead. Less than a generation later they had become the world's low-cost producer of many of the items in which they had started with a high-cost position (e.g., steel, ships, automobiles, and consumer electronics).

The criterion used by the Japanese in selecting which industries to emphasize or target is often loosely described as higher value added. This is true in a rough sense; after the fact, however, their criteria appear to have been more subtle, less mechanical, and above all appear to have required sophisticated judgments about the future. Shinohara explains:

> The two basic criteria to which the industrial structure policies adopted by MITI conformed . . . were an "income elasticity criterion" and a comparative "technical progress criterion. . . ."
>
> The "income elasticity criterion" provides a suggestion that an industry whose elasticity of export demand with respect to world real income as a whole is comparatively high should be developed as an export industry. . . .
>
> The "comparative technical progress criterion" pays more attention to the possibility of placing a particular industry in a more advantageous position in the future through a comparatively greater degree of technical progress, even if the cost of the products is relatively high at this stage. This term could be called the "dynamized comparative cost doctrine."[19]

The argument is not the same as pursuing higher value added per employee or higher technology sectors, as can be seen in the current U.S. context. Figure 2-12 shows U.S. industries ranked by level of R&D spending as a share of sales for the year 1979, with value added per employee for different industry groups stated in relation to the U.S. industrial average for the year expressed as 100. Value added correlates to some degree to level of technology, but the correlation is obviously weak. The correlation to the level of investment per employee is, however, much stronger. Literal pursuit of higher value added per employee in the U.S. context would put chemicals and oil refining above all other sectors, without adequate regard either for growth, technical prospects, or profitability. That these sectors could be high value added per employee and low profit at the same time should be noted. Literal pursuit of higher value added per employee would lead to gross misallocation of capital resources and to impoverishing the nation rather than improving its economic performance.

A STRATEGY TO CREATE ADVANTAGES—THE JAPANESE MODEL

The emergence of industries characterized by rapid growth, technical change, and declining costs opens the possibility of an industrial strategy for a nation as well as for a firm. A *firm* can accelerate its run down the experience curve through increasing its market share and hence its volume relative to competitors. Aggressive if not predatory pricing becomes a way to trade lower short-run earnings for a stronger, presumably more profitable long-run position. A firm can also accelerate its run down the curve by

Figure 2-12

Comparison of Value Added per Employee and Net Capital per Employee
in Manufacturing: United States, 1979 (100 = industrial average)

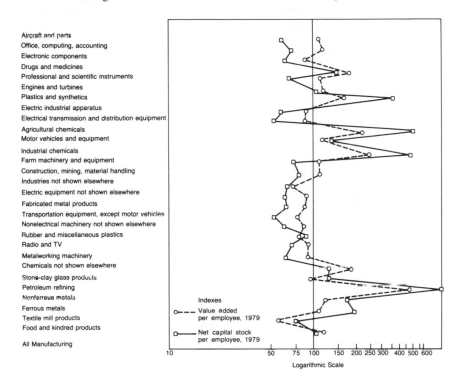

Source: CEC Associates, Manufacturing Industry Time Series, data prepared for the Department
of Commerce, Washington, D.C., July 1983.

acquisition of the latest technology, either through internal R&D or through
licensing from a competitor. A *nation* can build upon these ideas by protecting
the home market during the initial period of relatively high costs, by helping
provide low-cost, long-term finance to promote capital investment, and by a
variety of measures to maintain or promote the mobility of resources—both
capital and labor. In extreme situations in which the political motivation to
catch up allows government not only a visible hand but a heavy one, government can push firms toward accepting the latest technologies by setting

minimum sizes on new plants, thus requiring them to be brought rapidly to world scale. Excess capacity can be avoided by requiring firms to take turns building new plants, with the requirement that they supply competitors until they have had opportunity to build their own new facilities. A "very visible hand" has been described in the Japanese context as follows:

> The process is quite straightforward. Japan imports a technology . . . from the West. It then protects the industry in question from foreign competition to whatever extent and by whatever means may be required while it gains scale, experience, cost parity, and momentum in Japan itself—the world's second largest and fastest growing market, exporting aggressively, further enhancing its cost position. Gradually it converts a part of its cost advantage into improved product quality. At some point the Japanese competitor is able to offer a better product, profitably, and at a lower price. . . .[20]

Givens describes the Japanese practices as "a sophisticated strategy of selective protectionism." The sophistication is in protecting "a narrow moving band" that gradually moves up the technology scale. Successive industries are targeted and protected for a time. Once a superior position is achieved the protection is dropped.[21]

Selective protection is vital but only a part of the strategy. Without more detail, we cannot decide if the Japanese strategy is essentially an unfair trade practice or a more competitive, better strategy. The distinction is important. To see the Japanese strategy essentially as an unfair trade practice, for example, leads to demands that they change. To see the Japanese as having a holistic strategy of creating advantages rather than accepting the status quo is to recognize that their approach may be more competitive than ours. It also implies that they have little reason to change and are increasingly likely to resent demands that they do so. For the moment it begs the question of whether such a strategy would still be "better" if many, much less all, countries attempted to follow it.

Americans tend to be forced to one of two positions as they observe these developments in Japan. Economists steeped in a static theory that has no place for a strategy of creating comparative advantage claim that the Japanese are misunderstood, that there never was such a strategy, but even if there had been, it is a thing of the past. Business executives, who have a continuing awareness of the differences of doing business in competition with the Japanese, are inclined to dwell on those aspects of the Japanese strategy that are the most aggressive and not infrequently constitute unfair trade practices. American academics, for example, explain the demise of the U.S. television industry in terms of superior Japanese technology, typically treating the dumping and other unfair competition claims of U.S manufacturers as "legal harassment." They may even omit the fact that the importers were assessed $75 million in fines for dumping and criminal fraud. Industry executives, for their part, were slow to match an awareness of unfair trading practices with comparable recognition either of superior Japanese manufacturing practices or the strategy that was reshaping the structure of Japanese industry.

Targeting, or exerting a concentrated effort to catch up in a particular industry, is of course not a new idea. On the contrary, it has long been known as the infant industry argument. What is new, however, is applying the argument to build export-oriented industries rather than focusing on import substitution; to include a very broad range of industries instead of just a few; to achieve domestic rather than foreign control; and to systematically upgrade the portfolio of industries over time. The infant industry paradigm has traditionally been seen as a defensive response permitting a country to catch up in a sensitive area. As used by the Japanese it has become the paradigm for a broad-scale industrial offensive.

> In general, the nurturing of infant industries is limited to a certain period of time and to a certain number of industries. In Japan, however, these measures were across-the-board and applied to almost all industries. This Japanese-type of infant industry may not be admissible from the generally accepted premises of international economics, for one of its fundamental concepts is the international division of labor through free trade. Because of the vastly extended promotion of infant industries and across-the-board encouragement of exports, MITI's approach ran counter to the basic principles of modern international economics.[22]

The goal was to "strengthen the international competitiveness" of essentially all of the industries under MITI's jurisdiction by a set of incentives, through a consultative process in which MITI played a very influential but far from dictatorial role. In addition to the targeted incentives, the exchange rate was kept undervalued until 1971 and then allowed to rise only when there was no alternative. Probably of equal importance, but much less understood outside Japan, the results of its successful export promotion strategy were not allowed to accumulate as rising foreign exchange reserves. Instead, the Japanese began deliberately to accelerate their growth rate, starting in 1957, under the slogan "A hundred billion yen tax cut is a hundred billion yen of aid."[23]

Some American observers discount the Japanese claims of a program to build export competitiveness to the point of using familiar national income data to prove that it never happened. Thus, Japanese exports do not rise appreciably as a share of GNP, and they remain a smaller share than for a number of other (typically much smaller) countries. This argument misses the point. By deliberately accelerating domestic growth, the domestic market grew at about the same rate as exports, but at a rate twice that of Japan's leading competitors. Another argument, that Japan was not mercantilist because it did not accumulate foreign exchange reserves, also misses the point. Domestic growth was allowed to run as fast as it could, subject to a balance of payments constraint, until the early 1970s. Then, as domestic growth slowed, Japan began to accumulate the now familiar surpluses.

If one accepts that industries can be targeted and nurtured from infancy for the world market, that it can be done on a very broad scale, and that it need not result in balance of payments surplus if domestic growth is accelerated to generate offsetting imports, then one has the broad outlines of a supply-side strategy for rapid economic growth. Macroeconomic policy must help assure the savings necessary to finance the high levels of investment required to sustain it and accelerate growth to keep the external accounts in balance. And, as the economy approaches or reaches full employment, it is increasingly urgent to recognize that further progress comes from shifting resources from low-growth, low value-added sectors to higher-performance sectors. Mobility of resources is an essential ingredient of continued progress. Further, the capacity to mobilize and concentrate resources on key sectors permits the possibility of decisive breakthroughs, for a country as for a company or a military commander.

How aggressively a country wishes to use such ideas seems to depend on political priorities. How successfully it can implement them depends on translating them into a consistent, coherent strategy.

GROWTH/PRODUCTIVITY-ORIENTED STRATEGIES

The opportunity-oriented notion of competing in part upon created comparative advantage, selective protection, and "nurturing" is one vital component of an overall growth/productivity-oriented strategy. The other indispensable element is the goal itself; it can hardly be said too often that the goals drive a strategy. Full commitment to the growth/productivity goal means using the full mix of macro- and microeconomic policies in its pursuit.

Macroeconomic policies can contribute to long-term economic growth in a variety of well-known ways. One approach is creating or maintaining an undervalued exchange rate, which makes exports cheaper on world markets, helps boost profit margins, investment, and productivity. Undervalued exchange rates were part of the success stories of Japan and Germany in the 1950s and 1960s, and the loss of this favored position by Germany seems to be one of the major factors in its subsequent slowdown.

Using tax policy to promote savings and investment is an established way to increase supply. Tax-free savings accounts are an example of promoting individual savings, and accelerated depreciation is an approach to promoting both savings and investment by corporations. Tax policy may be able to stimulate supply through incentives for work as well as saving and investment, perhaps primarily by avoiding levels of taxation that act as disincentives.

Classic Keynesian demand management can also promote growth and productivity. For example, smoothing the business cycle reduces the depth of periodic recessions, thereby reducing business risk. Reduced risk promotes higher investment, and higher rates of investment help lift the potential growth rate for an economy. For a time Western Europe appeared to be benefiting from such a virtuous circle of steady, high growth accompanied by high levels of investment and rapid productivity growth. Unaccompanied by the notions of created comparative advantage, however, the economics of demand management have tended to focus on domestic demand. In this perspective, inadequate demand is cured by inflating the domestic economy— a policy that if pursued for long is the antithesis of the competitively oriented strategy followed by the Japanese. Politics leads to excessive reliance on domestic demand as a quick fix and to an inflationary bias over time.

Familiar sectoral approaches to promoting productivity and growth include development of infrastructure (e.g., canals, roads, railroads, airways, and communications systems), the educational system, and active promotion of research and development. Modification of microeconomic incentives is less tangible, but perhaps of equal importance. For example, "more years of schooling" implies one level of achievement; a curriculum oriented to specific skills and accompanied by a performance-oriented measurement and reward system implies a higher level. Likewise, while subsidies or rapid cost recovery for R&D are obvious approaches, increasing the rewards gained by the successful inventor or developer is probably more powerful. Directing rewards toward gains for the community or nation is not the same as directing them toward rewarding the individual. Hence, a long patent life increases the rewards for the inventor or the firm but not necessarily for the nation, since the patent may be licensed abroad and foreign firms and/or workers may capture much of the benefit. Licensing policy can influence the capture of these benefits by a country, typically at some cost to firms and/or inventors.

Public policy can also promote mobility in capital markets, labor markets, and product markets. A high capital gains tax, for example, retards the mobility of capital by exacting a high penalty from those who would move their capital from one successful investment in search of another. Reducing or eliminating such a tax promotes mobility, as was evident when the rates were lowered in the United States in 1978 (see table 2-2). Another way to promote capital mobility is taxing only on real or inflation-adjusted gains.

Financial guarantees, implicit or explicit, are a means of reducing risk, reducing cost, and increasing the mobility of capital. The Japanese have operated with a highly leveraged system that is offset by a system of guarantees—often only implicit—from the Bank of Japan to the big city banks to the big companies. This implies that there are administrative as well as market criteria for the allocation of credit, or in other words, an element of administrative credit rationing in the system. As part of a "developmental" strategy the effect is to promote mobility even if on "administered" terms, while as part of a distributional strategy the effect might well be the opposite. (A comparison of the Japanese and American capital markets and of their impact on the cost and availability of capital is the subject of chapter 10, by Philip Wellons.) Avoiding price controls, such as limitations on the interest that can be paid on various forms of savings, is another way to promote capital mobility.

Table 2-2
Venture Capital and Public Market Financing

Year	New Private Capital Committed to Venture Investment ($ millions)	Equity Capital Raised by Companies with Net Worth Less than $5 Million	
		No. of Offerings	Funds Raised ($ millions)
1969	$171	698	$1,366.9
1970	97	198	375.0
1971	95	248	550.0
1972	62	409	896.0
1973	56	69	159.7
1974	57	9	16.1
1975	10	4	16.2
1976	50	29	144.8
1977	39	13	42.6
1978	570	21	89.3
1979	319	46	182.9
1980	900	135	821.5

Source: Richard Bolling and John Bowles, *America's Competitive Edge* (New York: McGraw-Hill Book Company, 1982), 153.

Labor market mobility can also be promoted through public policy. Profit sharing, whether through stock ownership or through a system of bonuses paid proportionately to all levels of employees, allows compensation to vary with results and thus to create a system that automatically adjusts compensation. When accompanied by a commitment to lifetime employment in the firm, the system is relatively flexible, based on employment security rather than income security, and links the employee and the firm both in performance and in sharing the results. When, as is the case in many European countries, there are not only fixed wages but restrictions or high penalties on reductions in the labor force, labor market mobility can be sharply reduced. The likely result is increased reluctance to hire, an additional use of subcontractors, or less aggressive pursuit of opportunities.

Employment centers and retraining programs are familiar elements of a program to encourage labor mobility. The persistence of high levels of unemployment throughout the OECD area suggests, however, that these policies by themselves have only a marginal impact. Increasingly generous unemployment payments to help provide income security have the effect of reducing mobility by reducing the urgency of finding alternative employment.

Mobility in product markets can be facilitated by promoting ease of entry and exit. Deregulation of the airlines brought new, low-price, nonunion entries into the industry. Much the same is happening in trucking. The effect is to add new competitors and to change the nature of competition, a situation that in some respects parallels the entry of the East Asian Newly Industrializing Countries (NICs) into the American market.

Less obvious perhaps is the notion of "managed competition" as compared to maximum competition. With the former, a company might be encouraged to give up marginal products or product lines to concentrate on what it does best, while other domestic firms in the same industry would be encouraged to make similar concessions. The result would be a narrower line for all firms, permitting a higher level of resource commitment behind each remaining product market.

"Managed competition" requires government to play a role in mediating decisions about who would give up what, and it or an industry association would monitor compliance. This is similar to the portfolio management of a highly diversified multidivisional firm, involving government as a coach, broker, and referee. The continued industrial restructuring in Japan is a case in which government policies combine with corporate strategy to ensure rapid adjustment for targeted industries.[24] It contrasts sharply with American practice which assumes that the maximum degree of competition is best, even if that means five gas stations on a corner instead of four, with decisions to withdraw left to the competitors to be made in isolation.

Managed competition is a subtle concept, particularly at the national level. It conjures up the spectre of national planning, and the cumbersome hand of bureaucracy interfering in business affairs, in which it is often ill-trained, ill-informed, and ill-suited; there are endless examples of ill-fated interventions. Most of these unfortunate adventures, it should be noted, come from countries that do not have growth/productivity-oriented strategies, and where government is intervening not to promote long-term performance but to secure improved distributive justice measured in short-term gains. Successful management of competitive forces does not easily bring to mind a long list of examples in the North Atlantic area, despite the fact that a country like France has been perhaps as interventionist as Japan for a very long time.[25]

For government to intervene successfully usually does not depend on how refined the plans are or how expert the experts are but on the broad strategy that is in place. Security/distributional-oriented societies can hardly help but adhere to these same goals when they intervene in industrial affairs. As a consequence, they are more likely to focus on how the pie is divided than on what is necessary to increase its size, and in the process they may well inhibit instead of help its growth.

ECONOMIC SECURITY/INCOME DISTRIBUTION STRATEGIES

While some nations place high priority on baking more pie (that is, on measures promoting productivity and growth), others assume that the baking is best guided by the invisible hand, which leaves government free to place high priority on ensuring a minimum or fair share for everyone (that is, on measures promoting economic security and a redistribution of income via transfer payments).

The distinction between strategies is based on the political goals of the society, not on its performance. For example, it is not clear that income distribution in the distribution-oriented countries is more equal than in the productivity-oriented countries of East Asia. What is clear is that governments have accepted an ever-increasing responsibility for the income security of their citizens, for the redistribution of income, and for due process in attempting to see that all citizens receive the benefits to which they are "entitled." The contrast is as much one of process as substance, and of a shift of responsibilities away from the firm, the family, and the individual toward government. The countries that have focused on dividing the pie are those we know as the welfare states.

Over time, several characteristics of these welfare states have emerged. For one, their citizens continually expected more from government. As a result, the public sector continually assumed new roles, becoming responsible for a greater share of aggregate demand (see figure 2-13). Second, labor also expected more, and wages and salaries absorbed a larger share of national income (see figure 2-14). Third, although investment rose as share of GNP in many of the industrial countries during the 1950s and 1960s, by the early 1970s, in contrast with Japan and the NICs, it was stable or declining in

Figure 2-13

Total Outlays of Government as Percentage of GDP, Selected Countries, 1960-80

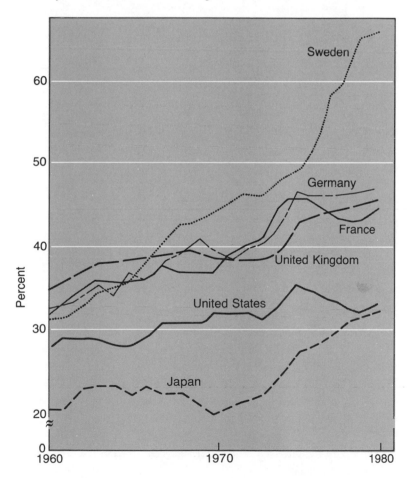

Source: OECD, *OECD Economic Outlook*, no. 32, December 1982.

Figure 2-14

Labor's Share of Total Domestic Factor Income

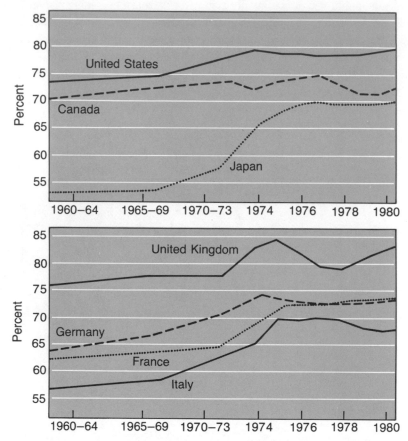

Source: Morgan Guaranty Trust Company of New York, *World Financial Markets*, May 1982, 3.

relative terms (see table 2-3), reducing the growth potential of these economies. Fourth, to sustain domestic demand and growing social programs in times of slack economic conditions, governments resorted to deficit financing. This policy was less and less effective in sustaining demand as all the industrial economies became more integrated in the world economy; inflating domestic demand led rapidly to rising budget deficits and balance of payments problems.[26] The problem was particularly acute in some of the smaller countries, where deficits have reached 15 percent of GNP (see figure 2-15) without achieving desired growth.

Table 2-3
Gross Fixed Capital Formation/GDP Selected Countries

	1960	*1970*	*1975*	*1980*	*1981*
United States	18%	17%	16%	18%	18%[c]
Canada	22	21	24	23	24
France	20	23	23	22	21
Germany	24	26	21	25	23
United Kingdom	16	19	20	17	16
Japan	30	35	32	32[b]	32
South Korea	11	24	26	31	27
Taiwan	17	22	31	na	
Hong Kong	21[a]	19	22	na	
Singapore	10	33	35	39	
Malaysia	11	16	25	29	32

Source: OECD, *National Accounts,* various issues.
[a]1961
[b]Share of GNP
[c]Includes government

An essential commitment of the welfare state is economic security for all, not just for the poor. The bulk of the budgetary cost for the welfare state in all industrial countries is for two programs that basically are not means tested: retirement and medical care. Table 2-4 shows relative magnitudes for the means-tested and other economic security programs in the United States. For those programs not based on a means test the essential criterion for eligibility is simply membership in the community.

With the spread of prosperity in the 1960s, there was a sustained increase not only in budgetary allocations to economic security programs but in the share of GNP committed to them (see table 2-5). The trend became, if anything, more significant in the 1970s, when for most industrial countries the only major budget categories to grow in relation to GNP were transfer payments to finance these programs and interest on public debt (see table 2-6).

Our key industrial competitors, notably the East Asians, have not made similar adjustments in their priorities, or at least not yet. While budget comparisons are not easily made outside of the OECD area or for Japan, a chart compiled by the International Monetary Fund (IMF) gives an idea of the order of magnitude of the differences (see figure 2-16). Japan has obviously increased its social security spending dramatically in the 1970s, but its unique budgeting system makes comparisons difficult.

Figure 2-15

Government Deficit as a Percentage of GNP, 1970-82

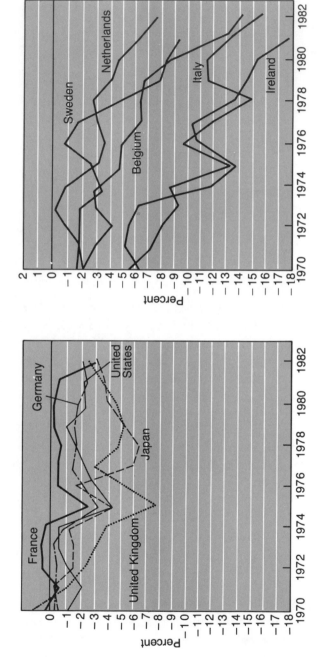

Source: International Monetary Fund, *International Financial Statistics*, September 1983; United Nations, *World Economic Survey*, New York, 1983.
Source: International Monetary Fund, *International Financial Statistics*, December 1982 and November 1983.

Table 2-4

Estimated U.S. Government Outlays, Comparison of 1980 to 1985 as Now Projected

	In Billions of Dollars			In Share of GNP[a]		
	1980	*1985*[b]	*1980–85 Change*	*1980*	*1985*	*1980–85 Change*
National defense	$123.9	$274.1	$+150.2	4.8%	7.0%	+2.2%
Benefit payments for individuals						
Need-related[c]	55.9	80.3	+24.4	2.2	2.0	−0.2
Non-need-related						
(social security, federal						
pensions, etc.)	227.1	380.1	+153.1	8.8	9.6	+0.8
Grants to state and local						
governments	57.2	53.6	−3.6	2.3	1.3	−1.0
Other federal operations	60.1	59.0	−1.1	2.3	1.5	−0.8
Net interest[d]	52.5	120.1	+67.6	2.0	3.1	+1.1
Total	$576.7	$967.2[e]	+390.5	22.4%	24.6%	+2.2%

Source: Peter G. Peterson, *New York Review of Books*, 2 December 1982. Reprinted with permission from *New York Review of Books*, Copyright 2 December 1982, NYREV Inc.

[a]Assumes real growth of 3–4 percent in 1983–85; 1985 GNP $3,935.4 billion versus Reagan's April 1981 supply-side target of $4,398.1 billion.
[b]Outlay projections are based on congressional action to date.
[c]In 1981 and 1982, the growth in these need-related programs was cut over twice as much as the non-need-related (10.1 percent versus 4.7 percent).
[d]For 1983–85, the interest-rate assumptions are those specified in the first concurrent resolution on the budget, declining to an average rate of 7.4 percent on new Treasury debt in 1985. If interest rates turn out to be higher, each percentage point over the entire three years adds about $8 billion.
[e]Reagan's April 1981 spending target for 1985 was $844 billion.

Expenditure numbers tell only part of the story. Social welfare expenditures must be financed largely through taxes on incomes and/or consumption. Rising income taxes reduce the returns to work and at some point tempt some members of society to do part or all of their work in the cash economy or even to leave the country. Rising taxes on consumption likewise become an incentive to move transactions into the cash economy.

Figure 2-17 shows how these forces have interacted over time in the United States. Real spendable incomes for those who worked roughly kept pace with the rate of increase of real spendable incomes for those receiving transfer payments until the mid-1960s. Since then a combination of more rapid increases in transfer payments plus their tax-exempt status led to a major shift: real spendable incomes for those not working continued to rise, while for the worker they peaked in 1972 and then began to decline. By the mid-

Table 2-5

Subsidies and Other Current Transfers as % of GNP

	1971	1972	1973	1974	1975	1976	1977	1978	1979	1980
Belgium	—	22.1	23.0	22.8	26.7	27.5	28.7	29.4	30.4	30.4
Denmark	19.4	19.4	20.0	22.5	23.1	22.8	24.1	25.3	26.1	27.7
France	—	—	20.8	23.0	24.5	24.4	25.5	26.7	30.5	31.0
Holland	—	—	30.2	32.8	36.7	36.9	36.2	37.7	38.3	38.8
Italy	—	—	19.3	19.5	22.4	22.4	21.5	26.0	25.7	27.3
Sweden	—	17.0	17.3	18.9	19.4	22.0	25.0	27.3	28.8	33.0
United Kingdom	15.4	16.3	16.1	18.6	21.1	20.1	19.9	19.8	19.2	19.9
United States	—	10.4	11.1	10.0	11.6	12.2	12.0	11.7	11.4	12.1
West Germany	12.4	12.1	12.0	12.9	16.1	15.8	16.1	16.0	15.6	15.3
Japan[a]										
South Korea	6.4	6.1	4.9	5.4	5.3	5.2	5.2	4.9	7.1	6.5
Singapore	—	2.8	2.1	0.9	1.5	1.2	0.9	1.0	0.7	1.2
Thailand	—	2.4	1.8	1.9	2.5	2.7	2.5	2.3	2.4	2.7

Source: International Monetary Fund
[a]Comparable figures not available

1970s, incomes based on Aid to Families with Dependent Children (AFDC) and unemployment benefits peaked, but retirement incomes continued their dramatic rise. Distributive priorities clearly took precedence over rewarding those who were baking the pie.

The connection between distribution-oriented strategies and economic performance is not easy to establish, despite the intuitive links suggested by figure 2-17. Michel Albert, former French commissioner for national planning, and James Ball, principal of the London Business School, have made such a link in their analysis of the relationship between incomes and employment as shown in table 2-7.

On the difficult question of the relationship between income and employment, this table speaks for itself: it shows that faced with a slowdown in growth, Europeans reacted in a very special manner, giving priority to individual income rather than employment.

In 1973 the difference from the average in the 1960s was 6% in Europe compared with 3% in the United States and less than 1% in Japan. It is easy to see how after the first oil price shock and the subsequent recession wage earners everywhere attempted to maintain the growth in their purchasing power in spite of the slowdown in growth. But they succeeded more in Europe where the difference reached 14% in 1975, than in the United States and Japan where it was only half this level (7%). This difference grew even more in the period between the two oil price shocks. The second oil price shock and the 1981-83 recession increased the gap. in Europe it is 7 to 8 points higher than in the United States. In Japan not only has the situation not deteriorated it has actually improved slightly. This is reflected in the vitality and competitive ability of Japanese firms which is linked to the effectiveness of their fight against unemployment. On the other hand it is clear that behaviour such as Europe has demonstrated marked by an enormous growth in individual income compared to GDP, indicates a preference for consumption to the detriment of investment and increase in the costs of undertakings which severely limit their ability to invest. Moreover, in view of the high level of wage costs, companies are attracted towards investments which save labour rather than investments which create jobs. This is particularly true in Europe since the tax and related charges added to salaries are the highest in the world and grew more rapidly than everywhere else—as we shall see—over the last ten years. Thus, the increase in individual incomes, which is excessive in comparison to the wealth produced, increases unemployment, reduces investment and compromises present and future growth.[27]

There are more direct, if perhaps less important, connections; for example, increasingly generous health insurance programs have led to more days lost

Table 2-6
Major Industrial Countries: Selected Components of Government Expenditure in Relation to GDP, 1965–79 (in percent of nominal GDP)

	Purchases of Goods and Services	Transfers and Subsidies	Interest on Public Debt
Seven major industrial countries[a]			
1965	19.2	8.5	1.8
1967	20.6	9.3	1.9
1969	20.0	9.7	2.0
1971	20.2	10.6	2.0
1973	19.4	11.1	2.2
1975	21.0	13.8	2.3
1977	19.9	13.8	2.6
1979	19.6	13.9	2.9
Four major European industrial countries[a]			
1965	19.2	14.3	1.7
1967	19.5	15.2	2.0
1969	19.2	15.4	2.0
1971	20.0	15.2	1.8
1973	20.2	16.0	1.9
1975	22.4	18.8	2.3
1977	21.0	19.1	2.7
1979	21.1	19.5	2.9

(*continued*)

Table 2-6 *(continued)*
Major Industrial Countries: Selected Components of Government Expenditure in
Relation to GDP, 1965–79 (in percent of nominal GDP)

	Purchases of Goods and Services	*Transfers and Subsidies*	*Interest on Public Debt*
United States			
1965	20.0	5.9	1.9
1967	22.3	6.7	2.0
1969	21.5	7.3	2.1
1971	21.2	9.2	2.2
1973	20.1	9.4	2.3
1975	21.3	11.9	2.5
1977	20.1	11.4	2.6
1979	19.7	11.0	2.8
Japan[b]			
1965	12.7	5.4	0.4
1967	11.9	5.4	0.6
1969	11.6	5.5	0.6
1971	13.0	5.9	0.7
1973	14.0	6.2	0.9
1975	15.4	9.3	1.2
1977	15.5	10.3	2.0
1979	16.2	11.3	2.7

Source: Organization for Economic Cooperation and Development, *National Accounts of OECD Countries*, vol. 2, *Detailed Tables, 1962–1979* (Paris, July 1981). (Table excerpted from *World Economic Outlook*, published by the International Monetary Fund, Washington, D.C., 1982, 191.)
[a]Weighted averages, with weights proportionate (in terms of three-year moving averages) to GDP valued in U.S. dollars.
[b]The data for Japan exclude some transfers for which data are not available for years prior to 1970. The combined value of these omitted transfers was equivalent to about ¾ of 1 percent of GDP in 1970 and to 1¼ percent in 1979.

due to illness, not fewer. The programs thus have a double cost, one measured in the budget and the other in the unmeasured disruption of work schedules. Thus in health insurance programs the critical element influencing days lost due to illness does not appear to be the amount of the benefit but the terms of eligibility. During the 1960s various European countries shifted from health plans in which the insurance coverage took effect on the fourth day of illness to programs that began coverage immediately on the first day, and all experienced a rise in days lost due to illness. The change was like offering "zero deductible" collision insurance on autos with no increase in premiums.[28]

For health insurance, the crucial change has been not so much the magnitude of the benefit, though it is not uncommon for the sick employee to receive 90 percent or more of pay during periods of illness, but the idea that the employee is entitled to a specified number of weeks of sick leave per year. If the system grants this entitlement, it is tempting to accept it. Enforcing a rigorous interpretation based on "sickness" is not only contrary to the spirit of the program, it is utterly impractical, since any doctor accepting the role of police officer risks losing some of his practice. As a result, the goal of increased health security has been translated into entitlement programs that in turn not only dramatically increase the economic costs of "illness," but do so in ways that are disruptive to productive activity.

Figure 2-16

Social Security and Welfare Plus Other Social Expenditures as a Percentage of Total Central Government Expenditures, Latest Available Year

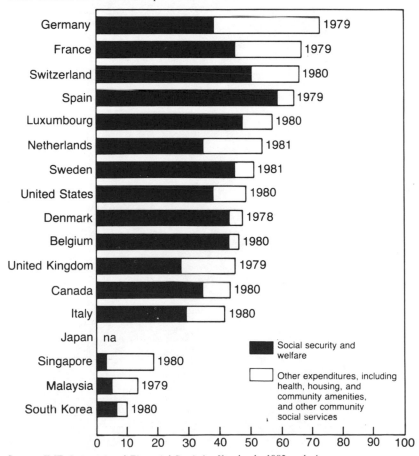

Source: IMF, *International Financial Statistics Yearbook, 1982,* vol. 4.

Figure 2-17

Indexes of Spendable Earnings for Workers and Various Social Benefit Payments to Nonworkers, 1950-81 (1950 = 100)

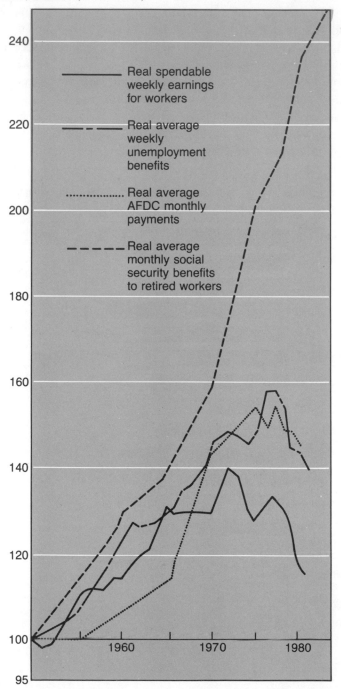

Table 2-7
The Rate of Unemployment and the Gap between Real Salaries and Real GDP per Person Employed

	Rate of Unemployment[a]			Difference between the Evolution of Real Wages per Capita and GDP in Volume per Capita[b]		
	EEC	U.S.	Japan	EEC	U.S.	Japan
Avg. 1961–70	2.1	4.6	1.2	100.0	100.0	100.0
1973	2.4	4.7	1.3	106.4	103.3	100.7
1975	4.1	8.3	1.9	114.0	106.5	107.2
1978	5.2	5.9	2.2	112.3	105.4	104.2
1980	5.8	6.7	2.0	113.0	106.8	98.7
1983 est.	10.8	10.1	2.4	116.8	109.2	97.9

Source: Michel Albert and James Ball, "Towards European Economic Recovery in the 1980s," European Parliament Working Documents, 1983–84, 7 July 1983, 11–12.
[a]Unemployed as % of total active population
[b]Index average 1961–70=100, wages per wage earner deflated by consumer price index and divided by GDP in volume per capita of active population

Similar distortions have occurred in other programs. Social security in the United States was originally a social insurance program with funding based on actuarial concepts, similar to a private insurance program. During the 1960s, however, benefits were increased much more rapidly than payments into the system, and during the Nixon administration the benefits were indexed. As a result, current beneficiaries receive far more than justified by their contributions, and current contributors have their payments used to finance retirees rather than to build the retirement fund for their later years.[29] Over time, an evermore generous notion of entitlement has turned a far-sighted and financially sound insurance program into one that not only places an unfair burden on the young to provide unwarranted benefits to those retiring, but inflates the cost of the system by having benefits so high that some people retire from one job to qualify as retirees, only to take another.

The minimum wage may have undergone a similar distortion. Originally designed to protect workers against unfair exploitation by employers, it was gradually turned into a vehicle for pushing up all wages. Because it was legislated, it did not have to be responsive to market conditions, and particularly to the need for wages to go down in a period of prolonged excess

Source: Based on statistics reported in (1) *The Economic Report of the President*, Council of Economic Advisers, Washington, D.C., February 1982, and (2) *Supplement to Employment and Earnings, Revised Establishment Data*, Bureau of Labor Statistics, Washington, D.C., August 1981, and (3) *Social Security Bulletin*, Social Security Administration, U.S. Department of Health and Human Services, May 1983.

labor supply. Thus, with some thirty million unemployed in the OECD area, and the prospect that the numbers may continue to grow, the minimum wage helps anchor wages and salaries at levels that are too high to clear the market. Part of the cost is borne by those without work and part by those who pay taxes to finance the unemployment compensation and relief payments. The rationale seems to be that, unlike other factors of production, labor is entitled to some minimum price (wage) below which it will not be allowed to fall, regardless of market conditions. France appears to be an extreme case in recent years (see figure 2-18).

While the United States has been less extreme than most West European countries in expanding the "sickness entitlement" across the private sector, and likewise less extreme than some in its minimum wage entitlement, it seems to have gone further in building the standard of living by promoting short-term consumer benefits at the expense of incentives to save and invest. Until the 1981 tax reforms there were "penalty taxes" on interest and dividends; the maximum rate went as high as 70 percent versus a maximum rate of 50 percent on earned income. Interest on consumer borrowing, however, was tax deductible—on a home mortgage, an auto loan, and even credit card purchases. The mortgage interest deduction was estimated to cost the Treasury $25 billion in 1982, and deduction of other consumer interest expense another $6 billion.[30] This presumably implicit U.S. policy of penalizing savings and subsidizing consumption would seem to be an important contributing cause to a national savings rate that was the lowest, by a wide margin, among the major industrial countries (see figure 2-19).

Giving high priority to distribution seems to lead to an increasing array of entitlements that have no necessary connections either to market realities or to individual performance. While proliferation of such programs is in part tied to national income levels, there is a distinct conceptual difference between the East Asians and the North Atlantic countries that Ezra Vogel has described in a comparison of Japanese and U.S. practices. He notes that health care and pensions rose rapidly in Japan during the 1960s and early 1970s, until they roughly approximated Western levels, but the programs did not proliferate nor was there a similar idea of entitlement behind them.

> Aside from health care and old age pensions, people do not have a sense of entitlement about welfare. There is a sense of stigma about accepting it, and it is given out very sparingly. The family (including relatives beyond the nuclear family) and the workplace are expected to bear a much bigger responsibility and to put aside funds for their own security.[31]

And, for the political leadership:

> The essence of the consensus is that the welfare state, with high welfare and high state burden as found in England, Sweden, and the United States, is

Figure 2-18

Index of Real Minimum Wages, Selected Countries, 1970-82

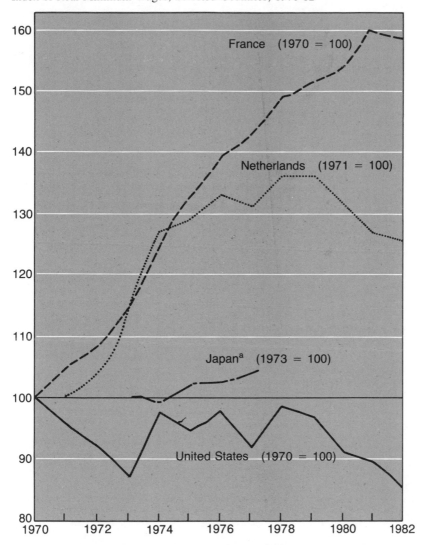

Source: U.S. Department of Labor, Wage and Hour Division, Washington, D.C.; United Nations, International Labor Office, New York, New York; Gerald Starr, "Minimum Wage Fixing," International Labor Office, Geneva, Switzerland, 1981; The French Embassy, Washington, D.C., *Annuaire Statistique de la France, 1982*, INSEE; The Japanese Embassy, Washington, D.C.; Embassy of the Netherlands, Washington, D.C.; Price Waterhouse, "Doing Business," various country series.

Note: The following countries do not have statutory minimum wages: Germany, the United Kingdom, Singapore, Hong Kong, and South Korea. Real minimum wages: minimum wages adjusted by consumer price index of individual countries. Nominal minimum wages in 1983:

United States	$ 3.35 per hour	Netherlands	2048.8 guilders a month
France	22.33 FF per hour	Japan	3,000.0 yen per day

[a]Data not available for Japan from 1977 to 1982.

Figure 2-19

Household Savings Ratios (net savings as a percentage of disposable income)

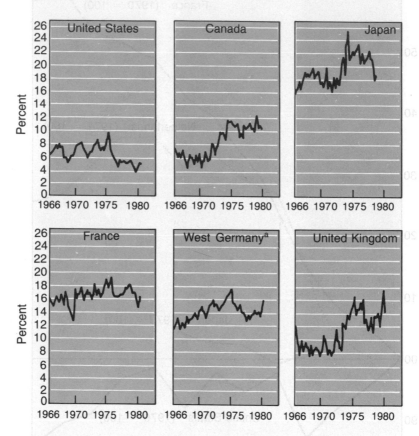

Source: OECD, *Economic Outlooks*, December 1980, chart Q, 139.
Note: Quarterly rates, seasonally adjusted, include private transfers to pension funds.
[a]For Germany, savings exclude retained earnings of unincorporated business.

undesirable . . . the basic rationale for the new consensus is understood by all in leadership positions and in muted form (in a period of low growth, with a heavily strained budget, funds are not available). . . . These leaders prefer to keep funds flowing into the productive sectors of the economy, to encourage the working place and the family to share welfare burdens, and to supplement private welfare with state funds only when it is essential to do so.[32]

Limiting the proliferation of programs and their budgetary cost is probably possible because large Japanese firms assume considerable responsibilities. This does more than relieve government of pressure to create new programs;

it connects eligibility to the financial success of the firm and to performance by the individual.

> Japanese companies concentrate their benefits in areas that will keep the employee attached to the company over a long period of time. Benefits in the United States include substantial sick leave, vacation time, and coffee breaks— benefits rarely provided by Japanese companies in comparable amounts. In contrast some seven percent of the Japanese population live in housing supplied by employers. An additional fifty percent . . . own the dwellings where they live, and over half that company employees borrow to buy housing is lent by employers.[33]

The Japanese government followed a similar pattern in dealing with companies and industries hard hit by the 1975 recession. Instead of making payments directly to unemployed workers, the government offered to pay half, or in the case of small firms two-thirds, on condition that the company retain the employees.[34] In this way, something is still expected both from the employee and from the firm, in contrast to American practice which relieves the firm of responsibility in favor of the government, which in turn creates an entitlement for the displaced employee.

> The government's policy of distributing wealth throughout society is not based on public welfare but on fine calibrations of wages, taxes, budget redistribution to poorer prefectures, and subsidies paid to farmers. People are not entitled to anything but the barest essentials unless they contribute to their groups. As a result, there is no sizeable group that feels indignant out of a sense of entitlement or self-deprecatory out of a sense of inadequate achievement.[35]

The Japan described by Vogel seems closer to an earlier America, in which the goal was equality of opportunity. The transition to the Great Society seems to have shifted that target to equality of outcomes or results, shifting more responsibility from the individual to the state. Much the same process has taken place in the Western European welfare states, but particularly in Scandinavia and the Netherlands. In the latter case, for example, students become eligible for the minimum wage at age eighteen, while studying, and in effect are guaranteed that wage for life whether or not they work.

In addition, Western ideas of individualism and rights to privacy mean that it is the individual who is entitled to the result, not the family, and that society rather than the family should bear primary responsibility of supporting not only those temporarily unemployed but those who have substandard incomes for prolonged periods (e.g., are eligible for relief or means-tested programs).

Over time, the distributional strategy appears to lead a nation not only away from a concern for productivity but to its opposite—increased dependency on the state to provide a living for a growing segment of the population. Essentially the individual has no performance requirement to establish eligibility; it is a right of membership. "Workfare" is considered demeaning in this scheme, and administrative cross-checks to avoid fraudulent benefit claims must follow the procedural safeguards of criminal law to avoid infringing on recipients' personal liberties.

Analyzing poverty programs' impact on poverty and labor force participation in the United States, Murray has found several trends that vary with those often reported. In fact, there are three rather than one notion of poverty, and the trends are different depending on which is used (see figure 2-20). "Official poverty" measures those families whose cash incomes fail to exceed three times the cost of an adequate diet. Official poverty has declined little since the advent of the poverty programs in the 1960s, a statistic that is frequently noted in the media. This should not be surprising, Murray points out, since many of the poverty programs provided payments in kind which are not counted in this measure. Using the concept of "net poverty," which includes noncash payments (e.g., food stamps) as well, poverty did continue to decline in the 1970s. And by this measure, the programs worked, though apparently less well than the economic growth and "trickle down" of the 1950s and 1960s.

However, "latent poverty" or the share of the population living below the poverty line except for grants from the government, began to rise with the expansion of the poverty programs in the 1960s (see figure 2-20).

> . . . how could it be that progress against official poverty and net poverty slowed or stopped when so much money was being spent for cash and in-kind transfers? The data on latent poverty provide one of the most important answers: Because latent poverty was increasing, it took more and more money in transfers just to keep the percentage of post-transfer poor stable. . . . The extremely large increases in social welfare spending during the 1970s were papering over the increase in latent poverty.[36]

A critical part of the explanation is that labor force participation among the poor began to drop with the advent of the poverty programs. While this shows up as a more rapid drop in black male participation in the labor force than white, and hence raises a question of race, Murray goes on to note:

> The explanation of the gap is not race, but income. Starting in 1966 low income males—white or black—started dropping out of the labor force. The only reason it looks as though blacks are dropping out at higher rates is that the blacks are disproportionately poor . . . the 1970 census data strongly suggest that middle and upper income males participated in the labor force at virtually unchanged rates since the 1950s, while the participation rate for low income males decreased slowly until 1966, and plummeted thereafter.

Figure 2-20

Three Measures of Poverty, 1950-80

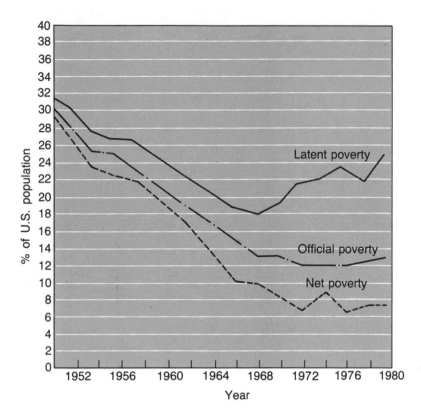

Source: Charles A. Murray, "The Two Wars Against Poverty: Economic Growth and the Great Society," *The Public Interest*, Fall 1982.

    This phenomenon needs explanation, for it was a fundamental change in economic behavior—participation in the labor market itself. . . . Without a doubt, something happened in the mid-1960s that changed the incentives for low income workers to stay in the job market. The Great Society reforms constitute the biggest, most visible, most plausible candidate.[37]

In pursuing the distributional strategy, government has little capacity and even less inclination to demand performance in return. It should not be surprising that this shifts the incentives to work among those who are poor and leads to increasing dependency upon the state; not the increasing independence and dignity that were the original hopes. The contrast with the vision of Lyndon Johnson, in 1964, is striking: "We want to offer the forgotten fifth of our population opportunity and not doles. . . . The days of the doles in our country are numbered."[38]

In addition to an unintended increase in responsibility because of increased dependency on government transfer payments and grants, government agencies become more focused on questions of equity and due process, as if substance—in this case baking the pie—were assumed to take care of itself. In a litigious society, in which government has funded numerous public interest law firms, various special interests can have a further impact on policymaking by attacking government agencies through the courts. In the United States, this means the courts are the final arbiters of equity and of due process, yet they have little if any mandate to strike a balance between performance and reward. The contrast between this and Japan, where even personal injury cases are typically settled without lawyers or courts, indicates fundamental differences in the concept of due process as well as the role of government.

Chalmers Johnson reminds us of the importance of both process and priorities, noting that Japanese "administrative guidance" by definition has no firm basis in law. Government, meaning principally the senior bureaucracy in Japan, is expected to lead or guide the community in pursuing a vision of the future that is best for all. The Japanese politicians are described as reigning more than ruling.[39] In common with the typically less democratic East Asian NICs, Japan may have more capacity to resist the tyranny of special interest groups and their self-interested search for increased distributional equity. Despite different histories, forms of government, and specific elements of their strategies, the development-oriented countries appear similar in process as well as substance, and quite distinct in both respects from those that are distribution oriented. A "strategy and structure" comparison may be an illuminating way to survey our major competitors.

THE MAJOR COMPETITORS AND THEIR STRATEGIES

If we were to schematize characteristic roles and institutional responsibilities for the development-oriented countries and those that give priority to economic security and income redistribution, a crude but suggestive contrast can be made (see table 2-8). The North Atlantic countries fall into one pattern and the East Asians into the other, suggesting that the developmental states differ from the distributional states in structure and process as well as strategy.

Figure 2-21 compares the major competitors' basic priorities, with government as a vehicle for redistribution on one axis and government as an

Table 2-8

Distribution and Development Strategies

	Distribution Strategy	Development Strategy
Security	*Economic Security*	*Job Security*
Responsibility	State	Employer
Coverage	Membership in society	Membership in firm
Eligibility	Membership entitlement	Performance
Government policies	Full employment	Stability/growth of firm
	Unemployment compensation	Retirement/health care
Financing	Unfunded liabilities	Funded and unfunded plan
Receiving unit	Individual	Individual or family
Distribution	*Redistribution by the State*	*Distribution through the Firm*
Responsibility	State	Employer
Criteria	Membership	Membership and performance
Means	Transfer payment	Salary and profit sharing
Financing	Tax and borrow	Corporate earnings
Wage policy	High minimum wage	Market clearing minimum wage
Savings		
	Subsidize borrowing	Subsidize savings
	Penalize saving	Penalize/restrict borrowing
Impact over Time		
Savings	Low savings	High savings
Wages	Rigid wages	Flexible wages
Labor mobility	Low mobility	High mobility
Responsibility for incomes	Increasing dependence on state	Family and firm retain high level of economic responsibility
Political priorities	Focus on due process	Focus on substantive performance

agency of development on the other. In this scheme it would be possible for a country to have balanced priorities either in the upper-left quadrant or in the lower-right, or unbalanced strategies in the other two quadrants.

Empirically it would seem that the United States and its major competitors

Figure 2-21

Country Strategy Matrix—A

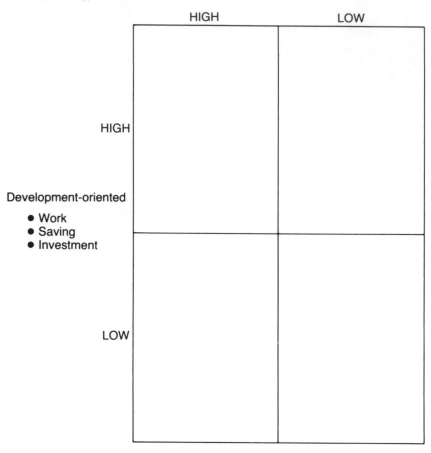

could be arrayed schematically as in figure 2-22, with the East Asians giving high priority to government's role in promoting development and low priority to a direct role in redistribution. The reverse appears to be the case for most of the North Atlantic countries, with France perhaps closer to a middle case prior to the advent of the Mitterrand presidency. The lower-right quadrant might include a number of less-developed countries in which government, although giving lip service to promoting both development and redistribution, seems more oriented to enriching an elite than to promoting either.

The upper-left corner is empty but has not always been so and need not remain so. In Germany, at the end of World War II, overtime wages were made tax exempt, there were large tax exemptions for interest earnings, and savings up to a limit could be deducted from taxable income. High levels of

Figure 2-22

Country Strategy Matrix—B

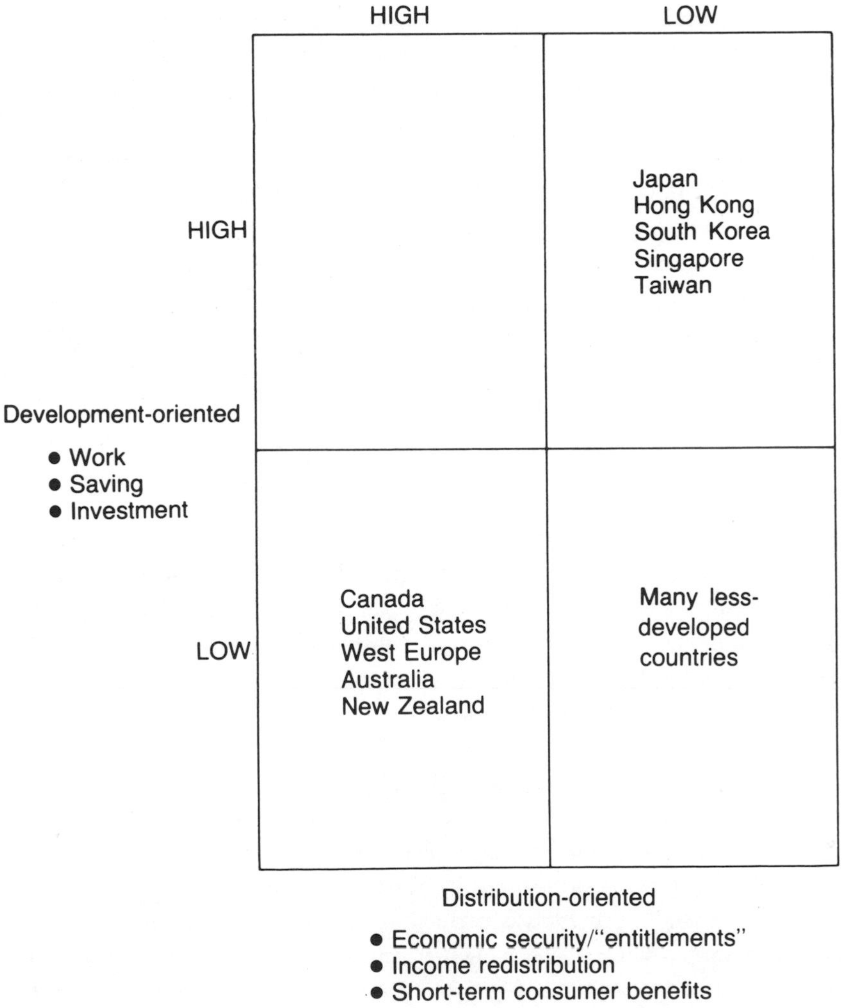

	HIGH	LOW
HIGH		Japan Hong Kong South Korea Singapore Taiwan
LOW	Canada United States West Europe Australia New Zealand	Many less- developed countries

Development-oriented

- Work
- Saving
- Investment

Distribution-oriented

- Economic security/"entitlements"
- Income redistribution
- Short-term consumer benefits

saving and investment were designed to create job security through an export-competitive society. Keynesian economics, with its emphasis on domestic demand management to promote economic security, was rejected.

Much of this changed after 1969. There was a half-hearted adoption of demand management economics and a proliferation of entitlements, such as the change in sickness eligibility, and a rapid rise in the cost of social programs. Elections in 1983 resulted in a coalition government which seems to aim to reestablish the previous balance of priorities, though only time will tell whether they will be successful.

Viewed in a very broad historical context, the trend appears to have been one of counterclockwise movement, with no significant examples of success in reversing the trend. The United Kingdom, for example, might have belonged in the upper-right corner in the mid-1800s, as Parliament repealed the corn laws and restricted or abolished the role of guilds to promote competition, the preferred means of promoting development (see figure 2-23). Even though government's role was indirect, Britain and then a number of countries in northwestern Europe and North America, saw establishing their infrastructure and encouraging competition as a strategy for promoting development. Government's role in promoting redistribution generally remained modest until the 1930s or even after World War II. Since the Depression, priorities have switched in one industrial country after another, until nearly all have become distributionally oriented welfare states.

This schematic representation is rough and has no single dimension with which to measure or place individual countries along either axis. With more research it might be possible to enhance its descriptive power by creating appropriate indexes that would allow gradations or perhaps a three-by-three matrix. As rough as it is, however, those familiar with the various countries have little difficulty agreeing on where to place them. It is a way to distinguish holistic strategies, and its empirical usefulness may be based largely on the premise that the differences between the strategic archetypes suggested by the matrix are far more significant than internal inconsistencies within any of the major countries.

For example, the United States is located in the lower left-hand quadrant with the European welfare states, despite the fact that the U.S. government makes a smaller claim on GNP than the other countries in the same quadrant. If we examine U.S. priorities, however, as expressed by share of the federal budget, the trend since 1960 is perfectly clear. Social programs have taken a steadily larger share of the budget, rising from about one-quarter to one-half since then (see figure 2-24). Until 1978 this shift was accompanied by

Figure 2-23
Country Strategy Matrix—C

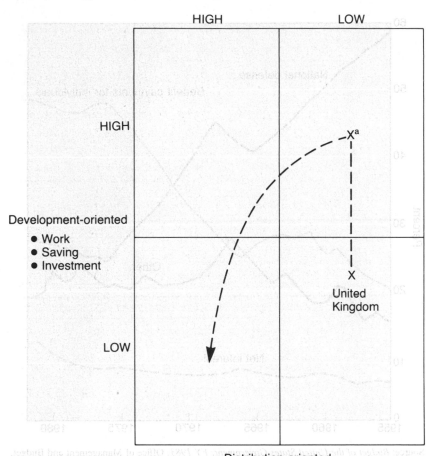

HIGH   LOW

HIGH

Development-oriented
● Work
● Saving
● Investment

X^a

X
United
Kingdom

LOW

Distribution-oriented

● Economic security/"entitlements"
● Income redistribution
● Short-term consumer benefits

^aCirca 1880

roughly corresponding cutbacks in military spending. Since 1978 military spending has been on the rise, but not at the expense of the key social programs—retirement and health care. We have chosen to have "guns and butter," but have not been willing to pay the full tax consequences. Instead we chose to finance the deficits first by the printing press and more recently

Figure 2-24

Federal Outlays as a Percent of Total Budget Outlays, 1955-82

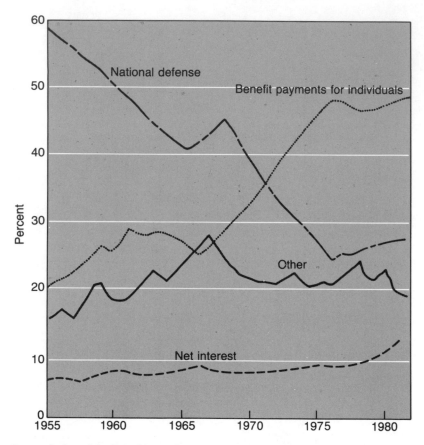

Source: *Budget of the United States Government: FY 1983*, Office of Management and Budget, Washington, D.C.

by borrowing abroad. Conservatives have put military spending ahead of competitiveness, liberals have put social spending ahead: neither conservatives nor liberals have yet done much to articulate the essential requirements of a competitive United States let alone how to get there.

The priorities are equally clear at the micro level. Real spendable income for those who work and produce has been allowed to decline, while all major categories who depend on transfer payments for the income have been well protected. Thus, as shown earlier in figure 2-17, benefits for the unemployed and those on welfare have occupied the middle ground, those on social security have done best, and those who worked have done least well. Government, it is clear, has given higher priority to enhancing and protecting the standard of living of those not producing than for those who do. In fact, it has been willing to raise the transfer payments far beyond its willingness to tax to finance them, thus increasing the unfunded liabilities to be paid for by the next generation.

The U.S. strategy is not noncompetitive with respect to others in the same general category. Indeed, the strength of the U.S. industrial portfolio suggests that the United States could continue its distributional strategy for quite some time before encountering a real "competitiveness problem" if it only had to compete with the other welfare states of the North Atlantic area. The competitive problem is due primarily to the emergence of new competitors whose principal strength is a more competitive strategy.

This suggests that international competition will increasingly be based on national strategies rather than resource endowments, and that countries with more competitive strategies are likely to have higher performance than others. It also suggests that each country will have to choose between becoming competitive, that is, having at least a rough balance between developmental and distributional priorities, or suffering in the competition.

In the U.S. context, moving toward a more balanced strategy would seem to require changes in priorities and process as well as substantive policy changes. It requires that public policy give much higher priority to growth and productivity than in the recent past, that we rebalance incentives among those who work and those who do not, and that we expect each generation to pay its own way rather than leaving an ever-growing bundle of debts for the next generation. Only with a change in priorities is there much chance that we can find effective ways to work within the fragmented, decentralized power structure through which the country is governed.[40] It would be a first among welfare states if a significantly more competitive industrial policy could be tacked on to the existing structure without such a change in priorities; it would also require a loosely structured government to effectively administer an internally inconsistent strategy: entitlement and nonperformance for the bulk of the economy, and the reverse for industry. Industrial policy is not likely to become an exception that proves the rule.

INDUSTRIAL POLICY

Not everyone sees it this way, of course. For some analysts industrial policy is an attractive alternative, whereby competitiveness can be dramatically improved without a basic shift in priorities and incentives. The idea is to apply the notion of targeting and creating comparative advantage within the existing system, carefully preserving the hard-won gains of the welfare state. In

In theory, the case for targeting or an active, sector selective industrial policy is simple and compelling. Those familiar with one of the strategy matrices, for example, the Boston Consulting Group growth/share matrix, will recognize it as promoting winners and cutting back on investments in low-growth areas. Or, using the scheme that organizes industries from high technology to low, it would be a strategy of systematically upgrading the portfolio as in the "Japanese model." Conceptually it can be likened to the application of product portfolio theory to the level of the nation state.[41]

A little reflection suggests some severe practical limits of targeting at the national level. Some of the easiest places to apply the concept, for instance, should be those countries, such as the various oil-producing states, that have a large, dependable cash flow that can be used to support investment in high-potential sectors. Some have had only a brief history of such wealth; others like Iran and Venezuela, countries that respectively compare in population with South Korea and Taiwan, have had this wealth for fifty years. It is enough to suggest the comparison: neither Iran nor Venezuela has remotely approached the industrial success of South Korea or Taiwan. To the contrary, easy if not windfall revenues have led to expanded spending in the public sector, inflation, failure to reduce the value of the currency accordingly, and manufacturing sectors that were barely able to export anything beyond petrochemicals and traditional items.

The Netherlands and Norway, advanced industrial societies with great oil and gas wealth, might have been expected to manage the transformation of public savings into productive investment. Again the story is one of rising public spending, inflation, an overvalued exchange rate, and decline of the manufacturing sector. Oil revenues have been used to support the distributional goals of the welfare state; the productive, competitive needs of the manufacturing sector have suffered.

Successful targeting seems to depend more on a broad commitment to productivity and competitiveness than on technical analyses of which industries to promote and which to exit. France has practiced targeting almost as long as Japan, beginning with similar concepts based on wartime rationing and using similar control mechanisms, including credit controls and administrative guidance. And, like Japanese firms, large French firms basically accepted that government should consult with industry and give guidance from time to time. For a variety of reasons the French results have been

modest.[42] There has been a much lower priority given to international competitiveness both at the political level and among key bureaucrats, notably
those at the ministry of finance. Savings were targeted disproportionately
toward losers because they were political problems, and toward housing, a
sure way to boost the standard of living.

The major premise of industrial policy advocates in the United States is
that the issue is the pattern of investment, not the amount, making the issue
essentially technical.[43] Central guidance of the pattern will yield a more
rational pattern. This overlooks why the pattern is the way it is, or why the
amount is as low as it is, both of which appear linked to the distributional
priorities. In particular, the need to reduce the cost and modify the criteria
for eligibility of social programs is denied. Somehow, we are asked to
believe, targeting can be carried on more rationally in the political spotlight
of a fragmented political system in which distribution has higher priority
than productivity, than it can in the obscurity of a multiplicity of corporations
in which the priorities are the reverse.

For example, in looking at various types of U.S. assistance to industry,
one can agree with Reich that "[t]he government . . . now spends five times
more on R&D for commercial fisheries than for steel and provides $455
million in tax breaks for the timber industry but none for semiconductors."[44]
One can also note subsidies for the maritime industry and tax breaks for the
oil industry, and one can see a pattern of favoring both sheltered domestic
industries and powerful political interests (see table 2-9).

However, subsidies, tax expenditures, and loan guarantees for the housing
industry dwarf the sector-specific advantages given to all the other industries
combined by several orders of magnitude. The tax expenditure that allows
the deduction of interest on home mortgages costs the government more than
all the grants for R&D assistance, all nonhousing subsidies, and all other
sector-specific tax expenditures combined. Do we consider this incoherence
based on politics, or is it a reflection of basic U.S. priorities that have favored
consumers over producers, and that have attempted to boost GNP by subsidizing consumption while assuming that productivity would take care of
itself?

Far from representing an aberration, these policies may represent a reasonably clear, if not always clearly articulated, strategy that is deeply rooted
in American assumptions about the competitive capabilities of American
private enterprise, the market system, and the proper role of government.
The R&D subsidies suggest that the United States has an energy policy, an
aviation policy, and a space policy, each of which is connected to defense

Table 2-9

Government Assistance to Selected Industries, Fiscal Year 1980 (in $ millions)

Industry	Type of Assistance				
	Research and Development	Other Direct Expenditures	Tax Expenditures	Procurement	Outstanding Loans and Loan Guarantees
Coal	$942	$120	$530	$0	$0
Forest products	14	130	455	49	0
Dairy	11	347	0	448	0
Nuclear	5,810	113	0	1,628	0
Cotton	8	232	0	0	0
Petroleum	273	174	3,350	3,733	0
Commercial fisheries	24	3	0	0	103
Maritime industry	16	585	70	4,075	6,342
Railroad industry	55	2,491	0	3	2,064
Housing industry	53	6,760	23,225	3,044	157,708
Automobiles and highways	108	1,394	0	1,217	940
Aviation	1,393	2,994	0	7,159	558
Steel	5	45	50	229	393
Semiconductors	55	0	0	4,600	0
Textiles	0	60	0	428	0

Source: Office of Management and Budget, budget of the U.S. government 1980; Congressional Budget Office, "Tax Expenditures: Current Issues and Five-Year Budget Projections for Fiscal Years 1981-1985," report to the Senate and House committees on the budget, Washington, D.C.; Office of Federal Procurement Policy, *Federal Contract Awards* (1979); General Accounting Office, *A Methodology for Estimating Costs and Subsidies from Federal Credit Assistance Programs* (1980). This table originally appeared in Robert Reich, "Why the U.S. Needs an Industrial Policy," *Harvard Business Review* (January–February 1982): 78. Reprinted by permission of the *Harvard Business Review*. Copyright © 1982 by the President and Fellows of Harvard College; all rights reserved.

concerns. Spending a few million more for fisheries than for steel seems trivial compared with the total spending for all sectors exposed to foreign competition. That, in turn, seems minuscule compared with the $25 billion "tax expenditure" for housing and the tens of billions added to economic security programs, like pensions and medical care, to index the benefits, but not the contributions, for inflation. The unevenness of the corporate tax burden, with sheltered domestic industries paying among the lowest rates, is but another example (see figure 2-25).[45]

The U.S. government's role has increasingly been to protect consumers via entitlements, and to create an ever-expanding array of regulations and burgeoning new regulatory agencies. Industrial policy has not so much been incoherent as one more manifestation of a basic distribution-oriented strategy.

Figure 2-25

The Huge Tax Gap among Industries

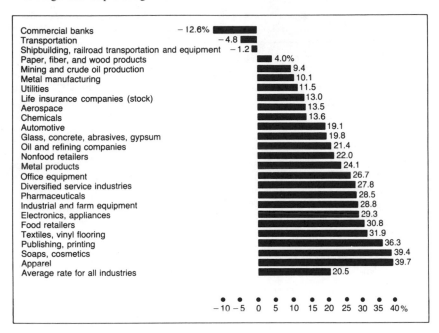

Source: *Dun's Business Month*, May 1983.
Note: Because of special breaks, the actual corporate tax rates paid in 1981 varied dramatically from industry to industry.

The emphasis on domestic social programs is likewise reflected in the dramatic growth of the social and environmental regulatory agencies during the 1970s (see table 2-10). Missing from the data are some indicators of public funding of public interest law firms and other grass roots agencies, which were created to lobby and to use the courts on behalf of various consumer interests.

The pattern of subsidies also appears to be consistent with the shift in educational priorities toward social objectives such as bilingualism and "levelling," and reduced emphasis on academic achievement. U.S. policies and institutions have given high priority to promoting economic security and increased equality of outcomes. We have shifted from the notion of "equality of opportunity" to the notion of "equality of results," with government giving much higher priority to promoting fair distribution of the pie than to promoting either the art or the effort of baking. From this perspective, the most

Table 2-10

The Growth of Federal Regulation in America: Personnel of Selected Agencies, 1935–77

"Economic" Regulation Agencies	1935	1945	1960	1975
Interstate Commerce Commission (1887)	1,093	1,817	2,409	2,142
Federal Trade Commission (1914)	527	484	756	1,569
Federal Power Commission (1920)	70	723	850	1,320
Federal Communications Commission (1934)	234	1,757	1,454	2,022
Securities and Exchange Commission (1934)	153	1,249	1,000	2,150
Civil Aeronautics Board (1938)	—	385	766	713

"Social" or "Environmental" Regulation Agencies	1970	1973	1977 *(est.)*
Equal Employment Opportunity Commission (1964)	780	1,739	2,377
Environmental Protection Agency (1970)	3,702	8,270	9,550
Occupational Safety and Health Administration (1970)	—	1,285	2,306
Consumer Product Safety Commission (1972)	—	579	890

Source: Budget of the U.S. government (Washington, D.C., various years), cited in Thomas K. McCraw, "Regulatory Agencies," *Encyclopedia of American Economic History*, vol. 2, ed. Glen Porter, 1980.

significant aspect of U.S. industrial policies is not their lack of coherence but their obvious and ever-increasing focus on short-term consumer benefits and their neglect of productivity and competitiveness. Changing this short-term consumption-oriented strategy significantly does not depend primarily on better analysis, or bringing the subsidies out in the open so the public can see and debate them to arrive at a consensus and a coherent strategy. Instead it depends on a change in priorities, specifically a willingness to reduce subsidies for consumption (e.g., the interest deduction on home mortgages), and a rebalancing of priorities in favor of work, saving, and investment.

The debate on U.S. industrial policy is clouded by the fact that those, such as Magaziner and Reich, who took a lead in pointing out our less-than-competitive policies, have built their notion of industrial policy on the premise that existing policies can be made more competitive by making them "more rational and more coherent" without a fundamental reordering of priorities, and particularly without the need for sacrifices in consumer subsidies or entitlements. Supply-side economics aims at a rebalancing of incentives with implied consumer sacrifices, Reich points out: the great merit of industrial policy is that "any such sacrifices may be unnecessary."[46] Supply-side economics calls for raising the level of investment, and thus, at least in the short term, reducing the level of consumption; the Reich and Magaziner notion of industrial policy emphasizes the "pattern" of investment on the grounds that the level is adequate. Industrial policy advocates would have us believe that if we were only more analytic in our approach, more explicit about who got how much in subsidies, and more open in how we conduct business in both public and private, we could, in essence, have all our consumption and all the investments we need—or have our cake and eat it too.

Industrial policy advocates tend to focus their comparisons on the North Atlantic area, and to note that many European countries have gone further with social programs than the United States, have more equal distribution of incomes, have more consensus, and have maintained their growth in productivity. A recent study done for the European Parliament paints a very different picture—one of self-inflicted competitive decline throughout Europe.[47]

There is little evidence that industrial policy has bloomed successfully in the climate of any welfare state. There is a good deal of evidence to the contrary. Over time it becomes another welfare program to help the disadvantaged who, in this case, rather than being supported in their existing activities should be encouraged to move to others. At the extreme, targeting becomes a panacea, no more deserving of serious attention than the Laffer curve of Reaganomics.

Targeting has been successful on a sustained basis only when it has been a part of a productivity-oriented development strategy. We need to turn our attention to comparing our strategy with those of our most successful competitors and to think holistically about reforms necessary to get our house in order. Excessive concern with the targeting issue is likely to lead us to focus our attention on retaliating against other countries for unfair trade practices or to create a social welfare program billed as a courageous new way for government to help build competitiveness. Unless our priorities change, revival of a "reconstruction finance corporation" would almost certainly create a new entitlement program and another competitive handicap. It should not require financial or technical wizardry to recognize that in an increasingly interdependent world economy our economy cannot meet its various commitments unless there are significant changes in political priorities—that is, a new emphasis on baking relative to distributing the pie.

IMPLICATIONS FOR INTERNATIONAL COMPETITION

Competition in the postwar trading system was envisioned as competition among firms, with governments establishing the rules and the enforcement process. It was an Anglo-American conception, consistent with Anglo-American conceptions of free markets, the invisible hand, and the limited state as the framework for domestic competition. That framework has now been challenged by a group of competitors that have found a positive role for the visible hand of government in creating comparative advantages and in promoting mobility of capital and labor in exploiting these advantages. Indeed the whole thrust of the foregoing analysis is that the competitive challenge comes from well-managed companies based in countries characterized by developmentally oriented national strategies.

How one views this challenge tends to be influenced by whether one is positioned with the challengers or the challenged: Shinohara speaks for the challengers.

> The major economic powers once held aloft a surrealistic and static concept of free trade, but in fact they colonized one country after another, under the ostensible pretext of free trade. . . .
> The lesson we have learned from the economic issue of trade frictions is. . . that perfunctory theories framed in a surrealistic and hypothetical world, in the years when Adam Smith and David Ricardo were predominant, are no longer workable. Recognition of this fact affords an unparalleled chance to ponder once again the way in which the principles of international behavior ought to be laid out in the economic sector.[48]

William Cline, speaking for the challenged, sees the issue quite differently.

> Analytically, there does seem to be a fundamental problem that might be christened "arbitrary comparative advantage." Increasingly, trade in manufactures among industrialized countries, even including the newly industrialized countries, appears to reflect an exchange of goods in which one nation could be just as likely as another . . . to develop comparative advantage, and the actual outcome is in a meaningful sense arbitrary. For a range of manufactured goods, it may be argued that "comparative advantage is made, not given. . . ."
> . . . The conditions of modern trade for a wide range of manufactures suggest that comparative advantage may be relatively malleable instead of rigidly predetermined by national endowments of resources and factors, and trade in this range of goods may be determined importantly by basic conditions of competition and market organization. Strategic behavior by nations and firms influences this trade, and rules of the game are essential if some countries (and firms) are not to be artificially disadvantaged relative to others.[49]

The central issue is that international competition is now influenced by national strategies as well as the strategies of firms. And the history of the last thirty years makes it clear that a developmental strategy based on mobilizing the resources of a nation to create comparative advantage in growth industries and industries in which technological change is rapid yields higher growth over the medium term than simply accepting advantages as "given." History also makes clear that a strategy that promotes mobility and/or limits the rigidities associated with entitlements allows a country to capitalize more rapidly on the advantages it creates.

As Cline notes, "strategic behavior" by nations influences outcomes. For those nations trying to catch up this means opportunity. For those in the lead, particularly those like the United States who are in the lead and who do not wish government to play a more active role in shaping business strategies, there is a substantive challenge of more competitive strategies and the related problems that are based in part on different working relationships between business and government. In these circumstances it is tempting to see the challenge as one to be met by new rules to limit the scope of such competition. At the extreme one can see the challenge emanating from unfair competition, to be dealt with essentially by better rules and/or more vigorous enforcement, rather than from better strategies that require restructuring priorities.

In one sense the search for new rules is desirable, in another it is naive and unrealistic. Competition among nations can take on a new aggressiveness that calls for not only new rules but more rapid enforcement to avoid a vicious circle of escalating frictions. The "rules," however, can hardly bridge the difference between two different ways to play the game. There is a risk that Americans will want to change the rules to outlaw what the new challengers consider essentials of a more competitive strategy through which they can catch up if not surpass the current leaders. In these circumstances, one is hardly likely to find a mutually agreed-upon set of rules.

It is as if the United States has been accustomed to fielding a football team of eleven rugged, "independent" athletes and watching them win game after game. Now, confronted by teams that have practiced their "plays" and are "coached" by their governments, the United States finds all the games' scores are closer and there are a disturbing number of losses. New rules and better enforcement can deal with some aspects of the situation, such as "unnecessary roughness" or "holding." But it is naive to think that our competitors should abandon plays requiring practice and coordination merely to fit our ideas of rugged individualism refereed by government: in other words, it is hard to see why "our rules" should prevail.

National strategies have been called the "new mercantilism," and perhaps this is appropriate.[50] What does seem clear is that when practiced by only a few countries they can be an avenue for catching up. Their impact on other countries seems to be a good deal less favorable. And, if practiced by all, the impact on the world economy is far from clear.

The implications for international competition are that there are three broad avenues into the future. (1) The welfare states might rebalance their priorities and become much more competitive using strategies like those pursued by Germany up until 1969. (2) The development-oriented states might become increasingly security oriented, and somewhat less competitive, thereby progressing into the upper-left quadrant of the matrix. (3) Or the welfare states might take the lead in restricting access to their markets, thereby reducing the competitive threat by restricting the roles of the most competitive players. A fourth option, movement by the welfare states to drastically curtail their entitlements and adopt strategies like the developmental states (i.e., move to the upper-right quadrant), simply is not in the cards. A fifth option, in which the developmental states shift their priorities to resemble those of the welfare states, is also not in the cards.

The only stable, mutually beneficial, and supportive outcome would seem to require that the major competitors find broadly similar strategies in the upper-left quadrant, the one area that is now almost empty. This would require that the leading developmental states take on more distributional responsibilities as direct state functions, and that the distributional states make many changes to achieve more balanced strategies.

Obviously the task will be much more difficult for the distributional states. In rebalancing their priorities they must in some real sense reverse direction and undo some of what has been labeled progress. This does not mean that they must turn the clock back on the social progress of the past 100 years, or even the past 20 years. What it does mean is that some of the extreme forms of economic security programs are too costly and antiproductive to be supported in an increasingly competitive world. The welfare states need to take a lesson from their rising competitors and shift toward employment security through the firm as a less costly and more effective form of security program. A rebalancing of duties and entitlements is an essential element of a more competitive strategy.

As the welfare states begin rethinking their strategies, it would be appropriate for them also to reconsider the rules and enforcement mechanisms of the trading system, if international competition is not to degenerate either into competition among increasingly aggressive strategies similar to an arms race, or into a "refusal to compete" based on increasing resort to protectionism. While industrial targeting is likely to be the focus of much of the rule making, it should not be allowed to obscure the fact that targeting is only part of the new strategies—and by itself is not normally a very successful part.

TENTATIVE CONCLUSIONS

International competition is increasingly being shaped by two competing national strategies, one focused on growth/productivity and external competitiveness and the other on domestic economic security and redistribution of income. The central premise of a developmental strategy is that a country, like a company, can accelerate its growth and performance by reshaping its resources in light of medium- or long-term market opportunities rather than by attempting to make the most efficient short-term use of existing resources. Thus Portugal, in the famous example, would be better off in the long term to reject the static, short-term notion of its comparative advantage in wine and aim to acquire and mobilize the resources necessary to compete with the United Kingdom in the industry in which growth and technological change are rapid, namely textiles.

The central premise of the distributional strategy is that free market outcomes, guided only by the invisible hand, yield the highest level of economic performance. Therefore, the essential role of government is that of a rule maker and referee whose responsibilities are to see that the market works, on the one hand, and that the pie is more evenly distributed on the other. Competitiveness depends essentially on business enterprise; social justice is the province of government.

From our present vantage point it seems clear that the nations with development-oriented strategies are gaining strength while the distribution-oriented countries are progressively losing strength. The basic reason for this difference in performance is not that some countries have more coherent strategies than others but that their priorities and underlying theory of competition are different.

The developmental strategy tilts toward governmental promotion of work, saving, and investment as principal means of promoting productivity; the distributional strategy assumes that productivity will be taken care of by market forces, and government tilts toward the promotion of economic security and income redistribution via an ever-increasing array of entitlements.

The developmental strategy is based on the premise that advantages can be created and that government can and should work with business and labor to help create them; the distributional strategy either does not acknowledge such an opportunity or believes it can be exploited by an isolated industrial policy which—unlike the remainder of the strategy—claims to be development oriented.

The U.S. strategy has been overwhelmingly distribution oriented and, like those of the other major North Atlantic countries, increasingly noncompetitive. It has created an ever-increasing array of rights or entitlements for which there are no corresponding duties or performance requirements. Entitlements reduce the incentives to work and save, and add rigidity to the system. In contrast, the "employment security" provided by the growth/productivity-oriented countries is less costly, less inhibiting for labor mobility, and has a more realistic balance of rights and duties. Over time our distributional strategy has relieved an ever-larger segment of the population of much of the responsibility for its own welfare and has induced an increased degree of dependence which has become an added burden on the productive part of the economy.

While the U.S. strategy is often characterized as incoherent and inconsistent, in fact it appears to be remarkably consistent—including trade, fiscal, regulatory, and labor policies as indicated in other chapters in this volume. Only very recently has there been the beginning of a small countertrend, notably the reduced capital gains tax, the elimination of penalty taxes on interest and dividends, and the opening of the tax-free savings accounts for retirement. These changes pale in the light of the 25 percent reduction in the income tax rates, a consumer-oriented tax cut sold as supply-side economics.

There are no technical solutions or quick fixes for the competitive problems of distribution-oriented nations like the United States. One commonly mentioned solution is to move up to higher technologies and thus escape the full force of the new competition. Unfortunately, the data suggest that the East Asian nations are moving up to higher technologies more rapidly than any of the older industrial countries, including the United States. In addition, it will be quite some time before the sheer volume of high technology exports can offset losses in older, mass production industries. Therefore, to be competitive the United States must aim to upgrade many of its traditional industries (e.g., autos and textiles) as well as pushing ahead at the top of the technological scale.

Some of the current enthusiasm for industrial policy regards it as a quick fix, as though it can be added on to the distributional strategy without a basic shift in priorities. None of the distributional states can point to much success from their various attempts to do so; for example, none has shown significant progress in upgrading its industrial portfolio the way the developmental states have.

Declining competitiveness is a particularly serious problem for the United States in view of its political, military, and economic commitments. The performance of the U.S. economy since the late 1960s has not been strong enough to support the costs of international leadership and simultaneous expansion of social programs at home. While this problem was masked for over a decade by the steady erosion of military spending, recent decisions have committed the United States to a major rearmament effort. There has been no corresponding moderation in the growth of the principal social programs—the so-called middle-class entitlements—namely pensions and medical care.

The conflict between ambitious commitments and limited means may lead someday to a dramatic event that will somehow resolve the issue. The more likely prospect, however, would appear to be a long, slow, irregular decline, in which a great deal of effort would be expended denying the problem, minimizing its seriousness, and doing little to solve it; that is, the United States could follow the lead of the United Kingdom. Faced with a similar situation after World War II, the United Kingdom gradually opted in favor of expanded social programs while allowing both its military power and its competitiveness to decline. While the consequences may have been serious for the United Kingdom, they were less serious for the Western Alliance because the United States gradually assumed the British role and many of its former international responsibilities. It is not clear that a similar option exists if the United States were to abdicate its military-political role in the next decade or two.

Like a successful company being chased by a rising competitor, the United States must first recognize that there is a real challenge. Nothing is more difficult for a country long-accustomed to being "number one." Even to entertain the question is to admit that time-tested axioms and traditions might have to change, and perhaps at a less leisurely pace than that to which our traditional position of leadership has accustomed us.

The challenge is before us: the starting point of an effective response is to admit the question of the competitiveness of the U.S. strategy for serious consideration.

Bruce R. Scott   143

progress in upgrading its industrial portfolio the way the developmental states
have.

Declining competitiveness is a particularly serious problem for the United

3
Sustaining U.S. Competitiveness in Microelectronics: The Challenge to U.S. Policy

William F. Finan
Annette M. LaMond

The U.S. semiconductor industry has recovered: near-term growth in de-mand is expected to soar about 20 percent in the mid-1980s; utilization of facilities is rapidly rising; profitability has been restored. The industry's future prospects, however, are less clear. It is possible that the Japanese semicon-ductor industry will surpass the U.S. industry by the end of the decade.

Policy issues surrounding the future of the U.S. industry differ from those that apply to other industries, for example, steel, textiles, and autos, in which the focus is on structural adjustment, that is, minimizing the costs of adjust-ment while permitting the gains from trade to enhance the overall efficient use of resources. In such situations the question is one of allocative efficiency: how will production be divided internationally? To this end, traditional U.S. trade policy has sought to achieve economically efficient outcomes within an international and domestic legal framework based on rules of fairness.[1] U.S. trade policy also interacts with U.S. antitrust policies, since it limits the type and degree of responses that U.S. firms collectively can make to foreign competition within the U.S. market.

In the case of semiconductors, several new competitive elements emerge. First, efficiency gains for the U.S. economy arising from the continuing development of new semiconductor products and processes are highly sig-nificant and therefore shift the policy emphasis away from a focus on allo-

William F. Finan is a special assistant to the undersecretary for international trade, Department of Commerce. Annette M. LaMond is a consultant specializing in industrial organization economics.

144

cative efficiency. Second, intergovernment rivalry between the United States and Japan has escalated in recent years. Both governments have stepped up their efforts to influence the competitive environment, but there are key differences. The Japanese government believes that the semiconductor industry is strategic, an essential part of the future industrial structure of Japan. The U.S. government perspective is less focused. The Department of Defense recognizes that microelectronic technology is important to our military strength and has acted accordingly.[2] U.S. trade policymakers seek to permit markets to allocate resources efficiently according to the rules of the trading system. To that end, U.S. trade policy has attempted to ensure Japanese firms access to the U.S. market and vice versa. To pursue that policy, the U.S. government has been drawn into a closer relationship with the U.S. industry as it tries to neutralize the strategic advantages that have been accorded the Japanese semiconductor industry by its government.

The problem, quite simply, is that the Japanese government has a coherent, strategic orientation toward its industry, and the U.S. government does not. We do not necessarily argue that such a strategic view be adopted by the U.S. government, that is, that the industry be accorded preferential treatment in capital investment or exemption from antitrust policies. Rather, the issue is how to ensure that actions by the Japanese government do not distort market outcomes. To the extent that the Japanese government's actions distort market outcomes, the dynamic benefits that flow to the U.S. economy may be lower than they would otherwise be. This is not a question of picking winners and losers. It simply recognizes that governments can influence market structure and firm behavior in ways that can have long-run detrimental outcomes for the United States.

INTERNATIONAL POSITION OF THE U.S. SEMICONDUCTOR INDUSTRY

The world market for electronics—including computers, telecommunications equipment, consumer products, industrial process control equipment, scientific instruments, and defense systems—has grown at an extraordinary rate for over three decades. As shown in table 3-1, the value of electronics products consumed in the United States, Western Europe, and Japan reached $200 billion in 1983, more than doubling the 1977 level. By the late 1980s, electronics is expected to generate over $400 billion in world sales, a figure that will place electronics with automobiles and oil as one of the world's leading industries.

Table 3-1
Major Electronics Systems Market Consumption, 1983 ($ billions)

	United States	Japan	Western Europe
Data processing systems, peripherals, and office equipment	$ 61.7	$14.0	$20.6
Consumer electronics	22.7	11.0	15.2
Communications equipment	8.3	3.0	11.1
Industrial equipment	4.5	4.1	3.0
Test, measuring, and analytical instruments	5.5	.8	1.2
Medical equipment	4.1	1.1	1.5
Automotive electronics	2.6	1.9	—
Power supplies	—	.5	.4
Total—all systems	$109.4	$36.4	$53.0

Source: *Electronics,* 13 January 1983.

At the heart of all final electronics systems are miniaturized electronic circuits imprinted on tiny chips of silicon a few millimeters across. In 1983, world consumption of these tiny chips reached nearly $17 billion, up from $2.5 billion in 1970. (See table 3-2.) By the end of the decade, consumption will reach $60 billion.[3]

The dollar value of semiconductor consumption, however, only partly reflects the central role that advances in semiconductor technology have played in transforming modern industrial society. The U.S. semiconductor industry's achievements in improving the speed and reducing the price of electrical functions have created dozens of new industries, from data processing and robotics to videogames. In three decades it has fundamentally altered communications, education, health care, recreation, entertainment, and work activity.

Table 3-2
Semiconductor Consumption by Market, 1983 ($ billions)

	United States	Japan	Western Europe
Integrated circuits	$7.5	$3.0	$1.8
Discrete	1.4	1.3	.8
Optoelectronic devices	.3	.3	.1
Total	$9.2	$4.6	$2.8

Source: *Electronics,* 13 January 1983.

U.S. semiconductor manufacturers have dominated the world semiconductor market from its inception in the early 1950s. In the late 1970s, however, the Japanese government, together with its major semiconductor firms, initiated an unprecedented drive to overtake the technological leadership of the United States in microelectronics. As a result, the Japanese have closed the technological gap with U.S. firms in advanced computer memories, a high-volume and rapidly growing product area in which the United States was dominant only five years ago. Japanese manufacturers are now striving to duplicate their success in commodity memory products in other key areas such as microprocessors and standard logic circuits.

In 1981, U.S. semiconductor firms still accounted for 61 percent of the $5.2 billion worth of integrated circuits (ICs) sold worldwide, but the Japanese industry had moved into a strong number two position with 32 percent of the world market, up from only 18 percent in 1972.[4] (See table 3-3.) Indeed, some forecasters predict that by 1985, Japan will pick up an additional two to three percentage points of worldwide market share.

Until recently, the Japanese semiconductor industry's export thrust was directed at the U.S. market. As shown in figure 3-1, Japan's balance of trade with the United States in semiconductors began to move in Japan's favor in the mid-1970s, the sharpest shift coming in 1979-81—a period that coincided with the completion of a major joint government-industry research project and the beginning of rapid expansion in the Japanese industry's production capacity. In 1978 the United States ran its first trade deficit in ICs with Japan.[5] By 1980, that deficit had reached nearly $300 million. Even in advanced metal-oxide semiconductor (MOS) ICs, in which U.S. firms were technology leaders, U.S. exports to Japan increased by only $25 million

Table 3-3
IC World Market Share Estimates of National Firms Based in the United States, Japan, and Western Europe (dollars in millions)

	1972		1979		1981	
United States	$958	73%	$4,856	68%	$5,215	61%
Japan	241	18	1,651	23	2,789	32
Western Europe	107	8	604	9	583	7

Source: Calculated from Dataquest (a market research firm) estimates of worldwide company sales
Note: Estimates include, at market prices, a company's internal consumption of semiconductors. However, the data exclude companies that manufacture semiconductors solely for their own use and thus make no sales.

Figure 3-1

U.S.-Japan Semiconductor Balance of Trade, 1975-82 (based on U.S. Department of Commerce figures)

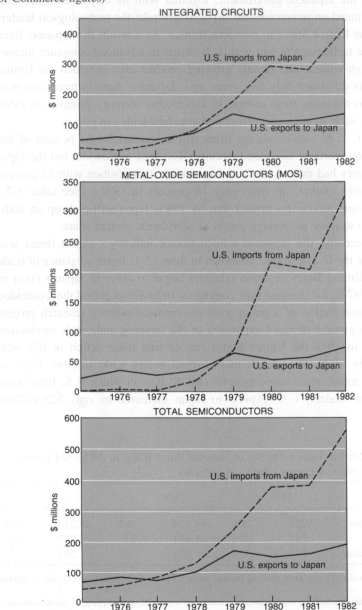

Source: Semiconductor Industry Association, *The Effect of Government Targeting on World Semiconductor Competition*, 1983.

between 1975 and 1980. Conversely, Japanese exports of advanced MOS ICs to the United States went from practically nothing in 1975 to $220 million in 1980.

As the trade figures suggest, U.S. firms have had little success in translating their technological leadership into a strong position in the Japanese market. Whereas in 1975 U.S. firms held 98 percent of the U.S. market for ICs and 78 percent of the Western European market, their share of the Japanese market was only 20 percent.[6] Many of the formal restrictions on sales and direct investment in Japan by foreign companies have been eliminated since the mid-1970s. Nevertheless, access to the Japanese market remains very difficult for foreign producers. Indeed, U.S. market share in Japan is actually lower now than before "liberalization" was undertaken.[7] Although the Japanese government has recently agreed to use administrative guidance to encourage domestic firms to buy more U.S. semiconductors, many observers remain pessimistic about the prospect that U.S. firms will be able to increase their share of the Japanese semiconductor market.[8]

In the past, U.S. semiconductor firms have offset the effect of their inability to penetrate the Japanese market with their strong sales position in Western Europe. U.S. firms currently supply half of Western Europe's total semiconductor demand and more than 60 percent of its IC consumption.[9] Recently, however, Japanese competition for European market share has increased dramatically as the major Japanese firms have moved to establish production facilities in Europe. By all reports, Japanese price competition in Europe is tougher than in the United States. Erosion of the U.S. industry's share in Europe has, in turn, heightened the importance of increasing U.S. access to the Japanese market—the world's second largest and fastest growing.

The competitive challenge that the Japanese have placed before the United States is perhaps best summarized by the massive increases in capital spending that Japanese manufacturers have sustained since the late 1970s. As shown in figure 3-2, the Japanese industry's capital investment growth rate has outpaced the U.S. industry's since 1980. Indeed, some observers believe that U.S. manufacturers may be underestimating how much added capacity and additional products the Japanese will be able to export in the years ahead.

THE SEMICONDUCTOR MANUFACTURING PROCESS

Semiconductor manufacturing is probably the most complex mass production process ever attempted. The success of the process is measured by yield,

Figure 3-2

U.S. and Japanese Semiconductor Firms' Worldwide Capital Investment Growth Rate

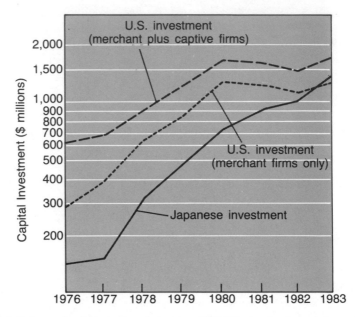

Source: U.S. International Trade Commission data (1976-78); Semiconductor Industry Association estimates (1979-83); and Semiconductor Industry Association, 1983.
Note: Figures for Japanese firms represent fiscal years beginning 1 April.
Yen conversion:
(1976–196.2:1) (1979–221.3:1) (1982–248.6:1)
(1977–165.9:1) (1980–224.8:1) (1983–235.0:1)
(1978–205.9:1) (1981–221.3:1)

that is, the percentage of initial product started into production that, after the last step of the process, tests out as acceptable product. Because of the complexity of the process, yields tend to be well below 100 percent. The industry operates with yields that would be unimaginably low for almost any other mass production process. For example, on complex new parts, yields initially may be as low as 10 percent. On simpler, mature products, the yields may be as high as 90 percent. By contrast, it would be unthinkable for a competitive automobile producer to simply discard one out of every ten cars produced.

A semiconductor device user, for a given level of performance, focuses on the cost per functional element as the determinant of which device will be used. Thus, manufacturers are continually pressing to lower the cost per functional element.

Lower costs per functional element are achieved over time primarily by two means. Within a given product generation, costs decline as productivity gains rise with increased yields. But there are practical limits. Once the process yield exceeds roughly 70 percent, there are likely to be only marginal improvements, and therefore only marginal reductions that can be achieved in costs.

To repeat the process, the next generation device must be put into production with a greater density of functional elements. Then the process of productivity gains is repeated—that is, not only including more elements per chip, but increasing the number of elements per unit area. Since 1970 the average size of functional elements on a chip has decreased by a factor of ten.[10] What is observed over successive generations is a steady decline in cost per function.

There is a systematic relationship between chip density and the cost per functional element. As shown in figure 3-3, manufacturing costs are aggregated into two groups: those that vary directly with chip density and those that vary inversely. Fabrication costs rise with density because producing chips with finer features requires more process steps and more processing

Figure 3-3

Relationships of Costs per Functional Elements to Chip Density

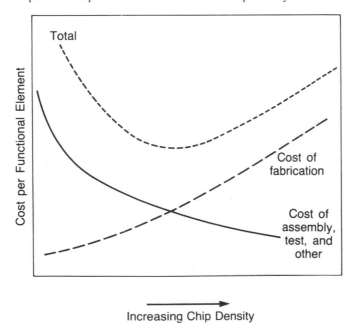

Increasing Chip Density

time. Testing and assembly costs typically decrease with density. Other costs per functional element, such as wafer preparation and materials cost, also decline with increasing density. On balance, increases in chip density are initially associated with decreasing costs. In addition, the cost curves for fabrication and assembly have shifted down over time, resulting in further reductions in the cost per function.[11]

Successive generations of semiconductor devices require increasingly capital-intensive production techniques. This trend translates into a larger capital investment for additional wafer fabrication, testing, and assembly facilities to achieve a given level of output. The result is a relative increase in the capital cost component of total production cost for a specific product per unit of output.

A look at the cost components for a particular product is useful to evaluate how the industry cost structure has been changing over time. Table 3-4 shows cost breakouts for a hypothetical U.S. facility manufacturing 64K dynamic random access memories (DRAMs), a high-volume computer memory device. At the plant level, semiconductor costs can vary by the type of process, the type of product, and the stage of the product's life cycle. The process is divided into four basic phases, though each stage, especially the fabrication stage, can have a large number of separate steps associated with it. The last column of table 3-4 shows the percentage of finished dies that are good at that particular stage. Overall, for case A, the yield is 22 percent, that is, 22 out of every 100 die started into the process are acceptable product. The ratio of capital to labor costs per unit of output is 0.48.

Learning economies or dynamic economies of scale occur as production experience cumulates. Table 3-4 (case B) illustrates how an improvement in yields from 40 percent to 70 percent due to learning effects changes the distribution of factor costs. There has been no change in underlying fixed or variable costs per unit. The overall yield has increased to 38 percent with the process becoming less capital-intensive on a per-unit basis, reflected in the decline in the capital-labor ratio to 0.35. Case C in the same table repeats the earlier example except that it assumes that the initial capital investment per wafer start increases by a factor of 2.5. (This increase in capital requirements is roughly the order of magnitude that the transition into VLSI will require.) In this case, over a third of total costs, 38 percent, are capital costs compared with 20 percent in case B. The capital-labor ratio more than doubles to 0.79.

These examples illustrate how changes in production parameters influence the cost structure. The dual effects of capital deepening and dynamic learning

Table 3-4
Cost Breakouts for a Hypothetical U.S. 64K DRAM Manufacturing Facility

A. Cost per Good Die—Recently Introduced 64K DRAM

Process Stage	Labor	Capital	Materials	Yield (%)
Fabrication	$0.35	$0.42	$0.46	80%
Wafer probe test	0.16			40
Assembly	0.17	0.04	0.07	90
Final test	0.27			75
Total cost	$0.95	$0.46	$0.53	
Cumulative yield				22%
Cost distribution	49%	24%	27%	
Ratio of capital to labor costs = 0.48				

B. Cost per Good Die—64K DRAM with Yield Improvement

Process Stage	Labor	Capital	Materials	Yield (%)
Fabrication	$0.20	$0.24	$0.26	80%
Wafer probe test	0.16	♦		70
Assembly	0.17	0.04	0.07	90
Final test	0.27			75
Total cost	$0.80	$0.28	$0.33	
Cumulative yield				38%
Cost distribution	57%	20%	23%	
Ratio of capital to labor costs = 0.35				

C. Cost per Good Die—64K DRAM with 2.5 Increase in Capital Investment

Process Stage	Labor	Capital	Materials	Yield (%)
Total cost	$0.80	$0.63	$0.33	
Cumulative yield				38%
Cost distribution	45%	38%	19%	
Ratio of capital to labor costs = 0.79				

Source: Adapted from estimates provided by Dataquest, Integrated Circuit Engineering Corporation, and conversations with semiconductor industry executives.

improvements in yields occur simultaneously as the industry expands. For the industry as a whole, the overall production cost structure is a result of these two dynamic elements. Within a particular generation of process and product technologies, the degree of capital intensity declines as yields increase in the fabrication stage of production relative to the yields of the other production stages. This results from the enhanced productivity of the most capital-intensive segment of the production process relative to the less capital-intensive stages. The capital intensity of the production technique for a particular product will thus decrease over time. But because successive generations of new products require more capital investment to decrease production costs per good die, successive generations of production facilities require an increasing scale of capital investment.

The trend toward greater capital intensity at the plant level has not resulted in an overall rise in capital requirements per unit of output for the industry. The following figures (from the Semiconductor Industry Association) show the ratio of sales per dollar of utilized gross fixed assets for U.S. IC manufacturers:

	1975	1976	1977	1978	1979	1980	1981	1982
Sales per $ of utilized gross fixed assets	2.8	2.7	2.4	2.1	2.5	2.7	2.6	2.0

The data do not suggest any clear trend toward capital deepening.

What is offsetting the move to greater capital investment at the plant level is a rising labor input at the front end of the production sequence—the design and development phase. The increasingly complex chips developed since the beginning of the large-scale integration era require a substantially higher amount of engineering design time. These two trends tend to offset one another so that capital requirements relative to labor requirements have not shifted substantially over time.

Nevertheless, these trends are changing several other characteristics of the industry. First, the minimum efficient scale of plant for the production of commodity devices is increasing as scale economies become more important. Second, due to the growing investment in design and development, firms are tied to a particular chip architecture for a longer time. Third, because of the combined effects of the above two factors, firms are witnessing a substantial increase in precommitment costs. To understand this concept, one must recognize that the product life cycles are relatively short—about two to five years. Management must decide for each new generation of product or process technology whether, based on past performance and future expectations, to continue to participate. For example, in semiconductor memories, there have been four generations of devices since 1970. At each crossover to a new generation, firms have had to decide whether to commit to participate in the next generation. This precommitment cost has been increasing substantially. A state-of-the-art production line that required an investment of only $1 million in 1965 today costs $60 million and is projected to cost $150 million by 1985. These increased equipment costs, combined with the greater investment in R&D required by each new generation of chip architecture, have substantially increased the risk associated with semiconductor invest-ment decisions at each crossover point.

There are a number of differences in the manufacturing strategies pursued by U.S. and Japanese semiconductor firms in their efforts to minimize total production cost per good die. To highlight the differences, table 3-5 provides a cost comparison for a major commodity device, the 64K DRAM. Cost differences would vary for other products, but the 64K DRAM market was critical to watch, since it was the largest single-product market in 1983.

The estimate for front-end costs of wafer fabrication in section A of table 3-5 suggests that the U.S. producers have a 20 percent cost advantage per wafer start over Japanese producers. Higher Japanese material costs arise, in part, from stricter purity standards for materials, which translate downstream into better yields in critical processing steps and, therefore, lower costs per good die. The capital cost component is higher because of the Japanese emphasis on process automation. Again this is a higher front-end cost dis-advantage which is offset by higher process yields. VLSI demands a defect-free environment to achieve high yields. Capital investments in automation reduce the number of operating personnel in the fabrication facilities and therefore decrease the defect rate per wafer start.

Section B of table 3-5 provides a comparison of U.S. and Japanese cost by stage of process. The Japanese accept a slightly larger die size (and the reduction in available die per wafer that results) because they need additional chip area for reasons partly related to their use of automation. They make up for the smaller number of die per wafer with higher yields in the assembly stage through automation. Whereas U.S. companies perform assembly off-shore in low-wage countries, most Japanese firms perform assembly of integrated circuit devices only in Japan or other developed countries. This leads the Japanese companies to try to minimize the labor cost component of assembly.

The net cost difference after accounting for the variations in yields and various process costs is quite small. Japanese factor cost per good die (line 14) is $1.90 versus $2.00 for a typical U.S. firm. Nevertheless, some observers place average overall yields at 40 to 50 percent for U.S. producers and over 60 percent for some Japanese producers. The figures in the paren-theses illustrate how a 40 percent cumulative yield for a U.S. firm, compared with a 69 percent cumulative yield for a Japanese firm, would still result in essentially equivalent costs per good die. What is important is that assuming comparable plant loadings, the Japanese facility has a higher rate of physical output, as shown in line 15. This translates into higher output per employee,

Table 3-5

Cost Comparison for U.S. and Japanese 64K DRAM

A. Components of Whole Wafer Cost ($ per wafer)

	United States	Japan
1. Materials	$32	$ 49
2. Capital (depreciation)	29	37
3. Labor	24	20
Total	$85	$106

Japan wafer costs ÷ U.S. = 1.25

B. Determination of Factory Cost

	United States	Japan
1. Wafer process cost	$ 85	$106
2. Wafer process yield	80%	95%
3. Yielded whole wafer cost	$106	$112
4. Die size (mil^2)	35,100	38,600
Total die/wafer	313	280
5. Wafer probe cost	$ 14	$ 12
Tested wafer cost	$120	$124
6. Probe yield	40%	52%
7. Good die	125	146
8. Cost per good die	$0.96	$0.85
9. Assembly cost	$0.20	$0.40
10. Assembly yield	90%	95%
11. Yielded assembly cost	$1.40	$1.32
12. Final test cost	$0.20	$0.20
13. Final test yield	80%	80%
14. Factory cost per good die	$2.00	$1.90
15. Cumulative yield	23%	38%
Number of good die	72	106
16. Gross margin	45%	40%
17. Final selling price	$3.64	$3.17
18. Total revenue	$262	$336

Source: Adapted from estimates provided by Dataquest, Integrated Circuit Engineering Corporation, and conversations with semiconductor industry executives.

and more important, greater market share for a given amount of fabrication capacity.

Also important to note is how the overhead structure affects the final price determination. The average U.S. gross margin is between 40 and 50 percent across all product types. Japanese firms, due to their willingness to accept a lower return on investment and the lower interest charges, have lower gross margins. Although table 3-5 shows a different final selling price (line 17) for U.S. and Japanese firms due to the different gross margin assumed, this could not happen in practice for a standard device like the 64K DRAM. As a consequence, U.S. firms must accept a lower gross margin, 37 percent in this case, to compete with the Japanese in this market. Finally, the total revenue per wafer start (line 18) shows that the Japanese firms can generate a larger cash flow than their U.S. competitors, despite lower gross margins and smaller numbers of initial available die.

Several factors, however, should be kept in mind regarding the cost comparisons in table 3-5. First, a number of key parameters are subject to wide variation across firms. Thus, these cost estimates should not be read as supporting the notion that either the U.S. or the Japanese industry has a decided overall cost advantage; it is quite the opposite. The relative cost situation is too close to say that one industry has the overall advantage. Second, exchange rate movements can affect which industry has a cost advantage at any given time because the two industries are so nearly even in overall costs. The yen/dollar exchange rate, for example, went from 231 in January 1982, to 270 in September, a 15 percent swing, and by the end of the year was nearly back at the 231 rate.

The unsettling aspect of the comparison shows up in lines 15 and 18. For a plant of identical capacity and loading, Japanese producers will obtain approximately 50 percent more good die and 50 percent greater overall revenue. U.S. producers would have to invest nearly 40 percent more just to achieve a comparable number of good die. Thus, despite the evidence that the U.S. industry is cost competitive with the Japanese industry today, the future is less favorable given the incessant pressure to achieve greater capital investment per unit output and the strategic value of such investment for maximizing sustainable yields.

U.S. INDUSTRY STRUCTURE: THE CHALLENGE
OF ADVANCING TECHNOLOGY

The technological base of the U.S. semiconductor industry has evolved dramatically since the industry's beginnings thirty-five years ago. It is useful to divide technological development of the industry into four phases. The first phase, which began in 1948 with the demonstration of the point-contact transistor at Bell Telephone Laboratories and continued through the 1950s, was characterized by the development of basic semiconductor technology. The second phase was ushered in with the commercial introduction of the

IC in the early 1960s. During this phase, which lasted through the early 1970s, the density of semiconductor elements on a single IC chip increased to as many as 100 logic gates—a level known as medium-scale integration. This progress in the direction of miniaturization gave rise to a wide variety of new devices, including the random access memory in 1970 and the microprocessor in 1971. The third phase, which began in the early 1970s, brought advances in large-scale integration (LSI)—conventionally defined as 100 to 1,000 logic gates or the equivalent—that resulted in a dramatic expansion in semiconductor applications and markets. Since the late 1970s, the industry has moved into a new phase—the very large-scale integration (VLSI) era in which tens of thousands of component elements are processed on a single chip.

Two important factors encouraged the development of the U.S. semiconductor industry. The first was the demand of the military and aerospace markets, which pushed the technology in the direction of miniaturization and of devices with higher performance and reliability. Government funding for the technological development of new and improved semiconductors during the 1950s and 1960s did much to encourage entry and to provide the industry with a financial base. Further, the military's willingness to pay a premium for quality and reliability helped the industry bear the cost of refining and debugging its products for price-sensitive, commercial applications.

A second major influence on the development of the industry and the diffusion of semiconductor technology was the establishment of liberal licensing policies by the industry's major technological innovators. Liberal licensing recognized the difficulty of maintaining industrial secrecy in the face of high mobility of engineers and scientists and wide availability of research results. Government antitrust policy, however, also played a significant role in encouraging liberal licensing. As a result of the AT&T Consent Decree of 1956, Western Electric was required to license all existing patents to domestic firms royalty free, and to provide future licenses at reasonable rates.[12] The Justice Department's role in stimulating AT&T's liberal licensing policy undoubtedly influenced other semiconductor firms to follow a similar policy.

The introduction of the IC in the early 1960s brought important changes to the semiconductor industry structure by widening the reach of semiconductor technology. As the number of IC users in the computer and industrial equipment markets increased, the semiconductor industry was thus able to reduce its dependence on military demand. In 1962, government procurement constituted 100 percent of the total value of U.S. IC sales; by 1972, government sales had fallen to 25 percent of the market, and computer and industrial sales had expanded to 65 percent of the value of domestic IC sales. See table 3-6 for a historical profile of the distribution of U.S. sales of IC devices.

By the early 1970s, new merchant entry encouraged by the proliferation of IC technology had produced a unique and highly competitive industry structure. Two different types of firms could be identified: (1) merchant producers and (2) captive producers formed by electronic systems firms. Together, these two types of firms ensured that a large number of participants would aggressively pursue new market and technological opportunities.

The semiconductor industry's structure has undergone substantial transformation since the advent of LSI in the early 1970s. As circuit density has increased and IC components have taken on an increasing number of system functions, the cost of efficient scale production at or near the frontier of semiconductor technology has soared. Semiconductor research and development costs, for example, have increased dramatically. During the 1960s, ICs were general building blocks that were incorporated into complex logic systems by systems designers with expertise in network theory, component properties, and practical knowledge of effective design techniques. The software costs associated with IC design were minimal. LSI fundamentally changed the design process as it became possible to put an ever-increasing number of transistors on a single chip and software became an integral—and rapidly increasing—part of IC design and cost. By one estimate, the man-hour requirements of circuit design increased more than fivefold over the 1970s.[13] Today, more than half the cost of new VLSI circuits is spent on

Table 3-6
Value of Total U.S. Sales of Integrated Circuit Devices, 1962–78

Markets	1962	1965	1969	1972	1974	1978
Government	100%	55%	36%	25%	20%	10.0%
Computer	0	35	44	40	36	37.5
Industrial	0	9	16	25	30	37.5
Consumer	0	1	4	15	15	15.0
Total U.S. domestic shipments ($ millions)	$ 4	$79	$413	$608	$1,204	$2,080

Source: Figures for 1962 are derived from John Tilton, *International Diffusion of Technology: The Case of Semiconductors* (Washington, D.C.: Brookings Institution, 1971). Figures for 1965, 1969, 1972, and 1974 from U.S. Department of Commerce, *A Report on the U.S. Semiconductor Industry* (Washington, D.C.: Government Printing Office, 1979), 102. Figures for 1978 are rough estimates based on figures in U.S. International Trade Commission, *Competitive Factors Influencing World Trade in Integrated Circuits*, publication no. 1013 (Washington, D.C.: 1979), 102; *Business Week*, 3 December 1979, 68; and "1980 Semiconductor Forum," *Rosen Electronics Letter*, 14 July 1980, 150.

software. Finally, as previously discussed, the cost of IC production capacity has also escalated as advances in LSI and VLSI have increased the complexity of production and test equipment.[14]

Entry costs rose dramatically over the 1970s as escalating research and production equipment costs increased the minimum efficient scale of fabrication. Increased capital requirements, coupled with changes in the late 1960s in the tax treatment of capital gains that reduced the availability of venture capital, resulted in a precipitous decline in the rate of entry after 1972. By one count, only four new firms entered the industry over the 1973-78 period—despite rapid market growth after 1975.[15]

Increasing investment requirements for the research and production capacity needed to support future growth also became a problem for existing merchant firms as the industry moved into the 1970s. In contrast to the large, diversified electronics systems producers, the merchants possessed more limited sources of internal funds and also faced less-attractive terms on external funds—problems compounded by the semiconductor industry's lower than average profitability. Indeed, cash-flow problems forced merchant IC producers to reduce capital expenditures as a percentage of sales during the 1975-77 period—a move that subsequently led to the industry's widely publicized capacity problems and provided Japanese producers with the opportunity to increase worldwide market share.

The increasing costs—and opportunities—of LSI technology also altered the strategic position of systems manufacturers who incorporated the merchants' products as intermediate inputs. As individual ICs took on the capability of complete electronic systems, systems producers felt compelled to integrate backwards into IC design and production as a means of incorporating proprietary designs, assuring a reliable source of supply, and capturing the increasing value added associated with the design and production of LSI circuits. Moreover, as LSI allowed system-level chips to be customized to specific applications, an increasing number of device types were needed by systems manufacturers, though the volume demand for any particular customized chip was low. These factors gave systems producers strong incentives either to acquire merchant firms or to create their own captive operations.

The capital constraints faced by the merchant segment of the industry, coupled with the systems manufacturers' incentives to respond to the evolution of semiconductor technology, thus led to a wave of mergers and acquisitions between IC producers and systems firms over the 1975-80 period. Foreign electronics firms played a major role in this trend due to the weakness of the U.S. dollar and the depressed state of the U.S. stock market in the late 1970s. Together, these factors made it cheaper for foreign firms to buy U.S. technology and market share through the purchase of existing companies than to build it through in-house development or by adapting the latest technologies. By 1980, at least fourteen independent merchant houses, including such market leaders as Fairchild and Signetics, had been acquired by foreign firms.

Growth in the systems firms' in-house IC design and production capabilities has paralleled the trend in semiconductor mergers and acquisitions. Captive IC production has risen continuously from 1970 to the present. Furthermore, over much of this period, captive manufacturing has grown faster than the merchant segment of the industry. By 1980, nearly fifty systems firms possessed either IC R&D, pilot production, or full-production capabilities, though fewer than twenty were actually engaged in full production.[16] Industry observers predict another steep rise in captive IC production by mid-decade, spurred by the home computer, office automation, and increased IC content in products such as automobiles and appliances. One market research firm predicts that captive producers will account for approximately 40 percent of all U.S. IC production by 1990, up from 30 percent in 1981.[17]

Despite the advantages associated with proprietary circuits, systems manufacturers facing the decision to manufacture VLSI circuits in-house must also weigh the disadvantages—substantial capital investment requirements, absence of a second source for critical IC designs, and difficulty in acquiring the expertise to make state-of-the-art VLSI devices on an efficient scale. Whether the captives continue to gain market share at the merchants' expense will thus depend on whether the merchants can supply large numbers of VLSI device types in low-volume runs. If merchant firms provide the necessary flexibility and service required by the nonstandard chip market, the captives' need to expand capacity to meet internal chip needs will be reduced.

A wave of new entrants specializing in the design or production of customized ICs has appeared. With the increased availability of venture capital following the 1978 revision of the capital gains tax law, approximately sixty such start-up companies have entered the custom segment of the industry since 1979.[18] Unlike the traditional merchants who must view their interests in terms of a spectrum of customers, the start-ups have attempted to offer customers an engineering-intensive relationship at whatever level is appropriate.

Some observers, however, are skeptical about the potential of these new entrants. They predict that start-ups are likely to fail unless they grow into complete semiconductor houses. For example, they question whether many of the start-ups will be able to generate enough cash to keep up with advancing technology, particularly as the cost of design automation tools and test equipment rises. Further, they note that, as chip design becomes more automated, firms will need increased volume to get a controllable process. Others question whether customers will be willing to put the heart of their systems in the hands of a small start-up company.

The start-ups are also beginning to encounter increased competition as the traditional merchants move more aggressively into the custom and semicustom business. Established firms—both U.S. and Japanese—are rushing to set up design centers, where customers can work with a chip supplier's engineers and software design tools. Moreover, during the recent recession, many merchant producers allocated idle fabrication space for outside foundry services, a trend that has led to an increasing number of captive design/silicon-foundry partnerships. Finally, increased competition promises to come from the captives themselves as they enter selected niches of the semicustom market in an effort to achieve economies of scale that will reduce the cost of chips consumed in-house.

Although there is no clear industry consensus on the extent to which stepped-up captive production and new custom design start-ups will affect the traditional merchant suppliers, most industry observers agree that the acquisition trend in the semiconductor industry will continue. As the industry moves from LSI to VLSI, the structure of the industry is changing. VLSI technology is forging new, tighter relationships between chip suppliers and users. Merchants and systems manufacturers are becoming increasingly interdependent, a phenomenon that is reflected in a wave of cooperative initiatives—major joint ventures, technology exchanges and ownership agreements among computer, communications, and semiconductor firms.[19]

At the same time, semiconductor manufacturers are also seeking new ways to share R&D costs among themselves, that is, through arrangements in which two or more companies independently develop individual parts in a family of chips. Such arrangements, which spread the risks of systems development and market penetration, have multiplied since the late 1970s. The costs of R&D and production capacity have become so high that such alliances are inevitable.

Cooperative approaches to basic semiconductor research are also increasing, thanks to a growing number of advocates in industry, government, and universities. Since 1982, major firms in both the semiconductor and computer industries have established cooperative research ventures as a means of better

utilizing R&D dollars and manpower. The first such venture, the Semiconductor Research Cooperative (SRC), was established in 1982 by the Semiconductor Industry Association as an affiliate nonprofit research cooperative
that will fund basic research at U.S. universities. The SRC, which now
includes most of the top-tier semiconductor manufacturers and nearly all
leading U.S. computer makers, hopes to have an annual budget exceeding
$30 million by 1985. Although the dollar magnitude of the SRC's research
funding is not great, it nevertheless represents a substantial increase in U.S.
expenditure on basic semiconductor research. In 1982, for example, the
National Science Foundation's budget for basic research in semiconductor
technologies was $7.5 million, and all semiconductor firms combined spent
only an estimated $20 million to $25 million.[20]

A second major joint research venture, the Microelectronics and Computer
Technology Corporation (MCC), was established in January 1983 by a group
of ten electronics firms led by Control Data. MCC will sponsor long-term,
high-level systems research in computers and software, that is, in microelectronics packaging, advanced computer architecture, computer-aided design
and manufacture, and software productivity. When fully under way in 1984,
MCC expects to support a research budget of $75 million to $200 million.
Unlike the SRC, MCC will develop technology for member companies that
will have initial rights to the technology developed and receive preferential
treatment.

The emerging semiconductor industry structure in the United States is fluid
and uncertain. Nevertheless, the way the U.S. semiconductor industry has
responded to the advent of VLSI technology underscores the strength of its
diverse industry structure, that is, its ability to generate a variety of approaches to exploit new technological developments. Merchant manufacturers
of commodity devices are seeking to grow larger and more diversified,
through both merger and forward integration, to increase their ability to
invest in R&D and production equipment. Smaller firms continue to develop
specialized product niches. Indeed, as many as 100 start-ups have entered
the industry since the late 1970s. Systems firms are moving to establish and
expand their in-house capabilities in microelectronics. With the settlement
of the IBM and AT&T antitrust cases, these two electronics giants will
continue to expand their influence on the industry's structure and competitive
position.

In contrast to the structural shifts transforming the U.S. industry, the
structure of the Japanese semiconductor industry has not changed significantly
in response to the development of VLSI technology. Six large firms—NEC,

Fujitsu, Toshiba, Hitachi, Mitsubishi, and Matsushita—remain the principal actors. One exception has been the movement by the largest Japanese producers to form relationships with the new VLSI design houses in the United States. The Japanese view these relationships as a way to overcome their weakness in establishing close customer-supplier relationships in the United States, as well as to gain access to U.S. design skills.

In the past, Japanese producers have been slow in adapting to major shifts in semiconductor technology. Although the Japanese electronics industry had mastered the mass production of transistors by the late 1950s, IC technology created new markets in the 1960s. Nevertheless, Japanese companies took nearly fifteen years to catch up and establish a significant position in IC technology. This said, the Japanese semiconductor industry today has vastly superior research strengths than it had a decade ago (see figure 3-4). In addition, the NTT research lab, a facility with close ties to most of the major semiconductor producers, is performing pathbreaking research in a number of technologies central to the industry's future development. NTT, in turn, feeds the results of its research directly to a favored subset of Japanese companies.

It is unlikely, therefore, that Japanese firms will fail to be a major factor in the major VLSI markets of the future. Rather, the equation will balance differently. The U.S. industry will have the advantage of diversity. The Japanese industry's strengths will center on their stronger financial base, which is capable of funding the scale of investment needed in the VLSI era, and on an integrated firm organization that links systems and component producers together.

ELEMENTS OF RIVALRY: POST-1977 COMPETITION BETWEEN U.S. AND JAPANESE SEMICONDUCTOR INDUSTRIES

The conditions of competitive rivalry faced by U.S. semiconductor producers—both domestically and internationally—were significantly changed by the emergence of Japanese firms as international competitors in the late 1970s. Before the advent of the Japanese, competitive success was based on product strategies that met four criteria: customer acceptance of product design; availability of second-source suppliers; aggressive pricing; and credible delivery commitments.[21] At the early stage of each successive generation, competition focused on product development. Several firms pursuing innovation strategies typically vied to have their product designs accepted by customers as the industry standard. As soon as a clear favorite emerged, other firms entered the race and adopted the standard design as second-source

Figure 3-4

Semiconductor Industry Research and Development: Japan and United States

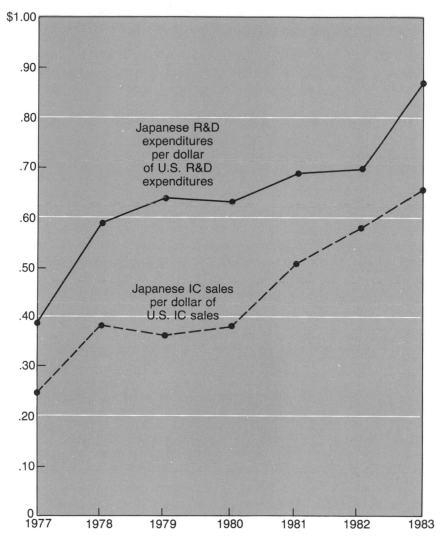

Source: Dataquest; *Japan Economic Journal*; BA Asia Ltd.; SIA.
Note: Japanese R&D totals exclude NTT and government-sponsored R&D.

producers. Through price competition, the introduction of improvements on the standard design, and the use of marketing and distribution strengths, these firms competed for market share in the new product area. Quality and reliability, though important, were secondary dimensions of firm strategy.

THE CASE OF THE DRAM

The Japanese assault on the DRAM market in the late 1970s added several new dimensions to the prevailing competitive calculus. As a high-volume, standardized product, the DRAM was an ideal first target for the Japanese. It allowed them to capitalize on their traditional strength (low-cost manufacturing) and to minimize their relative weaknesses (innovation and distribution/support services), while exploiting the financial constraints faced by U.S. producers.

High-volume products, such as MOS memory devices for computers, have great strategic importance to the international competitive position of the U.S. industry. The erosion of U.S. leadership in DRAMs is viewed with particular concern because they are the industry's highest-volume product. Sales of the 64K DRAM will reach nearly $1 billion in 1983, up from $100 million in 1981. Sales of the 256K DRAM, which is now being sampled, are expected to reach at least $2 billion per year by the late 1980s.

U.S. semiconductor producers, however, emphasize that more than profits is at stake in the DRAM business. The DRAM is a product that enables firms to reduce costs and enhance production in virtually all other semiconductor lines. Because of their high sales volume, DRAMs not only make possible economies of scale in overall semiconductor production, but lead the way technologically to greater IC density and complexity. As an area in which advanced production techniques have been honed and refined, high-volume memories stand on the cutting edge of semiconductor technology.

The Japanese entry strategy was based on a build-up of memory production capacity, which enabled them, through aggressive price competition, to gain a sizable share of 16K DRAM world sales and a dominant share of 64K sales. In doing so, Japanese producers underscored the importance of timely delivery—an element of strategy that had already been recognized as critical in the early phase of the memory market's development.[22] Indeed, since the introduction of the 64K DRAM, major Japanese producers have stressed their ability to deliver by announcing plans to add production capacity well in advance of demand.

In addition, Japanese DRAMs turned out to be of higher quality and reliability than U.S. chips, testifying to the Japanese industry's strength in high-yield mass production. Although knowledgeable observers emphasize that no mystery underlies the Japanese formula, in this area too, U.S. manufacturers were caught off guard. Until recently, all Japanese manufacturing equipment was imported from the United States. The Japanese simply added handling equipment, air purifying technology, personnel training, and comprehensive clean room control. New Japanese equipment suppliers provide state-of-the-art equipment, further supporting the manufacturing advantages of Japanese IC producers.

Finally, the aggressiveness of Japanese capacity competition has heightened the intensity of price competition in the memory market. When the 64K DRAM was introduced in 1980, few industry analysts expected 64K DRAM prices to fall below ten dollars until 1982; by the end of 1981, however, Japanese firms had begun to quote prices in the four- to five-dollar range.[23]

The entry of the Japanese into the DRAM market has forced U.S. manufacturers to reevaluate their competitive strategies on all dimensions—product and process innovation, capacity, quality and reliability, and price. If the circumstances of Japanese competition simply involved these factors, the role of the U.S. government would have been limited to the issue of technical superiority in microelectronics for reasons of national security. But the entry of the Japanese semiconductor firms also involved the question of strategic behavior by the government of Japan. Their industry promotion policies thus prompted a response by the U.S. government. What has resulted in the wake of the Japanese competitive thrust in memory chips is competition not just between firms of each national industry, but competition played out with the two governments as active participants. Both have attempted to shape the terms of the competitive environment but with different objectives, namely to obtain maximum strategic advantages in the Japanese case and to maintain existing advantages in the U.S. case.

THE CHANGING NATURE OF SEMICONDUCTOR RIVALRY

The advent of Japanese competition has changed the behavior of U.S. semiconductor firms both by intensifying competition along conventional dimensions, particularly R&D and quality, and by introducing new strategic factors, notably production capacity. With respect to research, for example, the U.S. industry has a history of an exceptionally high rate of investment in R&D, since performance advances for new devices relate closely to R&D efforts. U.S. IC producers have traditionally spent an average 8-9 percent of sales revenues on R&D. Even in 1975, a recession year for the industry, these firms sustained a rate of nearly 9 percent. To deflect the Japanese challenge, U.S. firms have intensified their efforts to maintain an overall lead in semiconductor technology. During the 1981-82 slowdown in sales, the U.S. industry thus pressed to maintain the absolute level of R&D spending at prerecession levels. The ratio of R&D to sales climbed from 9 percent in 1980 to 11 percent in 1981, to over 12 percent in 1982. The U.S. industry's increased commitment to research was a direct response to competitive pressure created by the Japanese IC firms, which spent an average 13-20 percent of sales on R&D between 1975 and 1982. Indeed, by 1982, the research expenditures of the Japanese IC producers nearly equaled those of U.S. merchant IC producers in absolute terms. Had U.S. firms simply maintained their previous R&D-to-sales ratios, U.S. merchant producers would have been outspent by as much as $125 million in 1982.

Japanese semiconductor firms have also heightened competition along the nonprice attributes of quality and reliability. Two points can be made about U.S.-Japanese attitudes regarding quality. First, since Hewlett-Packard's disclosure in 1980 that U.S. firms were behind in quality, U.S. producers' quality performance has increased dramatically. U.S. firms have given greater emphasis to tightening product compliance with specification standards. See, for example, table 3-7, which shows that U.S. suppliers of 16K DRAMs now outperform Japanese suppliers in terms of failure rate experience. In other product areas such as computer logic, in which Japanese firms do not concentrate their attention, U.S. producers are quality leaders. Second, by emphasizing a nonprice attribute, Japanese producers have attempted to compete without undercutting the prices of U.S. producers. This caution on the part of the Japanese companies is due to fears of having U.S. producers file a dumping case against them. Several episodes of price undercutting occurred in the late 1970s. The argument that Japanese chips were superior in quality allowed them to sidestep the dumping issue, since they could gain market share without having to be price leaders.

Another traditional attribute of semiconductor industry rivalry that has intensified since the advent of Japanese competition is signaling—the use of announcements of possible future actions to influence a rival's behavior in the market. At the firm level, the Japanese have typically used announcements to try to indicate to U.S. rivals to move out of the commodity DRAM

Table 3-7
U.S.-Japanese 16K DRAM Failure Rates (parts per million)

	1978	*1979*	*1980*	*1981*	*1982*
Japanese vendors	0.24	0.20	0.16	0.17	0.05
U.S. vendors	1.00	1.32	0.78	0.18	0.02

Source: Hewlett-Packard

business. For example, leading Japanese firms have announced additions to 64K DRAM production capacity well in advance of anticipated growth in sales. Similarly, Japanese firms have been highly aggressive in announcing complete development of 256K DRAM technology. Indeed, one of the most ambitious recent announcements by a Japanese firm came in August 1982, when NEC announced that it had developed the basic technology for the four-megabit DRAM—two generations removed from the existing commercial level of technology. Such signaling was intended to indicate to U.S. firms, which were just then vamping up 64K DRAM production, that the Japanese firms were going to press ahead so far and so quickly that U.S. firms should get out of the commodity memory market. (The signals may also have served to intimidate rivals within the Japanese market.)

The Semiconductor Industry Association (SIA), which includes all but one major U.S. semiconductor producer, has responded to the Japanese with its own signals. The first occasion came in 1979, when Japanese firms were pricing 16K DRAMs in the U.S. market below their home market price. After the SIA indicated its willingness to file a dumping complaint, Japanese firms altered their pricing behavior. More recently, the SIA threatened to bring a trade action against the Japanese industry over access to the Japanese market. Again, the threat was credible and negotiations were initiated to seek an appropriate remedy.

Although signaling usually is thought to be effective only when there are a relatively small number of firms in the market, the national industries of two countries clearly see the overall strategic nature of the competition and carefully evaluate and react to the moves of the other. Recent press accounts, for example, suggest that Japanese producers are holding back on mass production of 256K DRAMs, in part because of their concern that it would aggravate the current state of "trade frictions" between the two countries.

Finally, a new element that Japanese competition has introduced relates to production capacity. Like any cyclical industry, the U.S. semiconductor industry's utilization of available capacity varies over the business cycle. Prior to the advent of Japanese competition, U.S. firms expected that any excess capacity developed during a business downturn would be available at the next upturn. Because semiconductor demand is highly elastic, it was never questioned whether additional capacity would be needed; rather it was a question of deciding when to add capacity. Since internal cash flow was the primary way to fund capital expansion, significant capacity additions had to wait until profitability recovered after the recession. But the Japanese semiconductor producers pursued a different policy. In the 1974-76 period, they maintained a significant rate of capital investment. As a result, the U.S. industry found itself losing relative market share during the 1976-78 recovery. This strongly influenced the U.S. industry to sustain capital expenditures during the 1981-82 period, despite a weakened cash flow position. Table 3-8 compares the relative rates of capital investment of the two industries between 1975 and 1982. The result of the sustained capacity expansion was a significant deterioration in U.S. capacity utilization and profitability.

GOVERNMENT INVOLVEMENT IN RIVALRY

It is the element of Japanese government involvement that has caused the U.S. industry its greatest difficulties in the U.S.-Japanese battle for semiconductor market share. To understand why this is the case, some background is useful. For over a decade, beginning in the mid-1960s, the U.S. semiconductor industry prospered with little direct U.S. government support. It was in this period that it grew into an international industry dominating all the major markets in the world, with the exception of the protected Japanese market. Although the industry received significant government support, principally through military programs, during its early years, this was significantly reduced after the Minuteman missile program ended in 1964. By 1980, government procurement of semiconductors had declined to less than 10 percent of industry revenues.[24]

In contrast, the government of Japan has had a long-standing policy of encouraging the development of an internationally competitive semiconductor industry. Its support for the semiconductor industry takes place within a broad policy of promoting the development of those high technology sectors that are believed to be important for Japan's economic growth and international competitiveness. The leading proponent of support for high technology sectors is the Ministry of International Trade and Industry (MITI). MITI believes high technology industries can contribute to Japan's economic

Table 3-8

Capital Spending Relative to Sales: U.S. Merchant IC Producers Compared with Japanese IC Producers (%)

	1975	1976	1977	1978	1979	1980	1981	1982
U.S.	4.8	12.6	13.9	18.9	13.5	17.1	19.4	16.4
Japan	10.5	21.3	14.1	18.2	22.4	24.9	25.1	27.8

Source: SIA and MITI

growth because they are typically high value added, high productivity, and have significant linkages to other important sectors. The Japanese also believe that maintaining a strong international competitive position in manufactures is related to increasing their capabilities in high technology. First, it shifts their export base away from resource-dependent sectors. Second, learning and scale economies are important in many high technology sectors and generate improved efficiency over time. Finally, Japan's highly educated work force and the emphasis on quality are factors that provide it with an emerging advantage in high technology industries like semiconductors.

Beginning in the 1950s, within a broader policy of protecting Japanese industry from import competition and restricting foreign direct investment, the Japanese government offered additional support in the form of financial assistance, government direct support for R&D, and a liberal antitrust policy. A series of laws beginning in 1957 authorized MITI to exempt the computer/semiconductor industry from antitrust prosecution. Although extensive liberalization of trade and investment occurred by 1975, the government simply stepped up its financial aid and continued its liberal competitive policy. Between 1976 and 1982, the Japanese government provided at least $500 million in direct subsidies and soft loans to the industry. In addition, between 1971 and 1982, Japan Development Bank loans to the computer/semiconductor industry have been estimated at $2.5 billion. The government telephone monopoly, NTT, has been another important sponsor of VLSI research. Over the 1976-80 period, NTT invested $350 million independently of MITI's VLSI project.

By the late 1970s, the U.S. merchant semiconductor industry saw itself functioning in a highly competitive framework, bereft of government involvement, against large, vertically integrated Japanese firms allied with their government. Although the U.S. industry believed that commercial development of IC technology and markets had taken place optimally in the absence of significant government involvement, it saw the Japanese government as having introduced a new element into the competitive equation. From the U.S. industry perspective, the Japanese government was able to enhance the strategic power of its firms. What was needed, therefore, from the U.S. industry perspective was a credible U.S. government policy that could neutralize the Japanese government's role. The result, it was hoped, would be a restoration of the competitive framework in which rivalry among firms, independent of government support, determines market outcomes.

Despite the U.S. Defense Department's ability to direct substantial resources to advancing the state of technology, U.S. trade policy has become the instrument for addressing the problem of strategic competition with the government of Japan.[25] Because of aggressive lobbying by the industry, the U.S. trade policymakers are increasingly aware of the strategic aspects of the competition. In early 1982, for example, the U.S. Department of Commerce began an informal investigation into predatory pricing against Japanese 64K DRAM producers that was widely interpreted as a major signal threatening the Japanese producers with loss of access to the U.S. market. The U.S. government's objective was to attack those conditions of the competitive environment deemed to confer a strategic advantage on the Japanese producers, namely lack of access by U.S. firms to the Japanese market, Japanese competition policy, and government-sponsored financial incentives. Equally important was the signal to both industries that the U.S. government would henceforth be a player in the game.

The U.S. government's actions in the rivalry between the two industries do not imply it has decided to support the semiconductor industry as part of a strategic national industrial base. Rather, the United States has acted because the U.S. industry is viewed as an important political supporter of free trade. The actions of the Japanese government threatened to undermine that support because they are inconsistent with the liberal trade framework. This concern—and not necessarily a view about the long-run importance of the industry to the nation's economy—was what led U.S. policymakers to take action. This stands in sharp contrast to Japan's long-standing commitment to developing a national semiconductor industry based solely on its strategic importance.

1984 AND BEYOND: FUTURE PROSPECTS IN U.S.-JAPANESE COMPETITION IN SEMICONDUCTORS

Forecasting the future international competitive position of any industry is difficult. The dynamic nature of semiconductor competition, with its still-evolving process and product technologies, compounds the difficulty. Nevertheless, there are clear signs that the Japanese challenge will only intensify. As described earlier, the Japanese industry is now poised to overtake the U.S. industry (including captives) in both capital and R&D expenditures. One telling fact is that for 1984, the Japanese industry will add domestic assembly capacity equal to or greater than the U.S. industry's additions, excluding IBM. Likewise, in the absolute level of R&D, the Japanese industry is nearly equal to the U.S. total.[26]

There are several possible outcomes, any one of which could add to the problems the U.S. industry already faces.

- The U.S. industry may never regain a significant position in the commodity memory markets. Japanese producers are now beginning to make significant gains in other commodity markets such as microprocessors. These trends could suggest a U.S. industry gradually moving to a niche market orientation—a trend that would have adverse consequences on the industry's cost position and its ability to maintain technological leadership.
- The Japanese industry is trying to increase its market share in Europe at the expense of the U.S. industry. If successful, this would further accelerate the decline of the U.S. industry's worldwide market share. The U.S. industry could see its market position in both the United States and Europe shrink, while its position in Japan would remain relatively weak.
- The U.S. industry could lose its preeminent position in applied research. With the restructuring of AT&T, Bell Labs technology will be less and less accessible to outside firms. Meanwhile, in Japan, NTT has just opened a major R&D facility for LSI technology and is planning a substantial increase in its R&D activity in this area. The major Japanese firms are expanding their research laboratories.
- There is a shift in semiconductor process technology toward a technology called complementary metal-oxide semiconductor (CMOS). Because this technology has long been used in circuits manufactured for consumer electronic products, several Japanese companies are world leaders in the technology. How quickly U.S. firms can master CMOS technology will be an important issue.
- Although most semiconductors are fabricated with silicon, there is a growing role for nonsilicon technology. Especially important is gallium arsenide technology, which is highly desirable in communications and military applications. Japanese firms are world leaders in several of these important nonsilicon technologies.
- The U.S. industry appears to be falling behind the Japanese in capital investment. Given their differences in purchasing power for semiconductor equipment (some equipment can be 20-30 percent less expensive in Japan), it is likely that the Japanese industry is adding more capacity than the U.S. industry in absolute terms. Because Japanese firms get more physical output for a given increment of capacity, the Japanese industry is expanding its potential output at a significantly higher rate than the U.S. industry.

If either one or more of these events were realized, or if several of the adverse trends in technology or market share continue unabated, the U.S. semiconductor industry's prospects for retaining its world leadership would be diminished. To recognize where policy actions might be most beneficial, one can inventory U.S. strengths and weaknesses and compare them with Japanese strengths and weaknesses (see table 3-9).[27]

Against this background a number of questions emerge:

- How important is it that the U.S. maintain the merchant segment of its industry? Does the structure of the industry matter and should it be the focus of attention for policymakers? (Of course, the irony is that if the merchant segment falters, the United States would be relying upon two firms, IBM and AT&T, who have in the past been the subject of major antitrust cases.)
- Should the Japanese government's strategic objectives for this industry and the industrial organization of the Japanese semiconductor industry be concerns of U.S. policymakers?
- How can dynamic gains from technological advance be factored into policy decision making, which hitherto has principally focused on allocative efficiency?

Table 3-9
Comparison of U.S. and Japanese Strengths and Weaknesses

Strengths	
United States	Japan
Innovation	Labor cost (and stability of work
Venture capital	force)
Large domestic and foreign markets	Low capital cost
Diverse enterprises	Long-term view
	Dedication/attention to detail
	National strategy
	Quality
	Manufacturing engineering
Weaknesses	
United States	Japan
Capital costs	Closed system
Quality	Export dependence
Manufacturing innovation	Follower/copier philosophy

- Does it matter to downstream users of microelectronic devices whether they are sourcing those devices from a Japanese company that is also a competitor in the equipment market?
- Should the Department of Defense's VHSIC program, which is designed to ensure that national security interests in microelectronics are taken care of, also be aimed at ensuring that the U.S. lead over the Japanese industry is maintained? Specifically, should VHSIC funnel money into technologies and projects aimed at the commodity device market?

4

The Very High Speed Integrated Circuit Program:
Lessons for Industrial Policy

Michael Y. Yoshino
Glenn R. Fong

The Pentagon established the Very High Speed Integrated Circuit (VHSIC) program in 1979 to infuse research and development funds into the electronics industry. Government officials consulted extensively with industry leaders in formulating the program, and since that time industrial research has received constant guidance from government experts. Furthermore, industry participants have teamed up and coordinated their research efforts. Budgeted at $680 million over an eight-year period, VHSIC has awarded contracts to some twenty-five companies, from major computer manufacturers to merchant semiconductor firms.

The VHSIC program is *not* an attempt at industrial policy in the United States. But the program does contain important lessons for the making of industrial policy. Many features of the VHSIC program make it the closest American parallel to the collaborative government-industry programs in high technology pursued in Japan and Europe. Such collaborative programs are among the most intensive and challenging forms of industrial policy.

VHSIC's success in government-industry planning and industrywide support has not been inordinately dependent upon its attributes as a military program. Instead, the program highlights the importance of political and bureaucratic leadership, participatory consultation, technological competence, and institutional innovation—all factors directly relevant to industrial policy making in general.

Michael Y. Yoshino is professor of business administration at Harvard Business School. Glenn R. Fong is assistant professor of political science at the University of Illinois at Chicago.

LESSONS FOR INDUSTRIAL POLICY

The overall objective of the VHSIC program is to design and develop advanced integrated circuits highlighting specific military needs (most notably faster computational speed) and to introduce those circuits into military systems in a timely and affordable manner.[1] The technologies under development are comprehensive, ranging from system architecture to final chip test. The thrust of the program is to advance design concepts and process technology to develop high-speed integrated circuits with micron and submicron dimensions.

The program is organized into four phases, the first three of which are in sequence. Phase 0, completed in November 1980, was a study phase that defined the detailed approach for achieving the program's objectives and that prepared Phase I proposals. Fourteen prime contract bids were submitted for Phase 0 and nine awards amounting to $10.3 million were made to General Electric, Honeywell, Hughes, IBM, Raytheon, Rockwell, Texas Instruments, TRW, and Westinghouse (see table 4-1).

Phase I consisted of developing 1.25 micron circuitry and initial efforts to extend IC technology to submicron geometries. The nine Phase 0 contractors submitted bids for Phase I, and six awards amounting to $167.8 million were made in May 1981. Phase I work was conducted by Honeywell,

Table 4-1
VHSIC Bidders and Contractors[a]

	VHSIC Status	
PHASE 0	**PHASE I**	**PHASE II**
$10.3 million	*$167.8 million*	*$336.6 million*
March-November 1980	*May 1981-April 1984*	*1984-88*
GENERAL ELECTRIC		
Analog Devices		
Intersil		
Tektronix		
HONEYWELL	*HONEYWELL*	
3M	3M	
HUGHES	*HUGHES*	
Burroughs	Perkin-Elmer	
Signetics	RCA	
	Rockwell	
	Union Carbide	

(Contract Winners, listed in left margin)

[a] Prime contractors in italic letters; subcontractors in roman.   *(continued)*

Table 4-1 (continued)
VHSIC Bidders and Contractors[a]

	VHSIC Status	
PHASE 0 *$10.3 million* *March-November 1980*	**PHASE I** *$167.8 million* *May 1981-April 1984*	**PHASE II** *$336.6 million* *1984-88*

Contract Winners

IBM	*IBM*	
RAYTHEON Fairchild Varian		
ROCKWELL Perkin-Elmer Sanders		
TEXAS INSTRUMENTS	*TEXAS INSTRUMENTS*	
TRW GCA Motorola Sperry	*TRW* Motorola Sperry	
WESTINGHOUSE Control Data National Semiconductor	*WESTINGHOUSE* Control Data Harris National Semiconductor	

Losing Bidders

BOEING General Instrument	*GENERAL ELECTRIC* Analog Devices	
HARRIS ERIM Perkin-Elmer	Intersil Martin Marietta Tektronix	
SINGER American Microsystems Amhearst Systems	*RAYTHEON* Fairchild Varian	
WESTERN ELECTRIC Bell Labs	*ROCKWELL* Perkin-Elmer Sanders Associates	

[a] Prime contractors in italic letters; subcontractors in roman.

Hughes, IBM, Texas Instruments, TRW, and Westinghouse and was scheduled to be completed in 1984.

VHSIC Phase II is directed at (a) enhancing the yields of 1.25 micron technology; (b) rapidly inserting 1.25 micron circuits into military systems; (c) developing an integrated design automation system to standardize the computer languages being developed by VHSIC contractors; and (d) continuing the Phase I development effort to cross the one-micron barrier. At least $336.6 million will be allocated for Phase II efforts, and the work should be carried out through 1988.

Phase III runs parallel with the other phases and consists of many smaller, shorter-term efforts in specific technology areas designed to support the main program; $35.8 million has been awarded for fifty-nine Phase III contracts.

VHSIC is managed by the Department of Defense rather than by the military services. The program is a triservice effort in which the military departments (Army, Navy, Air Force) monitor VHSIC contractors on a day-to-day basis. The VHSIC Program Office, located in the Office of the Undersecretary of Defense for Research and Engineering (OUSDR&E), co-ordinates the three services, ensures technological commonality across the services, minimizes duplicative efforts, and prioritizes technical objectives.[2]

GOVERNMENT-INDUSTRY PLANNING

Two national security issues spurred DOD's initial thinking on the program. The first concerned a long-standing military problem that involved inserting advanced integrated circuits into defense systems on a timely and economical basis. This insertion lag between the commercial availability of an IC and its utilization in defense systems reportedly reached a twelve-year span.[3] The immediate stimulus for VHSIC's planning was an intelligence report in the fall of 1977 that suggested the U.S. military lead over the Soviets in microelectronics had diminished significantly.[4] Nevertheless, both the insertion lag and the IC gap were too amorphous to be held directly responsible for the construction of a program as ambitious and massive as VHSIC. The insertion problem had been long-standing and was insufficient on its own to generate a concerted response.[5] The reported shrinking IC lead over the Soviets was never substantiated even after intensive study.[6]

Transforming these abstract concerns into concrete policy action required much political and bureaucratic leadership and initiative. A handful of DOD officials determined many of VHSIC's key features in 1977 and 1978 including:

1. Funding the program at $100 million or more—setting VHSIC apart from all prior electron-device programs typically funded at no more than $5 million each;
2. Establishing high-speed computational throughput as the major technical objective;
3. Emphasizing lithography advances to achieve micron and submicron circuit features;
4. Investigating design approaches that would minimize circuit customization (e.g., standard cells and gate arrays);
5. Requiring system demonstrations of VHSIC circuits;
6. Pursuing several parallel circuit technologies (e.g., bipolar and complementary-metal-oxide-semiconductor);
7. Awarding contracts to many companies rather than a select few;
8. Setting off a diffuse technology support element (Phase III) from the mainstream industry effort; and
9. Determining that the program would be a triservice effort with management in OUSDR&E[7]

Important to VHSIC's planning was the willingness to seek out and incorporate industry advice. That industry and academic specialists readily provided such input is another major factor in accounting for VHSIC's successful formulation. Through 1978 the VHSIC office resembled a revolving door, as company after company contributed ideas on how the DOD program should develop. VHSIC organizers also made several cross-country trips for advice and information-gathering purposes.

Various defense agencies served as contact points for companies interested in VHSIC, especially the Defense Advanced Research Projects Agency, the Institute for Defense Analyses, and the three military services. Such multiple access points served VHSIC's planning well by promoting industry input. Indeed, the breadth of industry consultation probably enhanced industry support for VHSIC by creating at least the perception of political efficacy among companies.

One critical institutional link between government and industry during VHSIC's planning was the consultative forum provided by the Advisory Group on Electron Devices (AGED). Composed of preeminent industrial and academic specialists, AGED was used by VHSIC planners throughout the program's formulation.

In September and November 1978, two AGED Special Technology Area Reviews were organized to consult with specialists from Bell Labs, California

Institute of Technology, Carnegie Mellon, Clemson, Cornell, Fairchild, Hewlett-Packard, Institute for Defense Analyses, Jet Propulsion Labs, Johns Hopkins, Lincoln Labs, Massachusetts Institute of Technology, RCA, Research Triangle Institute, SRI, Stanford, Tektronix, Texas Instruments, TRW, University of California at Berkeley, and Westinghouse. In addition, representatives from thirteen companies were invited to make formal presentations on prospective VHSIC technology: Fairchild, GE, Hughes, IBM, Motorola, National Semiconductor, Raytheon, RCA, Rockwell, Sandia, Texas Instruments, TRW, and Westinghouse.[8]

These technical reviews dramatically illustrate both the openness of VHSIC planning to private-sector advice and the significant contribution that industry made to the structure and orientation of the program.[9] The AGED discussions are striking in that DOD officials sought out industry advice on such fundamental technical issues as:

1. The lithography approach to pursue (optical, X-ray, electron beam);
2. The lithography milestones to establish (1.25 micron versus submicron);
3. The types of circuit technologies to investigate;[10] and
4. The types of circuits to serve as test chips (dynamic random access memories, static random access memories, analog-to-digital converters, read-only memories, electrically programmable read-only memories, microprocessors, logic chips).

Industry input in general and AGED deliberations in particular contributed to the following five major features of the VHSIC program:

1. The enhancement of computer-aided design (CAD) into the program (CAD now accounts for 40-45% of VHSIC's budget);
2. The adoption of 1.25 microns as the program's intermediate milestone after the first three years;
3. The program's reorientation from a concentration on strict *device* technology to an emphasis on *system* needs and requirements in designing VHSIC circuits;
4. The vertical integration of the program, in which contractors are required to address nearly all aspects of VHSIC technology, from initial circuit design to system demonstration; and
5. The encouragement of multifirm VHSIC contract teams.

It is important to note that AGED's practice of conducting technical area reviews had begun only in the early 1970s, when a number of other significant innovations were introduced into the DOD electron-device program. Even so, until these reviews in late 1978, AGED had not held an area review in at least three years. The organization of the VHSIC technical reviews represents, therefore, an important institutional innovation that cannot be assumed to be standard operating procedure in the military world.

INDUSTRY SUPPORT

In 1979, thirty-two electronics firms submitted VHSIC Phase 0 bids, diffusing any fears that the program would not be supported by industry. Interviews with eighteen of these bidders reveal that military-related factors played only a limited role in company motivations to seek VHSIC participation.[11] National security concerns played almost no role in company decisions to support VHSIC. Only one company cited serving the nation's strategic military interest as a major reason for joining the program. Instead, commercial interests, in the broadest of terms, motivated industry participation.

In fact, DOD officials were aware from the beginning that the commercial payoffs from VHSIC would generate industry support for the program. During VHSIC's planning in 1978, DOD officials recognized that "one important side product of what DOD does should be to help U.S. industry."[12] VHSIC organizers were careful to explore commercial market "fallout" from VHSIC technology.[13] In mid-1979, when the first VHSIC contracts went up for bid, the deputy undersecretary of defense for research and advanced technology, Ruth Davis, wrote: "DOD judges that over 75% of the VHSIC program will provide either direct or indirect fallout to the consumer marketplace . . . many of the advantages of a DOD effort will still accrue to industry."[14]

Secretary of Defense Harold Brown met with industry leaders in 1981 to ensure that an adequate response would be given to the bidding for VHSIC Phase I contracts. In arguing for industry support, he stressed national interest and military necessity first and then the commercial and competitive benefit that would derive from VHSIC participation.[15] Hence, within DOD it was recognized that VHSIC could not be sold to industry on national interest alone or even in large part.

There is evidence, however, that a military-industrial complex "syndrome" has accounted for the support that VHSIC has received from one group of firms: the military systems houses—manufacturers of radar, electronic warfare, electro-optical, acoustic, communication and guidance systems for the military. Reflecting their dependence upon the DOD procurement market, these firms sought VHSIC participation to protect their military market positions and gain government contract money.[16]

In contrast, strictly commercial and competitive factors have motivated merchant semiconductor firms' participation. For IC makers and computer and semiconductor equipment manufacturers, a primary motivation for participation was that VHSIC was seen as augmenting existing mainstream technology efforts. Officials from Intersil, Motorola, National Semiconductor, Signetics, Control Data, Honeywell, IBM, Sperry, Perkin-Elmer, Varian Associates, and Bell Labs have stressed the "unbelievable match" between VHSIC's technical objectives and those of in-house technology programs. Under these circumstances, VHSIC participation was sought to supplement and accelerate these company efforts.[17]

It is no accident, of course, that VHSIC technology complemented mainstream commercial technology. Just as DOD planners recognized that VHSIC would be of commercial benefit to company participants, they took care to ensure that VHSIC research would not radically deviate from industrial research. As early as May 1978, VHSIC planners stipulated that "technologies employed [in the program] must be consistent with mainstream industry efforts. . . . Program goals must be consistent with the industry learning process."[18] During the Special Technical Area Reviews held in late 1978, DOD officials acknowledged the rationale for this requirement: "If [VHSIC technology is] not in the mainstream of commercial work we are going to lose it eventually."[19]

As previously mentioned, DOD officials have taken note of VHSIC's commercial payoffs and such payoffs have, in fact, played an important role in the decisions of firms to enter the program. IC makers, computer firms, and equipment suppliers have looked well beyond the military market in deciding to participate in VHSIC.[20] Commercial applications would seem to be a natural result of a military program designed to complement mainstream industrial technology.

In addition to the mainstream character of VHSIC technology and its commercial payoffs, two other factors emerged in the late 1970s to help IC makers and equipment houses be more receptive to VHSIC. First, capital requirements for both industries had been mounting dramatically. Start-up costs for a semiconductor facility rose from under $1 million in the 1950s to $10 million in 1970 to $30-40 million in the late 1970s.[21] Development costs for lithography and other semiconductor manufacturing equipment also skyrocketed.[22] VHSIC was well-timed as companies welcomed new sources of capital financing.[23]

Second, the program was also well-timed to help companies respond to the Japanese competitive threat in semiconductors. For instance, officials from one major merchant-semiconductor producer viewed their participation in the forward-looking VHSIC program as a means to counter the long-range microelectronics efforts pursued in Japan. Citing the Very Large Scale Integration project sponsored by the Ministry of International Trade and Industry between 1976 and 1980, a senior official of another merchant house acknowledged that his company welcomed any U.S. government effort, including VHSIC, that could enhance the long-term competitiveness of the firm. Other commercial IC producers have also cited competitive pressure from Japan as a reason for their VHSIC support.[24]

CONCLUSION

The preceding analysis reveals that VHSIC's status as a military initiative played only a limited role in accounting for two of the program's exceptional features: government-industry planning and industrywide support. The competent formulation of VHSIC depended upon the leadership and initiative of a handful of officials, widespread and intensive consultation between industry and government, and institutional innovation as represented by the organization of the advisory group's technical reviews. Computer manufacturers, semiconductor equipment suppliers, and especially merchant semiconductor firms were primarily motivated to participate in VHSIC for commercial and competitive reasons.

Military factors certainly underlie aspects of VHSIC's accomplishments: national security concerns initially motivated the program's conception and the program received support from traditional military contractors. But VHSIC's positive experience with government-industry planning and industrywide support has not been inordinately dependent upon its attributes as a military program. This does not imply, however, that resources are in place for establishing bona fide industrial policies in nonmilitary, commercial arenas. Still, policymakers might be heartened and possibly learn some valuable lessons from the VHSIC experience. The nonmilitary factors discussed in this chapter—participatory consultation, institutional innovation, technological competence—illustrate important requisites for the making of industrial policies in this country.

5

U.S. Competitiveness in Global Industries: Lessons from the Auto Industry

Malcolm S. Salter
Alan M. Webber
Davis Dyer

THE COMPETITIVE CRISIS

Recently, with moderating inflation and a temporary decline in energy prices, the long-awaited recovery of the U.S. auto industry has occurred, protected by Japan's "voluntary" export restraint program. This good news, however, does not necessarily herald a return to global competitiveness, and 1983's $6 billion industry profits should not be misinterpreted. Japanese competitors continue to make cars more efficiently than American automakers.

For more than fifty years, the auto industry has been at the center of the American economy. Roughly one out of six jobs has been connected to the industry; it has been a prodigious consumer of other industries' output, including steel (more than 20 percent), rubber (60 percent), aluminum (11 percent), ferrous castings (30 percent), glass and machine tools (20 percent). The auto industry has been closely tied to both energy use and its national policies. Increasingly, because of major purchases of services like health care and communications, and a rapid move into computers and microelectronics in the manufacturing process and the finished product, the auto industry has come to represent the hinge on the door of America's economy, as it swings from traditional manufacturing to services and high technology. Clearly, the size, scope, and position of the industry in our economy make its future competitiveness a matter of critical national concern.

Malcolm S. Salter is professor of business administration at Harvard Business School. Alan M. Webber and Davis Dyer are senior research associates, Harvard Business School. This paper draws upon research conducted by the Project on the Auto Industry and the American Economy. The authors wish to thank Mark Fuller for his contribution to the project.

At the beginning of the 1970s, Detroit could deliver a compact car on the West Coast for less than an equivalent Japanese model; by the end of the decade, the American automakers were at a 20-40 percent cost disadvantage, depending on the model. There is still a lively debate over the actual size of the total cost differential; lower Japanese wages and fringes explain only part of it. William J. Abernathy and Kim B. Clark have calculated a U.S.-Japan labor cost differential of about $1,700 per vehicle (using an average 1979 exchange rate of 220 yen/dollar). Harbour and Associates calculated that Japan's lower wages and fringes account for only $550 of the Japanese automakers' total cost advantage of $2,203 (assuming 235 yen/dollar). Harbour's calculations show that superior technology, better management systems, and union management relations account for most of the difference (see table 5-1).[1]

The recession of 1979-82 and high interest rates that drove industry volumes down to the lowest point in twenty years aggravated U.S. automakers' competitive position. Factory sales of passenger cars declined by a third between 1978 and 1982. As a result, each automaker experienced serious financial decay. In 1978, the year prior to the second oil shock, the Big Three (Ford, General Motors, and Chrysler) earned profits of $4.5 billion. Two years later, the Big Three booked $4 billion in losses. Despite substantial investment tax credits, they lost another $700 million during 1981 and 1982. Ford alone lost $3.2 billion from 1979 through 1982 (see table 5-2). While earnings declined, capital spending requirements increased, as the automakers tried to adapt to changing market needs. As a result, the three major U.S. automakers had a cash shortfall of $12.3 billion from 1980 through 1982. At GM, by far the strongest of the Big Three, cash generated from operations was only 25 percent of capitalized spending in 1982.

Predictably, working capital positions deteriorated and the companies borrowed heavily. At year-end 1978, the combined working capital of all four U.S. automakers (the Big Three plus American Motors) was $13 billion; three years later, it was below $2 billion. During 1982 Ford operated with negative working capital. Reliance on debt financing increased substantially. For the Big Three, long-term debt represented nearly 30 percent of the total (debt plus equity) in 1982, up from about 15 percent in 1978, when GM's ratio was under 5 percent and Ford's under 10 percent. In response to these trends, the two major rating services downgraded GM's and Ford's credit ratings, thereby increasing their financing cost disadvantage to Japanese competitors, who were burdened with far less debt, which they could finance at lower rates of interest (see table 5-3).

Table 5-1

The Japanese Cost Advantage for a Subcompact Vehicle

	U.S. Labor Cost per Vehicle	U.S.-Japan Difference
A. Abernathy-Clark Estimate of Labor Cost Differential		
OEM labor		
Hourly	$1,170	$ 673
Salaried	315	198
Purchased components	1,255	721
Purchased materials	171	98
Total labor cost	$2,911	$1,690
B. Harbour and Associates Estimate of Total Cost Differential		
Superior technology		$ 73
Better management systems		
Quality control		329
"Just-in-Time" production techniques		550
Materials handling engineering		41
Other (quality circles, job classification)		478
Total		$1,398
Union-management relations		
Less absenteeism		$ 81
More flexible relief systems and allowances		89
Union representation		12
Total		$ 182
Lower wages and fringes		550
Total cost advantage to Japanese		$2,203

Source: National Academy of Engineering, *The Competitive Status of the U.S. Auto Industry*, 1982, 172; and Harbour and Associates, reported in the *New York Times*, 16 February 1983. Copyright © 1983 by The New York Times Company. Reprinted by permission.

In addition, a relative disadvantage in product quality affected the competitive status of the U.S. auto industry. The Japanese again provide the baseline for comparison. Consumer surveys conducted by J. D. Powers & Associates as recently as August 1983 found that 50 percent of the new U.S.-made cars had problems on delivery, while 56 percent had mechanical problems after delivery. The comparative figures for Japanese cars were 36 percent and 39 percent, respectively. The percentage of respondents in this survey, who rated U.S. cars as giving "excellent" or "very good" value for the money, actually decreased from 1979 to 1983, while the comparable figures for Japanese cars increased (see table 5-4). Another Powers customer satisfaction index, in 1983, reported that nine of the ten highest-ranked

Table 5-2

Summary of Financial Results for the Big Three, 1973-83 (millions of dollars except for ratios)

	1973	1974	1975	1976	1977	1978	1979	1980	1981	1982	1983
General Motors											
Sales	35,798	31,550	35,725	47,181	54,961	63,221	66,311	54,729	62,791	60,026	74,582
Profits	2,398	950	1,253	2,903	3,338	3,508	2,893	(763)	333	963	3,730
Return on sales	6.7%	3.0%	3.5%	6.2%	6.1%	5.5%	4.4%	(1.4)%	(0.5)%	1.6%	5.0%
Ford											
Sales	23,015	23,621	24,009	28,840	37,842	42,784	43,514	37,086	38,247	37,067	44,450
Profits	907	327	323	983	1,673	1,589	1,169	(1,543)	(1,060)	(658)	1,870
Return on sales	3.9%	1.4%	1.3%	3.4%	4.8%	3.7%	2.7%	(4.2)%	(2.8)%	(1.8)%	4.2%
Chrysler											
Sales	11,667	10,860	11,598	15,538	16,708	13,618	12,002	9,225	10,822	10,045	na
Profits	255	(52)	(260)	423	163	(205)	(1,097)	(1,710)	(476)	170[a]	na
Return on sales	2.2%	(9.5)%	(2.2)%	2.7%	1.0%	(1.5)%	(10.9)%	(18.5)%	(4.3)%	1.7%	na

Source: Company annual reports

[a]Includes gain of $239 million on sale of Chrysler Defense. Results for 1983, wher available, are from corporate news releases.

Table 5-3

Comparative Financial Performance of Industry Leaders by Region[a] (%)

	1978	1979	1980	1981	1982
Return on Sales					
United States	4.1	2.4	(−3.9)	(−1.1)	0.4
Europe	1.2	1.2	0.6	0.0	–
Japan	4.1	3.3	3.8	3.4	3.2
Return on Capital					
United States	15.7	8.9	(−12.0)	(−3.5)	1.4
Europe	3.9	3.7	2.1	(−0.1)	–
Japan	14.4	10.9	12.9	11.0	9.4
Long-Term Debt as % of Capital					
United States	10.6	9.4	19.2	25.0	26.3
Europe	45.5	36.8	38.7	44.1	–
Japan	7.0	5.7	6.3	5.0	7.4

Source: Company annual reports

[a]United States = General Motors, Ford, and Chrysler; Europe = VW, Renault, and Fiat; and Japan = Toyota and Nissan.

Table 5-4

J.D. Power's Automotive Consumer Profile and Customer Satisfaction Index, 1983

	Domestic		Japanese		European	
	June 1979	Aug. 1983	June 1979	Aug. 1983	June 1979	Aug. 1983
Fuel economy[a]	11%	16%	51%	60%	40%	39%
Dependability/ minimal repairs[a]	28	24	18	30	20	25
Quality of workmanship[a]	20	21	25	41	34	42
Value for the money[a]	29	25	32	38	30	31
Had problems on delivery of car	—	50	—	36	—	47
Had mechanical problems after delivery	—	56	—	39	—	56
Definitely buy same make again	—	23	—	28	—	31
Median price paid for new car (average 1983 = $9,979)	—	$10,050	—	$8,610	—	$14,780

Source: J.D. Power & Associates

[a]Percentage of respondents rating manufacturers excellent/very good

producers were foreign. Out of the first fifteen producers recognized by U.S. car buyers for quality, only two were American (see table 5-5).

Complicating problems of perceived product quality was the declining relevance of U.S. automakers' traditional competence—the manufacture of large cars. In 1980, the year after the second oil crisis, 87.2 percent of U.S.-produced cars still had an engine displacement of over 2,000cc (77.8 percent by 1982). In contrast, both Japan and Germany concentrated most of their production in the 1,000cc to 2,000cc range (see table 5-6). With oil prices declining throughout 1983 and oil experts forecasting plentiful oil supplies

Table 5-5
Customer Satisfaction Index

1983			1982	
Rank	*Score*		*Rank*	*Score*
1.	159	Mercedes-Benz	1.	155
2.	137	Toyota	2.	149
3.	135	Subaru	5.	117
4.	124	Honda	3.	148
5.	118	Mazda	8.	107
6.	115	Volvo	6.	115
7.	114	Lincoln-Mercury	14.	92
8.	110	BMW	4.	126
9.	108	Saab		
10.	108	Porsche-Audi	11.	97
11.	107	Ford	18.	89
12.	103	Mitsubishi (sold by Chrysler)	12.	95
13.	101	Jaguar[a]		
14.	101	Nissan	9.	106
15.	98	Volkswagen	10.	102
16.	93	Dodge[a]		
17.	92	Oldsmobile	13.	92
18.	90	Chrysler-Plymouth	16.	91
19.	83	Chevrolet	17.	89
20.	81	Isuzu	7.	112
21.	81	Cadillac	15.	92
22.	80	Buick	19.	87
23.	77	Pontiac	21.	72
24.	76	American Motors	20.	81
25.	60	Renault	22.	59

Source: J.D. Power & Associates
[a]Did not make list in 1982

Table 5-6
Breakdown of Passenger Car Production by Engine Displacement, 1980
(% of national production)

	Below 1,000cc	1,000cc-2,000cc	Over 2,000cc
United States[a]	—	12.8%	87.2%
Japan	2.8%	91.5	5.7
Germany	—	81.6	18.4
France	15.9	70.8	13.3
United Kingdom	—	86.2	13.8
Italy	29.5	67.7	2.8

Source: *The Japanese Auto Industry Yearbook*, 1982; *World Motor Vehicle Data, 1983*, Motor Vehicle Manufacturers Association of the United States, Inc.; *Ward's Yearbook, 1983*.

[a]By the 1982 model year, U.S. automakers had reduced their production of cars with engine displacement over 2,000cc from 87.2% to 77.8% of national production. In contrast, Japanese automakers increased their production of cars with engine displacement over 2,000cc from 5.7% to 7.7%.

through the late 1980s, the U.S. consumer has once again begun purchasing larger cars, indicating that perhaps U.S. automakers' traditional competencies would still be relevant. However, this was only a partial indication. From 1980 to 1982, Japanese exports of "large" cars with engines over 2,000cc increased by 100,000 units, from just over 275,000 units to just over 375,000 units. The Japanese were clearly learning to play the Americans' own game.

Not surprisingly, U.S. automakers have been losing in the battle for the market share. Over the past decade, their domestic market share has fallen fifteen percentage points, reaching a low of 71 percent by early 1983, with most of the U.S. market share taken away from Ford and Chrysler (see table 5-7). On a worldwide basis, U.S. share fell from 27 percent in 1975 to 19 percent in 1982 (see table 5-8). Those eight share points were snatched up by Japanese and, to a lesser extent, German automakers. While the Japanese were adding manufacturing capacity, a peak of 270,000 U.S. autoworkers were laid off by 1982 (see tables 5-9 and 5-10). Although over half of these employees were recalled during the 1983 recovery, industry experts like Gerald Greenwald, vice chairman of Chrysler, claim that if Japan's restraints on exports to the United States were ended, that country's share of the U.S. market would jump to 40 percent, causing even more serious automotive unemployment.

Statistics revealing relative cost, product quality, and financial power are, of course, merely indicators of competitiveness or uncompetitiveness. Product cost and quality also are a function of corporate strategy and, in particular,

Table 5-7

Trends in Market Share—U.S. Passenger Car Market

	1970	1975	1980	1982	1983
General Motors	39.5%	43.8%	45.9%	44.2%	44.3%
Ford	26.5	23.2	15.8	16.9	17.2
Chrysler	16.2	11.7	7.4	8.6	9.2
AMC	3.1	3.8	1.7	1.0	0.5
Toyota	2.5	3.7	6.5	6.6	5.9
Nissan	1.8	3.5	5.8	5.9	5.7
Honda	0.1	1.2	4.2	4.6	4.4
VW	7.0	3.1	3.0	2.6	2.3
Other imports	3.3	5.7	9.1	11.9	10.5
Total imports	14.7	17.6	28.6	29.3	28.8

Source: Research Bernstein, corporate records, *Ward's Automotive Yearbook* (various years).

Note: Noncaptive imports not included in domestic market share. If included, Chrysler's and AMC's share in 1983 would be 10.3% and 2.5%, respectively.

Table 5-8

Trends in Market Share—Worldwide Motor Vehicle Production

	1960	1965	1970	1975	1980	1982
United States	48.3%	45.4%	27.9%[a]	27.0%	20.6%	19.0%
Japan	3.0	7.7	17.8	20.9	28.4	29.2
Germany	12.6	12.1	13.0	9.6	9.5	11.1
France	8.4	6.7	9.3	8.6	8.7	8.6
United Kingdom	11.1	8.9	7.1	5.0	3.4	3.2
Italy	3.9	4.8	6.3	4.4	4.2	4.0
Canada	2.4	3.5	3.9	4.3	3.6	3.4
Other	10.3	10.9	14.7	20.2	21.6	21.5

Source: Motor Vehicle Manufacturers Association of the United States, Inc.

[a]Depressed by GM strike

the many tacit and formal arrangements between management and labor that affect efficiency and workmanship. Arrangements between management and the government, whether voluntary or hostile, are also involved. When these relationships between management, labor, and government are in disarray, sooner or later the leading indicators of competitiveness will be affected.

We contend that not only are the relationships among the three major players in disarray, but they are also obsolete and have been for roughly twenty years. These outmoded relationships inhibit the U.S. automakers' ability to respond to the changes that times demand. Inadequate relationships between management, labor, and government are a principal source of the auto industry's competitive dilemma, and any long-term solution for the industry must take account of the three parties' need to adapt to a new environment.

TRADITIONAL COMPETITIVE ASSUMPTIONS AND BEHAVIOR

THE INDUSTRY DEVELOPS

Competition in the U.S. auto industry began at the end of the nineteenth century among individual entrepreneurs whose products made their names familiar: Henry Ford, Louis Chevrolet, Walter Chrysler, the Dodge Brothers,

Table 5-9
U.S. Auto Industry Employment[a]

	1978	1979	1980	1981	1982	% Change 1978-82
General Motors	611,000	618,000	517,000	522,000	441,000	−27.8%
Ford	256,614	239,475	179,917	170,806	155,900	−39.2
Chrysler	131,758	109,306	76,711	68,696	58,600	−55.5
American Motors	25,000	25,000	21,000	21,000	20,000	−20.0
Volkswagen	6,400	9,100	10,000	9,900	9,000	+40.6
Total	1,030,772	1,000,881	804,628	792,402	684,500	−33.6%

Source: Company annual reports and Transportation Systems Center, U.S. Department of Transportation.
[a]Totals include white collar and blue collar employees.

Table 5-10
U.S. Autoworker Layoffs from 1981 to 1983

	1981	1982	% Change vs. 1981	1983	% Change vs. 1981
Motor vehicle production	7,933,896	6,987,222	−11.9	9,204,456	+16.0%
Total layoffs	211,527	270,337	+27.8	108,200	−48.8
Indefinite	174,462	237,606	+36.2	107,700	−38.3
Temporary	37,065	32,731	−11.7	500	−98.7

Source: Data for 1981 and 1982 were compiled by Transportation Systems Center, U.S. Department of Transportation. Data for 1983 were compiled by *Ward's Automotive Reports*, as of the week of 30 December 1983.

Ransom Olds, David Buick, and others. Nonetheless, the basic structure of the auto industry as we know it today was almost in place by the eve of the Depression. As early as 1908, three of the automakers—Ford, GM, and the ancestor of Studebaker—controlled about 50 percent of the market. This economic concentration resulted from the ability to build cars on a massive scale, using methods pioneered at Ford, and the ability to cover the market nationwide with products that appealed to segments of the public, a strategy formulated at General Motors.

Relatively few changes occurred in production methods and product characteristics after the 1920s. The automakers' relationships with suppliers and dealers were refined in the same period, along with enduring behavioral patterns of pricing and profitability. The industry required heavy inputs of capital and labor. Auto company executives were responsible for enormous investments and had to manage large-scale production systems involving thousands of people. High-volume manufacture of a product as complex as the automobile, with thousands of interdependent parts and components, required management to pay careful attention to plant location, layout, and job design. Indeed, logistics, the coordinated scheduling and delivery of parts and components to the assembly line, became one of the fundamental managerial responsibilities in the business.

The primary ways in which the Big Three assured control over logistics included standardizing the layout of plants and streamlining production networks. They also gained control over logistics through vertical integration— the management of subsidiaries specializing in raw materials, and parts and components. This process began at an early date. By the end of World War I, for example, all of the large automakers built their own engines and axles.

The vehicles rolling off the assembly lines and out of the factories improved steadily from year to year, although the basic technological characteristics of the automobile changed little over time. However, Alfred Sloan's stunningly successful new strategy at GM fundamentally changed the nature of the automobile industry. Since the 1930s GM has controlled more than 40 percent of the American market; Ford and Chrysler never achieved more than 28 percent. Over time, U.S. auto companies grew more alike as they tried to emulate GM's market segmentation strategy and administrative practices, although GM focused on the higher end of each price segment of the market, Ford focused on the lower end, and Chrysler relied on low-priced, technologically innovative cars assembled largely from outsourced components.

Early in the development of the U.S. auto industry a predictable pattern of pricing began to emerge. General Motors set prices and the other companies followed. The result of GM's combined product and pricing policies was about a 20 percent annual return on investment over the years. The other automakers earned substantially lower returns and had considerably less flexibility in pricing. On the occasions when Ford or Chrysler announced prices for a given model and then were forced to lower them, it was typically a result of being undercut by General Motors.

Like so much else in the industry's history, dominant firm strategies, structures, and administrative practices emerged at an early date. As rival automakers were forced to match Ford's production system to remain competitive in the early 1920s, they felt obliged for similar reasons to follow many of GM's marketing, financial, and managerial leads after Sloan laid the foundations of his "modern" corporation in the early 1920s.

ORGANIZED LABOR RESPONDS

If the automakers had settled on enduring business methods by about 1930, it took several more decades to reach a working agreement with organized labor. Two preconditions had to be satisfied: labor had to win its rights in the eyes of management, and a balance of power between the two had to be struck. By the early 1950s both matters were resolved.

The American system of industrial relations was nurtured in the aftermath of the Great Depression. Before that, most efforts to organize unions in most manufacturing industries had been defeated by a combination of circumstances: management paternalism or intimidation, factional divisions in the American labor movement, and worker fear or indifference. The passage of the National Labor Relations Act in 1935, however, signaled that the government would support strong, industry-based unions.

The distinctive institutional characteristics of organized labor in the United States emerged in the 1930s in response to the fierce opposition of anti-union employers and the inability of welfare capitalism to preserve jobs and wages in the face of massive unemployment. Like the practices of the manufacturers, many of the features of organized labor remain unchanged today: industry-based unions, ideological conservatism, centralized "pattern bargaining" on economic issues but local bargaining on employment practices and working conditions, and generally adversarial relations between management and labor.

From the UAW's point of view, the ongoing struggles for legitimacy and internal control were only part of its early agenda. The UAW also had to define its own long-term objectives, and its eventual acceptance of managerial capitalism is another distinctive feature of American labor.

Walter Reuther presided over the UAW from 1947 to 1970. His success stemmed from his advocacy of programs that benefited the economic interests of the union membership and his ability to deliver at the bargaining table. His general philosophy was "full production, full employment, and full distribution." He repeatedly urged fair distribution of America's tremendous wealth among the people who helped create it. Yet although he insisted on workers' rights, Reuther embraced the American system of managerial capitalism wholeheartedly. For example, he acknowledged management's right to make decisions concerning new technologies and plant location and layout. However, he represented autoworkers' interests by pushing for a shorter working week to create more employment opportunities. Reuther sought standardized wages to remove wage cost as a source of competitive advantage. He also pursued protections for unemployed workers, health and safety benefits, and security at retirement through company-funded pensions.

Most of these points were embodied in a series of national contracts Reuther negotiated with the Big Three in the decade after World War II. Rising real wages for autoworkers were guaranteed, ensuring that they would rank among the highest-paid American workers. The national contracts further added premiums for night shifts and overtime, longer vacations, and other economic benefits.

After the early postwar years, local bargaining followed a relatively consistent pattern, confined within explicit economic bounds and supervised by the national union. Over time, UAW locals made a slow series of advances that severely circumscribed plant and shop-level managerial authority. In particular, the union gained control over training and apprenticeship, work scheduling, hiring, transfer and promotion policy, work assignments and jurisdiction, job descriptions and wage classifications and, occasionally, the type and amount of work that could be subcontracted.

In 1955 the UAW succeeded in establishing another distinctive practice, "pattern bargaining," which had a serious impact on the automakers. In bargaining years—after 1955 national contracts expired on the same day every three years—the UAW selected one of the Big Three as its primary target. Once agreement was reached with that company, the union negotiated similar terms with the other companies, including, eventually, the independent automakers and suppliers. Pattern bargaining had two effects. First, it greatly enhanced the negotiating power of the UAW, since the solidarity of every local union in the industry stood behind the national bargaining teams and greatly increased the potential consequences of a strike. Second, pattern bargaining widened economic disparity between the Big Three and the independent manufacturers, since the larger, more efficient companies could more easily absorb increased labor costs across greater sales volume.

In sum, the relationship between labor and management that developed in the United States from the 1930s through the 1950s never fully escaped its adversarial origins. The economic accommodation that was finally reached drove up costs at the same time that it solidified the wall between management and labor. In its effort to retain sole authority and responsibility for the company, management paid an ever-increasing price to labor. And labor, for its part, accepted its increasing wages and benefits without recognizing or assuming any responsibility for the competitive performance of the company.

THE GOVERNMENT INTERVENES

The federal government developed an ambivalent attitude toward the auto industry at an early date. On the one hand, the government had occasionally shown hostility toward big business since the nineteenth century. The antitrust laws were aimed at large companies and concentrated industries, and the Department of Justice and the Federal Trade Commission have kept a watchful eye on the automakers since the 1930s. On the other hand, the government quickly recognized the auto industry's economic importance. As an employer of hundreds of thousands, a large-scale consumer of steel, glass, rubber, and other basic products, and an important reservoir of engineering, research, and managerial talent, the auto industry occupied the center of America's industrial economy and became its major engine of growth. Not unlike other young industries during the early 1900s, it took root behind high tariff barriers (45 percent ad valorem until 1922, 25 percent until 1934, and 10 percent thereafter).

While federal antitrust actions and policies defined relations between automakers and dealers and constrained the automakers' ability to acquire suppliers and related businesses, the government avoided more drastic measures to increase competition. Despite frequent public cries to "break-up General Motors" in the 1950s and 1960s, the government did not force GM to spin off one or more of the automotive divisions. Moreover, the govern-

ment stood idly by while most of the independent automakers, including
Kaiser-Frazier and Studebaker-Packard, left the industry between 1953 and
1962. Indeed, by the latter date, American Motors remained the only producer of consumer vehicles other than the Big Three.

Federal management of the economy, which intensified during World War
II, affected the auto industry in several ways. The government's general
macroeconomic tools—taxes, interest rates, trade policies—and its laws regulating the nation's economic performance were not intended to favor the
auto industry more than any other. However, federal tax, energy, and road-
building policies did have the effect of encouraging the auto companies'
growth from the 1930s through the 1960s. The deductibility of interest
expense allowed by the federal tax code and the federally financed highway
program gave the public a strong incentive to purchase suburban homes and
second cars rather than city apartments serviced by public transportation.
The government intervened more directly in the auto industry during World
War II by regulating prices and wages. These powers, assumed first in the
1940s, have been exercised periodically since then—during the Korean War
and in the early and mid-1970s—with a marked effect on the auto companies'
pricing behavior. In addition, the government convinced the auto industry to
hold down prices on other occasions. In each instance of price restraint,
however, the automakers' profits remained healthy.

Federal intervention included laws and policies supporting unionization.
The Wagner Act, in addition to forbidding "unfair labor practices," also
established the National Labor Relations Board (NLRB) as an agency with
fact-finding and quasi-judicial powers. The NLRB certified union elections
and investigated unfair labor practices. The government subsequently provided arbitration and mediation services. In later years, federal employment
policies intruded on managerial discretion in various other ways: establishing
the minimum wage, limiting hours of work, defining compensation for overtime, defending rights of equal opportunity and affirmative action with special
provision for handicapped workers, regulating workplace safety, and requiring special arrangements for the funding and administration of pensions.

Government intervention in the auto industry moved to a new level after
the mid-1960s. To its existing functions as antitrust enforcer, industrial
relations monitor and mediator, and macroeconomic policymaker, the federal
government added a qualitatively different role: product regulator.

In 1966 Congress passed the National Highway and Motor Vehicle Safety
Act; in 1970 came the Clean Air Act; in 1975 the Energy Policy and

Conservation Act. The first two statutes created new federal agencies—the National Highway Traffic Safety Administration and the Environmental Protection Agency—with wide powers to define and enforce standards. Out of these new federal policies and agencies came hundreds of specific regulations with different timetables for auto company compliance. Federal policymakers, many without any experience in automotive engineering, concerned themselves with the details and specifics of product policy, from seatbelts to bumpers, from catalytic converters to exhaust systems, from engine specifications to materials characteristics. According to the U.S. Department of Transportation, 237 regulatory changes pertaining to automobiles and light trucks were created from 1960 to 1975.

The economic effects of the new regulations were staggering. By the mid-1970s, even conservative estimates of the costs of safety, emissions, and fuel-efficiency regulation reached hundreds of dollars added to new car sticker prices and billions paid out by the companies in capital investment. And these were only the direct costs. Major indirect costs included addition or retraining of engineering and managerial personnel, the creation of public affairs departments, expansion of Washington offices, and the acquisition of lobbying skills and techniques.

In sum, government's role in the auto industry had come a long way from the inconstant and indirect supports of the early years of this century. By the 1970s, government had become a powerful and constant participant in the industrial relationships affecting the automakers' competitiveness. It had learned how to use its investigative powers and hearings processes to catch and embarrass the automakers publicly. It had spawned new agencies and created new functions at an unprecedented pace, with little thought of coordination or cost. Most important, it had decided to make matters of public policy—safety, the environment, social justice, energy—high priorities without consideration of the costs or the competitive implications. As a result, government-mandated costs partly offset an advantage American producers might have enjoyed because of the declining value of the dollar during the 1970s. The gap between the price of imports and domestic cars did not narrow as rapidly as it otherwise would have, since American car prices rose annually, in part because of the costs imposed by regulations. While imports also had to introduce substantial changes to comply with new U.S. regulations, American-made automobiles required more design changes to comply with domestic regulations than did imported products, according to a 1977 study of imported automobiles by Harbridge House.

THE ADVENT OF GLOBAL COMPETITION

OVERVIEW

The attitudes and practices within the American auto industrial relationship seemed to matter little before the 1970s. Certainly, in the first twenty-five years after World War II, all parties—management, government, and labor—benefited from a relationship that was mutually supportive if increasingly irritable. Most important, because the competitive environment was largely limited to American companies, labor, and government, the quality of the relationship was essentially irrelevant. The automakers earned annual returns far in excess of typical manufacturing companies. The members of the UAW enjoyed rising real incomes annually and substantially increased benefits every three years. And successive governments, along with the public treasury, were beneficiaries of a prosperous industry that occupied the center of an expanding national economy.

During the post-World War II boom in the United States, domestic growth consumed most of the automakers' attention and corporate resources. Chrysler first expanded into Europe and South America and then retreated. While making investments around the world, GM's attention remained riveted on its large and growing share of the world's most important auto market. Ford, far more the global competitor than GM, tried hard to keep up with GM at home.

A low-cost, national energy policy that served to protect them from foreign producers whose cars were designed for markets where energy costs were high, reinforced the U.S. automakers' domestic focus during the postwar years. However, as the recovery of foreign auto industries accelerated during the 1960s, and as U.S. energy prices escalated during the 1970s, U.S. producers found themselves competing for the first time on their own turf with major European and Japanese automakers, whose products were now desired by the American consumer.

By the mid-1970s, the globalization of auto competition was an established fact. For decades the auto industry had been a "multinational" industry with national competitors, some of them subsidiaries of foreign owners, operating primarily in national markets. However, many economic and noneconomic forces, including increased intermarket homogenization, declining trade barriers and transportation costs, and increased opportunities to take advantage of lower wage costs and high market growth rates in different parts of the world, were transforming the auto industry into a global industry with international competitors operating in a world market. As marketing, production, product design, technology, supply, and finance became subject to worldwide economies of sales, competition in national markets increased, eroding the dominance of national producers. While some specific consumer preferences and government policies constituted continuing barriers to globalization, by the mid-1970s the manufacturing and assembly operations of major auto-makers were spread around the world (see table 5-11), and growth in both the share of total passenger car production exported and the absolute number of motor vehicles involved in foreign trade became an unmistakable trend (see figure 5-1 and table 5-12). A similar pattern emerged for such large components as drivetrains, power steering mechanisms, and engine blocks. As imports' share of the U.S. market surged into the country during the 1970s, the U.S. market began to look like other national markets despite its lower gas prices. (In 1977 U.S. retail gasoline prices were still about one-half those in Germany, France, Italy, and Japan.)

Although the two oil shocks of the 1970s accelerated the globalization of industry competition, U.S. automakers adhered to their traditional competitive strategies. Ford and Chrysler bet that a slightly down-sized fleet would dissuade U.S. consumers from buying the technologically differentiated, foreign-made cars that had been gaining market share during the 1970s. General Motors believed that its traditionally designed and manufactured Chevette could compete head on with the imports. Although it won many awards when introduced, the car ended up being heavily discounted in 1974 while some Japanese models were still selling at the premium established during the first oil shock. The industry's decision to make only incremental changes in design and manufacturing practices rather than a more sweeping overhaul of product strategy contributed directly to U.S. automakers' competitive decline. The continued emphasis on production volume rather than product quality also contributed to the decline. As domestic production of passenger cars increased by over 20 percent during the 1975-79 cyclical upswing in the economy, consumer perceptions of product dependability and "value for money" of U.S.-produced cars declined. Finally, attempts by General Motors to set up new plants in nonunionized areas of the country reinforced adversarial collective bargaining and relations with the UAW. Although GM managed to hold on to its market share, Ford and Chrysler lost share to imports. All three U.S. automakers ended up with positions of deteriorating relative cost and quality.

Labor followed management in missing the implications of a rapidly globalizing market. The UAW failed to perceive during the 1970s that their

Table 5-11
Major Manufacturing/Assembly Operations 1978–79[a]

	Japan	Korea	Australia	Indonesia	Iran	U.S.	Canada	Mexico	Brazil	Argentina	Nigeria	South Africa
General Motors	X	O	X		O	X	X	X	X			X
Ford	X		X			X	X	X	X	X		X
Chrysler	X					X	X	X				
American Motors						X	X					
British Leyland											O	
Renault			X		O	O		X		X		
Peugeot Citroen					O						O	
Volkswagen			X			X		X	X			X
Daimler Benz									X			
Fiat									X			
Alfa Romeo												
Volvo												
Saab									X			
Toyota	X	X	X									
Nissan	X	X	X					X				X
Honda	X											
Toyo Kogyo	X											
Mitsubishi	X		X									
Hino	X											

Key: X = existing major operation, O = potential major operation.
Source: Corporate reports
[a]Volume in excess of 10,000–20,000 vehicles/year

Table 5-11
(continued)

	U.K.	France	Belgium	Sweden	Germany	Spain	Portugal	Italy	Turkey	Yugoslavia	Romania	Poland
General Motors	X		X		X	O						
Ford	X		X		X	X						
Chrysler												
American Motors												
British Leyland	X		X									
Renault		X	X			X	O				X	
Peugeot Citroen	X	X	X			X					O	
Volkswagen					X					O		
Daimler Benz					X				O			
Fiat						X		X	X	X		X
Alfa Romeo								X				
Volvo			X	X								
Saab				X								
Toyota												
Nissan												
Honda												
Toyo Kogyo												
Mitsubishi												
Hino												

Key: X = existing major operation, O = potential major operation.
Source: Corporate reports
[a]Volume in excess of 10,000-20,000 vehicles/year

Figure 5-1

Share of Total Passenger Car Production Exported

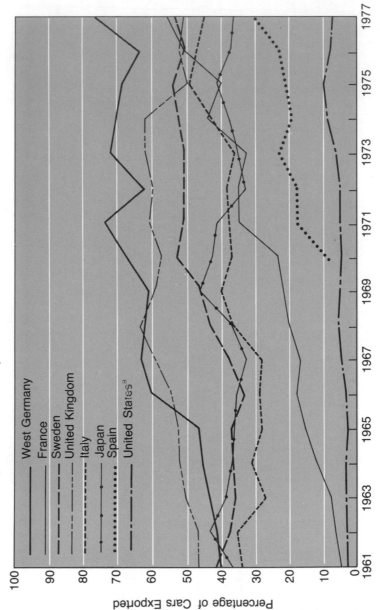

Source: Motor Vehicle Manufacturers Association of the United States, Inc.
[a]Includes trade with Canada

Table 5-12
Exports of Motor Vehicles for Selected Countries (in thousands)

	1950	1955	1960	1965	1969	1970	1971	1972	1973	1974	1975	1976	1977
United Kingdom	542	529	615	794	863	953	916	767	762	726	696	684	665
France	122	173	581	613	1,175	1,525	1,632	1,769	1,931	1,949	1,938	2,086	2,268
Germany	84	404	983	1,527	2,056	2,104	2,293	2,118	2,348	1,881	1,654	2,043	2,128
Italy	22	77	204	327	630	671	681	700	705	734	711	745	714
Sweden	3	q11	62	98	161	210	136	219	209	194	197	178	165
Spain	na	na	na	na	na	na	78	104	158	134	145	166	301
United States													
To Canada		36	32	53	353	300	414	467	564	677	681	694	708
Other		351	291	115	85	79	73	64	97	139	183	187	191
Total	252	387	323	168	438	379	487	531	661	816	864	881	899
Canada													
To United States	—	—	—	54	1,066	861	922	1,051	1,092	1,008	919	1,084	1,190
Other	34	18	21	49	58	68	65	51	31	55	87	104	127
Total	34	18	21	103	1,124	929	987	1,102	1,123	1,063	1,006	1,188	1,317
Japan	6	1	39	194	858	1,087	1,779	1,966	32,068	2,618	2,678	3,710	4,353

Source: Motor Vehicle Manufacturers Association of the United States, Inc.

monopoly on automotive labor in the U.S. market had ended. The substitution of foreign imports for American cars meant the substitution of foreign labor for American labor. But the UAW's demands for increased wages and benefits in 1979 and their opposition to revising work rules contributed to the decline of the U.S. auto industry's competitiveness. After two years of corporate losses, the UAW voluntarily agreed to reopen the contracts of Ford and GM and negotiated some economic concessions in 1982. With wage increases as high as 15 percent scheduled over the life of the contracts, however, the new agreements did little to reduce the cost advantage of Japanese automakers (see figure 5-2). Together, labor and management were able to improve the

Figure 5-2

Estimated Hourly Compensation of Production Workers in the Motor Vehicle and Equipment Industries (in U.S. $)

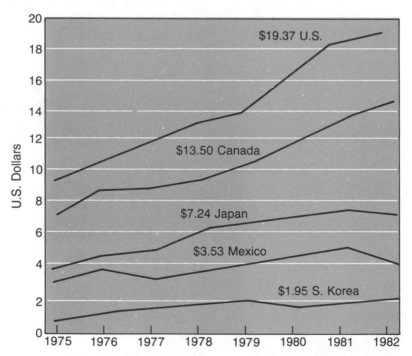

Source: U.S. Department of Transportation, *The U.S. Auto Industry*, 1980; U.S. Department of Labor, Bureau of Statistics, Office of Productivity and Technology, December 1982, unpublished.

Note: Changes in the dollar value of compensation is due to changes in the amounts of compensation and to changes in the value of the dollar. Hourly figures do not include all indirect labor costs. The dollar value of compensation has been estimated by using the average 1982 exchange rate.

relative efficiency of the U.S. manufacturing process, but the Japanese cost advantage is still substantial (see table 5-13). Although it was widely known that the rate of productivity increase of U.S. autoworkers was declining in the late 1970s (see figure 5-3), it came as a shock to many that Toyota could manufacture passenger cars with half as many labor hours per motor vehicle produced than GM.[2]

Government, too, failed to understand the full implications of globalization and increasing competition among countries for jobs. In countries where the auto industry was key to national economic development or stability, governments employed industry-specific policies such as accelerated depreciation, generous tax-free reserves, government-approved collaboration among automakers, and publicly funded research on auto technology to improve their competitive advantage. In the United States, however, the opposite was happening. Auto safety, fuel economy, and clean-air regulations paid no heed to economic consequences. Continued antitrust surveillance and legislation that prevented U.S. automakers from rationalizing their production systems on a worldwide basis constrained management rather than supported efforts to replace increasingly uncompetitive car lines and aging capital stock.

Overall, in the 1970s the U.S. auto industry, labor, and government showed a systemwide inability to adapt to the new competitive environment. The quality of the interaction between the three institutions once mattered little. After the industry globalized, however; these interrelationships became the key source of the auto industry's declining competitiveness. Traditional relationships locked management, labor, and government into a pattern of

Table 5-13
Comparison of U.S. and Japanese Manufacturing Systems, 1981

	United States	*Japan*
Parts stamped per hour	325	550
Manpower per press line	7–13	1
Time needed to change dies	4–6 hours	5 minutes
Average production run	10 days	2 days
Time needed per small car	59.9 hours	30.8 hours
Average daily absentee rate	11.8%	3.5%
Average annual employee turnover	1 per 7 workers	1 per 30 workers
Inventory/gross sales	16.6% (GM)	1.5% (Toyota)
Number of suppliers	Over 3,000 (GM)	300 (Toyota)

Source: Yoshi Tsurumi, "Japan's Challenge to the U.S.: Industrial Policies and Corporate Strategies," *Columbia Journal of World Business* (Summer 1982). Data drawn from reports of Harbour and Associates, Detroit, 1982, and computations by the authors.

Figure 5-3

Indexes of U.S. Productivity Output per Hour (1967 = 100)

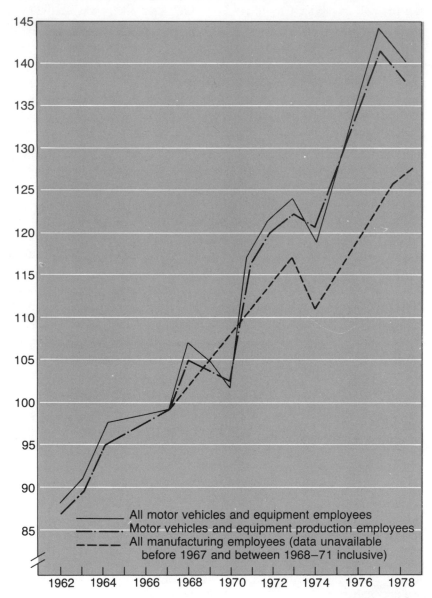

All motor vehicles and equipment employees
Motor vehicles and equipment production employees
All manufacturing employees (data unavailable
    before 1967 and between 1968–71 inclusive)

Source: U.S. Department of Labor

increasing costs, declining productivity, and ongoing adversarial processes, while foreign rivals—notably the Japanese—used the flexibility, efficiency, and pragmatism within their relationships to challenge the United States in the global competition.

Today a globalized market and deteriorated competitive position now require a fundamental reorientation of the strategic and operating assumptions that underlie the auto industry. The clear message is that the new competitive reality demands new strategies and administrative practices from automakers, workers, and the government to survive the high-cost, high-risk auto competition of the uncertain 1980s and 1990s.

THE AUTOMAKERS' STRATEGIES

Despite their many initiatives, no U.S. automaker has yet succeeded in developing an internally consistent, and therefore sustainable, strategy. Their basic dilemma is that the advantages secured in one area of business policy tend to be canceled or threatened by risks run in another. The cases of GM and Ford provide contrasting examples of this problem. Chrysler faces an even more difficult problem.

The differences between the responses of General Motors and Ford to international competition are significant. GM, a leader in introducing Quality of Work Life (QWL) programs into the auto industry, is now aggressively developing coalitions with Japanese and Korean automakers to supply completed vehicles and major components for a quarter of its product line, thereby risking inflamed relations with labor. Ford, on the other hand, appears to have made improved labor relations a top priority and has largely restricted itself from gaining the cost advantages associated with large-scale outsourcing from nonunion suppliers at home and even lower cost suppliers and subsidiaries in Japan and Mexico. In these respects, their competitive strategies are almost mirror images of each other.

Even if General Motors intends to become largely a designer and distributor of foreign-made, small cars in the United States, it needs the support of labor if it is to successfully recast its manufacturing methods, improve in-plant attention to quality, and contain the escalating manufacturing costs in plants producing its domestic cars. In light of the narrowly approved wage concessions in the 1982 GM-UAW contract, such support is by no means assured. Ford, which ran large cash-flow deficits in its North American automobile operations and more than doubled its debt from 1979 to 1982, needs to improve its relative competitive position (share, costs, and margins) if it is to keep its new relationship with labor from dissolving under the pressures of international outsourcing forced upon it by GM. Despite the current upswing in industry volume, this, too, is by no means assured.

Chrysler faces a different but related dilemma. The loan guarantees voted by Congress were intended to save jobs by saving the company, but employment has fallen at Chrysler by over 40 percent since 1979. In addition, these guarantees were contingent on two rounds of wage concessions from the UAW. Chrysler found itself in a situation in which it had to take money away from its employees, and at the same time eliminate more jobs and ask that remaining employees work harder and pay more attention to quality. Predictably, Chrysler workers have been intransigent in their demands for a return to wage parity with GM and Ford, threatening whatever cost advantage Chrysler may have compared with its larger competitors. As this labor cost advantage declines under the terms of the 1983 labor agreement and Chrysler's margins narrow, its financial capacity to invest in a new generation of automobiles will be severely constrained. Despite its startling comeback, Chrysler's ability to survive as a predominantly U.S.-based producer with a stable employment base remains highly questionable. Indeed, its return to modest profitability in 1983 masks enduring problems. The company has had to shrink down, focus on front-wheel drive, fuel-efficient cars and to rely upon foreign suppliers wherever possible to help it remain afloat. All this is at the present cost and future risk of labor's interests.

None of the Big Three can afford to live with its current cost structure. Each is restructuring the way it does business in the United States, retiring excess capacity and inefficient operations, automating its remaining facilities, and lowering its fixed costs by reducing the number of personnel and the level of vertical integration. The volume necessary for profitable operation has been cut: since 1979 the number of new car sales required for the industry as a whole to break even has declined from over twelve million to well under nine million. Although still committed to producing a wide line of autos in the United States, the Big Three are all relying on foreign auto manufacturers to provide components for new, smaller models. GM's joint venture with Toyota and, most likely, Isuzu, to provide small cars in the United States and Ford's recent decision to import a small, jointly produced Mazda from Mexico, are cases in point. Chrysler has imported fully assembled cars from Mitsubishi, its Japanese partner for over ten years; GM will soon do the same with its Japanese and Korean partners. If the razor-thin margin of success in ratifying GM's 1982 labor contract and the early defeats of Chrysler's 1983 contract negotiation are any indication, both will pay a high price in the form of deteriorating labor relations. Although work grievances decline in a period of high unemployment, it is inconceivable that lower manufacturing costs and higher product quality can come from factories populated by a disaffected work force. Ford, working hard to improve its relationships with the UAW, has been more cautious than its domestic competitors in pursuing this option. Such self-restraint will become increasingly difficult for Ford as its relative cost position deteriorates in the small-car segment of the market.

For the future, each of the Big Three will rush to complete the product revolution—the replacement of its pre-1979 fleet. In doing so, each competitor will continue to stress fuel economy, quality manufacturing, and vehicle electronics, including instrumentation and engine controls. In light of competition from foreign automakers, car prices will increase less than the inflation rate. Value received by the consumer will therefore increase. This is an encouraging picture, but not the whole one.

The Japanese cost advantage on a small car sold in the U.S. market still ranges from $1,500 to $2,000 depending on various factors. The automakers cannot escape continued pressure to restructure costs and raise productivity. Such a challenge will have two important side effects. First, it will require U.S. automakers to commit large amounts of additional capital as they struggle to reduce their manufacturing cost by converting to more fully automated factories. U.S. automakers will become even more capital-intensive and thereby vulnerable to economic downturns as an even greater proportion of manufacturing costs become fixed. Second, aggressive moves to restructure the cost position of the industry threaten to worsen relations with labor. The sustained emphasis on improving production economics will lock all three competitors into strategies that are inconsistent with the interests of the corporation's various constituencies. Although consumer value will increase, and some shareholders, managers, and senior employees will prosper, the interests of organized labor and affected regions will be jeopardized. Auto executives are fully aware of these conflicts, but there is little agreement among the Big Three as to how the conflicts should be resolved.

The problem for each of the Big Three is the sustainability of their strategy. For General Motors, which has considerably more flexibility and resources to draw upon than its domestic rivals, this issue rests largely in the political arena: How long will the UAW go along with a GM strategy that sources more and more product offshore with the promise of bringing it back to the United States some time in the future when economics permit? How long will Congress or a future administration wait before intervening in the middle of corporate investment decisions that affect the jobs and communities of their constituencies? For Ford, the sustainability issue is economic: How long can Ford hold out before GM's product strategy and the continued pressure from Japan force it to shift to more foreign-sourced vehicles? What happens to Ford's coalition-building efforts with the UAW in the event of such a strategic shift? And for Chrysler, economics and politics are both at issue: How long can the workers' demands be delayed? How long can the company market its line of cars without either overextending its product in the market or paying the enormous price of a complete redesign?

THE UAW'S RESPONSE

The crisis in the auto industry hit the UAW with devastating force. In 1978 U.S. automakers employed 1.03 million workers; in 1982, only 685,000. At the same time, UAW membership declined by 36 percent, from about 1.5 million to about 1.1 million. In mid-1983, some 250,000 UAW members were laid off indefinitely. The years since 1979 have been the worst since its establishment in the 1930s.

Reliable forecasts do not provide much hope for the future. According to estimates of the U.S. Department of Transportation, some 800,000 to 900,000 jobs in the auto and supplier sectors will disappear by 1990, even assuming that more cars will be produced in 1990 than in 1978. Of these job losses, 600,000 will be due to expected productivity gains of 5 percent per annum—not an unreasonable amount if production volumes continue to recover as many analysts expect. About 200,000 losses will be due to changes in vehicle design and consolidation of capacity. Another 50,000 to 100,000 jobs will be eliminated by announced outsourcing of about 2.5 million engines, 1.8 million transaxles, 1.3 million aluminum heads, 1.1 million CV joints as well as other miscellaneous parts such as smaller components and electronics. If the auto companies dramatically increase the foreign outsourcing of completely assembled cars for sale under their name plate, the employment impact could be greater. A good rule of thumb is that every one-million-unit fluctuation in sales and production will affect 150,000 to 200,000 jobs.

The union faces hard questions about its future. Should it bargain for higher incomes or more jobs? Will the auto companies allow it to trade wage dollars for jobs? In cooperating with management does it risk cooptation by management? Should it maintain the tradition of industrywide pattern bargaining or negotiate decentralized, company-specific contracts? Can it really expect federal intervention to halt the erosion of employment? How the UAW is currently thinking about these questions and behaving in response to the auto crisis flows out of its analysis of the problem.

The UAW leadership is confronting the difficult future of the auto industry with a united voice. Spokespeople for the union attribute the auto crisis to mismanagement by the companies and a reactionary government that refuses to counter "unfair" trade practices by the Japanese. UAW solutions to the auto crisis, accordingly, include a greater union participation in determining product policy and major investments, and a more interventionist role by the government to protect the American industrial base.

Asked how they think strategically about the future of the UAW, most union officers talk about using the means at hand—collective bargaining with the companies—to meet workers' long-term needs. After all, it was through collective bargaining that the UAW achieved high wages, seniority protections, a pension plan, unemployment benefits, generous vacations, an impressive array of medical and hospitalization benefits, dental care, even a prepaid legal plan. Collective bargaining, however, is a slow and unsteady process, complicated by traditional expectations and union policies. It is unlikely that a process used for so long to divide greater and greater spoils can be converted quickly to apportion diminishing rewards.

The auto crisis has affected the UAW's bargaining strategy and its long-term thinking in important ways. Most international union officers are knowledgeable about industry economics and are aware of capital investment needs and employment trends. Although the union agreed to economic concessions in 1980 and 1982, its future bargaining strategy calls for a recovery of many benefits foregone, increased job security, and greater access to managerial decision making. In bargaining toward these ends, however, the leadership must move carefully between the economic realities facing the companies and the economic demands of the rank and file. If the 1982 and 1983 contracts at Chrysler and early rhetoric surrounding the 1984 mediations at Ford and GM are reliable indicators, UAW leaders have decided to bargain for higher economic benefits even at the cost of many jobs.

Further, there is a growing recognition among top officials of the UAW that collective bargaining cannot, by itself, reconcile the concerns of workers with the competitive interests of employers. The Mutual Growth Forums and other joint committees made up of representatives of the companies and the union are one means of addressing the limitations of bargaining. Another is the union's emphasis on improving relations between the companies and the workers directly through Quality of Worklife programs (QWL) and Employee

Involvement (EI) programs. Both programs begin with the recognition that the traditional, authoritarian pattern of labor relations that developed in the auto industry is no longer suitable from the standpoint of human relations or competitive reality. QWL/EI programs represent the simultaneous attempts of labor and management to come to grips with "the Lordstown syndrome" and worker "alienation," on the one hand, and with declining productivity and product quality on the other.

However, after thirty-five years of escalating wages and benefits, auto-workers are unsure how to value such things as QWL/EI and Mutual Growth Forums. Although workers say that they want better relations with management and an end to capricious supervision, many do not see these as worth-while trade-offs for economic benefits. Nor are some workers willing to accept greater responsibility and pressure on the job.

QWL/EI and other efforts to transform industrial relations in the auto industry will be able to stave off immediate competitive threats. The UAW leaders understand this, and they are pursuing other answers to the auto crisis as well. To begin with, the UAW has intensified efforts to reduce its dependence on the auto industry by organizing employees elsewhere. Unfortunately, organizing—like collective bargaining—is an agonizingly slow process complicated by the activities of other unions, continued employer resistance, and the UAW's weak presence in areas outside the industrial Midwest. The UAW has also explored other ways of "diversifying" its membership. In the past several years, the union has affiliated with District 65 of the Distributive Workers of America, reaffiliated with the AFL-CIO, and held merger talks with the United Rubber Workers and the International Association of Machinists. The UAW's diversification strategy may serve it well in the long term. For the immediate future, however, the union is exploring political remedies for the auto crisis.

These political activities are unfolding along several lines. In several ways, the UAW is becoming a more open supporter of the Democratic Party (it endorsed Walter Mondale's candidacy for president) and its agenda of full employment policies including public works programs, retraining assistance, and funding for regional and community adjustment. Along with the AFL-CIO, the UAW campaigned actively on behalf of Democrats in the 1984 national elections. As for the immediate problems of the auto industry, the UAW is trying to shape globalization of the industry by urging passage of domestic content legislation and lobbying for the creation of a national industrial policy to promote the welfare of American industries, including autos, in global competition.

Critics of the UAW's political program charge that it represents, in effect, an attempt to persuade the public and the government to restrict managerial discretion of the automakers and to support its wage premium over nonunion and foreign workers. Whatever the merits of this change, it is clear that the UAW political program does not adequately address company-level and shop-level problems of competitive performance. Indeed, focusing on remedies at the federal level, the UAW's political strategy ignores serious causes and implications of the auto industry crisis.

The UAW, like management, is pursuing narrowly defined, largely self-interested goals, jockeying to improve its own institutional interests at the expense of the auto companies' long-run strength in the United States. But betting on the future shape of the auto industry is a high stakes game and, at the moment, management holds the better cards—the ability to shift capital to low-cost manufacturing areas, to substitute foreign components and fully assembled vehicles for domestic product, and to hold the UAW to a declining automobile employment base.

THE GOVERNMENT'S ROLE

Over the past eight years the government's auto policy has been marked by four characteristics. First, its approach to this bellwether industry has been dramatically inconsistent: neither the Congress nor the executive has been able to decide whether it wants to promote the industry or regulate it, shelter it or scold it. Indeed, on a philosophical level at the highest reaches of the government there is complete disagreement over whether having an "auto policy" is part of the problem or part of the solution.

Second, the government's interactions with the industry have been incoherent; they have not been directed at any clear purpose but rather have addressed a variety of goals, mostly related to social and environmental concerns.

Third, the government's policy toward the auto industry has largely been driven by short-term political considerations. It has been easier for the government to mobilize itself to bail out Chrysler or to pass a multibillion-dollar, short-term jobs bill as a response to unemployment than to focus on the longer-term economic factors that drove Chrysler to the brink or caused the widespread unemployment.

And finally, the government's interactions with the industry have almost routinely focused attention at the margins of the industry's problems and have addressed symptoms rather than causes. It is more than symbolic of the quality of thought in the government's auto policy that the issues that have dominated Washington-Detroit relations since the mid-1970s have been clean air, air bags, and unemployment relief.

If the past eight years have seen inconsistent auto policy from the government, the prospects for the immediate future appear no different: there is confusion and paralysis. Says a top lobbyist for General Motors, "I think in general the people in government don't know what to do. The past didn't work and we can't go back to it. Supply-side economics hasn't worked and it's very painful to go forward with that. I don't think people know where to go."

In this climate of uncertainty, the government is divided into two broad philosophical camps, varying in the analysis of the cause of the industry's problem and, therefore, in the recommendations for the solution. At the heart of the disagreement between the two camps is the issue of the source and significance of the current Japanese advantage in autos.

According to the prevailing macroeconomic wisdom, the Japanese have a competitive advantage in auto production based on factors such as labor wage rates, raw material and component costs, and technology. Following this analysis, the government has two options for auto policy. First, it can do nothing and disavow responsibility for the industry and its problems, accepting as inevitable the decline of the U.S. industry and putting as few obstacles as possible in the way. Says a Commerce Department official, "Unless the basic cost question is addressed, the auto industry won't be competitive. If the auto industry won't admit that twenty to thirty plants have to close, how can the administration go to Congress and ask for bills to deal with the problem?" Adds a Democratic congressman, "The government can't make management competitive or make labor accept lower wages. In more ways than not, the government is a bystander, hoping the industry will change its ways. Right now, there is glacial slowness because nobody wants to change. But the government is helpless."

A second course is for the government to focus on short-term relief— "burial insurance"—in two main areas: worker retraining and trade policy. These approaches acknowledge the Japanese advantage and attempt to cushion its impact by helping workers and slowing the rate of change. Thus far, most of the government debate and action has come in these areas: the $4.6 billion jobs bill passed in the spring of 1983, which includes $83 million in training funds for dislocated workers; the temporary "voluntary" restraint agreement negotiated with the Japanese; and the domestic content legislation being pursued in Congress by the UAW. Of the two forms of relief, trade policy is by far the more controversial, since protectionist measures do not comply with the guiding macroeconomic philosophy. Even some members of Congress who have supported the UAW effort are uncomfortable with the trade policy approach. Says a Democratic congressman, "I see local content as a cry for help. Voting in favor is more a statement to the Japanese than a real solution to our problem. But we don't have a real solution to our problem."

Analysts from the second philosophical camp see the source of the industry's problems differently and, therefore, offer a different prescription. According to this point of view, the Japanese do not have a natural comparative advantage in autos. Rather, over a period of more than thirty years, they have created a comparative advantage, using a mixture of public and private policy tools. Based on this analysis, the appropriate solution is to redefine the role of the government, allowing it to take the lead in shaping a U.S. response to the Japanese. Proponents of this approach call for a national industrial policy to counter the created competitive advantage of the Japanese. Legislation has been introduced to create a variety of mechanisms that would coordinate and direct government policies at the microeconomic level: a new version of the Depression-era Reconstruction Finance Corporation; a top-level tripartite Economic Cooperation Council; or an even broader-based Economic Policy Board. But like the macroeconomic approach, this alternative is not without its own serious questions. The first is whether, given the predominant macroeconomic ideology, there is any real likelihood that any of the measures being discussed could become law. A second question is which, among the many specific legislative proposals, would most effectively address the problems of the industry. All would merely graft a new function onto the top echelon without altering the deep-seated attitudes and institutions that constitute the abiding body of government. In spite of questions, however, these proposals are able to generate some support, at least in part because they offer an alternative to the business-as-usual philosophy of macroeconomics and the "burial insurance" of short-term politics. However, not all critics of the present course regard industrial policy as the solution. Says a top trade official, "The debate in the U.S. today is between anarchy and industrial policy—but those are not the only two options."

Most simply, in the near term this debate is not likely to produce a new government auto policy. From the government's point of view, enough short-term remedies have been applied to ease the immediate pain of unemployment for the workers and relieve the regulatory overload for the companies. The "voluntary" restraint agreement with the Japanese has brought some temporary breathing space from the pressure of imports; a 17.5 percent improvement in sales for the Big Three during 1983, with their vastly reduced breakeven points, has produced some real profits and further reduced the government's concern for the industry. Concludes a Commerce Department official, "We need a bigger crisis on our hands. It has to get worse before it can get better. Otherwise, the political system just won't spin out any new ideas." Ultimately, that may stand as a self-fulfilling prophecy.

THE SCENARIOS OF THE FUTURE

The emerging picture of an industry comprising players beset by conflicting internal policies and strategies likely to provoke further industrial discord is not an encouraging one. Not only are our industrial relationships currently in disarray, but the contributory factors are perpetuated. As a result, if the obsolete strategic thinking, attitudes, and institutions are not changed, the industry will face decay—disguised or undisguised.

Disguised Decay. In this scenario, a cyclical upswing in domestic sales, coupled with declining U.S. gas prices and resurgent consumer interest in highly profitable large cars, will fill up excess production capacity and put the major auto companies solidly back in the black. Protected by Japan's "voluntary" export restraint program, Ford and GM will once again be able to rely on internally generated cash flow rather than debt to finance their capital investment program. Liquidity will improve, dividends will be reinstated and increased, and managers will feel that their efforts during the previous five years have paid off, despite the protection provided by restraints on auto imports from Japan. Executive bonuses will return. The combination of reported profits, executive bonuses, and only limited increases in automotive employment will push the UAW to go for an increased share of corporate profits in the 1984 labor contract negotiations—a bargaining position justified as simply the reverse of the "equality of sacrifice" principle established in the 1982 negotiations. At the same time, the UAW will argue strongly for further constraints on outsourcing, plant closings, and the mobility of capital, as the offshore content for domestically built vehicles (currently 5-6 percent) gradually increases and as plans for importing more completely assembled small cars become public. The ensuing controversy over an economic package for labor and potential constraints on management discretion will lead to increasing hostility in the relationship between management and labor. Previous commitments to joint labor-management committees established under the 1982 contracts will wane. Novel and creative efforts to improve cost competitiveness and product quality in the plants will be jeopardized by a hostile work environment. The government will say that industry deserves whatever it gets. The fragile relationships between management, labor, and government will deteriorate swiftly during the next cyclical downswing. No enduring changes in the industrial relationships will have occurred.

Undisguised Decay. A sequence or a combination of two events—the end of the Japanese import restraints, argued strongly by GM, and a third oil shock—will lead to a new influx of imports totaling perhaps 40 percent or more of new car sales. GM will easily increase its proportion of domestically sold cars sourced from Japan to 25 percent. Ford will scramble to follow suit. Every U.S. automaker will effectively get out of the business of building small cars in North America. With balance sheets deteriorating once again and with our industrial relationships in complete disarray, management, labor, and government will reluctantly agree that something has to be done to keep the auto industry in the United States and to stabilize the economy of the industrial Midwest. "Sharing the poverty" schemes rather than programs for increasing competitiveness will become credible to the public and Congress. This will reinforce a downward spiral leading to even fewer jobs, another round of trade protection—this time including the Europeans, who have more automotive capacity for 1,000cc displacement cars than the Japanese—and disgruntled consumers and auto dealers. The prices of automotive stocks will decline at a rate commensurate with their recent increases.

WHAT IS TO BE DONE?

Two principal lessons emerge from the crisis in the U.S. auto industry and the initial attempts of management, labor, and government to deal with it. First, as long as the interests of the three parties continue to diverge, it will be impossible to maintain or improve the position of the auto industry in the new global competition. From this point of view, America's relatively high manufacturing costs and troublesome product quality are merely evidence of competitive disadvantage, not the causes. The primary causes are fractured relationships among the institutions of management, labor, and government.

A second lesson flows from the first and accents the urgency of the auto industry case. Unless the key industry players find a way to break out of the current pattern of industrial relationships, the U.S. auto industry will experience a further decay in its competitive position. The auto industry of Japan, which enjoys a more productive set of relationships, will continue to outperform America's auto industry.

The underlying message of both lessons is the same: only a system that integrates business, labor, and public policies in a coherent whole will promote the competitiveness of its companies. To be competitive, American management, labor, and government must reconstruct the rules, redefine the roles and responsibilities, and renegotiate the shares in the American system. For auto executives this means recognizing the legitimate interests of labor and government, seeing that it is better to deal with a strong union rather than one in disarray, and understanding the potential advantages of power sharing, information sharing, and job security. For the UAW this means recognizing that industrial competitiveness begins at the level of the firm, that the particular needs of individual firms merit attention, and that profit sharing coupled with wage restraint improves long-term employment prospects. For government, as well as for management and labor, it means recognizing that there is a proper role for government in the affairs of globalizing industries, despite the fact that many decisions are not government's to make and that government intervention as third-party neutral or provider of temporary slack may be required under certain circumstances.

The failure of management, labor, and government to understand this message has gradually eroded the equilibrium of the American system of industrial relationships and left it vulnerable to foreign competition. The result is that in the United States today, business policy, labor policy, and public policy reflect conflicting interests and opposing outcomes.

The policy dilemmas that afflict the U.S. auto industry can be broken. To do so requires accepting the notion of negotiated strategies, developing new institutional capabilities, and exchanging quid pro quos among management, labor, and government.

NEGOTIATING CORPORATE STRATEGY

Prior to the Great Depression most decisions of company policy and strategy were made by management. Since the 1930s, however, the free hand of management has been restrained as an increasing number of corporate activities have become subject to negotiations, either at the bargaining table or in the legislative arena.

In politically salient industries—in which the strategic behavior of corporations has a direct and heavy impact upon employment and the institutions of organized labor, regional economic health, the balance of trade, or national economic security—policy options and business decisions are being debated in forums outside management committees. In the auto industry, manufacturing policy and practices, outsourcing, and plant closing have all become agenda items for discussion between labor and management at forums or joint committees established by the 1982 national labor agreements. Forums also exist at the plant and shop-floor levels in the auto industry, where the work environment, product quality, and plantwide administrative procedures make up the substantive agenda. Some have been institutionalized like GM's Quality of Work Life groups and Ford's Employee Involvement program; others are ad hoc arrangements. In this latter category is the joint union-management team that planned the new "Buick City" facility in Flint, Michigan, that will merge Buick and Fisher Body plant operations and produce completely new front-wheel-drive automobiles for the 1986 model year.

Labor-management committees and negotiating forums operating over the past twenty years in other industries such as meat-packing, retail goods, and textiles—in which plant closings, the process of automation, domestic investment, and international trade have been key agenda items—show that the experience of the auto industry is not unique. In addition, government-initiated or -supported forums such as the steel tripartite committee and President Carter's auto committee, along with the recent development of sectoral advisory committees to the U.S. Trade Representative composed of management and labor representatives, indicate that support for experimental negotiating mechanisms at the national level is on the rise.

In light of these recent experiments and future prospects, the practice of corporate strategy can be seen as beginning to outrun established theory about management rights. In many politically important industries, especially those involved in global competition, senior managers are now faced with the task of negotiating the new "rules of the game" and their goals and resource requirements with other industrial actors such as labor unions and governmental bodies. Thus, traditional assumptions about managers' total control of corporate strategy are rapidly becoming out-of-date. The price of holding on to these outdated notions will increase as the success of international competitors, armed with strategies reflecting the interests of both their work force and government, continue to demonstrate that competitive advantage accrues to those industry players who can line up support for their basic economic goals and business policies.

DEVELOPING NEW INSTITUTIONAL CAPABILITIES

Attitude is one source of the auto industry's competitive dilemma—the blinding assumptions and blocking ideologies that have prevented the three sides from accomplishing the needed adaptations. The source is institutional. American management, labor, and government are still using the institutional capabilities and arrangements of fifty years ago to compete against the most modern systems in the world. Just as plant and equipment can become run-down or obsolete, so can the institutional arrangements that ultimately govern what goes on within the plants. One of the tragedies of the auto industry today is that Big Three management will spend billions of dollars retooling the machinery of production, but the process of information collecting and analysis of communication and negotiation will be largely dominated by the bureaucratic structures built around the litigious collective-bargaining process. The future competitiveness of the auto industry depends on the development of new institutional capabilities, on recognizing the power of information, particularly within the government, and on establishing new communication links between management, labor, and government through which trade-offs can be negotiated.

Information. To compete in global industries, American managers, workers, and government officials need more than ever to be focusing on a different set of information: data at the level of the industry and the company that track relative delivered costs, product quality, technology, domestic and world market share trends, the financial balance of power in firms, employment, and other indicators necessary to analyze the competitive strength of the industry and its companies. Nothing illustrates the importance and value of this kind of information better than the role played by the Transportation Systems Center (TSC) in the Chrysler bailout. Five government analysts operating in a think-tank environment were able to produce accurate, unbiased, credible data on the world auto industry, the American auto industry, and Chrysler. In a debate clouded by rhetoric and ideology, the TSC data base provided a neutral point of departure for real discussions: all sides agreed that TSC's numbers could be relied upon to measure the impacts of different proposals for dealing with Chrysler's problem. Ultimately, TSC's analysis—which literally took the issue down to the level of looking at the specific neighborhoods where Chrysler plants were located—transformed the congressional debate from an abstract argument about economic theory to a set of concrete issues that could be addressed by each side. It is precisely this kind of microlevel information that is needed today on an industry-by-industry basis to provide both an accurate yardstick for gauging the competitive position of America's global industries and a credible baseline for negotiating trade-offs acceptable to all sides.

For the past fifty years, the U.S. government has generally focused its economic data collection effort on macrolevel indicators: economywide or, at best, sectoral trends in employment, output, productivity, investment, and trade. Macrolevel data, by its nature, tends to level out the differences between companies and industries to read a trend line rather than a strategic position. As a result, macroeconomists from both political parties can agree that, based on their data, America does not have a competitive problem. For example, both Charles L. Schultze, chairman of the Council of Economic Advisors under President Carter, and Donald T. Regan, secretary of the Treasury under President Reagan, have agreed in almost the same words and with almost the same data that, "America has not been deindustrializing. Throughout the industrial world, economic performance in the 1970s did fall behind the record of the 1960s. But relative to the industries of other countries, American industry performed quite well by almost all standards."[3] The standards cited to prove the point are the usual macroeconomic indicators: production, employment, exports.

The problem with these conclusions about American industry is not that they do not fit the data. The problem is that it is the wrong data. The issues underlying competitiveness are not revealed by macroeconomic data. In fact, because of the purpose of macroeconomic data, competitiveness issues are more than likely to be obscured.

The fact is that notwithstanding the assurances of Schultze and Regan the federal government today does not know with any certainty how American industry stacks up in global competition, simply because the government has not been gathering the appropriate information. The limited capacity that has existed for collecting this level of information has had no support: the office in the Department of Commerce that has an industry-specific orientation has been reorganized three times under the past three administrations, shuttling around according to different reporting schemes; and TSC's auto analysis unit has all but been closed down.

Within companies and organized labor as well, there is the need for different and better information. In global competition, information is increasingly a source of economic power—a point underscored by Toyota's decision to set up its own international economics research center. Not only has the ability to collect, analyze, and act upon relevant information become an important source of competitive advantage, even more significant, the universe of what is relevant to the auto competition has expanded to include the realm of political economy as a major force in shaping the business environment. Today, governments around the world are interacting with each other and with their companies in unprecedented ways to influence the outcome of the increasingly high-stakes auto competition. Governments have adopted a variety of new roles: owner, planner, banker, regulator, investment manager, mediator, international representative. These interventions by foreign governments on behalf of their auto industries have added a dimension to the kinds of information American companies must consider in shaping their own strategies.

In effect, globalization has transformed the importance of information in the manufacturing competition and emphasized the critical importance of American management, labor, and government interacting as a system.

Communication Links. In addition to better information, new communication links are needed to give the three sides places to talk and negotiate the kinds of trade-offs that will promote competitiveness. The example of the auto industry suggests that neither collective bargaining nor congressional lobbying can effectively carry the full weight of negotiating. Instead, management, labor, and government need to experiment with new forums—ad hoc, issue-specific committees and ad hoc, industry-specific committees—up and down the system at all levels, to establish a steady stream of communication among the three sides.

Today the links that exist are handicapped. Long-standing institutional arenas such as collective bargaining and congressional lobbying are hard-pressed to adapt to the new needs. The collective bargaining process, for example, attempts to define terms of employment rights and of employees. Despite a long and growing list of collective-bargaining subjects, the institution of collective bargaining as we know it today cannot carry the full load of competitive adjustment in industries like autos.

There are several reasons. First of all, attempts to reduce all the rules governing a community like an auto plant or firm to fifteen or even fifty pages may retard adjustment rather than accelerate it. Not only is the nature of day-to-day relationships in the plant too complex to codify and regulate without bringing experimentation to a standstill, but entrepreneurial decisions in which labor may have big stakes do not necessarily coincide with contract negotiations. Second, rigidities in the process—such as episodic rather than periodic negotiations and complicated constituency politics at contract time—

tend to exclude flexible responses by the firm and the national union to changes in the competitive environment. Third, the inherently adversarial nature of the bargaining table means "getting away with as much as possible." This attitude of minimum obligation, often encouraged by the hostile environment surrounding negotiations, can erode competitive advantage in global industries like autos. Energy is misspent on extracting gains from one another rather than finding solutions to thorny competitive problems. While the recent economic downturn in the auto industry has led to important changes in the process and substantive results of collective bargaining—such as contract reopeners, a growing diversity in local agreements on work rules, company-specific bonus schemes, and weakened job control due to the rise of QWL programs—the adaptation of auto bargaining to its new economic environment will be a slow and arduous journey.

Similarly, the legislative process is not well suited to the need for negotiating industry-specific trade-offs. Legislatures are not the arenas in which those quid pro quos between management and labor that affect competitiveness can be exchanged. The trade-offs presented to Congress are rarely specific enough to help improve the competitiveness of a single industry or firm. In addition, Congress has a limited capacity to get agreement on industry-specific issues. Even in the case of the Chrysler bailout, a separate board (Chrysler Loan Guarantee Board) was required to work out appropriate adjustments and concessions by management and labor before the loan guarantees were actually extended. Finally, lobbying is by definition driven by self-interest. If the root of our competitive problem in autos and similar industries is the lack of overlap between the interests of management, labor, and government, then self-interested lobbying has little chance of narrowing the zone of controversy between the key industrial actors.

The solution is to create new forums outside the traditional arenas, where the sides can get together to discuss their problems and make new arrangements. In the past, other industries have responded to changing circumstances with closer communications and reciprocal trade-offs: meat-packing, textiles, and retail goods have all experimented with labor-management committees and negotiating forums. Similar experiments are now under way within the auto industry. QWL and EI programs are designed to improve communications at the shop-floor level. A notable example at the plant level is the labor-management team for General Motors that has cooperatively planned the new "Buick City" facility in Flint, Michigan. At the company level, both GM and Ford have committed themselves to broadly defined labor consultation programs that include systematic fact-finding on certain business developments of mutual interest to the union and the company, and the opportunity for top UAW officials to make direct presentations to the company board of directors. In the past, the government has even been willing to create new links, sponsoring or supporting tripartite committees for the consideration of specific industry problems—although with marginal results.

Ultimately, however, to be successful, these experiments need to be expanded, supplemented, and focused. The experience of Japan and Germany suggests that effective systems of linking institutions operate like the steps of a ladder, with rungs at each step of the system. These parallel links provide continuity within the relationships; they also provide greater focus to the discussions at each level. Thus, rather than having shop-floor workers and management debate the Japanese defense budget—as happened at one Ford Mutual Growth Forum—at each level the committees address issues that they can directly affect.

Thus far, the American experiments have suffered from inconsistency. The commitment to new linking institutions needs to be deepened and sharpened. The approach should be applied across the board, from top to bottom, so that shop-floor workers participating in quality circles can see mid-level managers and executives meeting with their union counterparts as a standard way of doing business. Moreover, the government must become a participant, without necessarily taking the lead. These links need not be tripartite; if only two sides are involved, that is all that is required. But competitiveness in the future will require a willingness to create these new negotiating forums in which the sides can meet and talk outside the channels used in the past.

Exchanging Quid Pro Quos. For negotiations to begin and have any chance of success, it is important not to lose sight of the real competitive situation facing the auto industry, the autoworkers, and the country: the Japanese still lead American producers in cost and quality; there will be fewer autoworkers in the industry in the future than there are today; and unless real changes are made, the country is at substantial risk of losing not only the auto industry but other important industries as well. It is against these harsh realities that negotiations must be cast.

The negotiated "answer" will not appear in this or any analytical treatment of the subject. There is no single formula for wages or productivity or trade or taxes that does away with the Japanese cost advantage or enhances American product quality or rescues autoworkers' jobs. But there are approaches to negotiating and specific issue areas that suggest the outline of a new alliance between management, labor, and government designed to promote America's competitiveness.

The needs of the auto companies at this time are discernible, particularly when measured against the foreign competition. They need to reduce the cost differential and improve quality. They need to develop greater flexibility in the introduction of new technology in their products. They need greater certainty in government policies that affect the business climate; energy cost and availability, the regulatory agenda, and macroeconomic policy. They need some measure of protection from the Japanese, in differing degrees. They need to rebuild their financial bases to sustain the next round of competition.

Just as clear are the needs of the autoworkers. They need work and some assurance of the amount of work they can reasonably expect in the future. They need incomes and benefits commensurate with the work they perform. They need training to upgrade their skills and retraining to provide new skills. And they need more participation in determining how they should perform the work of building cars.

Finally, the government has needs. It needs, among other things, a competitive auto industry, employed autoworkers, and new opportunities for unemployed autoworkers. It also has needs in social and environmental areas and internationally in trade and defense; some of these derive from and pertain to the auto industry and many extend far beyond it.

This is a set of needs and interests that do not line up—they never have here or in any of the competitor nations whose institutions and needs are similar to ours. Yet there are overlaps, and it is in these areas that quid pro quos can be negotiated.

For management, cost, quality, and production flexibility are a function of the relationship with labor. To make gains in these areas, management must seek from labor a relaxation in work rules and job classifications and a shift from pattern bargaining to some more decentralized, company-specific form of bargaining. At one time, pattern bargaining may have made sense; giving the industry a uniform wage price could eliminate the worst equipped employers, concentrate competition on securing the utmost efficiency of production, and provide more jobs with more security than otherwise. But with automotive unemployment as high as it is today and with the most efficient producer, General Motors, leaving the domestic labor market in search of lower production costs, the underlying logic of the pattern wage is becoming less relevant. In exchange, management must meet labor's needs: employment security for the core of the work force that can expect a future in autos; skills-upgrading so that workers can grow with the changing demands of increased automation and retraining for surplus workers. In addition, management must realize that it is in its own best interest as well as the interest of workers to cede greater responsibility and authority—greater power—to the workers at the shop-floor level. Finally, as part of the quid pro quo with labor, management should negotiate an economic bargain that includes profit- or gain-sharing as a way of reflecting the real role of the workers in the company's performance. This innovation, included in the 1982 national labor agreements, deserves increased emphasis on both sides of the bargaining table.

There is a similar package to be negotiated between management and government. For example, the federal government has yet to devise a national energy policy that gives either the automakers or auto buyers in the American market a clear signal about the price of gasoline—or even the direction of the price of gasoline—over the next five to ten years. In the area of trade, during the past six years the federal government has uncomfortably inched toward a more protectionist auto policy—first placing a high tariff on Japanese light trucks, then extracting a "voluntary" restraint agreement on Japanese autos. But this policy has been delivered with no enthusiasm by either the Carter or Reagan administrations, with no sense of what the government hopes to achieve by it or whether it is likely to continue to apply in the future. Nor did either administration attempt to use its trade policy as a bargaining chip with American automakers or the UAW. In short, it has been a trade policy without a context. To allow better planning for the future, the auto industry needs something more predictable from the government than Japan's voluntary export restraint program—and should negotiate for it.

The area of federal regulations has used up more energy and yielded less product than any other. Even the Reagan administration, which came into office committed to "getting government off the back of business," has landed squarely on the back of GM with a major, controversial lawsuit over product safety and has proposed new safety regulations for the industry as a whole. As a part of a negotiated package, management should recognize the anti-competitive effects of our current mode of regulation and create new forums in which to resolve differences.

Although capital cost or availability are not now central to the industry's competitive position, it is possible that members of the Big Three will want to look to the government as a source of capital—either for research and development or plant modernization—and will look for a more globally oriented antitrust policy. Finally, both management and labor need to gain the government's participation in devising and funding a coherent strategy to deal with the looming question of worker retraining.

In exchange for tailoring these policies to reflect the needs of the auto-makers, the government can expect the automakers to address its agenda of public interests. Chief among these must be investment in the United States in new plant and equipment and remodeled facilities.

The real dimensions of a package of quid pro quos could only emerge after meetings among the principals. Moreover, even such a package would not constitute "saving the auto industry." Rather, the process of negotiating corporate strategy is a dynamic one. A first round of negotiations might begin with and achieve only limited agreement on a limited agenda. But it would be a beginning, with real benefits for the industry. Over time, simply by working at it together, management, labor, and government could change their attitudes about each other and build new institutional capabilities. Together these three groups could find ways to modify their current industrial system to make it more competitive.

6

Textiles and Apparel:
A Negotiated Approach to
International Competition

Stanley Nehmer
Mark W. Love

The history of international trade and trade conflict in textiles and apparel exemplifies many elements of the growing challenge to American competitiveness in the world economy. These industries were among the first in the post-World War II period to experience increased international competition and the negative impact of a deteriorating trade performance. In general, shifts in competitive position and production capability away from the more mature economies toward the developing economies have progressed further in many segments of the textile and apparel industries than in most other industrial sectors.

In the past decade, a pattern of intensifying international competition has also emerged in other U.S. industrial sectors, whether labor-intensive, capital-intensive, or technology-intensive. The conventional wisdom that associated international competitive problems with a few mature, labor-intensive industries has given way to the recognition that no U.S. industry is immune.

A symptom of this decline in international competitiveness has been the U.S. departure from a strict free-trade posture in certain sectors, such as textiles and apparel, autos, and steel, which employ many people and are crucial to the socioeconomic well-being of numerous communities. These departures are often criticized as inflationary, harmful to our trading partners, and counterproductive over the long run, because they artificially sustain

Stanley Nehmer is president of Economic Consulting Services Inc. Mark W. Love is vice president of Economic Consulting Services Inc.

declining industries. Criticism of one such deviation from pure free trade—the Multi-Fiber Arrangement (MFA)—is either unwarranted generally, or is at least overly broad as applied to this specific agreement and industry. A system of managed trade such as the MFA offers a potential solution to other international trade conflicts caused by current trends in the world economy and the changing international competitive position of the United States.

Textiles and apparel constitute a significant albeit troubled portion of the American economy. Recently, for example, the nearly 34,000 widely dispersed plants in these industries had wholesale shipments of $100 billion (or 5 percent of all manufacturing), and directly employed 1.9 million workers (over 10 percent of all manufacturing) with another million in related fields. Competition among U.S. firms in both sectors has remained intense, with real wages and prices declining as companies scramble to maintain shares of a stagnating domestic market estimated to grow no more than 1.5 percent a year over the next decade.[1]

Despite impressive productivity gains, overall textile and apparel production has fallen behind manufacturing generally, prompting a 25 percent cut in the work force over the past decade. This employment decline has been particularly painful, both because of steady overall declines in manufacturing employment and because many employees are ill-equipped to shift to higher technology industries.

Some of these cutbacks have stemmed from rising imports over the last twenty years. With natural inputs widely available and local markets growing rapidly, many newly developing countries have targeted the labor-intensive textile and apparel industries for import substitution and export promotion programs. These in turn prospered on low labor costs, easily transferable technology, relatively low capital requirements, small economies of scale, minimal labor standards, population booms, as well as early U.S. foreign aid and cotton export subsidies. Thus, U.S. imports of textiles and apparel quadrupled between 1961 and 1972 from 306 million to 1.2 billion pounds, producing a trade deficit in the latter year of $2.4 billion (see exhibit 6-1).

The United States responded to such trade pressures by negotiating a series of multilateral trade agreements, culminating with the Multi-Fiber Arrangement (MFA) in 1974. The MFA, and its more limited predecessor arrangements on only cotton products, provided a multinational framework in which to manage international trade in textiles and apparel. By stabilizing world markets somewhat, the MFA has encouraged competitive responses by domestic manufacturers through investment, innovation, and consolidation. Long-term structural adjustment has continued without the massive dislocation that would have otherwise occurred. At the same time, the MFA has enabled developing countries' production and exports to grow significantly. Accordingly, the MFA, together with other activities such as management-labor joint research and automation programs, provides a possible model for other distressed American industries.

ROLE OF TEXTILES AND APPAREL IN THE U.S. ECONOMY

OVERVIEW

The American textile and apparel industries constitute a large, diversified manufacturing complex widely dispersed throughout the United States with the largest concentrations in the middle and south Atlantic regions. According to the most recently available *Census of Manufactures*, there were some 33,700 textile- and apparel-producing establishments in the United States, with 7,200 primarily engaged in producing textile mill products and 26,500 producing apparel products.[2] As recently as the 1960s and early 1970s, these firms directly employed up to 2.5 million workers. Even today they employ 1.9 million workers, or more than 10 percent of all manufacturing employment and nearly one-fourth of all nondurable manufacturing employment.[3] In addition, these two industries support an additional million workers in other sectors of the U.S. economy, including agriculture, manufacturing, construction, transportation, and services.[4] In 1981, total sales at the wholesale level were $100 billion, representing approximately 5 percent of the total value of shipments of manufactures.[5]

INDUSTRY STRUCTURE AND PRODUCTS

Despite wide diversity in the size and type of producing establishments in these industries and the thousands of different products manufactured, many sectors are closely integrated. Their output can generally be divided into four basic categories: (1) yarns and thread; (2) fabric; (3) textile mill products other than yarns, thread, and fabric, such as floor coverings, towels, and sheets; and (4) apparel-related products. Each step of the production process, from fibers to yarn to fabrics to apparel, relies on the demand generated by higher stages of processing for survival. Similarly, each step is dependent upon a secure, healthy, and diversified supply of inputs from other segments within the two industries.[6]

Textiles and apparel are among the most essential of all products. Demand is widespread and comes from nearly all segments of the U.S. economy—individual consumers, industry, and all levels of government—as well as foreign markets through exports.

The single largest component of final demand for the output of this industrial complex is apparel products, in recent years consuming about 40 percent of the total U.S. fiber output (by pounds). Another third of the output is turned into home furnishings such as carpets and rugs, draperies and upholstery, bed linens, and towels. Most of the remaining output goes into a wide variety of industrial applications and other consumer-type products, including tire cord and tire cord fabric, reinforced plastics, medical and surgical items, rope, cordage, footwear, luggage, umbrellas, tents, and bagging.

The concentration of both the textiles and apparel industries is generally low, compared to most other industries in the manufacturing sector. Barriers to entry, such as capital requirements and economies of scale are also relatively small, although of the two industries the textile industry has considerably higher capital requirements and greater economies of scale than the apparel industry.[7]

Historically both industries have been highly price competitive. This was confirmed in a 1978 study by the Council on Wage and Price Stability, which stated:

> The relatively rapid response of textile prices to changes in supply and demand conditions indicates that textile firms tend to be quite price competitive.
> The low seller concentration, low barriers to entry and long-run rates of return at the manufacturing level in the apparel industry suggest that the pricing behavior in this industry is also highly competitive and responsive to changing market conditions.[8]

PRICES

For many years, prices for textile and apparel products have increased far less than the overall inflation rate. Based on an index of 1967=100, for example, the producer price index (PPI) for textiles and apparel reached 204.6 in 1982, compared with 312.3 for all industrial commodities. Similarly, the consumer price index (CPI) for apparel was 177.0 in 1982, while that for all items was 289.1.[9]

Since the MFA was instituted in 1974, relative price trends have followed a similar pattern. Between 1974 and 1982, the PPI for textiles and apparel rose 58 percent, while the PPI for all industrial commodities rose 103 percent. The CPI for apparel rose 30 percent over this period, while the overall CPI rose 96 percent. This remarkable price performance is the result of several factors, including new materials development (e.g., man-made fibers), improvements in production process efficiency, and the pressure from import competition.

Although imports havé affected textile and apparel prices for many years, their role can be exaggerated. Normally, American retailers do not fully pass on the lower cost of imports to consumers but instead sell them at nearly the same price as locally produced articles, thereby reaping substantial profits. A 1977 study by the Library of Congress on imports and consumer prices concluded, in part, that "markup ratios on imports appear to be higher than those on domestic products, since the aim of the retailer is usually to sell identical or equivalent products at the same or approximately the same price."[10]

Retailers reportedly do offer bigger sales markdowns on imports than on domestic merchandise. Nevertheless, the beneficial price effects of imports to consumers are less than is often claimed.[11]

LABOR PROFILE AND PRODUCTIVITY

The work force in the textile and apparel industries consists largely of new entrants or older workers. Their median age in 1982 slightly exceeded that of all manufacturing employees, and they were also generally less well educated, according to the most recent census data.

The ratio of men to women in the labor force varies widely among different subsectors. Overall, however, women predominate in apparel production, accounting for about 80 percent of the work force versus about 50 percent in the textile industry.[12]

Diverse minority groups have always been heavily represented in these industries. Approximately 19 percent of the work force was nonwhite in 1982, up from 12 percent in 1968. This is considerably higher than the 12 percent in all manufacturing in 1982.[13]

In general, the textile and apparel industries offer proportionately more jobs, including entry-level positions, to less well educated, more disadvantaged groups in the United States than most other sectors of the economy. Studies show a relatively low degree of mobility among the social groups most heavily represented in the textile and apparel work force.[14] Moreover, the increasing use of computer technology in the production process, including robotics, has reduced the need for certain skills, leaving most textiles and apparel workers in less skilled positions, and reducing their job mobility.

Worker productivity in the textile and apparel industries has increased significantly in recent years, growing at a compound rate of 3.5 percent for textile workers and 2.3 percent for apparel workers between 1973 and 1981.[15] Productivity increases of textile workers exceeded those in all other manufacturing over the period; the rate for apparel workers also compared favorably.

Worker earnings have dropped sharply in the past fifteen years relative to both other manufacturing wages and inflation. Apparel industry hourly wages fell from 73 percent of all manufacturing wages in 1968 to 61 percent in 1982. The ratio for textile workers declined less, from 73 percent to 69 percent over the same period,[16] reflecting in part the relatively greater growth in the textile industries capital intensity and worker productivity, which have allowed greater wage increases. Since 1968, textile and apparel workers' real hourly wages have also declined by 5 percent and 16 percent, respectively. An apparel worker's average annual wages are below the poverty level for a family of four, and those of a textile worker are below the poverty level for a family of five.[17]

CAPITAL EXPENDITURES

The textile industry is more capital-intensive than the apparel industry and has become more so in recent years. In 1981, the most recent year for which official data are available, new capital expenditures in the textile industry reached $1.7 billion, versus $650 million in the apparel industry. By comparison, capital expenditures in all nondurable manufacturing totaled $65 billion.[18]

The difference in capital expenditures between the textile and apparel industries is reflected in their ratios of capital expenditures to value of shipments. In 1981, this figure was 3.4 percent for textiles, 1.9 percent for apparel, and 3.9 percent for all manufacturing.[19]

Capital expenditures per textile worker rose from $1,329 in 1974 to $2,542 in 1981, an increase of 91 percent. The capital expenditures per apparel worker have been considerably lower, $341 in 1974 and $599 in 1981, and rose by 75 percent over the period.[20]

PRODUCTION TRENDS

Textiles has trailed all manufacturing in growth of output over the last two decades (see table 6-1).

Table 6-1
Index of Production, Selected Years, 1961-82 (1967 = 100)

	Textiles[a]	All Manufacturing[b]
1961	72.4	81.8
1967	100.0	100.0
1974	122.8	120.6
1979	139.8	153.6
1981	128.1	139.8
1982	112.1	137.5

[a]Based on U.S. Department of Agriculture data on the poundage of total mill consumption of fibers as shown in *Textile Hi-Lights*, ATMI, Washington, D.C.
[b]Federal Reserve System data

Nevertheless, textiles has outperformed apparel since 1967, as the production of most major types of apparel has declined significantly (see table 6-2).

Table 6-2
U.S. Production of Apparel, 1967 versus 1981 (1967 = 100)

Apparel Type	1967	1981
Handkerchiefs	100.0	81.0
Gloves and mittens	100.0	89.0
Hosiery	100.0	134.6
Men's and boys' suit-type coats	100.0	96.6
Women's, girls', and infants' coats	100.0	122.9
Dresses	100.0	65.0
Playsuits, sunsuits, washsuits, etc.	100.0	88.6
Shirts and blouses, knit	100.0	254.8
Shirts and blouses, woven	100.0	82.4
Skirts	100.0	92.3
Suits	100.0	88.3
Sweaters	100.0	78.7
Trousers, slacks, and shorts	100.0	129.5
Body-supporting garments	100.0	72.5
Dressing gowns, robes, etc.	100.0	91.7
Pajamas and other nightwear	100.0	106.2
Underwear	100.0	94.3

Source: U.S. Department of Commerce, *U.S. Production, Imports and Import/Production Ratios for Cotton, Wool and Man-Made Fiber Textiles and Apparel* (Washington, D.C., 1978 and 1983).

IMPORT GROWTH

The American textile industry has been subject to international trade problems almost from its founding 200 years ago. In 1789, Samuel Slater came to the United States from England and within a year had established the American cotton textile industry at Pawtucket, Rhode Island. He had left England disguised as a farmer because, under the Mercantilist Doctrine then prevailing, the British government prohibited the emigration of skilled artisans, as well as the exportation of textile machinery or plans for such machinery. Samuel Slater had memorized the plans for the Arkwright spinning frame and recreated it in the first factory built in the United States. Although Slater pledged his workers not to build the frame themselves or to go into competition against him, Slater's efforts to maintain his monopoly failed.

In addition to the growing domestic competition among firms in the fledgling domestic textile industry, another kind of competition developed after the War of 1812. At that time, the American industry was faced with formidable competition from growing imports from the older, well-established British cotton textile industry. The infant U.S. industry asked for help to prevent market disruption, and Congress responded by enacting the Tariff Act of 1816, which established high protective duties on cotton textile (and some other) imports.

U.S. tariffs on textile and apparel imports have remained higher than those on other manufactured goods since the Tariff Act of 1930. This reflects both the economic and political importance of the textile and apparel industries in the United States and their high import sensitivity relative to other more capital-intensive American industries, which largely avoided import pressure until the 1960s.

The textile and apparel industries' relatively labor-intensive nature,[21] however, has meant that even high U.S. tariffs, estimated to be 20 percent on average, have failed to prevent domestic producers' being displaced by imports from an increasing number of developing countries.

Imports have grown rapidly for many reasons. First, the dissolution of the colonial system created a number of new, independent countries that sought their own economic development. Second, rapid growth in both the world's population and per capita income spurred worldwide consumption of textiles and apparel. At the same time, demand for these products in the United States, with its high standard of living, has not kept pace with worldwide consumption in recent years. Indeed, there was a small decline in per capita fiber consumption in the United States between 1974 and 1980.[22] This has magnified the effect of increasing foreign supplies on the U.S. market. Third, major advances in technology, the absence of major military hostilities on the scale of World War II, and the deliberate efforts by the free world powers to establish an open trading system have led to greater international interdependence, thereby vastly expanding international trade. Finally, the United States has itself sponsored the development of textile and apparel industries in other countries through direct foreign aid, U.S. funding of international development banks and organizations, and subsidies for U.S. raw cotton exports.

In addition to these economic and political developments, the nature of the textile and apparel industries has increased competitive pressures from other countries and made them the earliest industries to be developed almost everywhere. Demand for clothing ranks second only to food as a necessity for survival, thereby establishing a guaranteed market. The basic inputs for textile manufacture, such as cotton, wool, flax, and other vegetable fibers, have historically been indigenous to many countries. Others have received raw cotton from the United States under the P.L. 480 Program, which began almost thirty years ago and involves financing export sales of agricultural commodities to developing countries on easy credit terms.

Both textiles and apparel require less capital than most manufactures, making them logical choices for countries scarce in capital but rich in unskilled labor.[23] Apparel is even more attractive than textiles because its capital requirements are considerably lower, its labor content and value added are very high, and it has relatively fewer production economies of scale to hinder new entrants.

As a result, these industries are an ideal means for many developing countries to implement industrialization and import substitution policies and to obtain sorely needed foreign exchange. Despite a degree of natural competitive advantage, many of these countries have specifically targeted textiles and apparel for development, resorting sometimes to subsidies and dumping, and frequently to import restrictions, for broad social, political, and economic reasons.[24]

Thus, despite the existence of multinational arrangements designed to provide orderly growth in textile and apparel trade since 1961, U.S. imports have grown rapidly. In 1961, U.S. imports were 306 million pounds. Imports rose to a then record level of 1.2 billion pounds in 1972 before declining to 927 million pounds in 1974, the first year of the MFA.[25] However, imports continued to grow after 1974 and reached a record 1.7 billion pounds by

1982.[26] In 1983, imports rose to a new record of 2.2 billion pounds, far exceeding the 1982 level.

At the same time that imports have risen, the balance of trade in textiles and apparel has deteriorated sharply. In 1961, the United States had a textile/ apparel trade deficit of $191 million. By 1972, it had risen to $2.4 billion. The deficit for 1982 was a staggering $7.2 billion, and worsened by 33 percent in 1983, rising to $9.6 billion.[27] Since the early 1970s, most if not all of this deficit has been caused by trade in apparel, although a sharp deterioration in the trade balance in textiles occurred in 1983.

U.S. production, as measured by U.S. mill consumption of fibers, also grew during the 1960s, but at a much slower rate than imports. Moreover, absolute production has actually fallen since the early 1970s. Production rose from 6.5 billion pounds in 1961 to 11.6 billion pounds in 1972, but then fell to 10.1 billion pounds in 1982, a decline of 13 percent.[28] Total pounds of imports increased over the same period by approximately 40 percent.

The overall deterioration shown by these statistics masks wide variations among different segments of each industry. In certain product categories, domestic production has declined sharply; in other segments imports and domestic producers have maintained more stable market shares. In a few selected areas, such as carpets and rugs, the U.S. industry still dominates the market, holding a market share of approximately 98 to 99 percent. In fact, since carpets and rugs alone account for a large portion of domestic production,[29] removing this product category raises the remaining overall penetration levels of imports of textiles and apparel significantly. Thus, the textile and apparel complex has by no means experienced a uniform level of import penetration, although the aggregate trends reflect steadily increasing competition from foreign suppliers.

INTERNATIONAL RESPONSES TO TEXTILE AND APPAREL TRADE PROBLEMS

EARLY IMPORT CONTROL PROGRAMS

For nearly three decades national policy has sought to moderate the growth of textile and apparel imports, primarily through agreements with other governments. In its first response to disruptive trade during the post-World War II era, the United States and Japan agreed to a five-year aggregate annual limit, beginning in 1957, on cotton textile product exports to America, with ceilings for specific products. In that year, Italy also undertook to control its exports of certain cotton fabrics to the United States.

Despite short-term relief provided by such export controls, U.S. imports of cotton textile products grew sharply in 1959 and 1960 due to the rapid entry of new supplying countries, particularly Hong Kong. Thus, the pattern of sudden import growth and penetration by new suppliers first became firmly established between 1958 and 1960. This pattern was repeated with accelerating frequency in the next two decades, thereby thwarting bilateral attempts to deal with the problem in a reasonably effective manner despite the increasing scope and detail of restraint mechanisms.

In 1961 and 1962, two broader multilateral agreements were negotiated: the Short-Term Arrangement Regarding International Trade in Cotton Textiles (STA) and its successor, the Long-Term Arrangement (LTA). The LTA remained in effect for an initial five years and was extended in 1967 and 1970. During that time, cotton textile product imports grew constantly. Between 1962 and 1973, the last year of the LTA, cotton textile product imports rose from 310 million to 564 million pounds,[30] and U.S. production fell from 4.2 billion pounds to 3.7 billion pounds. Overall import penetration in cotton textile products reached 15 percent by 1972, and import penetration for many individual products was significantly higher.[31]

That thirty-three countries signed the LTA indicates the growing scope and volume of international trade in textiles and apparel during the late 1950s and 1960s. Moreover, under the LTA numerous countries besides Japan not only became major producers and exporters of cotton textile products but diversified into products made of noncotton fibers. The development and rapid growth of man-made-fiber textile products in the United States during the 1960s was paralleled by a rapid growth in U.S. imports.[32] From only 58 million pounds in 1960, such imports reached 628 million pounds in 1973, higher than cotton textile product imports in that year.

Thus, the growing problem of U.S. market disruption by imports had expanded along two dimensions—first, the number of supplying countries increased, and second, the number of products grew. The negotiation in 1971 of bilateral agreements on wool and man-made-fiber textile products with four major Asian supplying countries—Hong Kong, Japan, Korea, and Taiwan—first brought trade in noncotton products under an international mechanism of order and control.[33] The United States also negotiated a similar agreement with Malaysia, a smaller supplier. These accords expanded control over trade to products of cotton, wool, and man-made fiber, setting the stage for the more comprehensive Multifiber Arrangement in 1974.

THE MULTIFIBER ARRANGEMENT

The most recent, elaborate, and comprehensive attempt to deal with growing textile and apparel imports from less developed countries is currently extended until 1986. It is a multilateral agreement negotiated under the auspices of the General Agreement on Tariffs and Trade (GATT) and endorsed by about fifty countries. The MFA's purpose is to allow signatory countries to negotiate bilateral agreements between themselves and other countries to regulate trade in textiles and apparel. Normally, the major importers like the United States and the European Community initiate such talks. Bilateral agreements with twenty-five countries currently impose certain restraints on American imports of textile and apparel products of cotton, wool, and man-made fibers.

In addition to bilaterally negotiated limits, the MFA authorizes unilateral restraints against imports that disrupt or threaten to disrupt the U.S. market. These unilateral actions are permitted under Article 3, which requires consultations and establishes a formula for calculating the restraint level in the event such consultations are unsuccessful. This formula sets a minimum restraint at the level of actual imports or exports during the year ending two months before the consultation is requested.

Currently, U.S. bilateral agreements vary widely in the degree to which they actually inhibit growth in American imports from the individual countries and restrain individual products. In general, only a small number of highly sensitive products are subject to specific restraints that strictly limit the level of exports to the United States.[34] Bilateral agreements also provide for consultations if imports in product categories without specific limits begin to threaten or cause disruption in the U.S. market. In nearly all cases, however, these consultations take place only after actual import surges occur.[35] Moreover, most agreements automatically set new specific restraints 15-20 percent above actual trade levels.

The MFA has generally not been viewed by the U.S. government as an instrument to reduce or maintain existing levels of textile and apparel imports.[36] Rather, the MFA's stated aim is to promote the orderly growth of textile trade among countries, but on a sound, nondisruptive basis. This means, as a practical matter, that the MFA is governed by two somewhat contradictory propositions: first, that textile and apparel trade should increase, particularly to benefit developing countries, and second, that the growth of such trade should be controlled to ensure its orderly development.

The original MFA provided for a minimum annual growth rate of 6 percent for specific import limits negotiated between countries, in addition to other flexibility provisions. However, the growth of the U.S. market after 1974 was well below this minimum, and sharp declines in the U.S. market were actually registered in some years. This meant that imports captured a growing share of the domestic market. This inherent inequity not only caused continued market disruption in numerous product areas during the first four years of the MFA but led to calls for revision of the MFA.

As a result, incorporated in the first renewal of the MFA at the end of 1977 was language calling for "reasonable departures" from the import growth rate standard and flexibility provisions in particular cases.[37] This allowance for lower import growth rates and reduced flexibility in exceptional cases was reiterated in the protocol accompanying the second renewal of the MFA in December 1981.[38]

In 1980, Ronald Reagan promised, before his election, to relate the growth in imports to the long-term growth in the domestic market.[39] This commitment was in response to industry concerns over steady increases in import penetration despite the MFA and the threat of large additional imports from the People's Republic of China (PRC). The PRC had, in several years, grown to be one of the largest producers and exporters of textiles and apparel in the world and was becoming as large a supplier to the U.S. market as each of the traditional top three: Hong Kong, Taiwan, and Korea.

Since the president's commitment, the federal government has been prodded by the domestic industry to moderate imports from these four foreign suppliers more effectively and to relate the growth of total imports to that of the American market. However, aggregate imports rose sharply in 1982, despite the recession and declines in domestic production and surged again during 1983 well beyond 1982 levels.

EVALUATING THE MFA

LIMITS TO MFA IMPORT RESTRAINTS

No other U.S. industry adversely affected by import competition has received, or benefited from, an international agreement like the MFA. Despite the continued attrition of the textile and apparel industries, the MFA represents a unique and substantial effort to moderate the impact of imports, recognizing these industries' particular vulnerability and their importance to the American economy.

Despite some exceptions, overall increases in import penetration, market disruption, and job losses have continued since 1974, because the MFA is not a monolithic system of import restriction. Rather, the effectiveness of the MFA depends almost entirely on how the United States and other governments implement their rights and obligations under the MFA, particularly under bilateral agreements.

As a result, the quantity of total U.S. imports actually subject to binding restraints is quite small. Many major foreign suppliers, for example, have no bilateral agreements with the United States at all, and in 1982 these accounted for 28 percent of all American textile and apparel imports.[40] Even existing bilateral agreements do not subject the majority of product categories to specific import restraints, which are generally limited only to the most import-sensitive products (see exhibit 6-3). In addition, substantial growth rates frequently raise these limits. The historical norm has been 6 percent, although new agreements with the major suppliers have reduced this rate for some categories to a level more in line with long-term growth of domestic consumption.

Beyond the basic growth rate, a wide variety of provisions allow exporting countries to shift exports from one restrained product category to another in response to changes in U.S. demand. Moreover, specific limits are not reduced even when they are consistently underfilled by actual trade.[41] Thus, such restraints are often maintained and even increased each year to levels well above actual exports, giving exporting countries additional wide room for growth. As a result, imports can increase substantially despite specific restraints.

Finally, the removal of aggregate, overall import ceilings for each country may also have increased their flexibility.[42] These overall ceilings were traditionally included in most bilateral agreements, but have been dropped in recent negotiations in return for more restrictive limits on particular products. As a practical matter these overall ceilings were seldom reached by actual trade, but their removal may have given major country suppliers more mobility to move into uncontrolled product categories once specific restraints were reached on some products.

Given these limitations, it is hardly surprising that the system of bilateral agreements has only constrained trade moderately. Through the first nine months of 1983, for example, total American imports of textiles and apparel grew by 21 percent. This rate far exceeded growth of domestic consumption growth and spurred numerous requests for additional restraints. Nevertheless the surge in imports continues. The MFA's limited impact on trade is clearly apparent in the sharp increases in imports from Hong Kong, Taiwan, and Korea, countries that have the most restrictive bilateral agreements. As exhibit 6-4 illustrates, the quantity of U.S. imports from these countries rose 13 percent, 26 percent, and 27 percent, respectively, in 1983 compared with 1982.

TRENDS IN THE COMPETITIVE POSITION OF THE TEXTILE AND APPAREL INDUSTRIES

Textiles. Despite the continued long-term growth in import penetration since 1974, the MFA has provided a degree of predictability to the domestic industries that would otherwise have been absent. This relative stability has encouraged investment and adjustments, thereby strengthening the most competitive features of these industries.[43] This confidence has been substantially eroded by the import surge in 1983, however, and despite a major response by the U.S. government, many experts worry that this recent rise may not be temporary.

In 1974, the first year of the MFA, capital investment by the textile industry rose to a record $1.2 billion, from $1.1 billion in each of the two preceding years. After a sharp drop during the 1975 recession, capital expenditures reached $1.7 billion in 1981, an increase in real terms between 1975 and 1981. This increase nearly doubled capital expenditures per worker over the period and allowed textile workers' productivity to grow faster than that of any other manufacturing industry between 1973 and 1981.[44] These gains, in turn, contributed to the favorable trade balance in textile mill products that developed in 1974, after the consistent annual deficits in preceding years. This positive balance continued throughout the 1970s and peaked at $1,139 million in 1980 (see exhibit 6-1), led primarily by exports of man-made-fiber textile products.

These export surges and the positive trade balance in textiles were cut short by the dollar's sharp appreciation after 1980 and the continued development of foreign industries. The dollar's continued strength and the rise of textile imports caused a significant negative trade balance in 1983, compared with a small negative balance in 1982 (see exhibit 6-1).

Numerous technological developments have made the textile mill products sector more competitive.[45] In yarn production, improved opening, drawing, and spinning processes have increased labor productivity by decreasing the number of steps and amount of labor per specific level of output. Other recent innovations include new jet spinning (which eliminates several process steps and reduces space requirements, noise levels, and maintenance costs), and a new covered yarn system with the fastest production speed yet available.

The most extensive innovations have occurred in fabric production. In weaving, new missile, rapier, water-jet and air-jet looms are generally faster and more efficient than their predecessors and produce higher-quality fabric. They are also more expensive and less flexible, requiring more advanced support equipment and more skilled operators. Major technological changes have also occurred in both the knit and nonwoven fabric sectors. The non-wovens industry is technology-intensive, utilizing a wide range of inputs for products that not only compete with knit and woven fabrics but have many other end uses as well.

The textile industry has thus established a strong competitive position in world trade under the MFA. Viewed as a "sunset" industry only a decade ago, it is now one of the more vital parts of the American manufacturing sector. The dollar's recent rise, however, has temporarily reduced textiles' competitive strength internationally, along with that of many other American products.

Apparel. The apparel industry has not fared as well under the MFA. Since the early 1970s imports have shifted from textile mill products to higher value-added products. For example, apparel accounted for 41 percent of the total 1970 poundage of U.S. cotton, wool, and man-made-fiber imports and 42 percent in 1974. This ratio then rose to approximately 62 percent by 1982.[46] This relative shift away from textile mill products and toward apparel has occurred for various reasons.

First, apparel production has been and will likely remain more labor-intensive than textile production, giving lower-wage developing countries a greater advantage in these products. Second, apparel products are the most highly processed articles in the fiber/textile/apparel chain, so any labor and other cost advantages enjoyed by foreign producers will cumulate in the greatest cost advantage for apparel products. Third, apparel provides more foreign exchange per unit of production exported and thus motivates foreign producers to upgrade their product mix to the level that the MFA bilateral agreements constrain their exports. Fourth, the interchangeability of capacity among apparel products allows suppliers to shift product lines quickly to meet changes in demand or to circumvent restraints on particular products. Finally, apparel manufacturers have helped shift imports from textile mill products to apparel by offshore sourcing of apparel as well as fabric. This competitive response to increased import pressure has reduced domestic demand for fabric, reduced domestic production of apparel, and increased apparel imports.

The divergent trends of textiles and apparel imports do not mean that textiles are increasingly free from disruptive trade. On the contrary, apparel imports not only reduce the market for U.S. apparel producers but indirectly reduce their demand for domestic fabric and yarn. Thus, the textile sector suffers both direct competition from textile imports and indirect competition from apparel imports. The decline of U.S. textile production, as measured by U.S. textile mill consumption of fibers, from 11.1 billion pounds in 1974 to 10.1 billion pounds in 1982, roughly matches the rise of total textile and apparel imports from .9 billion pounds to 1.7 billion pounds during the same period.

The apparel industry has responded to this problem with the help of the unions, which have long encouraged changes in production process technology, despite their explicit goal of reducing the labor content of apparel production. In the past several years, for example, Draper Laboratories has conducted technological research under the auspices of the Tailored Clothing Technology Corporation. The Amalgamated Clothing and Textile Workers Union, several major fiber, textile, and apparel companies, the National Science Foundation, and the U.S. Department of Commerce have spent millions of dollars on this research, which is designed to automate the most labor-intensive elements of the sewing process for men's tailored clothing. (According to apparel union sources, only 25 percent of the labor required to make tailored clothing goes into actually sewing the garment, compared with 75 percent for handling.) Significantly, the union will be responsible, with management's cooperation, for compensating or relocating workers who may be displaced. The research is well advanced, with feasibility testing in apparel plants scheduled as the next step.

In addition to this specific research, other technological advancements have improved the presewing processes, including pattern grading, marker-making, and cutting. Computer technology has provided the primary gains in these areas and has also been used for programmable sewing machines, administrative functions, and garment design.

OVERALL TRENDS IN IMPORT MARKET SHARE BY TYPE OF FIBER

The MFA's effectiveness in limiting imports has also varied widely for the three major fibers. Cotton textile imports, for example, have grown rapidly despite the decline in overall consumption of cotton fiber, causing tremendous market disruption. Imports grew from 503 million pounds in 1974 to 904 million pounds in 1982, and record levels were forecast for 1983.[47] Similarly, imports as a percent of U.S. apparent consumption climbed from 6 percent in 1960, to 11 percent in 1970, to 24 percent in 1980 and to 29 percent in 1982.[48] These aggregate figures mask wide variations in penetration by product category, with certain types of broadwoven fabric, apparel, and made-up and miscellaneous products experiencing much higher import ratios.

By contrast, man-made fiber textile products have been somewhat more stable under the MFA. Rapid growth in 1969 through 1971 raised man-made fiber imports' market share to that of cotton products, but from 1974 to 1981 their share remained between 6 percent and 8 percent. In 1982, however, this ratio returned to 11 percent and should be considerably higher in 1983. Once again, much higher import penetration levels exist in certain categories, especially apparel products, than these overall averages imply.

Imports of wool textile products have achieved the highest market shares over the last decade, rising from 22 percent in the early 1970s, to 31 percent in 1978, 34 percent in 1982, and even higher in 1983.

While various segments of the domestic textile and apparel industries have suffered severe attrition due to increasing imports, their overall performance compares favorably with other labor-intensive industries not covered by the MFA. For example, the U.S. nonrubber footwear industry has experienced a long and rapid erosion of market share, production, and employment to imports. Between 1960 and 1982, import penetration rose from 4 percent to 60 percent, while production fell from 600 million pairs to only 331 million pairs and employment dropped from 243,000 workers to 137,000 workers.[49] Thus, the MFA has moderated the rate and degree of attrition of the textile and apparel industries that would otherwise have occurred and prevented these industries from suffering the precipitous decline that has characterized the footwear industry.

FUTURE OF THE MFA

ARE THERE ALTERNATIVES TO THE MFA?

The MFA has been criticized from all sides since its inception. To supporters, the MFA is inadequate; to detractors, it is a glaring aberration from free trade. For all the criticism, however, the MFA has existed for a decade and appears likely to survive for the foreseeable future.

The MFA's very size and scope reflect many years of painstaking negotiations on a massive scale, channeling a wide range of conflicting economic interests into a workable, albeit imperfect, solution.[50] International textile and apparel trade has grown greatly under the MFA and many developing countries have successfully expanded their industries. At the same time, mature economies have had a much more stable and predictable competitive environment than they would otherwise have had. As a result, the MFA remains in effect largely because the chief alternatives—free trade or unilateral controls—are unacceptable.

For the United States, eliminating all controls would cause rapid attrition among both the textile and apparel industries and their suppliers, with the likely loss of hundreds of thousands of jobs and thousands of firms in a short period.[51] Textile and apparel employees would face particularly acute hardships because of the American economy's ongoing shift away from basic manufacturing toward certain services and high technology sectors. This shift has exposed large segments of the labor force to long-term unemployment, particularly those workers with limited education, communication skills, or work experience.[52]

This incompatibility between currently unemployed workers and the type of jobs created by ongoing structural change suggests that eliminating the MFA would not have the dynamic employment benefits frequently attributed to free trade. In fact, available data indicate that expansion of trade could well have negative consequences. For example, the United States has registered a rapid deterioration in its trade balance in recent years. The administration projects that this trade deficit could perhaps be $130 billion in 1984. The trade sector thus constitutes a large net drain on the American economy and has a decidedly negative employment impact.

According to a recent report of the U.S. International Trade Commission, the United States had a net job displacement from 1982 trade in manufactures of more than 1,000,000 man-years.[53] On the basis of overall trade, the United States had a net displacement of 450,000 man-years, as agriculture and services fell far short of making up the deficit in jobs caused by trade in other sectors.

More troublesome is the growing job displacement caused by expanding trade with those countries that might benefit from the elimination of the MFA: Hong Kong, Taiwan, and Korea. Between 1978 and 1982, the volume of U.S. trade (imports and exports) with these three rose from $21.8 billion to $35.4 billion. However, this growth in trade resulted in a gain from exports of only 80,000 man-years for American labor, and a displacement from imports of 206,000 man-years.[54] These data suggest that any expansion of the trade sector resulting from the MFA's elimination would cause large net job losses and not the dynamic creation of new job opportunities.

In addition, there is no conclusive evidence that elimination of the MFA would, in fact, free up a portion of American's current expenditures on textiles and apparel for the purchase of products of other sectors. As noted, the price trends for textiles and apparel do not support the conclusion that the MFA has actually had much effect on raising prices to consumers above levels that would obtain otherwise. Even if there was some effect on expenditures by eliminating the MFA, the shift of such expenditures to other goods and services would likely offset only a small portion of the job losses incurred, because of the high relative labor intensity of apparel production and because a significant portion of such expenditures would be spent on imports of other products.

A recent analysis of Labor Department employment data indicates that the millions of jobs lost in manufacturing over the past several years have not yet been recovered in the current rebound and that a large portion will never be recovered. The alternatives for those unemployed, both currently and prospectively, are either permanent unemployment, withdrawal from the job market, or employment in low-paying service jobs (e.g., fast-food restaurants, gas stations, and retail stores), where wages are below employees' previous wages.[55]

No feasible adjustment or retraining programs have been devised that could even begin to address adequately the problems caused by the magnitude of U.S. job losses resulting from elimination of the MFA. The resulting dislocation, which would fall particularly heavily on hundreds of local communities, would impose enormous economic and social costs, thereby expanding the federal deficit.

Thus, eliminating the MFA would probably result in unilateral import quotas, which could be more restrictive and less flexible than the bilateral agreements currently in effect.[56] Moreover, under §504 of the Trade Agreements Act of 1979, any termination of the MFA prior to the final reduction (generally by 1987) of the rates of duty agreed during the Tokyo Round of the multilateral trade negotiations will automatically raise tariffs on textiles and apparel to those levels in effect on 1 January 1975.

ENHANCING THE VIABILITY OF THE MFA

Because of the deteriorating trade balance in textiles and apparel in recent years, pressures for increasing the effectiveness of MFA-negotiated bilateral agreements have grown. The continued import surge in 1983, despite a number of new import restraints in that year, undermined the federal government's credibility in preventing disruption from growing imports under the MFA.

Numerous reforms, however, could help maintain the MFA's viability in the current environment. First, a more systematic approach would supplement the bilateral agreements with global import ceilings, at least for the most sensitive products, thus reducing the likelihood of unpredictable surges from previously uncontrolled countries. Levels under the bilateral agreements could be subsumed under the global ceilings.[57] Second, restoring overall and group ceilings in bilateral agreements with individual countries could help limit disruptive import increases that exceed domestic growth. Third, administrative difficulties in monitoring imports could be alleviated by instituting import licensing to replace the current reliance on foreign government export controls. An import licensing system would improve U.S. ability to prevent various types of fraudulent circumvention of restraints. Moreover, an import licensing system could transfer to the United States any tariff effect of restricting imports away from foreign governments and industries, which currently allocate export authorizations to individual exporters and frequently tolerate the purchase and sale of such permits. The revenues generated by such transactions could be captured by the United States through the sale of import licenses and be used to assist the long-term adjustment of domestic industries.

EXPANDING THE MFA CONCEPT TO OTHER TRADE PROBLEMS

ADVANTAGES OF MANAGED TRADE

Because of the world dominance of America's industrial base after World War II, the United States benefited from adopting and promoting a strong free trade policy. Today the economic and political underpinnings of the prevailing free trade philosophy are beginning to erode, forcing a gradual reexamination of alternative policies. One obvious option is the selective management of trade on a multinational basis, as under the MFA.

The MFA has been designed to assure continued growth in textile and apparel imports, if justified by international competition. Moreover, this growth may even exceed domestic consumption, permitting developing countries greater access to the American market.

Import restraints are frequently criticized for "locking in" alleged inefficiencies in certain industries. However, the world abounds with countries that severely limit imports but nonetheless have very efficient and competitive industries.[58] Indeed, the United States' own textile industry has made great strides in international competitiveness because of the MFA.

Just as trade barriers do not necessarily promote inefficiency and international uncompetitiveness in industries of particular countries, industries that are internationally competitive do not necessarily thrive simply because of free trade and comparative advantage. Several of America's most successful export sectors—agriculture, commercial aircraft, semiconductors, computers, and defense products—owe much of their success to massive government subsidy programs or defense procurement.[59] Similar distortions of trade performance and comparative advantage have been and will remain endemic to many other countries as well.

Even from a global perspective, one cannot assume that the introduction of managed trade would necessarily lead to greater overall inefficiency. The world steel industry and the world footwear industry provide useful illustrations of this point.

One of the most dominant characteristics of the world steel industry is a pervasive system of massive subsidization.[60] Large portions of the steel industries of a number of countries would probably cease to exist if all subsidies were eliminated and some recent new capacity might not even have been brought on stream. Thus, the historical and current pattern of world production, prices, and trade flows can hardly be assumed to reflect a state of worldwide efficiency that would theoretically exist under a system of more perfect competition. The introduction of managed trade in this situation could as easily increase overall efficiency on a global basis as decrease it. At the very least, managed trade could prevent the United States from bearing an undue share of the burden created by trade flows that are predicated upon massive distortions in the world steel industry and market.

In the case of footwear, the world's markets are replete with a vast array of highly restrictive tariff and nontariff barriers. Since the termination by the United States of import relief for the American industry in mid-1981, the American market has been by far one of the most open in the world, a situation that existed even when the import relief was in effect between mid-1977 and mid-1981. In 1981, the U.S. International Trade Commission made the following assessment:

> An examination of the worldwide pattern of tariffs, quotas, taxes, and other barriers to trade in nonrubber footwear suggests that the United States is one of the most open markets in the world, despite its current import restrictions. Tariffs in other industrial countries are generally as high as or higher than those

in the United States, and many of these countries have imposed formidable nontariff barriers to footwear imports.

Developing nations also impose extensive restrictions on footwear imports. Except for Singapore and Hong Kong, which allow free trade in nonrubber footwear, Asian countries generally impose high tariffs and restrictions or outright bans on imports of these articles. Korea imposes import duties of 60 percent, and duties in Taiwan range from 25 to 85 percent. Similarly, with the exception of Argentina and Chile, duties in Latin American countries are high, and most of these countries impose prior deposit restrictions, import licenses, or other types of nontariff barriers.[61]

Once again, it is difficult to assert that current trade flows and production patterns necessarily reflect an efficient global allocat.on and utilization of resources. Managed trade could well represent an improvement of the present situation, or at least prevent the United States from bearing an unfair burden.

EQUITABLE SHARING OF NEGATIVE STRUCTURAL ADJUSTMENT

An MFA-type solution provides an equitable means of allocating negative structural adjustment more fairly among those countries that are less competitive. Political feasibility dictates that this burden be shared within an internationally negotiated framework. Such a process facilitates unpleasant decisions and moderates international competitive pressure, giving countries sufficient time to adjust and individual industries a more stable environment in which to plan their best investment strategies. Steel provides two illustrations of this type of joint adjustment: the recently established U.S.-European Community steel trade agreement and the European Community's carbon steel industry restructuring plan.

A MORE RATIONAL APPROACH TO WORLD INDUSTRIAL DEVELOPMENT

Another advantage of managed trade applies more fully to concentrated capital-intensive industries or high-technology industries with heavy R&D, and involves the pressure that could be brought to bear on countries to prevent unrealistic or overly ambitious investment in product areas already suffering from excess worldwide capacity. Frequently, developing industries are located in countries that already severely restrict foreign competition in their own markets, thus distorting local investment decisions. Moreover, certain countries, both developing and developed, target particular industries for development either for noneconomic considerations or to encourage selected goals (e.g., employment or market share) at the expense of others (e.g., profits or wages). Under a system of managed trade, there would be greater transparency of noneconomically based investment which could prevent actions that would unnecessarily worsen a trade problem.

Finally, an internationally managed trade program could potentially inhibit unfair trade practices, such as subsidizing and dumping.[62] Since growth in imports and import market share would moderate, the incentives for exporting countries to engage in these unfair economic practices might be reduced. Managed trade would also respond to the suspect pricing practices of industries in centrally planned economies, which the international trade community has not yet addressed adequately.

Given the contribution of the MFA to conflict resolution in the sphere of international trade, the question is whether, and under what circumstances, an MFA-type solution can be applied to other international trade conflicts.

At the outset, it should be noted that the usefulness and appropriateness of managed trade is not necessarily limited to mature, import-competing industrial sectors. Special problems exist for currently export-oriented, technology- and capital-intensive U.S. industries that are subject to unique pressures within the international economy. These pressures are usually not a function of free market forces and their impact on U.S. international competitiveness, but rather a function of market intervention by foreign governments.

Consequently, two sets of criteria have been developed, one that is relevant to mature, import-competing industries and one that addresses the special concerns of certain export-oriented U.S. industries currently possessing a degree of international competitiveness.

Mature, Import-Competing Industries. Several conditions must be met for a managed trade solution to apply in the case of an import-competing, mature industry:

1. The products in question must have widespread application in consumer or industrial applications.
2. With respect to these products, there must be significant production and production capacity in a number of countries.

3. Within this universe of the world's significant producing countries, there must be a persistent large imbalance of trade in the product between an identifiable group of importing countries and an identifiable group of exporting countries.

4. The importing countries must have experienced long-term stagnation or attrition of their industries, and suppression of investment below levels needed to modernize or optimally rationalize remaining productive facilities.

5. There must be ongoing disputes over international trade in the product in question involving a significant portion of both importing and exporting countries.

6. There must be one or more persistent inequities affecting relative international competitiveness and international trade among the significant producing countries. These inequities will usually involve wide differentials in production costs (e.g., labor cost), but may also be accompanied by widespread unfair trade practices (e.g., dumping, subsidization), wide differentials in the degree of market access to the significant producing countries, extensive participation in world trade by nonmarket economies, historical assistance by the United States and international organizations in the development of these industries in other countries, and other government intervention in support of the industries in numerous countries.

The following is a more detailed list of criteria expanding on the particulars of these conditions, recognizing that all criteria may not be applicable to all cases where a managed trade solution may be indicated.

INDUSTRY AND PRODUCT CHARACTERISTICS

1. Existence of significant-sized industries in a number of individual countries, size being defined in terms of the number of producing establishments or, in more capital-intensive industries, a significant level of production.

2. Significant regional or local economic dependency upon the industry within individual countries.

3. Existence of established, mature industries in several importing countries having comparable cost structures, and the existence of more newly established industries in exporting countries with a wide, absolute advantage in factor or input costs.

4. Significant, persisting world overcapacity, with stagnation in importing countries and growth in exporting countries.
5. Inhibition on investment in importing countries because of the price and volume effects of imports.
6. General availability of most product and production process technology throughout the world.
7. Widely used consumer or industrial goods involved.

LABOR CONSIDERATIONS

1. Significant levels of employment remaining in the subject industry in importing countries.
2. Significant noncyclical declines in the level of employment in the subject industry in importing countries.
3. Significant trade-induced structural unemployment due to limitations on alternative employment possibilities. Such limitations involve:

   - Inadequate growth or actual decline in comparable industries that could readily utilize the unemployed workers; and
   - Characteristics of unemployed workers that make available employment inappropriate, such as age, level of education, level of communication skills, immobility for social/economic reasons, and type of work skills possessed.

4. Wide absolute disparity in labor costs between importing country industries and exporting country industries.

INTERNATIONAL TRADE CONSIDERATIONS

1. General pattern of trade flowing in one direction from one group of producing countries (i.e., exporting countries) to another group of producing countries (i.e., importing countries), leading to persistent trade surpluses and deficits for each respective group.
2. Gradual acceleration of the generally one-way trade flow over time.
3. Ongoing international trade disputes between several exporting and importing countries involving the product in question.
4. A pattern of dumping, subsidization, or other unfair practices that affect world trade in the product, or extensive participation in world trade by nonmarket economies.

5. Discrepancies in the degree of market access among nations due to the relative level of formal and informal tariff and nonmarket barriers.

GOVERNMENT POLICIES

1. Current or historical government-aided or -sponsored industrial targeting programs in exporting countries.
2. Historical financial and technical assistance from the United States, other countries, or international organizations that aided the development of the industry in the exporting countries.
3. Significant differences between the laws and regulations of the importing countries and the laws and regulations of exporting countries regarding factors that affect costs of production (e.g., environmental standards, industrial health and safety standards).

Export-Oriented Industries. In the context of the application of managed trade, several critical differences exist for export-oriented industries, in comparison with more mature, import-competing industries. Primary among them is the present international competitiveness of such U.S. industries and the export success that has flowed from that competitiveness. The obvious pitfall of introducing managed trade in this situation is the potential inhibition of export success,[63] as well as the potential restriction of the natural flow of human resources and investment to these industries necessary to maintain competitiveness and to create new products and future exports.

A second difference is that international trade pressures on export-oriented industries do not stem directly from a combination of the inherent characteristics of the products or production process, differences in natural factor endowments among countries, and wide disparities in national income levels. Rather, these pressures flow from deliberate industrial strategies adopted by competing countries. These strategies represent government-sponsored market intervention designed to marshall resources not otherwise available to aid domestic industries. Such strategies may include direct government assistance in research and development, the pooling of capital and markets by several individual countries, the simultaneous restriction of foreign investment and the encouragement of technology purchases, export finance subsidies, performance requirements, liberal government regulations regarding industry structure and cooperation, or nonreciprocal access to domestic markets.

The source of trade pressures on export-oriented industries is thus considerably different from more mature, import-competing industries. Likewise, the prescription for their resolution and the application of managed trade must also be correspondingly different. However, the twin goals of managed trade remain the same, namely the minimization of disruption to existing industries and the continued promotion of international trade.

Although a principal sanction of an MFA-type solution for export-oriented industries would be potential restrictions of product markets, the focus of the arrangement would be on the actions and programs of participating governments that distort trade patterns. Such a managed trade arrangement would identify specific trade-distorting practices (e.g., export financing subsidies, performance requirements, restrictions on foreign investment, or restricted market access) to be avoided or controlled by all parties.

A surveillance body could be assigned the responsibility of monitoring such practices as well as trade flows among countries. A country would have the right to consult with any other country regarding any of the identifiable practices that are having or have had a damaging impact on its own given industry (either in the form of increasing imports into the country, a loss of exports to other markets, or lack of market access). If the consultations do not satisfactorily eliminate the offending practice in a short period of time, the injured country would be permitted to invoke appropriate sanctions (e.g., import controls or selective reciprocal behavior). Such a formalized arrangement would be designed to reinforce market forces in international trade in the given product with a minimum of government intervention in trade flows and a maximum of cooperation among signatory countries.

The following suggested criteria describe the conditions under which such a system of managed trade would apply to export-oriented industries.

INDUSTRY AND PRODUCT CHARACTERISTICS

1. Existence of significant-sized industries in a number of individual countries, size being defined in terms of the quantity and scope of products produced, the financial resources available to support research and development, and the amount of accumulated capital invested in the industry.
2. Relatively concentrated industries due to capital-intensity, the high cost of necessary research and development, and the related high risk of market success.
3. Heavy reliance of the industry on new technological developments not generally available.

4. Products having significant economic or strategic use, with widespread application in industry, defense, or research.
5. Products characterized by rapid technological change and short cycle of obsolescence.
6. Extensive internationl trade both among the major producing countries and between major producing and nonproducing countries.

INTERNATIONAL TRADE CONSIDERATIONS

1. Trade flows characterized by rapid expansion of demand as products are developed.
2. Rapid shifts in trade flows among countries related to rapid product cycles and success of individual countries in developing competing or new products.
3. Ongoing international trade disputes among producing countries.

GOVERNMENT POLICIES

1. A pattern of current or historical government intervention in and support of industry development.

CONCLUSION

As the foregoing criteria suggest, a system of managed trade is hardly appropriate for each industry or for every instance of international trade conflict. The application of managed trade is feasible only in the cases of significant industrial sectors making products heavily traded among numerous producing and consuming countries. Moreover, there must be a history of international conflict among the major countries producing and consuming the product, with no near-term prospects for resolution of the conflict.

Where the conditions do apply, however, managed trade must be considered an attractive means of ameliorating not only international economic and political conflict but their negative economic and political repercussions within individual countries. Indeed, a formal managed trade arrangement that replaces the often chaotic, uncoordinated, and widely divergent economic behavior and policies of individual countries could act to reduce uncertainty in world markets, reduce unnecessary worldwide redundancy in individual industries, and lead eventually to a more efficient, rational, and open trading system.

American political and economic leaders face tough choices regarding the present international competitiveness of our manufacturing industries. Ironically, the current problems largely result from the U.S. government's own past policies and reflect the success of such efforts to foster economic growth in our allies and trading partners. U.S. historical leadership here has flowed naturally from its international political and economic self-interest.

However, while American international political interests remain largely intact, the balance of our trade policies' economic gains and costs is no longer clearly positive. Relative stagnation in the United States and other advanced countries during the past decade has forced us to recognize that our resources for meeting domestic economic and social goals are limited. As a result, we must increasingly and more clearly evaluate the effects of our trade policy in relation to domestic economic needs rather than to global welfare or foreign interests. This is largely a political issue. When do the traditional trade policy's costs to the American economy outweigh the benefits of selected international objectives? Are there means other than trade that can achieve some of these objectives? The debate will continue to intensify, and exceptions to the U.S. traditional free trade posture, such as the MFA, will be a central topic.

Exhibit 6-1

U.S. Imports, Exports, and Trade Balances for Textiles and Apparel, Annual 1960-82 and January-September 1982 and 1983 F.A.S. Values ($ millions)

	Textiles			Apparel			Textiles and Apparel		
	Imports	Exports	Trade Balance	Imports	Exports	Trade Balance	Imports	Exports	Trade Balance
1960	na	na	na	na	na	na	886	618	-268
1961	na	na	na	na	na	na	773	578	-195
1962	na	na	na	na	na	na	1,013	580	-433
1963	na	na	na	na	na	na	1,074	583	-491
1964	na	na	na	na	na	na	1,132	681	-451
1965	na	na	na	na	na	na	1,342	640	-702
1966	908	554	-354	608	125	-483	1,516	679	-837
1967	812	531	-281	649	164	-485	1,461	695	-766
1968	963	522	-441	855	176	-679	1,818	698	-1,120
1969	1,019	576	-443	1,106	209	-897	2,125	785	-1,340
1970	1,135	603	-532	1,267	200	-1,067	2,402	803	-1,599
1971	1,392	632	-760	1,521	204	-1,317	2,913	836	-2,077
1972	1,526	779	-747	1,883	240	-1,643	3,409	1,019	-2,390
1973	1,568	1,225	-343	2,168	278	-1,890	3,736	1,503	-2,333
1974	1,621	1,795	+180	2,331	400	-1,931	3,952	2,195	-1,757
1975	1,219	1,625	+406	2,562	403	-2,159	3,781	2,028	-1,753
1976	1,635	1,970	+335	3,634	510	-3,124	5,269	2,480	-2,789
1977	1,772	1,959	+187	4,154	608	-3,546	5,926	2,567	-3,359
1978	2,200	2,225	+25	5,657	677	-4,980	7,857	2,902	-4,955
1979	2,216	3,189	+973	5,876	931	-4,945	8,092	4,120	-3,972
1980	2,493	3,632	+1,139	6,427	1,202	-5,224	8,920	4,834	-4,086
1981	3,046	3,619	+573	7,537	1,232	-6,305	10,583	4,851	-5,732
1982	2,807	2,784	-23	8,165	953	-7,212	10,972	3,736	-7,236
1983	3,225	2,368	-857	9,583	818	-8,765	12,808	3,186	-9,622

Source: U.S. government data in American Textile Manufacturers Institute, *Textile Hi-Lights*, various issues.
Note: Textile balance of trade equals exports minus imports.

Exhibit 6-2

Hourly Compensation Costs for Production Workers in
Textile Mill Products Manufacturing in Selected
Countries, 1979 and 1981 (in U.S. $)

	1979	*1981*[a]
United States	$5.78	$6.91
Korea	0.96	0.93
Taiwan	0.90	1.46
Hong Kong	1.32	1.58

Source: U.S. Department of Labor, Bureau of Labor Statistics,
Office of Productivity and Technology, unpublished data on the
Hourly Compensation Costs for Production Workers in Textile
Mill Products Manufacturing in 25 countries, 1975-81, April
1983.

[a]Data for 1981 are preliminary estimates.

Exhibit 6-3

The Number of Product Categories Subject
to Specific Restraint Levels in 1983

Brazil	4
China (PRC)	33
Costa Rica	1
Egypt	0
Haiti	9
Hong Kong	34
Hungary	3
India	10
Indonesia	3
Japan	11
Korea	42
Macau	22
Malaysia	14
Maldives	2
Mauritius	10
Mexico	14
Pakistan	11
Philippines	46
Poland	26
Romania	9
Singapore	22
Sri Lanka	17
Taiwan	34

(continued)

Exhibit 6-3
The Number of Product Categories Subject
to Specific Restraint Levels in 1983
(*continued*)

Thailand	22
Yugoslavia	2

Source: *Performance Report, Textile and Apparel Bilateral Agreements and Unilateral Import Restraints*, Office of Textiles and Apparel, U.S. Department of Commerce, Washington, D.C., July 1983.

Note: There are 109 textile and apparel product categories. There are a number of specific restraints levels that came into effect after publication of source.

Exhibit 6-4
U.S. Imports of Textiles and Apparel from Hong Kong, Taiwan, and Korea, 1982 and 1983 (quantity in millions of square yards equivalent)

	1982	*1983*	*Percent Change*
Hong Kong	843	952	+13
Taiwan	938	1,178	+26
Korea	764	968	+27

Source: *Textile and Apparel Import Report*, Office of Textiles and Apparel, U.S. Department of Commerce, February 1984.

7

Restructuring Petrochemicals: A Comparative Study of Business and Government Strategy to Deal with a Declining Sector of the Economy

Joseph L. Bower

Other chapters in this book assert that the United States is losing out in the battle among manufacturing nations. In some areas, however, the United States is winning because well-managed companies in the context of supportive government policies have done a good job. At the same time, in some countries, including Japan, efforts to help industry, of the sort often advocated currently in the United States, have not been successful. In fact, government interventions sometimes have led to a misguided development of industry and now may be slowing down or politicizing the response to changed economic circumstances.

The world petrochemical industry is an example. The U.S. producers have done well, exports have been high, and until the last decade, profits were good. Then as rising raw material prices changed the character of the business, the U.S. industry restructured; all but the strongest chemical companies exited. In Europe and Japan the story has been different: chemical companies with government support continued to enter or build capacity even as the successive oil shocks demonstrated that competition would favor those with cheap raw material. In Europe today an assortment of manufacturers fight for small pieces of market share and earn huge losses. In Japan, a dozen giants encouraged into place by the Ministry of International Trade and Industry (MITI) fight for position in a market half the size of Europe or the

Joseph L. Bower is professor of business administration at Harvard Business School.

263

United States, all of them handicapped by dependence on expensive raw material, all of them losing money.

Ideally, this chapter will be read as a cautionary tale by those eager to substitute elaborate government intervention for the working of the market. Evidence shows that the governments of France, Italy, and Japan bear significant responsibility for the poor economic condition that the companies experience today. Their policies of regional subsidies and encouragement of basic industry have resulted in a poorly located and configured chemical industry. If reducing excess capacity and rationalizing of industry structure are taken as performance measures, private action by firms in the United Kingdom and United States have produced the most impressive results. This has permitted firms in the United States and the United Kingdom, along with the Germans, to reposition themselves to do battle in the 1980s.

It currently appears that the commodity plastics business will move into the hands of (1) state-owned and privately owned oil companies with low raw material costs; (2) state-owned chemical companies with a tolerance for large losses; and (3) private chemical companies with strong technology and inexpensive chlorine. In turn, the traditional chemical companies have already shifted their portfolios to emphasize new, higher value-added products.

As a consequence, the United States on balance is expected to lose commodity chemical exports of $8 billion. At the same time, a wide range of new products should take their place along with royalties and other fees from the operations now being constructed with U.S. technology in the hydrocarbon-rich countries.

This evolution, which has taken place over several decades, reflects an apparently unusual combination of intensive competition among leading U.S. companies that have developed an extensive cooperation with government in areas like trade policy.[1] This chapter describes this evolution: the way an overcapacity problem has developed to plague the world's largest industry, petrochemicals; why there is a need for restructuring; how companies and governments have responded to this need; and what the implications of their response and the consequences appear to be.

THE WORLD PETROCHEMICAL INDUSTRY IN TRANSITION

OVERVIEW

It is estimated that the free world petrochemical industry in 1980 manufactured goods worth $390 billion (32 percent in the United States). Many of these industrial and consumer products require hydrocarbon gas or liquid as raw material, like polyethylene or polystyrene resin, which are, in turn, converted to film or foam used in trash bags and coffee cups. While many participants in the industry are engaged in the entire chain of activity from oil and gas exploration to the sale of consumer products, the industry proper is usually described as beginning with the production of primary aromatics and olefins from the feedstock, and ending with the manufacture of organic intermediates such as vinyl acetate, polyethylene, ethylene glycol, and nylon resin and fiber. The problem with this description is that ethylene glycol is both the material used by the final consumer as antifreeze and the raw material for polyester. Moreover, by-products of an intermediate stage may be recycled and used in an early stage.

The situation is even more complex: (1) there are generally several technological routes to a particular process. Indeed, improvements in process technology can be very dramatic, sometimes skipping several steps in an antecedent process. When such breakthroughs occur, much existing capacity becomes obsolete. (2) The facilities used to produce petrochemicals are large, expensive, and difficult to operate. A complete complex of ethylene cracker and derivative units will cost over $1 billion. Five years or more are needed to plan and construct a production facility, and during that time, technology, demand, and competition may change. (3) No two companies produce the same product mix. A minor by-product for one is often a core business of another. (4) The products are often hard to differentiate and easy to transport, hence the markets are global. Shifts in currency value are, therefore, of great importance to relative competitiveness. The rise of the dollar increased raw material costs for non-U.S. producers and the collapse of the French franc improved the competitiveness of French products as long as the government held the price in francs fixed.

For most countries, the development of a petrochemical industry was relatively recent and rapid. Plastics and synthetic fibers quickly penetrated the economy so that the ratio of industry growth to GNP growth was 1.3-1.5 during much of the postwar period. With steadily declining real costs to the user and an unending array of new applications, growth seemed limitless. The industry's original participants, the chemical companies, flourished and many others entered. In the United States, the oil companies saw an opportunity to invest their tremendous cash flow profitably, while numerous firms in mature industries such as shipping, tires, and steel saw an opportunity to escape secular decline. In Japan, each of the major industrial groups entered, sometimes with their long-established chemical producer (Sumitomo) and sometimes with a new organized venture (Mitsui Petrochemical). Then the original chemical companies followed, as did some oil companies. In Europe, the chemical companies were joined by oil companies, coal producers, and national governments seeking to stake out a claim in the new technology.

By 1972 the industry was crowded with giant producers poised to exploit the growth in demand. Then four major trends developed that converted this prospect from prosperity to catastrophe: feedstock prices increased, technology improved yields, the world economy entered a prolonged recession, and new sources of product loomed on the horizon.

Feedstock Prices. Prior to the escalation of oil and gas prices in the early 1970s, petrochemicals was a business of high fixed costs and low variable cost, roughly 70/30. By the early 1980s petrochemicals had become a high variable cost business with feedstock and fuel cost eating up a much higher fraction of the final price.[2] Variable costs reached 70 percent; total cost of a modern facility had increased; and the cost of debt was high.

A second major consequence of higher prices was that chemicals and plastics became more expensive relative to substitutes. For this reason, and because penetration of the economy had already been extensive, the relationship of chemicals growth to GNP growth fell from 1.3 to 1.0.

Technology. At the same time that companies were scraping around for cash flow, new technology emerged that made dramatically better use of feedstock, fuel, and facilities. A leading example of such a breakthrough was Union Carbide's development of a low-pressure route to linear low-density polyethylene (LLDPE). Since the new process was fuel efficient, and its capital cost was one-half a conventional facility, polyethylene producers all faced the potential obsolescence of their old capacity. Moreover, Dow, Du Pont, BP, and CdF Chimie all raced to the market with alternative processes.

Almost as challenging to capital budgets of companies under economic pressure were stricter laws about the production and disposal of toxic substances. Although the industry was supportive of improved health and safety, the diversion of scarce cash flow to modify new and existing facilities further depressed profitability.

Global Recession. A massive industry such as petrochemicals cannot grow when the GNP is stagnant. In the early 1980s the recession was especially punishing: prolonged slow growth, combined with decelerating penetration, higher yields, and new capacity in Europe—built to meet the optimistic forecasts made in the mid-1970s—resulted in very sick businesses. For those companies, such as Dow that financed new capacity with debt, or Du Pont and Occidental that financed acquisitions with debt, the low-growth and high-interest rates of the early 1980s were painful. Figure 7-1 shows Shell's summary forecast of the European situation—excess supply into the 1990s.

Sources of Supply. As if these three forces were not enough, OECD producers now faced new sources of supply. The nations that owned the feedstocks—the Arabs, along with Canada, Indonesia, Mexico, and Norway—were all moving to gather in some of the value added by building ethylene crackers and derivative units. These countries' plans are shown in table 7-1. Although construction of many of these units was postponed, in 1984 there was every reason to believe that when demand revives, these projects will be revived. From a global economic perspective, it makes sense that a business 70 percent dependent on fuel and feedstock develops where those raw materials are cheapest. All major studies of the industry's future trade pattern (e.g., Shell, U.S. Department of Commerce, French Ministry of

Figure 7-1

Ethylene Demand and Capacity in Western Europe 1972-90

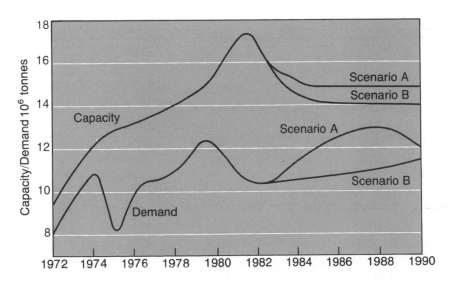

Source: Shell International Chemical Co., June 1983.

Table 7-1

Planned Petrochemical Capacity (in 1,000x metric tons)

	Ethylene	Low-Density Poly-ethy-lene	Poly-ethy-lene	High-Density Poly ethy-lene	Poly-propy-lene	Ethylene Dichloride and Vinyl Chloride	Styrene
Saudi Arabia	1,610	460	310	90		450	300
Singapore	300	120		80	100		
Indonesia	300	280		60		110	
Mexico	1,600	360					
Canada	2,000	910		375		190	507[a]

Source: *The Economist*

[a]Ethylbenzene (styrene's precursor)

Industry, Chem Systems) forecast a shift in ethylene and derivative trade flows. OECD producers are expected to lose markets to the Arabian Gulf and Canada.

Although only Japan is expected to become a major importer of ethylene or derivatives, the loss of export markets means that growth in demand for OECD producers will be further constrained. For major chemical exporters like Germany and the United States, the impact on companies and on the balance of payments can be severe. The U.S. petrochemical trade surplus in 1981 was $8.3 billion (10 percent of shipments). Nonetheless U.S. share of world organic chemicals[3] fell from 25.5 percent in 1970 to 16.9 percent in 1980. West Germany held just over 20 percent (see table 7-2).

THE NEED FOR RESTRUCTURING

The forces described above are large and sweeping in scope, battering even the giants that populate the industry. One would expect some attrition and that in time capacity would come into rough balance with demand—in a word, restructuring. This is one of the most important tasks a market should accomplish. But the fact is the industry has not behaved as one would have expected if only the market was at work. While some firms have exited the business, other companies have shown a substantial willingness to absorb major losses. This has been true of France and Italy where we have come to expect such things, and in Germany where we have not. And in Japan, where we expect order and coherence, there has been chaos—one chairman called

Table 7-2
Percentage Share of World Exports—Organic Chemicals[a]

Year	United States	West Germany	Japan	Netherlands	U.K.	France
1970	25.5%	20.7%	9.5%	8.8%	7.7%	6.6%
1971	21.7	20.3	11.4	9.7	8.1	6.5
1972	20.4	19.6	12.1	11.2	7.6	6.5
1973	20.1	22.0	8.3	11.9	8.1	7.5
1974	18.0	21.5	10.1	13.2	9.0	7.0
1975	19.6	20.4	10.2	12.0	8.3	7.2
1976	19.9	21.1	9.3	12.7	8.6	6.5
1977	19.8	21.5	9.6	11.5	8.9	6.9
1978	14.8	21.8	9.6	11.5	9.3	10.8
1979	15.8	22.0	8.0	12.0	9.6	10.8
1980	16.9	21.2	7.8	13.8	10.3	10.6

Source: International Trade Administration market share data; Bureau of Industry Economics, Department of Commerce.
[a]Percentage based on U.S. dollar value

it "stupid competition"—and lack of cooperation. The desire of major companies to bleed each other has been awesome.

Figure 7-2 reveals some of what has occurred. It traces the market share for manufacturers of high-density polyethylene (HDPE) in Europe, Japan, and the United States. In Europe, Hoechst is regarded as the leading producer, based on its market position and technology; it is equally significant that Sarda Polimeri and British Petroleum UK, which so markedly increased their share, are regarded as efficient but not leaders. Moreover, their new capacity was added when demand was stagnant.

A different picture can be observed in the United States, where certain chemical companies have lost position to others, but especially to the chemical company subsidiaries of oil companies. For example, the figure shows that U.S. chemical companies went from 70 percent of the market in 1960 to 32 percent in 1980. In the process, Grace, Monsanto, Celanese, and Hercules exited the business. Finally in Japan, the original three competitors now share the market with eight others, the smallest of which has significant absolute scale.

Thus, restructuring has been going on, but:

1. In addition to the number and size of the competitors, it has involved the kind of company participating. There has been a shift from private

Figure 7-2

Comparative High-Density Market Share

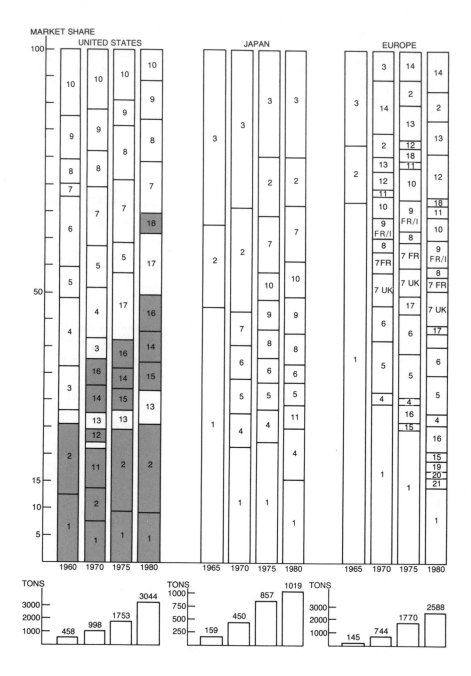

UNITED STATES   (shaded areas denote oil companies)

Key	Company Name	Type
1	National Petrochemical	oil
2	Philips	oil
3	Hercules	chemical
4	Celanese	chemical
5	Monsanto	chemical
6	W.R. Grace	chemical
7	Allied	chemical
8	Dow	chemical
9	Du Pont	chemical
10	Union Carbide	chemical
11	Sinclair	oil
12	Getty	oil
13	Chemalex	chemical
14	Amoco	oil
15	Arco	oil
16	Gulf	oil
17	Solvay	chemical
18	City Service	oil

JAPAN

Key	Company Name
1	Showa Denko
2	Nippon Petrochemical
3	Mitsui Petrochemical
4	Mitsubishi Chemical
5	Chisso Petrochemical
6	Mitsubishi Petrochemical
7	Asahi Chemical
8	Shin-Daikyowa
9	Nissan-Maruzen
10	Idemitsu
11	Tonen Petrochemical

EUROPE

Key	Company Name	Country
1	Hoechst	Germany
2	Dutch State Mines	Netherlands
33	Shell	UK/Netherlands
4	Calatrava	Spain
5	Huls	Germany
6	Ruhr Chemie	Germany
7FR	British Petroleum—France	France
7UK	British Petroleum—UK	United Kingdom
8	Rhone Poulenc	France
9FR/I	Solvay	(Italy and France)
10	Belgium Polyolefins	Belgium
11	Rumianca Sud	Italy
12	Sarda Polemeri	Italy
13	Montedison	Italy
14	Row-Shell & Basf.	UK/Netherlands/Germany
15	Wacker	Germany
16	Unifos	Sweden
17	ATO	France
18	Anic	Italy
19	Taqsa	Spain
20	Portugal Empresa de Polimeros	Portugal
21	Norpolefin	Norway

Source: McKinsey & Co. Chemical Industry Data Base; Mitsui & Co.

chemical companies toward state-owned enterprises and oil companies.

2. Despite the restructuring that has taken place, every forecast indicates that capacity will continue to exceed demand for a long time. Either the market is not working the way it is expected to, or it is taking a very long time to do its work.

THE RESPONSE BY COMPANIES AND GOVERNMENTS

During the period 1980-83, in response to the forces described, some 20 percent of OECD ethylene capacity has been shut down (but construction has continued in France and the United Kingdom). Derivative capacity has also been significantly reduced. Perhaps equally interesting has been the decline in the number of manufacturers.

COMPANIES

For the producers of commodity petrochemicals the recent period has been a disaster with huge losses with no prospect of an end to competitive pressures. When interviewed, top managers of the major companies of the industry reveal they *all* experienced the above problems in their current thinking about strategy. They knew their task was to reposition their company so that strength in feedstock, technology, product, or market could be translated into profit or they would have to exit. But accomplishing such a shift posed major problems:

1. Competition—there seemed to be too many firms with staying power.
2. Social obligation—in several countries, legal or moral obligations to the labor force or small customers seemed to block needed cost reductions and shutdowns.
3. State policies—either as owners or competitors, certain governments demonstrated a commitment to take a permanent significant position in the industry despite a weak initial—*or prospective*—economic base in the industry.
4. Finance—many of the moves that firms might wish to make required capital which they lacked because of the long period of losses, the high interest rates, and low stock price. External markets were closed and prices could not be raised to generate profit without a concerted suspension of competition.

5. Regulation—it has been traditional in the industrial markets of the West to form cartels when conditions made competition untenable and exit was unattractive or impossible. But the antitrust laws of certain countries and of the European Community hindered attempts to find cooperative solutions.

As they examined their portfolios, one firm after another recognized that they had to withdraw from all or part of the business. Others concluded that they must acquire their competition or remain ineffectively small. And still others sought profit in specialties or end-product businesses.

GOVERNMENTS

For several governments the crisis of the 1980s was not something to be ignored. In the 1950s and 1960s, several had intervened to stimulate the development of the industry. They were owners, bankers, or observer/ regulators of the industry. For them the existence and shape of their nation's petrochemical industry was an issue of national strategic significance, not merely corporate.

Moreover, in 1983 Europe's economy was reeling from the effects of the two oil shocks, the extended global recession, and high U.S. interest rates. In steel and fibers there had been concerted action to take capacity off the market so that the remaining competitors might survive. The European Commission's Industry Directorate under Viscount d'Avignon had supported two major restructurings by producers. And most of the major producers cooperated in subscribing to a detailed analysis of their problems by a private consulting firm, Chem Systems, that explicitly displayed their relative position, cracker by cracker and derivative unit by derivative unit on what were called "survival matrices."

In Japan, new leadership at the chemical desk in MITI collaborated with the industry structure council to study the apparently permanent weakness of certain depressed industries in Japan including aluminum, ferro alloys, fertilizers, fibers, and petrochemicals.

Inside the U.S. federal government, 1983 had the potential to become the year of petrochemicals, as studies of U.S. competitiveness and trade were conducted by the Department of Commerce, and the International Trade Council (ITC). There was also a major petrochemical dumping suit tried before the ITC and protectionist legislation filed in Congress.

For governments the problem was similar but not the same as for steel and fibers. Balance of payments and, perhaps, national security were involved, but the employment issues were quite small. Labor accounted for only 8-9 percent of chemical industry costs and consequently employment in the industry was less significant on a national basis. Nonetheless, regional issues could be important, as in Ludwigshaven, where BASF employed around 50,000 people.

The range of government response was dramatic:

1. France nationalized the entire French-owned portion of the chemical industry and regrouped the pieces into near monopolists. For example, Elf took over French production of all the commodity petrochemicals discussed, except for some units of CdF Chimie, which were also under consideration for movement to Elf.
2. Italy consolidated six companies into two, consolidated all of the commodity plastics save polypropylene into ENI, and reprivatized Montedison.
3. Germany's cartel office kept a close watch on the independent moves of gigantic BASF, Bayer, and Hoeschst.

IMPLICATIONS

1. Much of what happens in the industry can only be understood in terms of the desires and plans of nation states trying to improve their economic well-being by using their natural resources, their capital, and their buying power in a concerted, planned effort to help the nation prosper.
2. Good intentions are no more a substitute for good management at the state level than at the company level. But where a nation will borrow or print money to fund a corporate national champion, a well-managed private competitor can be hurt or destroyed. That is the dilemma of the Germans facing French and Italian competition.
3. Nonetheless, in petrochemicals, perhaps because employment is a less salient issue, raw material costs, technological advantage, or product development can neutralize the state's advantage. Without one of the three, there is every reason to expect that, left to themselves, privately owned competitors will withdraw in the presence of state-sponsored competition.
4. In the summer of 1983, governments were urging three different postures on the petrochemical industry: retrenchment with more imports, rationalization, or protection of the status quo. These positions

were built upon mixed foundations of ideology, analysis, and private self-interest.

5. For the United States, the position is extremely complex. The lowest-cost producer worldwide may well be Exxon, based in Scotland and Saudi Arabia. Among those most hurt may be American commodity chemical producers. But Union Carbide and others are well on their way toward turning parts of their companies into specialty/service businesses. Finally, the future of chemicals is expected to be in an entirely new set of materials. A move toward protection could very easily represent an investment in the past.

THE SITUATION IN THE MAJOR INDUSTRIAL NATIONS

The situation facing chemical company managements and national governments is better understood after a brief review of the industry's history and prospects in each of the major producing countries. When considering European countries, the role of the European Commission is also important.[4]

FRANCE

The French petrochemical industry developed in the shadow of the Germans almost as a by-product of the activities of coal, aluminum, textiles, and oil. Facilities were dispersed around the country near raw material or ports, and for many years, to reduce risk and capital required, most were conceived and managed as joint ventures.

The weakness of their industry and the French participants' preoccupations is important to keep in mind when considering the role played by the French government. At first, French governments left chemicals alone, except for the influence of regional policy that further fragmented the industry. More recently, French industrial policy has become more dirigiste, and the Ministry of Industry focused on the chemical industry. Government investments were needed if France was to have a modern French-owned chemical industry, yet most of its participating companies were weak. Since all the players were now government related through ownership or financing, nationalization was a more logical step here than elsewhere, and in the summer of 1983, the French petrochemical industry became fully nationalized. At the time, France had shut down fewer of its producing units than any of the other major countries, citing problems with the work force as the main reason.

The German chemical industry is unique: the three largest chemical companies in the world, BASF, Hoechst, and Bayer (with Conoco added, Du Pont is now bigger) are based in an economy one-third the size of the United States. A fourth large German company, Huels, is the chemical group of a partially government-controlled diversified energy group Veba/AG.

In 1983 BASF was a vertically integrated petrochemical, plastics, and fertilizer producer (50 percent of its sales), with important dye and consumer product businesses. Most of their European activities were carried on at a single integrated complex in Ludwigshaven that employed around 50,000 of the company's 116,000 personnel. With 18 percent of Europe's polystyrene market (number one), 14 percent of low-density polyethylene (number one), 8 percent of high-density polyethylene, and 11 percent polypropylene, BASF was the leading plastics producer in Europe.

Hoechst is the leading producer of HDPE in Europe, although its market share has eroded from more than 30 percent at the time of the first oil crisis to less than 20 percent today. It has the number two position in polypropylene, and strong positions based on good technology in polystyrene and polyvinyl chloride (PVC). Despite its strength, Hoechst's market position has eroded in the face of newly constructed capacity based on cheaper raw material. Losses have been serious. When the company's strategic planners review the corporate portfolio, they find a striking contrast between the strong competitive position and poor performance. It is widely debated whether Hoechst will exit one or more of its plastics businesses.

Of the three companies Bayer is the least involved in petrochemicals. It manufactures ethylene and low-density polyethylene in a 50:50 joint venture at Cologne with BP called Erdolchemie. The venture has operated near breakeven, but serves as an important source of propylene, and other hydrocarbons used by Bayer in its other chemical businesses. In the 1980s, reflecting its specialty-oriented product mix, it has been the most profitable of the three.

Veba AG is Germany's largest industrial enterprise and diversified group. It is 44 percent owned by the government. Chemische Werke Huels AG is owned 88 percent by Veba. Despite the poor performance of its chemical group, Huels is thought to be sufficiently strong financially to wait out the present crisis without exiting any of its positions.

As the largest market in Europe, Germany is a strong base for the leading exporters. Historically, Germany has penetrated the EEC and other countries, but exports are a lower percentage of sales than, for example, for the Dutch whose industry has been built primarily for export. In the last year, however, production, sales, and exports were down, while imports—especially from the Eastern bloc—increased 5 percent.

For various reasons, the Germans have headed the battle to cut capacity in commodity plastics without state aid. The Big Three companies are all privately held and leaders of the conservative business community. And though deeply involved in the German chemical industry association (VKE) and the Association of Plastics Manufacturers in Europe (APME), the company managements are very sensitive to the surveillance of the cartel office in Berlin. In a Europe rife with meetings in 1982 and 1983, there were no stories of discussions among the Germans.

ITALY

Traditionally, the Italian chemical industry was considered the "bad boy" of Europe, its producers expanding rapidly and dumping product. And the situation in the spring of 1983 was critical for the participants, the country, and for Europe. The state had restructured the industry into a giant, publicly owned bulk chemical and fiber company—Enichemica (ENI), and a giant, privately owned specialty, fine chemical, fertilizer and fiber firm—Montedison.

These two giants had formidable positions in all the major commodity plastics. If costs could be reduced, profitability might lie ahead and Italy could, for once, contribute to the stability of European chemical markets. Costs, however, were high because of excess labor costs, low productivity, and high interest expense. The new managements at Enichemica and Montedison faced formidable challenges as they tried to revitalize management cadres, lay off workers, and fight for major equity investments from a government under perpetual pressure from strong unions.

In the spring of 1983, the socialist minister of state participation announced that the plants' staff had to be reduced, and so the managements of ENI and Montedison—figuratively crossing their fingers and holding their breath—were proceeding to cut back capacity in ethylene and derivatives by 25 percent to 33 percent.

In short, Italy's more disciplined approach to the industry depended in part on the success of the Montedison strategy and in part on the ability of Enichemica's management to turn around a very uncomfortable mix of facilities, products, and people. This, in turn, depended on the government's willingness to fund both interim losses and investments in modernization and rationalization.

UNITED KINGDOM

The chemical industry in Britain is basically the result of four major developments: the building of Imperial Chemical Industries, Ltd. (ICI), followed by the decline of its competitive position in the 1960s and 1970s; the development of Shell's chemical activity; the development of Union Carbide and Distiller Ltd.'s chemical business and their acquisition by BP; the decision of Essochem to build a major olefin facility at Mossmoran, Scotland, based on North Sea gas in a joint venture with Shell.

From 1981 to 1983, industry capacity was transformed dramatically when ICI, the inventor of polyethylene, swapped its facilities for making that product with BP in return for the latter's PCV facility. Both proceeded to rationalize their positions with reductions, but the result was to leave Britain with fewer but stronger competitors.

British Petroleum is a 50:50 private-public corporation. Originally organized to control Britain's Middle Eastern exploration and production activities. It entered chemicals through a series of acquisitions; the inherited assortment of activities was a weak basis for competition. In 1979, BP proceeded with a series of studies, a reorganization, and some consolidation that reduced manpower from 18,000 to 11,000. In 1982, it became clear that more radical change was needed. BP had a very valuable asset, North Sea-based ethane; they were strong in polyethylene; they were too small in PVC and had to exit. Out of these assessments came the ICI deal. It was better to swap than scrap.

In 1926 a series of mergers produced Imperial Chemical Industries Ltd. Its line of explosives, dyes, fertilizers, and pharmaceuticals closely resembled the rival German companies. Cartel arrangements had enabled ICI to concentrate its activities on the United Kingdom, the Commonwealth, and to an extent, South America; Du Pont and its U.S. rivals held the U.S. market, while IG Farben and Solvay dominated the continent.

In 1983 the company had remained profitable over the entire previous decade, but profit before interest and taxation as a percentage of average assets employed had declined dramatically from 18 percent in 1973 to 7.4 percent in 1982. To deal with this decline, in April 1982 there was a dramatic shakeup and trimming of top management and corporate overhead, and then a tradition-shattering reorganization. Studies revealed that ICI possessed fundamental strengths in PVC but weakness in polyethylene. Division management reasoned that if they could exit polyethylene, they could reduce their need for ethylene. BP was approached and a deal was struck in June, with a 1 August completion date. Speed was considered essential. Externally, it was important to present a clear, worked-out package. BP and ICI each approached the Board of Trade and presented their case. In essence they said, "We have done our strategic planning, chosen to emphasize this business and exit that one. It is more economic and socially satisfactory if we trade our facilities than if we shut down." The deal was approved by the board, reportedly after Cabinet-level discussion.

Shell. Having entered olefins prior to World War II, Shell built olefin facilities in conjunction with refineries exploiting good feedstock situations provided by its producing and trading parent. From this sound position in olefins, Shell has built a base of commodity business on which it has sought to construct a portfolio of high value-added, more specialized businesses. Within commodities, they are more balanced toward propylene and its derivatives than other competitors, especially the other oil companies. Working in all private forums, the company has been prominent in efforts to get European companies to restructure the industry.

Thus, compared with France and Italy, the situation is closer to that in Germany, a result of private decisions taken by private companies. The major influence of the U.K. government has been its management of the North Sea gas resource, its monetary and trade policy, and its labor laws.

EUROPEAN ORGANIZATION

Europe has an old tradition of collective action expressed in the desire to set up cartels. At the same time, great private companies know they are in a near war to stay independent and beat back the socialist tide. Consequently, while collective action to deal with overcapacity in Europe is obviously useful, the British and Germans are reluctant, and they are the only two groups of financially strong and legally independent companies among the EEC states who could take part. It is against this ambiguous background that the Council of European Federations of Industrial Chemicals (CEFIC) and the European Commission should be considered.

CEFIC

In the fall of 1982, the leaders of two of CEFIC's more troubled groups—Jacques Solvay (Solvay) and Rene Malla (Rhone Pulenc)—approached Viscount Etienne d'Avignon of the European Commission's Industry Directorate and asked if he would organize a capacity reduction in petrochemicals of the sort arranged in fibers. D'Avignon said he would support such an effort but took exception to using the commission's offices. Instead, nine CEFIC members met with D'Avignon to discuss the problems. BASF and BP were not present, nor were Dow, Exxon, or any U.S. company.

A report was written and then circulated in April 1983. The British and Germans objected strongly to findings that proposed a cutback in activity proportionate with volume rather than in accordance with efficiency or some market-driven measure. At a meeting of the nine members in May the report was considered finished. Nevertheless, the members subsequently proceeded to work together, trying to find a cooperative basis for European restructuring.

THE EUROPEAN COMMISSION

Viscount d'Avignon has tried over the last several years to help the states of Europe deal cooperatively with the problems of industrial competition that are endangering the fragile European bonds. In one industry after another, companies have been unable to withstand the ravages of lower demand, increased raw materials and energy costs, social democracy in the work force and the tax system, and efficient competition from overseas—East Asia or the United States.

DG IV (Directorate General IV) is the directorate of the European Commission responsible for the enforcement of articles 85 and 86 of the Treaty of Rome—the Common Market's antitrust laws. Compared to U.S. law the provisions are quite tolerant of conversations and agreements among competitors—so that discussions of joint capacity cutbacks in the face of disastrous markets are legal. Conspiring to raise price or injure competitors is clearly prohibited, however, and there is some ambiguity as to DG IV's true policy. In 1984, DG IV investigated the BP/ICI deal, as well as an alleged conspiracy in polypropylene.

SUMMARY

As long as so many countries and strong, resourceful companies take part in the market, there will be an oversupply, and the European commodity plastic situation will be discouraging. However, some restructuring has occurred:

1. Private companies' own rationalization, for example, Shell, BASF, or the BP/ICI swap.

2. Government rearrangements of its interests followed by shutdowns, as in, Italy, or without shutdowns, as in, France.
3. The exit of multinationals from Europe such as Union Carbide and Monsanto.
4. A tendency for oil companies or their subsidiaries to take over the polyolefins business and the old-line chemical companies to dominate PVC and, to an extent, PP (polypropylene).

JAPAN

In the fall of 1983 there was an odd sight in Western Europe. The chief executives of twelve of Japan's leading petrochemical manufacturers traveled en masse around the continent visiting many of the major manufacturers just discussed. Leading the tour and making the arrangements was an official from the Japanese Ministry of International Trade and Industry (MITI), who described the event: "Our industry is in a very difficult situation with much overcapacity and too much competition. We could not get the companies to cooperate. We thought that seeing Europe's condition would persuade them of the structural nature of the crisis and that traveling together might help build cooperative relationships."

The source of Japan's concern was clear. There were as many large, powerful petrochemical manufacturers in Japan as in the United States, yet Japan's economy was half the size. Ethylene capacity was some 6.5 million tons against a requirement in 1982 of 3.6 million tons. The Industrial Bank of Japan estimated that the combined operating deficit of the petrochemical manufacturers was ¥400 billion (approximately $1.6 billion).

Japan's basic problem in this industry was that under MITI's guidance, capacity had been built in a series of *combinatos*, world-scale complexes of crackers and derivative units built next to refineries. During the early period of Japan's postwar growth, these joint ventures were required to assemble needed capital. To regulate the growth of capacity, a MITI-industry committee established minimum scale standards and growth forecasts. Companies wishing to enter the industry in order to justify entry were able to lobby for high demand forecasts. Within a combinato different companies managed different product units, ownership was complex, and rivalry among producers intense. These combinatos depended on naphtha from the refineries as feedstock.

After 1973, the industry entered a long period of depression. It was in this period that the companies first came under pressure as demand stagnated, imports strengthened, and naphtha prices increased. (Nonetheless, with plans made earlier, two firms built new complexes.)

The second oil crisis (1978) only heightened the problem, persuading at least some people that the industry faced long-lasting structural problems. Exports, which had peaked at 20 percent of production in 1977, dropped to 12 percent in 1979, while imports rose from 0.7 percent to 4.3 percent. The deterioration in Japan's basic position can be seen in table 7-3.

In this dismal situation Japan found itself with thirteen major producers of ethylene and derivatives at eighteen major petrochemical complexes. Around each complex was a host of plastic fabricators, some 23,000 altogether, employing 322,000 people (3 percent of all manufacturing). In 1981 pretax profits/sales for the eight largest chemical companies ranged from a high of 1.7 percent to a low of −1.1 percent. As noted already, losses in commodity plastics were catastrophic.

THE RESPONSE IN JAPAN

In this crisis situation, MITI was able to act. The distinguished Council for Industrial Structure set up a blue ribbon Chemical Industry Committee to examine the structure in the future. It made two basic recommendations:

1. Cost competitiveness should be recovered through energy-saving technology, diversification of raw materials, and disposal of inefficient capacity.
2. Excessive competition should be eliminated. MITI took a very strong role here, encouraging the companies to carry on discussions; leading the trip through Europe; and promulgating a very pessimistic view. (While the CIC called for a reduction of ethylene capacity to 4 million tons, MITI originally sought 2 million tons as a goal—the level based

Table 7-3
Comparative Feedstock Prices

Price	1973		1978		1981		1985 Est.		Saudi Arabia
	Japan	U.S.	Japan	U.S.	Japan	U.S.	Japan	U.S.	
Naphtha ¥000/ton	9		20		58				
Ethylene ¥000/kilogram	60	20	85	55	175	120	240	180	60

on "domestic naphtha"—but relented when pressed by the companies.) In MITI's view, Japan might be better to import basic derivatives at the distressed prices expected for the next decade.

To assist the companies MITI proposed a new law for the Restructuring of Depressed Industries. The following is quoted from a MITI description of the "Philosophy and Ideas of the Temporary Measure Law for the Structural Adjustment of Specific Industries":

Retreat and Revitalization

The law is in no way intended to protect the industries from the adjustment forces, including overseas competitors, but to encourage private enterprises to retreat–i.e., to dispose of the inefficient and obsolete facilities with no prospect of recovering economic viability. Under this law around 30 percent of present facilities are expected to be curtailed. At the same time, it purports to revitalize the remaining portion through innovative activities of businesses such as fuel conversion, sophistication of the products, R&D, and cooperation or consolidation of business. In this sense, the law embodies the idea of positive adjustment policy.

The director of the Industrial Structure Division of MITI's Industrial Policy Bureau offered the following explanation of this philosophy's evolution:

We are concerned that we have a number of industries that are fundamentally weak. The affected industries are petrochemicals, electric furnaces, pulp and paper, synthetic fiber, ferro alloys, chemical fertilizer, and aluminum. There were three reasons for the difficulty in these industries:

1. High energy cost, especially after the second oil shock.
2. Demand declined: this was a long-term structural decline. Demand got thinner and thinner.
3. There is excessive competition, I like to say "abnormal competition," because people don't know what excessive competition is. As a consequence, performance is poor. The costs are high and prices are low. Within a small market there are many fighting for increased share despite demand growth.

Competition is OK, it is reasonable in most cases. But we can judge the existence of excesses of competition from the outcome and by the structure. For example in ethylene there are twelve companies and a small demand. Abnormal competition is competition whose outcome is not good. Based on the recommendation of the Industrial Structure Council, we established a petrochemical industry advisory policy.

1. We want to reduce capacity to improve the demand supply situation. For example we want to scrap 40 percent of petrochemical capacity in three to four years.
2. In order to do that we have to consult so we had to exempt consultation and discussions from the antitrust laws. MITI can designate a process to do this.
3. In order to promote fair and reasonable competition MITI will encourage joint ventures and mergers.

We discussed all this in the Council and MITI took the results to the FTC. But the groupings created by the companies were a problem. The largest held greater than 25 percent of the market. So we set up a new clause. The company should bring a proposal to MITI and MITI would bring it to the FTC. This was the coordination clause. If the situation changes so that market share relationships are altered the FTC can comment to MITI. So for the first time we have coordination of industrial policy and antitrust policy.

For MITI the biggest issue is competition among the groups. We see competition dynamically in an international context. We are not concerned with concentration here in Japan because there is so much international competition.

We have made a clear, explicit international survey. Japan can survive as a smaller, more efficient industry. We don't seek to be a major exporter. We plan on a stronger role for international competition here in Japan. If European petrochemical industries can survive, Japan can, but we cannot compete with the United States.

This is a painful and long process. The companies must discuss inside their organization and create the right atmosphere. The Japanese petrochemical industry is in so much difficulty so may decide to rationalize very soon.

Employment will be a special problem. This is a very rapid scrapping of capacity, therefore it implies a very rapid cutting of employment in a company. This means transferring workers to other plants in the company or other companies in the group. But if cutting down is implemented there will be a real problem. The Ministry of Labour is considering legislation to promote retraining. (The Labour Union saw these issues in the Chemical Industry Council, but they also saw that if there was no action the industry would lose.) So in law the labour unions sought import relief. No one else wanted this, however, so the labour union's representative from aluminium said, "Scrap down, it's the second best solution."

There is considerable disagreement about the policy's potential success. The international press assumed the proposed reductions would take place, but some of the managers were less sure. The companies all intended to survive based on their strengths. Rivalry among the *zaibatsu*, reluctance of banks to take write-offs, reluctance of companies to lay off workers, and problems posed by relations with plastic converters exacerbated the resulting competitive climate. One top manager expressed his hesitation artfully: "I cannot say that there will not be a reduction in capacity."

There was a consensus, however, that the sales groups would form and help firm up prices. The idea was to divide up the manufacturers of each major product—that is, low-density polyethylene—into four groupings which in turn would negotiate price.

A model already existed, although there were considerable differences in its construction. In the summer of 1982, fourteen PVC manufacturers had succeeded finally in setting themselves up in sales groupings (and getting FTC approval of those groupings) and prices were firming. A somewhat different set of companies were involved whose leadership faced fewer problems of integration if they cut back. Also, PVC was not under the purview of MITI's basic chemical desk. And their customers tended to be larger and stronger. Still, the precedent of success was considered important.

In the spring of 1983 the companies were looking forward to improving prices. The various groupings were sorting themselves out and trying to determine how they would operate. The plan is shown in table 7-4.

Managers in the industry expected progress, despite anticipated difficulties. They had five years to reorganize, and rationalization was a prerequisite for international competitiveness. But closures posed problems that would have to be negotiated. Who would shut down? How would the thousands of small converters be helped? How would the companies be compensated for taking care of their workers? And how would the burden on the local communities be handled? Should the surviving companies help or should the government provide assistance? "Frankly," said one executive, "each company must work to survive. It must apply its own power and energy. Each company has its own strategy. The fact that oil prices are down helps provide time in the short run."

The companies thought they could predict the eventual outcome. Managers expected the product leaders in a field to emerge as the dominant forces: Mitsui Petrochemical and Showa Denko in high density; Mitsui Chemical, Mitsubishi Chemical, Showa Denko, and Sumitomo in low density; Nippon Zeon, Kanegafuchi and Shiantsu in PVC and so on.

This sense of direction was impressive given the disorder found in Europe, but it should not be exaggerated. The 1982 losses of Japan's polyolefin manufacturers were as bad as those in Europe—hundreds of millions of dollars for each firm. And MITI did not have the total confidence of the

Table 7-4

Proposed Selling Groups for Polyolefins

		Market Share		
Leader	Total	Low Density	High Density	Polypropylene
Mitsubishi	17	21	13	18
Showa Denko	25	26	38	19
Mitsui	22	19	30	22
Sumitomo	32	34	19	40
Imports	4	—	—	—
Total	100	100	100	100

manufacturers. After all, it was under their tutelage that the overbuilt combinato system had been constructed, and MITI had been unable to persuade
the FTC to accept the original plan for three (not four) sales groups. There
was, however, an agreed-upon diagnosis of the situation and some rough
goals. Most important, the Industry Structure Council's deliberations over
the course of 1982 and 1983 had been sufficiently publicized that a broad
political base existed for action if the parties involved could figure out how
to proceed.

Japan contrasts most dramatically with France, whose government tech-
nocrats had imposed structural change without a strategy or a political consensus. Japan had collectively worked out the strategy and built the consensus. It remained for their companies to formulate and negotiate a plan for
implementation.

THE UNITED STATES—THE WINNERS RECONSIDER THEIR FUTURE

In the United States, the petrochemical industry of the 1970s and early
1980s was a paradox—almost profitless prosperity. A number of giant,
technically innovative, and commercially sophisticated companies dominated
the industry. Strategic resource redeployment by the individual company
managements had resulted in much portfolio pruning; and the trade figures
reflected a steady ability of the U.S. manufacturers to penetrate foreign
markets (see table 7-5).

Of these exports, the biggest customer is Western Europe (30 percent),
Latin America follows (21 percent), and then Asia except Japan (12 percent),

Table 7-5
U.S. Trade (Exports-Imports) in Petrochemical Derivatives[a] ($ millions)

	1972	1977	1979	1980	1981	1982	1983
Chemicals and allied product	$2,150	$5,432	$11,250	$13,905	$13,634	$15,800	$13,500
Plastic materials and resins	382.5	950.9	1,936.9	2,440.0	2,366.4	2,003.8	2,000
Nitrogenous fertilizer	(3.8)	274	(29.1)	73.8	23	(110)	(216)
Pesticides	193.7	660.6	923.7	938	909	998	1,098

Source: Department of Commerce
[a]Respectively SIC codes 28, 2821, 2873, and 2879. Plastics materials and resins are closest to the products
studied. The other groups are included for discussion and contrast.

Canada (12 percent), and Japan (11 percent). (The biggest sources of imports are Western Europe, Canada, and Japan.)

Despite this evidence of success, the financial results of the companies over the last decade have been poor, with the exception of the post-1973 years when scarcities permitted prices to move up faster than cost. The lack of profitability needs to be qualified as well as explained. To begin, the post-1973 decade was a peculiar period during which few U.S. firms earned more than the cost of capital. Growth in demand slowed faster than supply; raw material costs soared; the cost of capital moved from negative to historic highs; and inflation undermined the strength of capital intensive industries that were pricing and accounting for depreciation based on historical cost.

But other more peculiar factors hurt the industry. It was infected with such severe competition that even during periods of product scarcity, price was often at marginally profitable levels based on historical costs. This was the result of three principal factors: entrants misunderstood the industry; competitors were exceedingly dissimilar and misunderstood each others' economics; and aggressiveness eroded value added in the chain of activities from raw material to the end user.

The final consequence of this intense competition has been exit. In the major commodity plastics, companies with good alternative opportunities (e.g., Dow in PVC) or very marginal positions (e.g., City Service in polyethylene) have left the business. Relative to Europe and Japan, whose companies began considering exit in the 1980s, these data show dramatic early moves.

As a result, the survivors have tended to perform notably better than their European and Japanese competitors. While they may not have returned the true cost of capital, they have been moderately profitable as the list of the eight largest chemical producers and chemical groups of oil companies indicates (see table 7-6).

THE U.S. RESPONSE

In contrast to the dire statements of early demise heard from executives in some U.S. industries in which trade patterns have shifted, the petrochemical manufacturers have stayed relatively calm. The Department of Commerce's increasingly sophisticated apparatus has prepared a competitive assessment of the industry and projects its future.[5] The abstract from the department's August 1982 report provides a good summary of the aggregate aspects of the situation:

Table 7-6
1981 Return on Operating Assets and Sales of Leading Chemical Producers (%)

Chemical Companies	Operating ROA	Chemical Sales	Oil Companies	Operating ROA	Chemical Sales
Dow	7.1	9.4	Gulf	—	2.4
Celanese	8.1	3.7	Shell	0.4	3.6
Union Carbide	9.7	5.6	ARCO	0.6	2.7
Allied	10.4	2.7	EXXON	5.5	8.5
Hercules	11.1	2.3	OXY	5.6	2.4
Monsanto	12.9	6.3	Mobil	6.8	2.3
Cyanamid	13.3	1.9	Indiana	7.6	3.1
Du Pont	14.0	12.2	Philips	9.1	2.5

Source: Department of Commerce

A major restructuring of the worldwide petrochemical industry has already begun and will gain in momentum over the next two decades. This will occur as the hydrocarbon-rich countries build facilities to utilize their presently wasted (flared) or underutilized natural gas for commodity petrochemical feedstocks, pricing these raw materials below world market levels to ensure the competitiveness of their national enterprises. The economics of such a strategy are overpowering, since the combined cost of fuel and feedstocks comprises from 35% to 80% of total production costs of most commodity petrochemical operations in the U.S. and other industrialized countries.

The decline in competitiveness of U.S. commodity petrochemicals is likely to be gradual, however, without crises that provoke calls for major government action to assist the industry. Still, the adjustment problems facing the industry will almost certainly lead to recommendations for government support of the industry in one form or another. . . .

The more important focus for the future is the opportunities arising in downstream specialty chemicals and pseudocommodity petrochemicals. Advances in technology and market needs for new, high performance materials will provide a new arena for intense international competition in the future among the U.S., Japan, and Western Europe. . . .

On the individual company management level, however, there are varying interpretations of "restructuring," beginning with the distinction between U.S. chemical companies and U.S. oil companies. Then there are differences in product mix. Finally, the parts of the federal system that we call government have also responded with their own strategies.

The Chemical Companies. The issue of restructuring is an old one for U.S. chemical manufacturers. They enlarged and succeeded before World War II or in the 1950s at the latest. In the 1960s, they experienced an attack from chemical groups of oil companies and others for whom raw material was cheap. After 1973, studies indicated that in commodity products, the oil companies, if well run, could achieve a fundamental strategic advantage. Analysis also showed that the long-term potential profitability of these businesses had shifted as potential value added shifted from 70 percent of sales price to 30 percent.

There were two basic responses to these analyses. Some companies chose to become oil companies. Using the leverage of debt with a negative real cost, Dow moved to acquire oil and gas properties in the Southwest and the Middle East. Most dramatically, Du Pont acquired Conoco. With the rise in interest rates, and the freeing up of feedstock following significant declines in the energy consumption worldwide, Dow has turned around and backed out of most of its "oil company" ventures. Having acquired important domestic reserves at a reasonable price, Du Pont is taking a long-term view.

The second response has been a selective approach to the commodity business. Following the logic of contemporary strategic thinking, companies focused the limited cash flow available from their current business mix on areas in which there was an opportunity to experience sustainable long-term profits and to grow. For all the chemical companies this has meant (1) an emphasis on new process technology; (2) upgrading of products through alloys, copolymers, and end-use products; and (3) an emphasis on new, higher-performance synthetics. When the basic raw material, technology, or commercial position has been strong enough, they have stayed to jockey for a position in the end game. But in every instance it has been a hard and costly fight.

The Oil Companies. For the oil companies, the chemical business has provided few returns for what appeared to be major investments. The general problem has been that chemical plants are often extremely difficult to run and chemical products hard to sell. Until oil companies developed the capability to build and run state-of-the-art plants and market the product skillfully, their presence was only disruptive. Even where they have mastered the businesses, they have faced tough competition from chemical companies that yielded market share grudgingly. The same tough markets and difficult economies also plagued the oil company's chemical subsidiaries.

Their ability to respond to the challenge from the Middle East is different. While Union Carbide can sell LLDPE technology to the Saudis, Exxon, Mobil, and Shell are in a position to help build and manage the plants. To an extent then, the oil companies *are* the competition from the Middle East.[6]

This idea becomes clearer if one considers who owns the projects planned for the Middle East and other hydrocarbon-rich nations (see table 7-7). The projects may pose problems as far as U.S. exporters are concerned, but they certainly look like important ventures for U.S. companies.

THE U.S. GOVERNMENT'S CHANGING ROLE

The U.S. petrochemical industry has had a long, close working relationship with the government, interrupted by periodic battles. The industry was encouraged to grow in numerous ways. After World War I, a tariff was erected to protect the infant dye industry from European competition—especially English and German. The American Selling Price System (ASP) guaranteed that imports could not sell lower than 8 percent above the average American selling price. The system remained in place until traded away during GATT negotiations prior to the Tokyo Round.

The development of synthetic rubber, plexiglass, and numerous advances in solvents, lubricants, gases, and weapons (napalm) were important contributions during World War II. Subsequently, national resource studies identified growth in synthetic fertilizers as a priority; the Korean War Defense Production Act then made accelerated depreciation available to all producers except Du Pont and Allied (then the dominant producers).

In fact, until environmental concerns became widespread, the industry was regarded as the same sort of benevolent example of bounteous "high tech" that computers are today. Accordingly, despite the fury of the Europeans, the ASP was retained during the Kennedy Round after eleventh-hour efforts by the industry restored the provisions.

In 1973, key company managers who had been involved in what was regarded as a narrowly avoided disaster of the Kennedy Round decided to create an umbrella organization, the Organization of Chemical Industry Trade Associations (OCITA). Founded in 1974, OCITA's rationale was to assemble a single industry position for the then upcoming Tokyo Round.

OCITA's leadership was in place just in time to take part in the industry sector advisory committees (ISACs) called for by the Trade Act of 1975. The organization's participation was particularly useful, since the U.S. Trade Representative (USTR) had divided the industry into three groups: chemicals and allied products (inorganics, organics, and fertilizers); rubber and plastics (including the polyolefins); and paints and coatings, which cut across the membership of the trade associations and the product lines of the major companies.

Table 7-7
Saudi Arabia Petrochemical Development Projects

Saudi Company and Partner	Products	Est. Cost	Status	Est. Completion Date
Saudi Petrochemical Co. and Shell (U.S.)	Ethylene, styrene ethanol, caustic soda, ethylene dichloride	$ 3 bil.	Detailed engineering and construction	1985
Al-Jubail Petroleum Co. and Exxon (U.S.)	Low-density	$ 1.3 bil.	"	"
Saudi Yanbu Petrochem Co. and Mobil (U.S.)	LDPE, HDPE, ethylene glycol	$ 2.0 bil.	"	1984
Arabian Petrochemical Co. and Dow (U.S.)[a]	Ethylene, LDPE and HDPE	$ 1.5 bil.	Negotiation of joint venture and engineering	1985
Saudi Methanol Co. and Mitsubishi Consort. (Japan)	Chemical grade methanol	$300 mil.	"	"
Eastern Petrochem Co. and Mitsubishi Consort. (Japan)	LDPE and ethylene glycol	$ 1.7 bil.	Detailed engineering and construction	1983
National Methanol Co. and Celanese (U.S.)[b]	Chemical grade methanol	$500 mil.	"	1985
Al-Jubail Fertilizer Co. and Taiwan Fertilizer Co. (Taiwan)	Urea	$400 mil.	"	1983

Source: Department of Commerce
[a] Dow Chemical withdrew on 30 November 1982. The Saudis, however, intend to proceed with construction and operation of at least portions of the planned complex using Union Carbide technology.
[b] Also Texas Eastern (U.S.)

The chemicals ISAC met twenty-five times a year for three years to find a limited list of products deserving protection on which very heterogeneous companies could agree. In the end, exceptions were negotiated for sixty to seventy products that constituted 70 percent of U.S. productive capacity. The American Selling Price System disappeared in the process, traded away for other concessions. Subsequently, OCITA has successfully taken part in a series of peacefully resolved negotiations with the European Commission. The association has filed a suit with the ITC charging Mexico with subsidizing exports. At the same time, legislation filed by Representative Gibbons of Florida seeks to make it possible to apply trade sanctions against imports that are successful because of others' targeted policies.

THE ITC REPORT

The ITC recently published an extensive report, *The Probable Impact on the U.S. Petrochemical Industry of the Expanding Petrochemical Industries in the Conventional Energy-Rich Nations*. Based on a study instituted in February 1982 on its own motion, "for the purpose of gathering and presenting information on . . . the effects of such expansion on the U.S. petrochemical industry," the conclusions are not very different from the Commerce Department study cited earlier—the U.S. trade position in commodity petrochemicals is likely to decrease substantially.

The report highlights the raw material price advantage of the energy-rich nations, noting that in almost all cases the prices are set by governments or government-owned producers (see table 7-8).

Table 7-8
Comparative Raw Material Prices, 1983

	Price/Metric Ton		
Area	*Ethane*	*Naphtha*	*Methane*
Canada	$ 80–100		$ 50–90
Mexico	45–65		20–30
Persian Gulf	20–30		0–30
Indonesia	20–30		0–30
United States	205–225	$275–285	205–230
Western Europe		320–330	215–230
Japan		340–350	310–320

Source: U.S. International Trade Commission (USITC) publication 1370

Table 7-9

Forecasted Price Differential of Basic Petrochemicals

	Price/Metric Ton		
Area	*Ethylene*	*Methanol*	*Ammonia*
Canada	$250–350	$100–150	$130–180
Mexico	230–270	100–140	125–165
Persian Gulf	300–340	110–150	140–180
Indonesia Gulf	355–395	125–165	170–210
United States	540–580	325–375	315–360
Western Europe	835–875[a]	380–420	400–440[b]
Japan	825–865[a]	355–395	355–470[b]

Source: USITC publication 1370
[a]Naphtha feedstock
[b]Methane to naphtha feedstock range

The consequent impact of feedstock prices expected in the 1985-90 period on the production cost of the three basic primary petrochemicals in a world-scale plant is estimated as shown in table 7-9.

The report then notes that for reasons of national development the new producers were likely to enter world markets faster than expected if they practiced something the ITC called "traditional entry"—growth solely in response to an "increase in the demand for that item." Apparently demand is not thought to depend on price nor tradition to be involved with past practices.

In fact, the report notes that new producers are likely to "depend upon advantages" (e.g., lower cost, linking petrochemical sales to access to petroleum reserves, cartels, and countertrade), and most production will be managed by state-owned enterprises. The impact of these developments is expected to vary from one product to another. Ethylene and its derivatives ought to be less affected because ethylene is hard to transport and derivatives are more complex to market. But the bottom line is an end to exports (see table 7-10).

In a brief note, the report indicates that lower-price petrochemical intermediates could help U.S. exports of final products.

THE DILEMMA FOR COMPANY MANAGERS

The changes described above pose dramatic choices for those managing the strategic development in the petrochemical producers. The options seem

Table 7-10
U.S. 1990 Trade Position

	Tons (in millions)
Ethylene and derivatives	1.3—(2.0)
Ammonia	(3.7)—(5.8)
Methanol	120 —(4.8)
Net dollar impact (1982)	($120 mil.)—($3.8 bil.)

Source: USITC publication 1370

to range from exit to aggressive expansion in an energy-rich nation, but also include merger, joint venture, specialization, and radical tailoring of product mix. Both the Department of Commerce study and the ITC report note the importance of a move toward "specialties" in the United States. Figure 7-3 reveals, however, just how dramatic a change is needed if a shift to specialties is to have any impact.

If the ten major commodity producers acquired the ten major specialty producers, the impact would be positive but negligible. Moreover, there is a more fundamental problem. If all the major producers shift to "specialties," these can quickly become commodities.

WHICH GAME TO PLAY?

The top management of most companies discussed in this chapter face several dilemmas:

1. The recession years and the apparent end of further penetration of the GNP by petrochemical substitutes, along with the growth of both capacity and the number of competitors, has resulted in no one's making money at current prices. To reach profitable prices, cooperation will be necessary—either to fix prices illegally or reduce capacity to bring it in balance with demand. Unfortunately, unless the agreement is enforced, individual companies have an incentive to cheat.

    In the United States, long-term losers quit—up to a point. Excess capacity still hangs over the market. But in Europe the biggest losers are often state owned and will not exit; to the contrary, they expand. Efficient private manufacturers do not wish to stand aside, so the competitive battle proceeds.

Figure 7-3

Margins for Industrial, Specialty, and "Combined" Companies (results second quarter 1982)

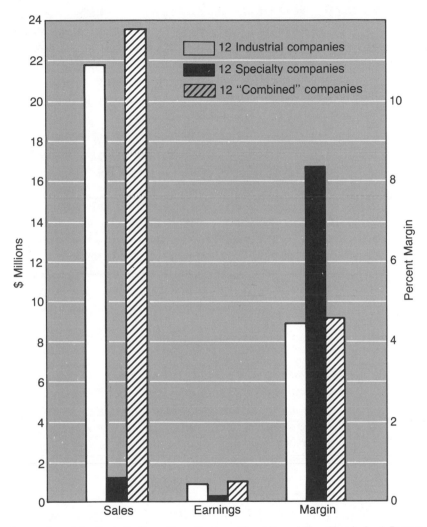

Source: Speech by Peter Godfrey, Chem Systems, "Specialty and Fine Chemicals, A Panacea for Profits?"

2. At the same time, company managers look ahead and realize that a) the world economy is likely to recover; b) there will be rationalization; and c) petrochemicals are one of the largest markets in the world. Some companies will be making commodity plastics and there are

potential profits. To compete, one must have the lowest costs and the best technology.

3. The governments of consuming and producing nations have multiple interests. In 1983, employment and balance of payments dominated most policy discussions. Japan had perhaps the most elegant attempt at a solution: they treated the worker as a fixed cost for the economy and sought to help companies maximize value added per worker. Restructuring the chemical industry required a transition period during which major companies could earn profits necessary to fund the migration to new higher value-added businesses.

   In Italy and France the government had intervened much more directly. Companies were reorganized and huge sums invested to build a world class, competitive industry. In Italy, workers had been laid off and plants closed, but in France it was not clear what would be closed or whether the government would even permit closings.

4. On the other hand, providing economic results that satisfied the objective of private capital markets for a return on investment competitive with other uses has led most managers to conclude that the government ought to be kept at arms' length. Otherwise, a government's natural desire to protect its political constituencies would interfere with the need to rationalize by shutting plants and laying off workers.

5. These dilemmas were also associated with different time pressures:

   a. *The day-to-day world of politics.* The morning's headlines and the evening TV news are important to the strength of a government and the position of individual politicians. Managers seeking to ally themselves with a government must have a very short-term view.

   If the government bank that owns your shares needs a dividend this month in order to shore up its balance sheet and perhaps the currency, then the opportunities in the capital budget to use those funds over the next year are irrelevant.

   b. But the *world of return on investment* is also demanding. Stock markets may have a longer-term view than the headlines, but they are only loyal to the last eighth of a point and have a healthy understanding of present value. If the cost of money is 15-20 percent, then commercial investment should yield that plus some premium—next year if not this one.

   c. In contrast is the *world of market share.* If there is a long-term future to a large market, then it may pay to stick out the period of low or cyclical returns during competitive battles to build up the cumulative experience and scale that results in industry domination. After all, if there is growth there may be positive cash flow, even if profits are meager. And over time, well-managed market share position will generate profit.

Each of these situations has its own logic. A management trying to compete in each one can develop a strategy that makes sense. The problem is that any move a company makes in one area is a move in all the others. What helps in one situation may well hurt in another. For example, one firm fights fiercely in an end game and finds other firms are uncomfortable dealing with it in a cooperative industry-level effort to develop a coherent aggregate position.

It would be difficult, but feasible, to approach these situations sequentially: conflicting demands can be met one after another. The problem is that all of these "games" are being played out simultaneously; there is no space or slack.

Under the circumstances, it is extremely difficult to move forward with any clear sense of direction. Some companies more or less ignore all but one of the games and treat other demands as if they did not exist or were unimportant. There are U.S. companies, for example, that treat all noneconomic problems as constraints affecting the simpler problem of maximizing return. Some European companies simply try to meet the objectives of employment and balance of payments specified by their government.

But most managers do struggle to move forward in several games at once by:

- cooperating while competing;
- shrinking while surviving;
- making profit while maintaining or increasing market share; and
- using government support to strengthen long-term international position while avoiding, when possible, short-term political costs.

STRATEGY IN A POLITICIZED ENVIRONMENT

The present situation is a war of attrition. Each day the action of a competitor or a government body poses serious problems. The aid of one's home government is tantalizingly attractive. But with support comes dependence and potential politicization. Even government-owned firms shun the direct intervention of political leaders when they can. Fundamentally, there is something unattractive to a professional manager about paying hard currency for feedstock, and managing a large, complex, high technology machine that produces a high-quality product, which is then sold at an economic loss.

For managers in such settings, every day is a battle. The best one can hope for is incremental progress on strategic matters, and a containment of political pressure at the boundary of the firm. Political coalition-building requires a kind of equity that defeats the selectivity in resource allocation, organizations, and rewards required for efficiency and effectiveness. For politicians, everything a company does can be traded away in day-to-day battles; executive position, local jobs, plant location, construction contracts, maintenance contracts, all kinds of equipment purchases and raw material sourcing bring benefits to someone. These benefits, rather than the needs of the firm, can become the central criteria by which action is guided in the politicized organization.

When a company can predict that its activities will be politically salient, it is possible to build defenses. Long-term costs of unwise proposals can be made visible. Politicians who disagree with a proposal can be alerted to the problem. More useful, carefully constructed working relationships can be built between the technical staffs of a company and relevant government counterparts. It is then possible to use company expertise to inform the public policymaking process.

The problem comes when the wind shifts so rapidly that one is caught unprepared. In the chemical industry the basic problem has been adjusting to a new set of circumstances in a situation in which many players

1. had inadequate capital to invest in modernization or new products;
2. had only recently perceived the structural nature of the problem;
3. could only get government help by reinvesting in mature areas where jobs would be maintained; or
4. were blocked from negotiating to stabilize markets and reorganize capacity for fear of antitrust prosecution.

In the United States, many of the leading firms have been worried that the economic recovery would take the pressure to exit off marginal producers. One manager put the point rather bluntly: "This recession has done what none of us had the courage to do for ourselves. Another year and we would have really cleaned up the industry." Privately, many managers have been appalled by the spectre of protectionist legislation.

IMPLICATIONS FOR GOVERNMENT POLICY

It is impossible to ignore the role of history in assessing the behavior and consequences described in this chapter. The British and especially the Germans developed early in chemicals and provided schools for engineers and managers. The strength of ICI, BASF, Bayer, and Hoechst today are attributable as much to this inheritance as to any recent move. The U.S. companies also became large early and enjoyed low-cost feedstock and a huge domestic market.

In contrast, France, Italy, and Japan entered chemicals, but especially petrochemicals, relatively late. The catch-up interventions of the Italian and Japanese governments stimulated their rapid growth of capacity, which is now excessively large and costly. The French government, the latest to discover petrochemicals, seems to have arrived on the scene to insure that billions of dollars would be invested in a declining industry remarkably vulnerable to competition from naturally favored sources of supply. While the Japanese and even the Italians have recognized that commodity plastics generate relatively low value added and few jobs, the French seem to be plunging ahead.

The U.S. government has played a reasonably constructive role over the industry's life, protecting its development during infancy, its exports during its preeminence, and now encouraging, by informed benevolent neglect, the migration of capital and management toward higher value-added materials that began in the 1960s as oil companies entered the field.

U.S. company managers have been remarkably sophisticated in devising a wide array of industry associations that are used for different purposes— from the Chemical Industry Institute of Toxicology, which studies toxic substances, to OCITA, the umbrella organization that has managed the industry's participation in trade negotiation. OCITA's working philosophy exemplifies what might be called an intelligent or constructively selfish approach to public policy. Although most large member companies are multinationals and all have product problems somewhere in their portfolio, they have taken the view that they must approach trade issues as U.S. companies, and they must not seek to protect inefficiency. While obviously U.S. government trade negotiators might disagree on their interpretation, these points appear to have provided a basis for building an effective coalition within an extremely heterogeneous industry. In turn, that coalition has been able to contribute its expertise and analysis to the formulating of policy in the U.S. Trade Representative and Department of Commerce and to making legislation in Congress. It is almost Japanese in character.

The problem today is to avoid what is almost special interest protectionist legislation and to recognize that the playing out of foreseeable economic shifts will cost the United States billions of dollars in trade in the commodity plastics. The question is not "how shall we prevent the loss?" but "is there a useful role for government institutions to play in facilitating the development of new materials and their markets?" For example:

1. Are patent laws adequate to protect process development associated with high-volume production of the raw materials?
2. Is there a way that the government could assist the funding of studies on toxicity?
3. Are there other areas in which methods for testing could be advanced?
4. Can government support for basic research in chemicals and materials be increased or made more effective?

In other words, the government might help by improving the context for product and market development. In considering such activity, the industry's associations again ought to provide useful guidance.

Inevitably, the temptation to provide more vigorous protection or assistance will exist. But here the record of the French, Italians, and Japanese should be clear. Unless a legislature has the discipline to produce something like the Basic Industry Restructuring Law, government ought to be an interested observer. What the United States does not need is a politicizing of the petrochemical industry.

8

International Competitiveness of American Industry: The Role of U.S. Trade Policy

Alan Wm. Wolff

Trade policies are directly related to issues of international competitiveness. With trade policies countries promote infant industries, support exports, and impede more competitive imports. Hence, to discover that American trade policy decisions have *not* been geared toward promoting the competitive position of the United States is striking and warrants explanation.

THE DETERMINANTS OF U.S. TRADE POLICY

The primary objective of American trade policy has been to create a single world market, free of barriers, discrimination, and subsidies. To this end, the U.S. government has devoted fifty years of unrelenting effort, from the passage of the Reciprocal Trade Agreements Act on 12 June 1934, to the present. U.S. policy is the antithesis of mercantilism. As a general policy matter it eschews government intervention in trade, either at the border or at the source of trade—at the point of manufacture.

The origins of this free trade policy are not hard to locate. Much of American trade policy of the last half-century can be read as a reaction to the enactment of the Smoot-Hawley Tariff Act in 1930. In that year following the collapse of the stock market, Congress began work on minor tariff legislation, and by the time it finished, it had granted protection to almost all domestic industries that faced import competition, placing U.S. tariffs at prohibitive levels.

Alan Wm. Wolff is a partner of Verner, Liipfert, Bernhard and McPherson, specializing in international trade and investment law. Contributions to this paper and to source documents from which parts of it were drawn were made by Thomas Howell, Lynn Holec, and William Noellert, all of Verner, Liipfert, Bernhard and McPherson.

Congress, which under the Constitution is accorded the commerce powers of the republic, in this case exercised this power without the active leadership of the president and with little awareness of the devastating effects its action would have on the world economy. The erection of this on average 50 percent ad valorem tariff wall was not planned; it was the result of political log-rolling of individual legislators, engaged in a beggar-thy-neighbor attempt aimed at preserving employment at home. The results were appalling. World trade quickly plummeted to a fraction of what it had been.

Congress never again exercised its broad commerce powers directly and has granted a succession of delegations of trade authorities to the president. A stark lesson had been learned about the enormous costs of yielding to protectionism. It is still feared that the imposition of any trade restrictions, particularly if Congress was a motivating force in seeking them, might herald the beginning of a broader protectionist wave. As a result, even trade measures that are clearly warranted to counter recognized foreign unfair practices, such as dumping and export subsidization, are more often than not labeled as protectionist by the press and academics, and are vigorously opposed.

It is not an overstatement to describe this basis of American trade policy as being almost religious. Protectionism is seen as an evil. This does not mean that protection is never granted, but no president feels good about doing so. There is still a strong moralistic opposition to the use of trade measures, regardless of the merits of an individual case.

A second basis for America's trade policy is provided by the economic theory of Adam Smith. In his simplified model of nations prospering by specializing in the exportation of goods in which they have a comparative advantage lies the theoretical basis often cited for seeking the opening of markets. There may be repeated departures from the American ideal of achieving global free trade, such as the formation of customs unions and free trade areas, and the granting of tariff preferences, but the core of U.S. policy continues to be a steadfast belief that achieving a completely unfettered market in which all Western nations participate fully will lead to maximum economic benefits for all. Departures from this vision have only reinforced America's impetus to global trade liberalization. For example, the negotiating authority granted to President Kennedy by the Trade Expansion Act of 1962 was justified as a means of diluting the harmful, trade-distorting effects of the European Common Market by reducing its Common External Tariff.

Theoretically, any trade liberalization is good. Adam Smith's heirs in each administration—residing primarily at the Treasury and the Council of Economic Advisors—would argue for the benefits of the *unilateral* removal of

U.S. trade barriers were it not for justifiable fears of a negative reaction from Congress, and indeed these economists argue for this approach despite its being politically unfeasible. In 1934, and ever since, Congress has agreed to reduce America's trade barriers on the condition that other countries grant American products reciprocal benefits. The president's authority to reduce tariffs was thus grounded solely in his being allowed to enter into international trade agreements under which U.S. and foreign barriers were to be simultaneously reduced.

These agreements created a counterweight to the imposition of protective measures. Thereafter, other than in narrowly defined circumstances, the imposition of trade restrictions would upset the balance of concessions and would risk corresponding (retaliatory) increases of foreign protection abroad. The imposition of new protective measures was no longer to be cost free. Through this process, an international trading system was created.

U.S. trade policy operates generally within the confines of the structure provided by the rules contained in trade agreements—originally a series of bilateral agreements, now largely superseded by the multilateral General Agreement on Tariffs and Trade (GATT). In this respect the United States is not very different from other major trading nations. However, American policy also operates under legal constraints of its own making. Even more determinative of U.S. trade decisions than international rules are the requirements of its domestic legal system. In this regard, America stands apart from all of its trading partners: it accords a dominant role to the rule of law in the setting of trade policy.

America relies on an elaborate system of legal rights and obligations enforceable by individuals because of a distrust of government prevalent in our country. For most of our trading partners, which have parliamentary forms of government, the discretion granted to government to consciously direct trade and structure the national economy is much greater. The party in power is given a mandate to govern, with scope for action that is much broader than that ever given the U.S. executive.

In America, the emphasis has been on the individual, who is invested with rights and given economic opportunities to exploit, by and large without the assistance of government. The role of government in the United States as it has evolved has not been to identify and support specific industrial goals. On the contrary, the primary motive for its interventions is to act as a neutral referee. Whether in the field of antitrust, consumer protection, or public safety, the purpose of government in the United States is to assure that broader public interests are not sacrificed in the pursuit of private entrepreneurial goals. Of all industries engaged in trade, only agriculture and arms are consciously nurtured and promoted.

Without an understanding of this profound difference between the United States and most of its trading partners, it is difficult to understand American trade policy. It is not an adjunct of any domestic program to preserve and enhance any particular industry, because there is no attempt made to foster any industry. It is foreign to American policymakers even to consider an appropriate industrial or trade profile for the United States. No U.S. government official seeks to determine what size steel or automobile industry the United States should have, nor whether America should have these industries at all. In its impassive role as referee, the U.S. government asks only whether an industry is facing unfair or injurious foreign competition, and if it is unfair or injurious, the government may provide a remedy, although it has a strong preference against doing so.

This impartiality about industry is reinforced by another part of the heritage of Adam Smith—a Darwinian notion that those competitors that are truly fit will survive on their own. To file an application for relief from international competition is viewed by some as an admission of failure, which the petitioner seeks to remedy by becoming a ward of the state. There exists an erroneous assumption that the conditions of international trade resemble those of domestic competition, either in terms of the structure of the market or of the nature of the competition. American trade policy officials tend to assume all too readily that failure of an American firm in international competition is attributable solely to faults of the firm's management rather than to the nature of international competition. Implicitly, a neutral stance on the part of government toward international trade problems is assumed to work in the international arena as it is supposed to work domestically: to promote the highest level of performance for the economy as a whole.

If American trade policy was to be judged solely by the trade measures taken, one might conclude that it was entirely erratic, a vessel taken here and there by random winds and currents. For trade officials, however, at least as a formal matter, there are certain proprieties to be observed; they would not want to be seen influencing which petitions are filed and which are withheld. Petitioners are to be treated equally, large and small alike, regardless of their importance to the economy, or whether the import restriction sought would fundamentally improve the situation of the petitioner. The trade actions themselves are almost never linked to any domestic program to improve the international competitive position of the U.S. industry. What is being dispensed is equity, not the promotion of industry. The common good is to be achieved by observing the rights of the individual. The nation is to be served, as it is in the workings of its domestic society, by individuals pursuing their legal rights—in this case, pursuing remedies designed to offset harm caused by foreign competition.

The great majority of those in this country who have worked with this highly legalistic system of "trade policy" formulation would defend it as preferable to the known alternatives. World trade has, after all, expanded greatly under the leadership of the United States during the last four decades. Moreover, it is a system that provides some equity and acts as an escape valve to relieve protectionist political pressures. In spite of the frustrations, there is often admiration in other capitals for a system that requires public proceedings, notice to those affected by proposed actions, an impartial weighing of evidence, and decisions on the record. Often actions are colored by politics, but a relatively high standard is maintained.

There are also, of course, domestic political exceptions to the quasi-judicial U.S. trade policy system. Two industries that stand in a class by themselves in these terms are textiles and apparel, and dairy products. In these industries, the number of domestic producers is large, their economic importance is great, and their geographic base is broad. Their political strength is correspondingly substantial. The result has been the maintenance of comprehensive import control programs, a status that other industries have aspired to but never achieved.

For other industries, the majority, there is a series of legal remedies potentially available. If an industry faces competition that deprives it of sales at home or abroad, it must find a category of actionable behavior within which to fit its complaint, and if it cannot, it has no choice but adjust to the competition, by becoming more efficient, by moving production facilities offshore, or by going out of business. Although trade officials may sympathize with an industry's plight, the U.S. government is disinterested as to which of the three actions is taken.

TRADE REMEDIES AND INTERNATIONAL COMPETITIVENESS

IMPORT POLICY

Each international trade agreement contains an escape clause. The theory underlying the escape clause is that the nation's contractual obligation to maintain reduced barriers at the border may result in injury to domestic industries due to a consequent increase in imports. The importing country is allowed to escape its obligations and to impose such temporary import restrictions as may be necessary to remedy the injury. Under the U.S. import relief law, the president, presented with an injury finding by the U.S. International Trade Commission, can impose increased tariffs or import quotas, or negotiate quantitative limitations pursuant to an orderly marketing agreement. Remedies may last for an initial period of five years with a possible extension for another three years.

The primary focus of the U.S. International Trade Commission's (USITC) inquiry is whether increased imports are in fact a cause of the injury at least equal in its effects to that of any other factor. The president considers this and other factors, such as the impact of import restrictions on consumer prices, the adverse reactions to be expected from exporting countries, and the efficiency of trying to generate employment through import relief (the consumer cost per job created). Whether the relief will be effective in promoting adjustment, what kind of effort is being made by the industry to adjust to import competition, and other considerations relative to the position of the industry in the nation's economy, although issues the president must take into account, are matters of strictly secondary importance, and are often only an implicit part of the decision-making process.

For trade officials, there are two factors that help them to abjure responsibility for the health of an American industry. First, because of the government's self-limiting role, officials are astoundingly ignorant of the facts surrounding the condition of any particular industry and of foreign competitors' particular advantages. Second, there is very little analytical capability to digest sectoral data of this kind, even if it were collected or available. Given that government trade officials are few and hard-pressed, and have about forty-five days from the receipt of a USITC finding of injury until their recommendation to the president, under current procedures there is very little time or capability to consider any detailed adjustment plan as part of the process of deciding whether or not to grant relief.

For their part, industries petitioning for relief generally do not present such a detailed plan of adjustment. There are a variety of reasons for this, one being antitrust laws. A coordinated approach for restoration of an industry to competitiveness would require close consultations among individual firms involving proprietary information needed to plan the rationalization of the industry concerned. Furthermore, firms' individual interests and positions often differ markedly: some are profitable, others are not; some import, others produce only domestically, and so forth. Moreover, a detailed adjustment plan must often rely upon increased revenues generated by virtue of the import protection. As a matter of practical politics, firms are reluctant to concede that there are substantial consumer costs associated with the relief sought. However, without consumer costs, increased revenues would be limited or nonexistent. While domestic industries talk somewhat obscurely of the need for a breathing space during which investment is likely to take place, details are usually not submitted, even confidentially. In part this is because no firm wishes to commit itself to its government to a particular course of private conduct.

Because government does not view its role as being responsible for strengthening the competitiveness of individual U.S. industries, it does not act as a catalyst for seeking industrywide solutions. No government official has a mandate to help the industry prepare an adjustment plan, nor would a government role of this kind be generally welcomed in the private sector. Thus, there are no detailed consultations between the firms, labor, and the government as to how relief would be utilized.

In general, however, there is a concern that unless relief is granted in a reasonable number of cases, pressure will build in the Congress to change the law to make relief more automatic. There is also a political equation that is peculiar to each case. Specific unions are involved, employment may be concentrated in the districts of key representatives or the states of influential senators, the number of workers affected may be large, alternative employment opportunities may be few, and inaction by the president might result in Congress seeking to legislate a solution of its own. On the other hand, every president tries to avoid appearing as a protectionist or adding inflationary pressures to the economy. He also considers the potential damage that might occur to relations with countries whose exports would be curtailed.

Domestic politics favors granting relief. General economic and diplomatic considerations oppose it. The result is generally a compromise that allows the president and Congress to move on to other issues. And when relief is granted, it more likely than not will bear only a tangential and accidental relationship to the future international competitiveness of U.S. industry in general or of the industry seeking a trade remedy in particular. Rather, relief will result from compromises between idealism and political reality and will serve other government goals such as avoiding an adverse impact on consumers or retaliation by foreign countries. It will also be a direct consequence of government's lack of both detailed knowledge about an industry and substantial analytical capability to choose an appropriate course of action. And most of all, relief will be the result of a philosophical repugnance by officials and businesspeople alike to governmental involvement in a cooperative process with industry to promote the fortunes of that industry.

The Shoe Case. Perhaps the most extensive effort by government to assist an industry occurred in the case of nonrubber footwear. The industry had clearly suffered injury due to imports. Fully one-third of the American plants producing footwear closed from 1968 to 1974. Taiwanese and Korean footwear exports to the United States had doubled. After being denied relief twice, the industry finally obtained quantitative limits on exports of Taiwanese and Korean shoes in 1977.

As part of this action, the Commerce Department engaged in a substantial effort to increase the chances for survival of smaller firms in the industry. Groups of firms were organized into limited cooperatives for the purchase of raw materials, for shipping, and marketing. Pledges were obtained from retailers to buy more shoes from domestic sources. The program was small in scope, but unprecedented in terms of an attempt at government-industry cooperation. The impact was highly limited.

What is perhaps most interesting is the choice of industry for which this effort was undertaken and the nature of the attempt. American shoe producers on the whole were not about to conquer foreign markets, nor even reconquer their own. One-third of the cost of a shoe is accounted for by labor, and 30¢/hour wages abroad were not unusual. Korean and Taiwanese costs could not be equaled by American producers. At the time, Italian, Spanish, and Brazilian shoes were setting style trends. The U.S. industry was becoming more highly concentrated, but the largest firms were not the object of government assistance. Some improvement was made, no doubt, in the fortunes of a few smaller-sized firms.

OTHER IMPORT REMEDIES

By far the most common U.S. trade actions result from petitions for countervailing and antidumping duties. These legal procedures are particularly well suited to America's form of trade policy. Here, an attempt at scientific inquiry can usually displace any broader considerations. All that is needed is an investigation of the amount of subsidy or of the dumping margin, and if an industry is found to be injured, a calculation can be made to offset the subsidy or dumping. The unfair act is to be precisely offset, the playing field made level again. The comparative health of the players is not at issue.

The range of inquiry is thus very narrow. Unfortunately, an industry's problems in international competition usually have many causes. Foreign governments usually do not confine their support of an industry to a single form of assistance. Import protection, waivers of antitrust rules, restrictions on the free transfer of technology, and preferential procurement are among the other tools of government programs that distort international competition.

A response confined to a countervailing or antidumping duty, unrelated to any broader objective, at best can remove a single distortion.

The striking inadequacies of the countervailing and antidumping duty laws were clearly demonstrated in two instances in which the problems of international competition have been most acute—consumer electronics and steel.

The Color TV Case. In the early 1970s, Japanese producers began to dump color televisions in the United States. Japanese home market demand was relatively limited due to the imposition of a substantial commodities tax and an archaic distribution system, among other reasons. There were other factors affecting the competition such as innovations in production technology. The U.S. industry was in obvious trouble.

An antidumping case was filed, and although the case resulted in a finding of dumping, no collection of duties took place for over a decade—an appalling display of governmental ineptitude. Further, the case was settled for a small fraction of the amount that the Treasury originally found to be involved. While some would ascribe the settlement to an elaborate conspiracy to obtain other trade negotiating objectives with Japan, the sad fact is that the case demonstrated nothing more than bureaucratic incompetency in calculating and applying dumping duties and the inadequacy of our legal system in trying to deal with international competition. The question for policymakers in a dumping case was not how to create an internationally competitive industry, it was how to maintain prices in the two markets at the same level.

In 1976, color television exports from Japan almost tripled. The then Japanese prime minister, Mr. Fukuda, apologized for the "torrential downpour" of these sets on the U.S. market. The domestic color television industry sought and in 1977 was granted import relief in the form of an orderly marketing agreement restraining imports from Japan.

The domestic industry then opened a second front. Zenith challenged the rebate on exports of the Japanese commodities tax as a countervailable subsidy. The Treasury, which at that time also administered the countervailing duty law, concluded that the rebate of indirect taxes could not be countervailed as a subsidy. This led to a second quasi-judicial inquiry entirely unrelated to the competition in television sets. For the U.S. government, the survival of the color TV industry was of absolutely no concern in the countervailing duty case. Rather, the outcome of the case was considered to be of enormous consequence because of the precedential effect it would have. If Zenith won, an offsetting duty would have to be placed on all imports in the amount of the indirect taxes—sales taxes, and the value added taxes (VAT) of Europe—rebated on them when they left their domestic markets.

Denied relief by Treasury, Zenith appealed to the courts. A curious, very American process was begun to settle this momentous issue of trade policy. Judges began an examination of an 1897 law to determine what that Congress sitting three generations earlier had meant by the statutory formulation "bounty or grant." Future world harmony and possibly the fate of the U.S. television industry (but this latter point was an element left unexplored) rested upon the result. The Supreme Court ultimately upheld the Treasury's ruling. This was undoubtedly the right result under the law, and necessary to preserve peace among Western trading nations. Yet there are trade distortions caused when some countries rely more heavily than others on indirect taxes. The problem in terms of international competition remained. The law functioned then and functions today independent of such concerns.

In 1983 litigation over the original color TV dumping case came to a close.[1] A dozen years had been spent in weighing various fair and unfair trade complaints. At no time was a comprehensive examination of the domestic industry's international competitiveness undertaken or was any plan of assistance implemented along with the relief. Imports had been restrained for a period. Patterns of investment and trade had been altered. But it would be hard to argue that those involved in the dozen years of trade litigation had spent their time to best advantage. It did not serve the domestic industry, the nation's economy, or even consumer interests well. Even for American trade negotiators, spending nine months of 1976-77 negotiating limits on Japanese television exports may or may not have been the right priority in promoting fairer competition between the two countries. Invoking a statutory right to a remedy substituted for any reasoning process about providing better or more appropriate remedies or otherwise safeguarding U.S. commercial interests. At best, the American effort can be seen as resulting in increased Japanese private investment in assembly operations in the United States. It was assumed that this served American interests.

Steel. The problems of the American steel industry antedate those of the color television producers: significant growth in steel import penetration began in the late 1950s. From 1950 to 1957, imports averaged about 1.7 percent of consumption. In 1959 this ratio jumped to 6.1 percent, largely because of a protracted strike in the steel industry. Imports increased steadily throughout the 1960s and 1970s and have recently been averaging 18–22 percent of apparent consumption. Increasing imports, a declining domestic growth rate for steel demand, and increasing labor productivity have led to a steady decline in employment in the American steel industry. While production and capacity in the United States grew only marginally over the years 1960 to 1981, the capacity and output of other countries expanded rapidly.

A variety of domestic and foreign causes have been found for the U.S. steel industry's decline in competitiveness. Studies of the relative international decline of the U.S. steel industry and the concomitant growth of imports point to such basic factors as a sharp decline in raw material, shipping, and unit labor costs of foreign producers relative to U.S. producers in explaining the shift in comparative advantage from the United States to other countries. The shift is also because of the difference in the government's role in the United States compared with government's role in other countries. Most nations have adopted programs to promote actively the international competitiveness of their steel producers.

No other country has adopted a stance that is basically adversarial toward its national steel industry. Abroad, government involvement is pervasive— in the form of quotas (in Japan until just a few years ago a near prohibition on imports existed), tariffs, preferential procurement, subsidies of all forms, and a variety of other measures to control trade. Government ownership extends to about 30 percent of free world steel production.

Alarmed at the rapid increase of steel imports, U.S. steel producers and workers began pressing for import protection in the 1960s. In the late 1960s the U.S. dollar became overvalued, the U.S. trade surplus disappeared, and trade became a national concern. In 1968, under threat of likely congressional passage of a steel quota bill, the Europeans and Japanese agreed to restrict their steel exports to the United States "voluntarily." In 1972, the U.S. executive branch renegotiated the voluntary agreements to last through 1974.

The international competitive problems of the industry continued despite the depreciation of the dollar. Imports remained a problem after the restraint agreements had lapsed. The industry initiated a series of legal actions designed to replace the restraints that had been inspired by threats of congressional action. In 1976, the American Iron and Steel Institute brought a section 301 complaint–a remedy discussed more fully in the following section– against the European Community alleging that the Community's restraint on Japanese steel was deflecting Japanese steel to the U.S. market. This complaint was ultimately rejected by the government on the ground that the allegation could not be substantiated.

Given a sincere (if not fully thought through) assurance from the U.S.

government that it would enthusiastically enforce the U.S. unfair trade statutes, in 1977 U.S. steel producers filed a series of twenty-three dumping
complaints against Japanese and European pricing practices covering a large
portion of these countries' steel exports to the U.S. market. The governments
of the exporting countries reacted hostilely to the prospect of the U.S.
imposing additional duties on so large a volume of their trade. At the same
time, the complexity of simultaneously conducting so many investigations
became apparent to U.S. officials. The early statements about "enforcing the
trade laws" had to be discarded as being overly simplistic. Under threat of
deteriorating relations with European governments and the Common Market's
Commission, President Carter put together a task force headed by then Under
Secretary of the Treasury Anthony Solomon to develop an alternative solution.

Solomon created a plan for monitoring the prices of all steel imports into
the United States against "trigger prices," with the promise of initiating
expedited antidumping investigations of any imports that entered the United
States below the trigger prices. Solomon's plan also recognized and attempted
to address some of the nontrade problems the U.S. steel industry was having
in trying to improve its competitiveness. It set up a Tripartate Advisory
Committee on steel composed of U.S. government officials, steelworkers,
and steel management to identify and suggest solutions to industry problems,
including taxation and environmental issues. No fundamental changes were
recommended regarding industry reorganization or structure. Moreover, the
committee had no authority to implement its recommendations, and although
some of its proposals have been adopted, many have never been implemented.

The trigger price system itself suffered from a number of flaws. Implicit
in the system was the acceptance of below fair value sales by those foreign
producers who were less efficient than the Japanese and who, but for the
system, would have had to sell at prices considerably above trigger price
levels. In addition, since the trigger price system was based on Japanese
production costs, it was more responsive to changes in the yen/dollar relationship than it was to basic changes in steel production costs. In 1979 the
yen/dollar movements reversed and the trigger prices failed to increase and
even decreased slightly during one quarter. Unfortunately, throughout this
period, U.S. producers' production costs continued to increase while domestic demand for steel was falling. U.S. producers were effectively experiencing a decrease in import protection at the same time that their position

in the home market was deteriorating. Imports of European steel remained high despite the fact that many European producers were much less efficient than the Japanese.

Ultimately this system proved unworkable. In March 1980 U.S. Steel Corporation filed numerous dumping complaints against the European producers. Again, the U.S. government was sincere in offering direct enforcement of the unfair trade statutes as the appropriate course of action. Again, European governments registered strenuous objections to the potential damage to their trade that would result from the dumping that duties would create. Lengthy negotiations ensued. U.S. Steel withdrew its complaints in favor of a strengthened trigger price system that was accompanied by a quantitative element. This revised system was implemented in October 1980 but ran into trouble almost immediately.

The U.S. market for steel was in a steep slump—particularly the steel sheet market, which was dependent on automobile production. U.S. prices for these and certain other products were below the trigger prices. Foreign producers found it difficult and frequently impossible to sell these products at the trigger price levels, a situation they found unacceptable. In mid-1981, steel was increasingly entering below the trigger price level. In November 1981, after import statistics had begun to substantiate the flood of imports, the U.S. government initiated seven unfair trade cases.

This was too little too late. With substantial subversion of the trigger price system, and what the U.S. steel industry saw as wholly inadequate enforcement efforts by the U.S. government, the trigger price system lost credibility. The industry filed 132 antidumping and countervailing duty complaints. The trigger price system was again suspended, never to be reinstated.

Again the U.S. government believed it could simply enforce the law. Again, serious protests were received from European governments. They pointed to severe unemployment at home and to adjustment programs that could not be accelerated without serious domestic political consequences. Moreover, the dumping duties were to be applied on a national basis—some European countries faring better than others. This was viewed as intolerable by the European Economic Community.

The Commerce Department began parallel discussions with the European Community and the U.S. steel producers about a negotiated solution to the trade problem. With the agreement of the European Community, the U.S. government imposed a system of agreed quotas for European steel, and the domestic steel industry withdrew its cases. During this period Japanese steel exports to the United States also appeared to have been subject to export restraint, but this was not pursuant to a formal or public proceeding in either country.

What is so extraordinary about this saga is that only a minute fraction of the attention devoted by the U.S. government to the problems of steel over the last seventeen years has addressed ways to enhance the industry's international competitiveness. Domestic government policies—pressing for early settlement to strikes, jawboning down price increases—have had adverse effects on costs and investment. Antitrust policies prevented restructuring. Tax policies were no match for the tax relief given by other governments. The government granted some protection from time to time, but selectively and sporadically. U.S. government policies have not resulted in a more efficient steel industry.

The lack of a connection between the competitive condition of the industry and the trade measures taken is strikingly illustrated by the fact that the current quotas on European steel are scheduled to terminate when the *European* firms are to have completed *their* adjustment and modernization in December 1985. (This is because the quotas are a substitute for countervailing duties. These duties end when the subsidies end: when European modernization is ostensibly completed.) Under the U.S. trade policy system, there is, of course, no domestic plan of modernization. Whatever occurs in this direction will be due to the efforts of individual companies investing as much as possible in a depressed market, with little in the way of new debt, equity, or retained earnings available as a source of finance.

U.S. public policies have not provided basic solutions for the American steel industry. With continued resort to the trade laws likely, and all parties maintaining their current ideological stances, U.S. trade policy will not prevent the continued erosion of this industry. What the government has done is reduce present political pressures. Its "solutions" do not provide for the future of the industry.

FOREIGN "UNFAIR" TRADE PRACTICES

When foreign governments intervene in the marketplace to promote particular industries, they employ a whole array of mutually reinforcing measures—subsidies, import protection, antitrust relief, favorable procurement, export promoting tax incentives, and so on. Some of the practices can be characterized as "unfair" in a traditional trade policy sense. However, our trade laws do not offer a coherent mechanism for responding to comprehensive national industrial promotion efforts. Under existing provisions, the foreign action must instead be dissected and fit into neat legal categories, such as dumping or countervailable subsidies. At best, this results in a fragmentary response to the problem and frequently in no response at all.

Industries whose problems do not fit more precise legal remedies have recourse to section 301 of the Trade Act of 1974. This is the president's broad discretionary authority to retaliate against foreign nations for their unreasonable, unjustifiable or discriminatory acts that burden U.S. commerce. This remedy suffers because its applicability is so extraordinarily broad and has so few guideposts for its exercise that it is almost never successfully invoked. With this statute, too, there is a pattern of failure to achieve and implement a coherent policy that would be of material assistance to American industry competing in a difficult world environment.

The government, with only two exceptions (both in agriculture) has remained passive in the use of section 301, awaiting the filing of private-sector petitions. The cases are not part of any government strategy. They have ranged from attempting to get a few refrigerators into Taiwan, steamships into Guatemala, soybeans into Spain, and citrus into the EEC. The emphasis placed on granting equitable treatment tends to replace any process of setting national priorities. Cases of little economic importance may be pressed as vigorously as those of greater significance.

The authority is both contentious—it is, after all, the president who is called upon to retaliate against the acts of sovereign governments—and ineffective. The cases tend to generate more heat than light. As there is no investigative staff, there is no detailed or probing investigation. A petitioner finds his own government highly skeptical of his petition's merits.

Section 301 demonstrates the inadequacy of trying to deal with problems of international competition as matters to be decided by a legal proceeding. In many instances a foreign government's action may not constitute clearly defined wrongful behavior under international agreements and domestic law, and yet substantial harm has been caused. Too often, once a tribunal's deliberations run their course with inconclusive results, the superficial inquiry ends, and concern dissipates until a new case is filed.

The Machine Tool Case. A good example of this is the case of Houdaille, a Florida manufacturer of machine tools, which brought an action against Japan's alleged "targeting" of its machine-tool industry that resulted in Japanese numerical machine tools capturing a major share of the U.S. market. Houdaille sought relief under an unused provision of law, Section 103 of the

Revenue Act of 1971, a similar remedy to section 301, except that the only relief permitted is the denial of the investment tax credit.

All of the failings of section 301 were found to exist in section 103. The government's internal debate focused on the "unfairness" of the measures taken to promote the Japanese machine-tool industry, the amount of subsidies given, and the extent of adverse effects on the U.S. producers. The burden of proof lay with the U.S. company, which produced reams of briefs on Japanese practices, in search of the "smoking gun" that would prove Japanese success was traceable to direct government funding. That the Japanese industry was successful in this competition was not in itself a consideration and little concern was manifested for the fate of the U.S. machine-tool industry.

Some facts were uncovered that were damaging to the Japanese position, but the benefit of doubt lay with the foreign country. Further, the relief sought was deemed too draconian to use. The U.S. government's investigation into the allegations was, of necessity, superficial—no teams of special investigators were available for assignment to this work. The strong bias in favor of letting the "market" decide who shall prevail, itself prevailed. Unless a specific injury due to a specifically actionable practice (a countervailable subsidy or dumping) is formally alleged under the appropriate procedure and can then be found to exist, the result is almost always inaction—and this was the result in the Houdaille case.

The trade association representing the machine-tool makers subsequently brought a national security case (under section 232 of the Trade Expansion Act of 1962) alleging that imports of machine tools were impairing U.S. national security. This statutory remedy has never been applied by the United States except with respect to oil imports. It is a very broad authority, with few standards, and therefore little accountability. While the GATT contains an exception for the imposition of national security import restrictions, the remedy is nevertheless viewed generally with repugnance by trade policy officials. There would be extreme reluctance, for all the policy and ideological reasons cited earlier, for a president to invoke this authority outside of extraordinary circumstances.

This does not mean that ultimately there will be no relief granted to reduce machine-tool imports. Whatever factors are causing the decline of an industry in this country relative to a foreign industry generally continue to have an effect. Market share erosion continues, and through an individual petitioner's perseverance, and without any governmental attempt to seek alternative solutions, a statutory trade remedy is often eventually found. But this is usually very late in the day, and the relief granted is very incomplete. It is most accurately described as symptomatic relief, not a cure. Thus, there is no particular likelihood, if past practice is a guide, that relief will result in enhanced international competitiveness of the U.S. machine-tool industry.

Semiconductors. The case of semiconductors illustrates even more starkly our trade laws' inability to offer a coherent response to a foreign government's promotion of its industries. The U.S. semiconductor industry has been widely cited as an unusually innovative, efficient, and competitive industry. In contrast to ailing U.S. industries like autos and televisions, the semiconductor producers have enjoyed a considerable degree of success in export markets—in 1982 they held over 50 percent of the world market. Nevertheless, this industry, too, has proved vulnerable to foreign government intervention.

Following the first oil crisis in 1973, Japan concluded that the key to its own national economic future lay in high technology, knowledge-intensive industries that required comparatively few imported raw materials. The Japanese government implemented a series of programs designed to accelerate and guide the development of these industries, which were already the beneficiaries of government protection from imports and investment and had been receiving some financial aid and antitrust relief for research and development in the 1960s and early 1970s.

In 1975, new government programs were launched which by the early 1980s would place Japanese semiconductor firms in a dominant market position in several advanced product lines; the U.S. semiconductor industry became concerned. Despite "liberalization" of the Japanese market in 1974-75, the U.S. share of that market remained stagnant, notwithstanding the opening of numerous local U.S. subsidiaries in Japan and generally superior U.S. semiconductor quality. Low-priced Japanese exports of 16K RAMs—then the state-of-the-art memory device—eroded U.S. firms' sales and were blamed for their serious operating losses.

Accordingly, the U.S. semiconductor firms formed a trade association in 1977 to look for answers to the Japanese challenge. They did not find satisfactory answers in the U.S. trade laws. Like other industries before them, they found that their problem did not fit into the neat legal compartments created by those laws. The countervailing duty law, for example, was of little use against Japanese R&D subsidies, which were moving the Japanese ahead technologically. Countervailing duties are determined according to the amount of actual subsidy allocated to individual products. In the case of semiconductors, the duty that would be imposed—a minute amount per device given the comparative size of the subsidy and the huge volume of semiconductor sales—would bear no relationship to the real-world business effects of the subsidies.

Similarly, despite very low pricing by Japanese firms selling 16K RAMs in the U.S. market, the antidumping laws were viewed as useless. For semiconductors, it is difficult to establish the appropriate allocation of R&D costs to a particular product line; moreover, in this industry, costs of production decline with extraordinary rapidity as learning efficiences are realized, making it difficult to establish the "average cost of production" for antidumping purposes before the product life cycle has run its course.

Questioning whether meaningful or appropriate relief would be available under the trade laws, the Semiconductor Association devised an affirmative program of its own to try to offset the Japanese government-industry efforts. An important part of this process involved convincing the U.S. government that a problem existed at all. At the same time, several industry-sponsored studies, coupled with growing realization of the strategic importance of the semiconductor and similar industries, generated sufficient concern in Congress to help pass legislation authorizing tax credits for increased research and development.

Tax credits for R&D, however, were not a match for Japan's development projects, and U.S. semiconductor firms considered filing a section 301 petition detailing actionable unfair trade practices. But what they sought from the U.S. government was partisanship in their favor, not an adjudication. In effect, the semiconductor industry was compelled to present a case to its government hoping that the problems that it detailed were sufficiently compelling to prompt government officials to put into place appropriate U.S. public policies.

With the support of the U.S. Semiconductor Industry Association, discussions were initiated between U.S. and Japanese governments, which led to an agreement to increase market access in Japan through long-term supplier relationships with Japanese industrial consumers. The Semiconductor Association has also attempted to counter the Japanese joint research efforts and to foster university training for engineers by establishing its own joint research endeavor, the Semiconductor Research Cooperative (SRC), in which participating firms pool funds to finance basic research at U.S. universities. The association is also seeking an array of new legislation—much of it designed to be part of an American response to Japanese promotional programs—including antitrust reform and improved copyright protection for semiconductor designs.

The progress that has been made, however, has not been a result of the American trade policy system, but has in fact been achieved despite its inadequacies. To be sure, the vagaries of the legislative process, coupled with the adjudicative posture of many within the executive branch, may still combine to frustrate the industry's effort to mount a comprehensive response to the Japanese semiconductor program. Even if the semiconductor industry's singular effort is successful, there is no guarantee that other U.S. industries confronted with similar problems can use the same approach with equal success.

EXPORT POLICY

American policy toward industrial exports differs from import policy primarily in terms of rhetoric. U.S. trade officials' speeches generally stress the importance of exports to the country: "one in every seven of our manufacturing jobs is related to exports"—but support of industrial exports as a whole is limited and is certainly not focused consciously on particular product sectors.

Besides general export promotion efforts, such as trade fairs, selling missions, and technical advice and information systems, some concrete support measures are offered. As part of the balance of payments program of the Nixon administration, the Domestic International Sales Corporation still survives as a modest export promotion measure. The U.S. government's direct export financing mechanism is limited, ad hoc, and reactive. The U.S. Export-Import Bank at best offers export credits on terms designed simply to match those being offered by other nations, and Eximbank's credits are granted only on a transaction-by-transaction basis, rather than systematically or on a sectorwide basis. Moreover, Eximbank's loan authority has been substantially reduced in recent years, and the bank has frequently (and inaccurately) been criticized by government officials as a drain on the taxpayer.

Not only does the United States have a comparative dearth of export-promoting policies, its laws and official policies have frequently served actually to retard the export competitiveness of our industries. The United States maintains tighter national security-related export controls on high technology products than any of its trading partners, and these controls extend not only to U.S. sales to the Soviet bloc, but to neutral third countries. In addition to national security export controls, the United States has, for foreign policy reasons, placed periodic embargoes on sales of U.S. products to several countries. While such actions and policies may be defended on grounds of foreign policy and national security, America's allies—and principal competitors—have not felt fettered by similar concerns and, as a result, U.S. industry is losing export sales to them. Foreign buyers committing themselves to the acquisition of major capital goods will increasingly prefer suppliers whose replacement components, software, and additional new equipment are not subject to interruption when international tensions increase.

The consequences of a continued lack of coherent export policy in a world in which national trade rivals pursue systematic export-promoting programs may result in a declining U.S. participation in export markets. Between 1975 and 1980 the United States suffered a decline in export market share in most of the major capital goods sectors in which official government export support is most pronounced (aircraft, industrial machinery, electric-power machinery and generating equipment, and machine-tool and metal-working equipment). While no single factor can wholly account for these market share reductions, these results suggest an urgent need to examine U.S. trade policy—or the lack of policy—from the standpoint of its effects on the export competitiveness of America's industries.

TRADE NEGOTIATIONS POLICY

After reviewing area after area of aimless drift in trade policy, it is refreshing to find at least one area in which America has a degree of strategic planning and excels in planning to a greater extent than any of its trading partners. Part of this success was accidental.

U.S. trade negotiators had always had some private-sector advice in major trade negotiations. In 1975 Congress legislated the creation of an unprecedentedly major private-sector advisory system for the Tokyo Round of Multilateral Trade Negotiations. The result was the establishment of forty-five committees and nearly 1,000 advisers. Representatives of a wide variety of interests were constituted as a top level committee to give broad policy advice. Industry, agriculture, and labor policy committees were also set up, supported by dozens of sectoral committees to provide technical advice. The trade negotiators, who drew all of their authority from Congress and would need to obtain congressional approval of all but tariff agreements if any negotiating results were to be implemented, had to formulate objectives with the advisers and report to them any failures to follow their advice. The advisers would then report their views to Congress at the time the agreements were presented to Congress for approval.

The political results were impressive. Congress, which had previously almost without exception rejected every trade agreement negotiated by the executive branch, gave a thumpingly lopsided endorsement to the Tokyo Round results—by a vote of 396 to 7 in the House, and 90 to 4 in the Senate. This was attributable not only to the political genius of U.S. Trade Representative Robert Strauss, but to the laborious process of private-sector consultation, in which the adversary relationship between industry and government was forgotten, and trade officials and industry representatives worked closely together to promote U.S. commercial interests.

No other government's negotiators had better information on objectives to be sought. Industry expertise was plentiful and was relied upon. Foreign barriers were identified, market opportunities assessed, and priorities established—a process foreign to all other areas of U.S. trade policy. One reason for establishing priorities was that even if academics would have preferred all trade barriers here and abroad be removed, this was not a realistic goal given national political realities. Therefore, specific objectives had to be established and negotiating priorities set. For a change, the international competitiveness of American industries was to be explored and exploited.

The setting of offensive and defensive negotiating strategy differed somewhat, however. Removal of export barriers would promote positive adjustment. U.S. import restrictions, however, were retained on a basis of sensitivity to imports to avoid dislocations. Older rather than infant industries retained protection. A regard for areas of greatest import sensitivity was the political price paid to allow major areas of protection to be removed in payment for removing foreign barriers to U.S. exports. However, an accurate assessment of certain U.S. import barrier's obsolescence allowed some cherished barriers to be traded off without significant harm to American industrial interests.

The private-sector advisory process that proved to be the strength of the U.S. negotiating effort in the Tokyo Round has not subsequently been used to help establish any other trade objectives. Formal private-sector advice is not sought for current trade issues either in import or export competition. The collaborative effort deemed appropriate for establishing defensive and offensive positions in the major "open seasons" for foreign and domestic trade restrictions, which occur once a decade in major multilateral negotiations, are somehow deemed wholly inappropriate for the individual decisions that make up U.S. trade policy between major rounds of negotiations.

The strategic thinking that characterizes a major trade negotiation is replaced with superficial philosophic, moral, and legislative judgments about specific trade issues. The collaborative relationship between industry and government is replaced with distrust and an adversarial relationship. An active leadership role of government yields to passivity and a reactive role. Drift replaces direction.

U.S. AGRICULTURAL POLICY

The reader may discount most of the foregoing if agriculture rather than industry is made the subject of this inquiry. The differences in the treatment given the two goods-producing segments of the economy are striking. Agricultural universities and research are government funded. Extension services bring new technologies to the farm. Support prices are set for major traded commodities, stocks carried, and farms, equipment, electricity, irrigation, and transportation financed. Plant and animal health is safeguarded. Export development is supported through marketing cooperatives, technical assistance, intergovernment minimum purchase agreements with nonmarket economies, and aggressive export financing. Foreign aid is used to distribute surpluses.

Knowledge substitutes for ignorance in government, from crop forecasts to conditions in any significant foreign market. The strengths and weaknesses of foreign competition are assessed. The agricultural community supports its voice in government, the Department of Agriculture, and is supported in return. Long-range forecasts are made, and production, distribution, and sales are encouraged.

Agriculture is still a market-driven sector of the economy, but the pervasive role of government is welcomed and contributes positively. The laissez-faire rhetoric is, if anything, stronger, but the private sector and the government work together in a complementary and highly successful fashion to promote in every way possible the international competitiveness of American agribusiness.

SOME SUGGESTED CHANGES IN APPROACH

In the case of agriculture there is little of the wavering uncertainty that characterizes industrial trade policy. While other policies occasionally override—President Ford's anti-inflation-motivated soybean embargo, and the ceiling on grain exports to the Soviet Union imposed by President Carter as a foreign policy sanction—these actions have provoked widespread domestic disapproval, particularly in the agricultural community, and would not be repeated lightly. As a political matter, industrial trade is far more easily restricted for foreign policy or national security reasons than is agricultural trade. The restrictions, once imposed, are more difficult to remove.

SOME SUGGESTED REFORMS

The absence of a process of setting priorities for industrial goods as opposed to agricultural commodities[2] is due partly to the fact that the production or export of industrial goods is itself not a serious national priority. The argument that America should seek open international markets for its industrial exports in pursuit of clearly defined national commercial goals, rather than for more abstract "broader" policy interests, has not found acceptance.

Underlying the U.S. government's reluctance to pursue American economic self-interest through a comprehensive trade strategy has been a tacit assumption that U.S. industries, for the most part, are competitively superior to those of our trading partners. U.S. policymakers have taken "a broader view" as advocates of free market noninterventionism, secure in the belief that U.S. industries could hold their own internationally without any government action, given only a reasonably level playing field.

That assumption probably once held some truth, but no longer. Industries have arisen in Japan, and more recently, in the newly industrializing countries of East Asia, that are as competitive or more competitive than our own. These industries, including the Korean steel and Japanese consumer electronics industries, are highly automated, well managed, technologically advanced, and have extremely low labor costs. Their product quality, more often than not, is superb. Moreover, they sometimes benefit from an array of government-aid measures designed to further enhance their competitive advantages. Faced with such formidable new rivals, America can no longer view with indifference the way in which the market is affecting the economic future of the country, if, when closely examined, the market is found to be far from free of distortions.

There is no reason why America's largely successful agricultural strategy cannot be matched by a coherent industrial strategy. Objectives of this strategy could include pursuing many of the principles that U.S. policymakers already endorse, but tempered with a degree of economic self-interest and informed realism that is currently missing.

The U.S. government should aggressively seek to take advantage of areas in which its industries are internationally competitive, ensuring open international markets for them. It should not hesitate to use the substantial leverage of its command to assure that competitive U.S. products enjoy full market opportunities abroad. If U.S. industries have lost their international competitiveness, there should be a national objective to restore that competitiveness if possible—not through import relief alone, but with rationalization programs if they are needed. If other nations seek to dominate international markets through major government promotional programs, the United States should respond with measures—such as matching subsidies—that deprive these promotional efforts of their appeal.

Moreover, at some point the United States must abandon its ideological excuses for continuing to ignore the fate of its major industries, and recognize that if it allows random events—including the policies of other nations—to control the destinies of its industries, some of these industries may become permanent wards of the state. An example of the need for a comprehensive inquiry into an industry's future is our automobile industry, in which a series of unrelated decisions has been taken. The largest of these was the imposition of quotas on Japanese shipments. Questions still remain: Ford and Chrysler have challenged the recently approved joint venture between General Motors and Toyota. In most Western industrial nations a proposed transaction of such significance might be an occasion for consultations involving labor, management, and government about the appropriate result for the economy as a whole. Instead, the inquiry in the United States was conducted by the Federal Trade Commission, an agency that does not possess the statutory mandate—or the inclination—to engage in a broad inquiry. Basic questions about the future of this industry will be resolved or left unresolved according to the narrow standards of the U.S. antitrust laws. The future international competitiveness of the U.S. automobile industry is not a question seriously addressed.

If the United States adopted a more enlightened approach, it would recognize that in the past the problems of ailing industries have been dealt with in a series of unrelated decisions in which import relief has been extended or withheld—with the one consistent element being the failure to link such relief with industrial renovation and reform. The U.S. government does not shrink from extending temporary protection to industries when political circumstances require it; however, it does not recognize that protection alone will not restore international competitiveness to an industry. More comprehensive measures, which may include industry restructuring (with some antitrust relief), phased capacity reduction, worker retraining, financial assistance, and technological and research and development aid, may be needed. The objective of such measures in all cases should not be to keep a moribund industry alive but to restore a noncompetitive industry to international competitiveness.

Implementating an affirmative national trade strategy means, first and foremost, pulling together the disparate strands that constitute current U.S. trade policy into a coherent whole. While there is an obvious need for some reorganization of the U.S. trade bureaucracy, with clear lines of authority for formulating *and* implementing trade policy, reorganization is not the most critical step. The U.S. government needs to develop the capacity to assess and evaluate industrial developments in this country and in other nations on an ongoing basis *before* major injury occurs to U.S. firms and workers. This means establishing a permanent staff of career experts with sectoral expertise—not only with the problems of U.S. industries, but with the industries and industrial policies of other nations so as to comprehend the realities of international competition.

It is noteworthy that those who formulate trade policy and negotiate for most of America's trading partners have spent their entire careers learning their profession. They are individuals drawn from the foremost rank of university graduates who have shown particular distinction thereafter. By contrast, the U.S. trade bureaucracy is staffed at the upper levels primarily by political appointees who may average eighteen months in office and who are often prevented by conflict-of-interest rules from being drawn from industry. There is a strong need to establish a professional career service in this country that will take a long-run view of our trade objectives. This service would have to find ways of being far more attractive than is currently the case if talented individuals are to be drawn in. This will mean providing adequate compensation and ensuring that these individuals are ultimately promoted to senior positions. At the same time, more professional exchanges with industry should be encouraged. This would give far better continuity than relying as heavily as the U.S. government does today on political appointees.

As important as the foregoing changes would be, of even greater importance is a change in the adversarial posture that exists between industry, labor, and government. The time has come to move toward a system in which consensus policies can be formulated. There is a strong need for a better method by which the private sector—both business and labor—can provide advice to and work with trade officials. If procompetitive policies are to be adopted, business, labor, and government must be able to meet together to discuss policy, share in trade remedy deliberations, and evaluate analytical work on U.S. and foreign industrial competitiveness. Otherwise there is no alternative but to leave in place the largely automatic and rigid legalistic trade policy system born in part of our distrust of government.

Clearly part of the solution would be to build a more cooperative and effective institutional relationship between Congress and the executive with respect to trade policy formulation. Too often, administration initiatives have failed simply because of inadequate advance discussion and consultations with appropriate members of Congress. Why did the Tokyo Round of multilateral trade negotiations receive an overwhelming vote of confidence from both houses of Congress, when most other executive branch trade discussions are regarded with criticism, skepticism, and hostility? Part of the answer is the fact that in the Tokyo Round broad negotiating objectives were set by the Congress, specific decisions were the result of intensive consultation, and no major step was taken without an opportunity for a full exploration with the congressional committees concerned. The private-sector advisers evaluated the results and made their views known directly to Congress.

No institutional framework currently exists for bringing the executive, Congress, and those in industry affected by public policy decisions together to formulate policy. This would not be difficult to do. If the straightjacket of automatic legal remedies is to be relaxed in favor of greater discretion, the means must be found to make officials more responsible to the Congress and the private sector. One means to do this would be to require annual approval of the general trade policy plan and priorities for the year by the House Ways and Means and Senate Finance Committees (akin to a parliamentary vote of confidence), after public hearings and the receipt of formal private-sector advisory committee advice. This would force closer coordination of all the actors involved in trade policy formulation.

These reforms are illustrative rather than comprehensive. The problems of international competitiveness extend beyond questions of trade policy formulation. Broad national policy designed to enhance technical education, the provision of grants to universities for the pursuit of basic research, programs for worker training and retraining, and additional tax incentives for research, development, and investment will each have their place.

With a politically more responsible system of trade policy formulation in place, it would be possible to undertake a basic overhaul of U.S. trade laws to make them more effective and responsive to international competitive realities.

Other measures will suggest themselves if and when U.S. policymakers are able to make the underlying philosophical change of attitude—namely that the international competitiveness of American industry is vital to the well-being of this country, the standard of living of its people, and its national defense. Paradoxically, only the successful pursuit of national economic self-interest will give the United States the means to keep its own market open, enable it to provide the necessary leadership to maintain a relatively open international trading system, and expand international trade for all participants. There will be little willingness by other nations to follow the lead of a country that is not an enormously strong competitor in its own right.

9

Technology as a Factor in U.S. Competitiveness

Harvey Brooks

Economic historians have long pointed out that since the early nineteenth century, superior technology has been a major factor in America's comparative advantage in world trade and in its higher average real wage levels.[1] Since 1880, U.S. manufacturing exports have been largely concentrated in new products that other countries either could not yet produce or had not yet begun to produce in quantity.[2] More recently, the product cycle theory developed by Vernon, Keesing, Hufbauer, and others has refined this idea.[3] According to their theory, to maintain its higher wage levels and living standards, the United States constantly has to develop new, unique products (or new types of tradable services) to exploit the temporary monopoly arising from their uniqueness: charging higher prices while not being faced with price competition. It is primarily this economic rent arising from innovation that enables U.S. producers to pay higher wages. By the time the new products or their production processes become standardized, and thus producible competitively in lower-wage countries, the United States would have developed improved versions of the products, more advanced production technologies, or entirely new products whose sales would be sufficient to offset the gradual loss of market for the more standardized items. In this theory, the rate of innovation in the United States must be fast enough to maintain and increase high-wage jobs more rapidly than they are lost through the transfer of older technologies abroad.

Because of this reasoning much current discussion of U.S. competitiveness focuses on our innovative capacity and on the state of our scientific and

Harvey Brooks is Benjamin Peirce Professor of Technology and Public Policy in the Kennedy School of Government and the Division of Applied Sciences at Harvard University.

technological infrastructure, which determines our future capacity for innovation.

For innovation to be economically significant, however, much more is needed than the capacity for originating new concepts and new ways of doing things. Implementing new concepts through successful commercialization, or through making them operational in the public sector, is as important, or sometimes more important, than originating the concepts. Since the end of World War II, where the first successful commercialization of a new technical invention has occurred has often been different from where it was conceived of first as an experimental model. During the periods of their most rapid economic growth, for example, Japan and Italy were the heaviest importers of licensed technology from the United States and were not major originators of new technology. Contrary to popular belief, the United Kingdom was not only a major source of basic science discoveries, it was also second only to the United States as the most prolific originator of significant industrial innovations. Yet most of these innovations found their major successful application elsewhere, chiefly in the United States. Jet engines and commercial jet aircraft are dramatic examples.[4]

Thus, the implications of innovation for competitiveness may depend as much or more upon the capacity to assimilate, adapt, and make operational new ideas and concepts from others as the ability to originate or invent them. It is in the ability to commercialize or operationalize new ideas before its competitors that America is losing its lead, even while it leads in the origination of new ideas, though not by as wide a margin as a decade ago. Indeed, the United States seems increasingly to serve as a world resource for new technical (and social and managerial) ideas that are being more aggressively and successfully pursued in other countries, especially Japan and the emerging "little Japans" of East Asia. If the United States fails to capitalize on its innovative ideas and realize the revenues from exploiting them, it will also gradually deprive itself of the resources it needs to continue generating new ideas. Meanwhile, other countries that currently appear less inventive will accumulate the resources that will enable them to become the primary locus of future innovations.

Two approaches are useful in assessing the state of U.S. innovation. The first is to examine various aggregate statistics on R&D performance, patent activity, technical manpower, industrial productivity, origination of major industrial innovations, or export market shares in high technology products. These aggregate measures do not support the extreme alarm being expressed on many sides over the decline in U.S. technical leadership.

The second approach is to examine the situation in specific industries or industry segments. Here the evidence of decline is much more alarming, as indicated in Bruce Scott's first chapter in this volume.[5] We are by now familiar with the dramatic turnaround in competitiveness that has occurred within a few industries in a very short time, particularly vis-à-vis Japan. The striking cases are, of course, automobiles and trucks, consumer electronics, steel, and machine tools. Somewhat less publicized are the cases of heavy construction machinery and some household appliances. More disturbing because of its implications for the future is the rapid growth of Japanese market penetration in semiconductors, particularly standardized memory chips such as the 64K RAM,[6] in robots, and in flexible manufacturing systems (FMC).[7] On the horizon also appears the spectre of "fifth generation computers," fine ceramics and high temperature materials in general, biotechnology,[8] possibly aeronautics, and commercial space-based communications and remote sensing services. In these high technology areas it is too early to judge how successful foreign efforts will be, but the signs seem more favorable for our competitors than would have been deemed conceivable just a few years ago.

The typical pattern of Japanese success has been rapid penetration of a narrow, but carefully selected, segment of a broad, expanding world market in which superiority in production efficiency, economies of scale, and exploitation of learning curve effects were particularly important. By expanding more aggressively than its U.S. competitors and anticipating learning curve improvements and economies of scale further into the future in its pricing strategies, Japan has been able to capture an important share of the market for selected products just behind the current technological frontier.[9] They have then broadened out from this point in the middle technology spectrum and moved gradually toward more sophisticated and higher value-added products in the same or a closely allied market segment. Willingness to plunge in and adopt a new technology on the basis of its ultimate promise before it was proven to be cost-effective has been combined with careful and thorough scanning of related world technological developments for their possible competitive threat or promise. Technology has played a more critical role in both government and industry planning in Japan than in other countries, especially the United States. There is evidence that U.S. companies have been caught completely by surprise by new technological developments in autos, machine tools, and consumer electronics because of a failure to monitor what the competition was doing worldwide. In Japan the selective use of all available policy instruments toward the single, overriding objective of international competitiveness has become an important ingredient of success completely lacking in the United States.[10] These instruments ranged from temporary protection of domestic markets to encouragement of company specialization and division of labor through cartel-like arrangements, all carefully orchestrated and timed according to a dynamic rather than a static assessment of the overall competitive situation.[11]

By contrast, U.S. technology policy has been oriented toward international economic competition more in rhetoric than in fact. Both our firms and our government, long accustomed to being the technological leaders in almost every field, have until recently measured their performance against domestic rather than foreign competitors. Technology has not been a key ingredient of policy decisions, and the dynamic nature of technological competition has been underestimated. Except in the field of specific defense technologies, decisions about protecting domestic markets from foreign competition are not made as part of a technology-promotion strategy as they are in Japan and in an increasing number of European countries (most notably France). We give lip service to the free market, but we use protectionist instruments as much or more than our competitors, largely as a case-by-case response to domestic political pressures rather than as part of a coherent strategy for gestating or nurturing future competitive industries.

AGGREGATE MEASURES OF U.S. COMPETITIVENESS IN INNOVATION

BASES FOR COMPARISON WITH OTHER COUNTRIES

Notwithstanding a widespread perception of declining innovativeness, it has been difficult to develop convincing quantitative measures of this phenomenon from aggregate statistics. A major problem is choosing a baseline against which to compare the current situation. The statistics most frequently quoted use the situation in the late 1950s or early 1960s as a standard of comparison. This was a period when most of the industrial world was still recovering from the devastation of World War II. Today's most formidable competitors, Germany and Japan, had suffered the highest degree of retardation of any of the industrial powers. In addition, both were just emerging from a period in which they had been politically enjoined from access to or development of important emerging technologies, such as nuclear energy and aeronautics, since they were considered militarily significant. A major purpose of postwar U.S. policy, including Marshall Plan aid and the promotion of multilateral free trade, was the economic and technological recovery of Europe and Japan. U.S. science support agencies, like the military basic research agencies and the Atomic Energy Commission (AEC), provided grants to overseas researchers and deliberately fostered the recovery of European and Japanese science. Though never explicitly stated, the purpose of these policies could hardly have been other than to close the gap in GDP per capita and in technical capability between these countries and the United States. Given the fact that our populations have comparable educational levels and similar political and economic systems, and that an increasingly open world trading system permits free movement of capital and knowledge as well as access to raw materials and energy, it is hard to imagine if anything could have preserved a dominant U.S. advantage over time.

The only factor that might have maintained U.S. dominance would have been an overwhelmingly superior innovative capacity. The United States began the postwar era with overwhelming technical dominance derived in large part from new technologies that had undergone forced development because of the war. Technological development was further nurtured by the political push of the Cold War and the military-technological competition with the Soviets. Until the early 1960s, military-technological developments probably had much more beneficial fallout for the civilian economy than was the case later, as the scale and sophistication of military systems began to diverge from what was applicable to civilian systems.

Through its continuing massive investment in defense R&D and through specific industrial policies for the defense industrial base, the United States continues to dominate in defense technology among its allies. Much of this technology, however, is now the elaboration of increasingly sophisticated, complex systems; only a relatively small proportion of expenditure on components and materials has significant applications in civilian industry. For example, the Very High Speed Integrated Circuit (VHSIC) program, reviewed by Yoshino and Fong in this volume,[12] is reminiscent of earlier defense-supported work in semiconductors, computer technology, and special materials such as titanium and composites. In fact, the VHSIC program and a few others in areas like Computer Aided Design/Manufacturing (CAD/CAM) and robotics supported by the Air Force have been partially sold to Congress on the basis of their potential contribution to the commercial strength of the United States as well as its national security. However, these programs are exceptions to the general rule that civilian spinoff is not considered seriously in the planning of defense R&D programs.

It is interesting to note that the dynamism in American technology during the 1950s and 1960s resembles the type we now observe in Japan, except that the latter is directed toward explicitly economic goals, while economic benefits were only incidental to ours. Indeed many of the elements of current Japanese industrial strategy were actually present in American strategy for the defense industrial base in this earlier era. The strategy included not only direct public funding of industrial R&D, but public procurement of high technology products to promote descent of the learning curve, special tax benefits, concessionary government-backed loans, and relaxation of the application of antitrust policies—to promote technological cooperation among firms and information sharing. These are all elements in current Japanese strategy.[13] In addition, the U.S. defense economy has been highly protectionist, with a preference for American firms and strict control over the entry of foreign defense products. The Pentagon also served as a sales agent for American defense products through its foreign military sales (FMS) program.

If the United States has lost its relative position in technology per se, one may ask whether it has done so to a greater degree than was inevitable, given the speed and ease of modern telecommunications, jet travel, and the growth of per capita income of our principal competitors.

As pointed out by Vernon,[14] until very recently, the gap in per capita income between the United States and other industrial countries meant that these countries had little incentive to develop products that would compete in the more affluent U.S. market, whereas U.S. products, through simplification and standardization, could increasingly compete in foreign markets. In addition, the size of the U.S. market generated economies of scale in production that gave American exports a price advantage against local producers in smaller foreign markets. In many cases this advantage was offset by trade barriers or high excise taxes in foreign markets, but in others it was not. This situation inevitably disappeared not only by the closing of the income gap but by the integration of the European market through the European Economic Community (EEC) and the remarkable growth of the Japanese domestic market. The Japanese market increased from less than 5 percent of the U.S. market in 1950 to more than 40 percent in 1980, and the EEC is now about equal in total market size to the United States market.[15]

In summary, the discussion of U.S. competitiveness, whether in terms of overall manufactured exports or in terms of its introduction of new technology in world markets, suffers from the absence of a base period that could be considered "normal." We could not have expected our competitors to accept the sort of dominant position that existed in the late 1950s, nor would that have been a reasonable goal for us. The real question is whether what we are seeing is merely the inevitable closing of a gap, or whether other countries, particularly in East Asia, are on a trajectory that is about to pass us and leave us in much the situation Britain now finds itself in.

THE AGGREGATE INDICES

International Trade in High Technology Products. One of the most frequently quoted measures of U.S. competitiveness in innovation is the balance of trade in high technology products. The classification of exports into high and low technology is usually based upon the ratio of R&D expenditures to sales or value added, or on the number of R&D scientists and engineers per 1,000 workers. In the studies used for the National Science Foundation (NSF) *Science Indicators 1980*, for example, technology-intensive industry was defined as industry classifications having twenty-five or more R&D scientists and engineers per 1,000 workers, and spending at least 5 percent of sales on R&D.[16] Other studies have used a breakdown into three categories, with industries spending more than 5 percent of sales on R&D categorized as "high tech."[17] There is an extensive literature on how to classify industries in this way, but for the most part, trade statistics are not too sensitive to the exact choice of boundary.

In high technology industry, the largest U.S. companies held 79 percent of world markets (including U.S. domestic) in 1959; this had dropped to 47 percent by 1978. Meanwhile, the market share of Japanese firms had increased fourfold.[18] Table 9-1 compares the worldwide market shares of the largest U.S. companies in four high tech industries in 1959 and 1978.

Table 9-1
Worldwide Market Shares of Largest U.S. Companies in High Tech Industries, 1959 and 1978

	1959	*1978*
Drugs and medicines	61.6%	35.0%
Chemicals	66.3	31.9
Electronic products	75.6	46.9
Aircraft and parts	78.3	53.2

Source: U.S. Department of Commerce, International Trade Administration, *An Assessment of U.S. Competitiveness in High Technology Industries* (February 1983), 53, table 27.

In terms of exports, the share of U.S. R&D-intensive goods in world exports declined from 31 percent in 1962 to 21 percent in 1977, while the Japanese share rose from 5 percent to 14 percent in the same period. These figures are frequently quoted to demonstrate the dramatic decline in U.S. competitiveness, even in its traditionally strong domain of R&D-intensive products; however, the decline in export share is actually less than the decline in the U.S. share of world GNP. Hence the true meaning of the statistic is difficult to interpret.

It is in low technology products that the U.S. competitive position has declined most dramatically and obviously. The U.S. trade surplus in R&D-intensive manufactured products, which increased by a factor of 6.5 between 1960 and 1979, was balanced by a deficit in non-R&D-intensive products which, from close to zero as late as 1964, rose to cancel the R&D-intensive surplus by the early 1980s.[19] In fact, beginning in 1981, the U.S. overall balance in manufactured goods turned negative rather rapidly, reaching a net negative balance of $28 billion annual rate, extrapolating from the first seven months of 1983. An equally disturbing indicator is the appearance of a large negative balance in high technology trade with Japan, beginning in about 1975.[20] Also significant is that both Japan and West Germany have been much more successful than the United States in selling high technology products in the most rapidly growing markets of the developing countries (LDCs). The U.S. share of the LDC market dropped from 46 percent in 1962 to 24 percent in 1977, while the Japanese share grew from 6 percent to 22 percent and the German from 11 percent to 14 percent.[21] It is well known that initial market penetration of high technology products creates a bias toward future purchases from the same source because of service requirements and successive generations of improvements or attachments.[22] If it is true that LDC markets will provide the major growth export markets of the future for technology-intensive products, Japan and Germany are clearly positioning themselves better than the United States to exploit these markets.

At the same time that the United States has been losing market share in high technology products in LDCs, it has absorbed a higher volume of LDC manufactured exports as a fraction of domestic GNP than any other industrial country.[23] To the extent that these exports from LDCs to the United States help finance their imports of high technology capital goods from other countries, the United States may be a double loser in the long run.

The term "technology-intensive" embraces a wide range of product characteristics from very advanced (and hence labor-intensive) to standardized (and hence, more capital-intensive). At the high end of this spectrum, products are usually sufficiently unique so that the demand for them is quite inelastic to price; this is what Vernon has referred to as the high end of the product cycle.[24] There is some evidence that the United States is competing most effectively in this domain, for example, custom microchips rather than standardized RAMs. By contrast, Japan has generally aimed to enter the market at a slightly later stage of the product cycle, when simplification and standardization are possible and competitive prices and production costs become a more important factor in market penetration. Japan has been able to move into the market for advanced products closer to the frontier of the product cycle by concentrating on reducing manufacturing costs and on quality standards for products first introduced to the market by U.S. firms. This strategy is well illustrated in Finan and LaMond's account (see chapter 3) of the history of Japanese penetration of the U.S. market for standard 64K RAMs.[25] A similar strategy is being followed for industrial robots.[26]

Nelson and Winter have developed a computer simulation model for "Schumpeterian competition," using an evolutionary theory, and their models may provide a clue to the reasons for the success of the Japanese strategy.[27] Under certain conditions, firms that follow an "imitative" R&D strategy may actually consistently capture market share from the technology leaders. Conducive to this are an environment of "public" science and technology external to the firms, which is advancing rapidly, and an aggressive investment strategy by the most successful firms. When investments by the successful firms are not restrained by fear of saturating the market, the leading firm in market share becomes one of the followers rather than the technological leader. The advantage of the imitator firm is presumably further enhanced if it is in a different country from the technological pioneer firm, where it may have access to cheaper capital for production or for market probing and expansion. This is a good model for Japanese-American competition in advanced technology.

International Trade in Services. A discussion of international trade in high technology must consider services and other "invisibles." To an increasing degree, services are dependent on high technology in transportation, telecommunications, and data management. The U.S. technological lead in these areas contributed to the development of a favorable balance of trade in services. Even the earnings from U.S. foreign direct investment can be considered as part of the "invisible" trade that depends on high technology, for U.S. foreign direct investment has been heavily biased toward high technology industries that are also major export industries.[28] Indeed, sales of foreign affiliates of U.S. firms accounted for $194 billion of revenue in 1977 compared with $96 billion in export sales.[29] Counting only foreign sales of manufacturing affiliates, total foreign sales are about twice exports.

Unfortunately, very little is known about the actual composition of the trade in services, and even the aggregate statistics are subject to gross uncertainties. During the 1977-80 period it is generally believed that the U.S. trade surplus in services grew rapidly and continuously, and, until 1980, it was enough to more than offset the growing but fluctuating deficit in merchandise trade. Between 1970 and 1980 the *cumulative* U.S. current account surplus topped $60 billion and was greater than that of any other country, despite the spectacular rise in the cost of oil imports and the growing merchandise deficit.[30] Since 1980 the surplus has continued but leveled off and was insufficient to prevent a $31.8 billion current account deficit for the twelve months ending February 1984, along with a merchandise trade deficit of $69.4 billion.[31]

Many high technology products, particularly in the computer/communications/office equipment sectors, are sold to service industries, and the fastest expansion in the service sector has been in the "integrative" part, which combines sophisticated information technology with marketing/management know-how.[32] Some estimates of the favorable U.S. trade balance in information-related services alone run as high as $40 billion.[33]

It is hard to estimate, however, how much of the U.S. surplus in services can be attributed to high technology and to what degree the surplus will erode as the foreign stock of information capital, often purchased from the United States, grows. Countries acquire their own information handling capability, and, as they do so, place restrictions on transborder data flows and integration of domestic information systems into multinational information networks.[34] The portion of earnings resulting from foreign subsidiaries may be somewhat more robust, but some is certainly interest on the foreign loans to LDCs from American banks, of doubtful future prospects. The earnings from foreign subsidiaries may be important in paying for the R&D costs of the U.S. parent firms, thus helping them to maintain their comparative advantage in world markets for both domestic and foreign sales.[35] In the case of the U.S. computer industry, for example, 37 percent of all earnings come from sales overseas.[36]

In general, the future of this rather ill-defined sector may be the hardest to predict. Its role in creating domestic employment is even more uncertain, since the services sector probably generates more overseas than domestic employment. Because of its apparent present robustness, the services trade is extremely important to watch as an indicator of future U.S. technological competitiveness. Very recently there have been reports of a decline in the U.S. services trade balance.

Balance of Trade in Royalties and Fees. In the early 1960s, under the impetus of European concern about the "technology gap,"[37] international payments for the use of patents, trademarks, copyrights, or proprietary know-how began to be used as a measure of relative innovative capacity. Such measures are open to criticism because much of the payment flow is for inventions or other knowledge licensed some time in the past. It may under-state the current rate of generation of innovations, especially for a country whose technological effort is growing rapidly.[38] Nevertheless, by this gross measure the United States appears to be doing well. At the end of the 1970s it was earning nine times as much as it was paying out in royalties and fees.[39] This ratio had scarcely declined since 1967 despite a large growth of the absolute balance. The balance also showed no signs of slackening growth as of 1979.[40] It is important to keep in mind that over 80 percent of these receipts are from U.S. affiliates abroad and are thus related to foreign direct investment and are not "unaffiliated transactions," that is, transactions be-tween independent firms. This means that the U.S. parents maintained an equity interest in the "intangible property" represented by the transferred knowledge. They could exercise some control over the competitive use of this knowledge. In the long run, however, a firm could maintain competi-tiveness without necessarily benefiting the competitiveness of the nation.

On the other hand, the Japanese ratio of receipts to payments showed a rapid approach toward balance during the 1970s, going from 0.2 in 1971 to 0.7 in 1981, indicating the rapidity with which Japan was shifting toward becoming a net exporter of new technology.[41] If allowances are made for the age of the licenses on which royalties were being paid, it is likely that Japan has a positive balance on the most recent licenses, which suggests that it is already a net exporter of new technology. Furthermore, because Japanese industrial policy still discourages foreign direct investment, it is likely that a much higher percentage of Japanese payments to other countries derives from unaffiliated transactions, giving Japanese firms much freer use of the technology licensed. They are thus in a position to capitalize on the trans-action by making further improvement innovations, a situation that is con-sistent with their general industrial strategy.

There is also a trend for U.S. firms to perform an increasing fraction of their R&D related to foreign sales in their foreign affiliates (average of 11 percent of total industrial domestic R&D expenditures in 1979). Moreover, the more R&D-intensive the firm, the sooner it is likely to transfer its technology abroad to an affiliate.[42] This trend could eventually reverse the growth of the U.S. surplus, although much of this technology transfer is probably essential in order to gain entry to foreign markets.

In summary, the balance of trade in royalties and fees is primarily an indicator of past U.S. success in innovation and lags considerably behind as an indicator of the current situation. Furthermore, it is an indicator of the generation, not the commercialization, of innovations in the United States. Indeed, with the growth of R&D expenditures and patenting rates in other countries, it is surprising that there has not been a decline in the ratio of receipts to payments for the United States. If we had been making as successful use of foreign inventions as foreigners had of ours, one would have expected a decline in the payment ratio as foreign economies and R&D expenditures grew relative to ours. It is also disturbing that, considering the lag in payments, the data reveal a startling Japanese surge in licensing receipts from abroad, thus confirming more subjective impressions about the shift of the world locus of innovation to Japan and ultimately to East Asia in general.[43]

Comparative Productivity Statistics. Perhaps the most frequently quoted statistic in support of a technological lag in the United States is our lower average productivity growth rate compared with almost all our competitors except the United Kingdom.[44] From 1960 to 1973 and from 1973 to 1980 the average annual growth in output per manhour worked in manufacturing has been less in the United States than in other industrial countries, although the gap in growth rates was smaller in the later period. Despite this the GDP per employed person, when adjusted for relative purchasing power in different countries, remains higher on average in the United States.[45] When one looks at specific industries, however, this does not provide much ground for complacency. The absolute level of productivity in Japan has overtaken that in the United States in a number of important industries. This level exceeds the United States in steel by 8 percent, in electrical machinery by 19 percent, in general machinery by 11 percent, in transportation equipment (mainly passenger vehicles) by 24 percent, and in precision equipment by 34 percent.[46] Not surprisingly, the industries in which the Japanese have been most successful in penetrating the U.S. domestic market are precisely those that enjoy a productivity advantage over their U.S. counterparts.

Whatever the source of the productivity lag, it is not of recent vintage. In the 1950s and 1960s it was usually explained by the fact that Europe and Japan were still catching up to best practice in the United States, but this explanation can scarcely apply when the "best practice" has clearly shifted to Japan.

The judgment of most observers is that in the particular industries cited above the Japanese advantage is more sociotechnical than technical.[47] However, "to the extent that a social behavior is operationally replicable and less than infinitely modifiable, it can usefully be treated as technology for many purposes."[48] In manufacturing processes particularly the organization and management of work and use of human resources may be as or more important than physical technology. A striking demonstration of this is provided by Garvin's recent study of a large number of Japanese and American manufacturers of room air conditioners.[49] Both the range of products offered and the manufacturing technology were quite similar for all the firms studied, yet Garvin found enormous differences in both product quality and labor productivity. Moreover, these differences could be traced directly to differences in work organization and managerial practices and priorities. The quality differences were considerably larger than those in productivity, but high quality and high productivity were positively correlated. In quality the average performance of the Japanese firms was literally hundreds of times superior to the average of the American firms, and there was no overlap in the distribution of product quality among firms in the two countries. A somewhat similar situation evidently exists in the automobile industries of the two countries,[50] although in this case there are somewhat greater variations in manufacturing technology, with the Japanese firms being somewhat more automated.[51] Even in this case, however, productivity differences are mostly accounted for by social and managerial factors such as the "just in time" inventory system.[52]

Manufacturing productivity is often taken as a proxy for the overall rate of technical change in the economy. However, productivity reflects only process innovation; that part of the innovation mix that leads to new or improved consumer products, for example, is not reflected in productivity statistics. Some have argued that the United States has emphasized product innovation much more than other countries; as a result, productivity measures alone may understate the rate of technical change in the American economy compared with others.[53] It is easy to see that some innovations may actually result in an apparent decrease in measured output. For example, durable consumer goods with a longer useful life, lower maintenance costs, or less energy consumption may provide the same service to consumers with less industrial output. A well-insulated house may be a net saving of GNP. As another example, safer consumer products or manufacturing processes that release fewer hazardous byproducts to the environment will reduce health care or environmental cleanup costs, and this will make an apparent negative contribution to output and probably to productivity. There are even those who believe that the productivity slowdown in the United States may be largely illusory for these reasons, and that it may be partially connected with the earlier market penetration of information technologies in this country.

It may be true that the United States, for a variety of historical reasons, has paid more attention to product innovation than to manufacturing innovation. During the entire postwar period, manufacturing engineering in the United States has had low status among the engineering disciplines and has been deemphasized until recently in the most elite engineering schools. This may result partly from the high fraction of the highest quality human resources devoted to space/defense activities in which manufacturing technology is of lesser importance. Also, there are short production runs in the most sophisticated defense and space products, which tends to make them intensive in the use of skilled labor and to offer relatively low economic returns to sophisticated manufacturing improvements. Interestingly enough, however, the biggest productivity gains come from those industries that are most closely related technologically to the defense/space cluster—computers, semiconductors, aircraft, electronic components, communications equipment, and so forth. A likely explanation may be simply the attraction of the best talent and some of the most venturesome capital and management to the civilian industries derived from the space/defense sector. Vogel has noted that in Japan there are many more graduate engineers, especially electrical engineers, on the shop floor in the Japanese machine tool industry than in the U.S. industry, which is largely populated by skilled artisans.[54]

We can conclude that lagging productivity growth in the United States is not *primarily* a symptom of a technological innovation lag, but derives more from managerial and broader economic and cultural factors, as suggested by Mills and Lovell.[55] There is evidence, however, that some of these factors are being corrected.

Investment in Research and Development. National investment in R&D is frequently used in international comparisons as a proxy for innovative effort. By this measure the U.S. can still be regarded as a world leader, at least in the "free world," although it has lost some ground in relative terms. The absolute level of U.S. R&D expenditures, when adjusted for purchasing power parity, was 1.5 times that of Japan, Germany, France, and the United Kingdom combined in 1977.[56] The United States had 1.3 times as many scientists and engineers employed in industrial R&D per 1,000 workers than in any one of these countries. To be sure, investment in industrial R&D grew much faster in Europe and Japan than in the United States from the late 1960s to the mid-1970s, but rates of growth in R&D expenditure have been roughly comparable since 1977. The U.S. *share* of R&D expenditures in the Organization for Economic Cooperation and Development (OECD) went from 68.7 percent in 1967 to only 49.7 percent in 1977 but has not slipped since. The number of scientists and engineers per civilian worker remained greater in the United States than in other countries. However, several of the latter were rapidly catching up to the United States during the 1970s.[57] By the early 1980s, both Germany and Japan were graduating more engineers (though fewer scientists) than the United States—Japan by a factor of nearly two to one.[58] However, because the growth of the number of graduates in other countries has been recent and rapid, its effects are not yet fully reflected in the stock of scientists and engineers in the labor forces of these countries. But unless the United States expands its development of technical people, it is only a matter of time before the stock of engineers and scientists in our principal competitor countries will surpass that in the United States measured as a proportion of the labor force. Moreover, this stock will be younger on average, and in consequence, possibly more innovative, more flexible, and more conversant with the latest advances.

Another frequently used index of innovation derived from R&D is the ratio of national R&D investment to GDP. By this measure the U.S. position appears less favorable. West Germany, for example, pulled slightly ahead of the United States in this ratio in 1977.[59] If civilian R&D expenditures only are considered (i.e., excluding government-funded defense and space R&D), then Japan, Germany, and the United Kingdom each passed the United States in the late 1960s (Japan, 1.9 percent; Germany, 2.1 percent; United Kingdom, 1.7 percent; compared with the United States, 1.5 percent in 1977).[60]

It is not clear, however, which of these measures is more relevant for estimating the effective innovative effort. If R&D was purely public and the results of R&D were freely and rapidly exchanged among all the R&D performers within a country, then the absolute level of national R&D expenditures would appear as the more meaningful index. One would have to assume that no cost or time delay was attached to the transfer of research findings between institutions—from academia or government to industry, or between different firms even in unrelated businesses. But in this model, for any purely national R&D expenditures to have any significance one would have to assume that the transfer of information stopped at national boundaries;

otherwise only the world investment in R&D would be significant, since anybody could tap into the world pool of knowledge for the purposes of innovation. In an opposite idealized model, one might assume that there was no exchange of results among performing firms. Therefore, there could be extensive duplication of effort. At the same time there would be the stimulus of competition, which might lead to covering more bets. If this model was strictly correct, then R&D investment relative to output or sales would be a more reasonable measure of innovative effort because there would be very little spillover of technical advance from one firm to another. The same would apply with even greater force to transfer across national boundaries. Thus R&D as a fraction of GNP might be the more meaningful index of innovative effort.

Clearly, the true measure of effective innovative effort must be somewhere intermediate between relative gross national expenditures for R&D and expenditures as a fraction of GDP. However, my own view is that relative total national R&D expenditures is probably the more meaningful index, since technical knowledge diffuses rapidly and easily, and the ease and speed with which this diffusion occurs has probably grown rapidly during the last two decades for both institutional and technological reasons. Because knowledge flows so readily across national boundaries, the commercialization of R&D results may be only weakly related to the purely national level of R&D, and this may become more true in the future.

The preceding argument over the meaning of national R&D investments reflects an ongoing policy debate about the relative roles of competition and cooperation in generating a high rate of innovation in industrial research. Some believe that competitive efforts are more creative because they assure more comprehensive exploration of all conceivable options and paths for progress. Concealing progress from competitors precludes "bandwagon" effects that would be operative in a more cooperative environment. Fear of what the competition may be doing can be a powerful spur to originality. Others feel that competition and its associated secrecy inevitably entail duplication of effort, which reduces the efficiency of the search process. The optimal tradeoff between competition and cooperation varies along the spectrum of activity from basic research to final product development, with wide sharing of findings being best near the basic research end of the spectrum and competition becoming more important as one approaches final application. But it is hard to get beyond these qualitative statements.

Many have argued that Japanese encouragement of cooperation among firms, especially in the early stages of development of an emerging technology, leads to much greater productivity in exploratory development than the more purely competitive situation that exists in the United States (outside the defense industry). There is a perception that Japanese industrial research is more productive per dollar than that in the United States largely because of this cooperative aspect.[61] Japanese firms, particularly in the early stages of an emerging technology, share information more freely than U.S. firms. With government encouragement they may even share markets for high technology products among themselves so that each firm can realize greater economies of scale and learning curve efficiencies by specializing in a particular product segment. Because of this perception, political attention in the United States has focused on the inhibiting effects of U.S. antitrust policy. Concerns about the legality of joint R&D ventures, it is argued, have inhibited desirable cooperation among firms. However, others have expressed doubts about the importance of this factor, maintaining that the stimulative effects of competition far outweigh the benefits of cooperation and openness, which can only too easily slip into a tacit cooperation in the avoidance of novelty.[62] Recently, the U.S. government has become more friendly toward cooperative R&D ventures, and this has resulted in a spate of cooperative ventures and consideration of legislation to make them easier to undertake and to protect them from legal attack.[63]

Bell Telephone Laboratories is frequently cited to illustrate the value of cooperative research and open sharing of information in the early stages of emerging technologies. Over the years BTL has been an unusually prolific source of fundamental industrial innovations. Because of a consent decree it has been forced to license its technologies widely and has developed a "culture" more akin to that of university research than other industrial research.[64] In this respect it has fulfilled a function in the development of American electronics and communications that is quite similar to the cooperation among firms fostered by the Ministry of International Trade and Industry for emerging technologies in Japan.

On balance, it seems that U.S. industrial R&D has been more duplicative than is optimal and that our innovative effort has suffered from an excess of competition exemplified in "me too" developments. This is hard to prove, however, especially since some of the difficulty is probably a product of the individualistic attitudes buried in our culture rather than of legal or political constraints.

It is also true that a steadily increasing investment in R&D probably generates more innovation per dollar than level expenditures, because continual increases allow greater flexibility in rapid deployment of resources to respond to new opportunities without requiring premature abandonment of efforts that are temporarily encountering obstacles or difficulties.

Patent Statistics. Patents have the advantage of being indicators of accomplishment much closer to final application; hence they are better measures of the relative state of technology as contrasted with science. Furthermore, novelty and originality have to be more formally documented for patents than they are for scientific discoveries.

During the 1970s U.S. patenting declined by about 14 percent, approximately tracking the decline of real R&D expenditures between its peak in 1967 and its minimum about 1976. Interestingly enough, this decline was entirely in patents assigned to institutions; patents assigned to individual inventors stayed constant at about one-quarter of all patents.[65] In contrast, patenting by Japanese citizens in Japan more than doubled in the same period, and patents awarded to Japanese inventors by the U.S. Patent Office increased fivefold from 1967 to 1978. Domestic patenting seems to track domestic R&D investment rather closely overall, even though there are large differences among industries in the apparent R&D cost of a patent.

The rate of foreign patenting in the United States also seems to reflect relative interest of the host country in the U.S. market, since it correlates quite closely with exports to the United States.[66] It is difficult to be certain, however, which is cause and which is effect, that is, whether high exports are the result of patents or whether the patents are a manifestation of successful penetration of the U.S. market.

There are also variations in the amount of patenting relative to R&D investment, though interpretation is complicated by a probable variable time lag between R&D and patenting. This makes it all the more remarkable that although Japan had only one-quarter as much industrial R&D as the United States in 1979, Japanese citizens were awarded almost as many patents in their own country as were American citizens in the United States. Since R&D was increasing rapidly in Japan, the actual R&D that produced the patents may have been much less than one-quarter the U.S. value, after allowing for the time lag between R&D and the granting of a patent. However, it is very difficult to compare the standards of patenting in the two countries, and therefore the above statistics cannot be used to draw strong conclusions about the greater effectiveness of R&D in producing technological innovation in Japan compared with the United States.

Furthermore, gross patent statistics do not tell us much about the economic significance of patents. Only a minuscule fraction of the 40,000 patents granted each year in the United States probably have any appreciable economic significance. A study conducted for the 1976 NSF *Science Indicators* by Gellman Associates[67] found that the United States produced forty-seven major industrial innovations (as judged by expert panels) in 1971-73 compared to 160,000 patents. The number of major innovations per 1,000 patents awarded to nationals varied from 0.08 in France to 0.49 in Britain, with the United States at 0.31 and Japan at 0.16. Considering the recent vintage of the Japanese R&D program, the number of major innovations attributed to the Japanese for a given level of R&D seems surprisingly high. Some question has been raised about the methodology of the Gellman Associates work, so too much weight should not be given to the statistics. The fact that the above statistics, soft as they are, confirm the widespread conventional wisdom about the cost effectiveness of Japanese R&D lends them some credibility that they might not have otherwise.

Pavitt and Soete have shown that among the industrialized countries there is a remarkably good correlation between national shares of total R&D expenditures and the national share of patents granted to citizens of the corresponding country by the U.S. Patent Office. This correlation remains true over time, at least for the time in which adequate internationally comparable R&D statistics have been kept.[68] Thus, relative national patent statistics do not yield much new information beyond that already given by comparative R&D statistics, except that the latter have been reliably collected only much more recently. Comparative patent statistics for relatively narrowly defined technology fields are now being developed and have at least the potential for being more revealing of the competitive technological positions of both firms and nations in particular industrial fields.[69] Campbell has recently argued that patent analysis can and should be developed as a tool for strategic technology planning both at the firm level and at the national level for key industries and product lines.[70] He suggests that it can be a sensitive means for anticipating national trends in technological competitiveness, before they show up either in the technical literature or in market performance. So far this tool has been little exploited in the United States except for the discussion of a few retrospective examples (e.g., catalytic converters for controlling auto emissions). Campbell suggests that both business and government should develop patent analysis as a tool for assessing future technological competitiveness much as financial analysis is used to assert current market competitiveness. Judging by their interest in the publications of the new U.S. Office of Technology Assessment and Forecasting of the U.S. Patent Office, the Japanese may be already pursuing this recommendation.

One of the most extensive uses of patent data has been made by a group at the University of Sussex, England, to assess trends in industrial competitiveness of the United Kingdom.[71] These authors have examined the relative number of patents taken out in the United States by several European countries and Japan and have attempted to correlate these with export shares (as a measure of comparative advantage) for some forty product groups. The results clearly document the relative decline of British industry as a source of world innovation and show a fairly good correlation between patenting in the United States and the world export shares of twenty-three out of the forty product sectors studied. As might be expected, the correlation is weakest or breaks down entirely for sectors in which natural resource endowments or relative labor costs would be expected to be most significant in determining comparative advantage. This is especially evident in traditional industries like apparel, but is also true in more technology-intensive industries such as paints, plastics, agricultural chemicals, and certain household durables, in which both the product and production technology are quite mature and thus are readily transferable to low labor cost regions. Since there is a general belief in the parallelism between the weaknesses of the British and American economies, this detailed study of British innovation may have significant implications for future developments in the United States. The existing data already clearly reveal evidence of the aggressive technology efforts under way in several Japanese industries known to be targeted for special stimulation by MITI or by industry-specific legislation.[72]

Scientific and Technical Manpower and the Quality of the Labor Force. Deploying scientific and engineering manpower in industry has followed fairly closely the national investment in industrial R&D. Between 1970 and 1979, science and engineering employment in the United States grew at about the same rate as the labor force as a whole, although the relative growth of S&E employment and industrial employment fluctuated over shorter subperiods.[73] However, the number of scientists and engineers engaged in industrial R&D, relative to the labor force, fell about 16 percent from its peak in 1963 to a minimum in 1975, largely reflecting the drop in federal government R&D expenditures accompanying the decline in space/defense R&D.[74] It took some years of growth in self-financed industrial R&D to overcome the slack demand for technical manpower. Since the economic recovery following the first oil crisis in 1973, particularly since 1976, the pattern of employment change has been quite complex.

From 1977 to 1980 the annual growth in employment of scientists, engineers, and technicians (SET) was 6 percent annually compared to only 1 percent for the labor force as a whole in manufacturing. As a result, SET employment, which constituted only 6 percent of the manufacturing labor force in 1977, accounted for 45 percent of employment growth during this period. SET employment as a fraction of total employment actually grew most in those industries experiencing a decline in overall employment. Thus in some thirteen industries experiencing a 3 percent decline in employment on average, SET employment increased by 11 percent during the same period. The largest increase in any one category was for industrial engineers, whose numbers increased at an annual rate of 25 percent.

This was a strong reflection of management's increased emphasis on manufacturing productivity and probably on quality control.[75] Thus the SET labor market was apparently responding strongly to the rising national concern with the drop in U.S. productivity growth and the challenge of foreign, mainly Japanese, competition in manufacturing technology.

There was also a rapid shift of SET employment into nonmanufacturing industry. The fraction of SET employment in the nonmanufacturing sector grew from 30 percent in 1970 to 37 percent in 1980. From 1978 to 1980 nonmanufacturing accounted for 60 percent of the growth in SET employment, principally in engineering and architectural services and in business services.[76] It appears that during the late 1970s, SET employment patterns were anticipating the restructuring of the economy toward services and also reflecting the upgrading of skill requirements in manufacturing. The "postindustrial economy" was more than a sociological hypothesis.

The rapid buildup of industrial R&D spending during the past five years, due to both industrial and government spending, has created a surge of demand for high-level technical manpower that has not been seen since the space/defense buildup of the early 1960s. This has continued with surprisingly moderate slackening even during the 1980-82 recession. It has resulted in severe shortages in some fields such as computer science and manufacturing engineering, especially for people with advanced training to the master's or doctoral level. In some areas of the country there has been an unprecedented flow of foreign-born scientists and engineers into the R&D work force. In engineering, for example, close to 50 percent of the Ph.D.s who graduated from U.S. engineering schools are foreign born.[77]

Among students in higher education, the fraction in engineering and science programs has been only 1.6 percent in the United States compared with 4.2 percent in Japan and 6 percent in the Soviet Union, with European countries being closer to the level of Japan than the United States. As long as participation in higher education was much higher in the United States than in the rest of the world, the lower fraction in engineering and science was of little consequence. But as the rest of the world has dramatically expanded access to higher education, it has begun to enjoy an advantage over us in the production of technical manpower.

In addition, the economic rewards in professional fields other than science and engineering have been such that the output of, for example, M.B.A.s and lawyers has each recently overtaken that of engineers.[78] Furthermore, one may speculate that lawyers and managers may keep a great many engineers busy in activities that do not contribute directly to industrial innovation, whatever other social values they may enhance.

There is now a widespread fear that if the U.S. economic recovery continues to pick up at the same time that the current military R&D boom continues, the competition for trained SET personnel between the civilian and military sectors will become increasingly acute. Because the defense/space sector is probably much less cost limited than the civil, it is feared that the most talented scientists, engineers, and managers will be attracted, gradually starving innovative capacity in the civilian economy, something many believe happened during the previous defense/space buildup of the immediate post-Sputnik era.[79] Defense and space are uniquely research-intensive as indicated by the fact that R&D constitutes close to 50 percent of total procurement in some industry categories such as guided missiles and spacecraft. Moreover, the character of some defense/space innovation is directly competitive with the most advanced parts of the civilian sector on which we may be dependent for future commercial leadership.

There is an intense debate about the SET labor market's efficiency, whether it can be relied upon to quickly relieve the current bottlenecks in the SET area. Many spokespeople for high technology industry are now expressing doubts, pointing to the long lag between demand and supply built into the educational pipeline, especially at the most advanced levels.[80] Furthermore, faculty shortages develop in exactly the fields that are in greatest demand by industry, thus amplifying the shortages of the most critical skills. Industry is criticized by educators for using up the "seed corn" from which the nation's capacity to stay at the forefront of technology ahead of its foreign competitors grows.

Others, however, believe that technical manpower in industry is currently used very inefficiently, perhaps a holdover from the days of surplus in the early 1970s. Industry, they say, "mines" the knowledge and skills acquired by recent graduates without affording them sufficient opportunity to continually upgrade their capabilities and keep up with the latest state of the art. They point to the high rate at which mature engineers abandon technical work, and the relatively early plateauing of the salaries of those engineers in industry who choose to remain primarily engaged in technical work.[81] They argue that, as already happens in the best-managed U.S. companies, the market can and soon will recognize this waste of human resources. It should become obvious that greater investment in retraining and upgrading of already employed engineers is more cost-effective than bidding up the starting salaries of fresh graduates or pressuring government to intervene to increase the supply of graduates through narrowly targeted subsidies to students and educational institutions. In this view, the labor market is likely to reach a better allocation of resources between the production of new graduates and the upgrading of the knowledge and productivity of existing SET personnel. As happened in the 1960s, the benefits of federal intervention may come too late to relieve the more serious bottlenecks.

Against the market argument lies the fact, or at least the belief, that the high mobility of the SET work force in the United States makes it more productive and creative. This means that investments in in-house training in industry are likely to benefit competitors as much as the firm that finances the training. Thus there is a large "positive externality" associated with in-firm training, and this externality must be recognized either by a public subsidy for training or by cooperative arrangements among all the firms in an industry to finance the training. However, the collective approach always runs up against the "free rider" problem, since any firm that opts out can still enjoy the benefits. In Japan and Europe, and in a few large high technology firms in the United States, where there are de facto lifetime employment policies, the benefits from investment by the firm in retraining are more readily captured by the investing firm, and such firms are apparently willing to invest more than the average in the education and training of their employees at all levels.

To some extent the problem is being addressed in the United States through competitive initiatives at the state and local level. Many states and even metropolitan regions are moving to develop comprehensive programs to stimulate the location and growth of high technology industry around local universities. Nearly all of these programs entail financial measures to assist advanced technical education in regional universities and technical schools.[82]

Thus, different localities are competing with each other, and in principle, this competition should lead to the most effective strategies' dominance. At the federal level, liberalization of tax benefits to corporations for contributions in kind to universities, or for cooperative programs with universities, has been advocated as a better strategy than targeted federal programs (other than the traditional and well-accepted support for academic basic research). The choice of targets is left either to industrial decision makers, or to local governments working closely with industry on the basis of a comprehensive regional industrial strategy. Massachusetts has been a leader, with its Bay State Skills Corporation.[83]

Many also point to the potential talent available from women and minorities. Women in particular are heavily underrepresented in science and engineering activities, especially engineering. Although the numbers are growing quite rapidly in terms of new graduates, the percentage of women in science and engineering occupations is very small compared to the percentage of scientists and engineers in the labor force as a whole.[84] Some ask if the excess capacity for training in graduate education, which is now being used for foreign citizens, should not be used instead for underrepresented groups in the S&E work force. Others would argue for a more strictly meritocratic approach.

Another area of concern relating to human resources is the American work force's general educational level, particularly as this affects its capacity to adapt to a rapidly changing environment of technology, market preferences, and foreign competition. Although a higher fraction of each age cohort graduates from high school in the United States than in any other country and there is greater participation in postsecondary education, there are serious questions about the *quality* of American public education, especially for science and mathematics, at all levels below the university. There have been extensive news reports about the low performance of U.S. high school students in science and mathematics compared with those in nearly all other industrial countries, particularly Japan.[85]

In the view of many, however, developing "human capital" on the job may prove to be even more critical than the level of formal education, although the two are in many respects complementary.[86] Excessive division of labor and rigid work rules and functional boundaries in U.S. factories frequently inhibit self-development on the job and decrease work commitment as well.[87] Overly fragmented division of labor affects the labor force's capacity to adapt to new technology and hence the economy's capacity to assimilate technological change. It is more difficult for an organization to adjust to changes in its environment, because every change requires either ad hoc retraining or a complex renegotiation of working assignments and usually both. Also, because they are less versatile, workers have trouble finding new employment in other jobs when the industries in which they work are declining due to technological change or foreign competition. The "deskilling" of jobs is often used as a short-term strategy to lower labor costs by using lower-paid labor and to achieve higher productivity through greater division of labor, but this usually results in creating shortages in certain critical categories of skilled labor for an entire industry. By "deskilling," these firms deplete the pool of skills available regionally on which all local industries depend for critical functions such as maintenance, experimental production, model shop work, and so forth.[88] The resulting scarcity of critical skills and consequent higher cost of some labor may offset the savings in other labor categories. By contrast, the Japanese labor system, for a variety of reasons, appears to result in a much better diversification of skills on the part of the individual worker and hence a more flexible and adaptable work force. At the same time, reassigning jobs and functions within the firm requires less elaborate negotiations between management and labor, in part because employment itself is more secure so that the worker has less vested interest in a particular tightly prescribed job function compared with his American counterpart.

SUMMARY OF CONCLUSIONS FROM AGGREGATE ANALYSIS

The preceding discussion suggests that the capacity for originating new and potentially competitive technology in the United States remains strong. Our national investment in industrial R&D exceeds that of any of our competitors by a large margin, and even when Europe is considered as a unit we are somewhat stronger. We are quantitatively much stronger in R&D than Japan, which is our most formidable competitor in the successful commercialization of advanced technology. It is apparent that, for a variety of reasons, the national investment in R&D may be more effective in producing industrial innovations per dollar of expenditure in other countries, especially Japan. One reason is that our competitors' governments take a more tolerant, or even supportive, attitude than our own toward cooperation among firms during the early stages of an emerging technological development. Another reason is that until recently foreign managements and governments have assigned a considerably higher importance to technology as the critical factor affecting future competitiveness and have, therefore, incorporated informed estimates of future world technological trends more intimately into their strategic planning and management philosophy. Japan especially has been sensitive to the importance of being first in an expanding market with high productivity and high reliability and quality of new products. It has frequently been prepared to sacrifice novelty and technical sophistication in the interests of reliability, excellent service, and rapid and sure delivery. These are all factors that relate not to the origination of new technology but to the tactics and strategy of its introduction to the market.

The fact that R&D has been expanding abroad until recently has probably made it easier for our competitors to shift priorities in response to new opportunities and environmental changes, so that an expanding R&D enterprise nationally may be inherently more productive per unit of expenditure than one in steady state or decline. In fact, in an economic situation in which comparative advantage is largely created by people, a growing system may have an inherent dynamic comparative advantage over steady state systems until it, too, reaches some form of saturation. In many ways this is a discouraging conclusion because it implies an inherent instability in competition, with success creating the conditions for more success and failure generating the seeds for more failure. In other words, the competition comes from countries and firms experiencing virtuous cycles in innovation and market penetration. The question then becomes whether this dynamic has any natural termination point before one side or the other of the competitive equation falls over the edge. The evidence on this `is not all in. In consumer electronics the disappearance of a whole industry has virtually already happened between Japan and the United States. However, the United States remains strong in the marketing, distribution, and service aspects of the field, and this probably provides a growing proportion of the employment in the industry worldwide. Generally speaking, patent, manpower, and royalty and fee statistics tell virtually the same story as R&D statistics, indicating that both Europe and Japan have been steadily narrowing the gap between themselves and us; but there is little indication in the aggregate data that they have overtaken us.

The overall educational level of the labor force, and the failure of management to organize work so that versatility and adaptability are developed on the job is probably a more serious problem for the United States in the long run than the current shortage of new graduates in some areas of engineering. The United States has been weak in upgrading its work force within the work environment and is not making efficient use of the human resources already available. In sum, the United States may have gradually lost the lead in human resources that it had developed during the postwar era as a result of much higher participation at all levels of education than our competitors. As participation rates became more nearly equal in other countries, the lower average quality of the American product became a more serious disadvantage, which was reinforced by lack of human development on the job. As technology became more sophisticated and the pace of change accelerated, this became more serious in its overall consequences for the economy, and the problem was further compounded by the preemption of so many of the highest levels of skills available by military and space R&D.

THE OUTLOOK

Aggregate analysis is not inconsistent with the widespread perception of a decline in U.S. innovativeness, but this decline does not appear sufficiently dramatic or serious in the gross statistics to explain the spectacular turnarounds that we have been seeing in important industries in only a few years. The gross statistics aggregated across large categories of industries conceal a great deal of detail about relatively narrow areas of activity in which dramatic decline is taking place over very short time periods. Where lightning strikes seems unpredictable from an overview of the economy as a whole or of very large industry groupings. The sources of decline appear different in each instance and often depend on the apparently accidental coincidence of several factors. The industries affected seem not to have fully understood the technological and market changes that were taking place globally in their industry, and the emergence of major foreign competition has caught them by surprise.

The U.S. government has frequently compounded the problem in two ways. Initially it has assumed that the industry was so robust that government did not have to worry about the consequences of its policies (e.g., regulation) for the future health of the industry. Later, when the industry began to show symptoms of trouble, government would simply accept a rather superficial and somewhat self-serving industry diagnosis of the situation and act in cooperation with the industry to deal with symptoms rather than underlying causes. In many cases, failure to understand what was happening in the technology was part of the problem, but the lack of understanding was sociotechnical rather than purely technical in nature. Frequently, short-term market signals and government policies actually led the industry to adopt strategies that, in retrospect, may have been contrary to its long-term interest. A classic example is the confusion of the auto industry about fuel-efficient cars. The long-term trends have been clearly toward higher fuel efficiency, lesser environmental impact, smaller size, and better durability, reliability, and maintainability. Yet neither the market nor government policies fully reflected these trends in the short term, so that the industry adjustment to them was uncertain. Statutory regulation of fleet average fuel efficiency combined with price controls on gasoline and, more recently, the world oil surplus have produced conflict between what the law specified and what the market demanded over extended time periods. In other cases, industries have adopted outsourcing policies to take advantage of low labor costs abroad when they might have done much better to start down the learning curve of automated production, which had much higher ultimate potential for cost reduction and especially for quality control and product reliability. When the United States has had superior technologies to offer, it has frequently been unable to get them into quantity production with good quality control and reliability ahead of its competitors.

The inability to adapt to the rapidly changing external environment has been most acutely felt in the parts of the overall innovation process that lie beyond R&D: the transition from R&D to production, the achievement of a reliable and consistent product output, concentrating human and other resources to satisfy rapidly expanding markets just a little ahead of competitors, using periods of slack demand to prepare the whole organization for the next period of expanding demand.

Yet the outlook may not be all bad. The R&D infrastructure of the United States is still unmatched in the world; however, it is burdened with responsibilities other than economic development, which are not borne in the same degree by its competitors, especially in military R&D including space. The United States has been inhibited from adopting protectionist or industrial policies available to its competitors because the political repercussions of such policies represent the greater of two evils. Our position of political leadership in the free world has prevented us from giving as much priority to our economic interests as has been possible for our allies. At the same time, the U.S. economy is beginning to respond to the new world environment, though the beneficial effects to our competitive position are not yet evident. Industrial investment in R&D has been remarkably robust through the severest recession in the postwar period. After a severe dip in the 1970s our schools are turning out more engineers, though not enough to meet demand in some critical areas. Public alarm over the parlous state of public precollege education has not yet turned into solutions, but public support for reform is available to be used constructively. American industry is rapidly waking up to the necessity of managing its human resources to assimilate and assist technological change rather than to resist it, and this will be greatly facilitated by a growing economy. In fact, our recovery in advance of the rest of the world may provide us with the opportunity to benefit preferentially from the virtuous cycle mentioned earlier. Although some of our loss of competitiveness undoubtedly owes much to the trade practices of our competitors, which are "unfair" by almost any standards, the major sources of loss of competitiveness lie in ourselves and not in others.

Changes are necessary. As long as capital for expansion to exploit rapidly opening markets is more expensive in the United States than abroad, we will fail to reap the economic benefits of innovativeness to the extent that we should. Either our competitors will reap those rewards, as Japan has, or our own firms will find it preferable to invest in production facilities abroad to make the products invented or designed in the United States. Thus the *country* may become less competitive at the same time that many U.S.-based multinational firms will become more competitive.

We must also be sensitive to the necessity of achieving the optimal balance between cooperation and competition in the innovative process, so that we get the most economic benefit from our national R&D expenditures. In applying our procompetitive policies, we should be primarily concerned with their effects on innovation rather than on firm size, market share, or even prices. Competition is important and beneficial to the economy; however, we should be prepared to compromise our ideological attachment to it when it inhibits innovation or wastes our technical resources through excessive duplication of innovative effort, especially in the development of "me too" products as has happened, for example, in pharmaceuticals and in personal computers. Finding the right compromise between cooperation and competition will not be easy. We have long recognized the need for some compromise (perhaps too much) in fields in which government is the principal customer, as in defense and space. We must now recognize its necessity in the commercial field.

10
Competitiveness in the World Economy: The Role of the U.S. Financial System

Philip A. Wellons

Compared with other countries, does the U.S. financial system on balance help the competitiveness of U.S. firms? How does a financial system "help"? It may affect the equation of risk and return for investors, increasing the volume of funds available to firms at a particular cost in ways that support those sectors of the economy exposed to foreign competitors or in ways that support the sunrise sectors rather than those on which the sun is setting.

Conventional wisdom holds that, to the extent possible in an integrated world market, the U.S. financial system helps U.S. firms, since it is the deepest and broadest in the world. Logically, four propositions support this view.

1. The U.S. financial market is the largest and most open in the world.[1]
2. The U.S. markets allocate and price most efficiently.
3. U.S. firms benefit financially from these markets.
4. The financial benefits aid the competitiveness of U.S. firms.

Set against this conventional view, however, is the compelling experience of the last few years. High real interest rates in the United States continue to generate enormous controversy about their cause and consequence. While much of the cause may lie in U.S. macroeconomic policy, the apparent difference in rates between the United States and other countries is persistent enough to suggest that markets are not fully integrated.

Two conceptual issues about the nature of the financial markets of the five biggest industrial economies, the Group of Five or G-5 (the United States, the United Kingdom, France, West Germany, and Japan), are important to

Philip A. Wellons is associate professor of business administration at Harvard Business School.

consider. The first involves the way each national market works. How free or managed is each domestic financial market? The second involves the extent to which national markets are distinct or integrated. Despite twenty years of reducing capital barriers, integration is still not complete, segments still exist, and questions remain about the impact of national barriers on capital movement.

These two issues address the question of whether industrial countries can manage their financial flows both at the border and internally. To the extent that they can manage both, one should see capital allocation and costs within the country that differ from other countries or the world market. Several questions arise. How do access and cost differ? Who pays? How? Most important, how significant are the differences to firms competing in world markets?

The picture that emerges shows very big differences in the financial systems of the G-5 countries, most notably Japan's in contrast to those of Europe and the United States. The biggest differences are in the financing of business, in the volume, and apparently in the cost of funds, both of which have important implications for competitiveness. Yet the financial systems themselves play a role in creating the differences: an analysis of their structure—particularly the segmentation and the share held by different intermediaries—reveals that funds are channeled in Japan and France in a way not found in the other G-5 countries. The fact that the channeling seems to have worked to enhance competitiveness in the one country more than the other is a function of what is called national strategy.

THE EXTENT OF THE PROBLEM

THE RELATIVE STRENGTH OF THE U.S. FINANCIAL SYSTEM

A closer look at some of the purported advantages of the U.S. financial system makes them less beneficial to U.S. firms. For example, as a share of GDP, U.S. financial stock ranks a distant second to Japan and was behind the United Kingdom until 1979 (figure 10-1). Relative to economic activity and, in a sense, to demand for finance, the U.S. markets are not the biggest. Despite the argument that market forces work most efficiently, if markets elsewhere are closed and managed, the cost of capital may well be lower there, giving foreign firms access to cheaper funds in their own homes.

Four recent studies have shown that the cost of capital in Japan is lower than in other industrial countries and that it is highest in the United States.

Figure 10-1

Total Domestic Debt as % of GDP
Total Domestic Debt and Equity as % of GDP

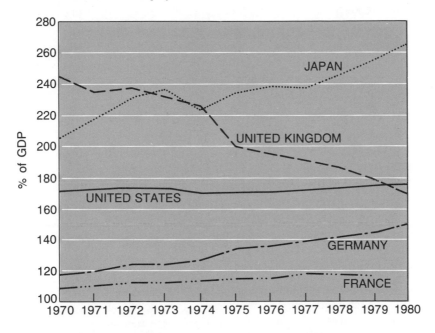

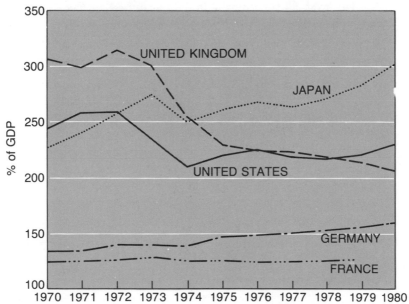

Source: Central bank bulletins of each country

Two studies examined the semiconductor industry. The first compared eight U.S. semiconductor producers with four Japanese firms in the same industry and concluded that the cost of capital for the Japanese firms was one-third less than for the U.S. firms: 10.9% compared with 17.5%.[2] The second concluded: "There seems to be strong evidence that the cost of corporate borrowing, correcting for inflation, in Japan was less than that in the U.S. during 1980 and 1981."[3]

Two studies compared capital costs nationwide. The first, comparing the United States and Japan from 1961 to 1981, found that the real costs of capital services were at least twice as high in the United States as in Japan during the period. Excluding depreciation, Japanese capital costs were negative while U.S. costs approached 14%.[4] Finally, a study by the U.S. Department of Commerce concluded that the weighted average cost of capital to industry in the United States was higher than in France, Germany, or Japan in 1981 and that the gap had worsened over the decade (see table 10-1).[5]

In short, in the face of conventional wisdom and the belief that capital markets are highly integrated, the studies conclude that the cost of capital in the United States is higher than elsewhere. That the studies disagree about the size of the difference is not surprising, given the state of the art and data limitations. However, all studies point in the same direction: there are basic differences in the cost of capital of the major industrial countries.

The greatest differences in cost of capital are between the United States and Japan, which is also our greatest trade competitor. In comparing these two countries, two major differences warrant explanation:

1. *Systemic differences.* Lower capital costs in Japan are made possible for users of funds in the entire economy by:
   a. reducing the rates on debt overall, which involves

Table 10–1
Average Weighted Cost of Capital to Industry (%)

Country	1971	1976	1981
United States	10.0%	11.3%	16.6%
France	8.5	9.4	14.3
West Germany	6.9	6.6	9.5
Japan	7.3	8.5	9.2

Source: U.S. Department of Commerce, *A Historical Comparison of the Cost of Financial Capital* (April 1983), 3.

      1. increasing savings without increasing the cost to the user;

      2. reducing the risk of the intermediaries; and

      3. insuring that intermediaries pass the lower cost on.

   b. reducing the risk associated with the firms that borrow, permitting very high debt ratios, which involves:

      1. reducing the vulnerability of the firms to downturns in the economic cycle; and

      2. reducing the cost to the firm of financial distress.

   c. reducing transaction costs associated with financing.

2. *Differences among individual firms.* In addition to having lower capital costs systemwide, Japan is said to target particular industries for beneficial financing. Since targeting itself is extremely difficult to demonstrate given the confidentiality of data, the important question is whether the means even exist by which Japan could target low-cost finance.

No single factor explains any of these changes in the cost of capital. The culture, institutions, government policy, and structure of the financial system all come into play. They seem to work most effectively in Japan, although some of the same factors exist in Germany or France. Perhaps the most important factor, however, is the continued ability of the country to sufficiently separate its financial system from the rest of the world to keep adequate control.

Before turning to the evidence for these conclusions, one other issue must be examined: it is not immediately apparent that finance affects firm performance. In some industries, finance is far from the most significant input. Labor costs, technology, quality, service, even exchange rates may account for major price differentials or may allow firms to differentiate the product in some other way. One example is the cash-rich firms in the pharmaceutical industry, for which marketing, not finance, is key. For industries of that sort, access to funds at a lower cost than one's competitor brings little advantage. However, in industries in which quality, technology, or service are so standardized that opportunities to differentiate are limited or absent, firms compete on price. Industries with high value added are capital intensive and thus are sensitive to capital costs. For new ventures, simple access to funds, regardless of cost, may make the difference between stagnation and take-off, allowing the new firm to build ahead to take advantage of scale to win market share. So, finance can be crucial for firms in industries that either are mature, have high value added, or are new.

The important point is that finance can affect firm performance in two ways: obviously, the cost of funds matters; equally significant for certain industries is the availability of funds. Both are subject to market forces. Both also could be expected to differ among countries even if the only relevant government policy was macroeconomic.

EXPLANATIONS OF ECONOMYWIDE DIFFERENCES
IN THE COST OF CAPITAL

FACTORS THAT REDUCE THE RATES FOR OVERALL DEBT

In various ways, a country like Japan induces its savers and intermediaries to accept real rates of return lower than they would accept without the inducements. It promotes savings with devices that do not raise the cost of funds to the user. It lowers the risk of placing savings with particular institutions and limits the ability of the intermediaries to capture the value added in the flow of funds. Each of these has the effect of lowering the cost of capital. The following sections examine how this works.

High Savings without Higher Cost to Users. Over the past twenty years, the country with the highest savings rate also offered investors the lowest return. Japan's high savings rate stands in particularly vivid contrast to that of the United States and Great Britain (see table 10-2). But Japan's investors reaped no special rewards for their performance. In a recent study of the real return on long-term bonds measured in local currency in the G-5 countries from 1960 to 1980, the United States about equals the United Kingdom and France, and falls far short of Germany. But for all, the returns far exceed

Table 10-2
Savings/GDP in G-5 Countries (%)

| | 1960–80 | | 1974–80 |
	Gross	Net	Net
Japan	34.5%	21.4%	19.5%
Germany	25.9	15.7	11.9
France	24.4	14.2	11.8
United Kingdom	18.7	9.4	7.0
United States	19.2	8.3	6.5

Source: OECD Historical Statistics, 1960–80 (1982).

Table 10-3
Compound Annual Yield on Long-Term Bonds,
1960-80, in Local Currency, Adjusted for
Inflation

Germany	3.04%
United States	1.07
France	1.06
United Kingdom	0.95
Japan	0.23

Source: Ibbotson, Carr & Robinson (1982); author's
calculations.

Japan. Somehow, the Japanese bondholders did least well (see table 10-3),
which should lower the cost of capital to the Japanese firms that issued these
bonds.[6]

Much of the explanation for Japan's high saving and low return lies in the
institutions and culture of that country. The structure of Japan's financial
system and of its society promotes savings and constrains consumption: the
absence of full pension and social security systems, lump-sum payments at
year end and at retirement at age fifty-five to sixty, encourage workers to
save. A worker who receives a large payment at the end of the year, rather
than in small installments throughout the year, is more likely to save it. A
worker with limited pension benefits is likely to save for the future. In a
sense, such a structure forces the worker to save. Large down payments on
mortgages and the absence of scholarships at private universities encourage
savings. The social organization helps to explain different patterns in the
supply and demand for funds. Other things being equal, a large pool of
savings ought to reduce the cost of capital and increase its availability.

Government policies are rarely neutral toward savings and consumption.
Tax policy, the typical tool to promote savings, is sometimes supplemented
by more informal techniques. Both Germany and Japan reward savers and
penalize those who borrow to finance consumption. In Germany, the taxpayer
may not deduct interest paid on consumer loans or on mortgages for single-
home dwellings (although favorable depreciation rates exist). However, tax
benefits—including tax-free savings to DM 612 a year—provided a "general
savings bonus" estimated by one study to equal 2.7% of all household savings
during 1975-78. In 1980, these "savings subsidies" began to wane.[7] Japan
goes even further: tax policies exempt income on post office savings accounts
up to a certain level (now the equivalent of about $13,000), after which

savers simply open new accounts at other post offices.[8] By law, the post offices also offer a rate slightly above that permitted to banks. Not surprisingly, the post offices command a higher share of household savings than do even the commercial banks.

It would appear that the U.S. policies encourage spending at the expense of saving. While the federal government exempts $100 in dividend income to each taxpayer, it exempts no interest income. It did offer special tax free "all savers" accounts up to $2000 at rates well below those offered on taxable government bonds, but with little success, since they appear to have encouraged switching accounts rather than saving more. By allowing unlimited deductions for consumer debt and mortgages, the government encourages consumption or investment in nonproductive activities. In this, the United States more closely resembles Britain.[9] Now, according to a recent study, U.S. marginal tax rates on household savings (debt or equity) are not substantially worse than those of the United Kingdom or Germany.[10]

Compared with the other countries, then, Japanese institutions and government policies encourage savings with a variety of carrots and sticks. The structure of the financial system, itself reflecting institutional evolution and government policy, also serves to limit the return available to the saver who is constrained to save. This has the effect of reducing the cost of capital to business.

In Japan, many dispersed small savers "bargain" with a few large banks. Like all the governments, Japan's finance ministry sets rates for deposits directly, or through lender cartels indirectly. Given the dispersal of the savers and the concentration of the banks,[11] it should not be surprising that the rates paid to savers are held low. That the big banks are always cash short and have to buy a substantial share of their resources from other financial intermediaries makes them vulnerable to these suppliers—not to the households— whose rates are set by the finance ministry. As the cash-short big banks need funds, and the call market rates skyrocket in times of tight money, it would appear that the smaller source banks have leverage. But a network of rules also limits the options of the smaller banks. The small number of big banks (only twelve account for over half of interbank uses) does not seem to be at the mercy of thousands of smaller ones.

What remains is to ensure that the big banks do not themselves capture the value added in the financial system but pass it on to the borrowers. Two factors are key: the structure of the financial system and the size and status of the users. Japanese intermediaries, which account for 80% of funding, lend in highly segmented markets. The big banks are twelve City banks, which alone account for over 30% of all intermediated credit and 40% of credit to business. Regulations hold them in relatively narrow service and geographic markets, within which there are enough banks to compete vigorously for share. Circumscribed, roughly equal in size, and sufficiently numerous to prevent the banks from managing the market themselves, the banks' resulting competition prevents them from retaining the value added.

The size and options of the large users give them further market power against the big banks. One large user is the government itself, which according to one study commands below market interest rates.[12] Among firms, the large ones should be quite powerful. They are more concentrated, have more alternative sources, and many have close equity ties with the City banks, ties that could hinder or benefit the firms. Another study found that in the mid-1970s the biggest group "pays a third less for its debt capital than those with less than ¥100 million in paid-in capital" and had done so for fifteen years.[13]

In sum, the big banks can squeeze savers, who have limited options anyway, but cannot count on high margins from powerful big borrowers. This suggests that in Japan the low-cost funds can be passed along to industry. Those who bear the cost are the savers, taxpayers, and, to the extent that they pay higher taxes, the consumers as well.

It is worth noting one other factor that is sometimes advanced to explain low capital costs in Japan: some see a low level of demand for funds relative to supply in recent years. Certainly economic growth has slowed, but the actual demand for credit has grown. In Japan:

- The government's demand for credit is strong and rising, both historically and relative to other countries (see figure 10-2).
- Business demand in Japan is twice as strong as elsewhere (see figure 10-3). Japan still invests much more than the others in machinery and equipment: 13.1% compared with a range of 7.3% (United States) to 9.7% (France), from 1960 to 1980.
- Consumer credit has been discouraged. Despite this policy, consumer credit in Japan is almost to equal that in the United States (see figure 10-4). In housing, Japan invests more than others: from 1960 to 1980, Japan invested more (6.5% of GDP) than the United Kingdom (3.4%) or the United States (4.5%). Some of this may be transitional as the Japanese economy evolves. Without the restraint, the growth would have been even stronger.

Japan does not lag behind other G-5 countries in demand for investment other than plant and equipment. Perhaps relative to the boom years of the

Figure 10-2

Government Debt as % of GDP

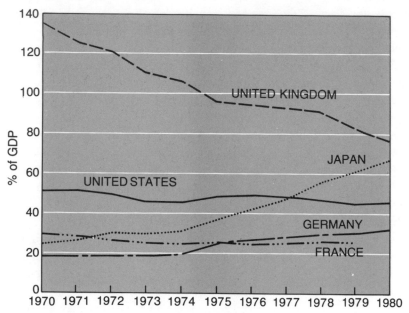

Source: Central bank bulletins of each country

Japanese economic miracle, up to 1973, demand for funds in later years was weak. Compared with other industrial countries, however, demand continues to be strong.

Reduced Risk in the Intermediaries. By reducing the risk that savers face when they place funds with intermediaries, governments reduce the cost of capital, since the premium demanded by savers is lower than it would otherwise be. Governments may do this in two ways: insurance or a guarantee is standard; in addition, as an intermediary, a government also reduces the risk for savers.

All governments offer some form of deposit insurance and provide an implicit guarantee that no big bank will be allowed to fail, but in France and Japan that guarantee reaches much farther than it does in Germany, the United Kingdom, or the United States. The effect on the capital structure of the banks, and hence on their costs, is striking. The French government implicitly guarantees the banks it owns. The Japanese government has permitted no bank to fail since World War II. Moreover, the small number of big banks, with their large and pivotal role in the financial system, means that in a crisis, a bank can be supported in a way that involves a relatively small number of players. The Japanese government can do this because of its deep involvement in the financial system. This permits equity/debt leveraging of 1:100 in Japan as well as France, compared with ratios of 4:100 or 5:100 in Germany, the United Kingdom, and the United States. The higher leveraging permits French and Japanese banks to offer funds at lower rates, thus reducing the cost of capital to borrowers. Short of a crisis, no one bears any actual cost; at the crisis, the parties negotiate.

The government itself is the largest single intermediary in Japan. Thousands of post office outlets, all under the control of the post office itself, collect almost 16% of all savings and 25% of all household savings, channeling them to the government first and to business and home buyers second. In addition, thousands of private agricultural cooperatives collect rural savings (amounting to 12% of all savings) and channel them through the Norin Chukin Bank, which they own but which is under the authority of the Ministry of Agriculture.[14] As the risk-free entity in the financial sector, the government

Figure 10-3

Business Debt as % of GDP

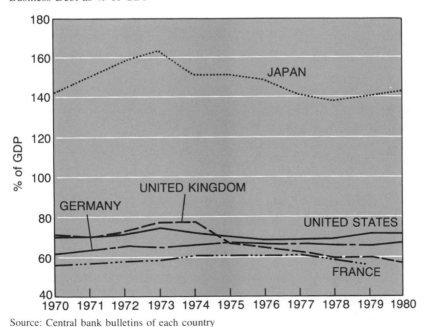

Source: Central bank bulletins of each country

Figure 10-4

Household Debt as % of GDP

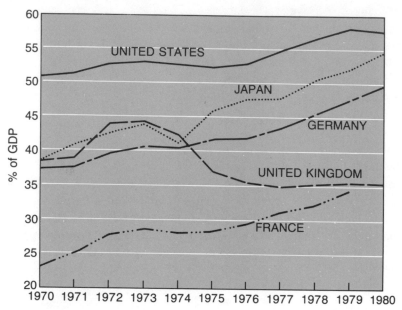

Source: Central bank bulletins of each country

in this role allows the saver to accept a lower return than it would require from a private intermediary. The government is in a position to pass this along to borrowers.

In sum, many factors exist in Japan—and some elsewhere—that would reduce the rate on credit throughout the economy. In Japan, it appears possible to increase savings without increasing the cost to the user commensurately. Others bear the cost. It also appears possible to reduce the risk associated with intermediaries, which accounts for much more of the financing than in the United States, for example. Until the crisis, no one bears an actual cost. Finally, the financial system is structured in such a way that the lower cost can be passed on to the large firms that are borrowers.

FACTORS THAT REDUCE THE RISK IN LENDING TO FIRMS

By reducing the vulnerability of firms to downturns in the business cycle and by reducing the cost of financial distress should downturns occur, it is possible to lower the cost of capital in advance of these events. Investors anticipate the reduced risk in their initial lending. They may permit higher leveraging, more short-term debt, or simply a lower risk premium. There are several ways in which firms become less vulnerable.

High self-finance is one way a firm may insulate itself from the costs of external finance, but it is expensive. To reduce costs, the firm looks outside. Firms in Japan draw 70% of their funds externally, more than twice the amount drawn externally by German firms (see table 10-4). External funding may come in the form of equity or less expensive debt. It may come directly from savers or indirectly through intermediaries such as banks and institutional investors. In Japan, for example, banks provide over half the external funds; in the United States, banks provide only about one-quarter.[15] Many argue that U.S. manufacturing firms rely on equity rather than debt because their vulnerability to deep recessions increases the instability of their earnings.[16] A vicious cycle is at work. Equally important is whether the external sources are public markets or administered.

By relying on administered markets rather than on public markets for debt and equity, firms reduce their vulnerability to recession and therefore reduce their cost of capital. Administered markets offer a much smaller number of players who can negotiate a coordinated response to a firm in financial difficulty during a recession. In the G-5 countries, investors in the public financial markets are too dispersed to do this. Yet in the United States, 47% of total financial stock in 1980 passed through the public markets, compared with 29% in Germany and 22% in Japan (see figure 10-5).

Of course, intermediaries must be able to administer, providing funds during a downturn that will enable the firms to weather the crisis. In the U.S financial system, there are too many players: 14,000 commercial banks, over

Table 10-4
External Funding of Business

External Sources as % Total Funds, Annual Average, 1970-80

Japan	70%
France	59
United Kingdom	58
United States	42
Germany	33

Source: OECD Financial Statements, Part III, 1982.

Figure 10-5

Sources of Funds for Government, Business, and Households (stock outstanding, end 1980)

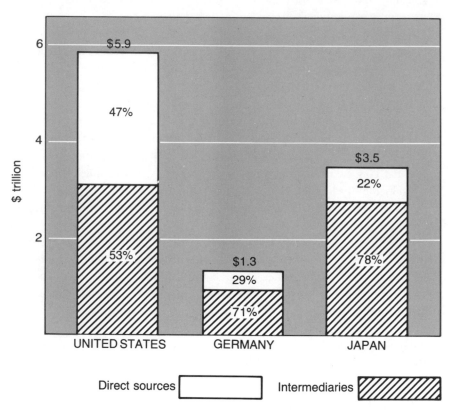

Source: Central bank bulletins of each country

4,500 saving and loan associations, almost 5,000 insurance companies. A firm may have scores of lenders, few of which see advantage in providing new funds to a troubled firm. The contrast with Japan is vivid. Only twelve City banks account for 40% of the lending to business (and a larger share to big business). Highly competitive as the banks are, the incentive to cooperate in crisis is supplemented by the means to do so and conventions that guide them. One important factor is the equity the banks hold in the firms.

Commercial banks in Japan and Germany hold substantial equity interests in firms, while those in France, the United Kingdom and the United States do not. In Japan, large industrial groups called *keiretsu* each revolve around a major City bank and a trading company. Despite conflicting evidence,[17] several aspects of the keiretsu relation provide lower costs to the borrower: banks redeploy liquid assets within the group; bank board members with real power shape management decisions, thus reducing risk, and monitor performance.[18] In a crisis, leadership falls to the bank with the closest ties. A similar rationale guides banks in Germany. Here is the convention that guides banks to cooperate. Here also is a factor that induces cooperation among debtholders and shareholders, so often missing in the United States: the big banks hold both debt and equity. They lack the incentive as lenders to place the burden of the loss on the shareholders.

Since investors understand this process in advance, they are prepared to accept higher leveraging or shorter-term debt, both of which would reduce the cost of capital. The high leveraging of Japanese, German, and French firms is commonplace (although the amount is disputed). The stock of business short-term debt in Japan was 110% of GDP in 1980, compared with a range of 25-40% in the other G-5 countries. All five had long-term debt in the range of 30-40% of GDP. Japanese firms could bear a much larger amount of short-term debt because the administered system that supplied it recognized that the firms' vulnerability to economic cycles could be reduced by an assured source of funding.

The same rationale governs firms actually in distress. Banks and other group members are expected, as shareholders, to help in times of crisis for the firm, thus reducing risk because there are fewer players with disparate interests.[19] In addition, in Japan the private sector needs to deal with only one regulator of the financial system, the finance ministry and the central bank, rather than multiple regulators with conflicting interests, as in the United States. The government lending agencies, also under the control of the finance ministry, have a stake in the outcome. With fewer players on the official side, the chance of misstep is further reduced and capital costs can reflect the benefit.

A further advantage of the administered system lies in reducing transaction costs. The arms'-length transaction itself costs more, in the abstract, than one in which the lender may obtain rewards in other ways than the payment of interest. The bank that also holds equity in the borrowing firm may take a longer view, accepting lower interest rates in return for an eventual appreciation in the value of the firm's stock. It may also have access to information unavailable to a lender, thus permitting it to share costs associated with the transaction.

SUMMARY

There are many ways in which capital costs can be reduced systemwide in a country like Japan. The rates on debt can be reduced overall by increasing savings without equally increasing the cost to the user; by reducing the risk of placing funds with intermediaries; and by assuring that the intermediaries pass the lower-cost funds on to the borrowers. The risk associated with companies can be lowered by reducing firms' vulnerability to restricted finance flows during a recession and by reducing the costs associated with actual financial distress. Investors would recognize these effects in advance and price lower accordingly. The costs of financial transactions may also be reduced.

The mechanisms that exist to reduce costs systemwide are numerous, ranging far beyond government policy or simply the equity interest a bank may have in its customer. These mechanisms include cultural and institutional arrangements and the structure of the financial system, as well as tax and regulatory policies.

When some form of subsidy goes to business, someone else must pay. Who does pay will depend on the mechanism that is used. The saver accepts lower returns in many cases but receives tax benefits in Japan for the use of certain institutions, in which case the taxpayer or higher-taxed consumer bears the cost. A regulatory system that segments the market so that it can be administered will have costs as well, which may be shared within the financial system or across the economy.

The foregoing discussion accounts for the lower cost of capital in Japan. Set against the range in capital costs found by the four studies, the economic and institutional logic suggests that the difference would be larger, not smaller, at the systemic level. There remains the issue of targeting.

THE ABILITY TO CHANNEL FINANCIAL FLOWS

Governments may also reduce the cost of capital for specific firms. The question is whether in crucial areas of economic activity, which could be housing just as much as competitiveness, the means (1) exist within the financial system and (2) are used to modify the mix of inputs to achieve a particular outcome.

At a strategic level, an analysis of the financial system's role in channeling funds is troublesome because in each of the G-5 countries thousands of institutions act as intermediaries. To maneuver such a behemoth toward national goals should require an explicit system of command or large, overt subsidies. Without the ability to command or reward, it should be impossible to "run things." Among the G-5, no government has so simple and obvious a system of command, not even France, where the government owns the banks. Among the G-5, many incentives designed to allocate credit are explicit and well known, like special-interest ceilings or tax relief to encourage housing. In each country, one sees the many intermediaries competing head-on and the political differences that keep them at loggerheads. That is, before the question of *whether* the financial system actually plays a subtle strategic role, there is the question of *how* it could possibly do so in a way not readily apparent. We need an institutional and economic rationale for the asserted control. This requires an analysis of the structure of the financial market in each country.

MARKET SEGMENTS AND SHARE IN THE U.S. FINANCIAL SYSTEM

Signals must be overt in public markets. In the United States, where half of all financial stock is from public markets (see figure 10-5), one must therefore look for overt signals. This is particularly true because the remaining funds are intermediated by thousands of institutions, difficult to administer in any subtle way.

To capture the complexity and diversity of the major groups of intermediaries, figure 10-6 identifies their share in each major market segment: (1) ultimate sources of funds—government, business, and households; (2) financial intermediaries; and (3) ultimate users—also government, business, and households. It is a snapshot of the assets and liabilities of the intermediary groups at the end of 1980.[20] Over 14,421 commercial banks (C), for example, held 35.5% of all sources of funds (3% is from governments, 5.6% from business, and 26.9% from households). The stock of outstanding funds is the outcome of strategic decisions over time, so it is more useful than the flow. Beyond the numbers, however, qualitative data are essential to understand the extent of the differences within and between the groups.[21]

Most striking in this picture of the U.S. financial system is the enormous number of institutions in each group, nearly 25,000 altogether. Within each group there is a hierarchy by size, of course. But even a firm with $60 billion controls barely 1.8% of all assets in the system. While the largest financial institutions in the world are in the United States, they are part of a system that dwarfs them. Depending on exchange rates, Bank of America and Citibank are larger than any other bank in the world. But though the top ten

Figure 10-6

U.S. Financial Intermediaries—Market Segments and Share (end 1980)
A. *The Markets for Deposits and Other Savings, Sources of Funds (Total Liabilities $3,225.8 Billion)*
B. *The Intermediary Markets*
C. *The Markets for Loans and Other Uses, Uses of Funds (Total Assets $3,382.9 Billion)*

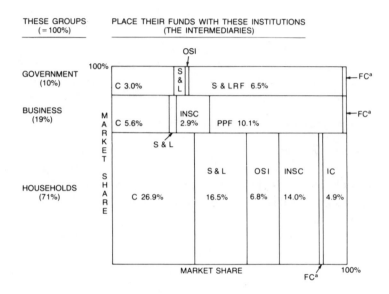

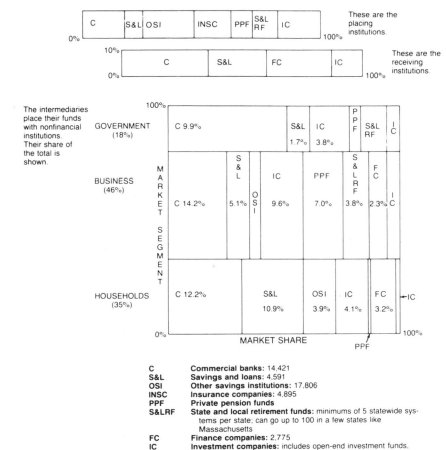

C   **Commercial banks:** 14,421
S&L   **Savings and loans:** 4,591
OSI   **Other savings institutions:** 17,806
INSC   **Insurance companies:** 4,895
PPF   **Private pension funds**
S&LRF   **State and local retirement funds:** minimums of 5 statewide sys-
          tems per state; can go up to 100 in a few states like
          Massachusetts
FC   **Finance companies:** 2,775
IC   **Investment companies:** includes open-end investment funds,
          security brokers and dealers, real estate investment trusts, and
          money market mutual funds

Source: Federal Reserve Board
[a]Less than 1%.

banks in the United States command 22% of the assets of all commercial banks, this gives them only 8% of total assets of the intermediated system (22% of [9.9% + 14.2% + 12.2%]). Coupled with the proliferation of financial institutions and the assault on regulatory barriers among the segments, the plethora of intermediaries in the United States suggests that they cannot be used in a subtle way to help achieve a national strategy.

If the U.S. government wants to influence lending it must use broad, public measures, and it does. According to a recent study, the housing industry received far greater government assistance than did any other of fifteen major industries. The U.S. government, using the financial system, gave 78% of its assistance to the housing industry, providing almost all its loans and guarantees to that one industry (see table 10-5). This is a strategy using the financial system in the most overt manner to promote housing, which is not an industry exposed to international competition.

MARKET SEGMENTS AND SHARE IN THE JAPANESE FINANCIAL SYSTEM

The Japanese system is strikingly different. At the point of distribution, a small number of banks allocate over half the intermediated funds, which account for almost 80% of all funds. In summary, two channels transfer Japanese savings:

Table 10-5

U.S. Government Assistance to Fifteen Industries (fiscal year 1980)

	Total Assistance		Of Which:	Tax
Industry	*($ bil.)*	*%*	*Loans and Guarantees*	*Expenditure*
All 15	$247	100%	68%	11%
Top 5 (in order)				
Housing	191	78%	64%	9%
Aviation	12	5%	a	0
Maritime	11	4%	3%	a
Nuclear	8	3%	0	0
Petroleum	8	3%	0	1%
Subtotal	$230	93%	67%	10%

Source: Robert B. Reich, "Why the U.S. Needs an Industrial Policy," *Harvard Business Review* (January-February 1982): 78; author's calculations.
a Less than 0.5%

- Among private institutions, thousands of small banks collect savings from households (part A of figure 10-7), channeling them—in part through interbank lending (part B)—to a small number of commercial banks (there are only thirteen City banks, if Bank of Tokyo is included). These banks lend to business (part C), mainly large firms.The government, not a factor in the deposit market, is a major segment in the loan market, as each group of intermediaries is required to invest in government securities.

- Among public intermediaries, thousands of post office outlets, all under the control of the post office itself, also collect household savings, channeling them to the government first and to business and home buyers second. Thousands of private agricultural cooperatives collect rural savings generated by government agricultural programs and channel them through the Norin Chukin Bank. Since rural demand for funds is limited, the Norin Chukin Bank deposits its excess funds with the City banks.

In Japan, seven kinds of institutions do most of the intermediating. Described in more detail in figure 10-7, they are City banks, long-term credit banks, trust banks, local banks, small business financing institutions, agricultural finance institutions, and the postal savings system. Although similar in powers and limitations, each group differs from the others.[22]

In searching for a means to target financial flows within a very complex financial system, one sees three kinds of power that could accomplish it if they worked in tandem: private market power, official market power, and regulatory power.

The Market Power of the Twenty-Three Largest Banks. Market power rests with the few City and specialized banks for three reasons: small numbers compared to thousands of savers (City banks, long-term credit banks, and trust banks number only twenty-three); proximity to the main borrowers (the keiretsu system described above); and control of about 40% of savings (many keiretsu firms keep their funds with their main banks). They do not compete head-on in all markets because of regulations that separate them by product and geography. Government policy is in part responsible for these three factors.

The Government as a Powerful Player. Through its postal savings system, the government is the largest single player in the market for deposits. Its size and position change the game for the other intermediaries. The postal savings

Figure 10-7

Japanese Financial Intermediaries—Market Segments and Share (end 1980)
A. *The Markets for Deposits and Other Savings*
B. *The Intermediary Markets–*Placing Institutions
*The Intermediary Markets–*Receiving Institutions
C. *The Markets for Loans and Other Uses*

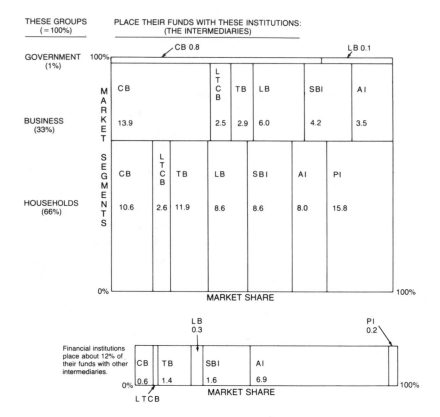

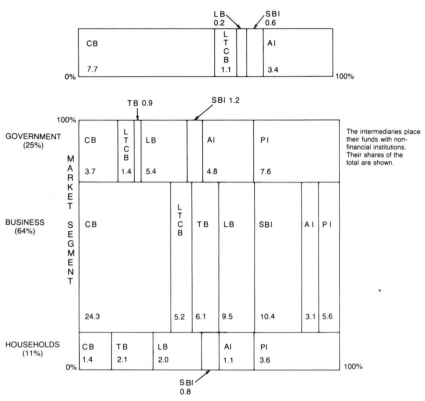

The intermediaries place their funds with non-financial institutions. Their shares of the total are shown.

MARKET SHARE

CB   **City banks:** 13 banks in major cities
LTCB   **Long-term credit banks:** 3 that lend long term
TB   **Trust banks:** 7 can be trustees
LB   **Local banks:** 63 are in the provinces
SBI   **Small business institutions:** 1,008 mutual savings and loans, credit associations, and credit cooperatives serve small firms
AI   **Agricultural institutions:** over 4,500 are agricultural cooperatives, their federations, and banks that gather farmers' savings and invest
PI   **Postal savings:** gathered through the Post Office and loaned by the trust fund bureau of the Finance Ministry

Source: Bank of Japan *Bulletin*

system flourishes with several competitive advantages created by government. These include a slightly higher interest rate that is tax free. In the deposit markets, therefore, the postal savings system is a formidable competitor of the City banks, which cannot even turn to the interbank market to buy deposits from the postal savings system as they can from the agricultural finance institutions. The competition changes to cooperation, however, in the loan markets. The savings raised by the post offices are transferred to the Ministry of Finance trust fund bureau, which allocates the funds. The funds go first to government users (see part C of figure 10-7); loans in the business segment support and supplement the banks' loans.

It is the government's role as lender that suggests its effect on the flow of funds. The direct role is small but apparently powerful. Only one-third of trust fund credit finances business; indeed, only 5.6% of the market (see part C, figure 10-7) reaches business from the government's own institutions, which include the Japan Development Bank (JDB), the Japan Export-Import Bank, and agencies to finance small- and medium-sized business. Few dispute that private lenders in Japan treat this lending as a sign that the firm or project has government support, which would reduce the risk of the credit. The issue is whether such an interpretation has much effect given the small size of the government credit.[23] It is worth remembering that the target is small (Japanese exports are only about 15% of GDP) and direct government lending is not the only available tool.

To the government's direct lending one must add the insurance function of lending by long-term credit banks,[24] another 5.2% of the market. The Industrial Bank of Japan, as the largest of the three banks, provided 12% of all investment in plant and equipment financed by banks in the year ending March 1982.[25] While there is no reason to believe that every loan was a signal to the banking community, its presence was substantial enough to have an effect, given this form of signaling.

The overall impact of the government exceeds its role as a direct lender but is closely tied to that role. Combined with the trust fund loans, the long-term credit bank loans accounted for 18% of all outstanding loans to business (see figure 10-7), and if the net flow of funds to business is considered, the percentage is higher. One cannot assume a harmony of interests between the finance ministry and the long-term credit banks (LTCBs),[26] but neither can one assume constant opposition. The point is not that the government gives all the orders, but that with its market power and power of command (see below), and given the small number of institutions involved (twenty-four account for 64% of all intermediated business finance), the government is in a position to influence the flow of funds. For example, one of the targets of the Japanese financial system is the government itself. A quid pro quo for protection of each group is that its members must buy an agreed share of new government bonds.

The Power of Command. As in all countries, the government in Japan regulates innumerable facets of the financial system. It limits entry and expansion, shapes geographic and product markets, and controls pricing directly and indirectly through cartels of the intermediaries. For example, the finance ministry approves the long-term prime rate that three long-term credit banks set acting as an official cartel,[27] and it helps decide where, outside the agricultural cooperative, the Norin Chukin Bank can invest its funds. Also, as planner, it helps set priorities without actually lending money.

The result is highly segmented markets in Japan. Competition across segments is limited though not lost. Competition within a market segment can be severe. The fact that twelve City banks are of roughly equal size suggests that they would compete aggressively against each other, as many observers confirm. Stiff competition among banks should itself permit lower capital costs to the borrowers. The government's ability to guide the flow of funds is critical.

Overall, the structure of the financial system—not simply the equity ties between banks and firms—appears to accommodate market power in a way that should reduce the cost of capital in Japan, improving its competitiveness. There are many reasons for this structure, some reaching far into the past and others reflecting recent government policy.

Today, the structure still appears to be amenable to subtle guidance in directions that conform to a national strategy that helps firms competing in world industries. Evidence suggests that these relations are changing, however. Competitive pressures due to slower growth in demand force City banks and local banks to vie for the middle-market firms. Cost pressures force City banks, which are liability poor, to search for cheaper deposits. Big borrowers' access to foreign funds reduces the power of their domestic banks. The opportunity to invest abroad increases the options of savers. Changes in the banking laws mean these opportunities now exist in a formal way. However, the finance ministry has kept informal controls strong and basic roles clear. It is problematic whether these controls can survive in the future as some of the enabling conditions erode. It is worth remembering, however, that the controls have survived other changes in the past, such as the entry of the commercial banks into international markets in 1970-71.

SEGMENTS AND SHARES IN EUROPE

Europe is different. The French banking system is nationalized but is not amenable to puppetlike control from the Banque de France and the Tresor. In fact, the monetary authorities use market mechanisms, such as credit ceilings, to manage the banking system. The line of official command is much more overt and direct in France than in the other G-5 countries, especially since the Mitterrand government took office. Nonetheless, although the potential exists, French firms have not been helped to compete in world markets.

Despite controversy in both Britain and Germany about the role of the financial system, there is little evidence to suggest channeling of the sort that may occur in Japan. Both systems have a few large deposit banks at the top, with close relations to major firms, but these banks are vastly outnumbered by the savings banks (called building societies in the United Kingdom), which have the dominant market share (see figure 10-8 for Germany). An analysis of market segments in Germany suggests that the dominant practices result in the preservation of market share among the groups. A recent study of British and German banks concluded that the banks had little effect on savings, noting that since 1975 the high savings rate in Germany fell, and the low rate in the United Kingdom grew, without change in the structure or behavior of the banking system.[28]

The main point of critics in both the United Kingdom and Germany is that the financial system favors the status quo, an issue discussed below. Given the distance that the governments of both countries maintain from their financial institutions, and the nature of their own economic strategies, their recent use of the financial system does not appear to promote competitiveness. To the extent government policy permits a status quo orientation, it may endanger competitiveness.

In short, while Japan and France both have the means to channel financial flows, Japan is far better situated to do so in a way that reduces the cost of capital and improves its firms' competitiveness. In the market segments, the Japanese groups have a more focused role. The specialized banks—some public, others quasi-public—have a century-old tradition that reflects a policy of rapid industrialization built around the need to channel funds within the economy. Today, the financial strategy draws on more than the simple U.S. distinctions based on geography or on commercial, investment, or savings banks. Government regulations assure margins and special privileges for each group; the government's ability to do this gives it the power to play one group against another and thus reduce the potential power of some of the large banks.

Of course, unequal or asymmetric relations found in Japan exist elsewhere. In Europe and the United States, big banks dwarf other financial intermediaries. Big banks buy money from others. Government regulations create significant barriers among market segments, and the banks try to keep the barriers that sustain them while removing those that are costly. It is a matter of degree. In Japan, the distinctions seem more pronounced and the opportunity greater for guidance through administrative action as well as through the action of the government as player.

While the evidence that Japan targets specific industries is ambiguous, analyzing the snapshot of the financial system suggests that this could be done in a very subtle way. The Japanese regulators are in a better position to enforce such a strategy than are the other G-5 regulators. Unlike Germany and the United Kingdom, the finance ministry and central bank are active. Unlike the United States, there are only two regulators; in the United States, the web of regulatory institutions almost defies unraveling. Unlike France, the Japanese authorities need not contend with a bank president appointed by the president of the Republic.

While a nation's financial system can be described as managed, in an integrated world economy that management should fail in the face of powerful market forces. Savers forced to accept lower returns at home would merely turn to foreign forms of investment that offered market rates. Intermediaries constrained in some way at home would turn abroad to escape. An essential component of any system that seeks to manage financing costs and flows is control at the borders. Yet the erosion of those controls has been the goal of major industrial states for at least the last twenty-five years. The dilemma is how the benefits of a system like the one described for Japan could survive in the increasingly integrated world of finance.

CONTROL AT THE BORDER: THE PREREQUISITE FOR CONTROL AT HOME

An essential part of any effort to manage the cost of capital at home is to keep control over the flow of finance in and out of the country. In restraining the outflow of capital, governments limit the opportunities of savers to invest, restricting demand in a way that serves to hold down the returns to savers and the cost of funds to borrowers. Many barriers exist to the free outflow of capital. The Germans have a queue for foreign bond issuers. The French

Figure 10-8

German Financial Intermediaries—Market Segments and Share (end 1980)
A. *The Markets for Deposits and Other Savings*
B. *The Intermediary Markets: Financial Institutions*
C. *The Markets for Loans and Other Uses*

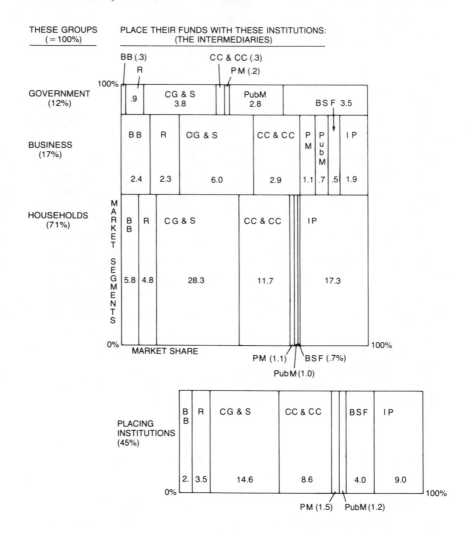

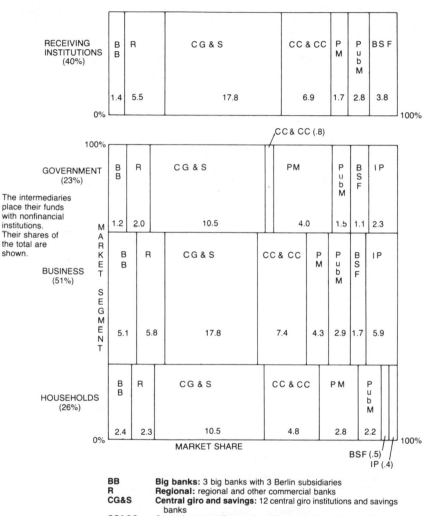

BB   **Big banks:** 3 big banks with 3 Berlin subsidiaries
R   **Regional:** regional and other commercial banks
CG&S   **Central giro and savings:** 12 central giro institutions and savings banks
CC&CC   **Central cooperatives and credit cooperatives:** 10 central institutions of credit cooperatives and 4,225 credit cooperatives
PM   **Private mortgage banks:** 25
PubM   **Public mortgage banks:** 13
BSF   **Banks with special functions:** 16
IP   **Insurance and pension companies:** 1,264 in 1978

Source: Bundesbank *Bulletin*

restrict franc loans to nonresidents, who may only borrow francs to finance the purchase of French exports. The Japanese go further: they control Samurai bonds, register foreign currency loans by Japanese banks, control foreign banks' operations in the domestic yen markets, and limit the use of the yen even by foreign central banks. Neither the United Kingdom nor the United States has clean hands: the British exchange controls and the U.S. interest equalization tax ended only ten years ago. Now, however, the two countries are more open.

These policies should affect the outflow of capital from each country. Since other factors—relative exchange rates and interest rates, for example— also affect the outflow, it is difficult to quantify the impact of the protectionist policies. One indicator is found in the extent to which nonbank residents of each country place deposits in international banks (see table 10-6).

Japan emerges as the country that differs substantially in the extent to which its residents place funds in international banks. As a share of GDP, foreign currency deposits by Japanese residents were a mere 0.06%, far outside the range of 0.56% to 1.27% for the other nondollar countries.[29] Japan also seems to have been most successful in preventing the yen from serving as a reserve currency: the ratio of domestic currency deposits to GDP and the ratio of domestic currency debt were both far outside the range for the other countries.[30] In vivid contrast, Japanese borrowers of foreign currency were well within the G-5 range.

Japanese residents have long been constrained in their ability to hold foreign currency deposits. There is no reason to suspect that Japanese residents require fewer foreign deposits than residents of the other industrial countries. Nor, given the strength and subsequent decline of the yen, can we assume that Japanese investors choose not to hold foreign currency deposits because of expectations about currency movements.

Although Japan's foreign exchange laws were formally relaxed on 1 December 1980, informal constraints have continued. Before that date, residents wishing to export capital needed the approval of the Finance Ministry. After that date they were allowed to invest abroad if they notified the Ministry of Finance twenty days in advance. The twenty-day delay had the effect, of course, of dampening speculative movements. The finance ministry, more- over, retained the power to suspend or modify this more liberal rule if "the transaction might adversely affect (1) domestic and international money markets; (2) Japan's international reputation; (3) Japan's industrial activity or the smooth performance of the economy; and (4) implementation of Japan's international agreements, international peace and security, or the maintenance of public order."[31]

Table 10-6
Nonbank Residents' Use of International Banks (outstanding, end 1980)

	Amount ($ billions)					Amount as % of GDP				
	U.S.	U.K.	France	Germany	Japan	U.S.	U.K.	France	Germany	Japan
Deposits										
In domestic currency										
abroad	$63.5	$2.7	$0.5	$3.3	$0.1	2.46%	0.63%	0.10%	0.50%	0.009%
In foreign currency										
abroad	4.0	5.5	3.7	3.7	0.7	0.15	1.27	0.78	0.56	0.060
at home		13.2	2.2	1.6			3.06	0.46	0.24	
Borrowing										
In domestic currency										
abroad	10.2	1.6	0.7	25.0	0.5	0.39	0.37	0.15	3.80	0.043
In foreign currency										
abroad	5.6	6.9	7.1	5.4	10.1	0.22	1.60	1.48	0.82	0.87
at home		22.6	8.0	1.7			5.23	1.67	0.26	

Source: Bank for International Settlements, International Banking Developments, second quarter 1983, table 7.

These new policies in Japan do not appear to have encouraged capital outflows immediately. Japan gradually relaxed its restrictions on cross-border capital movements and, during 1982, largely in response to high interest rates in the United States, net capital outflows were $12 billion, against annual average net inflows of $2 billion from 1976 to 1981. Since $12 billion is 1% of GDP, the swing is not trivial. As one would expect, there has been some opening, while Japan moved into current account surplus. The test will come when there is a threat to the balance of payments.

For countries to which trade is very important, the disincentive to integrating their financial market with the rest of the world is very strong. Japan, Germany, and France, have made it clear that they do not want their currencies to be reserve currencies and, therefore, the governments limit access to their currencies. Their fear is that, as nations with reserve currencies, they would lose control over domestic monetary policy, one component of which is interest rate management. The policy link to capital costs is strong.

The wide variety of ways in which capital costs are manipulated suggests a large gap exists between formally stating that a financial system is open to the world and achieving that goal. In finance, there is an equivalent to the nontariff barriers that stymie efforts to open trade. Numerous institutions tie the saver to its country. Relations among intermediaries or between intermediaries and those who use the financial services can be persistent when they are based on mutual benefit. A balance of power among groups of institutions will be hard to change if it is set by regulations that are designed to ensure the safety and soundness of a country's financial system. France's exchange controls are explicit. Japan's controls, which are much more complex, are likely to persist despite the appearance of change.

THE ADVANTAGES OF DIVERSITY: INNOVATION AND THE FINANCIAL SYSTEM

The previous analyses have suggested that the United States, far from having the cost of capital advantages commonly assumed to exist in such a large diverse financial system, in fact is at a disadvantage. At least Japan seems to be able to reduce capital costs systemwide and to channel funds to particular industries, since it controls its borders and has the infrastructure to manage financial flows inside the country. Yet it is clear that the Japanese are concerned about an advantage they believe the United States has: a financial system that promotes innovation from the bottom up.

THE U.S. ADVANTAGE

In comparison with other G-5 financial systems the United States has a major advantage in its venture capital firms. The U.S. stock of venture capital exceeds $10 billion, far surpassing Japan (estimates are about $130 million) and Europe (estimates for Germany are $300 million and for the United Kingdom, $1 billion). The number of venture capital firms in the United States exceeds 500, compared with about 30 in Japan (20 started since early 1982), 84 in the United Kingdom, 33 in France (by very broad definition), and 6 in Germany (5 of these were announced since June 1983).[32]

While venture capital will not invariably promote competitiveness, the consensus is that it has done so in the United States. Elsewhere, the ventures may be in services rather than in high technology, and the innovation may take place in larger firms (which is apparently the case in Germany).[33] In the United States, a government study concluded that "for each $1,000 of venture capital invested during the 1970s, an estimated $40,000 to $54,000 worth of productivity-enhancing products and services will be sold during the 1980s."[34] Although the $3 billion in U.S. venture capital investment during 1982 may seem small relative to the $444 billion in total investment, the payoff is big.

Two questions arise. First, does this advantage accrue to the United States because of the heterogeneity of the U.S. financial system? The other G-5 financial systems are shallower and, since equity plays a smaller role, lenders or government officials make more of the investment decisions. More cautious, they may have shied away from venture capital vehicles in the past. Second, should we expect the other G-5 countries to catch up with the United States in venture capital? In each country, agencies are urging the government to promote venture capital and, in most countries, the government has taken steps in that direction.

EXPLANATIONS OF THE U.S. LEAD IN VENTURE CAPITAL

The depth and sophistication of the U.S. financial system are certainly not the only factors in the development of venture capital in the United States. The entrepreneurial spirit found among certain groups of U.S. investors dates from the end of the nineteenth century and the wealth amassed then. The willingness of entrepreneurs themselves to take risks is not found abroad; in Japan and Germany, for example, both the security that comes from lifetime employment (formal or informal) and the hurdles to reentering the big companies if a venture fails to discourage mobility. The U.S. entrepreneur's willingness to share ownership of a venture is not echoed elsewhere; in France, for example, the owner of a small business wants 100% and will accept slower growth to keep it.

In addition, tax laws in the United States encourage capital investment more than have the tax laws in some of the other G-5 countries. One study plotted the decline and recovery of the U.S. venture capital market between 1969 and 1978. As the marginal tax rate on capital gains rose from 1969 to a high of 49.125% in 1976, new venture investment fell from $171 million in 1969 to $39 million in 1977. The Revenue Act of 1978 reduced the maximum rate to 28% and venture investment ballooned, reaching $570 million in 1978 and $900 million in 1980.[35] In contrast is the German tax law that until 1978 "favored the German preference for fixed-interest investments by taxing profits at the corporate level and then again as dividend income for the sháre holder."[36] Tax laws also create financial intermediaries that have no interest in ventures. Germany's *abschreibungs gesellschaften* (depreciation companies) offer individuals a chance to beat taxes by taking losses as their investments depreciate; they have invested up to DM 4.7 billion a year in ships or real estate. Today, however, depreciation companies may be less significant in deflecting investment from productive purposes.[37]

Investors themselves may prefer the security of bonds to the hazards of equity. In the words of one Frenchman, "Venture capital isn't natural here. Risk-taking is not the essence of French thinking. The incentives are important, but it's a question of mind over money. People won't bet on new companies. They prefer to buy bonds." Norms play a role, as do investor goals. In Germany, where many still see speculation as immoral, retirees looking for safe investments have put as much as DM 495 billion a year in savings accounts at banks. This vast pool of funds does not finance new ventures without 100% security.

That said, it is also true that the U.S. financial system promotes venture capital. The massive equity markets, and the over-the-counter market in particular, provide liquidity to investors that thin equity markets and shallow new OTC markets in Japan and Europe cannot offer.

Compared with their counterparts in Europe and Japan, the banks in the United States are much more willing to play a role in venture capital—mainly as lenders to new ventures but also as equity investors (through subsidiaries operating within a ceiling of 5% of capital). In this they were encouraged by the government, which created the Small Business Investment Company. With very few exceptions, the European banks have held their distance from venture capital and venture lending. Pushed by their governments in the mid-1970s, the French and German banks took small shares in joint-venture venture capital companies, which did little.

There are many reasons for the European banks' reluctance to act as venture capitalists. As lenders, they are cautious. They lack the skills needed to manage shareholdings. They apply tests of creditworthiness that are too stringent for new ventures, demanding security, demanding a track record rather than analyzing the market prospects, and requiring a high ratio of equity to debt despite the high leveraging of established firms (U.S. banks, however, require a still higher equity/debt ratio). As equity holders in large companies, the German banks are tied to existing firms. Even in Japan, the big banks have let the securities companies open most of the new venture capital firms, suggesting a reluctance to enter this market in force. Compared with the U.S. banks, the banks in the other G-5 countries are less prepared to finance new ventures. They will match each other's moves, as one would expect from oligopolists, but push no further.

PROSPECTS FOR VENTURE CAPITAL IN OTHER G-5 COUNTRIES

The governments of Europe and Japan have a long track record of promoting investment in small firms and new technologies. It is possible that their recent efforts are merely another turn of the same wheel, which did not move far in the past and will not in the future. Thus in France, the new over-the-counter market, designed for small companies with up to $5 million in capital, could be expected to succumb to pressure from the banks and other financial institutions to introduce bigger companies (the average equity of traded firms, already $27 million, is over five times the original ceiling). In Germany, despite pressure from the Ministry of Technology and the development/export credit bank, the finance ministry is reluctant to subsidize new ventures, in part because—with the German trade and current account in balance—it is hard to accept the argument that a problem exists. In Europe, the British have moved farthest but still have a long distance before they reach the United States.

The venture capital renaissance in Japan couples a sense of déjà vu with the intriguing question of whether a trade-off exists between a more centralized debt-dominated financial system and venture capital. Could a country manage its financial system in the manner discussed above and at the same time promote vigorous equity financing at the grass roots level? The recent venture capital boom is apparent: a Ministry of International Trade and

Industry (MITI) study showed growth of 43% in 1982 and 70% in 1983 (to about $166 million), as many more firms—some foreign—enter the industry. In November 1983, the finance ministry relaxed listing requirements for the over-the-counter market, permitting smaller firms to go public sooner. A "tenfold growth is looked for in the market over the coming five years, to take the leading twenty companies to total investments of ¥300bn ($1.2bn)."[38] If Japan succeeds, it will still be far behind the United States today. The fact that the recent growth is led by firms from the securities industry rather than banks suggests a new approach outside the debt-oriented system. If venture capital does not threaten management of that system, it can be expected to continue to grow. If it does pose a threat, it could well be dampened.[39]

In sum, the U.S. financial system contributes to the strength of venture capital here: necessary (without the equity orientation and the OTC market, other countries have not been able to follow the United States to now), but not sufficient (the tax law plays a central role). While other G-5 countries are trying again to replicate U.S. venture capital firms, those in Europe have major hurdles to cross. Japan may succeed in creating a smaller version of the U.S. system, but it should also run up against the demands of a more centralized system of financing. One possibility is that investment decisions even by venture capitalists in Japan would be made with an eye to the industries MITI, the Japan Development Bank, and the long-term credit banks support.

SUMMARY

As this review of venture capital in each of the G-5 countries illustrates, U.S. competitiveness appears to benefit from the depth and diversity of the U.S. financial system. Venture capital, however, is only a small part of industrial finance, and one is hard put to find other advantages. In some industries, access to finance and the cost of finance are not a major problem, but particularly with real interest rates high, finance has become important to competitiveness in a wide range of industries.

At the aggregate level, the difference in relative volume, and apparently also in cost, between Japan and the other G-5 countries is striking. In Japan, the stock of debt is twice as high as any of the other four countries and most is short term, which suggests a very different financial system. The cost appears to be substantially less than in the United States. Since each of the G-5 countries finances its industry with different institutions, mix of debt and equity, and incentives, one would expect the outcomes to vary as well. At each turn, however, Japan emerges as qualitatively distinct from its industrial peers. In addition to the cost and volume of funds, Japanese savers place less outside Japan and the Japanese system is much more concentrated.

Is capital allocated and priced in U.S. markets in a way that benefits U.S. firms and the country's competitiveness? Compared with Japan, the answer is no. There are two levels of differences.

Systemic Differences. Lower capital costs in Japan are possible for users of funds in the entire economy. While government policy plays an important role, it is not alone. Other factors include the structure of the financial system, the institutions, and even the culture of Japan. The cost is borne by other groups in the economy: savers, taxpayers, and consumers.

Japan is able to reduce the rates on overall debt in two ways. First, it increases savings without increasing the cost to the user. It promotes savings by increasing the cost of not saving, unlike the United States, and by offering tax incentives to savers, also unlike the United States. Given the structure of the financial system, savers' options are limited and the power of intermediaries that lend to business is augmented, unlike the United States, but not so much that they can keep the value added for themselves.

Second, it reduces the risk of the intermediaries. Japan's government stands behind its big financial intermediaries, notably the City banks, much more explicitly than does the U.S. government. The Japanese government is also directly involved as the single largest recipient of household savings. Both roles, by reducing risk to savers, reduce the cost of capital.

Japan is able to reduce in two ways the risk of firms that borrow. First, it reduces the firms' vulnerability to downturns in the economic cycle. Markets are administered, not public, so in a recession intermediaries can work together to supply funds to illiquid firms or to growing firms. This is possible because a small number of banks (twenty-three) provide the bulk of the funds at the aggregate level, governed by only one regulator. They can cooperate to assure continued financing. This prospect reduces the cost of capital in normal times in several ways: it permits higher leveraging and more short-term debt. Equity is more costly than debt, and long-term debt is more costly than short-term debt.

Second, it reduces the cost to the firm of financial distress. Three factors are important: the structure of Japanese financial markets, the single regulator, and the relations among banks and the firms they serve. If a firm approaches bankruptcy, the investors share a common interest in resolving its problems, since they are both lenders and shareholders. In the United States, conflicting interests prompt investors to nail the coffin shut. For Japanese investors, the prospect of this cooperation should reduce the risk premium they demand in normal times, thus lowering the cost of capital. Both permit much higher debt/equity ratios.

Japan is able to reduce transaction costs associated with financing. The same institutional network for debt and equity allows investors to share costs through wider sources of information and reap rewards in different ways at different times.

Differences among Individual Firms. The structure of the financial market in Japan also suggests that it is possible to channel the flow of funds to favored industries or firms. Of course it is always possible to do so in an overt manner: the United States targets housing, for example. Japan has the capacity to do so subtly: the twenty-three largest banks and the government have great power in the market, so they can lead; and the government continues to be a powerful regulator. When finance is channeled, the cost of capital is by definition lower for the target firms.

To maintain this sort of control over the domestic financial system, control over the border is extremely important. The options of savers and intermediaries must be limited. Japan appears to have succeeded in this respect into the early 1980s. The question remains whether its success can continue in the face of changes at home and abroad.

Here as elsewhere in the study of industrial policy and competitiveness, the core issue is the relative importance of market and nonmarket forces. Given the accusations by U.S. companies of Japanese industrial targeting, the evidence does suggest the financial system is managed to reduce the cost of capital at the aggregate level and for specific firms or industries. Japanese financial markets have been protected in ways that restricted savers' options to seek higher returns abroad and have been structured in ways that channeled funds from households around the country to big firms. The ability to manage the financial system to benefit firms in international markets persisted at least until the last few years, or long enough to finance a mighty industrial complex. Just as it is difficult to show such management in a definitive way, it is also difficult to say that it has ended.

For its part, the U.S. financial system continues to have major strengths: breadth, depth, and an orientation toward innovation not found elsewhere. Faced with a formidable competitor that has the power to channel finance to productive purpose, however, U.S. business could once again cry foul. But we should not overlook the critical fact that in Japan, sacrifice and internal competition also generate high savings, lower costs, and promote investment rather than consumption.

11
Saving, Investment, and Government Deficits in the 1980s

Benjamin M. Friedman

The current course of U.S. fiscal policy, including in particular the prospect of unprecedentedly large government budget deficits during the balance of the 1980s, poses a serious threat to the productiveness and hence to the international competitiveness of American business. This is ironic, since the arguments offered just a few years ago in support of some key elements of this fiscal policy stance portrayed them as highly beneficial to the U.S. economy's ability to supply goods and services. For the foreseeable future, however, the tax and spending policies now in place will probably lead to financial market conditions, including continuing high real interest rates, that will swamp whatever favorable supply-side incentives they entail. Their net effect will be not to spur but to retard new business investment in productive plant and equipment.

The most obvious damage done by this fiscal policy stance and the resulting impediment to business capital formation will be to slow the potential expansion of the U.S. economy (as measured by the growth of output, or real wages, or business profits) once the current recovery has returned the economy to full employment of its resources. In addition, however, the ability of American business to compete in world markets will probably suffer too. In the modern environment of continual rapid change in product mix and product design, competitiveness requires more than just keeping real labor costs low on a foreign exchange value basis. Industries, or even whole economies, that do not invest sufficiently to produce what markets demand, are unlikely to

Benjamin M. Friedman is professor of economics at Harvard University. The author expresses his gratitude to Diane Coyle and Ken Weiller for their research assistance; to the National Science Foundation and the Alfred P. Sloan Research Foundation for research support; and to George C. Lodge, Bruce R. Scott, and William C. Crum for their helpful discussions.

sustain competitiveness merely through adjustment of real exchange rates. Moreover, the same fiscal policy stance that constricts U.S. business investment will also maintain upward pressure on the dollar's international value, so that currency alignments will compound rather than alleviate the danger to competitiveness.

This set of outcomes likely to follow from a continuation of the current stance of U.S. fiscal policy bears attention, indeed warrants concern, for at least two reasons. The first, of course, is that it has strong implications for several potentially important aspects of business decision making. The second is that the situation is not without apparent remedy. Alternative fiscal policies may now lack adequate support, but support for alternatives in turn depends on how the consequences of current policy are perceived. Especially in light of the role that the business community has played in developing support for key elements of that policy enacted within the past few years, business leaders can hardly view tax and spending issues as beyond reach.

The U.S. government deficit poses a threat for the American economy's capital formation, and hence for its productivity and competitiveness, during the remainder of the 1980s. It is important to emphasize that the large deficits realized during the 1981-82 business recession, and in the early stages of the recovery from that recession, do not represent a problem in this context. With the current recovery proceeding vigorously into its second year, however, the proper focus of attention today is not yesterday's deficit but tomorrow's. What is extraordinary about the government deficits in prospect for the coming half-decade is not just that they will be so large, even in relation to the growing economy, but that they will reflect a fundamental imbalance between the federal government's revenues and its expenditures even at full employment.

CAPITAL FORMATION, PRODUCTIVITY, AND COMPETITIVENESS

Part of staying competitive is staying productive. The United States has traditionally enjoyed the world's most productive economy, but competitors abroad have steadily narrowed this gap by posting faster productivity gains on average over many years. At the same time, the American economy's rate of productivity increase has been slowing for more than a decade. The fact that other major industrial economies have consistently achieved higher investment rates than has the United States, and that the U.S. economy's own investment rate has fallen during the last decade, immediately suggests a key role for capital formation in this process.

Even so, the role of physical capital formation in enhancing business productivity turns out to be an elusive subject. At an intuitive level, the contribution of plant and equipment to business's ability to generate output from labor and material inputs appears obvious enough. Accounting for historical productivity trends in any precise way has always proved problematic, however, and the extra productivity growth likely to result from additional capital formation in the future is correspondingly difficult to quantify.

Table 11-1 summarizes the broad outlines of the historical relationship between productivity growth and business capital formation in the United States by presenting data for several measures of net capital formation, change in capital intensity, growth in productivity, and growth in real wages. In order to capture the two major breaks in the American economy's productivity trend since World War II, the table organizes these data into respective averages for 1948-65, 1966-73, and 1974-80. The table also shows the corresponding data for the recession and recovery years 1981, 1982, and 1983 individually.

The share of the U.S. economy's output devoted to net investment in business plant and equipment, beyond the mere replacement of depreciation and obsolescence, has historically been very low. In response to the overall climate of more rapid economic expansion in the 1960s, as well as to specific favorable tax legislation enacted early in the decade, the net business investment rate rose somewhat during the 1966-73 period. Since then, however, it has fallen back to or below the level prevailing in the 1950s. The 1.4 percent rate recorded during 1983 was the lowest experience in this regard since World War II. The growth rate of the economy's fixed business capital stock has shown a similar pattern, first increasing in the late 1960s but then slowing since the mid-1970s.[1]

Because capital is not the only input to the production process, what matters for productivity is not just the absolute growth of the capital stock but its growth in relation to labor (and, in principle, other noncapital) input. In addition to the decline in capital formation, as measured by either the investment share of total output or the growth rate of the capital stock, in the 1970s the American economy experienced an unusually rapid growth of its labor force. The maturing of the postwar baby boom generation, together with a sharp further increase in women's labor participation, added 24 million workers to the U.S. civilian labor force between 1970 and 1980. From the perspective of employment gains, the creation of 21 million additional jobs during these years surely stands as a remarkable achievement. Nevertheless, the combination of unusually rapid labor force growth and slowing business

Table 11-1

U.S. Capital Formation and Productivity Growth, 1948–83

	Net Investment in Plant and Equipment, as % of GNP	Private Net Fixed Non-residential Capital Stock	Net Capital Stock per Nonfarm Business Sector Worker	Growth Rate Productivity in the Nonfarm Business Sector	Productivity in Manufacturing	Real Wages in the Nonfarm Business Sector
Average, 1948–65	3.0%	4.2%	3.3%	2.7%	3.2%	2.4%
Average, 1966–73	3.5	4.9	2.0	2.1	2.8	1.6
Average, 1974–80	3.0	3.4	0.8	0.5	1.3	-1.1
1981	3.0	3.7	1.5	1.9	3.5	-0.6
1982	1.9	2.4	3.7	-0.1	1.2	1.6
1983	1.4	2.1	1.0	3.1	6.2	2.3

Source: U.S. Department of Commerce; U.S. Department of Labor.
Note: Capital stock data are in constant dollars; growth rates are in percent per annum.

capital formation almost halted the economy's historical trend toward an ever increasing amount of capital for each worker.

Together with this absence of much increase in capital intensity since the early 1970s, the American economy has also not experienced much increase in productivity. By the late 1960s, average labor productivity in the economy's nonfarm business sector had already slowed from the 2½–3 percent per annum trend that had prevailed in the first two postwar decades to about 2 percent per annum. After the early 1970s, however, productivity growth dried up almost entirely. Some of this slowing, like that of a decade earlier, represented the evolution of the economy's output mix away from manufacturing and other areas of traditionally rapid productivity growth into the service sector, for which productivity gains (at least as conventionally measured) are typically slower.[2] Even within the manufacturing sector alone, however—that is, wholly apart from effects due to changing output composition—the sharp slowing of productivity gains during the last decade is readily apparent.

Given these roughly parallel co-movements of capital formation and productivity growth, why is the linkage between the two still a subject of debate? The chief reason is that other explanations are also available. As table 11-1 shows, the more clearly apparent evidence of a relationship between capital formation and productivity growth comes not from the first break in the American economy's postwar productivity trend in the mid-1960s, but from the second one, in the early 1970s. During the most recent decade, however, there have been many developments at least potentially inimical to U.S. productivity growth, including higher energy prices, a less-experienced labor force, lower average utilization levels, reduced research and development spending, and more burdensome government regulation. Attempts to distinguish the respective roles of these different possible explanations of the U.S. productivity experience have, at least to date, proved inconclusive.[3]

Because of the intuitive logic stemming from the use of capital in the production process, however, and because of the potential ability of public policy to affect the nation's capital formation rate, business fixed investment has continued to attract widespread attention in the context of productivity objectives even without agreement on the relevant quantitative magnitudes. More than most of the likely causes of the post-1973 productivity slowdown, basic elements of macroeconomic policy can readily encourage business investment in plant and equipment, while adverse policy choices can just as readily work in the opposite direction. Further, because the American economy's net investment rate is so low—just 3 percent on average during the last thirty-five years—in principle, it is possible for policy actions to increase it by a large proportion without major costs in other areas.

International comparisons, especially relevant to implications for competitiveness, also support the idea of a significant role for capital formation in determining business productivity. The ranking of the major industrialized countries according to their respective net investment rates is essentially identical to the corresponding ranking according to their respective productivity growth rates (see table 11-2).[4] These data also can only be suggestive, but they again imply that maintaining a higher capital formation rate enables an economy to achieve faster productivity growth.[5]

If investment in business capital affects an economy's productivity, it is also likely to affect its international competitiveness. This proposition too may seem obvious enough at first thought, but in reality the connection between productivity and competitiveness is far from straightforward. To begin, there is no one-for-one connection—indeed, no necessary connection at all—between an economy's productivity trend and the associated trend of production costs to business. Wholly apart from the cost of material inputs, productivity gains lower unit labor costs only to the extent that producers do not pay them out in the form of higher real wage gains. Business may treat wages as fixed for a short time, but over longer periods labor is unlikely to go along with devoting all of the proceeds from productivity growth to lowering production costs and none to raising real wages. Indeed, in the

Table 11-2
International Comparisons of Capital Formation and Productivity Growth, 1971–80

	Net Fixed Investment as % of GNP	Growth Rate of Productivity in Manufacturing
Japan	19.5%	7.4%
France	12.2	4.8
Germany	11.8	4.9
Italy	10.7	4.9
United Kingdom	8.1	2.9
United States	6.6	2.5

Source: Organization for Economic Cooperation and Development
Note: Growth rates are in percent per annum.

United States (though apparently not in Japan or Western Europe), the pattern of real wage growth has closely tracked the pattern of productivity growth.[6]

Moreover, even that part of an increase in productivity growth left over to reduce production costs does not necessarily give business any advantage in international competition. What matters there is cost on a foreign exchange value basis, not cost in domestic currency alone. Sustained reduction over time of a country's costs of production, matched by no other changes, would lead its currency to appreciate, and that would partly offset the resulting cost advantage in comparison with foreign producers. Only to the extent that its exchange rate rises less than in proportion to the fall in production costs does any advantage remain.[7] Ignoring the effect of shifting exchange rates would be analogous to ignoring the effect of rising real wages.

If the response of real wages and of currency values is likely to offset much or all of the production cost advantage due to faster productivity growth, then what is the bearing of productivity growth (and hence capital formation) on international competitiveness? The connection is less direct than if real wages and exchange rates were constant, to be sure, but an economy enjoying faster productivity growth due to greater capital formation is likely to be more competitive nonetheless. International economic competition takes place only to a limited extent in markets for standardized products in which price is the only competitive tool. Instead, product mix and product design change rapidly in many markets, and being competitive means being able to produce the right product, with superior design, to capture market demand. Economies that are rapidly increasing production through investment in new plant and equipment are more likely to be able to do all this than economies that must continually retrofit old plant and equipment to function in new ways. In many cases, new products simply require new investment, and without the necessary capital formation business cannot compete at any price.

The linkages among capital formation, productivity growth, and international competitiveness are therefore more subtle than they may at first appear. There is reason to believe that they exist nonetheless, and that they are powerful. Although table 11-2 refers only to capital formation and productivity, and omits any measure of competitiveness, it is immediately apparent that the economies that have maintained the highest capital formation rates, and achieved the fastest productivity growth, have also done the best in international competition.

Increasing the American economy's low capital formation rate—low by the standard of international comparisons, or in comparison to the U.S.

economy's own earlier experience—offers one prospect for improving American competitiveness. The chief question is whether the nation's fiscal policy will encourage, or even permit, such an increase.

IMPACTS OF GOVERNMENT DEFICITS ON SAVING AND INVESTMENT

The most familiar way to address the question of the likely impact of sustained government deficits on an economy's capital formation is to explore the perspective provided by relationships among economic flows.[8] Table 11-3 summarizes the post-World War II balance between saving and investment in the U.S. economy by presenting data showing the economy's respective totals of net saving and net investment, together with the major components of each, expressed as percentages of gross national product. The table also includes, as memorandum items separate from these totals, corresponding data showing the economy's capital consumption and gross private saving (equal to net private saving plus capital consumption).

What stands out immediately in the upper part of table 11-3 is the relative constancy of U.S. net private saving (line two) in relation to gross national product. The economy's net private saving rate, consisting of personal saving plus corporate retained earnings, represents the share of total output that the private sector as a whole makes available to finance new investment beyond what is necessary simply to replace depreciating stocks of business and residential capital.[9] It is the starting point, therefore, in any analysis of prospects for net capital formation.

Despite substantial variation since World War II in such factors as tax rates, price inflation, real rates of return, and income growth trends—all of which could in principle affect saving behavior—the U.S. economy's net private saving rate has hovered near 7 percent throughout this period. (The postwar mean has been 7.2 percent, with a standard deviation around the mean of only 1.0 percent.) After correction for the influence of the business cycle, the net private saving rate has displayed no significant time trend during this period. It has varied in a modestly procyclical pattern, however, which accounts for the slightly higher than average saving rate during the 1960s and (in part) for the distinctly lower than average saving rate thus far during the 1980s.

If government budgets were always balanced (and if the foreign account were balanced too), the share of the economy's output available for net capital formation would simply be the share set aside as net private saving.

Given the experience since World War II, that would mean a relatively steady 7 percent of gross national product on average. In the presence of government surpluses or deficits, however, what is available for net investment is net private saving plus any government surplus, or less any government deficit.

As table 11-3 shows, in recent years public sector saving and dissaving have played an increasingly prominent role in affecting the U.S. economy's overall saving and investment balance. Since the 1970s, state and local governments, in the aggregate, have run ever larger budget surpluses on a consolidated basis, as current pension surpluses have grown faster than operating deficits.[10] By contrast, during this period the budget deficits run by the federal government have grown progressively larger in relation to gross national product.[11] These two trends have been in part offsetting, but increasingly unequal. By the early 1980s, the federal government's deficit had grown far beyond the aggregate surplus of state and local governments. The U.S. economy's *total* net saving, consisting of the relatively steady net private saving plus government saving or dissaving, has therefore declined sharply since the low-deficit days of the 1950s and 1960s.

The economy's total net *investment*, which differs from total net saving only by a fairly small statistical discrepancy, has of course declined in equal measure. Table 11-3 presents data for U.S. net investment, comparable to the data for net saving, and these too indicate a sharp decline in recent years. Because of a change from positive net foreign investment on balance before the mid-1970s to negative net foreign investment on balance thereafter, the deterioration of net *domestic* investment has been less severe than that of total net investment. Even so, net domestic investment has declined from 6.9 percent of gross national product on average during the 1960s to 6.2 percent on average during the 1970s, and only 3.2 percent thus far during the 1980s. All components of net domestic investment—business plant and equipment, residential construction, and business inventory accumulation—have shared in this decline.

In the context of this historical experience of the U.S. economy's balance of saving and investment, the implications of the current prospects for the U.S. government's budget deficit during the balance of the 1980s are clear enough. The Reagan administration has estimated that, under a continuation of current tax and spending policies (including the administration's defense program), the deficit will show little if any improvement during the next half-decade, averaging 5.4 percent to 6.8 percent of gross national product during fiscal years 1984-88.[12] Adoption of *all* of the tax and spending proposals submitted by the administration in its fiscal year 1984 budget would

Table 11-3
U.S. Net Saving and Investment, 1951–83 (% of GNP)

	1951–55	1956–60	1961–65	1966–70	1971–75	1976–80	1981	1982	1983
Total net saving	6.8%	6.9%	7.4%	7.6%	6.4%	5.7%	5.1%	1.9%	1.9%
Net private saving	7.2	7.1	7.8	8.1	7.6	6.5	6.1	5.3	5.8
Personal saving	4.7	4.7	4.3	5.0	5.6	4.2	4.6	4.1	3.5
Corporate saving	2.5	2.4	3.5	3.1	2.0	2.3	1.5	1.2	2.4
State-local govt. surplus	−0.1	−0.2	0.0	0.1	0.6	1.2	1.2	1.0	1.5
Federal govt. surplus	−0.3	0.0	−0.4	−0.6	−1.8	−2.0	−2.2	−4.8	−5.5
Total net investment	7.4	6.6	7.6	7.3	6.7	5.8	5.0	1.5	1.8
Net foreign investment	0.1	0.5	0.8	0.2	0.3	−0.2	0.1	−0.3	−1.0
Private domestic investment	7.3	6.1	6.8	7.1	6.4	6.0	4.9	1.8	2.8
Plant and equipment	2.8	2.6	2.9	4.0	3.1	2.9	3.0	1.9	1.4
Residential construction	3.4	3.0	2.9	2.0	2.6	2.4	1.2	0.7	1.7
Inventory accumulation	1.0	0.6	1.0	1.1	0.7	0.7	0.6	−0.8	−0.3
Memoranda:									
Capital consumption	8.5	9.3	8.5	8.4	9.3	10.5	11.2	11.7	11.4
Gross private saving	15.7	16.4	16.3	16.4	16.9	17.0	17.2	17.0	17.2

Source: U.S. Department of Commerce
Note: Data are averages (except for 1981–83) of annual flows, as percentages of gross national product. Total net saving and total net investment differ by statistical discrepancy. Detail may not add to totals because of rounding.

shrink the deficit sharply by 1988, but the greatest part of that deficit reduction would result from the "contingency tax plan" for which the administration never submitted legislation, and for which even the administration's own support is questionable at best.[13] Adoption of all of the administration's proposals *except* the contingency tax plan would still lead to a deficit averaging 4.3 percent to 4.9 percent during 1984-88. Similarly, adoption of all elements included in the First Congressional Budget Resolution for fiscal year 1984 *except* the unspecified revenue increases would produce an almost identical result.[14]

As table 11-3 shows, sustained government deficits of this magnitude in relation to gross national product will be unprecedented in U.S. peacetime experience. Despite the often expressed claim that the government's budget has always shown a large deficit, in fact persistent deficits larger than one-half percent of gross national product have been a feature of U.S. fiscal policy only since the 1970s. Moreover, until 1982 the deficit had exceeded 3 percent of gross national product only during 1975 and 1976, in the wake of the severe 1973-75 business recession. Analogous effects of the 1981-82 recession have now swollen the deficit to more than 4 percent of gross national product in 1982, and more than 5 percent in 1983.

Further, unlike the relatively isolated episodes of large deficits in the past, which largely reflected the shortfall of tax revenues and increase in transfer payments due to declining employment, incomes and profits in times of recession, the deficits now projected for the balance of the 1980s will increasingly represent a budget that will be unbalanced even if the economy is at full employment. In 1975 and 1976, for example, the actually realized deficits of $53 billion and $73 billion corresponded to high employment deficits of $15 billion and $21 billion, respectively. Similarly, in 1981 the budget would have shown a small *surplus* if the economy had been fully employed, and in 1982 the actually realized deficit of $128 billion would have been only $19 billion at high employment. By contrast, the administration's estimates, assuming no change from current tax and spending policies, show a "structural" component rising from $181 billion out of the total $249 billion deficit projected for fiscal year 1984, to $306 billion out of the $315 billion deficit projected for 1988.[15] In other words, the growing structural deficit will account for *more than all* of the projected growth in the actual deficit, as the economy returns to approximately full employment during this period.

The U.S. government deficits projected for 1984-88, therefore, will not just be large but, more important, they will indicate an extraordinary fundamental imbalance between the government's revenues and its expenditures. It is not possible to dismiss them simply by assuming that rapid growth will quickly restore the economy to full employment. The projected deficits increasingly are deficits at full employment, and in the absence of a return to full employment the deficits that actually emerge will be even larger. The issue now facing U.S. fiscal policy is not the familiar one of the role of automatic stabilizers, or even the desirability (or lack thereof) of temporary active deficits as discretionary stabilizers, but rather the effects of sustained deficits at full employment as a permanent feature of the economy's ongoing development.

Among the most important of those effects is the impediment that such deficits will place in the way of the economy's ability to undertake capital formation. If the deficit remains in range of 4-6 percent of gross national product, as now seems likely under either current policies or the proposed alternatives, it will absorb *more than half* of the private sector's normal net saving. In the absence of a vast expansion in government saving at the state and local level, the federal government's deficit will therefore keep the U.S. net capital formation rate depressed throughout this period.

Once the economy returns to (or nearly to) full utilization of its resources, this problem will bear little resemblance to the capital formation decline observed in the United States during 1981-83. With ample unemployed resources available throughout the economy, and the budget nearly balanced on a full employment basis, it is implausible to suppose that the federal deficit was responsible for the low rate of net capital formation during these years. The opposite is a better description, as weakness in the investment sector both fed upon and added to weakness elsewhere in the economy, and therefore caused tax revenues to fall and transfer payments to rise. An active (but temporary) fiscal response to the 1981-82 recession would have involved even larger deficits during these years, but would probably have led to more capital formation rather than less in the preponderance of industries in which inadequate product demand constituted the real impediment to investment.

As the economy heads toward full employment, however, the situation will change. Fewer unemployed or underemployed resources will be available. Product demand will not be weak. The source of the budget deficit will be not economic slack but a fundamental imbalance between the government's expenditures and its revenues. In the absence of some break from historical experience that is now difficult to foresee, the continuation of large government deficits under these conditions will then constitute a substantial impediment to capital formation.

In the context of the American economy's international competitiveness, it is also significant that the current and projected U.S. government deficits are unusually large not just by the standard of prior U.S. experience but by that of international comparisons as well. The comforting view that American deficits may be large but deficits abroad are larger, often heard during the 1970s, is simply no longer true. As table 11-4 shows, the U.S. government's deficit in relation to U.S. economic activity now exceeds comparable deficit measures for all of the other major industrialized economies except Italy. Especially in light of the international differences among saving rates shown in table 11-2, the U.S. economy can hardly afford the industrialized world's second largest government deficit.

Finally, an alternative form of analysis, based on stocks of debt obligations outstanding, further reinforces the conclusions reached above on the basis of the more familiar analysis of economic flows. One reason for going beyond this more familiar approach is simply to have an alternative analysis either to reinforce or to refute the results of the more conventional one. A perhaps more compelling reason, however, is the fear that well-known measurement problems may distort the meaning of changes over time in some of the flows that are most central to the conventional analysis. For example, public debt interest payments are likely to amount to some 3 percent of gross national product on average during 1984-88, a large amount in comparison to the average projected deficit.[16] Given prior and continuing price inflation, some part of these interest payments actually represents a repayment of debt principal, but how much? The alternative approach based on relationships involving the stock of debt obligations outstanding can avoid some of these problems. To the extent that nominal interest payments include repayment

Table 11-4
Government Deficits as Percentages of Gross Domestic Product

	1982	*1983*	*1984 Official Forecast*
Italy	11.9%	11.9%	12.1%
United States	4.8	5.9	5.1
Japan	4.1	3.4	2.5
Germany	3.5	3.0	1.8
France	2.6	3.4	3.5
United Kingdom	2.0	3.5	2.5

Source: European Economic Community; U.S. Office of Management and Budget.
Note: Estimates for 1984 are for full year.

of debt principal, for example, focusing on movements over time in debt stocks (relative to, say, gross national product), effectively compensates for this effect.

The key to the analysis of the implications of U.S. government deficits from this perspective is the close relationship of the *total* debt outstanding, issued by *all* U.S. borrowers other than financial intermediaries, to U.S. gross national product.[17] The U.S. economy's total debt ratio has displayed essentially no trend, and only a limited amount of cyclical variation, throughout the post-World War II period. More important for the purpose at hand, the stability of this relationship between outstanding debt and nonfinancial economic activity has not merely indicated the stability of a sum of stable parts. Neither private sector debt nor government debt has maintained a stable relationship over time to economic activity, but their total has.

The line at the top of figure 11-1 shows the total credit market indebtedness of all U.S. nonfinancial borrowers as of the end of each year since the Korean War, measured as percentages of fourth-quarter gross national product, as well as the corresponding total indebtedness as of midyear 1983, measured as a percentage of gross national product in the second quarter of the year. The lines below divide this total into the respective indebtedness of each of five specific borrowing sectors: the federal government, state and local governments, nonfinancial business corporations, other nonfinancial businesses, and households.[18]

The strong stability of the *total* nonfinancial debt ratio stands out plainly in contrast to the variation of the individual sector components. Although the total debt ratio rose sharply during the most recent business recession, as gross national product in the denominator weakened while substantial credit expansion continued, data for 1983 show a leveling off and suggest the beginning of a return toward the historical norm of about $1.45 of debt for every $1 of gross national product. The experience of a similar, though less pronounced, cyclicality in prior recessions also suggests that the 1982 bulge will not become a permanent interruption of the basic long-run stability. Moreover, the stability of the U.S. economy's total debt ratio is of longer standing than the three decades plotted in figure 11-1. As figure 11-2 shows, with the exception of a sharp rise and subsequent fall during the Depression (when much of the debt on record had defaulted de facto) and to a lesser extent during World War II, the total debt ratio in the United States has been roughly constant since the early 1920s.

By contrast, the individual components of the total debt ratio have varied in diverging ways both secularly and cyclically. In brief, the post-World War

Figure 11-1

Outstanding Debt of U.S. Nonfinancial Borrowers

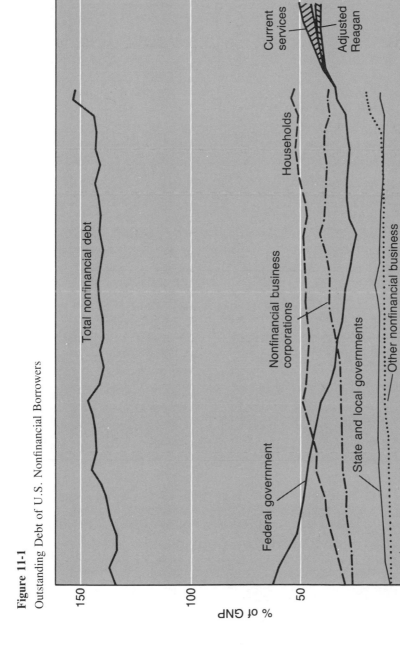

Source: Board of Governors of the Federal Reserve System

Figure 11-2

Outstanding Debt of U.S. Nonfinancial Borrowers

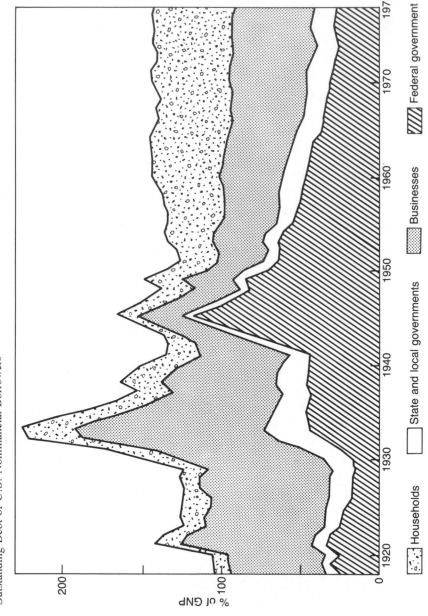

Source: Board of Governors of the Federal Reserve System

II secular rise in private debt has largely mirrored a substantial decline (relative to economic activity) in public debt, while cyclical bulges in public debt issuance have mostly had their counterpart in the abatement of private borrowing. Households have almost continually increased their reliance on debt in relation to their nonfinancial activity throughout this period. Both corporations and unincorporated businesses have also issued steadily more debt, on a relative basis, except for temporary retrenchments during recession years. State and local governments steadily increased their relative debt issuing activity during the 1950s and 1960s, but just as steadily reduced it during the 1970s. Finally, except for 1975-76 and 1980-83, years marked by large deficits due to recession and its aftermath, the federal government to date has reduced its debt ratio in every year since 1953.

Given the long-standing stability of the U.S. economy's *total* debt ratio, the evolution of the *federal government* debt ratio provides a useful perspective on the magnitude and import of the federal budget deficit. As figure 11-2 shows, since World War II the federal debt ratio has declined from a level in excess of 100 percent. Indeed, the 24-29 percent range in which the federal debt ratio fluctuated during the 1970s, and until 1982, corresponded favorably to the 27.4 percent value plotted in figure 11-2 for 1918. The past decade has already marked an important departure from prior experience, however. The years 1975 and 1976 were the first since 1953 in which the government debt ratio rose, and the renewed decline during 1977-79, which was subsequently reversed by the recession years 1980-82, was not sufficient to reduce the ratio to its 1974 low. The government debt ratio rose still further during 1983. Under any of the deficit projections just described, it will continue to do so for the foreseeable future.

This increase in the federal government's debt ratio is relevant to the implications of fiscal policy for private capital formation because, in the context of a stable economywide total debt ratio, it represents a useful summary measure of the net impact of federal deficits on the environment for private financing. If the government deficit were sufficiently small, or if either real economic growth or price inflation were increasing the gross national product sufficiently rapidly, then the government debt ratio would be falling—as it was, almost continuously, throughout the first three decades following World War II. Conversely, when the deficit is sufficiently large in relation to the economy's size and growth, then the government debt ratio will be rising—as it did during 1975-76, and has during 1980-83.

If the economy's total outstanding debt remains approximately stable in relation to gross national product over time, then a sustained movement in the *government* debt ratio implies an offsetting movement in the aggregate debt ratio of the *private* sector. A falling government debt ratio like that during 1946-74 implies a rising private debt ratio, while a rising government debt ratio like that during 1975-76 and 1980-83 implies a falling private debt ratio. The relevance, in turn, of a rising or falling private debt ratio for the economy's ability to undertake capital formation stems from the traditionally close connection in the United States between debt financing and net private investment, including both homebuilding and investment in new plant and equipment.[19]

In the absence of a major change in financing patterns, therefore, the economy's ability to achieve a greater capital intensity—that is, to increase its capital stock in relation to total output—depends at least in part on the private sector's ability to increase its debt in relation to gross national product. Over time, however, the private sector's debt ratio moves inversely with the government debt ratio. In the end, the rise or fall of the government debt ratio is therefore likely to be an important factor shaping the relationship between growth of the capital stock and growth of the economy's real output. As previously emphasized, changes in capital intensity in turn are likely to have an important bearing on productivity growth and international competitiveness.

As table 11-5 shows, not all industrialized economies share in equal degree the debt relationships documented here for the United States. In neither Japan nor Germany has total debt relative to economic activity remained flat as in the American economy. In Japan the trend increase was just over 1 percent per annum, despite occasional sharp bursts of growth as in the early 1980s. In Germany the trend increase has been more nearly 2 percent per annum, and almost 2½ percent per annum during the past two decades. More sophisticated statistical analyses that remove any time trends show strong evidence of systematically offsetting movements of public and private debt ratios in Japan, as in the United States, but to a much smaller extent in Germany.[20]

The shaded extensions to the "federal government" line plotted in figure 11-1 indicate the respective implications for the U.S. government debt ratio associated with the projected 1984-88 deficit paths described above. Under a continuation of current tax and spending policies, the government's outstanding debt will rise from 34.3 percent of gross national product as of yearend 1983 to 44.5-51.0 percent at the end of fiscal year 1988.[21] The upper shaded extension in the figure plots the government debt ratio range implied by this projection for 1984-88. The lower shaded extension plots the analogous range implied by projections corresponding to the adoption of all of the Reagan administration's budget proposals except the contingency tax plan. The resulting projected deficits imply increases in the government debt ratio to 39.5-42.4 percent at the end of fiscal year 1988.

The main point of the set of computations illustrated in figure 11-1 is that the ranges for both the "current services" and the "adjusted Reagan" deficit projections will continue to carry the government debt ratio further upward, instead of returning it toward the 24.8 percent postwar low reached in 1974, or stabilizing it at the 1982 level of 30.1 percent or even the yearend 1983 level of 34.3 percent. These projected further increases will raise the government debt ratio to levels last experienced two decades or more ago—the early 1960s under the adjusted Reagan projection, or the 1950s under the current services projection.

A sustained increase in the government debt ratio of anything like these magnitudes will be unprecedented in the U.S. economy's peacetime experience. If the economy's total debt ratio continues to remain near its historical norm, this increase in the government debt ratio therefore implies a comparably unprecedented decline in the private sector's debt ratio. As of yearend 1983, the debt ratios of the household and combined (corporate and unincorporated) nonfinancial business sectors were 52.6 percent and 53.5 percent, respectively—already down from 53.9 percent and 54.5 percent, respectively, at year-end 1982.[22] A decline of 15-25 percent, applied either to households or businesses alone or to both together, will represent a substantial readjustment. The market forces (chiefly high real interest rates) that constrain the private sector to limit its debt expansion to a slower pace than that of nonfinancial economic activity—and not as a temporary retrenchment in recession, but on a sustained basis at full employment—will probably also affect private sector capital formation.

Although a renewed depression of residential construction could perhaps be sufficient to reduce household mortgage borrowing by enough to absorb the entire required decline in the private sector's debt ratio, especially under the smaller "adjusted Reagan" deficits, even that extreme outcome would probably not permit any growth at all in the business sector's debt ratio—nor would sacrificing homebuilding to such an extent necessarily be desirable anyway.[23] More probably, business debt relative to income will also have to decline to make room for the ballooning federal government debt.

Without the ability to raise external funds in the credit market, the business sector will largely have to forego taking advantage of the recently legislated investment incentives unless it turns massively to equity financing—an un-

Table 11-5
Total Debt Ratios and Components, 1951–83

	United States			Japan			Germany		
	Total	*Govt.*	*Private*	*Total*	*Govt.*	*Private*	*Total*	*Govt.*	*Private*
1951	126.6%	63.7%	62.9%	na	na	na	82.7%	35.6%	47.1%
1952	127.8	61.5	66.3	na	na	na	81.8	32.2	49.6
1953	134.5	62.9	71.6	na	na	na	86.5	31.7	54.8
1954	136.8	61.5	75.3	na	na	na	91.7	31.6	60.1
1955	133.8	56.0	77.8	na	na	na	90.5	28.7	61.8
1956	133.4	51.9	81.5	na	na	na	90.5	26.7	63.8
1957	135.9	50.0	85.9	na	na	na	92.1	25.2	66.9
1958	137.3	49.5	87.8	na	na	na	94.1	24.6	69.5
1959	139.9	48.2	91.7	na	na	na	96.9	24.0	72.9
1960	144.0	46.8	97.2	209.6%	38.9%	170.7%	84.8	19.7	65.1
1961	142.0	44.9	97.1	202.1	32.5	169.5	89.7	19.8	69.9
1962	143.4	43.6	99.8	225.2	31.5	193.7	91.5	19.3	72.2
1963	143.7	41.5	102.2	225.8	26.3	199.5	94.9	19.5	75.4
1964	145.5	40.2	105.3	230.1	23.7	206.4	97.4	19.3	78.1
1965	141.2	36.6	104.6	236.1	22.7	213.4	100.9	19.8	81.1

(continued)

Table 11-5 (continued)

	United States			Japan			Germany		
	Total	*Govt.*	*Private*	*Total*	*Govt.*	*Private*	*Total*	*Govt.*	*Private*
1966	138.3%	34.4%	104.9%	223.5%	21.0%	202.5%	107.3%	21.0%	86.3%
1967	140.6	33.9	106.7	218.8	19.5	199.3	112.2	23.5	88.7
1968	139.1	32.5	106.6	204.3	17.7	186.6	105.9	22.2	83.9
1969	139.2	30.0	109.2	207.9	16.9	191.4	106.2	20.2	86.0
1970	141.9	29.8	112.1	210.4	15.0	195.4	106.4	19.1	87.4
1971	142.0	29.5	112.5	224.5	14.9	209.6	110.4	19.3	91.1
1972	140.3	27.6	112.7	228.6	15.9	212.7	114.6	19.6	95.0
1973	139.5	25.4	114.1	229.2	13.7	215.5	114.8	20.2	94.6
1974	142.0	24.5	117.5	221.9	15.5	206.4	116.8	21.4	95.4
1975	140.8	27.5	113.3	230.8	17.8	213.0	124.5	26.8	97.7
1976	142.6	29.1	113.5	239.7	20.7	219.0	127.1	28.4	98.7
1977	143.2	28.8	114.4	236.3	24.2	212.1	128.0	29.3	101.2
1978	141.1	27.6	113.5	242.2	30.4	211.8	132.2	30.4	101.8
1979	143.3	26.6	116.7	255.6	33.6	221.0	133.2	30.9	102.3
1980	143.9	27.1	116.8	261.6	37.0	224.6	134.3	29.9	104.4
1981	142.3	27.4	114.9	274.8	42.5	232.3	141.2	32.2	109.1
1982	151.5	31.9	119.6	282.7	45.6	237.1	147.4	35.5	111.9
1983	151.9	34.3	117.6	na	na	na	na	na	na

Source: Board of Governors of the Federal Reserve System; Bank of Japan; Deutsche Bundesbank.
Note: Data are year-end outstanding debt stocks, as percentages of fourth-quarter gross national product (seasonally adjusted at annual rate) for the United States and Japan, and as percentages of annual gross national product for Germany. Government category includes central government only.

likely prospect in light of long-standing U.S. business financing patterns. In terms of the factors directly confronting business investment decisions, the problem will be that the increased real cost of financing (and, for some companies, reduced availability) will outweigh the added attractiveness of new investment due to the large favorable tax changes. Under these conditions, business net capital formation will probably decline still further from the recent low level, once the surge associated with the rapid economic recovery toward full employment is over.

The conclusion of this analysis from the perspective of outstanding debt stocks, therefore, reinforces the conclusion reached above on the basis of relationships among economic flows. Unless an unforeseen change in traditional economic patterns occurs, the continuation of the large government deficits currently projected—even for after the economy's return to full employment—will substantially impede American economy's net capital formation.

SOME EASY BUT WRONG ANSWERS

When problems are as serious as the foregoing analysis indicates, there are rarely any easy answers. If there were, they would already have been adopted and the problem would not be so serious after all. Nevertheless, hard problems that are resolvable only by hard policy choices almost inevitably elicit suggestions that no such tough choices are necessary, either because some easy solution is readily available or because the ordinary course of events will provide one on its own.

The threat to American business capital formation posed by the U.S. government deficit in the 1980s is no exception. Three supposedly easy answers have dominated much of the public policy discussion of this issue to date.

Easy Answer #1 is that the lower tax rates legislated in the Economic Recovery Tax Act of 1981 will sufficiently stimulate personal saving to enable the economy to finance both enlarged government deficits and an increase in net capital formation.

Such an outcome is conceivable, of course, but it is unlikely for several reasons. To begin, theory alone cannot even indicate the *direction* of the effect of higher after-tax returns on personal saving.[24] The reason for this seemingly startling result is that higher after-tax yields affect the incentive to save in two potentially offsetting ways. Higher yields increase the reward, in terms of spending made possible later, for not spending today. This change in the terms on which consumers may substitute future for current spending increases the relative attraction of future spending, and hence unambiguously *encourages* saving out of current income. Higher yields also increase the rate at which savings grow, however, thereby making it possible to maintain desired spending levels in the future on the basis of less put aside today. This increase in lifetime total spending possibilities enables consumers to spend more both currently and in the future, and hence unambiguously *discourages* saving out of current income. Which of these two opposing effects is predominant can be determined only by resort to empirical evidence.

The problem here, however, is that the evidence on this question is ambiguous, to say the least. Many important economic relationships have theoretically undetermined directions as well as magnitudes, but in the case of the effect of after-tax yields on saving, the available evidence still provides essentially no ground for confidence about even the sign, much less the magnitude, of the net effect. Some studies have shown positive effects of a magnitude that would be meaningful in the context of the prospective deficit problem, while many others have shown no noticeable effect at all.[25] At best, relying on a large saving response to the 1981 tax changes is hardly a prudent basis for sound public policy.

Further, despite the rhetoric that accompanied it, the 1981 tax bill contained few specifically targeted saving incentives. The reduction from 70 percent to 50 percent in the maximum marginal rate applicable to "unearned" income was one such incentive; but it applies to relatively few taxpayers, and correspondingly accounts for only a small part of the revenue given up under the 1981 legislation. The new IRA and expanded Keogh account provisions are potentially even more important, but for many individuals they will only affect inframarginal rather than marginal saving flows (and hence, by the reasoning outlined above, will unambiguously *reduce* those individuals' total saving). By far the greatest part of the personal tax reduction enacted in 1981 and implemented during 1981-83 consisted of general across-the-board rate cuts, which are unlikely to have much impact on saving behavior even on the most optimistic rendering of the available evidence.

Finally, because the projected government deficits for the balance of the 1980s are so large, even a *doubling* of the personal saving rate—from the 1951-80 average of 4.8 percent to 9.6 percent—would merely finance the likely deficit, without leaving anything in addition to increase the economy's net capital formation. Only an increase in personal saving to magnitudes approximating the more outstanding countries abroad would meet both needs. Although the reasons why the U.S. personal saving rate is so low in comparison with the saving rates of some other countries remain imperfectly understood, they almost certainly involve some fairly fundamental aspects of societal arrangements rather than just marginal tax rates. Indeed, as comparisons like that in table 11-6 for overall marginal tax rates on corporate sector income indicate, the simple cross-country correlation of growth rates and marginal tax rates is more often positive than negative.

Easy Answer #2 is that a combination of large profits generated by the economic expansion and the liberalized depreciation allowances legislated in 1981 (though reduced somewhat under the Tax Equity and Fiscal Responsibility Act of 1982) will still provide American business with a sufficient internal cash flow both to boost the historically small corporate saving rate shown in table 11-3 and to enable business to undertake increased net capital formation, despite the likely reduction in its relative indebtedness as suggested in figure 11-1.

The problem here is that there is no one-for-one correspondence between increased business cash flow and increased net investment. At the most immediate level, the typical corporation is likely to pay out some fraction of the increased after-tax cash flow, either by raising dividends or by buying shares in other corporations in the course of mergers and acquisitions.[26] There has already been a substantial increase in merger and acquisition volume, although corporate dividend payouts usually respond to changes in cash flows only with a lag.

Further, even that part of the increased cash flow that corporations retain still does not bear any direct correspondence to overall business investment.

Table 11-6
Tax Rates, Economic Growth, and Capital Formation

	Overall Effective Marginal Tax Rate on Corporate Sector Income	Avg. Growth of Real Capital Stock in the Corporate Sector	Avg. Growth of Real Gross Domestic Product
Germany	48.1%	5.1%	3.7%
United States	37.2	3.7	3.5
Sweden	35.6	4.7	3.2
United Kingdom	3.7	2.6	2.3

Source: Mervyn A. King and Don Fullerton, *The Taxation of Income from Capital: A Comparative Study of the U.S., U.K., Sweden and West Germany* (Chicago: University of Chicago Press, 1983).
Note: Growth rates are averages, per annum, for 1960–80. Effective tax rates are based on average 1970–79 inflation rates.

As table 11-3 shows, net private saving in the United States is quite stable as a share of gross national product. This relative constancy suggests that, on balance, respective fluctuations in corporate saving and in personal saving about offset one another, as shareholders adjust their own direct saving to allow for the saving that corporations do in their behalf. More sophisticated econometric analysis confirms this result, typically indicating a personal saving response great enough to offset more than half of whatever variations occur in corporate saving.[27] The basic point is that what constrains net private investment (apart from government and foreign deficits) is net private saving, and rearranging the composition of net private saving is not the same as raising its total.

A closely related line of reasoning is that, because price inflation raises the effective tax rate on business investment, the recent slowing of U.S. inflation will reinforce the effect of liberalized depreciation allowances and hence boost business cash flows (and after-tax rates of return) still further.[28] In fact, however, the overall effective marginal tax rate on income generated in the U.S. corporate sector is relatively insensitive to inflation (see figure 11-3).[29] Inflation clearly distorts the *allocation* of capital by widening the dispersion among the different marginal tax rates applicable to different forms of corporate sector investment. At the average inflation rate prevailing in the United States during 1970-79, for example, the range of marginal tax rates on income generated in the U.S. corporate sector extends from −105 percent (that is, a 105 percent subsidy) on machinery financed by sale of debt to pension funds and used in the commercial sector, to +111 percent (that is, more than full confiscation of proceeds) on buildings financed by sale of equity to households and used in commerce or industry.[30] Nevertheless, inflation does not much affect the overall tax rate in a way that would plausibly reduce the *total amount* of capital formation.

Easy Answer #3 is that the United States can finance both its government deficit and its net capital formation with foreign capital inflows, as investors abroad increasingly see both high American interest rates and the stable American political and economic environment as strong attractions for their saving.

Further increases in foreign capital inflows, corresponding to a negative net foreign investment position in table 11-3, will no doubt occur. Indeed, for 1984 it is likely that such inflows will increase to 2 percent or more of U.S. gross national product, enough to finance one-half to one-third of the government deficit. Moreover, as the logic of the saving and investment balance summarized in table 11-3 suggests, such inflows constitute a direct

Figure 11-3

Overall Effective Tax Rate as Inflation Varies in Each Country

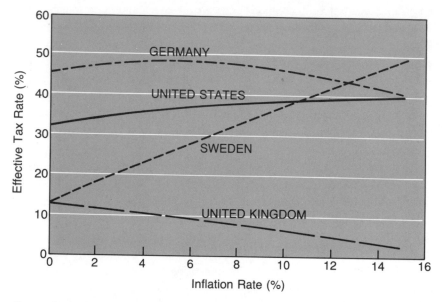

Source: From Mervyn A. King and Don Fullerton, *The Taxation of Income from Capital: A Comparative Study of the U.S., U.K., Sweden and West Germany* (Chicago: University of Chicago Press, 1983).

addition to the internally generated net saving available to finance both government deficits and private domestic investment. Why, then, are still further increases in foreign capital inflows not the most straightforward way to deal with the problem?

In the context of concerns about international competitiveness, foreign capital inflows score points only by giving away the game. An inflow of capital from abroad is simply the mirror image of a balance of payments deficit on current account. Foreigners hold an increasing amount of dollar assets (net of U.S. holdings of foreign currency assets) because Americans are buying more from abroad than foreigners are buying from the United States. The resulting imbalance of payments on current account inevitably makes foreigners net investors in dollar assets, and correspondingly, inevitably produces a negative U.S. net investment flow.

The direct counterpart to these capital inflows, therefore, is exactly the deterioration in U.S. net exports that has produced such widespread concern about American business competitiveness in the first place. The U.S. balance of merchandise trade has deteriorated from a seemingly invincible surplus before 1971, to a mixed pattern of relatively small surpluses and deficits during 1971-76, to continual deficits of $25-35 billion per year during 1977-82, to a record $61 billion in 1983.[31] Because of a positive balance in services, together with substantial net investment income, the U.S. current account balance is typically more positive than the merchandise trade balance by $30-40 billion per year. A current account deficit equal to 2 percent of gross national product, or more than $70 billion, as is likely for 1984, therefore means merchandise imports in excess of exports by over $100 billion. Hence, the U.S. merchandise trade deficit will almost certainly set a new record again in 1984. Capital inflows and current account deficits in the range of 5 percent of gross national product, as would be necessary to finance the entire U.S. government deficit during the remainder of the 1980s, would imply merchandise trade deficits of $250-300 billion per annum throughout this period—an enormous sum in comparison with the $261 billion of imports and only $200 billion of exports traded in 1983.

The chief market mechanism by which these large capital flows would have such devastating effects on U.S. net exports is the effect of real exchange rates on product demand and market share. If foreigners were willing to invest in the United States in such volume—and, just as improbably, if their governments were willing to permit it—their actions would further raise the international exchange value of the dollar after allowance for cross-country inflation differentials. The resulting higher real dollar exchange rate would in turn further erode the ability of American exporters to compete in world markets, and of a wide variety of other American businesses to compete against foreign producers for domestic sales. In large part, this process has already accounted for much of the accelerated decline of American competitiveness since 1980.[32]

In addition, if a policy of large foreign capital inflows was maintained for very long, it would sharply change still further aspects of the American economy's international economic balance, like the positive net flow of investment income. After all, borrowing from foreigners is fundamentally different from borrowing from ourselves. The total U.S. net international investment position—that is, U.S. holdings abroad less foreign holdings here—officially stood at $106 billion as of year-end 1983.[33] (After allowance for relevant "errors and omissions," the actual total was probably more like $100 billion.) Only a year or so of net capital inflow equal to the government deficit would entirely wipe out this net position, and subsequent inflows would increasingly make the United States a net debtor nation.

Solving the government deficit problem with foreign capital inflows would merely substitute a crowding out of the economy's foreign sector, via high real exchange rates, for the crowding out of the investment sector that would otherwise occur via high real interest rates. From the perspective of international competitiveness, that would be no solution at all.

In sum, none of these three "easy answers" represents an adequate response to the threat to American business capital formation posed by the U.S. government deficit in the 1980s. A hard problem requires harder choices.

CHOICES FOR PUBLIC POLICY

What options are available, then, for preventing the U.S. government deficit in the 1980s from having the adverse effect on American business capital formation, productivity, and competitiveness indicated by the foregoing analysis? One approach to the problem is to accept the deficit's inevitability and search for policy actions that will minimize its impact on net business capital formation. The other is to search instead for ways to reduce the deficit.

Apart from implications for the economy's foreign sector, discussed above, the main effect of sustained large government deficits at full employment will be to crowd out some combination of net residential and business investment. Because inventory accumulation is difficult to shrink below ½-1 percent of gross national product on an ongoing basis, the actual choice in this regard is between residential investment and business investment in plant and equipment. Homebuilding and business fixed investment have together accounted for some five-sixths of U.S. net capital formation on average over the last three decades (see table 11-3). Net investment in homes exceeded that in plant and equipment during the 1950s, but the reverse has been true since the late 1960s.

A policy of eliminating all or nearly all of the 2½ percent of total output that the United States devotes to net residential capital formation—a difficult and unattractive policy at best—would therefore shield business capital formation from much of the effect of the federal government deficits now in prospect for the remainder of the decade. In conjunction with a new inflow of foreign capital equal to 2-2½ percent of gross national product, for example, the complete elimination of net investment in homebuilding would suffice to absorb approximately all of the burden of financing the combined federal and state-local government sector during these years, thereby making it possible for business net investment to continue to claim the 3 percent share of total output that was typical during the 1970s. Such a result would not eliminate new residential construction altogether, of course. On average during the 1970s, net residential investment accounted for just over one-half of the total *gross* residential investment, with replacement of depreciating units accounting for the remainder.[34] Zero *net* investment would therefore imply slightly more than one-half as much residential construction activity as the United States has undertaken on average in recent years.

The analysis of the government deficit problem from the perspective of stocks of debt outstanding again reinforces the analysis of the economy's balance of saving and investment. As is clear in figure 11-1, the American household sector's outstanding debt bulks large in comparison to that of American business. Despite the common impression that a great deal of individual borrowing merely finances consumer spending, in fact, mortgage borrowing accounted for nearly two-thirds of all household sector liabilities outstanding as of year-end 1983.[35] Given the traditional importance of mortgage financing for new homebuilding, it is likely that a sharp reduction in residential construction activity would correspondingly reduce the household sector's relative debt position over time. A large enough reduction in the household debt ratio would in turn enable the government debt ratio to continue to rise without requiring any further reduction in the business sector's debt ratio.

At least three different sets of public policies, none mutually exclusive, could enforce this solution of shielding business capital formation from the domestic burden of government debt financing by placing that burden largely on the residential sector. First, to the extent that the large deficits now in prospect result from tax reductions for business, the current combination of tight monetary policy and loose fiscal policy works in just this direction.[36] The basic idea is that, while the resulting high real interest rates will discourage all interest-sensitive spending, specific business tax breaks can more than offset the negative effect on investment in plant and equipment. Overall, the net effect is to depress residential investment but not business investment.

A second route to the same result would be to rely on the tax system alone, coupling tax incentives that encourage business investment with tax changes that discourage residential investment. In light of the well-known nonneutralities in the U.S. income tax code that currently favor homebuilding and home ownership, such changes need not involve actual penalties. Instead, the mere elimination of some of the larger subsidies—for example, the exclusion from taxable income of imputed rent on owner-occupied housing, and the favored treatment of capital gains on home sales—would probably have a major effect on this direction.[37]

A third route for shielding business capital formation from the effects of government deficits, increasingly advocated in popular discussions, is to use direct government intervention in the credit markets to channel funds to business. Although advocates rarely describe the intent of such interventions in terms of shifting financial resources away from homebuilding, in the absence of an associated reduction of the government deficit that would inevitably be the end result. Here too, because of the proliferation in recent years of government mechanisms favoring housing, a milder form of the same policy action would be merely the elimination or reduction of some of the more important devices that now explicitly direct funds in the American credit markets toward the financing of residential investment. Federally sponsored credit agencies and mortgage "pools" now hold more than one-fourth of all home mortgages outstanding in the United States, and this share has been continually rising.[38] Moreover, their role in this market is especially important at times of high interest rates. Federally sponsored intermediaries accounted for 48 percent, 52 percent, and 100 percent of the total net extensions of single-family home mortgage credit during the "credit crunch" years of 1970, 1974, and 1982, respectively.[39]

In sum, ample policy actions are available in the United States that could diminish net residential capital formation, presumably even to the point of eliminating it altogether. The heart of this issue is not what is possible, but what is desirable. Recently legislated tax changes have sharply increased the attractiveness of corporate relative to residential fixed investment, but no U.S. Congress or administration has ever "declared war on housing"—not because that war is unwinnable, but because neither the majority of individual Americans nor many businesses have wanted to do so. A growing population has required a growing housing stock, and better housing for each family has always been central to American conceptions of a rising standard of living. Preserving productivity gains by a deliberate policy of failing to expand or improve the nation's housing stock would probably work, but it would constitute a sharp departure from past attitudes and actions.

The only other apparent course of action is to rethink once more whether the large U.S. government deficits now projected for the remainder of the 1980s are unavoidable after all. In terms of the balance of saving and investment, what is required is, at the minimum, to reduce the deficit to 2 percent of gross national product—in other words, about $84 billion on average during fiscal years 1984-88.[40] Deficit reduction of that magnitude would at least restore the availability of net private saving as it stood in the 1970s. Alternatively, in terms of the outstanding stock of U.S. government debt, returning the government debt ratio to its midyear 1983 level of 33.4 percent by the end of fiscal year 1988 would require shrinking the deficit to $118 billion on average during 1984-88, while returning the government debt ratio to an even 30.0 percent (the upper limit of its range during the 1970s) would require shrinking the deficit to $83 billion on average during this period.

Either cutting the absorption of net private saving to its 1970s level or stabilizing the government debt ratio at the upper end of its 1970s range would therefore require very major changes even in comparison with the Reagan administration's budget proposals, not to mention currently existing tax and spending legislation. The question that immediately arises is *what* changes. This crucial issue, however, is largely a matter of value judgments, not economic analysis.

The standard trio of suggested ways to reduce the federal deficit in the medium-run future includes cutting entitlement program benefits, slowing the scheduled acceleration in defense spending, and eliminating either the reduction in individual income tax rates that took effect in 1983 or the indexation of the tax code scheduled to take effect in 1985. The magnitude of the change involved in reducing the average 1984-88 deficit to the $84 billion level (or even $118 billion) is such, however, that no one among these three steps would by itself be sufficient. Table 11-7 shows a decomposition of the U.S. government budget position (including off-budget outlays) into components roughly corresponding to these three policy options, plus an additional expenditure category for net interest payments, measured throughout as percentages of gross national product. The table applies this decomposition to the actual outcomes for fiscal year 1970 (arbitrarily selected as a convenient benchmark), 1979 (the last in which the federal deficit did not exceed 2 percent of gross national product), and 1983, as well as to the projected average annual outcomes for 1984-88 on both the current services and the adjusted Reagan budget bases.

This decomposition shows that the substantial swelling of the U.S. government deficit as a percentage of gross national product during the 1984-88 period reflects a combination of (1) a reduction in revenues of about 1 percent in comparison with either 1970 or 1979; (2) an increase in defense spending of about 2½ percent in comparison with 1979, but not 1970; (3) an increase in net interest payments of about 1½ percent in comparison with either 1970

Table 11-7

Composition of U.S. Government Budget and Budget Deficit, 1970–88 (%)

	1970	1979	1983	Projected 1984–88
Revenues				
Historical/current services	19.9%	19.7%	18.6%	18.6–18.8%
Adjusted Reagan budget	—	—	—	19.2–19.4
Defense Expenditures				
Historical/current services	8.1	5.0	6.5	7.5–7.7
Adjusted Reagan budget	—	—	—	7.5
Net Interest				
Historical/current services	1.5	1.8	2.7	3.0–3.3
Adjusted Reagan budget	—	—	—	2.9
Other Expenditures				
Historical/current services	10.6	14.5	15.4	14.2–14.6
Adjusted Reagan budget	—	—	—	13.4–13.6
Deficit				
Historical/current services	0.3	1.7	6.1	5.5–6.8
Adjusted Reagan budget	—	—	—	4.4–4.8

Source: Office of Management and Budget
Note: Data are annual flows (for 1984–88 averages of annual flows), as percentages of annual gross national product. Military retired pay is included in "other expenditures," not in defense expenditures. Other expenditures include off-budget outlays.

or 1979; and (4) an increase in all other spending of about 4 percent in comparison with 1970, but not 1979. Such comparisons can never serve to resolve issues that depend so heavily on value judgments, of course, but they can at least place in perspective the nature of the policy choices to be made.

Finally, difficult as it would be to reduce the federal deficit to $83-84 billion on average during 1984-88, even this magnitude of budgetary change would still provide not *zero* absorption of private saving and a *falling* government debt ratio as in the early postwar decades, but merely a *2 percent* absorption of saving and a *stable* government debt ratio as in the 1970s— hardly an enviable era for federal budgets, corporate finance, net capital formation, productivity growth, and the American economy's international competitiveness. Setting the stage for a restoration of the more favorable pre-1970 environment appears to be beyond reach in the foreseeable future.

SUMMARY

The U.S. government budget posture now constitutes a major threat to the American economy's ability to gain in productivity and to regain its international competitiveness. Under either current tax and spending legislation or any set of alternatives now commanding serious support, the government deficit will remain unprecedentedly large during the balance of the 1980s. The unusual feature of this deficit is not just its size, even in relation to a growing economy, but the fact that it will persist even after the economy returns to full employment of its resources. In the past, large federal government deficits have mostly been a passive response to economic weakness. The deficits now projected for the remainder of the 1980s will, instead, increasingly represent a fundamental imbalance between the government's expenditures and its revenues.

Analysis of the U.S. economy's balance of saving and investment since World War II suggests that the continuation of large, sustained government deficits at full employment will stand in the way of an increase in the economy's already low rate of net capital formation. Without increased capital formation, gains in productivity and competitiveness will be difficult, if not doubtful. Deficits of the size now projected will absorb more than half of the economy's net private saving. Such a drain is warranted during times of business recession, when the private economy generates an excess of saving over investment anyway, but not on a continuing basis at full employment. In the absence of a break with prior experience that is difficult to foresee or consider likely, these deficits will constitute a major impediment to a continuing revival of U.S. net capital formation in the 1980s.

Analysis of the U.S. economy's stocks of assets and liabilities outstanding further supports this conclusion. Continuation of government deficits of the size now projected will lead to a rise in the government's outstanding debt, relative to nonfinancial economic activity, that will be unprecedented in U.S. peacetime experience. If the economy's total debt ratio remains approximately stable, as it has over many years, this rise in the government debt ratio means that the economy's private sector will not be able to increase its outstanding debt in pace with the economy's growth. Given the importance of debt in financing capital assets in the United States, this squeeze on the economy's private debt ratio also implies an inability to achieve any major increase in U.S. net capital formation during the remainder of the 1980s.

Several of the most familiar "easy answers" to this problem turn out, on reflection, not to be answers at all. Lower marginal tax rates at the personal level are unlikely to increase saving sufficiently even to finance the government's deficit, not to speak of an increase in net private investment. Business tax reductions, including especially the newly accelerated depreciation allowances, will probably not lead to very much increased business capital formation on a net basis. Larger foreign capital inflows are simply the mirror image of enlarged balance of payments deficits on current account—in other words, a worsening of the associated competitive situation rather than an improvement.

Only two solutions appear workable. One, highly unappealing, is to enact readily available measures that would sharply depress the homebuilding industry. Doing so would shield business capital formation, though hardly without both real and perceived ill effects. The other is to take the hard actions necessary to raise government revenues and reduce government spending sufficiently to shrink the deficit by about one-half in comparison to currently plausible projections.

12
Competitiveness: The Labor Dimension

D. Quinn Mills
Malcolm R. Lovell, Jr.

Successful enterprises require attention to both equipment and people, but in recent decades many American companies have invested too little in the former and have been inadequately sensitive to the latter. The result of this, combined with the increasing capabilities of our major trading partners and especially Third World countries, is that today our ability to compete in many international markets has greatly decreased. Physical investment by U.S. companies has not been low by U.S. historic standards, but it has been low by international comparison. Companies ordinarily do not measure investment in the human side of enterprises, but this investment has probably lagged behind some of our competitors as well. Measurement criteria for human resources are not clear.

The lack of capital facilities modernization—a managerial factor sometimes considered by economists to affect our competitiveness—has resulted in less effective manufacturing, and in lower-quality products, because new capital equipment is not neutral: it gives finer tolerances, better shaping, more certain molds and settings. It provides less range for error. Those companies that have not invested have fallen to the back of the competitiveness line.

The way we manage our human resources function and its impact on our competitiveness is less routinely considered. At the same time that investment in capital equipment lagged, many companies failed to maximize their investment in people, so that workers too have lost some of their competitive edge. Although wages in the manufacturing sector continued to rise during

D. Quinn Mills is Albert J. Weatherhead professor of Business Administration at Harvard Business School. Malcolm Lovell, Jr., is a visiting scholar at the Brookings Institution. The authors gratefully acknowledge the contributions of Rae Ann O'Brien, research associate, Harvard Business School.

recent years, this came in spite of poor productivity performance. That, in turn, gave a greater meaning to the already large wage gap between the United States and foreign competitors. Our system of collective bargaining, for both historical and institutional reasons, has contributed to increased labor costs and to inefficient work practices, which has led to a decline in the competitive capacity of the manufacturing sector. Partly as a result of this long-term decline, the United States is recovering from a period of high levels of unemployment, associated private and public costs, and a less certain future for a once rapidly expanding manufacturing labor force.

To a large degree American manufacturing is a victim of the success of various American foreign and domestic economic policies. Our foreign policy has encouraged the industrial development of the free world, and many nations we have assisted are now our competitors in manufacturing. With U.S. support, international lending has mushroomed, providing capital for industrial development abroad. These loans are best repaid in dollars earned in international trade, yet the strong dollar makes it more difficult for Third World countries to do so. Earnings from traditional exports on sale of natural resources or agricultural products must therefore be supplemented by those from manufacturers. American banks recognize that foreign nations need to earn dollars by shipping products to the United States to repay principal and interest in U.S. loans. Therefore, the money center banking community favors a strong dollar and accepts the consequence of declining U.S. manufacturing employment.

Our success in attaining socially desired goals has also contributed to current problems in the manufacturing sector. Rising living conditions in the United States have pushed our labor costs up, creating opportunities for foreign manufacturers. Quality of life concerns have lessened the commitment to unceasing labor. Attention to the environment has raised manufacturing costs, and some companies have abandoned plans for large, new, heavy industrial facilities. America has a higher quality of life than it did twenty years ago in terms of earnings, leisure, and the environment; as a partial consequence, it also has a restricted and more costly manufacturing sector. Short of abandoning these long-term social goals and policies, our society must consider other responses to meet the challenge of foreign manufacturers.

Although America does not have an explicit industrial policy, the majority of U.S. companies have pursued policies that have contributed directly to our long-term declining competitiveness. During the 1970s, companies minimized investment in their human and capital resources by maintaining a high employment, low productivity strategy regarding the labor force. In the short term, this minimized costs by avoiding large investments. An ample labor supply made this both possible and not too costly. High capital costs also contributed. The then prevalent management belief in industrial "life cycles"—that industries necessarily mature and lose competitive capacity— led management to "harvest" certain facilities, using a low investment strategy to fund investment elsewhere.

For a time, there were useful social results: national income rose and unemployment decreased. Eventually, however, the strategy collapsed, because a capital stock that was not updated combined with increasing problems of work force performance to yield low-quality, high-cost production. The United States became increasingly noncompetitive, with falling real wages and rising unemployment.

This domestic strategy made the United States vulnerable to competition from traditional European trading partners and to new, more imaginative competitors from Japan and emerging nations. The United States has come through a period in which its strongest international competition was from developed countries—Japan and European countries in particular. But we are entering a period in which the greatest challenges to U.S. manufacturing will be from extremely low-cost but increasingly capable and productive Third World labor, which may affect us as profoundly in the late 1980s as Japanese competitors did in the 1970s and early 1980s. It is as if a new national resource has been found—Asian labor—and manufacturers everywhere are now jockeying to see who will benefit and who will be damaged.

Low-cost Third World labor has existed for many years, but it has now taken on economic significance. Improvements in transportation and communication allow factories to be located in Asia and Latin America and equipped with up-to-date technology for production to be shipped to the United States for sale. The difficulties are being overcome: establishing plants, setting up distribution channels, and crossing language and cultural gaps.

Although economic development of the Third World has been a goal of both Democratic and Republican administrations for the past decades, we overestimated the obstacles. We believed that labor costs abroad would rise as economic development continued, despite the population dynamics of developing countries that suggested the opposite. We believed that the lack of indigenous natural resources would thwart economic competition, despite such glaring examples as Japan's ability to procure the petroleum to meet its needs. We believed that foreign companies would not be able to obtain needed capital to build an industrial base at the same time that U.S. banks were making international loans on increasingly favorable terms. We also were convinced that political instability abroad would disrupt economic development while at the same time our foreign policy of promoting political stability was meeting with some success. As a result, we failed to anticipate the competition we now face.

American companies manufacturing in the United States will have difficulty competing in this new world with our current quality and cost performance. Only modern equipment and a committed labor force will meet the test. If manufacturing is to continue on a large scale in the United States, productivity in our firms will have to rise to offset low labor and capital costs abroad. For the immediate future, retaining American jobs will depend in part on the rate at which we can automate our factories. It may appear in individual situations that new equipment is replacing people. But in a broader context, without new equipment even more jobs will disappear. For the next several years the number of jobs and the advance of automation are positively related and must be part of an overall strategy to regain a competitive position while attending to the inherent problems in making such a transition.

Fashioning a remedy for our decline in competitiveness that takes employment consequences into account will require the best thinking in the private and public sector. Industries within our manufacturing sector exhibit varying degrees of competitiveness and have differing capacities to respond. Sensitivity to these differences must be demonstrated, fine but critical distinctions must be drawn. The environment within which industries function has become increasingly internationalized and interdependent, and consequently, our macroeconomic policies, particularly international trade policy, are ever more directly linked to employment policy. William Brock, U.S. Trade Representative, recently stated that the United States will be incapable of sustaining a liberal trade position unless unemployment can be remedied.[1] He projected that a $70 billion trade deficit in 1983 will cost the United States two million jobs. The strong exchange value of the dollar has, of course, contributed to this trade deficit. But the less we rely on a weak dollar to regain our competitiveness, the lower inflation will be and the higher our standard of living.

Calls for an industrial policy have been made in response to our failing competitive position. Free trade advocates are right in the long run, yet they are naive about our competitors' short-run tactics and are reluctant to counteract if not to adopt their strategies. Rigid adherence to free trade policies may react against attempts to regain competitiveness in certain specific cases.

The U.S. government must, for example, be prepared to pressure the Japanese to open at least some of their markets to U.S. goods. Free traders also discount the human and political realities created by the transition problems in a U.S. economy open to foreign producers. It is the latter that we are concerned with: the employment consequences of our failing competitive position.

THE INTERNATIONAL CONTEXT

THE THREAT POSED BY LOW PAY ABROAD

Over the last several years the American business press has focused on the problem of competitiveness with our major trading partners—Japan in particular. However, Third World nations, both less developed and newly industrializing, also pose competitive challenges—not only to us but to Japan. This threat will increase as transportation and communications systems continue to improve, capital investment continues, and managerial and technical classes emerge in the Third World, creating a more stable environment that will permit the key resources of the Third World countries—low-wage labor—to emerge as a decisive competitive force. Korean construction companies, for example, have captured the Middle East construction market previously dominated by the United States. Similarly, these countries' low wages, with the current favorable rate of exchange they enjoy, offer a compelling opportunity for U.S. companies to shift production abroad, thus decreasing jobs for American labor at home.

Tables 12-1 through 12-5 document these labor cost challenges presented by our major trading partners and the Third World. Table 12-1 shows the gap in wages and benefits between the United States, Germany, France, and Japan for 1975 and 1982. As an aggregate, the U.S. compensation gap continues to widen in relation to France and Germany and remains about the same with Japan.

Compensation data for the developing countries of Mexico, Brazil, and Korea (table 12-2) reveal continuing wage costs challenges of a far greater magnitude. Wage differentials between the United States and Third World countries are at a ratio of 4:1, and in the case of Korea, 10:1.

The wage ratios in important industries like motor vehicle and equipment manufacturing (table 12-3) reflect an overall trend of increasing U.S. inability to compete on the basis of wages and benefits with either Western Europe and Japan or developing countries. In general, the same conclusions can be

Table 12-1

Compensation Gap between the United States and Major Trading Partners—
Production Workers in Manufacturing Hourly Compensation (Wages and Benefits)
(in U.S. dollars)

	1975	Percent of U.S.	1982	Percent of U.S.
United States	$6.35		$11.73	
Germany	6.19	97%	10.38	88%
France	4.58	72	7.96	68
Japan	3.05	48	5.80	49

Source: U.S. Department of Labor, Bureau of Labor Statistics, Office of Productivity and
Technology, unpublished data, December 1982.
Note: Changes in the dollar value of compensation abroad are due to changes in amounts of
compensation *and* to changes in the value of the dollar.

Table 12-2

Compensation Gap between the United States and Developing Countries—
Production Workers in Manufacturing Hourly Compensation (Wages and Benefits)
(in U.S. dollars)

	1975	Percent of U.S.	1982	Percent of U.S.
Mexico	$1.92	30%	$2.73	23%
Brazil	1.13	18	2.60	22
Korea	0.37	6	1.25	11

Source: U.S. Department of Labor, Bureau of Labor Statistics, Office of Productivity and
Technology, unpublished data, December 1982.
Note: Changes in the dollar value of compensation abroad are due to changes in amounts of
compensation *and* to changes in the value of the dollar.

drawn as from the aggregate figures of tables 12-1 and 12-2. The ratio of
U.S. compensation costs to those of its competitors remains so high as to
render almost meaningless the incremental percentage changes over the
seven-year period. The lower cost of building plants abroad has combined
with low wage scales to intensify pressure for U.S. motor vehicle and
equipment manufacturers to produce parts abroad, with the attendant cost
savings, and ship them back to the United States with a corresponding
continuing decline in U.S. employment levels in this sector.

A similar comparison of costs for production workers in iron and steel
manufacturing (table 12-4) manifests an even more dramatic profile of de-

clining U.S. labor cost competitiveness. In Germany, France, Japan, and Mexico, hourly compensation costs declined as a percentage of U.S. costs. In comparison to these countries, U.S. competitiveness based on compensation is substantially diminished in all cases.

Of course, conclusions drawn only from auto and steel data can be too sweeping. A high degree of concentration, market control, and historic dominance of world markets enabled companies in these industries to afford higher wages. Strong unions that organized a high percentage of the work force demanded and received wages substantially higher than for all manufacturing. Nonetheless, autos and steel serve as dramatic examples of overall trends.

Table 12-3

Hourly Compensation Costs (Wages and Benefits) for Production Workers in Motor Vehicle and Equipment Manufacturing (in U.S. dollars)

	1975	Percent of U.S.	1982	Percent of U.S.
United States	$9.44		$19.37	
Japan	3.56	38%	7.24	38%
Mexico	2.90	31	3.53	18
Korea	.50	5	1.95	10

Source: U.S. Department of Labor, Bureau of Labor Statistics, Office of Productivity and Technology, unpublished data, December 1982.
Note: Changes in the dollar value of compensation abroad are due to changes in amounts of compensation *and* to changes in the value of the dollar.

Table 12-4

Hourly Compensation Costs (Wages and Benefits) for Production Workers in Iron and Steel Manufacturing (in U.S. dollars)

	1975	Percent of U.S.	1982	Percent of U.S.
United States	$10.24		$22.20	
Germany	7.12	70%	11.68	53%
France	5.86	57	9.52	43
Japan	5.26	51	10.15	46
Mexico	2.27	22	3.28	15

Source: U.S. Department of Labor, Bureau of Labor Statistics, Office of Productivity and Technology, unpublished data, December 1982.
Note: Changes in the dollar value of compensation abroad are due to changes in amounts of compensation *and* to changes in the value of the dollar.

Table 12-5

Iron and Steel: Output per Hour, Hourly Labor Cost, and Unit Labor Cost for 1964, 1975, 1980—United States and Three Trading Partners (as a percentage of U.S. estimated)

	Output per Hour	Hourly Labor Cost	Unit Labor Cost (cost per unit of output)
1964			
Germany	55.5%	35.0%	64.0%
France	48.0	34.5	71.0
Japan	47.5	16.0	34.0
1975			
Germany	84.0	75.0	89.5 •
France	62.0	66.0	106.0
Japan	105.5	45.0	43.0
1980			
Germany	105.5	91.0	86.0
France	89.5	78.0	87.5
Japan	141.5	52.5	37.5

Source: Author's estimates based on unpublished data from U.S. Department of Labor, Bureau of Labor Statistics.

THE PRODUCTIVITY GAP

U.S. unit labor costs (cost per unit of output) also illustrate failing competitiveness. For example, between 1975 and 1980, Germany, France, and Japan decreased their unit labor costs in iron and steel in relation to those of the United States (table 12-5). Most dramatic is the emergence of Japan from a low productivity and low labor cost producer in 1964, to a moderate labor cost and high productivity producer in 1980. Japan has maintained its unit cost at between 34 and 37 percent of the United States for the seventeen-year period. This is a remarkable performance. Japan has seen its compensation advantage decline but has offset it by rapid improvements in productivity. Whether or not this is an explicit industrial policy, it is a very effective way to remain competitive in the international economy, and American companies must devise and implement a response.

Productivity trends also attest to flagging U.S. economic performance in an increasingly interdependent and internationalized world market. Between 1972 and 1981, both Germany and France more than doubled U.S. growth in output per hour (table 12-6). These increases were accomplished by a

Table 12-6

Manufacturing: Changes in Output, Employment, and Productivity in the United States and Its Major Trading Partners (percent change, 1972–81)

	Output	*Employment*	*Output per Hour*
United States	22%	5%	18%
Japan	73	1	77
Germany	17	−14	49
France	23	−9	46

Source: U.S. Department of Labor, Bureau of Labor Statistics, Office of Productivity and Technology, December 1982.

decrease in employment that, balanced against moderate but substantial increases in output, rendered productivity increases of 49 percent and 46 percent respectively. Although significant, those accomplished by Japan are even greater: during the same period, output per hour in Japan increased by 77 percent. Japan's productivity increases were accomplished by a 73 percent increase in output, three times that of the United States, Germany, and France, with an incremental increase in employment of only 1 percent.

In contrast, the United States seems to have had no concern for productivity at all. Output was up by 22 percent, a respectable amount in comparison with our European competitors, if not the Japanese. But to increase output we added employees, rather than cut back as in Europe; therefore, productivity increases in our manufacturing sector came in a poor second to European increases, and were almost a nonstarter compared with Japan's outstanding performance. Thus, although overall U.S. employment levels are higher than they would otherwise be, and we are now beginning to see some improvements in our productivity performance, the net effect of the productivity gap over the nine-year period has been a decline in the U.S. competitive stance.

HOW DEMOGRAPHICS DRIVE LABOR COST DIFFERENTIALS

Our competitors' increasing productivity relative to ours, combined with their lower compensation levels, constitutes a formidable advantage. The projected size of the Third World labor force when compared with ours is even more ominous for the U.S. competitive stance. The work force of the Third World is inexpensive, increasingly productive, and young; that of the United States has grown more expensive, less productive, and older.

Figure 12-1 shows the age profile of the U.S. and Mexican populations in 1980. The configuration of the Mexican population is representative of those of other Third World countries, with a majority of the population under the age of twenty-four and thus a large supply of young workers between the ages of sixteen and twenty-four with which to meet increasing manufacturing employment demands. In contrast, U.S. figures show the aging of the American population, with the highest population concentration in the prime ages of twenty-five to fifty-four. Projected U.S. labor force growth rates suggest these trends will continue. Although the number of young workers (sixteen to twenty-four) grew by 3.9 percent annually between 1965 and 1979, between 1979 and 1995, an annual percentage decline of .9 percent is projected. The number of workers of prime age (twenty-five to fifty-four) are projected to increase 2.3 percent annually.

These figures suggest both a potential shortage of younger workers in the United States and a plethora of older workers. Japan faces the same demographic profile as the United States and consequent challenge from the plentiful and low-wage work force of emerging nations. Between 1960 and 1981, Japan's labor force under age twenty-four decreased by 33.6 percent; concomitantly, the group over age forty-five increased by 53.7 percent.[2] In addition to the future competitive advantages that will accrue to developing countries as a result of these demographics, both the United States and Japan have already anticipated crises in the fiduciary integrity of their public pension systems and must devote greater proportions of national income to support pensioners. These costs will compound the difficulties of meeting low-cost Third World competition for the United States and Japan.

In addition to low labor costs and ready supply of labor in the Third World, the easing of foreign investment rules has proven a compelling lure for U.S. companies to move production facilities abroad. U.S.-owned assembly plants, for example located just over the Mexican border, provided approximately 124,000 new jobs to Mexicans in 1983.[3] Mexico has also recently relaxed its foreign investment rules to attract badly needed dollars.[4] If such foreign investment occurs, Mexico may join other Third World competitors whose rapid advances in manufacturing production capacity undermine the United States' historic strategy of competing on the basis of advanced engineering and management capabilities instead of labor costs. Steel imports, recently made subject to restraint agreements with the European Economic Community (EEC) and Japan, are now increasing from steel manufactures in Brazil and Mexico.[5] As capital shifts, the threat increases that the U.S. manufacturing sector will continue to contract.

Figure 12-1

Population Profile: Mexico, United States, 1980

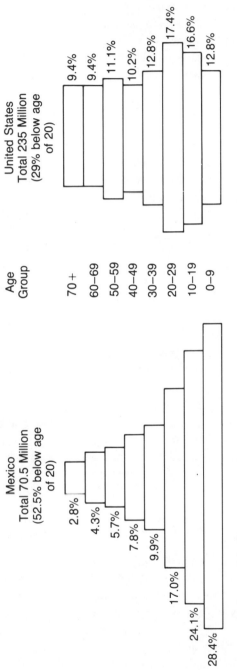

United States
Total 235 Million
(29% below age
of 20)

Mexico
Total 70.5 Million
(52.5% below age
of 20)

Age
Group

Age Group	United States	Mexico
70+	9.4%	2.8%
60–69	9.4%	4.3%
50–59	11.1%	5.7%
40–49	10.2%	7.8%
30–39	12.8%	9.9%
20–29	17.4%	17.0%
10–19	16.6%	24.1%
0–9	12.8%	28.4%

Source: U.S. Bureau of the Census

There is a general perception of the Third World as a homogenous whole, yet there are actually two tiers within it—"high wage" and "low wage" countries, relative to each other. The first tier has developed technical and management capabilities enabling it to win market share; the second tier will eventually pose a competitive threat to both the first tier and to industrialized economies. Mexico, with its average hourly labor costs of less than $1.00 (down from $1.65 in 1982 with the devaluation of the peso),[6] is on a par with South Korea, Brazil, Taiwan, Hong Kong, and Singapore; they, in turn, are struggling to compete with their even lower labor cost neighbors— Malaysia, the Philippines, Indonesia, Sri Lanka, and China.[7] Indonesian wage rates, for example, hover at an average of 40 cents per hour.[8] China, in particular, has put its labor cost advantage to use in a trade policy that tripled volume in the five-year period between 1977 and 1981.[9] Manufacturing exports now account for over half of this total, with an emphasis on light manufacturing that returns foreign exchange earnings more quickly than heavy manufacturing with relatively low investment.[10] Such capabilities have enabled China to win market share in apparel in the United States and Western Europe, and the same advantages may accrue as it develops other manufacturing sectors.

As Asian companies increasingly profit from their enhanced management capabilities, low labor costs, their countries' improved infrastructures, and demographic trends, they will be able to compete in world markets and provide financially attractive locations for the manufacturing facilities of U.S. companies. These newly industrializing nations have awakened to the potential of creating their own markets rather than continually depending on foreign aid. This dramatic change, no matter how desirable in the long run, causes short-term and perhaps permanent economic dislocation for industrialized nations.

THE RESULT OF FAILING COMPETITIVENESS: LONG-TERM MANUFACTURING DECLINE IN THE UNITED STATES

By nearly all measures, our manufacturing base is shrinking but in an unmanaged way, neither guided by strategy nor aimed at regaining competitiveness. The shape of our remaining manufacturing base is increasingly determined by obstacles facing the competition from abroad. High capital investment is required, for example, in chemicals; natural resources are necessary in paper and natural gas; transportation costs are important in cement; a short time from production to market is required for style in apparel. We will maintain industries like high technology only until production processes are rationalized and therefore exportable. The only other major countervailing force to the erosion of manufacturing sectors has been protectionist measures that affect automobiles, steel, and textiles. And although these have determined the perimeter of our shrinking base, Third World countries are increasingly overcoming these obstacles too.

The result of all these trends and factors has been long-term decline in manufacturing jobs as a proportion of the U.S. labor force and recently in absolute numbers. Figure 12-2 shows the actual decline in this percentage from 35.4 in 1947, to 21 percent in 1982. If this decline continues at the current rate, manufacturing would constitute only 13 percent of total employment in the United States by the year 2000. The impact on manufacturing employment may be mitigated by high economic growth and accelerated under conditions of low economic growth, but the direction of the projected trend line remains the same: downward and dramatically so.

These figures on manufacturing employment do not illustrate projections of overall growth in employment as a result of expansion in the service sector, which would offset declining manufacturing employment and lower the overall employment rate. Even if the total unemployment rate continues to decline, manufacturing employment will continue to decline as a percentage of total employment because its causes are cyclical and structural; both would have to be reversed to change the trends. The meaning of these trends in actual numbers of manufacturing jobs is shown in figure 12-3. Future projections are included in figure 12-3, depending on whether low or high economic growth occurs, and if there will be productivity increases driven by capital investment, which in the manufacturing sector means introducing robotics.

The rate of the introduction of robotics in the United States and the effect on employment levels in manufacturing remains to be determined. As of 1981, the United States had only 3.4 percent of the robots in use internationally.[11] Japan used 70.4 percent of the total of 67,435, which has been a critical factor in the soaring productivity increase in their assembly manufacturing.[12] The negative employment effects of the introduction of robotics in Japan have until recently been limited, apparently, by lifetime employment practices and the transfer of employees within the firm.[13]

Although the exact extent and impact of robotization on the United States in the future is unclear, the pressures to introduce robots to obtain further competitive advantages are large and growing. In the current context, robots are probably on the whole job-preserving, not job-replacing, in U.S. manu-

Figure 12-2

Projection of Current Trend—Manufacturing Employment in the United States as Percent of Total Employment

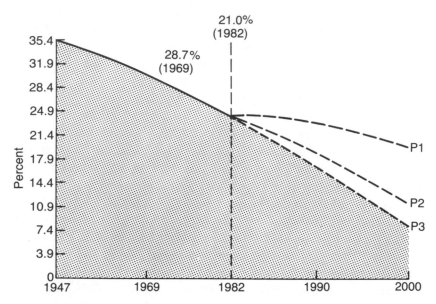

Source: Author's calculations

P1 *Competitiveness and high economic growth.* Tracks with some minor, judgmental modifications, the Bureau of Labor Statistics high economic growth rate for manufacturing to the year 2000. Manufacturing as a percentage of employment as forecasted by BLS is possible only with a combination of factors involving greater productivity resulting in part from improved labor-management relations and high general economic growth.

P2 *Competitiveness and low economic growth.* Tracks combination of BLS intermediate and slow growth rate. Manufacturing as a percentage of employment as forecasted by BLS with low-moderate general economic growth is possible only with a combination of factors involving greater productivity resulting in part from improved labor-management relations.

P3 *Noncompetitiveness.* Forecast based on continuation of present trends, although there may be short-term variations; for example, the present upturn in the business cycle. The course of the U.S. economy extrapolated from trend since 1947, which is associated with declining competitiveness in the last two decades.

facturing. White collar jobs in manufacturing and maintenance are preserved, although blue collar jobs may decline, since robotics raises quality, reduces costs, and thus preserves competitiveness.

Estimates suggest that as many as 50,000 to 100,000 robots may be introduced in the United States by 1990 (affecting directly 100,000 to 200,000 jobs in manufacturing), with a third to a half of these in the auto industry.[14] Others have speculated that the overall impact of the introduction of robotics, should it occur on a substantial scale, may not be nationwide, but would have a disproportionate effect on certain regions, most notably the Midwest, where there are high concentrations of certain types of industries, particularly metal working.[15] These industrial sectors are particularly ripe for robotization because of the structure of jobs in the industry and the intense competitive pressures under which they function.

Despite the uncertainty of factors such as robots, overall trends are clear. Taking the U.S. economy as a whole, the manufacturing sector constitutes not only a shrinking percentage of employment, but a smaller part of U.S. total output. Between 1959 and 1981, total output in the goods-producing industries decreased from 41.4 percent to 35.4 percent, while that of service-producing industries increased from 58.6 percent to 64.6 percent.[16] These

Figure 12-3

Projections of Current Trend of Manufacturing Employment in the United States (millions of jobs)

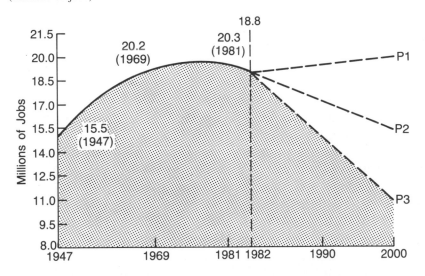

Source: Author's calculations

P1 *Competitiveness and high economic growth.* Tracks with some minor, judgmental modifications, the Bureau of Labor Statistics high economic growth rate for manufacturing to the year 2000. (See further explanatory note in figure 12-2.)

P2 *Competitiveness and low economic growth.* Tracks combination of BLS intermediate and slow growth rate. (See note in figure 12-2.)

P3 *Noncompetitiveness.* Forecast based on continuation of present trends, although there may be short-term variations; for example, the present upturn in the business cycle. (See note in figure 12-2.)

output trends were accompanied by corresponding changes in employment levels. In 1947, services constituted only 11.5 percent of nonagricultural employment. When services were combined with financial and government employment, the total was still only 28 percent. By 1981, services alone constituted 20.3 percent of total nonagricultural employment and reached 44 percent when combined with financial and government employment. A continuation of these trends would bring the total of services, financial, and government employment to 47 percent in 1990 and 52 percent by the year 2000.

Even these figures may overstate the number of manual jobs available in the manufacturing sector in the next decade. These projected figures are aggregated for manufacturing as a sector and do not speak to the distribution of white versus blue collar jobs within that sector. The ratio of nonproduction jobs to production jobs in manufacturing has increased since World War II, most dramatically in the larger firms. Robert Reich has estimated that between 1965 and 1975, the ratio of staff to production jobs in U.S. manufacturing companies has increased from 35:100 to 41:100.[17] Blue collar employment constitutes approximately 31 percent of the U.S. labor force today; by 2000 it will be 24-25 percent of total employment. Whether the primary effect of this is, as Reich has suggested, to create 364 steps to hire a new employee or to create a more productive, better-managed work force is still being debated. In either case, the immediate human impact is a further diminution of manufacturing jobs to meet the needs of those who have been and will continue to be displaced, and of new entrants to the labor force (although this group is growing smaller with the aging population).

If our present noncompetitiveness continues, the problem of the displaced worker will continue to grow with continuing layoffs. There are currently one and a half million displaced workers, and estimates project that as few as 100,000 or as many as two million will be added to their ranks. The number will be determined by the level of our economic growth, our competitiveness, and government trade policy, but will probably fall into the range of 250,000 to one million a year, on average. In years of business cycle recovery, such as 1983, the number will be lower.

The effect of these factors, combined with the recent recession, is a level of unemployment that reached nearly 11 percent early in 1983, although it has since declined to 8.0. Despite this substantial drop, both the administration and the Congressional Budget Office predict rates in excess of 7 percent through 1987. These unemployment figures, however, do not tell the entire story. They exclude approximately four million people not counted in unemployment tallies who have withdrawn from active job searches because they have become discouraged or have found part-time work when they desire full-time. The unmeasured effects of the loss of productivity due to underemployment are another cost of our current employment picture. These trends in measured and unmeasured unemployment are likely to continue, although perhaps at a slower rate.

JOBS IN A POSTMANUFACTURING ECONOMY

An American economy with fewer manufacturing jobs, however, is not necessarily one with high unemployment. Americans may find jobs in designing, financing, distributing, transporting, selling, and maintaining manufactured products, even if very few jobs are involved in actually fabricating or assembling products in this country. The Department of Labor has projected that by 1995, 28.5 million people will be employed in services.[18] Although the Bureau of Labor Statistics may underestimate the rate of growth of the number of new jobs, figures point to a transfer from higher-wage manual jobs to service jobs, in which the lower ratio of capital to employee may mean lower wages. The long-term aggregate impact on productivity as a consequence will depend, of course, on the distribution of growth among different service industries. Pipeline transportation and gas and electric utilities, for example, have a much higher ratio of capital stock to labor than do financial institutions or wholesale and retail trade.[19] It is likely, however, that if current noncompetitiveness continues, overall productivity will either not increase or will rise slowly in relation to our competitors. Over the long term, output per employee in services increases at a slower rate than output per employee in manufacturing.

The potential for job creation in nonmanufacturing, primarily the service sector of the American economy, remains strong, and the reduction in manufacturing job opportunities will not result one-for-one in increasing joblessness (whether due to layoffs or to the inability of new entrants to the labor market to find jobs). We will nevertheless have a persistent problem of joblessness in the range of 7-8 percent of our labor force at least through 1987.

But competition by American workers for newly created jobs in manufacturing will intensify as growing populations in emerging nations put pressure on the United States to increase immigration quotas and, failing that, continue to provide a growing number of illegal immigrants to a U.S. labor market that is already flooded with a labor force seeking manufacturing jobs. As a result, despite projections of a tight U.S. labor market, the lack of manufacturing jobs elsewhere in the economy paying comparable wages may result in a continuing problem of joblessness among its work force.

Much has been made of the potential for high technology manufacturing to absorb the employment slack in heavy manufacturing. Much will depend on how competitive we become. The high technology sector, though small, has a quickly growing output. However, the total number of jobs created will be fewer than half of those lost in heavy manufacturing between 1981 and 1990 if present trends continue.[20] Probably, by 1990, approximately five million high tech jobs will constitute 22 percent of all manufacturing jobs, 5 percent of all private sector jobs, and 4.3 percent of all jobs in the economy.[21] These figures are based on a high technology manufacturing job creation of only one million between 1979 and 1990. Further, those manufacturing jobs that are created will face the same competition from low-wage labor markets in emerging nations that have played a large role in the demise of heavy manufacturing jobs up until now. Atari and Apple, for example, have already announced plans to move parts of their production abroad. Hewlett-Packard predicts a faster growth in its overseas work force than in the United States.[22]

Although the potential for job creation in the service sector remains strong, earnings for some may be adversely affected. In 1982, average gross weekly earnings of production and nonsupervisory workers in manufacturing averaged $330.65 per week compared with $225.27 in services.[23] Other factors may complicate the transition from heavy to high technology manufacturing. The cost of education may be high, the foregone earnings during the period of retraining difficult to withstand, the new work culture too awkward an adjustment. These private costs must be combined with those the public bears in unemployment insurance, trade adjustment assistance and, if private and public job-related efforts fail, welfare costs.

ALTERNATIVE U.S. RESPONSES

At the end of World War II, the U.S. manufacturing sector had modern plants and top management talent. Domestic markets were almost entirely our own and foreign markets were expanding. The dollar was strong. International lending was minimal compared with today. All of this contributed to a strong and growing manufacturing sector. Now we are faced with old, inefficient plants and challenges to many of the assumptions upon which management decisions have been based. We are losing share in U.S. markets and face strong competition from foreign companies. A strong dollar now means we are losing export markets. For decades we viewed manufacturing employment as characteristic of our society: our labor laws are fashioned to fit manufacturing; our labor and management institutions are drawn from manufacturing. This is changing and we must be prepared to fashion a labor-management structure built on a different distribution of labor.

The United States is also faced with a low-wage, rising-productivity work force abroad. If this situation continues, we will have an economy with a larger percentage of the work force engaged in the design, finance, transport, distribution, sale, and service of goods rather than their production. Production would be limited to those manufacturing sectors in which automation and high levels of investment in capital equipment combine to keep labor costs low compared to our competitors' or to those sectors which remain competitive for other reasons. Although emerging areas of the economy would provide alternatives for employment for some undetermined percentage of those displaced, the nature of work in America would change dramatically.

How can the United States respond to the possibility of a continuing erosion in manufacturing employment, of a continual loss of competitiveness? What is the implication for employment levels, productivity, and living standards?

Competitiveness is not only a characteristic of our manufacturing sector as a whole, but of different industries, of individual companies, and even divisions of companies. We may think of a scale or spectrum of competitiveness, from high to low, with industries, companies, or divisions arranged along it, and with an average point for our goods-producing economy as a whole. Over time, the economy and each of its elements individually move along the spectrum. Table 12-7 presents a competitiveness continuum along which American companies fall, which in the aggregate, determines our national competitiveness. In recent decades, too many American companies, industries, and therefore, the manufacturing sector as a whole, have been shifting downward on the competitiveness scale.

Over time, different strategies have been adopted that have shifted our position on the continuum, our competitive stance worldwide, and our domestic employment levels and living standards at home. As the 1972-81 data show (table 12-5), we "harvested" U.S. manufacturing through a high-employment, low-investment strategy based on a strong market share. This strategy was necessarily time limited. U.S. markets were not protected, and with the development of new products and production processes abroad, low labor costs, and the introduction of new technology, foreign companies

Table 12-7
Competitiveness Continuum:
Employment Productivity and Living Standards under Conditions of High
and Low Economic Growth

High Economic Growth	*High Economic Growth*
Moderate Employment Levels	Moderate Employment Levels
Low Productivity	High Productivity
Moderate Living Standards	Moderate Living Standards
Noncompetitiveness ———————— (without protection)	Competitiveness ———→
Low Economic Growth	*Low Economic Growth*
Very Low Employment Levels	Low Employment Levels
Low Productivity	Moderate Productivity
Low Living Standards	Moderate Living Standards

increasingly overtook us in both foreign and domestic markets. During the period from 1978 to 1981, we altered the earlier strategy, or it was altered for us, as increasing production gave way to decline with continuing low productivity and employment. As a result, our manufacturing base eroded rapidly under the onslaught of increasingly effective foreign competitors. By 1981, pressure to take protectionist measures had mounted in the face of alarmingly high levels of unemployment. Import limitations were imposed on automobiles and steel to preserve jobs, as they had been on textiles. As a result of these measures, particularly voluntary restraint agreements with the Japanese, some protected industries appear to have survived the threat to their existence posed by foreign competition. The long-term prognosis is less certain.

Our recent circumstance consists of low productivity accompanied by falling production and employment in industries within our manufacturing sector (the left end of the continuum). There are degrees of applicability of this generalization across industries and across firms within industries. The scenario applies more directly, for example, to the steel, automobile, foot-wear, and apparel industries than to textiles, rubber products, chemicals, and high technology manufacturing. In periods of low economic growth, such as the current recession, this means very low employment and low living standards in industries overall and in varying degrees within the sector. This is the worst combination of any of the options presented. High economic growth would bring only moderate employment and living standards. In many ways our present course makes our living standards and employment levels most vulnerable to recessionary periods.

One response to our current situation could be to preserve production and employment in the United States through protectionism. This strategy would have a short-term positive effect on employment levels. However, low living standards would result under conditions of low economic growth, and low to moderate standards would result if high economic growth should occur. Such a strategy could also yield high-cost manufacturers, whose inefficiencies and lack of competitiveness in international markets would not be viable in the long run. This seems to have happened in Europe. Protectionism could also lead to reduced world trade, which, by limiting the flow of dollars abroad, could catapult into default the already precarious balance of payments of the Third World countries. The auto industry has provided a laboratory for observing protectionism at work. In part, as a result of protectionist measures, sales have soared. In response, the UAW is now asking for a share of the profits that have been generated behind a protectionist barrier and government financial assistance to one of the companies.

Regaining competitiveness means retaining production in the United States through a high productivity solution based on new technology and high worker commitment. This strategy is different from both a protectionist response and from current practices. It is superior because it yields the highest long-term results: employment levels, productivity, and living standards, regardless of whether the economy's macropolicymakers achieve their goal of high economic growth.

Within a competitive U.S. economy, introducing new technology manufacturing would be similar in some ways, but with critical differences, to the experience in agriculture. With automated farm equipment, people transferred out of agriculture, and productivity was increased dramatically. Agricultural workers were drawn from low productivity jobs on the farm to higher productivity jobs in the urban manufacturing centers. Introducing new technology in manufacturing would induce the transfer of people or their children from higher productivity jobs with higher wages to lower productivity and lower wage employment in the service industries. This scenario will be borne out unless there is a larger increase in capital/employee ratios in service than the historic trend suggests. Technological change also creates adjustment problems. Any long-run approach to the problem of introducing new technology must consider the impact on the lives of people who are affected in the short run and the costs, both private and public, of a jagged-edged transition.

WHAT DOES COMPETITIVENESS MEAN?

Although business, labor, and government would all agree that America should become more competitive, each of these actors in the economic system might have differing concepts about what "achieving competitiveness" means. Who is to define competitiveness—management, labor, government, stockholders? Does "what is good for GM" necessarily make the United States more competitive? Alternatively, does a prosperous work force necessarily mean a competitive American manufacturing sector? In the short run or the long run? By what mechanism is U.S. competitiveness to be enhanced and by what standard measured?

The concept of competitiveness used here is akin to that of a business person evaluating his or her firm's future viability. In the present, all financial measures may show good health; earnings are rising, sales are up. But the executive may know that his or her key competitor is about to leapfrog the current state of technology by introducing a new product that will put his or her company in a very difficult situation, one that several quarters hence will be reflected in a deteriorating financial position. Alternatively, an executive may see the company's stock take a beating, reflecting currently poor operating results. But he or she knows that the company will introduce new products, which will turn the current state of affairs upside down. In the first example, economic data are favorable, but the underlying competitiveness of the firm is deteriorating enormously. In the latter example, economic data are dismal, but the underlying competitive situation is improving. The same long-term approach is implicit in the definition of our national competitiveness.

This chapter has been directed at the employment consequences of competitiveness. For our purpose, enhancing competitiveness means a harmonization of profit and employment objectives and the reversal of trends indicated in figures 12-2 and 12-3 that is, the decline in U.S. manufacturing employment. This would not, however, necessarily be the standard by which companies doing business internationally would measure their competitiveness on a worldwide basis. For many companies that shift employment abroad, the nationality of the work force and the impact on American workers is not a main factor in their competitiveness formula.

As the number of multinational companies has expanded, they have increasingly encountered issues concerning employment in both industrialized host countries and less developed countries where national economic, political, and social conditions have functioned as a countervailing force to strictly economic considerations. Ironically, U.S. multinationals now face some of the same issues of national concern at home that they have successfully resolved abroad. Corporate competitiveness that involves production abroad may draw increasing criticism if unemployment levels remain high in the United States.

To the U.S. work force, competitiveness must necessarily involve the creation of jobs for U.S. citizens. Perhaps our work force will be indifferent to whether the employer is a Japanese, German, or American company and, consequently, indifferent to where the profits eventually end up. Sony or Motorola, Lever Brothers or Procter & Gamble, Shell or Texaco all offer employment. This would be an interesting counterpart to the concern of some managers to increase profits without regard to the loss of U.S. jobs. If our industrialized competitors decide to locate production facilities in the United States in an attempt to gain access to markets here, this would enhance U.S. competitiveness from the point of view of the work force, which would define the provision of jobs as an essential factor in the formula. U.S. companies, of course, would view such a development as a threat to, not an enhancement of, their competitiveness.

These competing definitions demonstrate the divergence of interest that exists in the national policy level when defining competitiveness from the perspective of the company or the labor force. The American work force could be competitive without benefiting American corporations, and our corporations could be competitive in the international marketplace without benefiting American workers. The latter seems more likely now than the former.

It is fashionable to insist that labor and capital have a mutual interest in making the United States more competitive. There is much truth in this observation, but also some exaggeration. Companies and unions are very different types of institutions: unions must represent today's workers, while capital has the option of looking to future markets. One serves the representational needs of its members; the other exists to create profits and thereby jobs. It is not surprising that at the bargaining table the parties get tangled in each other's different and sometimes opposing strategies. Despite these differences, a strong mutuality of interest exists at the plant level, where uncountered foreign competition can both put workers out of jobs and cost stockholders the value of their investment in the plant. And it is precisely this mutuality of interest, that if recognized by the parties, may alter the collective bargaining process so that the outcomes reflect not only the ongoing issue of the division of profits, but the viability of the firm in the long run.

But as one goes to higher levels of aggregation to the company level, the mutuality is weakened. A multinational corporation can abandon its American work force to set up production abroad, thus fulfilling the injunction of the nation's textbook writers on corporate finance for managers to maximize the value of the stockholders' wealth.

Alternatively, though not as clearly visible, American workers may support foreign-owned companies, and thereby foreign capitalists or governments, against our own corporations. American employees can provide greater effort and performance in their work for foreign-owned companies than for our own or agree to more favorable collective bargaining terms to attract foreign companies and jobs (e.g., Toyota-GM). Thus, foreign manufacturers may operate competitively in the United States when sometimes American manufacturers cannot.

We are beginning to see examples of this phenomenon—of foreign companies that take over unprofitable American plants and turn them into competitive powerhouses using American labor. Our commentators ordinarily ascribe this circumstance to the better skills of foreign managers. But these plants, though foreign-owned, are generally managed by Americans. Forced into a corner, the commentators then ascribe the foreign-owned but American-managed plants' success to superior foreign management techniques, which, for example, Japanese firms are said to instill in their American management and American work force.

SUMMARY

The competitive problems of American manufacturing in the international marketplace will not disappear with current economic expansion. A long period of inadequate investment, poor human performance, and low productivity are at the root of our problems, which have been exacerbated by the high value of the dollar in recent years. America has been losing share in total world industrial output for decades. Similarly, decades ago our domestic economic growth shifted from manufacturing to other sectors. In consequence, the percentage of our labor force employed in manufacturing has had a long-term decline since 1947, which is almost certain to continue even if the rate of decline slows. Today's recall of workers to auto plants may appear only a small upward deviation in the long, continuing decline of manufacturing in our economy. Alternatively, enhanced competitiveness may slow this trend.

The pressures that are causing American manufacturing's decline are increasing in intensity, not decreasing. The Japanese are as formidable competitors today as they have been in the recent past. Aided by the strong dollar, European manufacturers will be making greater inroads in U.S. markets, although they too face many competitiveness problems. But most significant, and emerging as perhaps the key dimension of the international challenge, is the appearance on the stage of international manufacturing of low-cost, Third World labor. American manufacturers confront enormous cost disadvantages in the world marketplace. Increasing access to capital and technology will enhance productivity in the Third World. Cost disadvantages will persist for decades, since they are rooted in the dynamics of population growth in different regions of the world.[24] The world is awash with people outside the narrow enclave of industrialized nations. The emergence of these citizens of the Third World into the international labor market in manufacturing is a major development that will pose a challenge to U.S.-based manufacturing for decades.

The challenge to American manufacturing is multifaceted: productivity, cost, quality, and long-lasting efforts to regain competitiveness may permit us to retain a large share of world manufacturing output, but at the price of a continuing employment decline in the manufacturing sector. Over the next several years in the world arena, employment in U.S.-based manufacturing is sure to decline. The question is what form the decline will take. Will it be a phased decline to which our work force can adapt?

A major implication of our analysis is that even under an equal and fairly administered system of international trade, the United States will do poorly in international competition. The differential in labor costs and the declining U.S. productivity advantage, coupled with the high cost of capital in the United States, means that the United States is disadvantaged in manufacturing over the long term, even if there was fair trade.

Potential conflict still exists between American companies that succeed in the world marketplace, by producing outside the United States and the interests of American workers seeking jobs. This may, however, be of only short-run significance. In today's very competitive world economy, with many American companies at substantial cost disadvantage, it is understandable that these companies should attempt to retain control of their market share (i.e., of the final customer) by cutting costs however possible, including locating manufacturing facilities abroad or subcontracting to foreign manufacturers. In the short term, this will cost jobs in the United States.

But in the longer term, technological developments may make it possible to integrate production once again in the United States. Highly sophisticated American-based plants should be able to hold their own in cost-effectiveness against competitors from abroad, in part because new technology is not only likely to be labor saving, but likely to produce new and better quality products. In the long term, this result will return to our country many manufacturing jobs and the potential for high-wage employment due to high capital per worker ratios in the new facilities.

Before this happy outcome, however, there are a few more years of difficulty in the international marketplace for America-based manufacturers. These difficulties, even if short term, require some response.

The challenge of American business and labor is clearly defined. Can we provide such improvements in productivity and quality that a higher degree of competitiveness can be achieved and a larger portion of the manufacturing market and employment retained? Do American labor and business have the desire and the resourcefulness to make the economic and institutional adjustments required to move to a less protected, more competitive position?

13

Enhancing Competitiveness: The Contribution of Employee Relations

D. Quinn Mills
Malcolm Lovell, Jr.

The challenge to the U.S. manufacturing community is to become more competitive. To do so, manufacturers must respond to the cost and quality challenges from both developed and developing nations with long-term efforts to regain our preeminence as efficient producers of the world's manufactured products. Various forms of protectionism must be abandoned as a long-term solution to the problems of our manufacturing establishment, and at the same time competitiveness must be elevated to a greater and more visible level as a factor in our economic and social policy agenda.

Historically, employment concerns have been one of the most significant forces driving national economic policy. It was the unemployment crisis of the 1930s that gave us Keynes's prescription for government spending as a core element of modern economic policy. Today's crisis is less severe than the 1930s, but the economy of that decade provides a harbinger of social and political upheaval if today's crisis is ignored or not effectively addressed.

In 1982, 22 percent of the U.S. work force, or some 26.5 million people, experienced some involuntary unemployment.[1] One result has been pervasive concern in our population about unemployment. If this and related uncertainties faced by working people are not recognized and diminished, U.S. economic policy will more likely be driven by these fears than managed in a way that enhances our competitiveness. It is within this context of an unsettled work force viewing an uncertain future, threatened managements

D. Quinn Mills is Albert J. Weatherhead Professor of Business Administration at Harvard Business School. Malcolm R. Lovell, Jr., is a visiting scholar at the Brookings Institution. The authors gratefully acknowledge the contributions of Rae Ann O'Brien, research associate, Harvard Business School.

455

facing continued loss of markets at home and abroad, and a government still seeking its proper role, that efforts to increase our competitive stance must be designed, articulated, and marketed to a broad range of constituencies. The challenge is great but there is reason for optimism.

In the unionized sector of our manufacturing industries, collective bargaining and emerging relationships based on joint problem solving may form a different system that addresses both the traditional needs of the parties and the long-term viability of the firm in the international market. The most promising development is management involving workers and unions more intimately in their long-term planning process and, in turn, unions and their members accepting the continued competitiveness of the company as being of greater importance than substantial increases in wages, benefits, and expensive work practices. It is possible that unions can win greater acceptance by management, the workers, and the public by sharing responsibility with management for the success (or failure) of America's industrial enterprise.

In the nonunion sector, which in the absence of collective bargaining agreements has historically had wider latitude than the union sector, experiments are being made in the reorganization of work. Enhanced competitiveness may be a critical by-product of these experiments at the firm level.

Efforts to regain competitiveness will ultimately succeed or fail on how well the union and nonunion sectors address the question of employment security for the work force and management. Without corporate concern for employment security, the commitment and imagination of those trying to design, produce, and manage products will necessarily be diverted and lost.

Government plays a role in helping to ameliorate the conflicts between the parties, socializing the cost of reemploying the displaced worker, and facilitating the achievement of those objectives shared by both management and labor that are in the public interest.

LABOR AND MANAGEMENT

Although only 20 percent of the total U.S. work force is unionized, levels of union representation in the manufacturing sector have historically been much higher—now approximately 40 percent. With the prevalence of union security provisions in most heavy manufacturing industries, this 40 percent figure also indicates the extent of collective bargaining agreements. Hence, decisions affecting the nature and size of U.S. manufacturing industries depend to a large extent on how management and labor fashion their relationship to either encourage or thwart efforts to be competitive. Designing effective solutions and, more critically, effectively implementing them, require the existence of strong partners capable of educating their constituencies with conviction.

But the results of bargaining between management and labor can be counterproductive if each side defines its objectives narrowly. If management sees its responsibility only as achieving profitability and if the goals of the workers are limited to improved wages, benefits, and working conditions, power relationships will continue to govern the outcome of the collective bargaining process. This has been the historic pattern. In the past, when U.S. manufacturers could sell their products at a favorable price, and competition was limited in most instances to American companies, the U.S. worker could, by the threat of withholding his labor, achieve substantial gains at the bargaining table. More recently, with the advent of greater foreign competition, companies have been able to wrest from unions concessions unimaginable in post-World War II bargaining.

A more cooperative approach requires a redefinition of the objectives of both management and labor. Traditional collective bargaining has failed to meet the needs of either management or labor now that competition has been internationalized. In a broad sense, in the past there was little difference to labor as an institution which company failed and which succeeded as long as they both were domestic producers. If there were to be 800,000 people working in the auto industry, their distribution among the various American companies was of little consequence to top union leadership. That has now changed. Labor, unlike capital, does not move easily across national boundaries. It now matters a great deal to union leadership at all levels whether an American producer succeeds or fails; each job lost to a foreign producer means one fewer job in that industry for an American worker.

Traditional collective bargaining in our large manufacturing industries has been generally sensitive to the economic health of an entire industry rather than to that of a particular company. Indeed, it has been the American labor movement's position that wages should not be a competitive factor among firms within an industry. Management, too, has readily agreed to collective bargaining formulas based on an industry's ability to pay. This did not imply acceptance of labor's contention that the cost of labor should not be a factor in competition. But management feared whipsawing—a union's achieving a concession from one company and then demanding it from all in the industry.

Just as organized labor did not want to have the wages and benefits of its members a factor in competition, companies as a matter of principle did not want to share the management function with unions. Concession in wages and benefits could be passed on, but concessions regarding who was running the shop, once made, were forever lost. Adversarial relationships, then, supported management's right to manage an industry, and pattern bargaining made it possible to "buy off" the union without seriously threatening any company's competitive position.

For the last fifty years, unions, with limited exceptions, have been equally reluctant to shift their emphasis to a larger participatory role involving areas traditionally within management's domain. The AFL was built on "bread and butter unionism": getting more of the economic pie for its members, not enlarging it. The typical role of much of American labor is to be an adversary to management. Unlike Japanese unions, American labor, with some notable exceptions, has sought not so much an accommodation with management as economic victories.

Just as American unions have had a long history as opponents of corporate management, business leaders have played at least an equal role in keeping the relationship adversarial. Most chief executives today are reasonably confident they could achieve greater competitiveness for their companies without a union. Management's opposition to unions has become more subtle but has been and remains effective. Unions once represented 37 percent of the total labor force—now it is down to 20 percent. Today, even in real terms, the number of union members has declined. Unions are losing more representation elections before the National Labor Relations Board than ever before, and decertification petitions are more frequently successful.

The law has been both a friend and foe of the labor movement. The AFL-CIO in recent years has vigorously maintained that U.S. labor law today is flawed in helping unions carry out the mandate of the 1935 Wagner Act. The Wagner Act preamble stated:

> It is hereby declared to be the policy of the United States to eliminate causes of certain substantial obstructions to the free flow of commerce and to mitigate and eliminate these obstructions when they have occurred by encouraging the practice and procedure of collective bargaining and by protecting the exercise by workers of full freedom of association, self-organization, and designation of representatives of their own choosing, for the purpose of negotiating the terms and conditions of their employment or other mutual aid or protection.

The heart of the act, Section 7, breathed life into the general statement of public policy embodied in the preamble by stating:

> Employees shall have the right to self-organization, to form, join, or assist labor organizations, to bargain collectively through representatives of their own choosing, and to engage in concerted activities, for the purpose of collective bargaining or other mutual aid or protection.

The Taft-Hartley Amendments to the Wagner Act, passed in 1947, fundamentally changed the policy enunciated in the Wagner Act. Section 7 was amended to provide that employees have the right to *refrain* from such activities and gave a list of union unfair labor practices with which to enforce the new language. As a result of Taft-Hartley, management's opposition to unions gained enhanced legitimacy through the employer free speech provisions of Section 8. Whereas the Wagner Act had extended to unions a means to win recognition in exchange for labor militancy, the Taft-Hartley Amendments took back a degree of this recognition. Thus, the never-resolved dispute over union recognition was institutionalized in American law.

The law provides that employees have the right to bargain collectively with management over the terms and conditions of employment, and these have increasingly become the boundaries of their interaction. Grievance procedures culminating in arbitration have evolved from informal alternatives to court litigation to proceedings typically supported by such legalistic trappings as opening and closing arguments and the submission of briefs. Both the time and the cost of arbitration have increased dramatically, thwarting the original purposes of the system: to make the process accessible to those directly involved—the company's labor relations advocate, the union representative and the grievant. Contracts have lengthened and emphasis has concentrated on the adherence to explicit rules and the implicit boundaries of past practice. During the life of the agreement, the major dynamic between labor and management has been the enforcement of individual rights under the contract's provisions. Concern for productivity and the competitiveness of the enterprise has been secondary.

In 1978, organized labor launched a major campaign of "labor law reform" to rectify what it considered an imbalance in the power between management and labor. At the height of the debate, large sections of the business community combined with the newly created National Association of Manufacturers' Council on a Union-Free Environment to oppose vigorously labor's campaign. Labor read this as a sign that even modest proposals would be contested. In an advertisement in the *Wall Street Journal* on 4 May 1978, then AFL-CIO president George Meany asked of the business community: "Do you want to destroy American trade unionism? Do you believe that labor-management cooperation in the workplace is improved through such attacks on the labor movement and its leaders?"

This attempt by the labor movement and the surprisingly vigorous and successful effort by the entire business community to defeat it intensified the adversarial relationship of the parties. Union leaders still carry the scars of the labor law reform battle. One can argue whether the diminished role of the union movement in the workplace is caused by inadequacies in the law, greater corporate sensitivity to the needs of its work force, a public image of unions tarnished by strikes in both the private and public sector, or by a concerted determination by well-financed managements to achieve a "union-free environment." It can not be disputed that bitterness persists which makes the reevaluation of roles and objectives more difficult and saps the desire to work toward a new and more cooperative relationship.

It is only recently apparent that the unions' success in wage and rules bargaining in some industries has rebounded to the disadvantage of many members. Instead of high living standards, many workers have reaped the unemployment line. This was not expected. Economic theory suggests that rising wages should have induced companies to make capital investments, thereby increasing productivity and justifying higher wages. Economic growth in the society as a whole would support higher employment via increased production volume. However, short-sightedness, noncompetitiveness, and inadequate capital investment left us with an engine for wage increases (collective bargaining) without offsetting productivity advances.

By 1982 the average wage increase negotiated by American unions came to 3.8 percent (down from 7.9 percent in 1981 and 7.1 percent in 1980).[2] In no postwar recessionary period had unions been forced to make concessions of the magnitude they were obliged to make in 1982 and 1983. These concessions often did not represent either an increase or diminution in the adversarial relations between the parties, but reflected changes in the economics of our manufacturing industries caused by foreign competition and the effects of deregulation on several industries. Unions made concessions, because if they did not, jobs would be lost that would not, in most instances, be taken up by other union members.

Thus the adversarial approach to collective bargaining failed to produce for workers when they needed it most. And it could be that the worst is yet to come—that in some instances the concessions may prove inadequate to make the company fully competitive, so that the job security workers thought they were buying by their concessions may be illusionary.

From management's point of view, reductions in the rate of wage increase not associated with worker dedication to continued cost and quality improvements frequently represented hollow victories. It is becoming increasingly clear to the managements of many companies that their ability to compete against the best of our foreign competition requires more than concessionary bargaining. It requires a willingness by all people at all levels of the organization to sacrifice short-term gain for the long-term economic health of the enterprise and a commitment to quality and productivity that is best volunteered rather than unilaterally demanded.

Given the bitter history of labor-management relations and the growing recognition that competitive companies of the future must have competitive labor costs and the enthusiastic cooperation of workers if they are to prosper, companies now face a hard choice. The ramifications of this will have major implications for American society. The choice for management is whether to (1) accept the union as an institution and to encourage the union to play a greater role in corporate governance; or (2) take heart from recent corporate successes in operating in a "union-free environment" and seek over time to end union influence in its establishments, utilizing the most innovative human resources management techniques laced with the fullest complement of anti-union maneuvers permitted by law.

Where unions are strong, as in the auto, steel, and communications industries, the second choice is not a real option for management. Indeed, companies in these sectors have already taken initial steps to reconstruct their relationship not only with their unions, but through them with the workers themselves. For example, in the auto industry, a five-cents-an-hour jointly administered fund was established to retrain workers, supplemental employment benefits were reinstated and extended when expired, and the fund was strengthened through additional contributions by both employees and the companies. At both Ford and GM, management agreed to a two-year moratorium on layoffs due to outsourcing. In the trucking industry, subject to increased domestic nonunion competition resulting from deregulation rather than increased foreign competition, the Master Freight Agreement provided for no wage increase in exchange for additional employer contributions to the pension, health, and welfare funds, and extended recall rights for laid-off workers. In electrical equipment, General Electric and Westinghouse agreed to a notification provision in cases of work transfer, plant closure, or the introduction of automated equipment; rate retention for certain classes of workers affected by transfer, subcontracting or new technology; and increased income security provisions for laid-off workers.[3] Long-term competitiveness will depend on such changes in the collective bargaining process, which encompass not only the division of the economic pie, but its continued existence as well.

MANAGING FOR COMPETITIVENESS IN THE UNIONIZED SECTOR

Because the obstacles to labor-management cooperation are so great—historically and ideologically based as they are—burgeoning efforts to forge a new relationship are impressive indeed. Historically, labor and management have opened discussions on subjects outside the confines of collective bargaining only in response to upheavals in their common environment such as war, depression, inflationary spirals, or the advent of technological change. The degree of cooperation has been in direct proportion to the perceived threat. None of these periods of cooperation, however, has fundamentally changed or diminished the curious balance of conflict and mutuality of interest that characterizes U.S. industrial relations.

Now the parties are faced with an external threat of the type that has previously fostered cooperation. This time, however, the threat is long term—a decline in the U.S. competitive position worldwide propelled by long-term foreign competitive advantage and international populations trends that will not be remedied by cyclical economic upturns. There will be no reprieve to allow the parties to return to their old adversarial ways.

The traditional arrangement between management and labor, as formulated in the early 1950s by the president of General Motors, called for the union to provide discipline and productivity from its members (see table 13-1). In exchange, management provided advances for union membership by way of increasingly favorable terms and conditions of employment. These material gains were also the major tools in unions' attempts to attract and maintain membership. Now, a new arrangement is emerging: the company requires not only discipline and productivity from the union but responsibility for quality and a commitment to the competitiveness of the firm as well. For its part, the union needs from the company an increased measure of employment security for its membership and a new leadership role based not on public victories founded on material gains but on consultation, information exchange, and notification mechanisms (see table 13-2).

Table 13-1
Fundamental Arrangements between Management and Labor

	Company Requires from Union	Union Requires from Company
Outdated Deal	1. Discipline 2. Productivity	1. Advances for membership 2. Public victories for leadership
Competitiveness Solution	1. Commitment to competitiveness 2. Responsibility for quality	1. Employment security for the membership 2. Acceptance of broader leadership role for the union

Table 13-2
Practices for Competitiveness

	Common Current Practice	*Requirements of a Competitiveness Solution*
UNIONS	— Uniform treatment of companies	— Individualized treatment by unions of companies in wages or working conditions or both
	— No identification with a particular company	— Concern for competitiveness of a particular company
	— Rule-making and enforcement	— Flexibility in order to provide greater efficiency
COMPANIES	— Interaction with rank and file left to union	— Better relations with the rank and file (a union can't deliver employee commitment)
	— Unilateral operational decisions	— Participative operational decisions
	— Protection of management prerogatives	— Delegation of responsibility and sharing information
	— Emphasis on income security	— Emphasis on employment security
	— Employment fluctuations used to control labor costs as business conditions and/or performance alters	— Compensation system possesses variability as business conditions and/or performance alters (i.e., competitiveness requires a greater flexibility in compensation to reduce employment variability)
GOVERNMENT	— Programs for the disadvantaged	
	— Programs for the cyclically unemployed that emphasize income support	
		— Programs for the displaced when objective is reemployment, not only income support

In practice, this means the overriding concerns of both parties will be their joint interest in the economic viability of the firm. Specifically, unions have traditionally sought to treat companies within an industry uniformly to prevent wages from becoming a competitive weapon between companies. With the industry fully organized, if one company failed, another unionized company would replace it. Today, if a unionized company fails, a foreign competitor, which American unions cannot organize, is likely to replace it. Hence, bargaining to regain competitiveness will mean a change from the present lack of identification with a particular firm to an understanding that employment security and the union's governance role are tied directly to individual firms. Unions may at first feel they have lost power in representing their members. In the long run, however, they will gain broader but more diffuse power to influence the most crucial variable of the relationship between management and labor: the survival of the firm and, consequently, the jobs of union members.

Management, for its part, will have to take the initiative to foster the new arrangement and begin to encourage better relationships with the work force and its unionized members. To establish employee relations systems to regain competitiveness, management will have to win the commitment to the enterprise's goals directly through its own actions. In part, this commitment can be won through a system of participative decision making to replace the traditional, unilateral method. Although this may appear to erode managerial power founded on the right to command, it offers a greater source of power: that borne of more informed decision making by including those who are involved in the production process itself.

For a century, protecting management prerogatives has been a primary corporate goal in its dealings with organized labor. The real question for the future is how management carries out *its* responsibilities; how imaginatively it exercises authority. In the process of protecting their authority in the past, managements have frequently failed to share information with the work force when such sharing might have enhanced the production processes. The more workers know about the reasons for their efforts, the more likely they are to work in a way that achieves those goals. The sharing of information and the delegation, not of the ultimate responsibility for decision making, but of broader discretion in the execution of the work tasks themselves, would better serve the human relations and consequently the profit concerns of the enterprise.

There are a few publicized success stories about changes in the collective bargaining system. General Motors at its new facility in Livonia, Ford through its Employee Involvement program, Procter & Gamble and Cummins Engine in their older plants have all made efforts that closely resemble the new interdependent system described. Others have been reluctant to make workplace innovations public and perhaps for compelling reasons. One observer has suggested that workplace innovations in human resources have offered such competitive advantages to companies that they are like trade secrets.[4] Other experiments, large and small, are proliferating and have been summarized elsewhere.[5] All of these experiments require a great deal of change from both management and labor. Both must move beyond measuring victories and losses only in terms of dollar-and-cent outcomes on contract terms, and management must invite the union and its members into an area it has historically protected.

Some unions will no doubt be threatened by the new areas of expertise required to function in this larger role. They are aware both of the difficulties facing them from their members' distrust of management and of the philosophic differences between the parties. Business unionism may now require different understandings not only of negotiations and grievance procedures but of the competitive stance of the firm and the competitive environment within which it provides jobs for union members.

Such changes will not be easy. Even when the parties have agreed that economic realities require a new approach, their respective constituencies are sometimes not ready to support them. In April 1983, for example, union members at Ford locations that were selected for an experimental lifetime employment plan failed to ratify the plan in a three-to-one vote. They reportedly felt it would overturn strict seniority provisions. A local president, describing his failed attempt to sell the package, commented, "I couldn't get people's attention to explain the issues. . . . I don't know how you ever get across to the common worker the changes which are happening in our industry."[6] Union leaders engaged in consultation, discussion, and agreement on competitiveness issues will continue to encounter difficulties, not the least of which will be selling these activities as legitimate to rank and file members, who may continue to demand from unions what the unions appeared to have promised—an ever-increasing standard of living, regardless of the long-term consequences.

Similarly, in steel, $3 billion in wage concessions was given in exchange for guarantees that savings would be invested here in the United States. When the U.S. Steel Company began negotiating a deal to import semifinished British steel rather than modernize its Fairless Hills plant in Pennsylvania, the Steelworkers spent over $350,000 on a critical ad campaign aimed to enlist the support of shareholders.[7] Such examples illustrate the distrust and suspicion that still exist on both sides and suggest that the transition for these industries will be difficult with no guarantee of success.

MANAGING FOR COMPETITIVENESS IN THE NONUNION SECTOR

Some executives in the manufacturing sector enjoy the secret dream of all managers—the freedom to manage in a union-free environment. In the unionized sector, labor-management relations to achieve competitiveness will involve trading off monetary gains for increased employment security and creating new areas of discussion traditionally outside the purview of collective bargaining. In the nonunion sector, employee relations managers have experimented with the reorganization of work. They have drawn on the work force's creative capacities, realizing both intrinsic value and the by-product of increased profits.

Although experiments with the reorganization of work cannot yet be described as extensive, their results are impressive. Companies have reported 15-20 percent increases in productivity when new, thoughtful work systems have been implemented. New work organizations are now in place in approximately 100 nonunion companies in the United States, most of which are small, with fewer than 300 employees.

These new forms of work organization (table 13-3) do not entail new institutional relationships as in the unionized sector, but instead a change in management style involving the delegation of more discretion to employees in the execution of their tasks. Narrowly specialized tasks are replaced by broadly defined ones; employees rotate among jobs instead of remaining confined to increasingly specialized, technical jobs; and teams with flexible assignments cover work projects rather than adhering rigidly to a formula set forth by rule book or overtime provisions. Compensation is by skills mastered, not job content; evaluation and supervision are conducted by the employee or by peers. A concern for the learning and growth needs of employees replaces the lack of career development frequently characteristic of traditional work systems. Although individuals' needs are not subsumed by the good of the group, the basic work unit is the team. Thus both individual recognition and group identification are present. And it is the team that runs its part of the business, based on the increased information available through the delegation of decision making and sharing of information.

Some who have studied work reorganization suggest that goodwill can, and should, replace money in the workplace. And it is upon this notion that efforts to reorganize work sometimes meet employee resistance and skepti-

Table 13-3
Alternative Work Systems

Traditional	High Commitment
Narrowly defined jobs	Broadly defined tasks
Specialization of employees	Rotation of employees through jobs
Pay by specific job content	Pay by skills mastered
Evaluation by direct supervision	Evaluation by peers
Work closely supervised	Self- or peer supervision
Assignment of overtime or transfer by rule book	Team assigns to cover vacancies
No career development	Concern for learning and growth
Supervisor deals primarily with employees as individuals	Supervisor deals with employees in a team
Employee is ignorant about the business	Team runs its part of the business

cism. Productivity issues (both quality and quantity) are sometimes obscured in the belief that work reorganization is the right thing to do to make the workplace more humane. Profit considerations are often left untouched. It is not clear that a happy worker is necessarily the most productive one. There are strong indications, however, that an *involved* worker is more productive and that the curious mixture of increased contentment and stress fostered by high commitment work systems enhances both product quality and quantity. These systems provide an opportunity to moderate short-run dislocations and, over the long term, to contribute to the economic viability of the firm.

Resistance to changes in work organization may come from both workers and management. Employees may wonder if the payoffs (both monetary and intrinsic) are worth the investment required to adapt to the new style. Managers may recoil from the new demands placed upon them. Those whose traditional accountability has been to the stockholders and investors and whose performance has been measured in large part by a showing on the quarterly earnings report may face difficulties. High commitment work systems will require a longer-range view of the corporate picture. Will stockholders and capital markets stay the course? Competing interests may be brought into sharp conflict, raising tough governance issues. As Kenneth Andrews has observed: "The rights of shareholders in large companies are as confused as their responsibilities. The managers of a large corporation sometimes think of it as their business, in which others, however much affected, should not meddle. Who owns the large, publicly held corporation is almost as hard to answer as who owns Harvard University; who runs either one is easier to answer."[8]

Some areas of mutual interest shared by management and labor have already been discussed. Another is the firm's viability in the long run, which may be at odds with investors' quarterly earnings agendas. Investors are consumed with the question of the distribution of wealth. Managers' and workers' livelihoods depend on wealth and job creation from investors' capital from which investors then derive their benefit.

Nowhere are the interests of management and labor so closely aligned and so at odds with that of investors than over the issue of employment security. No manager likes laying people off, and companies would prefer to be seen as offering continuous employment to competent members of their work force. And so, even without the restrictive legislation of Europe or the cultural values of Japan, some American companies have voluntarily adopted a range of strategies through which they assume responsibility for employment, or on a lesser scale, attempt to diminish the impact of unemployment. Among the first group are companies such as IBM, Hewlett-Packard, Upjohn, and the Norfolk Southern Corporation, which have successfully implemented policies demonstrating corporate interest in the long-term job security of the work force. Other companies have been deeply committed to employment security but have had to abandon that position, at least in part, because of foreign competition. In January 1983, for example, labor cutbacks began at Kodak that were "unparalleled in its 103-year history."[9] According to a *New York Times* report, Wall Street analysts favored the action.[10] In a pattern that has become more common, by October 1983, Kodak announced the need for further cutbacks—this time affecting white collar workers.[11]

Other companies lay people off but support public social programs and have their own adjustment programs, although they do not assume the responsibility of employment continuity to the same degree as the first group listed. Still others do not demonstrate support for any programs but instead lay people off when it appears to be required by business necessity or to offer a strategic business advantage. Atari, for example, recently laid off 2,000 employees at its Sunnyvale, California, location and shifted production to Hong Kong and Taiwan.[12]

HUMAN RESOURCES, COMPETITIVENESS, AND PUBLIC POLICY

Changes in public policy regarding workers adversely affected by competitive forces are necessary to diminish pressure for protectionist policies and to enhance cooperative labor-management efforts and work reorganization. Private and public efforts to deal sensitively with the problems of the displaced worker will temper demands for constraints on free trade. Although it would be naive to believe that even the most sophisticated program to help people relocate to new jobs would calm all concerns over the diminishing size of our manufacturing work force, without such efforts the pace of our move to a more competitive economy will be significantly slowed.

The costs associated with our declining competitiveness are substantial and fall unevenly across sectors and segments of our population. The costs of unemployment include the value of federal, state, and local payments and services as well as the cost of administering these and related categorical assistance programs. Assuming that the costs of job loss are symmetrical to those of job creation, a calculation of the cost of unemployment would also take as a factor the value added to the economy by the creation of a job. One set of calculations suggest, "the value . . . associated with each new job created in the private sector of our economy" averages $52,000.[13] Because of the structure of our unemployment insurance program, which is based on an experience rating for employers, the costs of the program fall most heavily on that sector of the economy that is least able to pay— manufacturing. Other sectors and industries such as insurance and banking are, to a degree, insulated from the direct costs incurred by our failing manufacturing sector. Despite the theoretical soundness of charging those who lay off employees for the adverse social consequences, the burden of this policy has become too heavy for an already failing manufacturing sector.

Unemployment figures, although frightening, show us only part of the problem. It is often assumed that the unemployed are adequately provided for by a network of income support programs. This is increasingly untrue. A report issued in September 1983 by the Brookings Institution compared the percentage of unemployed covered during recessions since World War II and concluded that the percentage of those covered by regular, extended, or supplemental unemployment insurance was lower in 1982 than any previous recession.[14] In 1975, 78 percent of unemployed were covered; in 1982, 45 percent. The Brookings study also found that in 1982 dollars, federal, state, and local governments paid less in unemployment benefits in 1982 when 10 million were unemployed than in 1978 when 7.6 million were jobless.[15] Twenty-two to 24 percent of all wage earners were unemployed at least once during the past year.[16] The average length of unemployment was nineteen weeks.[17] The private costs of joblessness are greater than official unemployment figures measure, and the public remedies have addressed only part of a larger problem.

Youth (ages 16-24) unemployment is not a new problem but has intensified over the past decade from an annual average rate of 11.9 percent in 1974 to 17.2 percent in 1983.[18] Youth unemployment deserves our special attention, since lack of opportunities to enter the labor force means that some youths will never get a first chance and may face a life of disadvantage as a consequence. Our young people should feel they have a stake in our system and a future within it.

The rate of unemployment, therefore, does not measure the extent of today's social and political problem. The underlying issue that will eventually shape economic and public policy is the insecurity and uncertainty that the rapidly changing labor market and high levels of unemployment evoke in the labor force. Continuing plant closings and layoffs caused by foreign competition, although not so severe in aggregate now that the recession is ending, nevertheless contribute to a high level of anxiety among all employees. Rapid technological change adds a further dimension, causing people to worry that they will be replaced by a robot or by a younger person with different skills. Middle-aged and older workers fear they will lose jobs or be forced into early retirement. As the work force ages, a larger proportion of workers becomes subject to these fears.

To reduce these uncertainties, Congress and state legislatures are already debating a variety of proposed new regulations on business. Some would limit a firm's discretion in adjusting to its economic environment through, for example, plant closing legislation. Two states—Maine and Wisconsin— have already passed plant closing legislation, which requires companies to give sixty days' notice of intended closings. Maine's law, passed in 1971 and strengthened in 1981, also has a statutory provision for severance pay— one week for affected workers with three years' seniority.[19] Federal proposals for plant closure notification surface periodically and one bill is now pending. William Winpinsinger, president of the International Association of Machinists, has proposed a system to arbitrate plant closings: "If the panel found that a firm could profitably continue operations, it could recommend a federal court injunction to prevent the shutdown."[20] Other proposals, such as the video display unit (VDU) bills, would put restrictions on new technology, or would require companies' products to contain a certain percentage of U.S.-made components.

Protectionist measures are increasingly associated with these proposals to regulate company actions. Major interest groups are abandoning their commitments to free trade and lobbying Congress to do likewise. The U.S. government today gives lip service to trade liberalization but may be forced, step by step, into an increasing web of protectionism unless other ways to counter foreign competition are devised. In autos, domestic content legislation and reciprocal action against foreign trade practices increasingly draw serious public debate. At the beginning of April 1983, President Reagan, in an attempt to aid Harley-Davidson, dramatically increased the tariffs on large motorcycles. Orderly market agreements for nonrubber footwear and televisions and "buy America statutes" promulgated by the states are additional examples. Other mechanisms have been added to the repertoire of protectionist measures. The trigger-price mechanism (instituted in 1978 for steel and suspended in 1982), "voluntary" quotas in autos, orderly market agreements (voluntary export quotas) in footwear, the Multifiber Arrangement in clothing and textiles, and various antidumping provisions have, for longer or shorter periods of time, provided trade protection. In steel, tariffs, and now four years quotas, have thrown a protectionist shield around our declining steel industry. These measures exist despite indications that the public maintains a strong belief in the value of free trade, not so much as a theoretical matter, but rather, to have continued access to lower-cost, high quality imported goods.

Unionized American workers no longer see their own interests furthered by a liberal trade policy. For the first ninety years of its existence, the American labor movement supported free trade. In the 1920s and 1930s, and in the Smoot-Hawley legislation, manufacturers pushed for protectionism while organized labor supported free trade and the resulting access to cheap foreign goods. But a drive toward protectionism appeared from those sectors of the labor movement subject to increasing foreign competition. This support began to grow in the 1970s as jobs in other sectors were lost to foreign encroachment. By the late 1970s, the AFL-CIO reversed its position, providing a ready constituency for each protectionist measure. To the extent that labor is unable to protect the interests of its members through collective bargaining, political solutions will be sought. In the present context this will mean increased pressure for protectionist measures, more generous entitlement programs for worker protection, an "industrial policy," and a larger government role in the private sector.

Industry too, when faced with a declining inability to compete internationally, may cling even more closely to its historic protectionist approaches, looking to the government for loan guarantees, subsidies, and bailouts.

The government's major role outside macroeconomic policy may be to help eliminate or reduce the severity of the constraints that discourage or interfere with achieving greater competitiveness. In the human resources area, the major constraints, of course, are the threats to job security in industries that must move to new technology and make use of the lowest-cost and highest-quality components, whether made in this country or elsewhere. Government programs to help the displaced worker find new employment are a vital part of an overall effort to deal with the job security question which, if ignored, will serve to increase pressure for protectionist measures to preserve jobs.

FACILITATING ADJUSTMENT TO CHANGE

It is difficult to know the exact number of workers currently displaced or to predict how many will be displaced in the next decade. Employment and unemployment figures do not reveal all such displacements. Gross unemployment figures, for example, may not detail displacements by company, area, or skill, or when laid-off people are replaced by an equal number of workers in other locations, industries, or types of jobs.

The Congressional Budget Office's estimates of displaced workers range from 200,000 to 2,000,000 a year, depending on the definition of displacement. Marc Bendick of The Urban Institute, using an extremely limited definition, estimates only 90,000 displacements annually. Kenneth McLennan estimates that even in a year of serious recession, 80 percent of job losers can expect eventually to return to their same employer.[21] In 1982, when approximately four million people lost their jobs without recall, this calculation would yield a displaced worker pool of over 800,000. Other economists predicting rapid and extensive technological change and a more rapid reduction in our manufacturing work force produce numbers approaching those at the high end of the Congressional Budget Office's forecasts.

Even using the more optimistic forecasts of overall unemployment for 1984 through 1990, an estimate of 500,000 displaced workers per year is probably reasonable. Such a figure, though small as a percentage of the work force, is sufficiently large to build support for constraints on the competitive process. The number is also small enough so that an intelligently conceived employment and training program geared to the needs of the displaced or dislocated workers could improve prospects for eventual reemployment at a relatively modest cost.

Currently, there are four programs that serve the nation's unemployed but fall short of meeting the needs of the displaced workers: the Trade Adjustment Assistance Act, the Unemployment Insurance program, the Employment Service, and the Job Training Partnership Act.

In 1962 President Kennedy proposed the Trade Adjustment Assistance Act (TAA) in return for which the AFL-CIO supported his free trade policies. This program, which certified no workers as eligible for benefits in its first seven years, almost matched in the last nine months of 1975 the total number approved as eligible since the program's inauguration. From 1979 through the end of 1982, 974,997 workers received cash benefits under the program, totaling over $3.3 billion.[22] Although program participants were eligible for training and other services, almost all of the appropriated funds were used for income support. Ironically, the program, by supporting workers for substantial periods of time, discouraged many unemployed people from seeking new work. Indeed, over 60 percent of those drawing trade adjustment assistance benefits did return to their former employer.

The program today has been reduced in size and its eligibility significantly tightened. Although the 1984 Reagan budget calls for $29 million for training costs to be available under the act, the program remains basically an income transfer exercise, providing little incentive or assistance to the worker who will have to find new employment at another company, in a different industry, or in another area.

A fundamental weakness of the TAA Act, in addition to its emphasis on income support rather than a comprehensive effort on reemployment, is its narrow definition of eligibility. An individual permanently displaced from a job by the introduction of new technology so that an employer may become more competitive would not be eligible for trade adjustment assistance unless the firm had already been injured by foreign competition. The program thus provides a means of reacting to, not anticipating and meeting, competitive challenges. This concept is too limited to meet the needs of American workers in almost all walks of life whose jobs may be lost so that their companies can become more competitive and can survive economically.

Other income support, employment, and training programs are just as unsuccessful as the Trade Adjustment Assistance Act is in helping displaced workers find new employment. The Unemployment Insurance program has been designed basically as a mechanism to serve the cyclically unemployed, those who will normally return either to their former job or to a similar one with another company. The job search requirement is generally weak and not designed to aid or encourage an unemployed worker to develop and follow a thoughtful relocation effort. The addition of the Extended Benefits Program in those states with unusually high unemployment, and the Federal Supplemental Compensation program to provide benefits beyond those to which unemployed people would normally be entitled, are at best stop-gap income support efforts and at worst an encouragement to delay seeking reemployment.

The Unemployment Insurance program, developed in the 1930s, has served the country well over the last fifty years, providing temporary support to the cyclically unemployed. An additional new strategy is needed, however, to augment the U.I. system, providing not only a safety net but a ladder by which an unemployed person can climb to new employment.

Recognizing the need to do more for the unemployed than provide income support, the Reagan administration in 1983 recommended to Congress that the unemployment compensation law be amended to encourage states to allow monies in their unemployment insurance trust funds to be used for other than benefit payments. Partly because of the substantial deficits in many of the state trust funds, and partly because of management and labor reluctance to tamper with the unemployment compensation system's primary emphasis on income support, the administration's proposal has aroused little enthusiasm.

A better performance from our publicly funded job placement program should also be expected. The Public Employment Service, created in 1933, is a federal-state system of local employment offices that helps workers obtain employment and helps employers secure labor. Only 5 percent of recent hires in the labor market obtain employment through the service, with private agencies accounting for slightly more than that amount. The E.S. has been criticized throughout its history. Attempts to provide greater service to the disadvantaged without lessening attempts to place U.I. recipients and new entrants to the labor market have frequently resulted in reduced service to all. A recent evaluation of the Employment Service by SRI International found it to be only marginally effective, although the estimated increase in earnings of referred applicants was found to be greater than the estimated cost of providing a referral. The study cited an average $120 in earnings increases compared with the estimated cost of $80 per individual referred, with the placement of women accounting for the entire gain.

Critics suggest that Employment Service's major flaw is its responsibility to both the state and the federal governments. Others blame contradictory mandates from Congress and an entrenched bureaucracy for the mediocre performance of the agency. In any case, the United States spends over a billion dollars a year to maintain the Employment Service, and its rejuvenation should be a prime public policy target. Any program redesign should dovetail with other existing programs aimed at facilitating the match between workers and the labor market.

The Job Training Partnership Act, Title II, is the recent replacement for the Comprehensive Employment and Training Act (CETA). Title III provides funds to states to help displaced workers find employment. This title was inserted in the legislation more as an acknowledgment of a problem than as a comprehensive solution. It does not provide a timely link between the unemployment compensation system and whatever new services states may provide. Its funding level of $200 million and its funding source from general revenue create problems in developing a long-term strategy that would bring together in a comprehensive package income support, job search assistance, mobility allowances, and retraining for all who need these services. Basic to a more effective strategy is a program aimed at maximizing the transition to new employment rather than creating an unending income support system. Indeed, an effective system could reduce income support costs by speeding the process by which people find new employment.

Just as there are substantial costs to society from protectionist measures and policies that discourage competitiveness, there are costs that must be carefully evaluated in the prolonging of unemployment by programs that reduce the attractiveness of available employment. The policies we are recommending should, over time, reduce unemployment costs to employers and the public.

NEW PUBLIC POLICY INITIATIVES

Concern over worker displacement has been inadequate, and existing public efforts to cause the labor market to function more efficiently and humanely are insufficient. Helping the American displaced worker to adjust rapidly to market and technological change will be a continuing need in our society, and new public policy initiatives of adequate magnitude must be undertaken.

In formulating these policies, there are a number of factors to consider. Whatever initiatives are agreed upon should be supported by an independent tax base to ensure continuity. Existing income support and employment systems should be simultaneously strengthened and utilized. Ultimately, however, since the displaced workers themselves will bear major costs associated with their unemployment and have the most to gain from their own reemployment, they must be given individual choice in the basic decisions made in any adjustment assistance program. Because the incidence and timing of unemployment are difficult to predict—potentially affecting anyone, anywhere—a program to assist displaced workers must cover everyone who is involuntarily displaced. Programs should be attractive to participants but not so generous as to appear superior to a job reasonably suited to their skills, training, and experience. And perhaps most crucial, program design should encourage the earliest intervention possible to speed the reemployment process.

While it is clear that new displaced worker programs will not eliminate the fear of economic redundancy, they will be a constructive move toward a more competitive, less protectionist posture for our manufacturing sector. It is unlikely that any new adjustment assistance effort would win back labor support for a liberal trade policy. It would, however, strengthen the argument of those who wish to minimize restraints on open competition and demonstrate a sensitivity to the legitimate fears of American workers, who are currently expected to bear a disproportionate share of the economic burden of competitiveness.

SUMMARY

Improved competitiveness can be achieved through more imaginative and effective management of our human resources in both the union and nonunion sectors. The closer we can move toward a competitive stance, the higher our living standards, employment levels, and productivity will be. These three factors will be enhanced even if we move to a more competitive stance under conditions of low economic growth. The country is unlikely to accept a definition of economic competitiveness that does not acknowledge jobs as well as profits. It is also unlikely to acquiesce quietly to the erosion of our manufacturing base, which would make us only consumers of manufactured goods produced abroad by foreign companies.

Unionized companies in the manufacturing sector can achieve long-term competitiveness only with the support of their workers and the unions representing them. How companies address the difficult problems they face in this regard will be an important determinant of their success in the marketplace.

New economic and institutional relationships can encourage employees, unions, and managements to broaden the area of mutual problem solving to encompass the economic viability of the firm as well as the more traditional concerns. These new relationships will have to overcome substantial impediments. Not the least of these will be legalistic models imposed on a process that evolved from the participants' desire to maintain control over a private and voluntary rule-making relationship. A new construct will be required that lessens the reliance on the adversarial relationships fostered by the law, and promotes the needs of labor and management to consider the implications of their actions for competitiveness.

All of this will be more difficult now that the labor union as an institution appears more threatened than at any time since World War II. Organized labor has failed to convince most managements that it can help enlarge the size of the economic pie. More important, it has not convinced the American public that it represents more than a narrow, parochial interest. Now that its membership is declining, organized labor must get its message to the majority of workers if we are to retain a strong, vibrant union movement within a highly competitive manufacturing sector. Labor leaders will confront some difficult issues. They will have to recognize the importance of a competitive industrial sector and that protectionism in its many forms will work against the best interests of its members and the country in the long run. Further, unions will have to persuade a larger percentage of the work force that they can advance long-term worker interests as well as provide short-term economic advantages.

The stakes are high, not only for labor leaders, but for American democracy. Economic power over time will be abused if it is not tempered, and the American labor movement plays a pivotal role in assuring that the needs of workers, not just the needs of capital, are well represented. Without free trade unions to balance economic power, workers will look even more to the government to protect their interests. In the long term, the degree of management's freedom to act for all parties at interest in an enterprise—workers, stockholders, investors, and the public—with minimum government intervention depends on the existence of private institutions that bring into balance the interests of the society as a whole.

In the unorganized sector, management will continue to experiment with innovative human relations strategies to gain worker commitment to increased quality and efficiency, upon which employment security will be based. Employees in both organized and unorganized plants will have to respond with a sustained commitment to enhanced competitiveness.

The effects of noncompetitiveness pervade the entire work force, potentially affecting all members, who fear that years of work have failed to ensure both employment security and economic security for their families. Because of this, the more the displaced worker is recognized and provided for through both public and private initiatives, the less companies and unions will join together to support protectionist measures in an effort to protect jobs. Increased employment security in the work force will also lessen opposition to new technology, which may appear to threaten jobs, but which in the longer run is essential if we are to compete with the labor forces of foreign nations.

Government plays an important role. Public policy initiatives to ease the human impact of our transition to a more competitive economy will be necessary to augment company and individual efforts. They will also serve to diminish the pressures on the parties that may produce crisis reactions rather than creative solutions. Our present programs, primarily designed to address the problems of the short-term, cyclically unemployed, are ill-equipped to aid the displaced worker who must move to a new job, industry, location, or occupation. Wise and careful intervention on behalf of those who are and will be displaced is, after all, both a private and public responsibility from which all of us will eventually benefit if competitiveness is recaptured.

14
The Pursuit of Remedies

George C. Lodge
William C. Crum

The United States' ability to compete in the world economy has eroded significantly over the past two decades. While this decline has been most dramatic in the steel, automobile, consumer electronics, apparel, and machine tools industries, it is also reflected in various aggregate measures, such as America's falling share of world GNP and exports, deteriorating merchandise trade balance, reduced profitability and productivity growth in manufacturing firms, and widespread plant closings, bankruptcies, and unemployment. Moreover, our situation will probably worsen over the long run if left unattended, despite the 1984 cyclical upturn in domestic production.

These trends are alarming, especially since many of them have followed any mere return to post–World War II "normalcy" and have predated the dollar's high value over the past four years. Staying competitive is now more important than ever, given our increasing dependence on international trade. One-sixth of all domestic manufacturing jobs depend directly on exports, for example, and more than 70 percent of American goods are effectively exposed to foreign competition.[1] Other nations, however, especially Japan, continue to move into higher technology and value-added sectors, often by exploiting American inventions and upgrading their products within existing industries, partly in response to "voluntary" import quotas.

Our chief competition now comes less from traditional rivals than from five East Asian nations—Japan, Taiwan, South Korea, Hong Kong, and Singapore—which in 1983 together accounted for over half of our trade deficit and exported more merchandise to the United States than Western

George C. Lodge is professor of business administration at Harvard Business School. William C. Crum is an Associates Fellow at Harvard Business School. The authors wish to thank Professors Norman Berg, Harvey Brooks, and Bruce R. Scott for their help with this chapter.

479

Europe, Canada, OPEC, or the rest of the world. As Bruce Scott has demonstrated, these countries have achieved high investment and productivity growth rates by adopting national development strategies to mobilize resources and foster work incentives in response to long-term market opportunities. By contrast, our more pluralistic pursuit of wide-ranging diplomatic and domestic goals has handicapped our ability to compete effectively and made us resort to ad hoc trade restraints.

To date, the symptoms of our declining competitiveness have been partly masked by some fundamental demographic changes in American society. As the "baby boom" generation matured and more women worked during the 1970s, the increase in the employed portion of our total population helped keep real income per capita rising for a while, even after pretax weekly earnings began falling with the continued shift out of manufacturing into lower-paying trade and service jobs.[2]

If these trends continue, however, the United States will face prolonged high unemployment, a stagnant or declining real standard of living, and possible social unrest. Growth in some high technology and service industries may mitigate the adverse effects of our overall decline but will not offset them completely. Ultimately, even our national security could be undermined due to cuts in funding for defense or the loss of productive capability. Yet despite the high stakes involved, we seem unable, like Britain before us, to fully acknowledge our problems or to agree on why we are losing our competitive clout so quickly.

To regain our competitiveness, America must adopt its own national strategy. Such a strategy, however, must rest on a wide social consensus and fit with our institutional norms; it cannot be imposed effectively by fiat from on high. Many of our past policies have deliberately favored short-term consumption over long-term investment, while relations between government, big business, and labor have been extremely adversarial. Overcoming these obstacles will thus require a broad-based and persistent educational campaign.

To illustrate how far the United States currently is from having a competitive strategy, we shall briefly review some of the main actions taken to date and the major proposals before Congress in 1983. The most appealing remedy to many legislators has been some form of protectionism, which might actually make our ailments worse, not better. We will then suggest that to regain our national competitiveness, government, business, and labor leaders must inspect a number of cherished but partially antiquated assumptions about international trade, domestic government, management-labor relations, and the rights and duties that accompany membership in American society.

PROBLEMS AND RESPONSES TO DATE

Our competitiveness has deteriorated for a variety of reasons. Some have involved past actions, such as the reconstruction of Europe and Japan after World War II, and are now irrevocable. Others flow from international wage differentials, the diffusion of advanced technologies, and the development of foreign infrastructures. But even if the decline in American competitiveness has been partly due to our own, often well-intentioned policies or to external changes we could not control, a mixture of antiquated economic theories, incoherent government policies, ineffective management-labor practices, and unrealistic priorities continue to undermine our already precarious position in the following ways.

Obsolete notions of static comparative advantage and a predisposition for open markets induce policymakers to naively pursue unilateral free trade and to underestimate the effectiveness of foreign national strategies that subsidize exports and actually create competitive superiority in select sectors. Some economists are acknowledging that much trade among industrial countries is based more on dynamic learning curve effects and scale economies than on fixed resource endowments, but their new models have not yet been fully integrated into a broader theory of general applicability. As a result, trade officials often lack a clear conceptual framework for setting long-term priorities, and promote exports of citrus fruit and beef, for example, more than those of semiconductors.

Meanwhile, afflicted but politically salient industries have forced the federal government to provide protection, either in the form of import restraints, or subsidies and loan guarantees. Sometimes, as with textiles and apparel, these policies may provide a breathing spell, enabling firms to retrench more efficiently and/or increase their competitiveness through renewed investment and technological innovation. In other cases, such as steel and perhaps autos, the long-term effects of ad hoc protectionism are less clear. When the government does give aid, it often acts too late to have an optimal economic impact and fails to obtain any real promise of improvement or reform from management and labor.

Apart from ad hoc protectionism, U.S. trade policy has consisted largely of legalistic attempts by private parties to force other nations to play by our rules, by eliminating subsidies and halting "unfair" practices. Foreign firms and governments are strongly committed to their own strategies, however, and, perhaps sensing our reluctance or inability to enforce international agreements, have resisted pressures to change with blanket denials and effective lobbying. In practice, therefore, as Alan Wolff has shown, U.S. trade policy has had little impact on, or relationship to, American competitiveness and may actually have hindered it.

Erratic controls on exports to the Soviet Union and its allies further inhibit billions of dollars of current or potential overseas sales by American firms and deter joint operations with European suppliers, as much to satisfy transient foreign policy goals as to preserve our true long-term national security interests. At the same time, the United States is losing its capacity to produce machine tools, specialized bearings, and certain classes of electronics, partly because there is no monitoring, no data base, and no coherent system in place to predict critical needs. The Department of Defense has increased funding for research in a number of high technology areas, but it remains unclear whether these programs will enhance commercial competitiveness in a cost-effective fashion, or simply achieve primarily military goals by diverting scarce talent away from the civilian sector.

Our fragmented governmental system is designed to reflect the public will while preserving individual rights, but it often promotes costly legal adversarialism and denies public officials access to the expertise and data they need to make sound decisions. Over the past decade, the federal government has improved its analytical capabilities by strengthening both the Office of Management and Budget and the Office of the U.S. Trade Representative, but there is a long way to go, especially given the lack of any national consensus about the proper balance between defense and domestic programs, and the impact of each on our competitiveness. In David Stockman's words, "The budget system is not the problem. The problem is that this democracy is somewhat ambivalent about what it wants. . . low taxes and substantial public spending."[3]

Past antitrust standards have apparently deterred export activities, discouraged industry cooperation, and failed to adequately reflect the effects of foreign competition when evaluating combinations of domestic firms seeking economies of scale. In response, Congress has strengthened the exemption for export trading companies, while the Reagan administration has proposed granting limited antitrust immunity for joint research and development projects and revised its merger guidelines to give greater weight to overseas production; the ultimate effects of these initiatives, however, are still unclear.

Other federal regulations have also been based on a presumption that American industry was competitively unassailable. The cumulative effects of these policies, many of which had undoubted merit, and their ad hoc implementation have helped raise American production costs above those of our competitors. The federal government has recently reduced its regulatory hold over certain select industries, such as banking, trucking, and commercial airlines, and has tried to make remaining rules more cost effective. While the results seem promising to date, experts still debate the long run consequences of these actions and how much further these trends should go.

State and federal governments have occasionally tried to stimulate corporate cash flow and reinvestment through various means, including tax cuts, investment credits, loan guarantees, accelerated depreciation schedules, safe harbor leasing, and tax-exempt municipal development bonds. While these policies no doubt improved some firms' liquidity, the benefits of such poorly focused subsidies may have been outweighed by their overall costs to the public in the form of budgetary deficits and higher interest rates, which, as Benjamin Friedman has shown, inadvertently crowd private borrowers out of our capital markets, and overvalue the dollar, thereby overpricing American exports.

Although our basic science programs and inventive capacity remain strong according to Harvey Brooks, our ability to implement commercially new ideas has not kept pace. As technology and capital become more internationally mobile, foreign competitors increasingly treat much of our research and development as a "public good" to be adapted and exploited for their own purposes. Congress has responded by granting a tax credit for R&D and by passing the Stevenson-Wydler Technology Innovation Act to create centers affiliated with local engineering schools. Also, President Reagan has proposed strengthening process patent rights significantly.

Educational practices at both the primary and secondary levels have failed to produce the skills needed for industrial rejuvenation and have caused "a rising tide of mediocrity that threatens our very future as a nation and a people," despite extensive federal funding through direct grants, the GI Bill, and recent Guaranteed Student Loan Programs. However well intentioned, the lack of effective qualification criteria for the individual and institutional recipients has greatly swollen the cost of such programs and has apparently produced too many lawyers and not enough engineers. Recent studies have recommended an extensive overhaul of our educational system, with proposals ranging from longer hours and merit pay for public teachers to computer-aided instruction and tuition vouchers for private schools.[4]

Collective bargaining habits and attitudes increase the cost of labor negotiations, distort market signals, impose systemic rigidities (such as pattern bargaining and inflexible work rules), and generate lasting ill will and employee alienation. Management and labor in some industries such as automobiles have sought to restrain expenses and to innovate, by adopting or strengthening profit sharing, job security, and quality of work life programs. These reforms can improve morale and thus productivity, but their progress has been slow and uncertain, as Quinn Mills and Malcolm Lovell, Jr., have demonstrated. Given such changes, the traditional purpose of a union—to bargain collectively in an adversarial relationship with management—is increasingly questioned as workers participate more directly in certain managerial decisions. At the same time, many unions' ability to represent their members effectively seems threatened both by company-sponsored decertification campaigns, and by the National Labor Relations Board's enormous backlog, which all too often chills the free exercise of employees' statutory rights by delaying their enforcement.

Tax and income programs favor consumption over savings, raise the cost of capital relative to our competitors, and skew its allocation into comparatively unproductive sectors of the economy, as Philip Wellons has argued. Various governmental programs also help unemployed workers cope with the effects of uncompetitiveness but do relatively little to solve their underlying adjustment problems. Some arguably even reduce people's short-run incentives to seek alternative employment, without providing any real lasting security.

This partial list of responses leaves us with a pessimistic conclusion: although government, business, and labor have taken some promising initiatives, most of these remain halting and incomplete. Furthermore, there is still no consensus on the underlying cause of our competitive difficulties: the lack of an adequate national strategy that sets goals and priorities to invigorate our manufacturing base. There is even less agreement about the scope or urgency of any appropriate remedies.

SOME CONGRESSIONAL PROPOSALS

While we have generally refrained from advocating specific remedies in this book, preferring instead to first diagnose our competitive problems, current proposed solutions show how political leaders perceive our country's situation, and how their perceptions may constrain our options. We should, therefore, consider some of the major proposals before Congress in January 1984 as part of the problem to be diagnosed. These proposals fall into four general categories: laissez-faire, the space-shot approach, protectionism/retaliation, and structural reform.

LAISSEZ-FAIRE: SOUND MACROECONOMICS IS ENOUGH

Many economists seem to agree with Charles Schultze, former chairman of the Council of Economic Advisers, that "getting America's monetary and fiscal policies in order is far more important than any conceivable set of new industrial policies."[5] Citing the failures of more active "targeting" programs in Western Europe, these economists argue that we should confine legislative activity to small-scale, ad hoc tinkering or further deregulation, while tacitly letting private interest groups set national priorities via informal bargaining, much as they always have.

Martin Feldstein, when he was chairman of the Council of Economic Advisers, basically concurred with Schultze. Neither the administration nor Congress, however, could agree on how to scale back unrealistic social and military spending to what we can afford or to boost competitiveness so that we can afford more. Despite President Reagan's professèd commitment to budget cutting, the federal government's expenditures in 1983 reached about 24 percent of the gross national product, the highest level in decades. Moreover, the budget deficit may well average about 6 percent of GNP over the next five years, which is roughly equal to our traditional net private savings rate.[6] The fiscal reform that Schultze and other economists recommend is thus not happening and is not likely to happen soon, though public pressure to revise our tax system is slowly rising. The nation appears locked into the same "guns and butter" policies that had such a devastating effect during the late 1960s and seems unable or unwilling to adjust its priorities to its productive capabilities. We can hardly be consoled by observing that most of Western Europe is in even worse shape.[7]

Critics of this mainstream macroeconomics position argue further that waiting for the economy to achieve some long-term equilibrium ignores the likelihood of continuing shocks from abroad and would impose enormous and inequitably distributed adjustment costs, thereby making some sort of political action virtually inevitable. Since foreign governments—and even our own—have traditionally influenced economic development in various ways, the issue should turn more on pragmatic questions of institutional competence than on any ideological aversion to government per se.

THE SPACE-SHOT APPROACH

Some feel that the only effective way to deal with our government's inertia and fragmentation is to focus on a "big idea," such as the Apollo Project, and hope that our competitiveness problems will be solved through serendipity. Such an approach would let us mobilize resources for a politically acceptable cause, like improving our transportation infrastructure or reforming the educational system, which would indirectly raise future commercial productivity. Senator Slade Gorton (R-Wash.) has proposed providing over $50 million a year for studies to improve manufacturing. Similarly, Congressman John J. LaFalce (D-N.Y.) and Congressman George E. Brown, Jr. (D-Calif.) have advocated a National Technology Foundation and an Industrial Extension Service to fund and facilitate the development of engineering innovation. Symbolically, President Reagan's sole reference to American competitiveness in his 1984 State of the Union address arose from his proposal for a manned space station.

Another variant of the space-shot approach focuses on protecting American national security. The Department of Defense, for example, expects to spend about $32 billion in 1984 on research and development in high technology industries. This program, driven both by the threat of Soviet arms and the fear that other nations, especially Japan, are gaining a lead on new defense technologies, includes $500 million for very large-scale integrated circuits, $250 million per year for advanced lasers, and $40 million per year for fiber optics. In addition, the administration has announced a five-year, $1 billion program designed to maintain U.S. leadership in "supercomputers."

Such proposals may individually have merit; many wonder, however, if they can actually succeed, now that the commercial uses of new technology are not as closely associated with defense needs as they once were. Some also worry that these programs are not truly cost-effective or sufficiently comprehensive in scope and may encourage unproductive collusion by industries exempted from antitrust review.

PROTECTIONISM/RETALIATION

Knowledgeable observers believe that a majority of Congress favors some action to protect American industry or punish foreign competitors. In 1983, for example, the Senate passed a bill, S.144, proposed by Senator John C. Danforth (R-Mo.) that would authorize the president to retaliate more forcefully against other nations' unfair trade practices. Representative John P. Murtha (D-Pa.) has introduced even stronger legislation to apply countervailing duties to offset a broad range of foreign government export promotion schemes, including upstream subsidies and special credit allocation. This bill would, in effect, punish any country found targeting if its practices threatened to materially injure an American industry. In addition, various domestic content bills, sponsored by Representative Joseph M. Gaydos (D-Pa.), would limit the sale of certain foreign auto and steel products in the United States unless they were substantially manufactured here. Given the erosion of the old free trade coalition composed of labor, consumers, multinational corporations, and academia, these remedies are gaining supporters and have only been staved off by President Reagan's opposition, Japan's timely concessions in certain key sectors, and the current economic recovery.

Critics of protectionism worry that it would increase inflation and partly insulate inefficient industries, thereby delaying the painful adjustments required to recover long-term competitiveness. They also fear that erecting import barriers would antagonize our trading partners, undermine our diplomatic alliances, and provoke retaliation just as the Smoot-Hawley Tariff Act did in the 1930s. Therefore, although selective temporary restraints could conceivably induce reforms at home and force open markets abroad, such devices should only be used sparingly as part of a total strategy, with a full appreciation of all potential risks and costs.

STRUCTURAL REFORM

There is growing interest in reforming the federal government's decision-making system so that it can deal more coherently with America's competitiveness problems. The Office of Technology Assessment put the case for such "structural reform" succinctly in its *Report to Congress on International Competitiveness in Electronics*:

> People can and will argue endlessly about the successes and failures of industrial policies in other countries, but the primary lesson to be drawn from foreign experience is simply this: *industrial policymaking is a continuing activity of governments everywhere.* In the United States, industrial policy has been left mostly to the random play of events. Improvement is clearly possible; policymaking can be a purposeful activity characterized by learning from past experience within a framework of empirically based analysis. Developing a more effective industrial policy for the United States must begin in this spirit, while recognizing that the process is inherently political. There is no one thing that the federal government can do that will make a big difference for the future competitiveness of the U.S. electronics industry, but there are many specific policy concerns that deserve attention. Only by linking and coordinating these more effectively can the United States expect to develop a coherent and forward-looking approach to industrial policy. Until the nation begins this task, American firms will continue to find themselves at a disadvantage when facing rivals based in countries that have turned to industrial policies as a means of enhancing their own competitiveness.[8]

The actual proposals vary greatly and their advocates span most of the political spectrum.

Basically, these proposals seek to reorganize traditional interest group pluralism to achieve a consensus more in keeping with the national interest than that of any particular clique. They assume that the government's micro-policies are so profuse and uncoordinated as to constitute a macro problem. Therefore, structural change is required: innovation in what Frank A. Weil, a former undersecretary of commerce, calls "political architecture." President Reagan himself has acknowledged the possible need for reform by appointing a Commission on Industrial Competitiveness, while leading Democrats have also advocated various consultative mechanisms.

Several proposals seek to coordinate our domestic and international policies within the executive branch. Senator William V. Roth, Jr. (R-Del.) has introduced a bill, S. 121, to establish a new Department of International Trade and Industry, combining the Office of the U.S. Trade Representative and elements of the Department of Commerce. An amendment to his bill would also create an Office of Competitive Analysis to assemble and analyze data more strategically. Similarly, Congressman Don Bonker (D-Wash.) has sponsored a bill to establish a Department of Commerce and Trade and create a special Office of Assistant to the President for International Trade.

Others have suggested strengthening the existing Office of the U.S. Trade Representative, while still keeping it as a separate, elite agency to avoid diluting its effectiveness. Alternatively, two recent bills advocate supplementing existing trade mechanisms by establishing ad hoc boards to develop adjustment plans and evaluate trade barriers that adversely affect troubled industries. Under H.R. 4531, introduced by Congressman LaFalce, for example, the chairman of the International Trade Commission would appoint an Adjustment Plan Board, consisting of industry leaders and cabinet officials, to recommend reductions in excess capacity, technological improvements, new products or designs, management and productivity changes, and government policies—all with an explicit exemption from federal or state antitrust laws. H.R. 3681, sponsored by Congressman Stewart B. McKinney (R-Conn.), would authorize Congress to establish a Transitional Industries Trade Board by joint resolution, to be appointed by the president and to recommend revisions of GATT, increased tariffs or import quotas, regulatory relief, assistance to displaced employees, and/or support from the Export-Import Bank or Overseas Private Investment Corporation.

Others prefer some form of permanent tripartite advisory council representing labor, business, and government, with regional or sectoral subcouncils. H.R. 3443, introduced by Congressman Timothy E. Wirth (D-Colo.), would appropriate $20 million annually for a nine-member board serving staggered six-year terms with the support of a staff Bureau of Economic Analysis and Policy. Similarly, the Senate Democratic Caucus has recommended a twenty-member Council on Economic Competition and Cooperation to provide a forum for debate and a biannual report. Also, Congressman Bonker has suggested establishing an Industrial Competitiveness Council.

Some people doubt that such advisory councils can be successful unless backed up by some form of development bank. Weil has advocated a semi-autonomous Federal Industrial Coordination Board modeled on the Federal Reserve System, which could provide up to $6 billion in loans, loan guarantees, and tax incentives. The board could also exempt certain agreements from the antitrust laws and administer various antidumping and countervailing duty laws. He feels that such an institution could make our national policies more coherent and preserve future commercial opportunities, but only if it has the knowledge, money, and power to induce change without being captured by short-run political interests. Congressman Stan Lundine's (D-N.Y.) bill, H.R. 2991, would establish a similar twenty-member Economic Cooperation Council and a National Industrial Development Bank which could raise and lend its own funds, and guarantee up to $24 billion in U.S.-backed loans to firms unable to meet all their financing needs in the private market. Also, Congressman LaFalce has introduced H.R. 4360 and 4362, which would create a fifteen-member Council on Industrial Competitiveness and a Bank for Industrial Competitiveness, to invest in and lend to firms in mature or emerging industries, guarantee U.S.-backed loans totaling $17 billion, and borrow up to five times its paid-in capital. A related bill, H.R. 4363, would stimulate financing for small businesses by creating a Federal Industrial Mortgage Association to buy, insure, and resell pools of industrial mortgages to institutional investors.

All these proposals for structural reform and greater coordination raise the following issues:

1. Where should such structural changes take place: in the executive branch, the legislature, somewhere in between, or outside in some semiautonomous niche like the Federal Reserve Board?
2. What should be their orientation and scope? Should they be concerned with long-run, comprehensive issues of national strategy, necessarily holistic, looking for the relationships between macro policies and micro interventions? Or should they be relatively short run, focused on putting out fires more efficiently?
3. How much information should they have? What kind of knowledge

is required to think coherently about the United States in the world economy? What interconnections need attention, and how much data should be publicly available, either at the time or later?

4. How much money—if any—should be at their disposal and how should it be spent? Should such funds come from general revenues or more specialized sources?

5. How much power should they have? Should they have enforcement and control functions? What should be the standards for judicial review, if any?

6. Should there be a part-time or full-time staff? What sort of qualifications should its members have? Who should appoint them, and for how long?[9]

Many oppose such structural reform, partly because of their traditional assumptions about the proper role of government. Some critics fear that any new agency or bank will inevitably be captured by special interest groups and forced to subsidize politically powerful but noncompetitive sectors of our economy. They argue further that similar targeting efforts elsewhere have either largely failed, as in Europe, or have rested on a complex combination of cultural, historical, and institutional factors, as in Japan, which cannot be easily replicated here.[10] Others, such as Scott, accept the need for greater coherence and dialogue but feel that these proposals rely too much on procedural devices, without also addressing the substantive short-term sacrifices required to increase our nation's investment, productivity, and growth. Thus, while greater coordination is clearly desirable, any form of centralized "planning" could actually make matters worse if badly done.

ELEMENTS OF AN EFFECTIVE STRATEGY

Whatever the individual merits of most of the proposals now before Congress, they do not by themselves change the fundamental assumptions and priorities that have caused America's competitive failure. A national strategy to reverse our decline must address these issues directly, while avoiding the costly ambivalence and inadvertence that have handicapped our responses to date.

Part of our reluctance to act decisively stems from the complexity and interdependence of our problems, and from the differing needs of various industries and firms in our economy. In the automobile industry, for example, the large number of components and need for quality control makes labor relations and employee morale a key success factor. By contrast, in the petrochemical industry, the relatively high variable costs of fuel drive firms toward countries richly endowed with raw materials, even though interference from certain governmentally controlled companies may delay effective restructuring. Similarly, in a labor-intensive but widely dispersed industry like textiles and apparel, a multilateral approach to managing trade may make both political and economic sense, given the employees' inability to find similar work elsewhere and the need to stimulate reinvestment to preserve at least some domestic operations in the face of large retailers' willingness to buy from offshore sources. And in semiconductors, the industry's rapid technological turnover has, at times, made joint R&D, access to equity financing, and government procurement crucial for obtaining economies of scale. Indeed, as John F. Welch, Jr., chairman of General Electric, has pointed out, many large, diversified firms find that even their own internal divisions each require different management practices and governmental policies to thrive.[11]

Clearly there is much to be done by many players in government, business, and labor unions, given the differing problems of various industries, firms, and even divisions. A more fundamental obstacle, however, is that some of the actions required to regain competitiveness challenge deeply held notions about the proper roles of our institutions and their relationships to one another. As a result, the debate to date on potential remedies has been hampered by widespread miscommunication and ingrained beliefs. As long as the cures appear worse than the disease, influential commentators may prefer to deny or downplay crucial aspects of our crisis, rather than join any new consensus for change.

Many proponents of structural reform, for example, see industrial policy largely as a cost-free "add on," whereby the government can do a better job without significantly changing the consumption-oriented policies that have hindered our competitive performance in the past. Arguing that our aggregate savings and investment rates are adequate, although misdirected due to private-market imperfections, some seem to suggest that we can regain our long-term fitness largely by taking supplemental vitamins, without extended dieting and exercise. By contrast, critics with a greater stake and deeper faith in free enterprise often acknowledge the need for wage restraint and increased savings, but frequently prescribe such austerity only for others, while offering little in return themselves.

The evidence and analysis in this book suggest, however, that we can solve our competitiveness problems effectively only by adopting a national strategy that is *holistic, coherent, flexible*, and *balanced*: holistic in embracing all the interrelated political, social, and economic causes of deterioration; coherent in pursuing various goals and priorities; flexible in fitting particular remedies to the ailments that they are designed to cure; and balanced in curtailing the postwar tilt toward short-term consumption in favor of longer-term gains. This implies three principal points for public policy. First, we must understand that the United States has a strategy that has become progressively uncompetitive and favors short-term benefits at the expense of future prosperity. Second, we must correct this imbalance both in macroeconomic policies and in those areas that affect industries generically, such as trade, antitrust, finance, technology, training, and employment. Only after these issues have been addressed should we undertake governmental programs aimed at particular sectors or firms. Third, since changing the thrust of these macro and generic policies will be both systemic and painful, we must perceive the full range of effects and share the burdens fairly.

For example, the United States—unlike Japan—has traditionally relieved business of any responsibility for employment security, assigning the task to the government. Our government, however, has for the most part preferred to alleviate unemployment through income maintenance policies or temporary public works projects. Competitive pressures are now forcing us to limit such programs, but this curtailment will be socially unacceptable unless we provide income another way—through private employment. This approach will focus more on corporate management, on personnel and investment decisions, and thus on the whole matter of corporate governance. Here again we can see the systemic nature of strategy and the need to consider the full effects of what we do.

Similarly, we must regain parity with our major competitors in the cost and availability of capital by overhauling our tax system to reduce the deficit, while stimulating savings and productive investments and also limiting existing subsidies for "frivolous" consumption. A sales or value-added tax on nonessential domestic purchases, for example, could raise substantial sums without penalizing exports. Alternatively, an indirect consumption tax—levied on income less savings and investments—could eventually increase capital formation and still retain progressive rates based partly on people's ability to pay. Finally, a flat tax might not only encourage compliance by reducing current rates and applying to real, rather than nominal, interest income and capital gains, but also actually expand total receipts by eliminating most deductions, including those for business entertainment and for interest payments on consumer loans (except those on inexpensive first homes).[12] Unlike some earlier tax cuts, these changes need not deprive the treasury of revenue overall, since the purpose is less to give the wealthy a windfall than to alter the incentives under which they consume or invest. We should also revise our approaches in many other generic policy areas, from trade to education, before asking the government to target more actively at the industry or firm level.

To be implemented effectively, this strategy must be based on a broad social consensus and match our institutional norms; it cannot be imposed by force against the majority's will. In the 1960s, for example, France had an elegant strategy designed by some of its sharpest minds, but the resulting plans failed largely because they did not fit the country's true situation, values, and needs. Arguably, our own national traditions, both as practiced and perceived, make any successful strategy difficult to achieve. Many of our policies have heavily favored consumption over investment, while relations between government, big business, and labor have been highly adversarial. To overcome these obstacles, we will therefore need a broader and deeper understanding of our current problems, and a greater willingness to bear the short-run costs of austerity more equitably.

THE PROSPECTS FOR CHANGE: OLD ASSUMPTIONS AND NEW REALITIES

As the preceding chapters imply, the continued erosion of American competitiveness could cause high unemployment, a stagnant or even declining real standard of living, demands to reduce our foreign commitments, and social unrest. Although a unilateral resort to protectionism may seem tempting to preserve some jobs in certain industries over the short run, it might also reignite inflation, provoke retaliation abroad, and threaten the collapse of the world financial system as debtor countries default, unable to expand their exports.

Such a scenario may seem unduly alarming to some, particularly those savoring the long-delayed beginning of our cyclical recovery in 1983. Jobs could well continue to grow in certain service sectors or high technology fields, and our social system might survive sustained unemployment and stagnant living standards for quite a while. Why not just hope for the best and hold off making any real changes?

Unfortunately, the cost of such complacency will be high. Most of the factors reducing our national competitiveness are likely to persist and get worse—not better—over time. They may be temporarily alleviated by a cyclical upswing but will surely return to plague us during subsequent down-turns. We need to begin reexamining and reforming our national strategy now to make it more competitive. To do so, however, we must shed certain ideological blinders and, in particular, revise four pervasive assumptions in light of the new underlying realities.

THE UNITED STATES IN THE INTERNATIONAL TRADE SYSTEM

The Assumption. The position of any nation in world trade depends largely upon its natural resources, its population, and its capital. A somewhat static notion, this idea led many Western observers to conclude, for example, that Japan at the end of World War II was doomed to remain poor and could only develop by making maximum use of its major resource: cheap labor.

According to this Ricardian theory, countries should specialize in products requiring the natural inputs with which they are most endowed. Mutually beneficial trade can then occur among numerous private companies, with prices set by supply and demand, provided governments keep trade free and open through multilateral agreements.[13] In this way all economies will even-tually grow and prosper, although some may suffer greater adjustment costs due either to more volatile business cycles or occasional shifts in marginal productivity.

The Reality. The static notion of comparative advantage no longer adequately explains international trading patterns. As Bruce Scott has pointed out: "Un-willing to accept the conventional Western idea that their role is to specialize in goods based on cheap labor . . . the East Asians have forged a dynamic theory of comparative advantage that allows them to allocate human and financial resources toward jobs with high value added in growing industries and, for example, to succeed in steel despite a lack of both coal and iron."[14]

By using systematic government policies, Japan has moved its economy from labor-intensive products such as textiles, to capital-intensive goods such as television sets and automobiles, into the advanced technology sectors of electronics, semiconductors, and computers. Many other countries are fol-lowing Japan's example. Although natural resource endowments still influ-ence each nation's competitiveness in certain sectors, for example, agriculture and petrochemicals, successful countries have learned how to *create* com-parative advantage through a global strategy that also considers intangible assets, like a well-trained work force, and future economic trends based on a product's income elasticity and rate of technological change.

Under such circumstances the old premise of free trade is in many ways a delusion. Governments are directly concerned with the outcomes, not just the rules of trade, and they manage their national portfolios by designing policies and institutions both to achieve competitiveness and to ease the costs of industrial transition within their borders.[15]

The alternatives for America are thus either to devise a national development strategy or to continue to resort to various ad hoc devices to protect its weakening industries from overseas competition. Our ambivalent attempts to force foreign countries to abandon their policies and to play by the old rules of free trade have not worked well and it is unlikely that they will.

For example, in 1982 the domestic steel producers' attempt to use U.S. countervailing duty laws to prevent European governments from subsidizing their own industries evolved into a multilateral agreement under which the latter promised to limit their steel exports to 5.5 percent of the American market. If such international negotiations will determine the size and nature of world steel production, then our government must also consider other issues about the proper scope of the U.S. industry, the costs of retrenchment, and the national interest concerning imports (presumably Mexican steel is preferable to Korean, at least until the Mexicans pay their bank debts).[16] To bargain successfully about such global trade flows, we must design a national strategy that is accepted and sustained by business and labor. This brings us to the next assumption, about the role of government.

THE ROLE OF GOVERNMENT

The Assumption. Americans have traditionally adhered to the belief of John Locke and the founding fathers that government is a necessary evil, to be minimized whenever possible. Its chief purposes are to protect citizens' property and enforce their contracts, without favoring private factions unduly, but it should neither plan nor even be very coherent, except, possibly, when it undertakes a war. Rather, it should be checked, balanced, and separated, so it will respond only to crises and broad-based coalitions.[17]

Although periodically questioned in practice by activists in American history like Alexander Hamilton, Nicholas Biddle, and Franklin Roosevelt, this aversion to any centralized, powerful government remains strong today. For example, President Reagan stated in his 1981 inaugural address that "government is not the solution to our problem; government is the problem."[18] Similarly, Chief Justice Burger recently noted with approval that "[t]he choices. . .made in the Constitutional Convention impose burdens on governmental processes that often seem clumsy, inefficient, even unworkable, but those hard choices were consciously made by men who had lived under a form of government that permitted arbitrary governmental acts to go unchecked."[19] Accordingly, as Samuel Huntington wrote, "Because of the inherently antigovernment character of the American creed, government that is strong is illegitimate, government that is legitimate is weak."[20]

The Reality. Our traditional emphasis on interest group pluralism and preference for a limited state has, ironically, created a very large, interventionary and expensive government. It has also spawned a vast array of transfer payments, subsidies, and credit programs, as well as environmental, tax, and monetary policies that restrain savings, investment, and industrial growth, but whose impact on U.S. competitiveness is seldom fully assessed. As federal policies increasingly affect America's trade prospects, the government now must recognize all the consequences of its actions, choose priorities among many desirable goals, and create a consensus to implement its choices. Government does not need to be bigger; rather it must partially change its nature and purpose by becoming more coherent, as it did, for example, during the past decade when Presidents Carter and Reagan centralized regulatory authority in the Office of Management and Budget. Although the United States as a whole has not yet grasped the need for a competitive strategy, a number of business and labor leaders clearly have perceived this new reality.

For all its reliance on ad hoc solutions, our government has had an underlying strategy of sorts, though this has naturally remained implicit, given our aversion to any form of explicit "planning." Its chief goal has been short-term consumer welfare: a higher standard of living through deficit-financed subsidies to consumption and easy access to low-priced imports. Meanwhile, numerous East Asian nations have adopted longer-term strategies to raise their standard of living by encouraging savings, investment, and productivity.

Our fear of centralized planning has caused the United States to shun government "credit allocation" and to leave such matters to the supposedly free capital markets. But consider the reality. In 1982, the Council of Economic Advisers reported that of the $361 billion raised in U.S. credit markets the previous year, $86.5 billion involved federal government loans, guarantees, and subsidies for housing, farmers, ailing steel and auto firms, and so forth. The council complained that "increasingly political judgments, rather than marketplace judgments, have been responsible for allocating the supply of credit" and then suggested a formal "Federal credit budget."[8] Similarly, the Congressional Budget Office found that government aid to business in 1984 will total $131.9 billion, apart from the $140 billion spent by the Department of Defense on goods and services, and the $110 billion that will go to individuals for medical and housing subsidies.[21] None of these expenditures is primarily designed to foster national competitiveness.

Arguably, the U.S. government cannot choose winners and losers. But it may already be doing so, favoring the losers over the winners. To ensure America's future competitiveness, should not we distinguish, for example, between tobacco growing, semiconductor manufacturing, and shoemaking? The free market/limited state advocates would say no, but reality suggests that a limited amount of "industrial triage" may be preferable to our exclusive reliance on the current pork barrel system.

Under our federal system the executive branch is not only separated from Congress and the courts, but is also fragmented among numerous agencies and departments. Trade and adjustment policy, for example, is made in countless places throughout Washington: Defense, State, Commerce, Treasury, Agriculture, Labor, the Senate, and the House. The Office of the U.S. Trade Representative (USTR) is theoretically designed to coordinate all these matters, but it can only do this with a strong presidential endorsement, which has been lacking in recent years. Meanwhile our competitors proceed more deliberately.

While renovating this system is difficult, given the power—and value—of the old ideal of the limited state, the government's role may now be permanently shifting. Over the past several years, for example, the Environmental Protection Agency has experimented with a system of "controlled trading" to allow existing manufacturers to sell their emission rights to potential new entrants in each region, subject to an overall ceiling. By adopting this holistic, coherent, and flexible approach, the government can alleviate many health hazards, while letting firms minimize their overall compliance costs.

There are probably many other areas of our economy in which the government can better reconcile public needs with private incentives through such innovative policies, but it will need the close collaboration of business and labor, particularly big business, which is heavily engaged in world competition. Business and labor have the primary skills needed to compete successfully, but their competencies will be handicapped unless nourished and legitimized by government's authority. The workings of the advisory committees to the USTR in the 1979 trade negotiations showed that such a consensus could be developed.

MANAGERS AND MANAGED

The Assumption. Under the old notions of property rights and freedom of contract, owners could dispose of their businesses as they wished, and hire and fire employees at will. At first, work contracts were individualistic, and the owners' right to dictate the terms was constrained only by the market for labor. As managers replaced owners in large, publicly held companies, however, their obligation shifted to maximizing the economic benefits for an increasingly distant and anonymous group of shareholders, often over the short run. With the rise of trade unions, the contract in many companies also became more formal and bureaucratized, with its terms set through collective bargaining and private arbitration.

The Reality. Once again, the old assumption has become at least partly obsolete. The institutionalization of the stock market has hampered managers' ability to assess the owners' wishes accurately, and frequently has driven them to "play to the mercurial tics and prejudices of a small cadre of stock price influencers' shifting ideas of value rather than value itself."[22] Those who refuse often risk having their companies taken over and being fired.

Furthermore, as companies increase their debt and suffer greater financial distress, debtholders have often become as important as shareholders. State and federal governments have also imposed various demands, as shown by recent safety and environmental regulations, and proposed plant closing laws. Meanwhile, courts and administrative agencies have begun restricting management's right to terminate employees without "just cause," prompting over 200 companies to rewrite their personnel manuals and establish in-house grievance systems, to forestall lawsuits and restrain irresponsible supervisors.[23]

Finally, various factors have changed the relationships between managers and managed. The old hierarchical separation of supervisors and workers has become costly. With rising levels of education, for example, employees often obtain greater fulfillment by becoming involved in the decisions directly affecting their work. New technology can thus be introduced more smoothly and efficiently if workers are consulted beforehand and allowed to help manage the new procedures.

In many industries, the old conception of managerial prerogatives and adversarial relationships has driven labor costs per unit of output far above those of foreign competitors, causing industrial deterioration and unemployment. Some unions have recently recognized the need for wage restraint to preserve jobs. But they are unwilling to check their adversarial proclivities fully without greater consultation about such management decisions as investment, profit sharing, employment security, and even executive salaries. Why should an auto or steelworker, for example, take a pay cut if the funds saved thereby will be used to raise top management's compensation or to diversify out of the industry?

In a wide variety of ways and for many reasons, therefore, the old notion of contract is being supplemented by a new one of consensus. Managers and managed often have mutual interests that are far greater than their conflicts. Both, at least theoretically, have a stake in their company's survival. As a result, they have embarked on numerous programs ranging from Quality of Work Life and Employee Involvement in the auto industry to employee stock purchases. Such transactions frequently cost less than shutdowns; employees who own the firm will sacrifice to make it competitive. Board membership in these new companies is sometimes shared by managers and workers, suggesting that the rigid separation implied by these old words may no longer always be appropriate.[24]

The significance of these changes for managers and unions is radical and profound. The old bases of authority for each have eroded, while the new ones are still forming. Some critics wish to limit unions substantially, because they believe the unions' old adversarial stance proved counterproductive. Unionization has declined to less than 20 percent of the American work force for a number of reasons, including illegal discharges by employers.[25] At the same time, thoughtful managers know that their right to manage comes partly from those they manage. But how then will employees organize to express their interests? Can there be any lasting consensus without a labor movement?

The competitiveness of American enterprise seems to depend on new conceptions of corporate governance. In Japan, shareholders are relatively unimportant and the relationships among banks, government, managers, and managed are carefully balanced to achieve growth and competition. How will the United States respond? Much of the current debate about "inside" and "outside" directors, shareholder democracy and the like in the United States seems appropriate but somewhat remote from our most pressing problem.[26]

RIGHTS AND DUTIES

The Assumption. Since the Great Depression, our society has accorded its citizens certain rights and entitlements from the federal government. Many of these are inherent in membership in the American community and do not depend either upon the whims of charity or on any productive performance by the recipients. They include, for example, rights to income, health, education, employment, pensions, and more. During the last two decades this social "safety net" has grown enormously as new programs were added and their benefits were indexed to inflation. We as a nation implicitly assumed that the economy could afford to pay for these expanded rights while at the same time meeting increased obligations for defense, environmental protection, and industrial reinvestment. By contrast, people's duties were largely left to their individual consciences and good sense.

The Reality. By 1984 these rights, particularly those not tied to a means test, were consuming about one-half of the deficit-plagued federal budget. Moreover, if left unattended, the situation will clearly worsen as our population ages. We must now recognize that, however well intended, many of these programs incur mounting unfunded obligations, divert wealth unduly to politically powerful groups, and may actually diminish some able-bodied recipients' willingness to work. Whereas the provision of certain civil rights facilitates the efficient allocation of resources, these "middle-class entitlements" hinder investment, and so competitiveness. Thus, the escalation of such transfer payments can actually erode the economy's long-term capacity to provide them.

If the community provides its members with rights, it now must require duties as well, such as the obligation to work hard and well, or to share fairly the burden of austerity imposed by our declining competitiveness. Having an acceptable process for defining and enforcing these rights and duties is thus crucial for our long-term economic health.

During the early 1980s, for example, some governmental leaders and social commentators diligently reminded citizens of their duty to work and admonished them to stop relying on public welfare. This advice, however, generally came from the rich and strong to the poor and weak, and sometimes had a taint of self-interest.[27] Other political leaders have responded that the greater good might also require limits on tax deductions for interest payments on consumer loans, which help the wealthy buy fur coats, yachts, and vacation homes.

Nowhere are duties more urgent than in our legacy to our children. Each generation has an obligation to pay for what it consumes, lest its successors be subject to taxation without representation. Yet the escalating federal debt, together with the appalling interest payments required to service it, will force those who come after us to repay lenders—foreign and domestic—for much of what we now enjoy.

Competition, as we have seen, has also forced many managers and their employees to redefine their respective rights and duties, and to share more fairly both the pain and the gain of their mutual undertakings. Will these changes and the promising new relationships associated with them last and contribute to national productivity, or will they wither at the first brief return to prosperity? The answer depends on how well the leaders of government, business, and labor cooperate and on how imaginatively they work to design solutions to the difficulties of adjustment. Take, for example, the layoffs that often follow unavoidably from consolidations and renovations carried out to regain competitiveness. What can we do as a nation with the unemployed, short of preserving sinecures through shortsighted protectionism? There seem to be three choices, since few today would question the right of even the idle to survive. Government can pay them to be unemployed or hire them to perform public works. Neither of these options has been entirely satisfactory, so we turn to the third, which resembles the Japanese approach: government can coerce or subsidize firms to hire and retrain those out of work so that they can contribute to more viable industries. Such a solution, however, will force us to redefine the respective roles and relationships of government, business, unions, and individuals.

CONCLUSION

As this book has shown, America's ability to compete in international trade has declined alarmingly over the past twenty years. As of 1984, much of the popular discussion of this topic has either focused on sectoral symptoms (e.g., in autos or steel) or sought panaceas in the current recovery and perceived positive prospects of certain service and high technology industries, thereby denying the systemic nature of our problems. While such growth may temporarily ease our social pains, it cannot be relied upon as a sustainable cure or even as an effective narcotic. Rather, we must shake off our complacency, recognize that many of our policies and practices have become progressively uncompetitive, and take immediate steps to avert a future crisis.

The preceding chapters all suggest that to solve our competitiveness problems effectively we must adopt a national strategy that is holistic, coherent, flexible, and balanced. Only after we have reformed our aggregate fiscal and monetary policies and our "generic" approaches to such things as trade, antitrust, savings, investment, technology, training, and employment should the government consider direct targeting of particular industries or firms on an ongoing basis.

To be implemented successfully, however, such a strategy must also rest on a broad social consensus and be compatible with our institutional norms; it cannot be dictated from on high. Our own national traditions, both as practiced and perceived, make an effective strategy hard to achieve. Changing these ingrained habits will therefore be difficult and painful, requiring both a sustained educational campaign and a fair sharing of all the initial burdens and eventual benefits.

In conclusion, the strength and prosperity of the United States depend upon how quickly and how well we understand the reality facing us, inspect the old assumptions that have controlled our conduct, and adopt new ones better suited to meeting the challenges of foreign competition. Delay will weaken our capacity to provide all Americans with the standards of living they have come to expect, and consequently will threaten our political and social fabric. It will also erode our capacity to defend ourselves and our allies against aggression and thus further jeopardize the attainment of a more stable and peaceful world. Only by carefully pursuing our enlightened self-interests can we achieve a more efficient, safe, and humane future.

Contributors

BRUCE R. SCOTT is Paul Whiton Cherington Professor of Business Administration at the Harvard Business School. He was one of the principal architects of Business, Government, and the International Economy, a required course that analyzes national economic strategies. Subsequent work includes course modules on Japan and France and related *Harvard Business Review* articles. From 1963 to 1968 he studied the influence of the French government on French industry. This work resulted in the volume, *Industrial Planning in France* (1969).

GEORGE C. LODGE is professor of business administration at the Harvard Business School. He teaches Business, Government, and the International Economy in the Advanced Management Program and Human Resource Management in the M.B.A. program. He was a political reporter and columnist for the *Boston Herald* before entering government service, where he was director of information of the U.S. Department of Labor, and assistant secretary of labor for international affairs. He is the author of numerous articles and books including *Spearheads of Democracy, Engines of Change: United States Interests and Revolution in Latin America, The New American Ideology,* and *The American Disease.*

JOSEPH L. BOWER is professor of business administration at the Harvard Business School. He has taught courses in Business Policy and Business, Government, and the International Economy, and has served as head of the Business Policy Course and chairman of the General Management Area. He has published widely in the fields of development of corporate strategy, and organization in multibusiness and multinational companies. He is the author of *Managing the Resource Allocation Process,* which won the McKinsey Foundation award for the best book on management in 1971, and *The Two Faces of Management: An Approach to Leadership in Business and Politics.*

HARVEY BROOKS is Benjamin Peirce Professor of Technology and Public Policy in the Kennedy School of Government and the Division of Applied Sciences at Harvard University. He is also professor of applied physics on the Gordon McKay Endowment and former dean of the Division of Engineering and Applied Physics. Most recently, he was a consultant to the Organization for Economic Cooperation

503

and Development for the report, "Science and Technology Policy for the 1980s," and was a member of the National Academy of Sciences Panel on Advanced Technology Competition and the Industrialized Allies and of the National Research Council Committee on National Urban Policy. He has also served on the president's Science Advisory Committee and the National Science Board.

WILLIAM C. CRUM is an Associates Fellow at the Harvard Business School and was the project administrator for the colloquium. A former teaching fellow at Harvard College, he holds an M.B.A. from Harvard Business School, and a J.D. from Harvard Law School.

DAVIS DYER is an associate editor of the *Harvard Business Review* and senior research associate at the Harvard Business School. He is the coauthor of three books: *Renewing American Industry* (1983) with Paul R. Lawrence, and two forthcoming volumes—one on the auto industry and the American economy with Malcolm S. Salter, Alan M. Webber, and Mark Fuller, and one on the reorganization of the Bell System under deregulation. He holds a Ph.D. in history from Harvard University.

WILLIAM F. FINAN is a special assistant to the undersecretary for international trade, Department of Commerce, and is primarily responsible for policy development for high technology trade. He has also been vice president and principal consultant at the Technecon Analytic Research, Inc., Director of the Wharton Econometric Forecasting Associates, and staff economist for the Committee on Finance of the U.S. Senate.

GLENN R. FONG is assistant professor of political science at the University of Illinois at Chicago. He was a postdoctoral research fellow at the Harvard Business School. He holds a B.A. in political science from the University of California at Berkeley, and an M.A. and Ph.D. in government from Cornell University. His research and writing is in the area of the politics of trade and industrial policy.

BENJAMIN M. FRIEDMAN is professor of economics at Harvard University. He teaches macroeconomics and monetary economics and conducts a seminar on monetary and fiscal policy. He has worked with Morgan Stanley & Co., and the Board of Governors of the Federal Reserve System, the Federal Reserve Bank of New York, and the Federal Reserve Bank of Boston. He writes on monetary economics, macroeconomics, and economic policy and is the author of *Changing Roles of Debt and Equity in Financing U.S. Capital Formation*.

ANNETTE M. LAMOND is a consultant specializing in industrial organization economics. She holds a B.A. degree in economics from Wellesley College, an S.M. degree in management from the Massachusetts Institute of Technology, and a Ph.D.

in economics from Yale University. She is the author of several books and articles, including a forthcoming book on the competitive status of the U.S. electronics industry to be published by the National Academy of Engineering.

MARK W. LOVE has been vice president of Economic Consulting Services, Inc., since 1979, having previously served as assistant to the director of Economic Consulting Services of Wolf and Company since 1976. He has written extensively on international trade issues involving the U.S. manufacturing sector, including government studies on the use of export trading companies to enhance U.S. exports of textiles and apparel.

MALCOLM R. LOVELL, JR., is visiting scholar at the Brookings Institution. He was undersecretary of labor from September 1981 to early 1983. Prior to that he was president of the Rubber Manufacturers Association. He served as assistant secretary of labor for manpower from 1970 to 1973 and was appointed by President Ford to the National Advisory Council on Vocational Education. Lovell was graduated from the Harvard Business School with an M.B.A. in 1946.

D. QUINN MILLS is Albert J. Weatherhead Professor of Business Administration at the Harvard Business School and is a member of the Organizational Behavior/ Human Resources Management Area of the school. He has taught Personnel, Labor Relations, and Government Relations in many of the school's programs. He helped administer wage and price controls during the Nixon and Ford administrations in 1971–74. He was the labor arbitrator on the building of the Trans-Alaska pipeline. He is a member of the National Commission on Employment Policy by appointment of the president.

STANLEY NEHMER has been president of Economic Consulting Services, Inc., since the firm's organization in July 1978. Prior to that date, he was a principal of Wolf and Company and served as director of Economic Consulting Services after his retirement from the U.S. government in February 1973. Before joining Wolf and Company, Nehmer served for over seven years as deputy assistant secretary of commerce and director, Bureau of Resources and Trade Assistance. He was in charge of the Commerce Department's work on key industries, including the trade adjustment assistance program for firms. He was chairman of the U.S. government's Interagency Committee for the Implementation of Textile Agreements and of various industry advisory committees. He has spoken and written extensively on trade, finance, energy, and other resources matters. In 1972, Nehmer received the annual award of the textile section of the New York Board of Trade for his distinguished service to the nation in the field of textiles.

MALCOLM S. SALTER is professor of business administration at the Harvard Business School, teaches courses in general management, and serves as head of the

Business Policy Teaching Group. He is an authority on the problems of managing diversified companies and is currently leading a major research and course development project on the auto industry and the American economy. Professor Salter is coauthor of *New Alliances, Policy Formulation and Administration, Merger Trends and Prospects for the 1980s, Diversification Through Acquisition,* and many articles addressing general management seminars for companies in the United States and abroad.

ALAN M. WEBBER is a senior research associate at the Harvard Business School and is the coordinator of the school's Project on the Auto Industry and the American Economy. Prior to that he was the special assistant to the secretary of transportation, Department of Transportation, responsible for overseeing auto industry analysis and transportation capital investment strategy.

PHILIP A. WELLONS is associate professor of business administration at the Harvard Business School and teaches Business, Government, and the International Economy in the M.B.A. program. Before joining the Harvard faculty, he worked for the Development Center of the Organization for Economic Cooperation and Development in Paris doing a study of borrowing by developing countries in the eurocurrency market. He is the author of *World Money and Credit: The Crisis and Its Causes.*

ALAN WM. WOLFF is a partner of Verner, Liipfert, Bernhard and McPherson, and specializes in international trade and investment law. From 1977 to 1979, he was U.S. deputy special representative for trade delegations in negotiations with our major trading partners, including Japan and the European Community. He chaired a senior coordinating group on U.S. economic relations with Japan and played a leading role in seeking greater access to Japan for U.S. exports. In January 1979, Wolff was elected to be the first chairman of the Twenty-nation International Steel Committee of the Organization for Economic Cooperation and Development.

MICHAEL Y. YOSHINO is professor of business administration at the Harvard Business School and has taught International Business and Business Policy in the M.B.A. and executive programs of the school and in company-sponsored programs in the United States, Europe, and Japan. He is a member of the editorial boards of the *Harvard Business Review* and the *Strategic Management Journal.* He is the author of numerous articles and books, the most recent of which is *The Japanese Trading Company: Strategy and Structure.*

Notes

INTRODUCTION NOTES

1. Under this definition, our national competitiveness might be fostered by certain domestic practices (e.g., improving infrastructures or nurturing infant industries), just as it might be undermined by other countries' policies (e.g., predatory pricing). But, over time, a nation whose basic industries can only survive with the aid of substantial import restraints or artificial subsidies is not competitive; rather, it is either insulated from true competition or operating at an overall loss.

2. Most of America's recent surplus balance in services consists of investment income. According to the Council of Economic Advisers, for example, the U.S. net surplus in traded services of $33.2 billion in 1982 reflected $27.3 billion of net investment income and only $7.8 billion of other net services (including fees and royalties), plus $.2 billion net surplus for military transactions and less a $2.1 billion shortfall for net travel and transportation receipts. See *The Economic Report of the President*, transmitted to the Congress, February 1984, 332.

3. See Bruce R. Scott, chapter 1, this volume, figures 1-7 and 1-8; D. Quinn Mills and Malcolm R. Lovell, chapter 12, this volume.

4. Otto Eckstein, *Report on U.S. Manufacturing Industries*, Data Resources, Inc., January 1984, 187 and 189. Also, compare Benjamin M. Friedman, chapter 11, this volume, on the difficulty of measuring service sector productivity.

5. Cf. the Annual Report of the Council of Economic Advisers, in *The Economic Report of the President*, transmitted to the Congress, February 1982, 178-79.

CHAPTER 1 NOTES

1. See Robert Z. Lawrence, "Changes in U.S. Industrial Structure: The Role of Global Forces, Secular Trends and Transitory Cycles," paper prepared for the Symposium on Industrial Change and Public Policy, Federal Reserve Bank of Kansas City, August 1983; Charles L. Schultze, "Industrial Policy: A Dissent," *The Brookings Review* (Fall 1983): 3-12; and Council of Economic Advisers, *The Economic Report of the President*, 1984, 88-94.

2. The argument is sometimes made that service exports can and should replace the export of goods as the United States becomes a more service-based economy. This line of reasoning seems ill-advised for three reasons. First, the distinction between manufacturing and services is often artificial (as in data processing or telecommunications) and the development of one is often tied to the development of the other. Second, much of the new service activity would be at risk were it not for the proximity of the associated manufacturing activities. Could the United States expect to lead in computer software without a strong thrust in hardware, for example, or in telecommunications services. Third, the accounting system has significant distortions that probably underestimate service exports—particularly in new areas such as data banks in the United States—but that also classify royalties and other fees based on manufacturing activities abroad as service income. The important point is the linkage between manufacturing and services, not the accounting distinctions of "either-or."

3. Otto Eckstein, *The DRI Report on U.S. Manufacturing Industries* (New York: McGraw-Hill Book Company, 1984), in collaboration with Data Resources, Inc., Boston, Massachusetts.

4. Council of Economic Advisers, *The Economic Report of the President*, February 1983, 56.

5. Ibid., 58-59.

6. Ibid., 79.

7. Ibid., 80-81.

8. Ibid., 53.

9. Michael Albert, *Un Pari pour L'Europe* (Paris: Editions du Seuil, 1983), 16.

10. Robert U. Ayres, *The Next Industrial Revolution* (Cambridge, Mass.: Ballinger Press, 1984), 11.

11. Council of Economic Advisers, *The Economic Report of the President*, February 1984, 260.

12. For a recent example of this approach, see chapter 3 of the Council of Economic Advisers, *The Economic Report of the President*, February 1983, or Lawrence, "Changes in U.S. Industrial Structure," 32.

13. Council of Economic Advisers, *Economic Report*, February 1983, 67.

14. Ibid., 53.

15. Lawrence, "Changes in U.S. Industrial Structure," 29.

16. William Abernathy and Robert Hayes, "Managing Our Way to Economic Decline," *Harvard Business Review* (July-August 1980): 67-77; Ira Magaziner and Robert Reich, *Minding America's Business* (New York: Harcourt Brace Jovanovich, 1982), 117; and Robert Reich, "The Next American Frontier," *Atlantic Monthly* (March 1983): 52. For a similar analysis of the decline of British industry vis-à-vis Germany, see R.J.S. Hoffman, *Great Britain and the German Trade Rivalry* (Philadelphia: University of Pennsylvania Press, 1933), 73-105.

17. Eckstein, *Report on U.S. Manufacturing Industries*.

18. See David A. Garvin, "Quality on the Line," *Harvard Business Review* (September-October 1983): 64-75.

19. Robert Reich, "Why the U.S. Needs an Industrial Policy," *Harvard Business Review* (February-March 1982): 74-81; and Reich and Magaziner, *Minding America's Business*, 341.

20. Reich, *Harvard Business Review* (January-February 1982): 80. Reprinted by permission of the *Harvard Business Review*. Copyright © 1982 by the President and Fellows of Harvard College; all rights reserved.

21. Ibid., 79.

22. Ibid., 80.

23. Brian Atherton, in conversation with Michael Houser, *Euro Asia Business Review* 2 (1 November 1983): 48-49.

24. Donald Morse and Edward Olsen, "Japanese Bureaucratic Edge," *Foreign Policy* (Fall 1982): 172.

25. Chalmers Johnson, *MITI and the Japanese Miracle* (Palo Alto, Calif.: Stanford University Press, 1982), chapter 1.

26. Lawrence, "Changes in U.S. Industrial Structure," 18.

CHAPTER 2 NOTES

1. Richard Caves and Ronald W. Jones, *World Trade and Payments* (Toronto: Little, Brown & Co., 1981).

2. Caves and Jones, *World Trade*, 115.

3. For other discussions of the inadequacy of the theory of comparative advantage in depicting aggregate trade flows of manufactured goods, see John Zysman and Laura Tyson, *American Industry in International Competition* (Ithaca, N.Y.: Cornell University Press, 1983); Paul Krugman, "New Theories of Trade Among Industrial Countries," *American Economic Review*, Papers and Proceedings, May 1983.

4. Caves and Jones, *World Trade*, 116.

5. Regina Kelly, *The Impact of Technological Innovation on Trade Patterns*, U.S. Department of Commerce, Bureau of International Economic Policy and Research, ER-24, December

1977. See also Chase Econometric Associates, Inc., *Long-Term Interindustry Forecast and Analysis*, December 1983. This recent study produces a similar ranking using 1977-79 data.

6. Based on data presented in "An Assessment of U.S. Competitiveness in High Technology Industries," prepared by the International Trade Administration for the Cabinet Council on Commerce and Trade, table 23, October 1982, A42-43.

7. Almost all of the gains had been achieved by 1970, as shown in chapter 1, figure 1-17, this volume.

8. "The Competitiveness of the European Community Industry," Commission of the European Communities, Brussels, 5 March 1982, 15-16.

9. Miyohei Shinohara, *Industrial Growth, Trade and Dynamic Patterns in the Japanese Economy* (Tokyo: University of Tokyo Press, 1982), 88.

10. Centre des Etudes Prospectives et D'Informations Internationales, Paris, France.

11. International Monetary Fund, *International Financial Statistics* and UNCTAD, *Handbook of International Trade and Development Statistics*, as cited in Roger Cass, *The World Economy* (Santa Barbara, Calif.: NAE Research Associates, 1983). For an earlier comparison, see also David B. Yoffie, *Power & Protectionism* (New York: Columbia University Press, 1983), 214.

12. Earlier discussion on dynamic comparative advantages may be found in (1) Bruce R. Scott, "Can Industry Survive the Welfare State?" *Harvard Business Review* (September-October 1982); (2) John Zysman and Stephen S. Cohen, *The Mercantilist Challenge to the Liberal International Trade Order*, a study prepared for the use of the Joint Economic Committee, U.S. Senate, 97th Cong., December 1982; and (3) Robert Reich, "Beyond Free Trade," *Foreign Affairs* (Spring 1983).

13. Ernest Gellner, "Scale and Nation," *Philosophy of the Social Sciences* 3 (1973): 15-16, as quoted in Chalmers Johnson, *MITI and the Japanese Miracle* (Stanford, Calif.: Stanford University Press, 1982), 16.

14. Shinohara, *Industrial Growth*, 24.

15. Zysman and Cohen, *The Mercantilist Challenge*, 10.

16. Charles L. Schultze, "Industrial Policy: A Dissent," *Brookings Review* (Fall 1983).

17. Yoshizo Ikeda, "Japanese Industrial Policies," address given at John F. Kennedy School of Government, Harvard University, 11 October 1983. See also Shinohara, *Industrial Growth*, chapters 2 and 3.

18. OECD, *The Industrial Policy of Japan*, Paris, 1972, 15.

19. Shinohara, *Industrial Growth*, 24 25.

20. William L. Givens, "The U.S. Can No Longer Afford Free Trade," *Business Week*, 22 November 1982, 15.

21. Givens, "U.S. Can No Longer Afford Free Trade"; and Shinohara, 48-49.

22. Shinohara, *Industrial Growth*, 49.

23. Johnson, *MITI and the Japanese Miracle*, 16.

24. For an analysis of the "controlled competition" evidenced in Japan, see Zysman and Cohen, *The Mercantilist Challenge*, 11-24, and Zysman and Tyson, *American Industry in International Competition*.

25. Bruce R. Scott, "How Practical is National Economic Planning?" *Harvard Business Review* (March-April 1978): 131.

26. Michel Albert, *Un Pari pour L'Europe* (Paris: Editions du Seuil, 1983).

27. Michel Albert and James Ball, "Towards European Economic Recovery in the 1980s," European Parliament Working Documents, 1983-84, 7 July 1983, 11-12.

28. Typically, governments do not publish data on work days lost to illness, in part because there is an implication that one is collecting and publishing data on absenteeism, and not just on illness. Nevertheless, senior business executives who have examined their company records tell a consistent story. Prior to the change in eligibility, days lost due to illness were typically in the range of 3-4 percent of the workweek. After the change, the figure climbed gradually to about 10 percent, rising first in urban areas where there was more anonymity and also in unpleasant or difficult occupations. A longtime member of the cabinet of the Federal Republic of Germany noted that Germany had not only shared this experience, but that in industries such as mining and steel the days lost went as high as 15 percent following the change in eligibility for sickness benefits.

The economic impact of these days lost is even greater because they are not randomly distributed. They tend to be concentrated on Mondays and Fridays, still more before and after major holidays, and especially at the end of the year when the combination of poor weather, holidays, and the highest marginal tax rates have a combined effect. While the prolonged nature of the recession has reduced these rates in some countries to more like 8 percent, even the latter figure is very large when compared with the often-cited comparisons of days lost due to strikes, which are, with rare exceptions, a fraction of 1 percent of the workweek.

29. Peter G. Peterson, "Social Security: The Coming Crash," *The New York Review of Books*, 2 December 1982.

30. Senate Finance Committee, U.S. Congress, *Estimates of Federal Tax Expenditures for Fiscal Years 1981-1986*, 1981.

31. Ezra F. Vogel, *Japan as Number 1, Lessons for America* (Cambridge, Mass.: Harvard University Press, 1979), 189.

32. Ibid., 185-86.

33. Ibid., 191.

34. Ibid., 192.

35. Ibid., 201.

36. Charles A. Murray, "The Two Wars Against Poverty: Economic Growth and the Great Society," *The Public Interest* (Fall 1982): 10.

37. Murray, "Two Wars Against Poverty," 13.

38. Lyndon B. Johnson, quoted in the *New York Times*, 21 August 1964, 1, as cited in Murray, "Two Wars Against Poverty," 9.

39. Johnson, *MITI and the Japanese Miracle*, 243-74.

40. Joseph L. Bower, *The Two Faces of Management* (Boston: Houghton Mifflin Co., 1983).

41. Scott, "Can Industry Survive the Welfare State?"

42. John H. McArthur and Bruce R. Scott, *Industrial Planning in France* (Boston: Harvard Business School, 1969), chapter 3.

43. Robert B. Reich, "Why the U.S. Needs an Industrial Policy," *Harvard Business Review* (January-February 1982): 74-81.

44. Ibid., 76.

45. "Corporate Taxes: Why Some Firms Pay Less," *Dun's Business Month*, May 1983, 36-42.

46. Reich, "Why the U.S. Needs an Industrial Policy," 75.

47. Albert, *Un Pari pour L'Europe*; and Albert and Ball, "Towards European Economic Recovery."

48. Shinohara, *Industrial Growth*, 118-19.

49. William Cline, *Reciprocity—A New Approach to World Trade Policy?* (Washington, D.C.: Institute for International Economics, September 1982), 39-40.

50. Zysman and Cohen, *The Mercantilist Challenge*.

CHAPTER 3 NOTES

1. See the chapter by Alan Wolff for a detailed review of U.S. trade policy goals.

2. See chapter 4 by Yoshino and Fong, this volume.

3. Worldwide semiconductor employment over the same period is likely to double to 500,000.

4. Semiconductors are divided into two major categories: discrete devices and integrated circuits. Market share in integrated circuits, the newer and more rapidly growing product category, provides a better measure of competitiveness than either semiconductors as a whole or discrete devices. The focus throughout the chapter is thus placed on integrated circuits rather than the broader semiconductor classification.

5. U.S. Department of Commerce, *U.S. Industrial Outlook, 1982*. The U.S. Department of Commerce statistics may underestimate U.S. exports to Japan to some degree because U.S. firms export to Japan from their offshore facilities as well as directly from the United States.

Similarly, some U.S. firms, notably Texas Instruments, operate manufacturing subsidiaries in Japan that export semiconductors made in Japan to the United States. Nevertheless, the Commerce Department's measures of the trade balance in semiconductors do not include semiconductor components in electronic equipment imported into the United States from Japan. In 1978, for example, the value of the semiconductor content contained in electronic equipment exported by Japan to the United States was almost three times the value of visible component exports. See *World Semiconductor Industry in Transition 1978-1983* (Cambridge, Mass.: Arthur D. Little, 1980).

6. U.S. Department of Commerce, *A Report on the U.S. Semiconductor Industry* (Washington, D.C.: Government Printing Office, 1979).

7. The Semiconductor Industry Association estimates that the U.S. share of the Japanese IC market dropped to 12 percent in 1981. Semiconductor Industry Association, *The Effect of Targeting on World Semiconductor Consumption* (February 1983), 72.

8. The results of the agreement are likely to be masked by the condition of today's semiconductor market. With orders for semiconductors running ahead of the ability of all the world's manufacturers to produce them, Japanese electronics firms are more than willing to buy parts wherever they can get them. What concerns U.S. producers now is not a lack of Japanese orders, but the fear that if they increase their manufacturing capacity in an effort to supply Japanese customers, they will be left with excess capacity in another year or two when Japanese manufacturing capacity also has expanded or when the next downturn occurs in the cyclical semiconductor industry.

9. Semiconductor Industry Association, *Effect of Targeting*, 74.

10. Progress toward increasing the number of circuit elements per chip was spurred by the development of metal-oxide semiconductor (MOS) technology in the 1960s. Although MOS circuits are slower than bipolar devices—the dominant semiconductor devices of the 1950s—they consume less power and dissipate less heat. Consequently, MOS technology permits a denser packing of circuit elements, and MOS circuits have therefore tended to lead the way down the miniaturization trajectory. In addition, the low power consumption of MOS devices made possible portable products like electronic calculators and electronic watches, which must use power sparingly to give satisfactory battery life. In contrast, the high-speed characteristic of bipolar technology makes it relatively more attractive for applications involving real-time signal processing, such as radar and communications equipment.

11. Fabrication costs per functional element are lowered by moving to increasingly expensive production equipment that can achieve finer patterns but at the same time significantly increase productivity. Assembly costs per unit are lowered as automation increases productivity. Partially offsetting these trends is the need for clean-room manufacturing facilities with fewer particulate impurities.

12. In 1949, the Justice Department initiated an antitrust suit against AT&T that sought to separate Western Electric from the Bell System. Although the 1956 consent decree left Western Electric within AT&T, Western Electric was required to administer the licensing of Bell Laboratories' patents in a way that made the technology available to both domestic and foreign firms.

13. Gordon E. Moore, "VLSI: Some Fundamental Challenges," *IEEE Spectrum* (April 1979): 30-37. The main thrust of VLSI technology will be to fabricate as many transistors and other circuit elements as possible on a chip. However, the major changes will come not in the manufacturing processes but in the technologies needed to design the chip and its package. Given the complexity of VLSI chips, the industry is intensifying its efforts to automate the IC design process. Design automation will, in turn, transform the industry away from a commodity orientation to a value-added, engineering service business.

14. "Semiconductor Makers Facing Costly Choice on Equipment," *Wall Street Journal*, 15 October 1982. In addition to increased product sophistication, inflation has also driven IC production equipment prices up sharply. From 1975 through 1980, for example, the price of a wafer fabrication module increased at an annual compound rate of nearly 40 percent and is expected to continue at that rate through 1985. See U.S. Department of Commerce, *U.S. Industrial Outlook 1981*, chapter 26.

15. This drop in the rate of entry has also been attributed to the fact that the increasing complexity of design and production process has made it far more difficult for a small number

of employees to establish a viable and highly competitive advanced production capability. Richard C. Levin, "The Semiconductor Industry," in *Government and Technical Progress: A Cross-Industry Analysis*, ed. Richard R. Nelson (New York: Pergamon Press, 1983), 29.

16. Integrated Circuit Engineering Corporation, *Status 1983: A Report on the Integrated Circuit Industry* (Scottsdale, Arizona: ICE Corporation, 1983).

17. Ibid. This percentage could be much higher if one or two major merchant producers are acquired by companies that choose to focus production on in-house systems needs rather than on those of the open market.

18. "Do-It-Yourself Chips: A New Case of Startup Fever," *Business Week*, 21 March 1983. Most of these start-ups have focused on a product called a gate array—a chip that consists of a standardized grid of transistors that are connected in the last processing step to give the chip a unique design for performing a specific task. Others, however, offer standard cell designs in which a custom chip can be designed more easily by putting together functional blocks of circuitry from standard cell "libraries" stored in a computer memory. Many industry observers foresee fully custom chips displacing both approaches as more sophisticated computer-aided design tools become available.

19. One widely publicized example is IBM's recent purchase of a 12 percent stake in Intel for $250 million—an amount that nearly equaled Intel's combined 1982 spending for capital investments ($130 million) and R&D ($130 million). Intel has thus obtained valuable support without being controlled by IBM, and IBM has stated that the stock purchase was made as an investment and to strengthen Intel as an IBM supplier.

20. "Chipmakers Pool Their Research to Stay Competitive," *Business Week*, 23 May 1983.

21. For discussion of pre-1977 competition in several major semiconductor product lines, see Robert W. Wilson et al., *Innovation, Competition, and Government Policy in the Semiconductor Industry* (Lexington, Mass.: D.C. Heath & Co., 1980).

22. Robert W. Wilson's study of the 1970-78 period emphasizes the importance of delivery: "Timely delivery is frequently worth more to customers than new-product features or an edge in price or reliability, because most users of integrated circuits insert them into equipment in assembly-line factory operations. Integrated circuits are intermediate goods that must be delivered on time to avoid costly assembly-line shutdown. Since delivery problems usually result from production yield problems, delivery is clearly affected by variables throughout the firm. Firms that can control their operations carefully enough to assure good delivery gain an advantage over firms that cannot." Wilson, *Innovation, Competition, and Government Policy*, 80.

23. The Semiconductor Industry Association has estimated that the average DRAM price per bit in mid-1981 was 39 percent lower than the level prices were expected to be, given actual cumulative volume and the observed historical relationship between cumulative volume and price. Semiconductor Industry Association, *Effect of Targeting*, 41.

24. In the late 1970s, the Department of Defense became concerned over the U.S. industry's declining interest in fulfilling DOD needs. The Yoshino-Fong chapter discusses this issue and the program that it spawned, the Very High Speed Integrated Circuit (VHSIC) program. Although the VHSIC program was not originally conceived as a response to emerging Japanese competition, DOD officials have subsequently pointed to Japanese gains as one of the justifications for VHSIC.

For a theoretical discussion of firm rivalry in which governments perceive themselves as being in competition with each other for profitable international markets, see James A. Branden and Barbara J. Spencer, "Export Subsidies and International Market Share Rivalry" (unpublished paper, Queens University, 1982).

25. It should be noted that DOD's VHSIC program has not served as a credible threat to the Japanese. This is due to the nature of the membership of the VHSIC contractor teams, VHSIC's objectives, and the fact that portions of VHSIC research are being performed in university environments open to the Japanese.

26. Given the close relationships between NTT's LSI laboratories and the major Japanese semiconductor producers, the R&D performed at these facilities is actually a resource for the entire Japanese industry to draw upon. Neither IBM nor Bell Labs makes its research available to other firms on the favorable terms that NTT does.

27. This list is, in part, prepared by Erich Bloch, vice-president, IBM.

CHAPTER 4 NOTES

1. The following description is based upon: Committee on Assessment of the Impact of the DOD Very High Speed Integrated Circuit Program, *An Assessment of the Impact of the Department of Defense Very High Speed Integrated Circuit Program* (Washington, D.C.: National Academy Press, 1982); Larry W. Sumney, "VHSIC Status and Issues," 1981 VHSIC Conference, unpublished report; and "The VHSIC Program: Review and Status," 15 October 1982, unpublished report prepared by the VHSIC Program Office.

2. Key figures in the establishment of the program were (in descending hierarchical order): Harold Brown, secretary of defense (1977-80); William Perry, undersecretary of defense for research and engineering (1977-80); Ruth Davis, deputy undersecretary of defense for research and advanced technology (1977-79); Leonard Weisberg, director, electronics and physical sciences (1975-79); Larry Sumney, staff specialist for electron devices and VHSIC program manager (1977-82).

3. Committee on Assessment, *An Assessment of the Impact*; Glenn W. Preston, *Large Scale Integrated Circuits for Military Applications* (Arlington, Va.: Institute for Defense Analyses, 1977); Leonard R. Weisberg and Larry W. Sumney, "The New DOD Program on Very High Speed Integrated Circuits (VHSIC)," paper presented to Government Microelectronics Applications Conference, 14 November 1978; VHSIC documentation.

4. Personal interviews with government officials.

5. Committee on Assessment, *An Assessment of the Impact*, 6-7.

6. Personal interview with government official.

7. Based on personal interviews with government officials; also VHSIC documentation and Weisberg and Sumney, 14 November 1978.

8. VHSIC documentation.

9. The following two paragraphs are based upon VHSIC documentation and personal interviews with government and company officials.

10. The technologies investigated were bipolar, N-channel metal-oxide-semiconductor, complementary-metal-oxide-semiconductor, and silicon-on-sapphire.

11. The eighteen bidders interviewed, classified according to type of firm, were: (a) military systems houses: GE, Hughes, Rockwell, Sanders Associates, TRW; (b) merchant semiconductor firms: Analog Devices, Intersil, Motorola, National Semiconductor, Signetics, Texas Instruments; (c) computer manufacturers: Control Data, Honeywell, IBM, Sperry; and (d) semiconductor equipment manufacturers: Perkin-Elmer, Varian Associates. For analytical purposes, the eighteenth company, Bell Labs, can be classified with merchant semiconductor firms. Bell's position toward VHSIC parallels that of IC makers.

12. VHSIC documentation.

13. VHSIC documentation.

14. Ruth M. Davis, "The DOD Initiative in Integrated Circuits," *IEEE Computer* (July 1979): 78.

15. Personal interviews with government and company officials.

16. Personal interviews with company officials.

17. Personal interviews with company officials.

18. VHSIC documentation.

19. VHSIC documentation. This discussion reflects on the debate, often with VHSIC as a battleground, over whether military technology diverges from commercial efforts. A number of firms, notably Intel, declined to participate in VHSIC because such a divergence was perceived.

Experts cannot agree on this issue. From a nontechnical point of view, the entire debate may be misguided. The question is almost assuredly not an "either-or" matter. Furthermore, advocates should consider the short-term versus long-term distinction. A short-term divergence may, for instance, contribute to long-term objectives. Such circumstances would seem to apply to much of Japanese industrial policy.

It is important to note that the VHSIC program was designed to avoid divergence from commercial technology and that the significant portion of the American electronics industry that joined the program sees no divergence. Most of these companies would not have been interested in the program if it aimed solely at developing military-specific technology. VHSIC technology is seen as generic rather than a dead-end military affair.

20. Personal interviews with company officials; also David H. Moore and William J. Towle, *The Industry Impact of the Very High Speed Integrated Circuit Program: A Preliminary Analysis* (The Analytic Sciences Corporation, 15 August 1980).

21. Dataquest, *Semiconductor Industry Service*, 15 June 1980, 1.5-7; Robert W. Wilson, Peter K. Ashton, and Thomas P. Egan, *Innovation, Competition, and Government Policy in the Semiconductor Industry* (Lexington, Mass.: D. C. Heath, 1980), 167.

22. *Business Week*, 23 May 1983, 83.

23. Personal interviews with company officials.

24. Personal interviews with company officials.

CHAPTER 5 NOTES

1. Lest one think that a change in exchange rates would solve the cost problem, Ford's internal studies have shown the impact of the value of the yen on the relative delivered cost of Japanese autos in America. According to Ford, Japan's delivered cost advantage (*exclusive* of Japanese commodity tax rebates and U.S. tariffs) varies from $2,100 at 250 yen/dollar to $1,900 at 220 yen to $1,400 at 185 yen. Thus, even assuming a radical upward shift in the dollar value of the yen, U.S. automakers will continue to have substantially higher production costs than the Japanese.

2. According to Chrysler's controller's office, a total of eighty-seven hours was required to manufacture a small car in the United States in November 1982. The comparable hours in Japan were estimated at thirty-five, for a Japanese advantage of fifty-two hours.

3. Speech delivered as part of J.A. Vickers Lecture Series, University of Kansas, 14 October 1983.

CHAPTER 6 NOTES

1. U.S. Department of Commerce and U.S. Trade Representative, *Industry Consultations Program Sector Profiles* (1983), 356.

2. U.S. Department of Commerce, Bureau of the Census, *1977 Census of Manufactures* (Washington, D.C., 1980).

3. U.S. Department of Labor, Bureau of Labor Statistics, *Employment and Earnings* (Washington, D.C.).

4. *The Dependency of the U.S. Economy on the Fiber/Textile/Apparel Industrial Complex*, prepared for the American Textile Manufacturers Institute (ATMI) by Economic Consulting Services Inc., Washington, D.C., January1981.

5. U.S. Department of Commerce, Bureau of the Census, *1981 Annual Survey of Manufactures* (Washington, D.C., 1983).

6. A detailed examination of the interrelationships among sectors of the textile and apparel industries is provided in *Fibers/Textiles/Apparel: A Unified Industry Dealing with the Import Problem*, prepared for the ATMI by Economic Consulting Services Inc., Washington, D.C., October 1980; and *The Competitive Status of the U.S. Fibers, Textiles, and Apparel Complex*, National Academy of Engineering and National Research Council, National Academy Press, Washington, D.C., 1983.

7. This general statement does not apply evenly across the board to all segments of these industries. In addition, some of the most recent technological innovations in apparel production process involve costly capital equipment, investment in which is limited to the largest apparel producers.

8. Council on Wage and Price Stability, Executive Office of the President, *Textiles/Apparel, A Study of the Textile and Apparel Industries* (Washington, D.C., July 1978).

9. American Textile Manufacturers Institute, *Textile Hi-Lights* (Washington, D.C.).

10. U.S. Congress, House Subcommittee on Trade of the Committee on Ways and Means, *Library of Congress Study on Imports and Consumer Prices*, Ways and Means Committee Print: 95-43, 19 July 1977.

11. This situation points up a major difference between the fiber/textile/apparel complex in the United States compared with that in Japan. Trade in these products is determined to a large extent by retailers in the United States. In Japan, the man-made fiber producers control, to a major extent, the production and distribution not only of the fiber they produce but also the textile mill products and apparel produced by themselves and, more important, by others in Japan and elsewhere in East Asia.

12. Department of Labor, *Employment and Earnings*.

13. Ibid., and unpublished data from the Bureau of Labor Statistics.

14. *Impact of Import Penetration on Labor in Selected U.S. Industries and Related Problems of Adjustment*, prepared under contract for the U.S. Department of Labor by Economic Consulting Services Inc. (Washington, D.C., October 1978).

15. U.S. Department of Commerce, *1983 U.S. Industrial Outlook* (January 1983).

16. Department of Labor, *Employment and Earnings*.

17. The U.S. government has established the poverty level for families of four and families of five at $9,862 and $11,684, respectively. See U.S. Department of Commerce, Bureau of the Census, *Money Income and Poverty Status of Families and Persons in the United States: 1982*.

18. U.S. Department of Commerce, Bureau of the Census, *1981 Annual Survey of Manufactures* (Washington, D.C., April 1983).

19. Ibid.

20. Ibid.

21. In 1980, production worker wages in the textile and apparel industries accounted for 16.2 percent of the value of shipments, compared with 11.7 percent for all industries (excluding petroleum and coal products). See *1981 Annual Survey of Manufactures*.

22. Per capita fiber consumption (in the form of textiles and apparel) in the United States increased between 1974 and 1979, from 21.9 kg to 23.3 kg, then declined to 21.1 kg in 1980, according to unpublished data of the Food and Agriculture Organization of the United Nations.

23. Exhibit 6-2 provides a comparison of average hourly labor costs in the United States and selected major developing country exporters of textiles and apparel, which reflects the dramatic labor cost advantage of these countries.

24. A description of such practices in two of the world's largest exporters of textiles and apparel is provided in the U.S. Department of Commerce's *Country Market Survey* of the textile and apparel industries of Korea and Taiwan:

> "The development of the Korean apparel industry has been controlled and planned by the Korean Government to fit import substitution first and export objectives second. The apparel industry, especially on the export side, is designed to be the primary consumer of products that the Korean textile industry produces so as to complete the vertical integration of the industry. It is sheltered by unbreachable nontariff barriers and is the beneficiary of frequent government incentives in the form of international marketing assistance, tax credits, and direct aid." (See U.S. Department of Commerce, *Country Market Survey-Apparel Korea*, December 1979.)

> "It [the textile and apparel industry in Taiwan] is organized to be self sufficient and an important earner of foreign exchange, through exports. Participation by Taiwan authorities, in all aspects of the industry, is well established. . . . Currently imports of most textiles and apparel for sale in the domestic market are restricted. The importing of textiles for prompt use in the manufacturing of goods to be sold in the export market is permitted on a carefully controlled, import permit basis." (See U.S. Department of Commerce, *Country Market Survey-Textiles Taiwan*, May 1980.)

An additional summary of some of the more obvious trade restrictions in many developing countries appears in U.S. Department of Commerce, *Foreign Regulations Affecting U.S. Textile/Apparel Exports* (August 1981).

25. Textile and apparel products covered by the MFA are limited to those made from cotton, wool, and man-made fiber, which account for the vast majority of trade and U.S. production of textiles and apparel.

26. U.S. Department of Agriculture data and *Textile Hi-Lights*. Measurement of imports under the bilateral agreements and the restraints on imports provided thereunder are normally

expressed in square yards equivalent, or SYE, and actual units of quantity. Pound measurements are used here for comparison with domestic production, since no measurement of the total square years equivalent of domestic production is available. One should note that the square yards equivalents of a pound of cotton, a pound of man-made fiber, and a pound of wool vary widely.

27. U.S. Department of Commerce, Office of Textiles and Apparel; and *Textile Hi-Lights*.

28. *Textile Hi-Lights*.

29. Carpets and rugs accounted for approximately 15 percent of total U.S. mill consumption of fibers in 1982. See *Textile Organon*, Textile Economics Bureau, Inc., New York, N.Y.

30. *Textile Hi-Lights*.

31. U.S. Department of Commerce, *U.S. Production, Imports, and Import/Production Ratios for Cotton, Wool and Man-Made Fiber Textiles and Apparel* (Washington, D.C., 1978 and 1983).

32. Nevertheless, in terms of quantity the United States was a net exporter of man-made fiber products until 1969, which contributed to the exclusion of such products from bilateral agreements until 1971.

33. Negotiations with these countries took two years to conclude. Japan consistently refused to control its exports of man-made fiber textiles and apparel, even though it had already entered into agreements with eleven other countries restricting its exports to these markets. See "Japan's Trade and Investment Policies—Challenge for the United States," speech to the American Management Association by Stanley Nehmer, deputy assistant secretary of commerce, 17 March 1971.

34. The method of control used by the United States to implement the specific restraints does not involve import licenses, but rather relies primarily on export controls by the foreign country. U.S. Customs permits imports of articles under specific restraints from the participating country to enter on a first-come, first-served basis, as long as the articles are accompanied by documentation of valid export authorization.

35. In response to the problem, the United States has established an authorization system with Hong Kong, Korea, and Taiwan, the three top foreign country suppliers. This system has improved the U.S. government's ability to anticipate import trends, but the system retains an automatic 15 percent bonus, or uplift feature, in setting new specific restraints.

36. President Kennedy directed in 1962 that the LTA be administered to maintain penetration (the ratio of imports to domestic consumption) at or below 6 percent. However, this directive was never implemented. See R. Buford Brandis, *The Making of Textile Trade Policy 1935-1981*, American Textile Manufacturers Institute (Washington, D.C., 1982).

37. General Agreement on Tariffs and Trade, *Protocol Extending the Arrangement Regarding International Trade in Textiles*, Geneva, 14 December 1977, paragraph 5.3.

38. Ibid., 22 December 1981, paragraph 9.

39. Letter from Ronald Reagan to Senator Thurmond, 3 September 1980. This commitment appears to have been diluted recently in a speech by President Reagan on 20 September 1983, when he said, ". . . our administration will strive to work toward an ever closer relationship of textile imports and domestic market growth, consistent with our existing international obligations." Weekly Compilation of Presidential Documents, vol. 19, no. 38, 26 September 1983.

40. U.S. Department of Commerce, International Agreements and Monitoring Division, Office of Textiles and Apparel, International Trade Administration, *United States Textile and Apparel Trade* (August 1983).

41. The protocol extending the MFA on 22 December 1981 specifically noted the problems caused by significant differences between negotiated restraint levels and actual imports, which allowed for sharp and substantial increases in imports from one year of shortfall to the following year, if limits are filled to the base restraint level and flexibility provisions are utilized. Mutually satisfactory solutions to this problem were allowed in the protocol.

42. These overall ceilings meant that whether or not certain product categories were restricted, total exports of textiles and apparel from a country could not exceed the overall ceiling.

43. The record of investment by the textile mill products sector and the judgment of decision makers in the industry clearly support this relationship. The bilateral agreements on wool and man-made fiber textiles and apparel negotiated with Japan, Korea, Taiwan, and Hong Kong in

1971, three years before the MFA went into effect, contributed to the confidence of the industry in its future and its subsequent investments.

44. Other measures of the significant improvement in the productivity of the textile mill sector and its shift to greater capital intensity can be found in value added per employee and net capital stock per employee. Data for 1967 and 1979 show the following:

($ thousands)	1967	1979
Value added per employee	$8.76	$21.28
Net capital stock per employee	7.51	26.20

45. This discussion of technological developments was drawn from *The Competitive Status of the U.S. Fibers, Textiles, and Apparel Complex.*

46. *Textile Hi-Lights.*

47. These trends partly reflect the MFA's special consideration to cotton textiles from cotton-producing countries. See article 6 of the MFA and paragraph 12 of the protocol extending the MFA, 22 December 1981.

48. These and subsequent import penetration figures are taken from *U.S. Production, Imports and Import/Production Ratios for Cotton, Wool, and Man-Made Fiber Textiles and Apparel.*

49. Based on data available from the U.S. International Trade Commission, the Department of Commerce, and Footwear Industries of America, Inc.

50. Criticism has been levied about the expensive and cumbersome nature of the MFA, because of the lengthy negotiations and the government bureaucracies needed to administer the program. However, the main cause of the expense, bureaucracy, and cumbersome nature is the piecemeal approach that has historically been taken, and the attempts by the federal government to make the MFA as unrestrictive as possible. A vastly streamlined and less expensive system of administration could be readily developed, consisting of global quotas, with allocations of quotas by country and by product based on historical trade. However, it is the very desire of the federal government to maintain as open and flexible a system as possible that has largely created the expense and complexity of the system.

51. One estimate of employment losses in the U.S. apparel industry alone under free trade is 570,000 jobs by 1990. This estimate is provided in Donald B. Keesing and Martin Wolf, *Textile Quotas Against Developing Countries,* Trade Policy Research Centre (London, England, 1980). The authors are strongly against continuation of the MFA.

52. During the 1975 recession, the unemployment rates for nonfarm laborers and machine operators rose to 16 percent and 15 percent, respectively, which were far above the unemployment rates for other types of occupations, which ranged from 3.0 percent to 8.5 percent. This pattern has continued ever since, despite economic recovery during some years. In 1982, 19 percent of nonfarm laborers and 18 percent of machine operators were unemployed, far higher than other occupations which had unemployment rates generally well below the 10 percent average. See *Employment and Earnings,* and U.S. Department of Commerce, *Statistical Abstract of the United States 1982-1983.*

53. U.S. International Trade Commission, *U.S. Trade-Related Employment,* publication 1445 (October 1983). The ITC admits it understated the job displacement caused by U.S. imports of apparel. See Appendix C of the ITC report.

54. Ibid.

55. "Jobless-Rate Dip Said Masking Bigger Woes," *Washington Post,* 19 August 1982, D8.

56. It is possible that unilateral import quotas could also result not from termination of the MFA but from the failure of the MFA, as implemented, to prevent growing market disruption. In such a case, the MFA would be terminated after, and not before, unilateral import quotas would be established.

57. Such a system has been established by the U.S. government with regard to imports of specialty steel. Global ceilings have been established for three specialty steel products, orderly marketing (bilateral) agreements with certain countries have resulted in the allocation of parts of the global ceilings to such countries, and all other foreign suppliers may ship on a first-come, first-served basis under the remainder of the global quota.

58. A review of historical Japanese formal trade barriers and industrial targeting practices is provided in U.S. International Trade Commission, *Foreign Industrial Targeting and Its Effects on U.S. Industries, Phase I: Japan*, publication 1437 (October 1983). In 1982, Japan had the second largest GNP in the free world, yet imported fewer manufactures than Canada or the Netherlands, both with far smaller GNPs and population:

	1982 Imports of Manufactured Goods (billions of U.S. $)	1981 GNP (billions of U.S. $)	1981 Population (millions)	1981 GNP per Capita (U.S. $)
Japan	30.3	1,186	118	10,080
Canada	41.1	276	24	11,400
Netherlands	32.9	168	14	11,790

Source: *1983 World Bank Atlas*, The World Bank, and *International Economic Indicators*, U.S. Department of Commerce, Washington, D.C.

59. One estimate claims that defense funding accounts for one-third of America's research and development. See *Proposed Changes in Domestic Policies to Improve U.S. International Competitiveness*, prepared for the Coalition of International Trade Equity by Control Data Corporation, March 1983.

60. Documentation of such subsidies can be found in a series of determinations in recent years by the International Trade Administration of the U.S. Department of Commerce in countervailing duty investigations of imports of various steel products from a variety of countries.

61. U.S. International Trade Commission, Report to the President on Investigation no. TA-203-7 under Section 203 of the Trade Act of 1974, *Nonrubber Footwear*, publication 1139 (Washington, D.C., April 1981).

62. Managed trade would not eliminate these practices, of course. Despite the MFA, the U.S. government frequently finds that textile and apparel products are being dumped or subsidized. These practices continue largely because of competition among countries within restraint levels or in uncontrolled product categories. Managed trade, however, can reduce the extent of such practices.

63. Many countries already maintain restrictive tariff and nontariff barriers on U.S. exports of many products in which the United States is highly competitive.

CHAPTER 7 NOTES

1. The Europeans and Japanese have argued that U.S. competitiveness is based on subsidized raw material prices. In fact, the U.S. industry is built on ethane, which permits a simpler, less sophisticated chemistry to be exploited, in comparison with the naphtha-based chemistry of Europe and Japan. This difference seems to have been far more important than any alleged effect of regulation on the price of ethane, a point that has been accepted in a series of GATT negotiations.

2. In the United States between 1970 and 1980 feedstock cost rose 585% and product prices 161%.

3. A more inclusive category than petrochemicals.

4. Because of space limitations, Belgium (Solvay and Petrochime) and Holland (DSM) have not been included.

5. U.S. Department of Commerce, Office of Competitive Assessment, Assistant Secretary for Productivity, Technology, and Innovation, "The Medium to Long-Range International Competitiveness of the United States Petrochemical Industry: A Competitive Assessment."

6. In the summer of 1983 the Aramco partners were thought to be threatened by the emergence of a Swiss-based Saudi trading company, selling Saudi crude directly to OECD customers and the spot market.

CHAPTER 8 NOTES

1. A related antitrust case, alleging a conspiracy on the part of Japanese producers, continues.

2. There are exceptions to this rough dichotomy. Occasionally, America's preoccupation with legal rights substitutes for sound judgment in the areas of agricultural interests as well. The United States has brought a GATT case against Japan for a number of residual agricultural quotas, seemingly because they are not justified under the GATT rather than that there is strong commercial interest to be served in prosecuting these cases. In this process, Japanese resentment is provoked, more valuable U.S. export goals are ignored, and the chances of success are nil in terms of obtaining valuable additional market access.

CHAPTER 9 NOTES

1. Richard R. Nelson, "'World Leadership,' the 'Technological Gap,' and National Science Policy," *Minerva* 9 (July 1971): 386-99.

2. Raymond Vernon, "International Investment and International Trade in the Product Cycle," *Quarterly Journal of Economics* 80 (May 1966): 190-207.

3. References given in Nelson, "World Leadership," footnote 3, 387.

4. John Newhouse, *The Sporty Game: The High Risk Competitive Business of Making and Selling Commercial Airliners* (New York: Alfred Knopf, 1982).

5. Bruce R. Scott, "American Competitiveness: Concepts, Performance, and Implications," chapter 1, this volume.

6. See William F. Finan and Annette M. LaMond, "Sustaining U.S. Competitiveness in Microelectronics: The Challenge to U.S. Policy," chapter 3, this volume.

7. Ezra F. Vogel, "Machine Tools and Robots: Auxiliary Industry," draft chapter for forthcoming book; cf. also, U.S. Department of Commerce, International Trade Administration, *The Robotics Industry* in series *High Technology Industries: Profiles and Outlooks*, April 1983; Ralph Landau, *The U.S. Position in World Markets: The Effect of Technology on Selected Industries*, adapted from a keynote address presented at the 50th Anniversary meeting of the Accreditation Board for Engineering and Technology, Colorado Springs, 28 October 1982, printed in the Proceedings, cf. especially 34-38.

8. U.S. Department of Commerce, International Trade Administration, *The Computer Industry*, series on *High Technology Industries: Profiles and Outlooks*; H.K. Bowen and J. Pask, eds., "Ceramic Science and Technology in Japan," *American Ceramic Society Bulletin* 61, no. 9 (September 1982); U.S. Congress, Office of Technology Assessment, *Commercial Biotechnology, An International Analysis*, Report OTA-BA-218, January 1984 (Washington, D.C.: GPO, 1984), cf. especially chapter 1, Executive Summary.

9. K. Imai and A. Sakuma, "An Analysis of Japan-U.S. Semiconductor Friction," *Economic Eye, a Quarterly Digest of Views from Japan* 4, nos. 13-18 (Tokyo: Keizai Koho Center, Japan Institute for Social and Economic Affairs, June 1983); cf. also John Zysman and S. Cohen, "Double or Nothing: Open Trade and Competitive Industry," *Foreign Affairs* 6, no. 5 (Summer 1983).

10. Zysman and Cohen, "Double or Nothing"; also Zysman and Cohen, *The Mercantilist Challenge to the Liberal International Trade Order*, prepared for U.S. Congress, Joint Economic Committee, November 1982.

11. See Bruce R. Scott, "National Strategies," chapter 2, this volume.

12. See Michael Y. Yoshino and Glenn R. Fong, "The Very High Speed Integrated Circuit Program: Lessons for Industrial Policy," chapter 4, this volume.

13. Imai and Sakuma, "An Analysis of Japan-U.S. Semiconductor Friction."

14. Raymond Vernon, "Technology's Effects on International Trade: A Look Ahead," in *Emerging Technologies: Consequence for Economic Growth, Structural Change, and Employment*, ed. Herbert Giersch, Institut fur Weltwirtschaft an der Universitat Kiel (Tubingen, West Germany, J.C.B. Mohr [Paul Siebeck], 1982), 145-66.

15. Ibid., 158.

16. National Science Board, *Science Indicators 1980* (Washington, D.C.: National Science Foundation, 1981), 31; see also NSF, *Research and Development in Industry, 1977* (NSF 79-313), 56-57; NSF, *Research and Development in Industry, 1978* (NSF 80-307), 22, 32.

17. U.S. Department of Commerce, International Trade Administration, *An Assessment of U.S. Competitiveness in High Technology Industries* (February 1983), 41, especially footnotes 1, 5.

18. Ibid., 53, table 27.

19. Ibid., 32, figure 1-12.

20. National Science Board, *Science Indicators 1980*, 33, figure 1-14.

21. Ibid., 34, table 1–11.

22. M. Therese Flaherty, "Determinants of Market Share in International Semiconductor Markets," commissioned paper for the Panel on Advanced Technology Competition and the Industrialized Allies, National Research Council, 1982, available from National Academy of Sciences.

23. "The United States and the World Economy," briefing paper distributed to Panel on Advanced Technology Competition and the Industrialized Allies, NAS/NRC, July 1982.

24. Vernon, "International Investment."

25. See chapter 3 this volume.

26. Vogel, "Machine Tools"; Landau, "U.S. Position in World Markets"; U.S. Department of Commerce, International Trade Administration, *High Technology Industry, Profiles and Outlook: The Robotics Industry* (April 1983).

27. Richard R. Nelson and Sidney G. Winter, *An Evolutionary Theory of Economic Change* (Cambridge, Mass.: Harvard University Press, 1982), 289-301.

28. Harvey Brooks, "Policies for Technology Transfer and International Investment," chapter 12 in *The New Atlantic Challenge*, Richard Mayne, ed. (London: Charles Knight & Company, Ltd., 1975), 157-79.

29. The Labor-Industry Coalition for International Trade, *International Trade, Industrial Policies, and the Future of American Industry* (Washington, D.C., April 1983).

30. "The United States and the World Economy," briefing paper.

31. "Economic and Financial Indicators, Trade, Exchange Rates, and Reserves," *The Economist*, 10-17 February 1984, 98.

32. "The United States and the World Economy," briefing paper.

33. Geza Feketekuty and J.S. Aronson, "The World Information Economy," draft paper, to be published.

34. Oswald H. and Gladys D. Ganley, *To Inform or Control? The New Communications Networks* (New York: McGraw-Hill Book Company, 1982), 83-95.

35. National Science Board, *Science Indicators 1980*, 24; also, Gellman Research Associates, Inc., *Indicators of International Trends in Technological Innovation*, report prepared for National Science Board, *Science Indicators 76*.

36. U.S. Department of Commerce, International Trade Administration, *High Technology Industry, Profiles and Outlook: The Computer Industry*, 52, table 2.

37. National Science Board, *Science Indicators 1980*, 25.

38. Ibid., 25, footnote 101.

39. Ibid., 228, table 1-18.

40. Ibid., 25, figure 1-10.

41. Japan Institute for Social and Economic Affairs, *Japan 1983: An International Comparison* (Tokyo: Keizai Koho Center, 1983), 18, figure 4-7.

42. National Science Board, *Science Indicators 1980*, 28, and 232, appendix table 1-23.

43. Gene Gregory, "Japan: New Center of Innovation, Evolving from Imitator to Inventor," in *Speaking of Japan*, vol. 3, no. 18, 2-9 (Keizai Koho Center, Japanese Institute for Social and Economic Affairs, June 1982).

44. Robert Z. Lawrence, "Changes in U.S. Industrial Structure: The Role of Global Forces, Secular Trends and Transitory Cycles," paper prepared for the symposium on Industrial Change and Public Policy organized by the Federal Reserve Bank of Kansas City at Jackson Hole, Wyoming, 25-26 August 1983.

45. National Science Board, *Science Indicators 1980*, 221, table 1-11.

46. Lawrence, "Changes in U.S. Industrial Structure."

47. Harvey Brooks, "Social and Technological Innovation," chapter 1, 1-29, in *Managing Innovation: The Social Dimensions of Creativity, Invention, and Technology*, ed. S.B. Lundstedt and E.W. Colglazier, published with the Aspen Institute of Humanistic Studies and the Ohio State University (New York: Pergamon Press, 1982).

48. National Science Foundation, Division of Industrial Science and Technology, Productivity Improvement Section, *The Process of Technological Innovation: Reviewing the Literature* (Washington, D.C.: NSF, May 1983).

49. David A. Garvin, "Quality on the Line," *Harvard Business Review* (September-October 1983): 65-75.

50. Alan Alshuler and Daniel Roos, *The Future of the Automobile: Global Crisis and Transformation*, chapters 7 and 8 (Cambridge, Mass.: MIT Press, forthcoming 1984).

51. Malcolm S. Salter and Alan M. Webber, "U.S. Competitiveness in Global Industries: Lessons from the Auto Industry," chapter 5, this volume.

52. W.J. Abernathy, chairman, Automobile Panel, Committee on Technology and International Economic and Trade Issues, National Academy of Engineering, *The Competitive Status of the United States Automobile Industry* (Washington, D.C.: National Academy Press 1982), cf. chapter. 6, pp. 90-108, esp. table 6.7, 106.

53. Albert Rees, chairman, Panel to Review Productivity Statistics, National Research Council, *Measurement and Interpretation of Productivity*, cf. esp. chapter 9, "International Comparisons of Productivity," also chapters 5 and 6.

54. Vogel, "Machine Tools."

55. D. Quinn Mills and Malcolm Lovell, Jr., "Competitiveness: The Labor Dimension," chapter 12, this volume; also Mills, Lovell, "Enhancing Competitiveness: The Contribution of Employee Relations," chapter 13, this volume.

56. Lawrence, "Changes in U.S. Industrial Structure."

57. National Science Board, *Science Indicators 1980*, 7, figure 1-3.

58. U.S. National Science Foundation and U.S. Department of Education, *Science and Engineering Education for the 1980s and Beyond* (Washington, D.C.: GPO, 1980).

59. National Science Board, *Science Indicators 1980*, 7, figure 1-3.

60. Ibid., 9, figure 1-4.

61. Gregory, "Japan: New Center of Innovation."

62. Transcript of presentation by William F. Baxter to the National Association of Manufacturers (Washington, D.C. Prototypists, Inc., 10 May 1983).

63. J.C. Miller III, "Antitrust, Innovation, and Productivity," Statement to Subcommittee on Monopolies and Commercial Law of the House Committee on Judiciary, 14 September 1984.

64. H.W. Lane, R.G. Beddows, and P.R. Lawrence, *Managing Large Research and Development Programs* (Albany, N.Y.: State University of New York Press, 1981), cf. 100-121; Hendrik W. Bode, *Synergy: Technical Integration and Technological Innovation in the Bell System* (Murray Hill, N.J.: Bell Laboratories [privately printed] 1976).

65. National Science Board, *Science Indicators 1980*, 112, figure 4-11.

66. Ibid., 225, table 1-15.

67. National Science Board, *Science Indicators 1976* (Washington, D.C.: National Science Foundation, 1977), 199, table 1-17; cf. also Gellman Research Associates, Inc., *Indicators of International Trends*.

68. Keith Pavitt and Luc Soete, "Innovative Activities and Export Shares: Some Comparisons Between Industries and Countries," in *Technical Innovation and British Economic Performance*, ed. Keith Pavitt (London: The Macmillan Press, Ltd., 1979), 38-66.

69. U.S. Department of Commerce, Patent and Trademark Office, *Technology Assessment and Forecast: Tenth Report* (Washington, D.C.: GPO, November 1981).

70. Richard S. Campbell, "Patent Trends as a Technological Forecasting Tool," unpublished paper (Battelle Pacific Northwest Laboratory, Richland, Washington, 1979).

71. Pavitt and Soete, "Innovative Activities."

72. U.S. Department of Commerce, Patent and Trademark Office, *Technology Assessment*; *Summary of Japanese Public Law #84*, provided to National Research Council Panel on Advanced Technology Competition and the Industrialized Allies, 26 May 1981.

73. National Science Board, *Science Indicators 1980*, 129, figure 5-3.

74. Ibid., 129, figure 5-3; 9, figure 1-4; 92, figure 4-2; 54, figure 2-4.

75. National Science Foundation, "Manufacturing Employment Becomes Increasingly Technological," *Science Resource Studies Highlights*, Document No. NSF 83-303, 10 March 1983.

76. National Science Foundation Report NSF 82-331, *Changing Employment Patterns of Scientists, Engineers and Technicians in Manufacturing Industries: 1977-80* (Washington, D.C.: National Science Foundation, October 1982).

77. National Science Foundation, *Science Resource Studies Highlights*, Document No. NSF 81-316.

78. David Ragone, private communication, based on American Council on Education, *1981-1982 Fact Book*.

79. J. Herbert Hollomon and Alan E. Harger, "America's Technological Dilemma," *Technology Review* (July-August 1971): 31; also, Harvey Brooks, "What's Happening to the U.S. Lead in Technology," *Harvard Business Review* (May-June 1972).

80. Winthrop Knowlton et al., Harvard University, Center for Business and Government, "Invitational Conference, Higher Education and Economic Development," 25 March 1983.

81. Lotte Bailyn, "Resolving Contradictions in Technical Careers," *Technology Review* (November-December 1982): 41-47.

82. Robert Pear, "States Fostering High Technology," *New York Times*, 16 August 1983, A1, A21.

83. Bay State Skills Corporation, public relations kit distributed to Kennedy School of Government, Business and Government Seminar, 27 January 1984.

84. National Science Foundation, *Science Resource Studies Highlights*, Document No. 80-316.

85. Torsten Husen, "Are Standards in U.S. Schools Really Lagging Behind Those in Other Countries?" *Phi Delta Kappan Journal* 64, no. 7 (March 1983): 455-61.

86. Harvey Brooks, "Technology, Competition and Employment," in *Robotics: Future Factories, Future Workers*, ed. R.J. Miller, special issue of *The Annals of the American Academy of Political and Social Science* (November 1983): 115-22; H. Brooks, testimony to Subcommittee on Science, Research, and Technology of the Committee on Science and Technology, U.S. House of Representatives, 97th Cong., 1st sess., 10 September 1981. Hearings on *The Human Factor in Innovation and Productivity* (Washington, D.C.: GPO, 1981), 78-91; S.B. Lundstedt, E.W. Colglazier Jr., eds., *Managing Innovation: the Social Dimensions of Creativity Invention and Technology*, published with the Aspen Institute of Humanistic Studies and the Ohio State University (New York: Pergamon Press 1982), cf. esp. H. Brooks, chapter 1: "Social and Technological Innovation," 1-29.

87. D. Yankelovich, H. Zetterberg, B. Strumpel, and M. Shanks, *Work and Human Values: An International Report on Jobs in the 1980s and 1990s* (New York: Aspen Institute for Humanistic Studies, September 1983).

88. Maryellen Kelley, "Computer-Controlled Machines and the Disruption of Workplace Productivity: Establishing a New Labor-Management Relationship," paper prepared for a meeting on "Technology and Competition: Their Impact on Labor/Management Roles and Relationships" under auspices of Harman Program, Kennedy School of Government, Harvard University, 19 April 1983, to be published as a Kennedy School Discussion Paper, 1984.

CHAPTER 10 NOTES

1. Supporting this view are findings by some that the U.S. bond and equity markets at the end of 1980 made up half the total world bond and equity markets. The U.S. bond market was 21% and its equity market was 37% of world markets totaling $5.8 trillion. Roger G. Ibbotson, R.C. Carr, and A.W. Robinson, "International Equity and Bond Returns," *Financial Analysts Journal* (July-August 1982): 61.

2. Chase Manhattan Bank, *U.S. and Japanese Semiconductor Industries: A Financial Comparison*, prepared for the Semiconductor Industry Association (9 June 1980). For the cost of equity capital, Chase calculated the risk-free rate, the market risk, and the risk premium for the

company. Much of the difference in capital costs was due to the high leveraging of Japanese companies.

3. M. Therese Flaherty and Hiroyki Itami, "Financial Systems and Capital Acquisitions," project on U.S.-Japanese Semiconductor Industry Competition, Stanford University (1982).

4. George N. Hatsopoulos, *High Cost of Capital: Handicap of American Business*, a study sponsored by the American Business Conference and Thermo Electron Corporation (26 April 1983). Using a methodology that drew on the work of Dale Jorgenson, the group related financing to different kinds of investment (such as fixed assets, inventories, and net receivables), which carried different marginal costs due to inflation, taxes, and depreciation. The more common approach, particularly for businesses, would separate the cost of liabilities from the cost of assets.

5. U.S. Department of Commerce, "A historical comparison of the cost of financial capital" (April 1983), 12. The Commerce Department calculated the pretax cost and value of long-term debt, short-term debt, and equity, and adjusted for the marginal tax rates in each country. Commerce used nominal calculation because it affects tax deductions, uncertainty that firms can earn high nominal returns, and depreciation allowances.

6. Roger G. Ibbotson, R.C. Carr, and A.W. Robinson, "International Equity and Bond Returns," *Financial Analysts Journal* (July-August 1982): 61. While it is true that individual savers do not buy these bonds, the differences illustrate the returns to debtholding savers. Obviously, tax differences will affect the impact on the issuers.

7. Mervyn A. King and Don Fullerton, *The Taxation of Income from Capital: A Comparative Study of the U.S., U.K., Sweden and West Germany* (Chicago: University of Chicago Press, 1984), 334.

8. Chalmers Johnson, *MITI and the Japanese Miracle* (Stanford: Stanford University Press, 1982).

9. U.K. policies that allow only £.70 in tax-free interest on savings accounts but do not even assess tax against pension funds do not increase savings but do affect their allocation among institutions (building societies benefit, for example). Until 1981, Germany subsidized 40-50% of savings, giving premiums for savings in banks and for those contributed by employers. Economists Advisory Group Ltd., *The British and German Banking System: A Comparative Study* (United Kingdom: Anglo-German Foundation, 1981).

10. King and Fullerton, *Taxation of Income*, appendix A, 577.

11. The structure of the Japanese financial system is discussed in detail later in this chapter.

12. Stephen Bronte, *Japanese Finance: Markets and Institutions* (London: Euromoney Publications, 1982).

13. Richard E. Caves and Masu Uekusa, *Industrial Organization in Japan* (Washington, D.C.: The Brookings Institution, 1976), 37.

14. See figure 10-7.

15. See Flaherty and Itami, "Financial Systems" citing Soichi Royama, "A Perspective of Comparison of Financial Institutions," *Contemporary Economics* (Summer 1981), in Japanese. Since 1973, some large, successful companies have increased their dependence on self-finance in Japan.

16. See for example O. Eckstein, C. Caton, R. Brinner, and P. Duprey, *Report on U.S. Manufacturing Industries* (Boston: Data Resources, Inc., November 1983), 49. They also argue that the U.S. tax laws are "less favorable to debt financing in manufacturing" than in other industries.

17. Caves and Uekusa, *Industrial Organization in Japan*, 37. The authors found "no evidence that group membership raises a firm's rate of profit" and indeed that "group firms probably make higher average payments for borrowed capital than do independent companies." See 77 and 82.

18. Flaherty and Itami, "Financial Systems."

19. Ibid.

20. Note that assets and liabilities are not identical. The data in these charts, which report only domestic accounts when known, come from various sources. Careful judgments about the users of various instruments were needed to classify assets and liabilities, but not all could be assigned.

21. Merely to know that a financial system is concentrated, of course, does not prove it is being managed. If in a country a small number of intermediaries raise a large share of funds or lend a large share, they could help to frame or implement a national strategy without publicized directions from the government. Their small numbers might also augment their power in dealing with the government, leading either to a stand-off or to their taking the lead. In either case, however, trade-offs among groups or their members could be negotiated in private. In this sense, the management of the financial system could be quite subtle. Alternatively, if in a country each group had many members, no clear boundary on its services, and no large share of a segment, big hurdles would impede use of the financial system in any but the most overt manner.

22. Two small groups are omitted because of inadequate data: trading companies and insurance companies. The seven groups examined here are particularly important for business finance. From 1976 to 1980, the seven provided 83% of the net industrial funds in the country. The other sources were: equity markets (8% of net industrial funds), corporate bond markets, 4%; insurance companies, 3%; and government special loan account, 2%. Since financial institutions operate in the equity and bond markets, some of these other sources are captured in the figure. The intermediaries accounted for about 33% of the value traded in the industrial bond market and 33-40% of the number (not the value) of listed shares. *Industrial Bank of Japan Handbook* (Tokyo: IBJ, 1982), 108-109, 204, and 298.

23. Some observers note that during the last twenty years much of the JDB's lending has financed shipping and electrical utilities, rather than the exposed industries; these observers have concluded that its impact on industrial policy must be small, Philip H. Trezise, "Industrial Policy is Not the Major Reason for Japan's Success," *The Brookings Review* (Spring 1983): 13. Actually, JDB lending has gone through several phases since 1952, only the earliest of which concentrated on key heavy industries. However, in the fiscal year ending March 1981, 49% of JDB credit funded "energy resources and technology," *Business Week*, "Japan's Strategy for the 80s," special issue, 14 December 1981. In a study of the trust fund to 1977, while only about 7% financed "industrial development," about 17% financed trade and 40% financed small and medium industry; E. Sakakibara, R. Feldman, and Y. Harada, "The Japanese Financial System in Comparative Perspective," a study prepared for the use of the Joint Economic Committee, U.S. Congress, 12 March 1982, 44. The last category is important: "roughly 60% are subcontractors that contribute so much to Japan's competitiveness" ("Japan's Strategy," *Business Week*, 9).

24. Sakakibara et al., "Japanese Financial System," 54. Participation of a long-term credit bank in a loan consortium gave a de facto government guarantee to the project involved, making it possible for the private corporation in the project to socialize the risk.

25. Industrial Bank of Japan, 1982 annual report, 17.

26. See for example, a study by Andrew Spindler published by The Brookings Institution in March 1984.

27. Bronte, *Japanese Finance*.

28. Economists Advisory Group, *The British and German Banking System*.

29. Because of the role of the dollar as a banking currency, it is necessary to exclude U.S. residents from the comparisons.

30. The low rate of French franc deposits abroad—nevertheless a multiple of the Japanese—reflects a prohibition against most uses of francs outside France.

31. International Monetary Fund, *Annual Report on Exchange Arrangements and Exchange Restrictions, 1981* (Washington, D.C.: IMF, 1982), 241.

32. Sources include unpublished research by Werner von Guionneau (Harvard Business School); Yoko Shibata, "Securities houses lead boom in venture capital in Japan," *Financial Times*, 8 September 1983, 23; "Chassez le fonds propre," *Le Nouveau Journal*, 4 June 1983, 8; "A guide to development and venture capital facilities," *Investors Chronicle*, 11 February 1983 (United Kingdom); and author's interviews in Europe. Definitions of venture capital investment and institutions vary widely. In a narrower study, the Bank of England focused on "fast-growing, innovating companies . . . in risky, high technology" and found some 130 venture capital firms in the United States with investments of $3 billion compared with about 24 in the United Kingdom with investments of under $200 million. Bank of England, *Quarterly Bulletin* (December 1982), 511.

33. According to a study by the Kreditanstalt fur Wiederaufbau, a larger share of its assistance in 1981-82 sponsored the innovation of new procedures and new products in large firms than in small, annual report, 1981, 36.

34. U.S. General Accounting Office, "Government-Industry Cooperation Can Enhance the Venture Capital Process," Report to Senator Lloyd Bentsen, Joint Economic Committee, GAO/ AFMD-82-35, 12 August 1982, appendix 2, 8.

35. Richard Bolling and John Bowles, *America's Competitive Edge* (New York: McGraw-Hill Book Company, 1982), 153.

36. John Tagliabue, "West German Venture Capital," *New York Times*, 6 June 1983, D7.

37. According to an official in the German finance ministry (a) the change in the tax laws about three years ago limited the deductible loss to the amount of the investment (with exceptions for shipbuilding, over half of which is financed by big, publicly traded firms); (b) the recession slowed the appreciation in the value of buildings; and (c) included in the DM 4.7 billion in Bauhaven modellen are legitimate purchasers of homes and flats (which also makes it hard to get support from the housing minister for changes in the law).

38. Shibata, "Securities houses lead boom."

39. There could be reasons outside the financial system that discourage venture capital. For example, firms may not want to lose key employees to new ventures.

CHAPTER 11 NOTES

1. Another important factor during this period was the surge of pollution control investment during the late 1960s and most of the 1970s. Net investment in air and water pollution abatement plant and equipment increased fairly steadily from .04 percent of gross national product in 1961 to .27 percent in 1975, and then declined to zero percent in 1983. Of the $3.1 trillion net stock of fixed nonresidential capital owned by the economy's private sector at year-end 1983, $92 billion consisted of air and water pollution abatement plant and equipment; U.S. Department of Commerce.

2. The service sector accounted for 31 percent of U.S. gross national product in 1950, 38 percent in 1960, 43 percent in 1970, and 47 percent in 1980; U.S. Department of Commerce.

3. For example, Edward F. Denison attributed only a negligible amount of the post-1973 slowdown to reduced capital inputs. "Effects of Selected Changes in the Institutional and Human Environment Upon Output Per Unit of Input," *Survey of Current Business* 58 (January 1978): 21-44; "Explanations of Declining Productivity Growth," *Survey of Current Business* 59, pt. 2 (August 1979): 1-24; *Accounting for Slower Growth: The United States in the 1970s* (Washington, D.C.: The Brookings Institution, 1979). His analysis left more than two-thirds of the slowdown unexplained, however, and he concluded, ". . .I do not know why the record turned out so badly after 1973. . . ." (from "Explanations," p. 5). Similarly, Barry Bosworth concluded, "I am as puzzled as everyone else about why productivity growth has slowed so sharply; but it would appear under normal accounting procedures, that capital formation is not contributing much to the story," from Barry Bosworth, "Capital Formation and Economic Policy," *Brookings Papers on Economic Activity* 2 (1982): 285. John W. Kendrick attributed a somewhat greater role to reduced growth of capital input, especially in comparison with 1966-73, but still attributed most of the slowdown to other factors; see John W. Kendrick, "Productivity Trends and the Recent Slowdown: Historical Perspective, Causal Factors, and Policy Options," in *Contemporary Economic Problems in 1979*, ed. William Fellner (Washington, D.C.: American Enterprise Institute, 1979); and "International Comparisons of Recent Productivity Trends," in *Essays in Contemporary Economic Problems: Demand, Productivity, and Population*, ed. William Fellner (Washington, D.C.: American Enterprise Institute, 1981). Martin Neal Baily has argued that, because of increased obsolescence due to higher energy prices, conventional estimates overstate the existing post-1973 capital stock, so that analysis based on these estimates understates the role of reduced capital in causing the productivity slowdown; see Martin Neal Baily, "Productivity and the Services of Capital and Labor," *Brookings Papers on Economic Activity* 1 (1981): 1-50.

4. These data are not fully comparable to the measures in table 11-1. Unlike in table 11-1, the net investment concept here includes residential construction and inventory accumulation, and the productivity measure is output per hour rather than output per worker. The conclusions in the text are unaffected by these differences.

5. The reverse line of causation is also entirely plausible. Under several familiar theories of saving behavior, rapidly rising real incomes will lead to high saving rates, at least until consumers are sufficiently confident of the prevailing income growth trend to incorporate it in their assumptions about future incomes. Because of the fundamental equality between saving and investment, such behavior will deliver high investment rates also, unless government deficits or international capital outflows absorb the saving. The two directions of causation here need not be mutually exclusive. See, for example, James S. Duesenberry, *Income, Saving, and the Theory of Consumer Behavior* (Cambridge, Mass.: Harvard University Press, 1949); and Milton Friedman, *A Theory of the Consumption Function* (Princeton, N.J.: Princeton University Press, 1957).

6. Jeffrey D. Sachs has argued that the difference between the United States and other industrial economies in this regard is due to differences in labor market institutions. "Wages, Profits, and Macroeconomic Adjustment," *Brookings Papers on Economic Activity* 2 (1978): 269-319.

7. Similarly, currency appreciation in the absence of falling production costs (relative to production costs abroad) can importantly damage a nation's competitiveness. Exactly this combination of events has affected the U.S. economy since 1979. For an analysis from this perspective, see Paul Krugman, "International Aspects of U.S. Monetary and Fiscal Policy," *The Economics of Large Government Deficits* (Boston: Federal Reserve Bank of Boston, 1983).

8. This section draws on my earlier research; see Benjamin M. Friedman, "Debt and Economic Activity in the United States," in *The Changing Roles of Debt and Equity in Financing U.S. Capital Formation*, ed. Benjamin M. Friedman (Chicago: University of Chicago Press, 1982); "Money, Credit and Nonfinancial Economic Activity: An Empirical Study of Five Countries," mimeograph, National Bureau of Economic Research, 1982; "Managing the U.S. Government Deficit in the 1980s," in *Removing Obstacles to Economic Growth*, ed. Michael L. Wachter and Susan J. Wachter (Philadelphia: University of Pennsylvania Press, 1983); "Implications of the Government Deficit for U.S. Capital Formation," *The Economics of Large Government Deficits* (Boston: Federal Reserve Bank of Boston, 1983).

9. Personal saving includes saving by unincorporated businesses. Corporate saving is adjusted to remove artificial profits due to the use of first-in-first-out inventory accounting, and artificial profits (or losses) due to accounting depreciation allowances greater than (or less than) true economic depreciation.

10. The data exclude accrued pension liabilities, however, so that the pension surpluses reported here do not imply that these governmental units are funding their pensions in excess of accruing liabilities.

11. The data in table 11-3 measure the deficit on a National Income and Product Accounts basis, which excludes off-budget outlays. Hence these data understate the post-1979 deficit increase.

12. Here as well as later in this chapter the range given represents the administration's (higher) deficit estimate presented in February 1983, along with its budget proposals (*Budget of the United States Government–Fiscal Year 1984*), and its (lower) estimate presented in July 1983 (*Mid-Session Review of the 1984 Budget*). The more recent projections foresee smaller deficits than the earlier ones, in part because they incorporate the 1983 Social Security legislation but also because they are based on more optimistic assumptions about economic growth. The more recent estimates ignore the repeal of tax withholding on interest and dividend payments, however. The most likely outcome is somewhere between the two projections, and probably closer to the more recent (lower) estimate; Office of Management and Budget.

13. The contingency tax plan, as proposed in the February 1983 budget message, would have consisted of a 5 percent surcharge on the individual and corporation income taxes plus a $5 per barrel excise tax on oil, to take effect on 1 October 1985, if other developments did not independently reduce the fiscal 1986 budget deficit to 2½ percent of gross national product or less, if the economy were growing, and if Congress adopted specific expenditure proposals.

The administration subsequently deleted the contingency tax plan from the budget message proposed in February 1984.

14. See U.S. Congress, Congressional Budget Office, *The Economic and Budget Outlook: An Update* (August 1983). The two sets of proposals lead to almost identical budget outcomes for 1984-86; the Congressional Resolution did not extend to 1987-88. Although the budget *totals* are about the same, the composition of expenditures proposed by Congress differs sharply from that proposed by the administration.

15. These estimates correspond to the earlier (and larger) projections cited above; see again footnote 12. The administration did not calculate new high employment estimates as part of the midsession review.

16. U.S. Office of Management and Budget.

17. The reason for excluding the debt of financial intermediaries is simply to avoid double counting.

18. The source for the data plotted in figure 11-1, as well as in figure 11-2, is the flow-of-funds accounts compiled by the Board of Governors of the Federal Reserve System.

19. The nonfinancial corporate business sector, which typically accounts for three-quarters of all U.S. investment in plant and equipment, relied on external debt financing for 64 percent of its total net sources of funds on average during 1956-80; Board of Governors of the Federal Reserve System. This percentage presumably understates the importance of external funds in financing *net* investment. Within this period business corporations' reliance on external debt has shown an irregular but nevertheless increasing trend. Unincorporated businesses financing new plant and equipment and households financing new homebuilding have also relied heavily, and increasingly, on borrowed sources of funds.

20. See the evidence presented in Friedman, "Money, Credit and Nonfinancial Economic Activity."

21. The explanation and sources given in footnote 12 apply here also.

22. Board of Governors of the Federal Reserve System.

23. Mortgage debt typically comprises nearly two-thirds of all debt owed by U.S. households. As of year-end 1982, mortgage debt accounted for $1.2 trillion out of total liabilities of $1.9 billion for the household sector; Board of Governors of the Federal Reserve System. See also the further discussion below.

24. For a rigorous presentation of this argument, see Martin Feldstein, "The Rate of Return, Taxation, and Personal Saving," *Economic Journal* 88 (September 1978): 482-87.

25. For examples of each result, see Michael J. Boskin, "Taxation, Saving, and the Rate of Interest," *Journal of Political Economy* 86 (April 1978): 53-527; and Philip E. Howrey and Saul H. Hymans, "The Measurement and Determination of Loanable-Funds Saving," *Brookings Papers on Economic Activity* 3 (1978): 655-85.

26. Acquisitions effected by stock purchases constitute the most straightforward way for the U.S. corporate sector to pay out returns to shareholders without subjecting those returns to the "double taxation" usually involved in paying dividends.

27. An early example of such a result is Franco Modigliani, "The Life Cycle Hypothesis of Saving and Intercountry Differences in the Saving Ratio," in *Induction, Trade and Growth: Essays in Honour of Sir Roy Harrod*, ed. W. A. Eltis, M. Fg. Scott, and J. N. Wolfe (Oxford: Clarendon Press, 1970).

28. A prominent example of this argument is Martin Feldstein and Lawrence Summers, "Inflation, Tax Rules, and the Long-Term Interest Rate," *Brookings Papers on Economic Activity* 1 (1978): 61-109.

29. Figure 11-3 is reproduced from Mervyn A. King and Don Fullerton, *The Taxation of Income from Capital: A Comparative Study of the U.S., U.K., Sweden and West Germany* (Chicago: University of Chicago Press, 1983). The strong sensitivity of the tax rate to inflation in Sweden is mostly a consequence of laws governing the taxation of Swedish insurance companies.

30. Ibid.

31. U.S. Department of Commerce.

32. See again, for example, Krugman, "International Aspects."

33. U.S. Department of Commerce.

34. Ibid.

35. See again footnote 23. Moreover, the great majority of households' remaining liabilities consist of debt financing either automobiles or other consumer durables. The National Income and Product Accounts definition of investment, used in table 11-3, excludes consumer durables. The discussion in the text therefore focuses on the option of crowding out homebuilding, but not, for example, new automobile purchases. Deliberately crowding out the automobile sector is a further conceivable alternative, but (at least to the author's knowledge) no one has seriously suggested doing so.

36. Martin Feldstein, for example, has argued for a combination of tight monetary policy and loose fiscal policy along just these lines. Feldstein, "Tax Rules and the Mismanagement of Monetary Policy," *American Economic Review* 70 (May 1980): 182-86.

37. The deduction from taxable income of mortgage interest is a further subsidy in the absolute sense, but not relative to other forms of investment. The U.S. tax system is unusual in permitting this deduction without limit.

38. Board of Governors of the Federal Reserve System.

39. The mortgage market receives, as a net addition to available funds, less than all of the credit provided by the sponsored credit agencies and mortgage pools if they in turn sell their securities to investors who would otherwise have held deposits in mortgage lending institutions; see the analysis of this effect in Dwight M. Jaffee and Kenneth T. Rosen, "Mortgage Credit Availability and Residential Construction," *Brookings Papers on Economic Activity* 3 (1979): 333-76.

40. Here and later in this chapter the deficit calculations in the text are based on the more optimistic economic forecast given by the Office of Management and Budget in the midsession review; see again footnote 12.

CHAPTER 12 NOTES

1. William Brock, U.S. Trade Representative, National Commission on Employment Policy, Washington, D.C., 15 September 1983. The $70 billion figure refers to merchandise imports over exports.

2. Japan Federation of Employers' Associations (NIKKEIREN), *Report of the Committee for the Study of Labor Questions: Toward the Solution of Accumulated Problems* (1983), 13.

3. Toni Mack and Jessica Greenbaum, "Constructive Criticism," *Forbes*, 23 May 1983, 50.

4. Lynda Schuster, "Mexico Eases Foreign Investment Rules, But Investors Still May Be Hard to Attract," *Wall Street Journal*, 20 June 1983, 31.

5. Samuel Brittan, "A Very Painful World Adjustment," *Foreign Affairs* 61, no. 3 (1983): 562.

6. Mack, "Constructive Criticism," 50.

7. "The Four Dragons Lose Their Fire," *Business Week*, 28 March 1983, 64.

8. Ibid.

9. "China's Rapid Trade Growth and Impact on the World Economy," *Federal Reserve Bank of New York Quarterly Review* 7, no. 4 (Winter 1982-83): 41.

10. Ibid., 45.

11. Japan Federation of Employers' Associations, *Report of the Committee*, 11.

12. Ibid.

13. Ibid.

14. Bureau of National Affairs, *Daily Labor Report*, no. 96, 17 May 1983, A-4.

15. Bureau of National Affairs, "Statement of Robert U. Ayres, Professor of Engineering and Public Policy, Carnegie Mellon University," *Daily Labor Report*, no. 54, 18 March 1983, F-5.

16. Bureau of National Affairs, *Daily Labor Report*, no. 91, 10 May 1983, G-2.

17. Robert B. Reich, "The Next American Frontier," *The Atlantic Monthly*, March 1983, 51.

18. *Time Magazine*, 30 May 1983, 64.

19. Bureau of National Affairs, *Daily Labor Report*, 10 May 1983, 62.

20. *Business Week*, 28 March 1983, 85.

21. National Commission on Employment Policy draft, "Changes in the Workplace," 42.

22. *Business Week*, 28 March 1983, 85.

23. U.S. Department of Labor, Bureau of Labor Statistics, *Employment and Earnings*, vol. 30, no. 5, May 1983, 77.

24. It should be emphasized that this conclusion is *not* based upon uncertain projections of future population growth rates. Instead, nearly all persons who will enter the world's labor force between today and the year 2000 are already living. To calculate the increase in the labor force one need only age today's children automatically and adjust for retirements or deaths. The United Nations study has calculated that 750 million people will enter the world's labor force by 2000, and of these, 90 percent will be in the Third World.

CHAPTER 13 NOTES

1. Bureau of Labor Statistics, *Daily Labor Report*, no. 154, 9 August 1983, 2.

2. James Parrott, "Bargaining Against a Bleak Backdrop," *The AFL-CIO Federationist* 90, no. 3 (14 May 1983): 2.

3. *AFL-CIO News*, 14 May 1983, 6.

4. White House Conference on Productivity, Cooperation in the Workplace Teleconference, April 1983-September 1983, Conference Comment no. 179, Ed Dulworth, 29 July 1983.

5. For example, see Irving H. Siegel and Edgar Weinberg, *Labor-Management Cooperation: The American Experience* (Kalamazoo, Michigan: W.E. Upjohn Institute for Employment Research, 1982), and U.S. Department of Labor, Labor Management Services Administration, *Resource Guide to Labor Management Cooperation* (Washington, D.C.: GPO, 1982).

6. Bureau of National Affairs, *Daily Labor Report*, no. 55, 21 March 1983, A-15.

7. *Wall Street Journal*, 7 June 1983, 1.

8. Kenneth R. Andrews, "From the Boardroom: Rigid Rules Will Not Make Good Records," *Harvard Business Review* (November-December 1982).

9. Eric N. Berg, "Shrinking A Staff the Kodak Way," *New York Times*, 4 September 1983, 1.

10. Ibid.

11. "Kodak to Reduce Work Force by 800 at Two Locations," *Wall Street Journal*, 25 October 1983, 12.

12. *Wall Street Journal*, 27 June 1983, 5.

13. Gellman Research Associates, "The Value of A Newly Created Job," unpublished paper.

14. Peter T. Kilborn, "Study Finds Low '82 Level for Unemployment Claims," *New York Times*, 9 September 1983, D-17.

15. Ibid.

16. *Business Week*, 23 May 1983, 37; Bureau of Labor Statistics *Daily Labor Report*, no. 154, 2, 9 August 1983 (22%).

17. *Business Week*, 23 May 1983, 37.

18. Department of Labor, Bureau of Labor Statistics, Boston regional office, telephone interview, 22 February 1984.

19. Nancy Folbre, "Plant Closings, Maine Style," *Boston Globe*, 17 May 1983, 3.

20. "Legislation on Plant Closings Sought to Protect Workers," *AFL-CIO News*, 7 May 1983, 3.

21. Kenneth McLennan, "Policy Options to Facilitate the Reemployment of Displaced Workers," unpublished draft.

22. Sam Bryant, supervisor of special programs, U.S. Department of Labor, Washington, D.C., telephone interview, 6 December 1983.

CHAPTER 14 NOTES

1. C. Fred Bergsten, "International Economic Relations," *TransAtlantic Perspectives*, February 1982, 2; and Ira C. Magaziner and Robert B. Reich, *Minding America's Business* (New York: Random House, 1983), 32.

2. Council of Economic Advisers, *The Economic Report of the President*, February 1984, 222, 253, 254, and 258; and the Bureau of Labor Statistics, *Handbook of Labor Statistics*, Bulletin #2175, December 1983, 159 and 204-206.

3. Peter W. Bernstein, "David Stockman: No More Big Budget Cuts," *Fortune*, 6 February 1984, 56; also see Executive Order #12291 of 17 February 1981, printed in *The Federal Register*, vol. 46, no. 33, 19 February 1981; and George C. Lodge and William B. Glass, "U.S. Trade Policy Needs One Voice," *Harvard Business Review* (May-June 1983): 75.

4. National Commission on Excellence in Education, "A Nation at Risk: The Imperative for Educational Reform," Washington, D.C., April 1983; also "Can the Schools Be Saved?" *Newsweek*, 9 May 1983, 50-58.

5. Charles Schultze, "Industrial Policy: A Dissent," *The Brookings Review* (Fall 1983): 11.

6. Council of Economic Advisers, *The Economic Report of the President*, 102-111, 220, and 305.

7. See, e.g., M. Albert and R. J. Ball, "Towards European Economic Recovery in the 1980's," Report to the European Parliament, 7 July 1983, English edition, 10-17.

8. U.S. Government Printing Office, November 1983, 19-20.

9. Frank A. Weil raised many of these points at the Industrial Policy Seminar at Harvard University on 5 November 1983.

10. See, e.g., J. L. Badaracco, Jr., and D. B. Yoffie, "Industrial Policy: It Can't Happen Here," *Harvard Business Review* (November-December 1983): 96; and Chalmers Johnson, *MITI and the Japanese Miracle* (Stanford, Calif.: Stanford University Press, 1982), 305-324.

11. John F. Welch, Jr., "Quality Recovery For World Competitiveness," *Financier*, April 1983, 40-44.

12. See, e.g., David Warsh, "Debate Over Tax Reform Finally Takes Center Stage," *The Boston Globe*, 29 April 1984, A77, A84.

13. David Ricardo, *The Principles of Political Economy and Taxation* (London: J. M. Dent and Sons, Ltd., 1926), 77-93.

14. Bruce R. Scott, "Can Industry Survive the Welfare State?" *Harvard Business Review*. (September-October 1982): 72.

15. John Zysman and Stephen S. Cohen, *The Mercantilist Challenge to the Liberal International Trade Order*, a study prepared for the Joint Economic Committee of the U.S. Congress (Washington, D.C.: U.S. Government Printing Office, 1982), 4.

16. Thomas F. O'Bayle, "U.S. Steel Files Actions Against Three Nations," *The Wall Street Journal*, 11 November 1983, 56.

17. James Madison, "The Social Foundations of Political Freedom," *The Federalist Papers*, #51 (New York: Pocket Books, 1964), 121.

18. Quoted in 17 *Weekly Compilation of Presidential Documents*, no. 4, p. 2, 20 January 1981.

19. *I.N.S. v. Chadha*, 103 S. Ct. 2764, at 2788 (1983), holding unconstitutional a section of the Immigration and Nationality Act that allowed either house of Congress to overturn the attorney general's decision to let a deportable alien remain in the United States.

20. Samuel Huntington, *American Politics: The Promise of Disharmony* (Cambridge, Mass.: Harvard University Press, 1981), 39.

21. Council of Economic Advisers, *The Economic Report of the President*, February 1982, 94; and "Federal Support of U.S. Business" (Washington, D.C.: U.S. Government Printing Office, January 1984), ix-xiv, 40.

22. John Schnapp, "Who For the Pedestal Now?" *The New York Times*, 11 July 1982, section III, 2.

23. Anna Cifelli, "Rolling Back the Freedom to Manage," *Fortune*, 19 January 1984, 90-94.

24. See, e.g., George C. Lodge, *The American Disease* (New York: Alfred Knopf, 1984), chapter 9.

25. Compare Robert M. Kaus, "The Trouble With Unions," *Harper's*, June 1983, 23-35, with Paul Weiler, "Promises To Keep: Securing Workers' Rights to Self-Organization Under The NLRA," *Harvard Law Review* 96 (June 1983): 1769-1827.

26. See, e.g., Victor Brudney, "The Independent Director—Heavenly City or Potemkin Village," *Harvard Law Review* 95 (1982): 597; and Richard R. Ellsworth, "Shareholder Wealth, The Cost of Capital and Competitive Decline," draft, 22 May 1984.

27. William Greider, "The Education of David Stockman," *The Atlantic Monthly*, December 1981, 27, 50-54.

INDEX

This book was set electronically from the authors' word-processing diskettes. The typeface is Merganthaler Times Roman, originally designed by Stanley Morison for *The Times* of London in 1932. The book was printed by offset lithography on acid-free paper.